The United States in the World

The *United States*

A HISTORY OF

HOUGHTON MIFFLIN COMPANY   BOSTON   TORONTO

GENEVA, ILLINOIS   PALO ALTO   PRINCETON, NEW JERSEY

in the World

AMERICAN FOREIGN POLICY

H. William Brands

Texas A&M University

VOLUME II

Sponsoring Editor: *Sean Wakely*
Senior Development Editor: *Fran Gay*
Senior Production/Design Coordinator: *Pat Mahtani*
Senior Manufacturing Coordinator: *Priscilla Bailey*
Marketing Manager: *Rebecca Dudley*

Cover credit: Three Allies in Cairo by William H. Johnson, ca. 1945. *National Museum of American Art/Art Resource*
Cover design: *Dragonfly Design, Ron Kosciak*

Printed in the U.S.A.

Library of Congress catalog card number: 93-78669

ISBN: 0-395-62181-X

3456789-QF-02 01 00 99 98

Contents

                                                                       v

Chapter 10
Mugged by Reality, 1937–1945   131

Chapter 11
The Struggle for a New World Order   181

Chapter 12
The Rise of the Third World, 1950–1962   222

Maps

Preface

This book adopts a global approach to the study of the history of American foreign relations. Two reasons motivate this approach. The first is historical: for the greater part of the existence of the American republic, the world has had a much larger impact on the United States than the United States has had on the world. Understanding relations between Americans and the rest of the world requires close attention to developments in the rest of the world.

The second reason is contemporary: at no time has an understanding of the foreign side of American foreign relations been more important than during the 1990s. The bipolar framework of international affairs that grew out of the Second World War has collapsed, and no compelling framework has emerged to replace it. Countries that did not exist in 1945 clamor to be heard. Nations leveled by the war have regained their former stature. Ancient rivalries suppressed during the Cold War have burst forth again. Economics and technology have evolved in ways unforeseen fifty years ago. The United States remains the single most powerful nation on earth, but Americans increasingly find themselves having to take account of the wishes and demands of people in other countries. Understanding America's present and shaping its future require understanding those wishes and demands.

The global approach of this book assumes the form, most obviously, of a more thorough treatment of developments in other countries and in the world at large than generally appears in texts on American diplomatic history. Where other books have planted their readers, so to speak, in Washington, or at least within the United States, and directed readers' attention outward to the world beyond American borders, this book conceptually locates readers somewhere above the earth, where they can see the entire planet; and while it keeps America always in the picture (a conceptual possibility if a geographical improbability), it allows them a much broader view.

Adopting, as it does, the world as its frame of reference, this book concentrates on large issues of world affairs. Sometimes this concentration comes at the expense of what might be called more traditional elements of diplomatic history. When, for example, considerations of space have dictated a choice between detailing the negotiations leading up to a particular treaty and sketching the evolution of the global balance of power, the latter has won out. Similarly, items often considered extrinsic to conventional diplomatic history—intellectual and technological developments, trends in the world economy, cultural influences on the actions of peoples and governments—receive substantial attention here. America's relations with foreign countries have reflected much more than what diplomats and governments said to each other, and histories of American foreign relations should reflect this fact.

Organization of the Book

The book is divided into two volumes to correspond to the typical two-semester course. The first volume covers the period from the colonial origins of the United States to 1914; the second volume (which overlaps the first by one chapter) covers the period from 1895 until the present. The first two chapters of Volume I lay out themes that have characterized American foreign relations for two centuries and place the creation and early evolution of the United States squarely in an international context. Subsequent chapters trace the conflicts between an expanding United States and the great powers of Europe, as well as between the United States and the lesser powers of the Americas and the aboriginal inhabitants of North America. The transformation of the American and world economies during the late nineteenth century, the emergence of nationalism and other ideologies in Europe and elsewhere, and the effects of these developments on American foreign relations are treated in the last three chapters of Volume I.

Volume II describes the rise of the United States to global dominance at the midpoint of the twentieth century and its relative decline since. Europe's two great wars play a central role, as do the long-running revolution in China, the emergence, eclipse, and re-emergence of Japan, and the transformation of large parts of the nonindustrial world. Several chapters discuss the assorted ideological reactions to modernization, particularly fascism, communism, and religious fundamentalism. The last chapters of Volume II chart the disintegration of the post-Second World War order, including the sudden and spectacular collapse of the Soviet Union and its Eastern European empire. The last chapter also covers the Persian Gulf war of 1991 and other recent developments.

Pedagogical Features

While the text of the book carries the story line and analysis, additional features of the two volumes provide guideposts to students. Each chapter contains a chronology of important events of the period in question; these often go beyond the narrative to lend additional context to the events described there. Maps orient students geographically; in keeping with the overall approach, the maps stress international and global developments. Each chapter concludes with numerous suggestions for additional reading, from broad-gauged surveys and synthetic works to detailed monographs. Reproductions of photographs, paintings, and cartoons convey images words cannot so easily capture.

Instructor's Resource Manual with Test Items

An *Instructor's Resource Manual with Test Items,* prepared by Donald Rakestraw of Georgia Southern University, provides teaching ideas and test questions as additional resource material for instructors. The manual includes for each text chapter a chapter summary, lecture suggestions, classroom discussion questions, class activities, term paper topics, approximately twenty-five multiple-choice questions, and five essay questions.

Acknowledgments

Although the title page of this book lists but a single author, no work of this scope is really the work of one person. The book would not have been possible without the assistance of those hundreds of historians, economists, political scientists, and others who have investigated particular events in greater detail than this author ever could have and who have recorded their conclusions in books and articles (many of which are listed among the suggested readings). Nor would this book have acquired its present form without the patient reading and careful commentary of the reviewers to whom earlier drafts were sent. These include:

Richard A. Harrison, Lawrence University
Sandra M. Hawley, San Jacinto College
Lawrence S. Kaplan, Kent State University
Thomas R. Maddux, California State University, Northridge
Robert J. McMahon, University of Florida
Margaret R. Morley, Northern Arizona University
Donald A. Rakestraw, Georgia Southern University
William Stinchcombe, Syracuse University
William Stueck, Jr., University of Georgia

Finally, special thanks go to Frances Gay, Senior Development Editor at Houghton Mifflin, for her work on the manuscript.

H W B

The United States in the World

Chapter 7

Democratic Imperialism, 1895–1914

T he twentieth century started early for the United States. The opening gun was the outbreak of war with Spain in the spring of 1898, though the war was merely a symptom of something larger. Americans had fought Europeans before: the British twice and the French once. Each fight had been a stiffer contest than the bout with Spain proved to be. Nor were the stakes of the Spanish-American War especially vital. Some American property in Cuba had suffered damage in the preceding turmoil, but hardly enough to warrant a war. Had the McKinley administration chosen to ignore Madrid's ill-treatment of its Cuban subjects, Americans might simply have gone on about their affairs; other imperial powers routinely oppressed their colonials. For America's part, Washington had nothing to boast of in its treatment of native Indians.

The significance of the Spanish-American War lay in the fact that it represented a willingness on the part of the American government and the American people to use American power for purposes not immediately related to American security and to do so at a great distance from home. This was what most plainly distinguished the twentieth century in American international relations from the eighteenth and nineteenth centuries. Americans had not shied away from the use of force during the earlier period, but force had always borne a direct and obvious connection to vital American interests. During the Revolutionary War, America's national existence was on the line. During the undeclared naval war against France in 1798–1800, Americans fought to avenge past attacks on American shipping and prevent future attacks. The War of 1812 had a variety of causes, but they clustered around a felt need to enforce respect by the British for American rights and interests. The other foreign war to date—the Mexican War—had less to do with American security than the others, but took place right next to the United States.

Although the Spanish-American War started over events in Cuba, some of the most important fighting occurred halfway around the globe in the Philippines. By carrying the contest to the Philippines, the American government signaled America's intention to join the ranks of the world's great global powers. The joining did not come without complaints: from the Filipinos who resisted the extension of American control over their islands, from American anti-imperialists who denounced the establishment of an American empire in the far Pacific, and from Americans generally who believed that the warnings

Chronology

1895   Venezuelan crisis with Britain; Cuban war of independence breaks out; radio telegraphy invented

1898   Spanish-American War; Hawaii annexed

1899   Philippines annexed; Philippine war begins; first Open Door note; Samoa partioned between United States and Germany; Boer War begins

1900   Boxer Rebellion in China; second Open Door note; first radio broadcast of human voice

1901   Platt amendment to Cuban constitution; Hay-Pauncefote treaty with Britain; oil discovered in Texas

1902   Anglo-Japanese alliance

1903   Panama gains independence with American help; Hay-Bunau Varilla treaty with Panama regarding canal

1904   Russo-Japanese War begins; Roosevelt corollary to Monroe Doctrine

1905   Taft-Katsura agreement with Japan; Treaty of Portsmouth between Russia and Japan

1906   American troops occupy Cuba; Algeciras conference regarding Morocco

1907   "Gentlemen's agreement" with Japan; J.P. Morgan stops run on U.S. gold supply; Roosevelt sends fleet on around-the-world cruise

1908   Root-Takahira agreement with Japan; Henry Ford introduces the Model T car

1909   Payne-Aldrich tariff

1910   Japan annexes Korea; Mexican revolution begins

1911   Qing dynasty in China falls

1912   U.S. troops land in Nicaragua; Sun Yatsen founds Guomindang party in China

1913   Balkan war

1914   American troops occupy Veracruz; First World War begins; Wilson proclaims neutrality; Panama Canal opened to traffic

of George Washington, Thomas Jefferson, and John Quincy Adams about keeping clear of entanglements with other countries and peoples still ought to guide American foreign relations. The complainers lost this round of the debate, as, for most of the twentieth century, would those who advocated a modest and circumscribed role for the United States in world affairs.

The energies of the United States for the first decade and a half of the twentieth century continued to concentrate on East Asia and the Caribbean basin. In East Asia, the American government sought to prevent any other country from gaining inordinate influence. The term "open door" catch-phrased the policy devised to prevent such a happening. The policy had both political and economic connotations and referred especially to China. Politically, the Open Door aimed to keep China from being partitioned among the European imperialists and perhaps Japan; economically, it attempted to forestall the closing of China to American trade by the Europeans or Japanese.

In the Caribbean basin, the policy of the United States had the same overall objective as in Asia—maximizing American influence against competing claims—but employed quite different tactics. If the label Open Door captured the American approach to Asia, "closed door" could have summarized American policy toward the Western Hemisphere. First by the Roosevelt corollary to the Monroe Doctrine, and subsequently by the "dollar diplomacy" of the Taft administration, the American government attempted to secure much of Latin America as a United States sphere of influence. Only in Puerto Rico did Washington explicitly colonize territory to its south, but American leaders acquired influence in many parts of the region that made formal control almost superfluous.

That the United States did *not* claim more territory—Cuba being the most likely candidate—resulted from two factors, one that reflected well on America's national conscience and one that did not. Many Americans felt it unbecoming, indeed disgraceful, for the country that had invented modern democracy to forcibly deny other countries the right to govern themselves. This strain of thinking had been evident earlier in American history, notably during the Mexican War; but it gained adherents and influence during the controversy that followed the Spanish-American War. This appeal to America's better nature did not prevent the annexation of the Philippines and Puerto Rico, but it did help prevent the emergence of a full-blown American colonialism. The anticolonial factor that did not reflect well on Americans had also been evident during the nineteenth century. Many opponents of an American overseas empire shrank from association with the dark-skinned peoples such an empire would include. The majority of those who felt this way did not have much use for African-Americans in the United States, and they thought that (white) Americans would only be asking for more trouble to take other colored people to their bosom.

Underlying the controversy over America's new role in international affairs were fundamental questions of how to reconcile democracy with global power. Could a democracy rule an empire and remain a democracy? Were spheres of

influence more compatible with democracy than outright colonies? What obligations did a great democracy have to its colonies or to the countries within
its sphere? What effect would America's new role in the world have on its
institutions at home? Americans wrestled with these questions at the beginning
of the twentieth century; in one form or another, they have been wrestling with
them ever since.

Cuba Libre!

Although Grover Cleveland could interpret Britain's agreement to submit the
Venezuelan dispute to arbitration as a diplomatic triumph, the Democrats remained in the ditch the depression of the 1890s had got them into. Foreign-
policy successes almost never make up for domestic debacles, and they did not
for the Democrats in Cleveland's day. The presidential campaign of 1896
turned on a homegrown issue: silver. The Democratic candidate, William Jennings Bryan, knew almost nothing about international affairs (which nonetheless would not disqualify him, older and only slightly wiser, from being named
secretary of state in 1913); but Bryan did not bother with foreign affairs, instead training his booming voice on what he discerned as America's need to
debase the currency by remonetizing silver. Bryan naturally did not put the
matter so directly—but the Republicans did. Republican candidate William
McKinley promised sound money, meaning gold, and a return to prosperity.
The voters preferred McKinley's promises to Bryan's.

McKinley entered the White House with no compelling agenda for international affairs (in fact, so leery was he of seeming forward on foreign topics that
when visiting Niagara Falls he refused to walk more than halfway across the
bridge connecting the United States to Canada lest he be the first president to
leave American territory while in office). McKinley initially thought it would
be enough for him to get the American economy back on track again. But
events overseas—and reactions to those events in certain American quarters—
soon demanded his attention.

The most pressing of these events took place in Cuba. Early in the nineteenth
century, when most of the rest of Spain's American empire was breaking free
of the mother country, Cuba had remained loyal. The Cubans' loyalty did not
indicate so much a deep-seated affection for Spain as an attachment to the
prosperity the island was enjoying. The anti-French revolt in Haiti, which had
contributed to Napoleon's decision to get rid of Louisiana, sparked protracted
unrest that destroyed Haiti as a major sugar producer; primacy in sugar production shifted to Cuba. The Cuban population grew tremendously, as did
Cuba's wealth. A large portion of both consisted of the slaves who worked the
sugar plantations. Elsewhere in Latin America, independence from Spain had
produced strong pressure for emancipation of the slaves. Cuba's slave holders
had no desire to give up their slaves or the riches the slaves were bringing them;

Looking neither like a warmonger nor particularly like an imperialist, William McKinley was accused of being the one and convicted himself of being the other. *Brown Brothers*

they sought to avoid the pressure for emancipation by eschewing independence.

But the slaves, predictably, did not like the situation, and on several occasions during the first half of the nineteenth century, they rose in rebellion. None of the rebellions succeeded, but they did rattle the Cuban status quo. Over time, the dissatisfaction spread to other groups in Cuba, including the Creoles (Cubans of Spanish descent), who held most of the positions of power in the island—and only some of whom owned slaves. The Spanish government was growing increasingly corrupt, and decisions affecting Cuba often were dictated by court politics in Madrid. When a sharp economic depression in the 1860s added to Cuba's distress, a group of Creoles decided that continued loyalty was costing too much, and they determined to split from Spain. In 1868 they declared Cuba's independence and prepared to defend it by armed struggle.

The Spanish government responded to the declaration by sending a huge army to Cuba: ten times the size of the force it had sent to deal with the revolts in all of Spanish America earlier in the century. For ten years, war—labeled the Ten Years' War—ravaged the island and exhausted both the Cubans and the Spanish. Finally in 1878 the two sides called it quits. Madrid granted greater autonomy, short of full independence, to the Cubans; the Cubans pledged continued allegiance to Spain.

If conditions in Cuba had always been as pleasant as in this drawing, there probably wouldn't have been uprisings there or a war between the United States and Spain. *The Bettman Archive*

As part of the peace package, Spain freed Cuba's slaves. Emancipation was designed to win the gratitude of Cuba's large black population, which to some extent it did. But it had the additional effect of cutting the Creole slave holders' last tie to Spain. Formerly independence had threatened to deprive the planters of their slaves; now, with their slaves lost, independence held no such threat.

Moreover, Cuba was falling into the American economic sphere. During the latter half of the nineteenth century, American investors purchased farms and other property in Cuba, slowly at first and then faster. By the mid-1890s Americans had sunk some $50 million into Cuba's economy. American interests gained control of the Cuban sugar industry, aided by the McKinley tariff of 1890, which eliminated duties on sugar imports to the United States from Cuba (while applying duties to Hawaiian sugar). Cuba became the third leading supplier of foreign goods to America (after Britain and Germany). The United States was far and away the largest market for Cuban exports.

The growing American stake in Cuba caused Americans to pay more notice than before when the Cuban independence movement revived in 1895. The chief revivalist was José Martí, a Cuban exile who after the Ten Years' War had spent more than a decade in New York writing and agitating in favor of Cuban independence. In the spring of 1895, Martí and a small band of followers landed on the Cuban shore and once again raised the banner of revolt.

Though Martí was killed shortly thereafter (he would become a hero to subsequent generations of Latin American revolutionaries), the insurgency grew swiftly.

Spain's response to the renewed revolt could hardly have been more inept. The Spanish employed tactics that were harsh enough to alienate most of the Cuban people but not harsh enough to stamp out the insurgency. The most infamous tactic was that of *reconcentrado*, a brutal, albeit logical, effort to terminate the guerrilla activities of the insurgents. The insurgents attempted to blend in with the population at large while staging nighttime raids and hit-and-run ambushes. The Spanish forces, led by General Valeriano Weyler, countered by concentrating the Cuban peasants into camps where they could be closely supervised and by declaring much of the rest of the countryside a free-fire zone. Anyone found outside the camps was assumed to be an insurgent and could be captured or killed summarily. Not surprisingly, the *reconcentrado* policy made Spain many enemies. Ordinary people who merely wished to be left alone were uprooted and treated as criminals. Conditions in the camps were miserably unsanitary; thousands of Cubans died of disease.

The Cubans' plight quickly became a hot issue in the United States. Part of the reason was that the fighting between the Cuban insurgents and the Spanish troops destroyed American property: American businesses and individuals who saw their investments torched wanted the war to end. If neither the Spanish nor the Cubans could put a finish to the fighting, then perhaps the United States should step in. Another part of the reason for the American interest was the brilliant success with which the Cuban insurgents broadcast their propaganda in the United States. Building on the contacts José Martí and others had established during the 1880s and early 1890s, the rebels made sure that their side of the story was carried by most important newspapers in the United States.

It helped the cause of the insurgent propagandists that American newspapers, especially in New York City, were engaged in fierce battles for readers. The battles reflected recent changes in printing technology that allowed newspapers to be printed more efficiently and sold more cheaply than before. But the new presses cost money, and publishers sought to recoup their investment by attracting advertisers to their papers. The advertisers demanded large readerships: hence the newspaper wars. William Randolph Hearst and Joseph Pulitzer, whose papers dominated the New York market, were happy to publish the most lurid stories about Spanish atrocities in Cuba. The tone of Hearst's *New York Journal* was typical when it described General Weyler as a "fiendish despot" and an "exterminator of men." The *Journal* added, "There is nothing to prevent his carnal animal brain from running riot with itself in inventing tortures and infamies of bloody debauchery." If the characterizations were overdrawn and the stories were not always entirely true, Hearst and Pulitzer persuaded themselves that moderation and scrupulousness did not sell papers.

President McKinley, pressured by his Republican capitalist friends with Cuban connections and by an American public opinion that increasingly backed the Cuban insurgents against Spain—and finally by American expansionists who hoped to add Cuba and perhaps other Spanish possessions to American territory or at least an American sphere of influence—began speaking out. McKinley did not want war if war could be avoided. The American economy was finally beginning to recover from its disastrous slump, and the president did not wish to do anything that might shake the confidence necessary for the recovery to continue. In December 1897 he called on Spain to pay heed to the legitimate demands for more self-government, and he suggested that the United States might feel obliged to intervene if the situation in Cuba did not improve. But he resisted demands from warhawks for American belligerency, and he refused to grant diplomatic recognition to the insurgents' provisional government.

The situation in Cuba did not improve. It only got worse. Loyalists in Cuba (that is, opponents of Cuban independence), resenting what they saw as American meddling, attacked American property and threatened American nationals. McKinley responded by ordering an American battleship, the *Maine*, to Havana in January 1898. This infuriated the loyalists even more. In February an explosion tore through the hull of the *Maine*, killing hundreds of American sailors and sending the ship to the bottom of Havana's harbor. Although the cause of the explosion was unknown at the time (much later an investigation called it an accident), fire-eaters in the United States immediately pinned the blame on Spain and the loyalists. "Remember the *Maine!*" resounded across America.

A Spanish diplomatic (or rather undiplomatic) blunder increased the momentum toward war. The Spanish minister in Washington, Enrique Dupuy de Lôme, wrote a letter to an associate in the Spanish government describing McKinley unflatteringly as a "bidder for the admiration of the crowd" and predicting that the Americans could be appeased with reforms that were more cosmetic than substantive. The part about McKinley wishing for popular admiration was true enough—as it would have been true of nearly any politician. But diplomats are supposed to be more tactful than to say so, at least in correspondence that might be pilfered by enemies. The insurgents got hold of de Lôme's letter and leaked it to American newspapers. The uproar against Spain grew louder than ever.

McKinley was not one to buck a strong tide, and despite persisting reservations about the wisdom of war, he issued an ultimatum to Spain that proved to be more a justification for American intervention than an honest effort to end the fighting in Cuba. The most important part of the ultimatum implied that Spain must grant Cuba independence.

The Spanish government had numerous problems of its own, and for it to knuckle under to the American demands almost certainly would have been politically fatal. For a time the Spanish government looked to the other European powers for help. Public opinion in Europe toward American meddling in Cuba ranged from disappointment to outrage; almost no one took the Americans at their word regarding concern for the welfare of oppressed Cubans. Among some of the European governments there existed strong sentiment in

Though the cause of the explosion that sank the *Maine* was unknown, the chief effect was soon apparent: increased shouting in the United States for war against Spain. *The Bettman Archive*

favor of warning the Americans off. Germany's Wilhelm saw a conspiracy between the Americans and the British to aggrandize themselves at the expense of the rest of the world and considered American pressure on Spain to be part of the plot. Wilhelm declared that it was "high time" the monarchs of Europe jointly offered their assistance to Spain "in case the American-British Society for Theft and Warmongering looks as if it seriously intends to snatch Cuba from Spain."

Unfortunately for Spain, the other powers did not agree with Wilhelm (neither did all of Wilhelm's own ministers). None of the other powers wanted to see the United States take Cuba, and none particularly wanted to see Spain humbled. But neither did any of them especially desire to tangle with the Americans over an issue that was peripheral to essential European interests. Britain was having more trouble than ever in southern Africa, where the Germans were still aggravating the situation; the British and French were at loggerheads in central Africa and were about to go to the brink of war over a spat at Fashoda on the upper Nile; the British, Germans, French, and Russians were fretting over the Japanese and each other in northeastern Asia. Although the Europeans made a largely pro forma gesture of urging moderation on the

Americans, they refused to offer Spain the sort of support Madrid needed to withstand the American pressure. The British, most notably, refused to jeopardize their recently improving relations with the Americans. British prime minister Salisbury thought the Spanish government hoped to get the British navy to do Spain's dirty work and thereby spare Spain the trouble; he declined the honor, saying that the British should resist entreaties "to offer ourselves as candidates for the post of Archibald Bell-the-Cat."

When the Europeans left Spain to its own devices, and when Madrid refused to grant Cuba independence, McKinley on April 11 asked Congress for authorization to employ military force against Spain. "The present condition of affairs in Cuba is a constant menace to our peace," he said, exaggerating. Congress granted the president's request, and shortly thereafter Spain and the United States traded war declarations.

The Spanish-American War

The war against Spain came at a convenient time for the McKinley administration and the Republicans. The party of the administration had elections coming up in the fall, and though it seemed almost impossible that the Republicans would do as well this time as in their thorough trouncing of the Democrats in 1896, the war would be a good issue to campaign on.

It would be, that is, if the war went quickly and well. Skeptics had reason to doubt that Spain would be a pushover. The oldest among the naysayers could remember the Mexican War and how the American army had needed two years to get the overmatched Mexicans to give up. Middle-aged doubters recalled that both sides in the Civil War had expected that contest to be far shorter than it proved to be. Spanish power was not what it had been, but it was not obviously something to sniff at either. Americans attacking Spanish forces in Cuba would be mounting a difficult amphibious operation, the likes of which no living American soldier had ever accomplished (nor any dead ones, for that matter).

The skeptics turned out to be wrong, however, and the American contest against Spain turned out to be not much of a contest. Although the Spanish navy looked reasonably strong on paper (much the way the Mexican army had looked in 1846), its ships were old and poorly maintained. The smaller American navy was newer and faster and packed more punch—chiefly because of the influence of A. T. Mahan and his disciples on congressional appropriations during the 1890s. The American army was typically unready for war when Congress declared it, but the overall fighting capacity of the United States enormously exceeded that of Spain. And a generation of young men weary of hearing their fathers and grandfathers talk about the glorious days of the Civil War, when men were really men, flocked to arms to test their mettle.

Theodore Roosevelt desired more than most others of his generation to prove his manhood. Many American leaders (and many more leaders of other

Theodore Roosevelt was never happier than when contemplating the glories of war. *Brown Brothers*

countries) have sought the fruits of war, but the majority of them would have preferred that the harvest not include all the killing and dying that war inevitably brings. Roosevelt adopted the—thankfully uncommon—view that war is to the nation what calisthenics are to the individual: a means of eliminating flab and toning muscles. "No triumph of peace is quite as great as the supreme triumphs of war," he declared; and he spoke glowingly of that moment in the warrior's life "when the wolf begins to rise in his heart."

As soon as Congress declared war against Spain, Roosevelt began rounding up a volunteer cavalry unit. Several years earlier he had spent time in Dakota Territory, where he was smitten by the romance of the American cowboy; now he contacted some of his old partners and talked them into taking their ponies and six-shooters to Cuba to clean out the dastardly Spaniards. He also lined up some polo-playing buddies from his days at Harvard. This unusual mix gathered at San Antonio before moving to Florida, where Roosevelt and fellow officer Colonel Leonard Wood pulled strings to get the Rough Riders, as they called themselves (having rejected other monikers proposed by the press, such as "Teddy's Terrors" and "Teddy's Texas Tarantulas"), booked onto transports for passage across the Florida Strait.

Well they might have wanted to get out of training camp and into combat. Battle deaths in the Spanish-American War were very light as wars go: less than four hundred Americans fell to enemy fire. American soldiers faced far greater danger from tropical diseases contracted on the way to the battlefield than they did once they got there. Ten times as many succumbed to malaria, yellow fever, and dysentery as to Spanish bullets and bayonets.

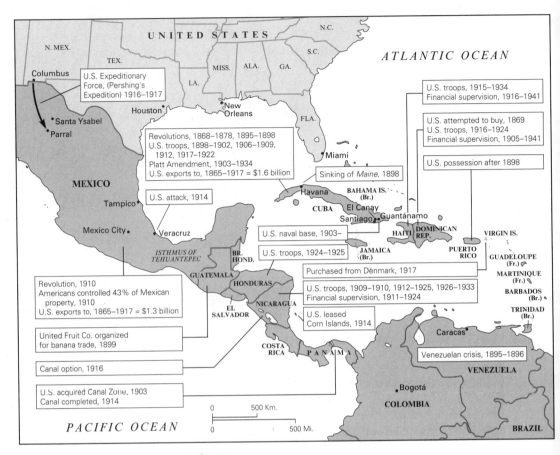

Central America and the Caribbean

Outfitting the troops (many in wool winter uniforms since there were not enough summer khakis to go around), arranging for provisions (including, as it turned out, some poisonously putrid meat that laid hundreds of American soldiers low), training the men (using officers who had not seen regular combat for more than thirty years, if at all), putting them up (in camps that often showed an abysmal ignorance regarding basic principles of cleanliness), and transporting them to Cuba (several weeks into the Caribbean hurricane season) required until the middle of June. During the latter part of that month, some eighteen thousand troops of the American expeditionary force landed in Cuba. The Spanish commander on the island chose not to challenge the landing, preferring to save his troops for later battles.

When those later battles came, their results showed that he should not have waited. At San Juan Hill (where Roosevelt and the Rough Riders gave a good account of themselves), El Canay, and, ultimately, Santiago, American forces soundly defeated the Spanish. The capture of Santiago in July, shortly after the American destruction of the Spanish fleet harbored there, effectively ended the Cuban phase of the fighting, although the details of an armistice required another month to work out.

Part of the reason for the delay was that the war had spread far beyond the Caribbean. Despite the fact that the situation in Cuba had dominated headlines in the United States, American military strategists well understood that a declaration of war against Spain would make Spanish possessions around the world fair game for American soldiers and, especially, sailors. Before the war started, the Navy Department had formulated contingency plans for dealing with the Spanish; the plan in effect at the time of the war's outbreak called for the American Asiatic fleet under Commodore George Dewey to steam to the Philippines and destroy the Spanish naval squadron at Manila.

As soon as the fighting commenced, Dewey weighed anchor from Hong Kong, where the British had been kind enough to allow him to provision, and set off for Manila. On arrival, he engaged the handful of Spanish ships in the bay and destroyed them within a matter of hours without loss of American life or craft. By noon on May 1, Dewey commanded the waters near the Philippine capital.

Conquering the land in the area and in the rest of the Philippines was much harder and took far longer. Dewey had to wait for reinforcements of ground troops to arrive from the United States. The outcome was never in doubt: since American ships controlled the approaches to the Philippines, Dewey could ensure that American reinforcements got through and Spanish reinforcements did not. The only question was how much resistance the Spanish would put up.

Actually, there was another question as well. For several years the situation in the Philippines had mirrored the situation in Cuba: local nationalists, upset at their treatment as inferiors by the Spanish colonial authorities, had waged a revolt. But in the Philippine case the revolt had fizzled out just before the United States declared war on Spain. The leader of the insurgents, Emilio Aguinaldo, had surrendered and gone into exile.

The onset of hostilities between Americans and Spanish seemed to Aguinaldo an opportune moment to resume the fight for Philippine independence. He hurried to intercept Dewey, about to embark for Manila, and hitched a ride back home. Because Dewey lacked ground troops, the American commodore calculated that Aguinaldo might help speed Spain's surrender by remobilizing his freedom fighters. Confusion later clouded the issue of what sort of bargain Dewey and Aguinaldo struck: Aguinaldo claimed that Dewey promised to support Philippine independence in exchange for collaboration against the Spanish; Dewey denied doing any such thing. No paper trail traced the negotiations, such as they might have been. Aguinaldo said that when he had suggested something in writing, he had been assured that the word of an American naval officer was guarantee enough. Traveling aboard an American warship, still separated from his fighting forces, the Filipino leader was in no position to insist.

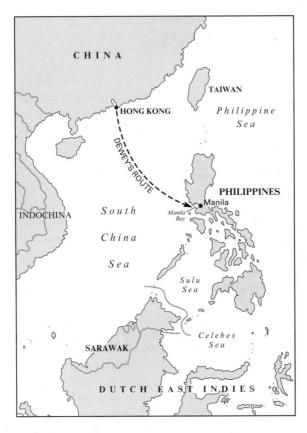

The Philippines During the
Spanish-American War

During the several weeks after Dewey's victory in Manila Bay, Aguinaldo's troops succeeded in wresting control of most of the Philippines from the Spanish. At the beginning of August, only the city of Manila remained in Spanish hands. By this time sufficient numbers of American ground forces had arrived to allow a landing and an attack. The Spanish found themselves confronting two armies: the American and the Filipino. The two armies were now cooperating only in the sense of sharing Spain as an enemy; the Filipinos had caught on that the Americans might have aims in the Philippines besides Philippine independence, while Dewey took care not to make any (more?) commitments binding the United States past the end of hostilities against Spain.

The Spanish commander, weighing considerations of Spanish honor and his own, judged that it would be less humiliating to acknowledge the termination of more than three hundred years of Spanish rule in the Philippines by handing his sword to a general of the United States army than to surrender to the rebel Aguinaldo. The Filipinos guessed that something like this might happen, and they assaulted the city. The Spanish stoutly resisted the Filipino attack but offered only token opposition to a simultaneous American assault. After a cu-

Dewey's victory at Manila in 1898 was almost as easy and one-sided as this
illustration suggests. *The Bettman Archive*

rious battle in which the Spanish barred Manila's front gates to the Filipinos
even as they let the Americans in at the back, the Americans wound up in
possession of the city, and the Filipinos wound up frustrated. Rendering the
whole affair more ironic was the fact that the battle of Manila, like the 1815
battle of New Orleans during the War of 1812, took place after the diplomats
had negotiated a formal end to the fighting. In this case, however, the delay of
the news was deliberate, or at least the result of a deliberate act, rather than
the consequence of a technological shortfall: Dewey earlier had cut the telegraph cable in order to disrupt Spanish communications.

Getting from the armistice of August 12 to the Treaty of Paris of December
10 required much talking and evaluating of options. The principal American
options involved how much to claim as spoils of war. At the beginning of the
conflict, American anti-imperialists, who doubted warhawk claims of solicitude for the welfare of oppressed Cubans, had called the war faction's bluff
and inserted into the war resolution an amendment barring the United States
from annexing Cuba. The war advocates had to accept the Teller amendment (named for Colorado Republican senator Henry Teller) or else admit the

selfishness of their motives. They ground their teeth and went along with the maneuver.

But they had their revenge regarding the Philippines. It had not occurred to Senator Teller to include that distant archipelago in his disclaimer; as a result, the McKinley administration enjoyed the option of taking title to the Philippines from Spain. McKinley evidently struggled with the issue before deciding that he ought to exercise the option. The alternatives were not especially promising. To leave the islands in Spanish control would create a tumult in the United States. If the Spanish had not been fit to govern Cuba, what fitted them to govern the Philippines? Besides, though American casualties in the Philippines had been relatively light, the McKinley administration would have had serious problems justifying those casualties and the expenses of the Philippine campaign if it merely restored the status quo.

Granting the islands independence made sense to many Americans but not to the administration. McKinley and his advisers contended—with good reason—that given the predatory atmosphere of the times, an independent Philippines would not last long. Germany already was lurking in the area. Japan was likewise seeking to extend its grasp. Britain or France might move simply to preempt Germany, Japan, or each other. Some persons suggested Philippine independence under an American protectorate. This suggestion presupposed greater altruism than Americans possessed toward the Filipinos: it would saddle the United States with the liabilities of defending the Philippines against foreign attack without availing the United States of the benefits of ownership. The protectorate proposal went nowhere.

The administration settled on annexation. American navalists, led by Mahan, liked annexation because it gave the United States control of Manila Bay—and, even better, the deeper and more protected harbor of Subic Bay. Commercial expansionists saw the Philippines as an entrepôt to the Orient, especially to the China market. (Just weeks earlier, amid the applause for Dewey, the navalists and commercial expansionists had finally persuaded Congress to annex Hawaii.) Missionaries—Protestant missionaries, that is—viewed the Filipinos, 90 percent of whom were Catholic, as constituting a field of souls awaiting harvest. McKinley later claimed to have arrived only reluctantly at his decision to annex. He said he had sweated and prayed over the issue long and hard before receiving divine guidance. "There was nothing left to do," he said of the islands and their inhabitants, "but take them all, and educate the Filipinos, and uplift and civilize them."

Inducing the Spanish to agree to American annexation of the Philippines was not particularly difficult, since Spain had few cards left to play. To soften the blow, the United States agreed to pay Spain $20 million, in keeping with the American diplomatic conceit that the United States never stole, only purchased, territory. The Paris treaty also transferred Puerto Rico and Guam, two islands that had similarly escaped the attention of Senator Teller, to the United States. Last but certainly not least, the Spanish consented to clear out of Cuba.

The Wages of Empire: The Philippines

The 1898 Treaty of Paris was hardly the last word on the issue of Philippine annexation. The Senate still had to approve the treaty, and approval was no sure thing. While the war was going on, the glorious news from the front drowned out the complaints of American anti-imperialists, but once the shooting stopped and the bargaining began, the anti-imperialists commenced a campaign against annexation. The anti-imperialist movement was a diverse coalition, including Republicans (Teller and Massachusetts senator George Hoar, among others), Democrats (most conspicuously William Jennings Bryan, the past and twice-future presidential nominee), captains of industry (steelman Andrew Carnegie) and of labor (Samuel Gompers of the American Federation of Labor), denizens of the ivory tower (Presidents Charles Eliot of Harvard University and David Starr Jordan of Stanford), journalists (E. L. Godkin of *The Nation* and Carl Schurz of *Harper's*), other writers (Mark Twain), and many more besides.

Some of the anti-imperialists made their case on the ground that an American takeover of the Philippines would deprive the Filipinos of their right to govern themselves; but this argument did not persuade very many people since it seemed to imply that the Filipinos would do a better job governing Filipinos than Americans could. To most Americans, such a contention sounded absurd. How could Filipinos, who had no tradition of self-government, know as much about governing as Americans, who had been running their own affairs for more than a century—and were Caucasians to boot?

Besides, selfless arguments almost never win in American politics (or the politics of other countries). Americans (and other people) considering a particular course of action want to know what is in it for them. Regarding the Philippines, the anti-imperialists replied: Nothing but expense and worry. To take the Philippines would cost Americans piles of money at the least. The United States would have to increase the size of its army and navy and prepare to fight the Germanys and Japans of the world. If war preparations did not suffice to warn off aggressors, the cost would escalate much further as Americans died defending Filipinos. Such entanglements were what the sages of American foreign relations—Washington, Jefferson, John Quincy Adams—had warned about from the start. Adams, in particular, had also warned that enlisting in the causes of others would corrupt American institutions, demoting liberty as an American priority and elevating force. The anti-imperialists considered this the most pernicious effect of annexation. Endlessly they recited the example of republican Rome, which had lost its virtue when it acquired an empire. An imperial America might gain the world but would lose its soul.

The anti-imperialists slipped from this high moral ground when some among them injected the specter of race mingling into the debate. What in the world did America need with millions of colored people, they asked, when it had not figured out what to do with the colored folk it already contained? American blacks at least had a chance of making something of themselves, being surrounded by the higher civilization of whites; Filipinos, in their backward native environment, would be nearly hopeless. Furthermore, if the Spanish experience afforded any example, annexation would invite miscegenation. Filipinos might be happy and pleasant people by their own standards, many Americans conceded. But would you want your daughter to marry one?

The imperialists rebutted each of the anti-imperialist arguments. Depriving Filipinos of the right of self-government was no more serious than depriving children of the right of self-government. Someday the Filipinos would be able to look after themselves; in the meantime, the United States was justified in acting in loco parentis. An imperial policy would be expensive but no more expensive than a policy that ignored America's global interests. Whether the anti-imperialists liked it or not, the world was an increasingly competitive place, and those who did not join the competition would find themselves at the mercy of those who did. By fearing for America's republican future, anti-imperialists betrayed a lack of confidence in the strength and resilience of democracy. American democracy had survived repeated foreign and domestic crises, including a civil war; it would not be destroyed because the American flag waved proudly in the breeze over some islands far away. Nor would the political attachment of the Filipinos to the United States corrupt American society. And who said anything about marrying?

The imperialists won the debate, but not by much. And their victory only followed a torpedoing of the anti-imperialist case by one of the antis' leaders, William Jennings Bryan. Though Bryan had convincingly lost the 1896 presidential election to McKinley, he was an unregenerate optimist and hoped to even the score in 1900. Bryan wished to clear the deck of the Philippine issue, which he throught would cloud the campaign. Besides, as he pointed out, if the Senate rejected the Paris treaty, America would remain technically at war with Spain, an awkward situation for both countries. By accepting the treaty, the Senate could detach the issue of the Philippines' future from the issue of the war with Spain. Then the American government could deal with the Philippines on that country's separate merits.

From this combination of reasons, Bryan directed his followers in the Senate to support the Paris treaty. The Bryanite votes provided just the margin the McKinley administration needed for victory. Yeas outnumbered nays by 57 to 27—1 more yea than the necessary two-thirds. On February 6, 1899, six months after the fighting ceased, the Spanish-American War formally ended.

It ended not a moment too soon. Several hours before the Senate approved the Paris treaty, a new conflict broke out in the Philippines. For some time after the August battle of Manila, the Filipinos had hoped that the Americans would live up to their democratic traditions and grant Philippine independence. Filipino diplomats traveled to Washington to make their case to McKinley and then to Paris to urge their views on the American negotiating team. They contended that Spain could not convey ownership of the Philippines to the Americans since Spain had never acquired legitimate title; title remained with the Filipinos, as title to any country invariably remains with that country's inhabitants. All the Filipino envoys got for their trouble was a runaround by the McKinley administration; the administration had decided to annex, and that was going to be that.

But the Filipinos had not exhausted their arguments. Unheeded in Paris and Washington, they took to the mountains of the Philippines to continue the debate with bullets. Ignoring injunctions to lay down their arms, they launched a war of independence against the Americans.

The Philippine War, the direct result of the Spanish-American War, lasted far longer than that conflict and produced much more in the way of death and destruction. The majority of the deaths and most of the destruction befell Filipinos, a fact that did little to endear America's new subjects to their new rulers. After unsuccessfully challenging the Americans in regular combat, the Filipino soldiers adopted a guerrilla strategy. Like most guerrilla contests, this one brought out the worst in both sides. Filipino fighters requested, then demanded, the support of Filipinos living in the countryside. If they did not receive enough of it fast enough, they punished the laggards, often harshly. The Americans discouraged Filipinos from assisting the guerrillas, by means including torture. The technique that gained the greatest notoriety was the "water cure," in which a subject being interrogated was forced to swallow more water than his stomach could hold and then had his stomach pummeled or kicked until he chose to cooperate with the interrogators, or occasionally died. Ironically for the Americans, and tragically for the Filipinos, the American military commanders in the Philippines felt themselves compelled to resort to the same reconcentration tactics the Spanish had used in Cuba, and which Americans had condemned as barbarous. The results of the American policy in the Philippines, in terms of lives lost among the persons reconcentrated, were comparable to those of the Spanish policy in Cuba.

Gradually most of the Filipinos decided that they could not win and that continuing the war compared unfavorably to accepting American rule. American officials made this decision easier than it might have been by offering educated Filipinos, even some who had taken part in the fighting, a share in the islands' government. This policy of attraction drew all but the hardest core of the nationalists out of the mountains and back into civilian society; by 1901 the resistance had lost most of its energy. When Aguinaldo fell into an American trap and was captured, and soon thereafter publicly swore allegiance to the American government, the fighting all but ceased. What little resistance remained caused the Americans no trouble.

Progressives and Imperialists

The American policy of coopting the Filipino nationalists was not entirely cynical. Despite Americans' preoccupation with what served American interests, they were not immune to considerations of what might benefit the Filipinos.

The good of the Filipinos never weighed more in the scales of American policy making than the good of Americans, but when American interests did not dictate one course of action over another, Filipino interests sometimes tipped the balance.

Besides, Americans at the turn of the twentieth century were sufficiently self-centered to believe that what served American interests usually served Filipino interests as well. Rarely in history have American leaders been so sure they knew what ailed humankind and how to fix it. The period of the presidencies of Theodore Roosevelt, William Howard Taft, and Woodrow Wilson was the great age of progressivism. The progressives came from both major political parties and from various occupations, but they all believed that the ills of life in a modern industrial society could be substantially mitigated by intelligent people acting through government on behalf of society as a whole. The progressives placed much store in education, being convinced that understanding a problem was halfway to solving it. They revered democracy, often saying that the cure for democracy's shortcomings was more democracy. They were whiggishly optimistic, judging that nearly any problem could be cured by progressive legislation or other social action. On the whole the progressives were a pretty sunny bunch of confident, energetic, and capable people.

But there was also a darker side to progressivism. When progressives touted education, what they often had in mind was not an open-ended seeking after truth but an instilling of the values of well-educated America into less fortunate groups. The progressives particularly targeted recent immigrants, who brought their own sets of values and customs across the ocean with them. The progressives promoted education as a means of "Americanizing" such people: that is, making them over in the pattern of the progressives. When progressives glorified democracy, they had a particular kind of democracy in mind. Not for them the democracy of the urban political machines, of Tammany Hall and its imitators in other cities, despite the fact that the big-city bosses (or often their front men) were duly elected and reelected by their constituents. The progressives had a much more genteel vision of democracy: they conceived of scrubbed and schooled voters casting their ballots against Boss Tweed and his henchmen and in favor of good-government reformers—candidates much like progressives themselves. The progressives were optimistic, yet not uniformly so. Certain social problems might be too much for people to solve of their own free will. In such cases, people could use the assistance of the strong arm of government coercion. The movement to prohibit alcohol, for instance, represented an effort by progressives (and others) to enforce respectable middle-class behavior on working-class, tavern-frequenting types.

It was no coincidence that the same period that saw the blossoming of American progressivism also witnessed the flowering of American imperialism. Much of what the imperialists were trying to accomplish abroad, in places like the Philippines, was what the progressives were trying to accomplish at home. In fact, many of the most imperialistically minded American leaders were also the most progressively minded. Albert Beveridge purpled the Senate chamber with a rousing proannexation speech during the debate over the Philippines;

Beveridge later helped organize the Progressive party. Teddy Roosevelt, that advocate of the martial virtues, wielded his Big Stick as energetically against corporate malefactors at home as against rival foreigners abroad. William Howard Taft, the first American governor-general of the Philippines, as president busted even more trusts than Roosevelt. Woodrow Wilson belonged to the wrong party to be an overt imperialist (Democrats attacked imperialism in large part as a means of breaking the Republican lock on the presidency); but in intervening in the Mexican revolution, in the First World War in Europe, and in the Russian Revolution, Wilson showed himself to be as militantly assertive as the most flagrant American imperialist. Historically, Wilson is commonly considered the greatest progressive president.

"Progressive" has never been a dirty word in American politics; "imperialist" usually has. Yet in certain respects, American imperialism was simply American progressivism gone international. Chronologically, progressivism began at the level of the cities, where reformers took on corrupt bosses and graft-ridden machines. Progressivism advanced to the state level when civic reformers realized that state governments set the tone and the ground rules for much of what went on in the cities. After reform slowed at the state level and the progressives discovered that many problems were too big for the states to handle, progressivism hit the national stage. Finally, progressives—especially progressive presidents Roosevelt and Wilson—became convinced that the realm of international affairs had to be progressivized if America as a nation were to live in peace and prosperity. Roosevelt's corollary to the Monroe Doctrine conferred on the United States police power for the Western Hemisphere, imposing American ideas of order and fair dealing on America's neighbors; Wilson led Americans to war in 1917 to make the world, as he put it, "safe for democracy."

China and the Open Door

American progressives looking for evidence that the world required remaking did not have to look any farther than China—which admittedly was rather far from the United States in miles but which with ongoing improvements in ocean travel and telegraphic communications increasingly seemed part of America's Pacific neighborhood. (Upon American annexation of the Philippines, East Asia became even more a part of America's neighborhood.) China during the late 1890s was nearly at the end of its rope. The rope in question was quite long, stretching back more than 250 years as it related to the current Qing (or Manchu) dynasty and more than 2,000 years as it related to a unified China under a central authority. As the nineteenth century drew to a close, both the Qing dynasty and the concept of a unified China were at serious risk. Since the Taiping Rebellion of midcentury, China had continued its slow process of disintegration. The presence of foreign merchants and soldiers in the treaty ports exacerbated the process by capitalizing on China's weakness to extract and enforce concessions. The Chinese were of two minds regarding contacts with the Western countries. Some Chinese sought to shut the Westerners out entirely; others argued for using Western technology to defend China against the West. The latter group, waving the banner of "self-strengthening," gained the upper hand during the 1860s and 1870s and adopted a program of importing selected Western products, studying Western languages and ideas, and building a Western-style army and navy.

But Chinese conservatives opposed the self-strengtheners. To some extent, their opposition reflected an honest Confucian regard for precedent. It would be unfilial of the emperor, they said, to alter traditions established by his predecessors; it would be equally unfilial of the Chinese people at large to overturn the ways of their ancestors. To some extent, the conservatives' opposition reflected the natural inclination of those in power to resist whatever might diminish their power. Getting ahead in Chinese officialdom was a trying process, and having invested their careers in learning to play by one set of rules, Qing bureaucrats were reluctant to see the rules change. Against this entrenched opposition, the efforts of the self-strengtheners made progress only slowly.

Too slowly, as it turned out. Japan's defeat of China in the Sino-Japanese War of 1894–1895 precipitated a psychological crisis in China. To have to bend to the will of the Westerners had been hard enough for Chinese to accept, but to be humiliated by Japan, which for centuries had existed in China's shadow, was too much to bear. The terms of surrender included, besides the acceptance of Japanese primacy in Korea, the loss of Taiwan to Japan and an indemnity that amounted to three times the Chinese government's yearly revenues.

The European powers had attempted, with some effect but not enough for the Chinese to notice, to get the Japanese to soften their demands. No love of China motivated the Westerners; they simply wanted to prevent Japan from taking so much from China that there would not be anything left for anyone else. Japan's pressure on China prompted the Europeans to increase their own pressure; as they did so, it looked as though China might go the way of Africa, sliced into pieces by the imperialists.

Chinese reformers made a last-ditch effort to salvage their country and their culture from the barbarian assault. A group of several hundred examination candidates (bureaucratic hopefuls) petitioned the Guangxu emperor to make major changes in China's system of education, economy, and government. The emperor mulled the matter over—for three years—and agreed to implement many of the reformers' demands.

But conservatives retreated only to counterattack. They persuaded the young emperor's aunt, the empress dowager Cixi, to force her nephew into premature retirement. She then threw her support to the standpatters, leading to the rout of the reformers. Many fled to other countries; some died on the barricades.

American leaders observed China's vicissitudes with concern. Although the China market had never lived up to the expectations of American merchants, they continued to hope it would. But clearly it would not if the Japanese and

Beijing looks calm in this picture, but the troop column that these American soldiers were part of had to fight its way to the city in 1900 to relieve the foreign community trapped there in the Boxer rebellion. *The Bettman Archive*

the Europeans partitioned the bulk of China into colonies or exclusive spheres of influence. Therefore, the merchants opposed such partitioning. Meanwhile, American missionaries kept the attention of another influential sector of the American public—evangelical Christians—focused on events in China. The missionaries did not like to see the Chinese victimized by European and Japanese imperialists; in addition, the missionaries suspected that if the Europeans and Japanese partitioned China, they would not leave much room for American missionaries.

Both the merchants and the missionaries appealed to Washington to do something to prevent the sundering of China. Like all persuasive arguments in matters of foreign policy, this one joined self-interest to altruism. Preserving China from the imperialists would benefit both American merchants, who could continue to hawk their wares in China, and American missionaries, who could continue their efforts to save Chinese souls. It would benefit the Chinese, who would be able to buy American products and join American churches and who did not want to have their country stolen out from under them by the foreign imperialists.

The merchants' and missionaries' arguments found a sympathetic hearing within the McKinley administration. McKinley's secretary of state was John

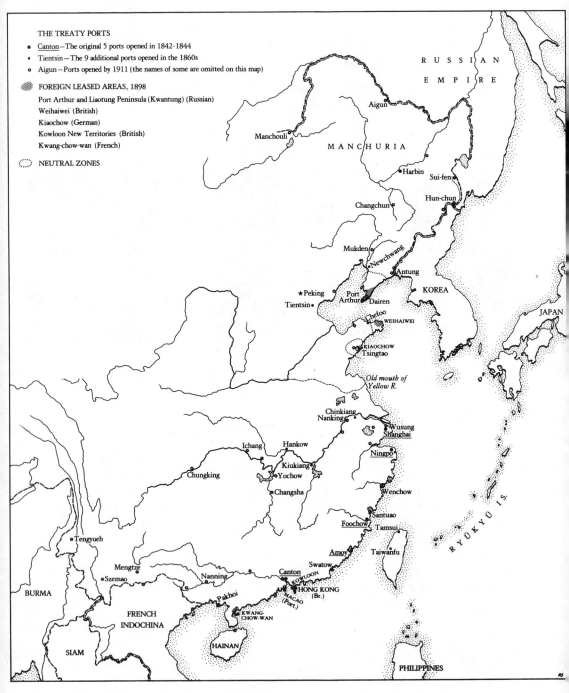

THE TREATY PORTS

- Canton—The original 5 ports opened in 1842-1844
- Tientsin—The 9 additional ports opened in the 1860s
- Aigun—Ports opened by 1911 (the names of some are omitted on this map)

FOREIGN LEASED AREAS, 1898

Port Arthur and Liaotung Peninsula (Kwantung) (Russian)
Weihaiwei (British)
Kiaochow (German)
Kowloon New Territories (British)
Kwang-chow-wan (French)

NEUTRAL ZONES

East Asia in the Late Nineteenth Century

Hay, formerly personal secretary to Abraham Lincoln and a man who had cut his teeth in government during the tenure of the archexpansionist and Pacificist (as definitely distinguished from pacifist) William Seward. Hay proposed a strategem reminiscent of the promulgation of the Monroe Doctrine. Hay had reason to believe that the British would support a warning to the other powers to lay off of China, just as the British had supported the Monroe administration's warning to lay off of the Western Hemisphere. Hay's reason for this belief was that the British had broached the idea of just such a warning, much as they had broached the similar idea in Monroe's day. And just as John Quincy Adams and James Monroe had declined a joint Anglo-American statement in 1823, leaving the British to recognize their own interests in the affair, so John Hay and William McKinley decided to go it alone in 1899 and let the British tag along.

The vehicle Hay chose to declare the American policy was a diplomatic note circulated to the governments of the great powers. This first Open Door note started its rounds in September 1899 and declared American adherence to the principle of "equality of treatment of all foreign trade throughout China." Tariffs, transportation charges, and the like should be the same for every comer. The point was to prevent the powers from enforcing spheres of economic interest in China to the detriment of merchants from the United States. Hay requested that the powers announce their backing for such a policy of fair dealing.

It was a clever ploy. Hay knew the British would accept the Open Door principle; they had indicated as much, and with all their troubles in South Africa and elsewhere, they did not want to have to join a scramble for China. The Japanese were still trying to digest their meal from the Sino-Japanese War and were not itching for a tussle with Westerners just yet. The French were fairly well satisfied with the colonies they had recently seized in Indochina and were not eager to push north. Although the leaders of Britain, Japan, and France did not appreciate Hay's putting words in their mouths, none sufficiently opposed the American position to denounce it publicly. Their diplomats muttered in their beards, producing equivocal replies that committed them to nothing—but allowed Hay to claim their assent.

Russia and Germany caused more worries. Both countries had recently grabbed bits of Chinese ocean frontage, and both seemed hungry and aggressive enough to try to grab more. But as things happened, neither St. Petersburg nor Berlin cared to start something in East Asia that might spread to other regions, particularly Europe, where the balance of power was growing more precarious by the day. With a conspicuous lack of grace, the Russians and Germans acquiesced in Hay's statement.

Hay had little time to congratulate himself on his shrewdness. As rulers beleaguered at home so often do, the Chinese empress dowager tried to shift blame from herself to outsiders. She joined forces with a xenophobic secret society known as the Boxers and in 1900 declared war on foreigners in China. The Boxers killed those foreigners they could catch in the countryside and then marched to Beijing to besiege the foreign quarter there. A massacre appeared imminent. But the foreigners dug in and managed to keep the Boxers at bay. The Western and Japanese governments hastily put together a rescue force, including American troops pulled from the Philippines, and directed the rescuers to fight their way to Beijing from the sea. They succeeded in doing so, lifting the siege after two months with little additional loss of foreign life, but more than a little of Chinese.

With large numbers of foreign troops now on the ground in China, and with the foreign governments hopping mad, partition appeared more probable than ever. This was especially true in light of the fact that the foreign governments could reasonably claim that the Chinese government no longer possessed the power to enforce its own laws, including those that should have protected foreign nationals.

As before, John Hay sought to prevent such a fate befalling China—and American interests there. In July 1900 he circulated a second Open Door note, which amplified the first and explicitly called for continued "Chinese territorial and administrative entity": in other words, no partition.

As before, the Europeans and the Japanese acceded to the American position, less out of respect for the Americans or the Chinese than out of fear of each other. To them, China just was not worth fighting over at this stage.

The McKinley administration's establishment of the Open Door policy toward China had two effects. The first was to put the other great powers on notice regarding where the United States stood with respect to China. From the narrow perspective of 1900, it did not really matter much where the United States stood; Americans were not ready to put steel and lead behind their views on China. Yet for future reference this was worthwhile knowledge.

The second effect was to delude the American people into thinking that their country exercised more power in East Asia than it actually did. The Republicans were not above claiming a moral and diplomatic victory for the McKinley administration: the administration had spoken forthrightly in defense of China, and the other powers had backed off. *Post hoc ergo propter hoc.* Gradually at first, but significantly over time, Americans came to consider themselves the protectors of China. This attitude and the fact that it was based on specious reasoning eventually had very large consequences.

No-Fault Imperialism: Latin America

American policy toward East Asia was in the classical tradition of power balancing, of keeping competitors at bay by keeping them preoccupied with each other. Wars do not usually happen when two opponents are evenly matched or think they are; governments tend not to start wars they might lose or even need a long time to win. (Civil wars and revolutions—conflicts fought by entities other than sovereign governments, at least on one side—are a different story.) Wars usually break out when one country thinks itself sufficiently stronger than its rivals that it can defeat them fairly easily. Sometimes such countries are wrong; the bad guessers lose or expend an excessive amount of energy winning. The point of power balancing is to keep potential enemies from getting too confident. This was the approach the British took in Europe through most of the nineteenth century, and it was the American approach in East Asia at the beginning of the twentieth.

The other common way to prevent wars is for one country to be so much stronger than all its rivals that none of the rivals will risk crossing it. If governments do not like to start wars they *might* lose, they like even less to start wars they are *sure* to lose. No country has ever established hegemony all around the world; the best any country has been able to manage is regional hegemony. During the heyday of the Roman empire, the Romans controlled a big territory centered on the Mediterranean; within this region there prevailed a *pax Romana,* or Roman peace, the result of would-be upstarts knowing that Rome's legions would quickly quash any peace breaking.

The Monroe Doctrine represented an effort by the United States to establish hegemony—a *pax Americana*—in the Western Hemisphere. The effort lacked teeth until late in the nineteenth century, but by the time of the Venezuelan boundary dispute and the Spanish-American War, it was starting to bite. The war with Spain demonstrated that the United States was far and away the dominant military power in the Americas. The chief question that remained was what the United States intended to do with its dominance. Washington annexed Puerto Rico, making it an American colony. As for Cuba, the precipitant of the war and the prize of the Caribbean, that island's fate was complicated by the self-denying Teller amendment.

When the war ended, American forces occupied Cuba, effectively controlling as much of Cuban life as the officers of the occupation chose to. American authorities were pledged to Cuban independence, but they were determined to take their time delivering it and to ensure that Cuban independence would not damage what they conceived to be American interests in the area. Partly because of the existence of the Teller amendment, and partly because the Cuban revolutionaries were exhausted after years of battling the Spanish, no insurgency against the American occupation developed, such as in the Philippines. The Americans had promised to go home and leave Cuba to the Cubans; until the Americans showed plainly that they were reneging on their promise, there was no percentage in picking a fight with them.

The American occupying force was commanded by Roosevelt's friend General Leonard Wood, and it set about putting Cuban life on a soundly progressive footing. The first order of business was repairing the damage wrought by war and Spanish neglect. This required time but was well under way within a couple of years. As part of this reconstructive effort, Wood's engineers and doctors (Wood himself had an M.D.) undertook to wipe out yellow fever by attacking the mosquitoes that transmitted it. American educators revamped the school system the Spanish had left behind, making it possible for millions of Cubans to learn to read and write ensuring that what they read—at least in the schools—instilled the values of middle-class America. Although instruction took place in the Spanish language, many of the texts were translations of books written for students in places like Boston and Kansas City.

Wood and the Americans sought to foster conditions that would produce political stability in Cuba, which in turn, they believed, would produce economic stability and growth. Cuban prosperity and happiness, to the American way of thinking, depended on close economic ties between the United States and Cuba. The American economy at this time was one of the wonders of the world; by hitching a ride with the Americans, the Cubans likewise would enjoy the benefits of economic advancement. Cuba should be opened to American investment, which would provide jobs for Cuban peasants, besides guaranteeing continued American interest in Cuba's security and welfare.

Wood oversaw the gathering of a Cuban constitutional convention that had the purpose (for the Americans) of making sure that the good work of the occupation forces would not be undone by Cuban carelessness and (for the Cubans) of convincing the Americans to leave sooner rather than later. The constitution the conventioneers drafted met the Americans' requirements— which was not particularly surprising, since Wood kept them writing until they came up with a document he and his superiors in Washington liked. The final draft included provisions that closely circumscribed the independence the Teller amendment was supposed to have promised the Cubans. The most important provision was the so-called Platt amendment (named for American senator Orville Platt of Connecticut but actually composed by Secretary of War Elihu Root), which gave the United States the right to intervene in Cuba to preserve Cuban independence, to defend lives and property, and generally to look after American security needs. Most Cubans disliked the Platt amendment for obvious nationalistic reasons; but if such was the price of ending the American occupation, they were willing to accept it.

America's limited grant of independence to the Cubans left the United States in a position other imperialists could only envy (and attempt to emulate, as some did). By relinquishing authority over the day-to-day running of Cuban affairs, Washington absolved itself of responsibility for what befell the Cubans. Were Cubans poor? That was not America's problem. Were Cuba's leaders corrupt and brutal? Tough luck. But by retaining ultimate power over Cuba's foreign and economic policy, Washington ensured that American interests were well looked after. Did foreign powers threaten America's favored position in Cuba? Cite the Platt amendment and the Monroe Doctrine and chase them off. Did some Cuban government threaten the security of American investments in Cuba? Send in the marines.

Responsibility without power is an unenviable combination: you get blamed for problems you have no way of fixing. Responsibility with power is a fairer deal: you have to cope with the problems, but you have tools for doing so. Power without responsibility—what the United States enjoyed in Cuba—is what only children and great powers can get away with: you do what you want and let others clean up the mess you leave behind.

The American domination of Cuba soon came under political assault in the island. Most Cubans objected to the duress under which the Cuban constitution had been written and contended that the Platt amendment had no validity. A 1903 trade treaty between the United States and Cuba, which slashed tariffs between the two countries and tied the Cuban economy more closely than ever to the American economy, raised additional objections. Cuba was dependent on the United States not only politically, the critics charged, but also economically. Easy access to the American market for Cuban sugar was a mixed blessing at best: though it provided jobs for Cubans, it warped the Cuban economy by pushing it toward the production of a single crop. American investors bought up a great amount of farmland in Cuba and planted it to sugar, displacing producers of food crops, who in any event were being undercut by cheap imports from the mechanized farms of the United States. Cuban industry did not stand a chance against competition from American factories. Boosters of close Cuban-American economic relations might point out that the average income of Cubans increased with increasing trade between the two countries, but the critics countered by contending that averages masked wide disparities between the few wealthy of Cuba's cities and the many poor of the countryside. Besides, the economic colonization of Cuba by American capital was too high a cost to pay for marginally higher incomes.

Cuban resentment at American influence led to protests against the government the departing American troops left behind. That scandals and corruption surrounded the activity of the government did not help matters. In 1906 a rebellion broke out. President Taft responded by ordering American forces back to Cuba. A former judge himself (his real ambition, later achieved, had always been to be Supreme Court chief justice rather than president), Taft appointed a Minnesota judge, Charles Magoon, to head a provisional Cuban government. Somewhat like Solomon, Magoon offered to split the spoils of office between the leaders of the rebels and the incumbents. Unlike the real mother in the Solomon story, the rebels and the incumbents accepted Magoon's offer.

In buying off the insurgents, Magoon paved the way for the withdrawal of American troops, which took place early in 1909. At the same time, however, he helped institutionalize corruption in Cuban politics. Cubans dissatisfied with the status quo came to see that although the United States would tolerate no serious revolution–making in Cuba, Washington would not object to spoilsmanship and pocket lining by those in office. So the pockets got lined, and the revolution got postponed.

Cuba felt the weight of American hegemony more directly than any other Latin American country, but it was not alone in the kind of treatment it received. During the early years of the twentieth century, the United States broadened and deepened its influence in the southern two-thirds of the Western Hemisphere. In the rest of Latin America, as in Cuba, what Washington desired most was stability, usually defined to mean security for American investments and the prevention of undue European influence. These two objectives meshed with each other: conditions that jeopardized American investments usually jeopardized European investments as well, tempting European governments to act as bill collectors for their nationals and otherwise try to increase their influence.

Although Theodore Roosevelt and his associates in the executive branch of the American government were progressives, they were also Republicans. This implied that they placed great importance on contracts and financial obligations. If Latin Americans borrowed money, they ought to pay it back; if they resisted paying, they ought to be made to. Roosevelt had a hard time complaining too much when the Europeans dunned tardy regimes, even by threat of military force.

But such threatening violated the Monroe Doctrine. Roosevelt would not have been Roosevelt had he not insisted that other nations respect this hoary article of American international relations. To square the two principles—that governments ought not to be allowed to default on debts and that the Europeans ought to observe the Monroe Doctrine—Roosevelt devised a principle of his own. In 1904, following some brusque treatment of Venezuela by Germany, France, and Britain and concurrent with an impending default by the Dominican Republic, the president enunciated what came to be called the Roosevelt corollary to the Monroe Doctrine. The Roosevelt corollary asserted that to prevent other countries from enforcing proper behavior on the Latin Americans, Washington would undertake the duty itself. The United States would exercise an "international police power" to see to it that the Latin American countries met their obligations.

Predictably, most Latin Americans did not acquiesce kindly to the idea of the United States acting as the cop of the Western Hemisphere. They had not liked the idea of European intervention either, but most people, when given a choice, prefer bullies who live far away to ones who live next door.

As always, though, there were persons willing to adjust to the new power reality to claim a piece of the action. The Roosevelt corollary led to American military intervention in several countries—Cuba, Haiti, the Dominican Republic, Nicaragua, Honduras, Mexico—during the next three decades. In each country American officials looked for and eventually found locals who could accomplish, for a while anyway, the delicate feat of appeasing Washington without thoroughly alienating the masses of people in their own country. Those who undertook this assignment commonly comforted their consciences with the typical collaborator's rationale: that somebody has to do it, and if not me, then probably someone worse. They comforted their bank accounts by skimming taxes and shaking down officeholders. The American government usually looked the other way unless the grafting got so bad that the grafters' opponents took up arms. Then Washington sent in the marines and found a new set of collaborators.

There was one problem with the policy outlined by the Roosevelt corollary, though; it required too much effort on the part of the United States. Roosevelt himself never complained about the effort; he liked the exercise. But to many Americans, there seemed something incongruous about American troops acting as collection agents for European bankers. The Europeans made money off their loans, while American taxpayers picked up the tab for the cost of collection.

Roosevelt's successor Taft, who was smarter than most people gave him credit for being, had a better plan. Washington should encourage the Latin Americans to curtail their financial obligations to Europe in favor of closer ties to the United States. In particular, the Latin American governments should retire their European debts by taking out loans from American banks. This way the profits from the loans would flow north instead of east across the Atlantic, and there would be fewer objections in the United States to using American force to collect late payments. In fact, if Washington played its hand shrewdly and used American money to back regimes that arranged their priorities correctly—placing prompt payment at the head of the list—intervention might rarely be necessary. Moreover, the expansion of American loans and investments would contribute to hemispheric solidarity—always important in Washington's thinking—and encourage development of the Latin American economies. Economic development would benefit both the Latin Americans, who would see their living standards rise, and American farmers and manufacturers, who would watch their exports to Latin America increase.

Taft and Secretary of State Philander Knox practiced this dollar diplomacy toward several countries of Latin America (and less successfully toward East Asia). The best example of how the policy worked involved Nicaragua. In 1909 the Nicaraguan government of José Santos Zelaya faced a revolt by the numerous persons and groups he had antagonized during the course of his dictatorial rule. The Taft administration disliked Zelaya's policies, which included close financial connections to Europe; Zelaya had equally little use for Taft's policies. The decisive break between Washington and Managua came when Zelaya ordered the execution of a pair of Americans caught with the rebel forces. Washington responded by severing diplomatic ties to Zelaya's government and by providing support to the rebels, who proceeded to defeat Zelaya's troops and take power.

The Taft administration then resumed diplomatic relations with Nicaragua, now headed by the friendly and cooperative Adolfo Díaz, formerly an employee of an American company in Nicaragua. Díaz reversed his predecessor's pro-European policies, granting Americans favored treatment and borrowing from American banks to pay off his country's European creditors. When a new group of rebels rose up against Díaz in 1912, the United States again intervened, but this time on the side of the government. Washington sent marines to put down the revolt and safeguard Díaz—and American investments and loans.

The Big Stick and the Big Ditch: Panama

Although Americans tended to think of Latin America as a whole—for the purposes of the Monroe Doctrine, for instance—in practice the American government has always paid closest attention to Mexico, Central America, and the Caribbean basin. One reason for this extra attention has been proximity: people are naturally concerned about what happens nearby. The other reason has been the long-standing American interest in canal transit between the Atlantic and the Pacific. From the early nineteenth century onward, it was clear that any such canal would be built in Mexico or Central America; ships approaching or leaving the canal would pass through the Caribbean. The canal would be vital to the economic health of the United States, and American naval vessels would need to traverse the canal. (The perceived need for a canal increased greatly during the Spanish-American War when the battleship *Oregon* had to go clear around South America to get from the American west coast to Cuba and almost missed the fighting.)

After early flutters of interest in Mexico's Tehuantepec isthmus, Nicaragua and Panama (the latter still a province of Colombia) had become the prime possibilities for an interocean canal. The French trencher Ferdinand de Lesseps, fresh from his triumphal excavation of the Suez Canal, started slicing across Panama in the late 1870s, but mountains, jungles, and yellow fever forced him to abandon the project. The attention of canal builders then shifted to Nicaragua. The shift occurred, not because the Nicaraguan route was easier, shorter, or less expensive, which it was not, but because the French company that held the rights to dig in Panama wanted an extortionate price for surrendering those rights.

At the turn of the twentieth century, the French company's board of directors hired two agents, French engineer Philippe Bunau-Varilla and American lawyer William Cromwell, to represent the board. Bunau-Varilla and Cromwell first convinced the board to cut the asking price by more than half, to a mere $40 million, and then convinced the American Congress to authorize payment of $40 million for the rights.

There were two flies in the ointment, however. The first was Britain, which by the 1850 Clayton-Bulwer Treaty possessed a veto right over a Central American canal. The Roosevelt administration swatted this fly by negotiating a new treaty, the Hay-Pauncefote pact of 1901, which allowed the United States to build (and fortify) a canal on its own.

The second fly was the Colombian government. The Colombians did not want to approve the transfer of canal rights to the United States, chiefly because the French company's concession would expire in 1904, causing the rights and the $40 million or whatever the rights were worth to revert to Colombia. Bunau-Varilla and Cromwell were painfully aware that their hopes for a commission would expire at the same time; they redoubled their lobbying efforts.

At this point, their interests and those of the Roosevelt administration, which wanted to get started digging a canal as soon as possible, fell into line with the interests of nationalists in Panama. Colombia's hold on Panama had never been very firm; from Colombian independence in 1821 through the end of the nineteenth century, various Panamanian factions had averaged almost one rebellion against Colombian rule every year and a half. At the beginning

By the time they got to the bottom of this mountain range, some of the engineers and construction workers were wishing the great canal had gone through Nicaragua rather than Panama. *AP/Wide World Photos*

of the twentieth century, a bitter civil war wracked Colombia, encouraging the Panamanians to try again.

The Roosevelt administration likewise encouraged the Panamanians. When Bunau-Varilla told Roosevelt in the autumn of 1903 that an uprising was near, the president hinted strongly that the United States would look favorably on self-determination for the Panamanian people.

This was good enough for Bunau-Varilla, who relayed the message south. In November the rebellion began. American warships conveniently positioned nearby—under the terms of an 1846 treaty granting the United States transit rights across Panama—made sure that Colombia was unable to land troops to quell the uprising. (It was one of many ironies in the affair that the 1846 treaty had been designed to protect Colombia, then called New Granada, against outside aggression; now it was being invoked against Colombia.) Two days later Washington extended diplomatic recognition to the new government of Panama. Secretary of State Hay and Bunau-Varilla quickly devised a treaty by which the American government would guarantee Panama's independence and pay $10 million at once and $250,000 per year in exchange for rights to a ten-mile-wide canal zone across Panama.

The affair turned out well for all involved except Colombia. Panama got its independence, although later it would have second thoughts about relinquishing control of the canal zone. The United States got its canal—the Senate ratified the Hay–Bunau-Varilla Treaty at the beginning of 1904; construction commenced a few months later; and the canal opened to traffic in 1914. Bunau-Varilla and Cromwell got their commission. Indeed, the two agents got more: Bunau-Varilla went on to serve as the Panamanian minister to the United States, while Cromwell was appointed Panama's fiscal representative in the United States, a post he held for more than thirty years.

Though Roosevelt was mightily pleased with the outcome of the affair, the president could not escape a certain nagging of conscience regarding his role in fomenting a revolution against the Colombian government. At a cabinet meeting shortly after the event, he strenuously supported his actions—against no particular challenge. "Have I defended myself?" he demanded of those present. "You certainly have, Mr. President," Elihu Root replied. "You have shown that you were accused of seduction, and you have conclusively proved that you were guilty of rape."

Roosevelt Wins Peace Prize!
(Japan and Northeast Asia)

The Panama Canal's primary importance was economic. It speeded water transportation from one coast of the United States to the other and from some foreign countries to some American ports. Its secondary importance was strategic. It allowed the American navy to conserve ships by making it easier to shift vessels from the Atlantic to the Pacific and vice versa. (The fact that the canal had to be defended, thus adding to the navy's tasks, partially offset the convenience it afforded.)

The strategic element increased in significance during the ten years of the canal's construction. In Europe, the Germans were acting more bellicose by the month, causing the European powers to divide into two armed camps: Germany and Austria-Hungary against Britain, France, and Russia. The slightest incident, it seemed, might precipitate a bloodbath. If war came, the United States would be hard pressed to stay out. As during the Napoleonic wars, the belligerents doubtless would try to prevent American merchants from trading with the enemy; should Washington aggressively defend American neutral rights, somebody was bound to get provoked. At one point, the danger of war grew so great that Roosevelt felt obliged to intervene diplomatically, urging the French and Germans to settle their differences (over Morocco, in this case) peacefully; the resulting Algeciras conference of 1906 lessened the tension but did not resolve the underlying troubles.

The situation in Asia seemed equally threatening. The vultures continued to hover over China's barely breathing hulk. As soon as one landed, it appeared, the rest would surely move in. Japan was the likeliest candidate for first on the ground. Since the Sino-Japanese War of 1894–5, Japan had continued to expand its influence on the Asian mainland. Japan's industrial revolution was under full steam; like the other industrial nations, Japan was looking beyond its borders for markets and sources of supply. The Japanese labored under severe domestic deficiencies of iron ore and the kind of coal needed for steel production, but there was plenty of both on the Asian mainland—hence Japan's desire for a sphere of influence there. Korea had been the logical first component of a Japanese sphere; the Chinese province of Manchuria seemed the second. Despite the modest success of a yen diplomacy analogous to what Americans were practicing in Latin America, the Japanese felt that their position in northeastern Asia was insufficiently secure; Tokyo intended to remedy the insecurity.

To this point, none of the Western powers with interests in Asia considered Japan a major threat. Worrisome, to be sure: Japan's quick defeat of China demonstrated that the Japanese were stronger than the Westerners had thought. But China in the 1890s might have been knocked over by a feather, and the Japanese army and navy had yet to clash with the forces of an industrialized country. Nor had Japanese troops shown that they could stand up to white men in battle.

The Russians, in particular, underestimated the Japanese. The government of Czar Nicholas had designs of its own on Manchuria and Korea. The Japanese until now had not much objected to Russian activities in Manchuria, but when the Russians tried a ruble diplomacy in Korea, Tokyo got testy. The Japanese offered Russians a deal: Japan would stay out of Manchuria if Russia would stay out of Korea. The Russians greedily and imprudently declined the deal, hoping to win both Manchuria and Korea. The Japanese took offense; Japanese leaders judged that the Russians, with a huge and undeveloped empire of their own in Siberia, were unfairly trying to bottle up Japan.

To break the bottle the Japanese struck out militarily. Without warning or formal declaration of war, they attacked the Russian Pacific fleet. Shortly thereafter they sent ground troops smashing into Korea. By the time St. Petersburg regained its balance, the Japanese had entrenched themselves in key positions throughout the Korean peninsula.

The American government had been watching the events in Northeast Asia with mounting concern. When the war began, the Roosevelt administration quietly applauded the Japanese, deeming Russia the bigger threat to the stability of the region. But the rapidity and completeness of the Japanese victories on sea and land alarmed Washington. The goal of American policy was balance, and an overpowerful and overconfident Japan would jeopardize the balance. Before the Japanese could add to their victories over the Russians, Roosevelt offered to mediate. He invited Japan and Russia to send representatives to America—to Portsmouth, New Hampshire—to talk peace.

The Russians accepted with a sigh of relief. Not only were they losing, but the military reverses had helped touch off a revolution that was rattling the china in St. Petersburg even as the Japanese were rattling St. Petersburg in China.

The Japanese accepted, too, though with a show of reluctance. In command of the situation on the ground and hoping for a rich peace treaty, they played hard to get. In their coyness, Japanese leaders led the Japanese public to expect a big indemnity, which would go far toward assuaging the pain of those who had lost loved ones in the fighting. Behind their hesitation, however, Japan's leaders were happy enough to stop shooting and start talking, for they were almost out of ammunition and money, and they wanted to settle before their shortages became obvious.

Roosevelt, aware of Japan's predicament, quickly let Tokyo's envoys know that a large cash settlement was unrealistic. Russia was down but not defeated, and if allowed time to mobilize its massive resources, Russia might make Japan wish it had been more reasonable. With a conspicuous lack of grace, the Japanese negotiators accepted Roosevelt's argument. They persuaded the Russians to consent to Japanese control of Korea and forced Moscow to pull Russian troops out of Manchuria, but they dropped their demand for an indemnity.

For his part in writing the Portsmouth Treaty, Roosevelt won the recently created Nobel Peace Prize. That such an admirer of war as Roosevelt should win the peace prize was only slightly more incongruous than that the prize had been established by the inventor of dynamite. The prize proved to be about the only thanks Roosevelt got for his pains. The Japanese especially complained about being coerced by the American president into accepting an unfair settlement. It was a classic case of buck passing: the Japanese government found it easier to tell the Japanese people that the Americans had cheated them out of their indemnity than to own up to the fact that the government itself had exaggerated the likelihood of getting such an indemnity. Fortunately for the government, but unfortunately for Japanese-American relations, the Japanese people channeled their disappointment and anger eastward across the Pacific.

The Japanese did have other, legitimate causes for feeling angry at America. In the first decade of the twentieth century, anti-Asian agitation again cropped up, again in California. In 1906 the San Francisco school board voted to segregate children of Asian descent from Caucasian children—on the model of what schools in the American South were doing to children of African descent. The Japanese considered this a slap in the face and protested vociferously to Washington. Across Japan noisy and sometimes violent anti-American demonstrations, which the government did nothing to discourage, became regular political events.

Roosevelt deplored the action of the San Francisco board—What did those yahoos think they were doing, meddling in foreign affairs?—but he had no constitutional authority to overturn its decision. Instead he invited the board members to Washington for a stern lecture on American national interests and on how those interests were larger and more important than the parochial concerns of San Francisco parents. Yet notwithstanding his expostulations and the prestige of his office, Roosevelt got results only when he offered the Californians something concrete. In 1907 the president negotiated a "gentlemen's agreement" with the Japanese by which Japan suspended most emigration to the United States in return for San Francisco's consent to rescind its segregation order.

The accord solved the immediate problem but left some ominous loose ends. Most disturbing was the tendency of politicians on both sides of the Pacific to use the other country as a scapegoat. Demagogues in California blamed the troubles of American workers on Japanese immigrants; demagogues in Tokyo blamed shortcomings in Japan's foreign relations on American obstructionism.

While this tendency—an amalgam of racism, xenophobia, genuine griev- ance, and cheap politics—came to constitute one of the hardiest features of transpacific affairs during the first four decades of the twentieth century, Roo- sevelt succeeded in keeping it mostly in check. In fact he negotiated some hard- headed and realistic agreements with the Japanese. In 1905 William Taft, then Roosevelt's secretary of war, traveled to Tokyo and met with Japanese foreign minister Katsura Taro. The meeting produced a memorandum outlining each country's acknowledgment of the sphere of interest of the other: the United States recognized Japanese hegemony in Korea, while Japan forswore any de- signs on the Philippines. The Japanese valued the Taft-Katsura agreement for ratifying their gains in the war against Russia; Americans liked it because it removed—if the Japanese could be believed—the primary military threat to the Philippines. The removal of the Japanese threat was especially important to Washington because American taxpayers were showing a reluctance to fund the Philippines' defense.

Three years later, the Roosevelt administration concluded another agree- ment with the Japanese. This agreement, the Root-Takahira Accord of 1908, followed a visit by the American navy to Tokyo. The voyage of the "Great White Fleet" (named for the color of the ships rather than the sailors) was a bold public relations maneuver by Roosevelt, who desired to remind the Jap- anese that the United States was a military power to contend with in Asia. The president sent all sixteen battleships of the American navy on a round-the- world cruise, with stops at strategic ports of call. Congressional critics charged Roosevelt with wastefulness and recklessness: the voyage was wasteful, the critics said, because it cost lots of taxpayer money; it was reckless because it placed all of America's largest naval eggs in one basket. Moreover, for a time that basket would be in the home waters of sneak-attack-specialist Japan. In an effort to prevent the voyage, Congress refused to appropriate necessary funds. Roosevelt responded by sending the ships halfway around the world with the funds on hand and daring Congress to let the vessels rust in the Indian Ocean. As Roosevelt guessed, Congress capitulated.

The show of force impressed the Japanese, contributing to a subsequent Jap- anese naval build-up; in the shorter term it encouraged Tokyo to conclude an accord with Washington further delineating the respective interests of the two countries in Asia. By the Root-Takahira agreement, the United States and Ja- pan accepted the status quo in the region and reaffirmed respect for the prin- ciples of the Open Door in China. There was an implicit contradiction in the pact, however, for the status quo included a de facto sphere of Japanese in- fluence in southern Manchuria and thereby violated the Open Door. But diplomats get paid for facility in elastic language, and the importance of this accord rested less in what it said than in what it symbolized—namely, an effort by the two parties to deflate the belligerent rhetoric between them and to accommodate the interests of both. The accommodation did not last, and the rhetoric eventually reinflated, yet the accord provided something of a breathing spell.

Wilson and the Mexican Revolution

The Republicans of the Roosevelt-Taft era had better luck bargaining with the Japanese and Russians than with one another. Not long after Roosevelt reluctantly retired at the beginning of 1909, biting his tongue for having said he would consider his first three years in office as a full term under the George Washington two-term rule, he and Taft, his hand-picked successor, had a falling out. The falling out gave rise to a three-way race for president in 1912 and consequently to the election of Democrat Woodrow Wilson.

Wilson had no experience in international relations when he was elected; but he did not think that the standards of human conduct in Afghanistan, Argentina, or Angola ought to differ much from those in his home state of New Jersey. Given the opportunity, he planned to attempt to enforce those universal standards.

Wilson got his first opportunity after a revolution erupted in Mexico. In 1908 Mexico's long-time dictator Porfirio Díaz fell prey to the illusion that often afflicts rulers who suppress dissent: he began to believe his own propaganda and think that the people actually liked him. Díaz asserted that Mexico was ready for democracy; he would allow the formation of an opposition party. Díaz's opponents took him at his word and organized to contest the presidential election of 1910. At first Díaz ignored the chief opposition candidate, Francisco Madero, but when it became evident that Madero had a large following, the dictator arrested him. Madero spent the election in jail, while Díaz declared himself the victor by an overwhelming margin.

Thinking Madero harmless, Díaz released him. Madero skipped across the Rio Grande to Texas, where he began plotting a revolt. He gathered supporters, denounced the recent elections as rigged and invalid, and bestowed on himself title of provisional president of Mexico. Returning to Mexico, he issued a call to arms against the Díaz regime.

The initial response proved disappointing, so Madero decided to go back to Texas for a while longer; but his example encouraged others to challenge Díaz. The most important challengers were Pascual Orozco and Pancho Villa in the northern state of Chihuahua and Emiliano Zapata in the southern state of Morelos.

Díaz was old—eighty years—and did not relish the prospect of fighting off several contenders at once. Judging Madero the least radical of his opponents, the octogenarian abdicated in Madero's favor and fled to Europe.

To this stage, the Mexican Revolution suited the American government well enough. Despite early friendliness toward American investment, Díaz recently had attempted to counter what he saw as excessive American economic influence in Mexico by favoring British investors over American in granting concessions and other commercial opportunities. The Taft administration, busy pursuing dollar diplomacy policies elsewhere in Latin America, saw events in Mexico under Díaz moving in just the wrong direction. Washington winked at Madero's revolution-organizing efforts in Texas, and American officials shed no tears on Díaz's departure.

But Madero turned out to be a disappointment. Although he was no radical—the real radicals were Zapata and his followers—Madero legalized labor unions and allowed strikes, which disconcerted American business interests. Worse, he failed to get a grip on the political situation in Mexico and lost ground to Zapata and the genuine revolutionaries. Washington began wishing Díaz had never left. The American ambassador in Mexico City, an ardent conservative named Henry Lane Wilson, actively conspired with Madero's right-wing enemies.

The strongest and most ruthless of the right wingers was General Victoriano Huerta, who staged a coup that toppled and then killed Madero. By this brutal deed, Huerta hoped to stop the revolution in its tracks. Instead he caused it to mushroom. Zapata's peasant armies intensified operations in the south; Villa's cavalry rode roughshod across the mountains and deserts of the north. A third Huerta opponent, Venustiano Carranza, also attracted a large following. Carranza's group called itself the Constitutionalists and demanded restoration of constitutional government.

It was at this point that Woodrow Wilson assumed the presidency of the United States. Although the other great powers had extended diplomatic recognition to the Huerta regime, Wilson refused. Standard—but not completely uniform—international practice had been to apply a simple, pragmatic test in determining whether to recognize a new government. Did the government really control the territory of the country in question? Aspiring governments were always claiming to be in control even when they were not; what other nations needed to know was whether a particular claimant could control what went on inside its territory.

A second aspect of the recognition test concerned obligations to other countries. When governments negotiate treaties, incur debts, and the like, they do so not simply for themselves but for their nations. Governments may change—by election, coup, revolution—but the obligations remain. (Differences on this point provoked much of the dispute between Alexander Hamilton and Thomas Jefferson regarding the appropriate American response to the French Revolution during the 1790s, particularly whether the Franco-American treaty of alliance of 1778 still applied.) If such were not true, other governments would refuse to make long-term commitments, and the better part of international relations would grind to a halt. (The worse part—war—would go on about as usual.)

Generally, governments had not concerned themselves about the methods by which other governments came to power or kept themselves in power. For the purposes of diplomatic recognition, moral or ethical tests had been the exception rather than the rule. There were two reasons for this agnostic attitude. The first had to do with the nature of the international political order. After hundreds of years of dynastic, religious, and ideological wars, the powers of Europe during the nineteenth century arrived at the principle that what happened inside a particular country was the concern almost solely of the government of that country and its people. Painfully and slowly, the powers agreed not to meddle in each other's internal affairs. If Britain wanted a constitutional monarch; France, a president; and Russia, a czar, that was the business of each country alone. The practice of recognizing governments on the basis of effective sovereignty and fulfillment of international obligations reflected this hands-off attitude.

The second reason was that judging the moral character of a government is a nearly hopeless task. What constitutes unacceptably immoral behavior in a government? Executing traitors? Waging war against small, weak neighbors? Suppressing dissent or preventing secession? Few countries, and none of the great powers—whose actions effectively established the rules for the rest—could bring a spotless record on such matters to the bar of international justice. For decades before the American Civil War, most governments of the world considered slavery inhumane and oppressive. The American government did not. Establishing moral standards for one's own country is hard enough; establishing them for another country, which may have an entirely different cultural background, is almost impossible.

But it did not seem impossible to Woodrow Wilson. The American president refused to recognize the Huerta government of Mexico, complaining that Huerta had seized power over the dead body of his predecessor Madero. It did not improve Huerta's prospects of gaining Wilson's favor that the Mexican revolution continued unabated. Although Wilson was hardly an agent of American owners of Mexican property, the president could not help being concerned about the future of a large amount of American foreign investment. Many of the property owners—along with Ambassador Wilson—advocated recognition of Huerta. But President Wilson was never very good at accepting others' advice, and he did not in this case. He shortly fired the ambassador.

The president did not content himself with denying recognition to Huerta. He actively maneuvered to have the general deposed. He pressured the British to withdraw their support from Huerta. London reluctantly did so. The chances of war in Europe were growing greater all the time, and as they had since the mid-1890s, the British appreciated their need to be on good terms with the Americans.

Britain's backing away undermined Huerta's financial position and thereby weakened his power base. Whereas leaders of popular uprisings can run low-budget revolutions (peasant guerrillas work cheap), right-wing movements require regular infusions of cash (to pay troops whose loyalty to the usually elitist reactionary leadership groups generally has to be bought). Huerta grew desperate for revenues and suspended payment on Mexico's large foreign debt. This further lost him favor with the British and other creditors and cleared the way for Washington to turn the screws still tighter.

Wilson did so by tilting toward Carranza in the ongoing civil war. Early in 1914 the president authorized shipments of American weapons to Carranza's forces. Huerta responded by looking for additional arms of his own. Germany, happy to make trouble for the British and their American friends, offered to supply such arms. When Wilson learned that a German ship bearing weapons was approaching the port city of Veracruz, the president ordered American marines to occupy the town.

The landing followed a fabricated, or at least much embellished, incident that already had Mexicans fuming at American arrogance. A handful of American sailors on shore leave at Tampico had tried the patience of the local authorities, as sailors on leave often do, and had wound up in jail, again as they often do. The men were detained briefly, and then released.

But instead of treating the affair as part of life on the waterfront, American officials acted as though it was cause for war. The American commander on the scene demanded a formal apology and a twenty-one-gun salute to the American flag. Wilson backed the demands, even the ridiculous second one. In addition, the president prepared Congress for war with a sermon on the need to insist on respect for the United States in relations with Mexico, especially with the scoundrel Huerta.

Wilson's highhandedness antagonized many Mexicans who otherwise had little good to say about Huerta. The American president's order to occupy Veracruz, an action that produced sharp fighting and hundreds of deaths, mostly Mexican, antagonized many more. Those antagonized included Carranza, who refused to be a pawn in Wilson's game and who in any event could not afford to appear less zealous in defense of Mexican honor than Huerta.

Wilson now realized that he might have gone too far. He agreed to a proposal by Argentina, Brazil, and Chile to stop the fighting between Americans and Mexicans and start talking. Yet the talking failed to find common ground between Wilson and Huerta, which was not surprising since Wilson's terms still included Huerta's ouster.

Carranza, also invited to talk, spurned the South Americans' offer. He wrapped himself in the Mexican flag and declared that he had nothing to say to foreign invaders of Mexican soil. Carranza could afford to stand on principle: the revolution was going his way. Indeed, by July 1914 Huerta was on the run. He left for Europe before the month ended—arriving just as the tension among European powers finally burst into war. In August, Carranza assumed control of the government in Mexico City.

Carranza's victory might have solved Wilson's Mexican problems if Carranza had managed to solve his own. In particular, Carranza had to figure out how to deal with the other revolutionary factions in Mexico. He failed, at least at first. Pancho Villa refused to accept Carranza's right to govern, as did

Zapata. The two men led their troops against Mexico City and forced Carranza to flee. Ironically, Carranza took refuge in Veracruz, which Americans had evacuated just a few weeks earlier.

At the beginning of 1915, however, Carranza staged a comeback. His generals drove Villa and Zapata out of the capital. Villa retreated to the north, where he resumed his guerrilla campaign; Zapata headed south, back to his stronghold in Morelos.

After the outbreak of the war in Europe, Wilson had difficulty concentrating on events in Mexico. During the spring of 1915, the European war approached the United States, despite the president's efforts to keep clear. In May, the Germans sank the British liner *Lusitania* with more than one hundred Americans aboard. Under the circumstances, Wilson hoped to liquidate America's involvement in the Mexican revolution as quickly as possible. To this end, he extended de facto (informal) recognition to Carranza's government. The implication was that de jure (formal) recognition would soon follow.

Pancho Villa upset Wilson's plans. Villa realized that American support would probably make Carranza invincible, and he attempted to create a rift between the Americans and Mexico's new government. In March 1916 Villa launched a terrorist attack on Columbus, New Mexico. The attackers killed seventeen Americans and outraged public opinion across the United States. Wilson immediately ordered the American army to go after Villa.

Carranza initially acquiesced in the American border crossing; but as Villa danced about the countryside of northern Mexico, General John ("Black Jack") Pershing's expedition grew larger and more intrusive. Carranza came to believe that Wilson had something in mind besides punishing Villa: he feared that the American president wanted to undo various of the reforms of the revolution that threatened the value of American investments. Wilson *did* want to do precisely that, though how badly he wanted to remains unclear. In any event, Carranza warned the Americans back and sent troops to reinforce the warning. The American and Mexican contingents skirmished, with casualties in the dozens. A bigger clash appeared imminent. Villa looked on in delight.

Unfortunately for Villa's chances of displacing Carranza, the Germans chose just this moment to get particularly ugly. In January 1917 Berlin decided on war against American shipping in the North Atlantic. Once the new policy took effect, Wilson would have almost no choice but to declare war on Germany. For four years Wilson had tried to keep the United States out of war; now he certainly did not want to get America involved in two of them.

At the end of January 1917, Wilson announced that he was canceling the Pershing expedition. By early February, the American troops had left Mexico. A few weeks later the American government acquired a copy of the so-called Zimmermann telegram, which included a proposal by the German government to the Mexican government for an anti-American alliance. The scheme was almost absurdly unrealistic (a simultaneous offer to Japan to switch sides in the war from the British-French-Russian camp to the German-Austrian-Turkish had only a slightly better grip on reality), and the Mexicans were not seriously tempted. But Wilson did not want to take any chances. During the first half of 1917, his representatives mended fences with Carranza, and in August of that year Washington extended full de jure recognition to Carranza's government.

*   *   *

It was a measure of the importance and power of the United States that Germany went to improbable lengths to start a brush fire on America's southern border before attacking on the Atlantic front. A decade and a half into the twentieth century, the Germans recognized that American strength could well determine the outcome of the world war.

This recognition, and more particularly the reality it reflected, was something new in the history of American international relations. Through almost the end of the nineteenth century, the United States had been a regional power at most, gradually extending its control across the North American continent to the Pacific, and later spreading its influence throughout the Western Hemisphere, but having little impact on the world beyond. At the very end of the nineteenth century, America's horizon of power expanded across the Pacific, encompassing the Philippines. American officials proclaimed an Open Door for China, and during the early years of the twentieth century they undertook to prevent Japan from getting overly powerful in Northeast Asia. At the same time, Washington deepened its position in Latin America. The United States made a formal protectorate of Cuba and informal protectorates of most of the other countries of Central America and the Caribbean. America built a canal across Panama and stamped its mark on the Mexican revolution. But Europe, still the center stage of great-power rivalry, remained essentially beyond the area most Americans considered vital to their country's safety and welfare.

This opinion would soon change. In 1914 Americans were halfway (conceptually, not chronologically) to a redefinition of their international interests. At the time of their country's birth in the late eighteenth century, most Americans were happy to control merely their own small corner of the Atlantic world; by the middle of the twentieth century, they would consider the entire planet their bailiwick. At that latter date, a few Americans would look back fondly to the days when they had to worry about only North America or even the Western Hemisphere. But most would find the idea of global power irresistibly alluring.

Sources and Suggestions for Further Reading

The Spanish-American War and the events surrounding it have been the subject of scores of books. H. Wayne Morgan, *America's Road to Empire* (1965) is succinct; Frank Friedel, *The Splendid Little War* (1958), has lots of pictures; David F. Trask, *The War with Spain in 1898* (1981), is comprehensive. Other useful volumes are Ramón Ruíz, *Cuba: The Making of a Revolution* (1968); Louis A. Perez, Jr., *Cuba between Empires, 1878–1902* (1983); Lewis L. Gould, *The Spanish-American War and President McKinley* (1982); Julius W. Pratt, *Expansionists of 1898* (1936); David Healy,

U.S. Expansionism: The Imperialist Urge in the 1890s (1970); and Ernest R. May, *Imperial Democracy* (1961).

On the Philippines, start with H. W. Brands, *Bound to Empire: The United States and the Philippines* (1992); and Stanley Karnow, *In Our Image: America's Empire in the Philippines* (1989). Then proceed to Stuart Creighton Miller, *"Benevolent Assimilation": The American Conquest of the Philippines* (1983); and Peter W. Stanley, *A Nation in the Making: The Philippines and the United States, 1899–1921* (1974). The opposition to annexation of the Philippines is detailed in Robert L. Beisner, *Twelve against Empire* (1968).

American policy toward China is the subject of works cited in the previous chapters, as well as of Thomas J. McCormick, *China Market: America's Quest for Informal Empire, 1893–1901* (1967); Charles S. Campbell, *Special Business Interests and the Open Door Policy* (1951); Michael H. Hunt, *Frontier Defense and the Open Door: Manchuria in Chinese-American Relations, 1895–1911* (1973); and Marilyn B. Young, *The Rhetoric of Empire: American China Policy, 1895–1901* (1968).

Regarding the Caribbean basin, Dana G. Munro, *Intervention and Dollar Diplomacy in the Caribbean, 1900–1921* (1964), is solid. David G. McCullough, *The Path between the Seas: The Creation of the Panama Canal, 1870–1914* (1977), is lively. David F. Healy, *The United States in Cuba, 1898–1902* (1963), examines the first American occupation of the island; Allan R. Millet, *The Politics of Intervention: The Military Occupation of Cuba, 1906–1909* (1968), examines the reprise.

American relations with Japan play a large role in Howard K. Beale, *Theodore Roosevelt and the Rise of America to World Power* (1956), which is also the best book on the inimitable Teddy as a maker of foreign policy. Akira Iriye, *Pacific Estrangement: Japanese and American Expansion, 1897–1911* (1972), looks at the growing friction between the two Pacific powers, as does another book by the same author: *Across the Pacific: An Inner History of American-East Asian Relations* (1967). Roger Daniels, *The Politics of Prejudice* (1962), discusses the anti-Japanese movement in California. Eugene P. Trani, *The Treaty of Portsmouth* (1969), recounts the negotiations that ended the Russo-Japanese War.

American troubles with Mexico are explained in Robert E. Quirk, *An Affair of Honor: Woodrow Wilson and the Occupation of Veracruz* (1962); P. Edward Haley, *Revolution and Intervention: The Diplomacy of Taft and Wilson with Mexico, 1910–1917* (1970); Larry D. Hill, *Emissaries to a Revolution: Woodrow Wilson's Executive Agents in Mexico* (1973); and Mark T. Gilderhus, *Diplomacy and Revolution: U.S.-Mexican Relations under Wilson and Carranza* (1977).

Chapter 8

To Right the Balance of the Old, 1914–1920

During the second decade of the twentieth century, the United States abandoned the principle of nonintervention in European affairs that had guided it from the early years of independence. The abandonment came hard; American leaders and the American people struggled mightily to hold fast to the advice of George Washington, Thomas Jefferson, and John Quincy Adams. But they eventually let it go, convinced that America's increasingly global interests required defending even at the cost of entanglement in Europe's affairs.

It had been America's good luck that for a century Europeans had figured out how to solve their most pressing international problems peacefully. Such conflicts as the Crimean War (1854–1856) and the Franco-Prussian War (1870–1871) stayed relatively small and uncomplicated by the ideological issues that had made the wars of the French Revolution so violent and all-consuming. Nor did a would-be continent conqueror like Napoleon arise to force the countries of Europe to line up behind or against him. Under these circumstances of comparative calm, American leaders faced little temptation to get involved in European affairs. Such insight as was required to stay out mostly entailed the if-it-ain't-broke-don't-fix-it variety. The United States would have required genuine fools to meddle where there was no reason to meddle, and though geniuses were scarce in American international relations during the period between 1815 and 1914 (Adams and maybe William Seward), outright fools were even scarcer.

Consequently, the noninvolvement in European affairs on which many Americans liked to congratulate themselves was really nothing to boast about. As soon as temptation arose in the form of another major European war, the United States started sliding into temptation. In less than three years, the neutrality of more than a century vanished, replaced by a belligerence so vehement as to astonish even some of those who supported it.

Yet habits of six generations die hard, and as peace returned to Europe, Americans returned to America in spirit as well as body. Many began thinking that participation in the war had been a mistake. In fact, it had not been—not, that is, according to the criteria that have generally guided American foreign policy. But because Americans were new at the game of European affairs, and

Chronology

1914	American troops occupy Veracruz; First World War begins; Wilson proclaims neutrality; Panama Canal opened to traffic
1915	*Lusitania* sunk; Wilson approves loans to belligerents; U.S. troops to Haiti
1916	House-Grey memorandum; Pershing chases Villa in northern Mexico; American troops to Dominican Republic
1917	Zimmermann telegram from Germany; Russia Revolution commences; United States enters world war
1918	Wilson's Fourteen Points; Brest-Litovsk treaty takes Russia out of the war; Allied and American interventions in Russia; armistice ends fighting in Europe; influenza pandemic
1919	Paris peace conference produces Treaty of Versailles; Senate rejects treaty
1920	Senate again rejects Versailles treaty

because the game had changed fundamentally in ways even Europeans themselves did not understand, this misconception was understandable. It took another quarter century and another major war to clear it up.

The Origins of Europe's Suicide Attempt

The deep roots of the First World War ran to the breakup of the Roman empire, when the last approximation to unity the continent had enjoyed disintegrated. Over the next millennium and a half, the different peoples of western Europe forgot they once had spoken a common language (Latin—the best educated among them, anyway) and shared a common political allegiance. The Protestant Reformation severed the ties of religion that had held them together, and the rise of the nation-states dissolved the dynastic glue that had kept such transnational entities as the Holy Roman Empire more or less intact.

Ironically, given that political fission established the fundamental preconditions for the First World War, a form of political fusion was the more proximate cause. The peace that followed the Napoleonic wars was primarily the result of a comparatively even balance of power among the main potential mischief makers of the continent. Britain was the most active in trying to maintain the balance, throwing its support to this side or that depending on the relative weights of the others. Britain's success owed much to the fact that the biggest of the others, notably France, Austria, and Russia, balanced themselves fairly evenly. It usually required only a British thumb on the scales, rather than both feet, to keep things in line.

The situation changed with the unification of Germany after the Franco-Prussian War. The rise of Wilhelm's and Bismarck's reich produced a new element in the heart of Europe that tended to disrupt the balance. On unification, and with continuing industrialization, Germany became potentially the strongest power on the Continent, one that Britain would have difficulty counterbalancing. Britain's recognition of this fact was what had prompted London's recent efforts to cultivate friendly relations with the United States. It also produced the most striking realignment in western European politics since the turn of the millennium: the Franco-British security alliance, or Entente Cordiale, of 1904. The French had already fashioned (in 1894) an alliance with the Russians, a pact that likewise signaled the fear felt by Germany's neighbors. For its part, Germany took comfort in an alliance with next-door Austria-Hungary and a looser and shorter-lasting link to Italy.

The emergence of this system of alliances exacerbated two sources of European instability. The first was the imperialist race for colonies and spheres of influence in the nonindustrialized regions of the world, especially Africa and Asia. The two leaders in the race, Britain and France, were arrayed on one side of the alliance divide against two recent challengers, Germany and Italy. As a result, efforts by Britain and France to keep Germany and Italy out of Africa, for example, added to tensions arising from troubles in Europe. By the same token, annoyances in Europe added to Italian and especially German feelings of being unfairly treated in Africa.

The second source of instability had to do with the so-called nationalities question. Although Germany and France still disputed the ownership of the border region of Alsace and Lorraine (in German hands since 1870), most of the frontiers in western Europe occasioned little disagreement. The British lived in Britain and the French in France, with neither side claiming title to lands of the other. (The Hundred Years' War of the fourteenth and fifteenth centuries had been fought over this issue.) In central and eastern Europe, however, borders and sovereignty remained topics of continual dispute. The empire of Austria-Hungary seethed with plots and insurrections designed to deliver power to whatever nationality was doing the plotting. The Russian empire similarly comprised a variety of peoples who did not appreciate having to pay respect and taxes to the czar. The nationalities issue would not have been a major international problem except that the great powers often used it as an excuse for meddling in other powers' affairs. The Russians purported to speak for Slavs everywhere; the Germans did likewise for Germans outside the fatherland. Needless to say, the governments of the countries where these Slavs and Germans lived did not appreciate the attention their subjects received from St. Petersburg and Berlin.

In the second decade of the twentieth century, the term *subject* was a more apt description of most Europeans than *citizen*. Genuine democracy had arrived in France and Britain around the beginning of the century, as political reforms enacted earlier resulted for the first time in the election of large

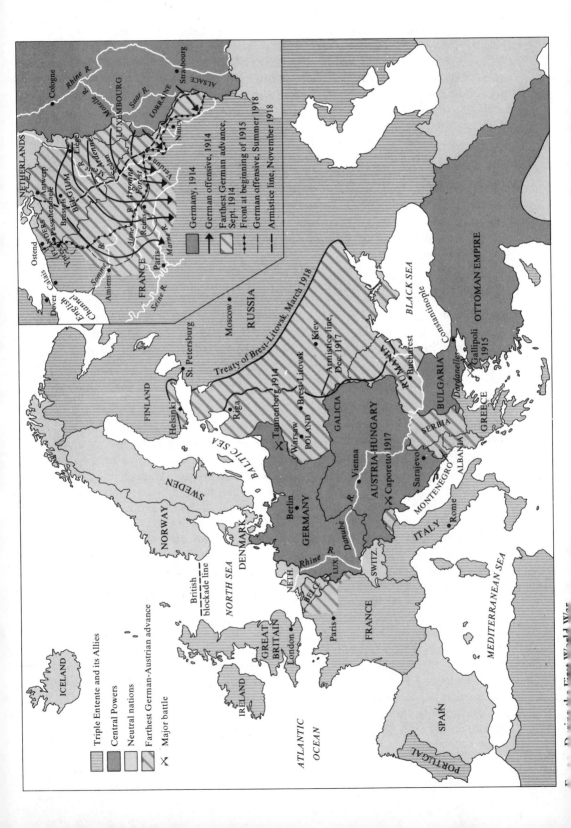

Europe During the First World War

Legend (inset, upper right):

Germany, 1914
German offensive, 1914
Farthest German advance, Sept. 1914
Front at beginning of 1915
German offensive, Summer 1918
Armistice line, November 1918

Inset place names (Western Front):

Cologne · Rhine R. · NETHERLANDS · Ostend · Dover · Calais · English Channel · Antwerp · Brussels · Liège · BELGIUM · FLANDERS · Passchendaele · Ypres · Meuse R. · Moselle R. · Saar R. · LUXEMBOURG · LORRAINE · ALSACE · Strasbourg · Nancy · Verdun · Argonne Forest · Ardennes · Reims · Aisne R. · Marne R. · Somme R. · Amiens · Seine R. · Paris · FRANCE

Main map legend:

Triple Entente and its Allies
Central Powers
Neutral nations
Farthest German-Austrian advance
✕ Major battle

British blockade line

Main map place names:

ICELAND · IRELAND · GREAT BRITAIN · London · ATLANTIC OCEAN · NORWAY · SWEDEN · FINLAND · Helsinki · BALTIC SEA · NORTH SEA · DENMARK · NETH. · BELG. · LUX. · Paris · FRANCE · SWITZ. · SPAIN · PORTUGAL · MEDITERRANEAN SEA · ITALY · Rome · Rhine R. · Danube R. · GERMANY · Berlin · POLAND · Warsaw · Brest-Litovsk · ✕ Tannenberg 1914 · Riga · St. Petersburg · Moscow · RUSSIA · Kiev · Treaty of Brest-Litovsk, March 1918 · Armistice line, Dec. 1917 · GALICIA · AUSTRIA-HUNGARY · Vienna · ✕ Caporetto 1917 · RUMANIA · Bucharest · Sarajevo · SERBIA · MONTENEGRO · ALBANIA · BULGARIA · GREECE · Dardanelles · Constantinople · Gallipoli 1915 · OTTOMAN EMPIRE · BLACK SEA

numbers of candidates unabashedly championing the interests of common people. Italy embraced democracy a little later—just in time for the world war and the postwar reaction to snuff it out. But Germany was essentially undemocratic: despite democratic forms, real power rested with the emperor and chancellor and the officer-aristocrats who controlled the army. In Austria-Hungary, the nationalities issue had frozen the machinery of government: the dominant elites lorded over the rest, rendering democracy a dead letter. Russia was not quite a lost cause for democracy: the revolution of 1905 had frightened Nicholas into allowing the creation of a parliament, the Duma. Yet the Duma's powers were severely circumscribed, and the czar still ruled as an autocrat with an absolute veto.

Educated Americans were aware of the growing tension among the great powers of Europe and their separation into armed camps. American orators praised American wisdom in staying out of Europe's squabbles. A few farsighted persons recognized the stake America had developed in European stability and understood the ill effects a European war would have on American commerce. But the large majority of Americans did not believe that keeping clear of a European conflict would present any insurmountable problems. For a century, since the days of Napoleon, Americans had held aloof from Europe's troubles; there seemed no compelling reason they should not continue to do so.

The Struggle for American Neutrality

When the European tensions erupted into war in August 1914, few Americans found cause to change their minds. If anything, the outbreak of the war reinforced the idea that insanity inspired European diplomacy. The June 1914 assassination of Austrian archduke Francis Ferdinand by a Serbian nationalist in the Austrian-controlled city of Sarajevo hardly gave Americans cause to complain of a peculiar European predilection toward violence: assassins had claimed the lives of three American presidents in living memory. But the sequence of events that led from the assasination to the war re-convinced Americans that Washington and Jefferson had been correct about the dangers of alliances. Austrians demanded the right to investigate the Sarajevo murder within the borders of Serbia—a blatant affront to Serbian sovereignty. The Austrians doubtless intended for Serbia to refuse the demand so as to give them a pretext for slapping down the Serbs, who were inflaming the nationalities problem in the southern portion of Austria-Hungary by agitating for South Slavic self-determination under Serbian leadership. Germany, Austria's ally, encouraged the Austrians to recklessness by promising support in any trouble that ensued.

The Serbs dealt a joker by appealing to Russia for protection, and the Russians played it. The Russians warned Austria not to try to intimidate their

Francis Ferdinand became famous for getting assassinated and thereby triggering the First World War. His wife was killed also but remained obscure. *The Bettman Archive*

fellow-Slav Serbs. Because Germany was backing Austria, Russia had to prepare for war against Germany as well as against Austria. This caused all the machinery of the alliance systems to kick into gear. If Russia went to war, France had to be ready to do so; if France and Russia went to war, Britain had to get set.

The state of military technology at the time contributed to the momentum toward war. Although warfare was becoming mechanized, draft animals still did a large part of the transporting of supplies and equipment that war requires. Preparing for war necessitated commandeering horses and mules, gathering fodder, and moving animals and feed to where they would be needed once the shooting started. Similar considerations applied to the soldiers who would do the shooting. It was an intricate process and a slow one. If war appeared at all likely, governments had to start mobilizing at once. But mobilization, however defensive it might have seemed to the mobilizer, looked threatening to the mobilizer's neighbors. They felt the need to mobilize if they had not mobilized already. The original mobilizer took this as justification for what it had already done and reason to do more along the same lines. What had begun as a precaution became a provocation; a defensive move became offensive. That the side that started a war might gain a substantial advantage, in terms of military momentum and concentration of forces, by doing so added to the precariousness of the situation. As soon as any party decided war was inevitable, or even probable, that party felt an almost overwhelming compulsion to strike first. Wars always dirtied hands; if getting in the first blow helped guarantee victory, the additional dirtying that striking the first blow caused would not much matter.

Europeans in 1914 were in no mood to shy away from war. Except in distant and relatively small-scale colonial wars, their young men had never had the chance to kill for God and country. Consequently, the martial profession enjoyed a mystique often lacking when eye patches and missing limbs are a common sight and young women cannot find husbands. Junior officers had long chafed at their rare promotions; war would break the logjam that kept colonels at that rank for decades. National honor bruised easily; militant jingoes and superpatriots were thick on the ground.

Those who desired war in the summer of 1914 got their wish. Ultimatums elicited counter ultimatums, and mobilization counter-mobilization. After six weeks of rising tension and excitement, war came in a rush. On July 28 Austria declared war on Serbia. On August 1 Germany declared war on Russia. On August 3 Germany declared war on France and mounted an attack through neutral Belgium. On August 4 Britain, citing Germany's violation of Belgian neutrality, declared war on Germany. By the middle of August, most of Europe was at war.

The war spread beyond Europe a week later when Japan, an ally of Britain since 1902, declared war on Germany, in small part from loyalty to Britain and in large part from a desire to divest Germany of its holdings in East Asia and the Pacific. Ottoman Turkey entered the fighting in November 1914 on the side of Germany and Austria and against its traditional rival Russia. German and Austrian ally Italy initially sought to sit out the conflict, declaring that its alliance was only defensive; by 1915, however, Italian desires to win territory controlled by Austria caused Rome to declare war against its former allies.

As is usually the case, the governments going to war thought the fighting would be brief. The German general staff looked to the example of Bismarck's quick victories in the 1860s and early 1870s and assumed they could match him. They failed to foresee the development of trench warfare, with the advantage it gave to defenders. The French made the same mistake. France's aggressive young officers preached the gospel of attacking at all times and all places. When their attacks failed and their offensives bogged down in the mud, they were left without a strategy.

Partly because the war promised at first to be short, most Americans initially did not feel called on to take sides. On the contrary, prudence seemed to dictate withholding judgment. The war would be over soon; life would go on. There was no point in alienating either side.

Although this widespread conviction that the war was Europe's problem and should stay that way was the most important factor in American neutrality during the first phase of the fighting, there were others. Woodrow Wilson and the Democratic party had political concerns. Elected chiefly for his stands on domestic issues, Wilson was intent on pushing his progressive legislation through Congress. A bill creating a Federal Trade Commission—a centerpiece of the president's consumer protection reforms—had worked its agonizing way through the congressional mill and was on the verge of passage. What would become the Clayton Antitrust Act, the first significant antitrust measure in over twenty years, was right behind. Wilson—a political scientist by training—recognized that Congress works best when its attention is focused on one set of issues; he feared that as soon as the lawmakers started debating issues of war and peace, their concern for domestic reform would fly out the window.

Economic considerations also argued for American neutrality. At the time the war began, the American economy was in recession; American farmers and manufacturers could reasonably expect that the fighting in Europe, by disrupting markets and supply networks and increasing demand, would raise prices for the goods they produced and help restore prosperity to the depressed sectors of the economy. Indeed, the mere threat of war during the summer of 1914 had already sent commodity prices soaring. If the United States stayed neutral, American suppliers stood to make money trading with both sides. If the United States entered the war, suppliers would lose their customers on the other side and would incur the risks related to belligerence, including loss of cargoes and ships.

Consequently, Wilson's August 4 proclamation of American neutrality elicited overwhelming support in the United States. Congress did not have to concur in the declaration, though it would have. Elaborating on his neutrality decision, Wilson urged his compatriots to be "impartial in thought as well as in action." The president fully understood that the war in Europe involved the ancestral homelands and therefore potentially the sentiments of tens of millions of people in America (the census of 1910 showed that more than 23 million Americans out of a population of 92 million were either immigrants from the European countries at war or the children of such immigrants). It would be difficult for recent immigrants and their children not to cheer for one side or the other. Congress reflects, albeit imperfectly, the desires of the American people, and it would be a short step from cheering for one side to underwriting or arming that side. Furthermore, because Americans traced their ancestry to both sides of the conflict, energetic partisanship might well spill over into the domestic arena and poison the atmosphere in America.

For several months the temptation for the United States to take sides remained minimal. The German invasion of neutral Belgium marked the Germans as apparently more ruthless than their enemies but not sufficiently threatening to American interests to warrant a strong American response. By the time the fighting season ended in November 1914, the line separating Germans from French and British had stabilized more or less where it would remain for the next three years, running south from Ostend (of Ostend manifesto memory) to within about sixty miles of Paris and then turning east toward Verdun and the German border. The French suffered the heaviest losses of the war's first year: during this period nearly half of all French families lost a son or husband in battle. The British took heavy losses as well; in the defense of Ypres alone, the British expeditionary force lost fifty thousand troops. Germans survived the year in substantially better shape: striking first had paid off. Germany's worst casualty figures would come in the last year of the war.

By the beginning of 1915, the two sides were starting to see that they had locked themselves into a war of attrition. The Germans would not quit because they were winning; the French would not quit because one-tenth of their territory was occupied by German forces. What remained was to see which side would first lose the will to keep fighting. Both sides adopted a strategy of pounding the enemy's lines with intense artillery fire (in one battle the French allotted nineteen shells per meter of the front) before sending the infantry over the top of the trenches into the no–man's land between the trenches. Success was measured in hundreds of meters of advance, losses in hundreds of thousands of deaths.

One of the reasons the Europeans had expected a war to be short was that they could not figure out how their countries could afford a long war. When countries industrialize, they specialize, and when they specialize they become dependent on foreign suppliers and customers. The opponents of corn law repeal in Britain in the 1840s had predicted that Britain would find itself dependent on farmers living in other countries. They were right, as the American Civil War, during which the British people's appetite for northern wheat had helped negate British industry's appetite for southern cotton and prevent British recognition of the Confederacy, had demonstrated. When Germany and France industrialized, they, too, tied themselves into an international network of supply and demand. In the years prior to 1914, many forecasters predicted that a prolonged war between the great powers would shatter that network and cause the European economies to grind to a halt. Furthermore, a war among the industrialized powers would be enormously expensive. The treasuries of the belligerents would soon run dry. The belligerents would be bankrupted and thereby forced to settle their grievances diplomatically.

This conventional wisdom underestimated the possibility of external financing of hostilities. In particular, it neglected the possibility that American bankers would provide the cash Europeans needed to keep their soldiers supplied with shells, bayonets, and potatoes after their governments ran out of money. Such was exactly what happened starting in 1915.

Wilson allowed the loans reluctantly. As a Democrat and a moralist besides, Wilson considered himself above the petty property-mindedness of his Republican predecessors. He believed that he dealt in higher principles than the balance sheets of the country's corporations. Yet not even Wilson could ignore the health of American big business, if only because when corporate America coughed, working-class America—a prime Democratic constituency—took sick also. The outbreak of the European war had instantly strengthened the American economy. Orders from the belligerents for everything from cotton

and leather to machine tools and medicines allowed farmers to pay old mort-
gages and build new barns, factory owners to recall workers and add shifts,
shipbuilders to lay keels and buy steel, merchants to extend hours and expand
inventories. As is so often the case, the misfortune of the belligerents was the
good fortune of the neutrals.

But the buying that fueled the American recovery depended on the purchasing power of the belligerents, and as the war lasted into 1915, this purchasing
power weakened. The treasuries of Germany, France, and Britain reached their
limits, and the finance ministers of those countries began scrambling for ways
to keep the needed supplies flowing in. The most obvious way was to borrow
the money; the most obvious lender was the United States, which was making
a killing (the metaphor was not too strong for many Europeans resentful of
the profits American firms were reaping from the war trade) while Europe
suffered. American bankers were happy to lend the money. Just as the war had
raised the price of pork bellies and potassium nitrate, it raised the price of
money—in other words, the interest rate. Besides, governments are generally
good credit risks; when they get in trouble financially, they can raise taxes.
They can also default, but they usually do so only under the direst circumstances since default scares away prospective lenders and makes future borrowing problematic.

At most times in its history, the American government has regulated lending
to foreign governments; it did so in 1915. Accordingly, American bankers had
to gain the permission of the Wilson administration to float loans across the
Atlantic. Secretary of State William Jennings Bryan opposed the loans. Ever
since the 1890s, when he had stumped the country campaigning for president
against the gold standard, Bryan had distrusted Wall Street and the American
financial establishment. Then, Bryan's distrust had been based largely on instinct. Now logic complemented his instinct, as he warned against sending
money to the belligerents. "Money is the worst of all contrabands," Bryan told
Wilson, "because it commands everything else." At present the Europeans were
dependent on the United States; yet if Americans lent heavily to Europe, de-
pendency would flow in the opposite direction. Others besides Bryan repeated
the old chestnut about how when you owe the bank ten thousand dollars, you
have a problem, but when you owe the bank ten million dollars, the bank has
a problem. Once the Europeans went heavily into debt to American financiers,
those financiers would put tremendous pressure on the American government
to take action to safeguard their loans. Perhaps if the bankers spread their
loans equally to both sides in the war, the pressure would cancel itself out.
Perhaps—but the people of the United States should not count on being so
lucky.

Sophisticates sneered at Bryan. They laughed at his attempts to introduce
prohibition into American diplomacy by banning alcoholic beverages from
State Department receptions. Yet Bryan was shrewder than they thought, and
he ignored their insults—as he had during an earlier encounter with the visiting
Japanese admiral Togo Heihachiro, the hero of the Russo-Japanese War. Bryan

had caused flutters among American protocolists when he resolutely refused to toast Togo with champagne at an official dinner. Raising his glass to the visitor, Bryan proclaimed, "Admiral Togo has won a great victory on the water, and I will therefore toast him in water. When Admiral Togo wins a victory on champagne, I will toast him in champagne."

Woodrow Wilson saw the shrewdness in Bryan and recognized the power of Bryan's argument against American loans to the belligerents; but Wilson understood that a decision against the loans would exact a cost as well. Without the money, Europeans would stop buying American goods. The economic recovery that was swelling American incomes and employment would falter. Holding Congress and the White House in Democratic hands in 1916 would be difficult if the economy stumbled. Even if Wilson himself had not paid attention to such mercenary matters, his advisers and congressional allies did, and they communicated their worries quite clearly.

The president initially took a half step in the direction of approving loans. He let sellers of American products arrange financing with American lenders for their European customers. In doing so, he ensured that the loans were directly tied to sales of American goods.

But this procedure satisfied neither the American producers and lenders, who chafed under the restrictions, nor the Europeans, who needed money in bigger doses than Wilson's approach allowed. Both groups increased their pressure on the Wilson administration to lift the restrictions and allow American financiers to sell European government bonds in the American financial market. Eventually Wilson gave in to the pressure. In September 1915 he allowed the bond sellers to begin shipping American money to Europe.

It was perhaps the most portentous decision Wilson ever made. Although in principle the administration's policy favored neither the Allied powers (Britain, France, and Russia) nor the Central powers (Germany, Austria-Hungary, and Turkey), in practice it tied the United States closely to the Allies. Britain, the traditional naval superpower, controlled the seas; this being the case, it was far easier for American merchants and shippers to do business with Britain and France than with Germany. When the war began in 1914, American businesses sold twice as much to British and French customers as to German. During the next two years, as the Allies blockaded the Central powers and British naval superiority took effect, exports to Britain and France tripled, while exports to Germany dried up almost completely. As a result, American loans to the Allies outstripped loans to the Central powers by a margin of ten to one.

If not for the big jump in sales to the Allies, American merchants would have been quite upset at Britain's blockade of Germany. They were upset enough as it was, and so was the Wilson administration. The British, following their own example of the Napoleonic wars, ignored the niceties of international law in shutting down neutral trade with the Central powers. For the first several months of the war, London paid lip service to neutral trading rights even while violating them. By the middle of 1915, however, it had dropped most of the pretense of respecting neutrals' rights, and British commanders began seizing nearly everything bound for Germany they could get their hands on.

The British seizures were exactly the sort of thing that had caused great friction between the United States and Britain at the beginning of the nineteenth century, contributing eventually to the War of 1812. The Wilson administration never seriously considered declaring war on Britain for these latest violations of American neutrality, but it did lodge vigorous protests with the British government. Of greater significance, the British violations irritated many Americans and made it difficult for the administration to draw closer to Britain and France against Germany.

Yet German violations of American rights were eventually more serious and significant. Britain ruled the waves but not what went on beneath the waves. The major new naval weapon of the First World War was the submarine, which the Germans built and deployed in large numbers. The submarine, or U-boat, somewhat evened the odds at sea between Britain and Germany. Submarines were cheap, stealthy, and deadly, and when commanded by daring officers, they could wreak havoc on enemy shipping. In presubmarine days, the process of capturing a merchant vessel was gentlemanly and usually bloodless. A warship trained its guns on the merchantman and ordered it to stop; the merchantman had no reasonable recourse but to do as told. Submarine technology changed the strategy of interdiction. The submarines were small, flimsy, and slow, and their commanders could not offer merchant captains the privilege of surrendering without risking getting their submarines rammed, shelled (many merchantmen were armed), or outrun. Nor could submarines pick up survivors in the event of a sinking. Crowded with their own men, they had no room for extras. German submarine commanders fell into a shoot-on-sight strategy, not because they were more barbarous than their British counterparts, but because their technology severely circumscribed their available courses of action.

The technological excuse was cold comfort for the relatives and friends of those killed by German torpedoes. During the first several months of the war, while Germany's surface fleet at least gave the British a contest, the German high command kept its submarines in check. But by early 1915 the British fleet had largely cleared the open ocean of German surface vessels, and Berlin placed greater reliance on the U-boats. In February Germany declared a "war zone" around the British Isles in which enemy ships would be subject to attack without warning. At the same time, Germany warned neutral nations to keep their ships clear of the zone lest they be attacked by mistake—a possibility increased by the British habit of disguising their merchant vessels with neutral flags.

Dozens of British ships fell victim to German torpedoes during the subsequent weeks, but it was not until May 1915 that Americans took particular notice. In that month the British passenger liner *Lusitania* departed New York with nearly two thousand persons aboard. The ship also carried a cargo of ammunition bound for the British army. At a time when German submarines were scoring daily hits on freighters bound for England, the British hoped Ger-

This notice appeared in New York newspapers on the day the *Lusitania* set sail for England. *UPI/Bettman*

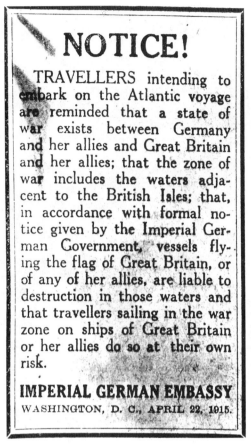

NOTICE!

TRAVELLERS intending to embark on the Atlantic voyage are reminded that a state of war exists between Germany and her allies and Great Britain and her allies; that the zone of war includes the waters adjacent to the British Isles; that, in accordance with formal notice given by the Imperial German Government, vessels flying the flag of Great Britain, or of any of her allies, are liable to destruction in those waters and that travellers sailing in the war zone on ships of Great Britain or her allies do so at their own risk.

IMPERIAL GERMAN EMBASSY
WASHINGTON, D. C., APRIL 22, 1915.

mans would let a passenger vessel through. The German government warned Americans to stay off the ship, taking out advertisements in American newspapers for the express purpose. But if the ads scared away some Americans, almost two hundred others decided to take their chances on what promised to be an exciting voyage through the war zone. They were reassured by the speed of the *Lusitania*, by its great size, and by design features calculated to make it nearly unsinkable.

As good (or bad) as their word, the Germans torpedoed the *Lusitania* off the coast of Ireland. More than 1,000 individuals died, among them 128 Americans. The *Lusitania* sinking triggered outrage across America and cast into tragically bold relief the difference between Britain's sins on the high seas and Germany's. British transgressions violated property rights: someone had a cargo or a ship impounded. German transgressions violated human rights: people died violent deaths. International lawyers and German diplomats might argue that violations were violations and that German violations were not all

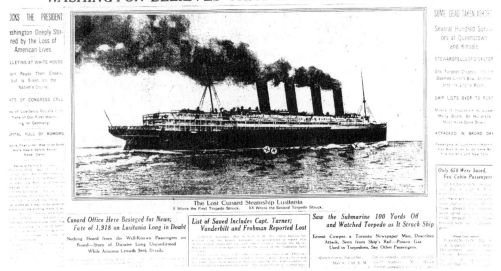

"All the News That's Fit to Print." **The New York Times.** EXTRA 5:30 A M

VOL. LXIV No. 20939   NEW YORK, SATURDAY, MAY 8, 1915.—TWENTY-FOUR PAGES.

LUSITANIA SUNK BY A SUBMARINE, PROBABLY 1,260 DEAD; TWICE TORPEDOED OFF IRISH COAST; SINKS IN 15 MINUTES; CAPT. TURNER SAVED, FROHMAN AND VANDERBILT MISSING; WASHINGTON BELIEVES THAT A GRAVE CRISIS IS AT HAND

The Lost Cunard Steamship Lusitania

X Where the First Torpedo Struck.   XX Where the Second Torpedo Struck.

Canard Office Here Besieged for News;
Fate of 1,918 on Lusitania Long in Doubt

List of Saved Includes Capt. Turner;
Vanderbilt and Frohman Reported Lost

Saw the Submarine 100 Yards Off
and Watched Torpedo as It Struck Ship

The sinking of the *Lusitania* brought the world war home to Americans in a way nothing else had. *AP/Wide World Photos*

that different legally from British violations; but emotionally and politically the two kinds were worlds apart.

The uproar in America that followed the *Lusitania* sinking forced the Wilson administration to take stronger action than the president might have taken on his own and definitely stronger than Secretary Bryan thought prudent or just. Wilson demanded that Germany recognize the right of neutrals to cross the ocean unmolested, that it renounce submarine warfare against unarmed vessels, and that it pay reparations to the United States for the deaths it had caused. Bryan objected to this course. The secretary of state asserted that the British invited such disasters as that of the *Lusitania* by shipping munitions aboard passenger vessels. The United States government had an obligation to warn Americans to stay off British ships if the British were going to engage in such cynical actions, but it had no obligation to protect Americans who ignored such warnings. There was a war on, and Americans had better watch where they went. When it became clear that the president was determined to send a harsh note to Berlin, Bryan insisted that at the least a corresponding note complaining of British violations of American rights be sent to London.

To do otherwise would open the Wilson administration to charges of favoritism toward the Allies and might well lead to war.

Wilson rejected Bryan's advice, and the secretary of state soon resigned. Nature abhors vacuums, and so do bureaucracies. Bryan had not even caught a train back to his home state of Nebraska before two ardently pro-Allied advisers filled his place. Robert Lansing took over the State Department. Lansing came from a family that specialized in producing secretaries of state: his father-in-law, John Foster, had been secretary of state under Benjamin Harrison; his nephew, John Foster Dulles, would be secretary of state under Dwight Eisenhower. Lansing felt a community of interest with British diplomats and government officials, many of whom he knew personally. At the same time, Lansing despised and feared the Germans, whom he knew more by reputation (a reputation at least partially manufactured by Britain's propaganda bureau) than by experience. Lansing believed that the United States could survive and prosper in a world where Britain, perhaps with the help of France, played the leading role in Europe. He did not think the United States could do well in a world where Germany dominated Europe.

Edward House was just as determined as Lansing that Germany not win the war. "Colonel" House, as he was commonly known despite having neither a military nor a Kentucky background, was Wilson's closest adviser. House held no official, permanent position; a wealthy man, he could afford to work with Wilson simply for the satisfactions of being close to power. Like Lansing, House believed that the United States had to be prepared to enter the war if necessary to prevent a German victory. The thought of an Allied victory alarmed him not at all since the foreign policy aims of Britain and France broadly paralleled those of America—or so he judged during the period before American entry into the war.

From the autumn of 1915, the United States moved steadily closer to war. After the *Lusitania* sinking and the August 1915 torpedoing of the British liner *Arabic,* in which two more Americans perished and which the Wilson administration similarly protested, Germany pledged to refrain from attacking unresisting passenger liners without warning and without providing for the safety of passengers. For a half year Berlin honored this pledge. In March 1916, however, a German U-boat torpedoed the French channel steamer *Sussex,* injuring several Americans and scores of others. The Wilson administration complained vigorously against both the injuries and the apparent violation of the earlier pledge. (In fact, the sinking probably resulted from mistaken identity.) Wilson demanded that Germany promise not to attack either liners or freighters. Germany, not willing to risk bringing the Americans into the war at this stage, backed off once again. Berlin agreed not to sink unresisting liners or freighters without warning and safety provisions. However, the promise contained a condition: that the United States insist that the Allies respect neutral rights, including the right to trade with Germany.

Germany's *Sussex* pledge marked the onset of several months of superficial warming in German-American relations, but the chilling continued at a deeper level. As the fighting persisted in Europe, Americans were increasingly drawn toward the Allies. A variety of factors accounted for this. Economically, American trade with the Allies and American loans to the Allies linked the prosperity of the United States to the success of the Allies. Culturally, Americans felt closer to Britain than to Germany; many more Americans traced their ancestral roots to the British Isles than to Germany (though Irish-Americans resentful of British control of Ireland often cheered British battlefield reverses). Politically, Americans preferred the democracies of Britain and France to the autocracies of Germany and Austria-Hungary. Strategically, the Central powers seemed more threatening to American interests than the Allies did. The United States had lived with a powerful Britain for nearly 150 years, and though the experience had produced tension and once war, for almost a generation Britain had been on good behavior. Britain was a known quantity. Germany was largely unknown, but what *was* known did not appear promising. For nearly a half century since unification, the Germans had rocked the boat of international affairs, repeatedly pushing the powers to the edge of war. Now war had come, and Germans had acted abominably, from the moment they crushed neutral and defenseless Belgium, through their atrocities on the high seas. If the British were a nation of shopkeepers, as Napoleon had said, the Germans were a gang of militarists.

During 1916 Wilson's pro-Allied advisers, especially House, worked to attach the United States even more closely to Britain and France. Wilson still hoped to keep America out of the conflict. The president sincerely feared the consequences of taking America to war; he rightly predicted that once the nation went to war, its tolerant and progressive impulses would largely disappear, replaced by harsher feelings. In addition, Wilson did not care to run for reelection in 1916 on a war platform. Foreign wars have never sold well from the back of a campaign train, and Wilson was not the salesman to create the exception to the rule.

But events conspired to draw the United States in. At the beginning of 1916, House traveled to Britain for discussions with British foreign secretary Edward Grey. Ostensibly House was investigating the prospects for American mediation leading to a peace accord, but the principal result of the talks was a memorandum describing the American position on the war in terms that favored the Allies. The House-Grey memorandum recommended that the Wilson administration propose a peace conference at a moment opportune to Britain and France; if Germany refused, the United States would probably enter the war on the side of the Allies. If Germany accepted the American proposal but stonewalled at the conference, the United States would leave the conference and join the Allies.

On its face the House-Grey memo committed the Wilson administration to nothing. In its original form, it included enough "probablys" to allow the president all the wriggle room he needed, and Wilson himself added a few more. Yet the memo showed active cooperation at nearly the highest levels between the American and British governments, something that definitely did not exist between Washington and Berlin. American neutrality was a thing of the past. American belligerence now appeared increasingly likely.

The memo—or rather the favorable American attitude it signified—encouraged Britain to tighten its blockade of Germany. Critics of Britain, including many in the United States, contended that Germany had no monopoly on human rights violations: the British blockade was an attempt to starve an entire nation. By the nature of things, children and old people were the first to succumb to malnourishment and disease—a situation the German government did not alleviate when it reserved much of the available food, clothing, and medicine for the military. Yet in the politics of war, sheer numbers of dead mean almost nothing. Although the torpedoing of the *Lusitania* and the other ships the German submarines sank killed far fewer noncombatants than died of hunger and disease in Germany, the disasters at sea made much more dramatic news and caused Germany to appear far more brutish than Britain.

The Wilson administration continued to protest British violations of American rights, but it never evinced sufficient seriousness to cause London to alter its policy significantly. As had been true a century before during the struggle against Napoleon, the British judged their nation's survival to be at risk. In such a crisis they had few compunctions about bending international law. The only important question was whether Americans would be sufficiently provoked to do something about it. The House-Grey memo and similar signals from Washington demonstrated that Americans would not.

Wilson's reelection in November 1916 brought war closer still by removing some of the restraining influence of public opinion. During the campaign the Democrats boasted, "He kept us out of war," as part of an effort to distinguish Wilson's policies from those recommended by Republican nominee Charles Evans Hughes, who advocated a tougher line against Germany. Wilson's campaign strategy narrowly returned him to the White House; at the same time, it provided him with more political maneuvering room than he had previously enjoyed. Like other second-term presidents, Wilson now looked to history, rather than the next election, for vindication.

Three developments of early 1917 increased the chances of American intervention on the side of the Allies. In January Germany's military leaders chose to gamble the fate of their country on one last roll of the dice. They prepared a major offensive designed to crack the Allied resistance in France and force the British and French to sue for peace. Success would depend on the inability of Britain and France to make up for losses; this in turn would depend on cutting the Allies off from their American suppliers. To effect the cutoff, German submarines would sink all American shipping that came into the cross hairs of their periscopes.

German civilian officials greeted this plan with skepticism. Would not the sinking of American ships bring the United States into the war? Would not this simply compound Germany's problems? Generals and admirals tend to get promoted for being optimistic in military matters, rather than otherwise, and Germany's military leaders dismissed the civilian complaints as defeatist. Maybe the Americans would enter the war, but on recent experience it would take them months to decide to do so. Moreover, they were not ready to fight.

At least a year would elapse before American soldiers would make any difference on the ground in Europe. By then the war would be over.

The civilian government in Berlin finally agreed to the military's plan, chiefly because the civilians did not have any better ideas for breaking the stalemate. On January 31, 1917, Berlin announced that German submarines would begin attacking all shipping, belligerent or neutral, that approached Britain. The Germans, in announcing their decision before attacking, were not merely being considerate. The Atlantic Ocean is a big place, and the Germans knew they could never hit all the American ships trying to get over. They intended to scare as many as possible into not leaving American ports in the first place. At the least they would frighten the maritime insurance companies, which would raise premiums or suspend coverage, thereby keeping some ships in port. The tactic worked, and many ship owners decided not to risk the voyage.

The second important event of this period was the publication of the Zimmermann telegram, the message from the German foreign minister calling on Mexico to join an alliance with Germany and tempting Japan to jump from the Allied side in the war to Germany's. Until now such support as had existed for American belligerence on behalf of the Allies was concentrated primarily on the East Coast. Westerners felt far from the fray and relatively apathetic. In Texas a large contingent of German-Americans actively opposed aid to the Allies. The Zimmermann telegram went far toward reversing this situation. By hinting that a Mexico allied to a victorious Germany might regain the territory it had lost to the Americans during the Mexican War seventy years before, the German government immediately outraged Texans and other residents of the Southwest. By trying to entice the Japanese into switching sides, the Germans reminded Californians and other West Coasters how much they feared and disliked the Japanese. Never had a German victory seemed so ominous.

The third important event of the period was quite possibly the single most momentous event in twentieth-century world history. In March 1917 the Russian Revolution began. The revolution took place in two stages, the first in March, the second in November. (The Russians, using the old Julian calendar, called these the February and October revolutions.) The first stage of the revolution accomplished the overthrow of the czarist regime and its replacement by a republican government headed by Alexander Kerensky.

The toppling of Nicholas solved a problem that was vexing the Wilson administration. After the German declaration of submarine warfare and the publication of the Zimmermann telegram, war increasingly seemed the only option for the United States. But Wilson, in keeping with his desire to chart American policy according to Presbyterian mores and progressive ethics, wanted to make it a fight of good against evil. Britain and France had compromised themselves in the conflict but not disqualifyingly so; both countries were liberal democracies and therefore made fit associates for the United States. Czarist Russia, in contrast, was a lost cause. The country was the most backward in Europe; its people were ignorant and were oppressed by both the crown and the superstition-driven Orthodox hierarchy. How the United States

Even in the midst of revolutions there is a lot of standing around. This crowd is waiting for something to happen in Moscow in 1917. *The Bettman Archive*

could in good conscience fight alongside such a country was more than Wilson had been able to figure out.

If necessary, he probably would have been able to do so; but the February revolution saved him the trouble. Overnight Russia joined the ranks of the democracies, so that the Allies all wore white hats while the Central powers wore black.

A final consideration prompted Wilson to decide in favor of intervention. What with the world war and the Russian Revolution, it was clear to all concerned that the shape of world affairs was changing decisively. Wilson believed it imperative that the United States have a role in the shaping. Until now he had thought diplomatic means might suffice to achieve that role; as recently as December 1916 he had called on the two sides to state their war aims and offered to mediate a settlement. But the subsequent events, especially Germany's declaration of unrestricted submarine warfare, demonstrated that diplomacy could not do the job. Force was required. Wilson was determined that the United States have a seat at the peace conference that sooner or later would follow the fighting. If American intervention was the price of admission to the peace conference, Wilson was prepared to pay.

On April 2, 1917, following the sinking of four American merchant vessels by German submarines, Wilson asked Congress for a declaration of war. In keeping with his desire to use American intervention as a device for reordering world politics, the president asserted that the United States would be fighting not only for American interests but also for the welfare of humanity. The world, Wilson said, had to be made "safe for democracy." Congress responded with great fervor, granting Wilson's request by the largest margin to date in the history of American warmaking. The Senate approved the war resolution by a vote of 82–6, the House by a margin of 373–50.

Over There

Although Wilson took the United States into the war on the side of the Allies, he refused to link America too closely with Britain, France, Russia, and Italy. Wilson disagreed with the other great historical figure of the war decade—Russia's Vladimir Lenin—on just about everything else, but he concurred with Lenin's suspicions regarding Allied war aims. Lenin interpreted the war as being a struggle among the capitalist classes of Europe (and now America) for control of Europe and the colonial empires. Wilson would have put the issue differently, but the president likewise saw the self-interest that lay behind the Allied coalition, self-interest that extended beyond Europe to the far corners of the earth. On this account he refused to sign any treaties of alliance with Britain, France, Russia, or Italy. The United States fought the war as an "associated" rather than an "allied" power.

Wilson's uneasiness was well founded. Most of the time the Allied leaders were polite enough to humor Wilson in his idealism, but they had no illusions about making the world safe for democracy or any other airy abstraction. The British prime minister (since late 1916) was David Lloyd George, a lapsed radical whom the war had converted into an unblinking pragmatist. His attitude toward the fighting was summarized in his response to idealists who went off to battle declaring that this was the war to end war; Lloyd George predicted that the next one would be, too. He offered no apologies for putting Britain's interests above everyone else's or for placing the crushing of Germany at the head of the list of British priorities.

The French prime minister (since the autumn of 1917) was Georges Clemenceau, like Lloyd George a onetime leftist who had seen the error of his ways and swung hard to the right. He considered such a shift entirely natural. When afterward told that his son had just joined the Communist party, Clemenceau replied, "My son is twenty-two years old. If he had not become a Communist at twenty-two, I would have disowned him. If he is still a Communist at thirty, I will do it then." Clemenceau entered office at a time when many in France were saying that they had had enough of the war and wanted to quit. Clemenceau quickly put a stop to this defeatist drivel by throwing dissenters in jail (as Lloyd George was doing in Britain). Again like Lloyd George, Clemenceau defined war aims in a thoroughly practical fashion. Defeating Germany, forcing Germany to pay for the destruction it had caused, and preventing Germany from undertaking similar action in the future were his goals. Clemenceau felt no compulsion to save the world; with Lloyd George, he thought Wilson a little loony on the subject but not unlike many

Lenin plots the destruction of czarist Russia and the creation of the Soviet Union. *The Bettman Archive*

other Americans. Clemenceau described America as "the only country in history to have passed from barbarism to decadence without experiencing civilization."

Yet while the British and French governments dismissed Wilson's ideals, they happily accepted American troops. Not that they expected the Americans to work miracles: as did the German high command, British and French strategists believed that the outcome of the war might well be decided before the Americans arrived in large numbers. And it did indeed take the Americans some time to get to Europe. A few units reached France during the summer of 1917, and during the autumn American strength on the Continent continued to mount. But it was not until the beginning of the fighting season in 1918 that the Americans were prepared to deliver really telling military blows against the Germans.

The question of how quickly the Americans would arrive injected one unknown into the strategists' equations; changes in military technology injected others. By 1917 military thinkers and tinkerers were beginning to discover how to neutralize the big advantage defenders had enjoyed over attackers in the current war. The introduction of poison gas by the Germans in 1915 had momentarily promised to break the deadlock of trench warfare, but problems vexed its use, including the fact that it often tended to blow back in the faces of attackers. The gas attacks did cause serious damage: as many as a quarter of American casualties during the war resulted from gas. But the difficulties involved in the use of gas prevented it from having a major strategic impact. In late 1917 the British rolled out a more decisive weapon: the tank. The tank—a mobile pillbox that the British had been experimenting with for some time—solved the problem of troops having to expose themselves to enemy fire while crossing the barren ground between trenches. Although the infantry would still have to do most of the heavy fighting, the armored divisions could slice through the enemy lines and create openings for the foot soldiers to exploit.

The adaptation of aircraft to military use portended an even greater revolution in war fighting than the tank. In 1914 airplanes had been hardly more than toys. They were novelties that often killed their makers but had little effect on anyone else. Yet by 1917 both sides were finding dozens of military uses for these devices that lifted their operators out of the mud and added a third dimension of movement to fighting that had stalemated in two. At first the airplanes did better what balloons had been doing for years: looking down on enemies from above and locating vulnerable points. From spotting vulnerabilities to attacking them—with hand grenades, then with larger bombs and wing- and fuselage-mounted machine guns—was an obvious step. In the autumn of 1917, the Germans took another step, one that carried them to a thoroughly modern conception of air power. They staged a series of raids against the population of London. The idea was to carry the war to the enemy's home and demoralize the enemy's people.

Military planners would require an additional generation and another world war to integrate tanks and airplanes fully into their destructive schemes; during the First World War the new inventions served chiefly to inject some motion into what had been a very static conflict. With the opposing sides so evenly balanced, a little advantage for one side or the other could have a large effect, and in certain battles the new weapons determined the difference between victory and defeat. These weapons also threw off the planners' timetables.

Political developments, especially in Russia, likewise fouled up forecasting. In the autumn of 1917, Lenin's Bolshevik party staged a coup that ousted Kerensky and left Lenin in control of Russian affairs—to the extent anyone was during the next few turbulent years. Having preached that the war was a capitalist plot against the proletarians of the world, and that socialists should have nothing to do with it, Lenin immediately set out to end Russian participation. He probably would have done so even if ideology had not pointed him in that direction since weariness with the war had been a prime cause of dissatisfaction with the czar's government and subsequently with Kerensky's.

Awkwardly, though, at the time the Bolsheviks took power, the Germans held a large portion of Russian territory. To quit the war would probably mean conceding control of this occupied territory to Germany. When Bolshevik negotiators raised the question with German representatives in December 1917, the latter confirmed that such was precisely what quitting the war would mean. The Bolsheviks squirmed for several weeks, then walked out of the peace talks. The Germans responded by taking more Russian territory. In March 1918 the Bolsheviks accepted Germany's terms in the treaty of Brest-Litovsk.

By leaving the war, Russia allowed Germany to move hundreds of thousands of troops from the eastern front to the west. They arrived just in time for what Berlin hoped would be the war-winning offensive. The German offensive began in March 1918 and lasted into the summer. Spurning the need for reserves, the Germans threw everything they had into the battle for northern France. They drove the French back toward Paris and the British toward the English Channel. (See map, page 48.)

The Allied lines bent alarmingly, but they did not break. Although the Americans were not completely responsible, their presence afforded the British and French greater flexibility in meeting the German onslaught than otherwise would have been possible. As important as anything, the appearance of the Americans bolstered morale in Britain and France. For the British and French, the worst was over: the Allied side would get stronger with each passing month. Conversely, the Americans' appearance cracked Germany's spirit: the Germans knew that with each passing month their chances of victory diminished.

Just because the end was in sight did not mean it was particularly close. Getting there required lots of bloody fighting, in which the Americans took full part. During June 1918, they fought at Château-Thierry, blunting a last-ditch German drive toward Paris. In July they launched a counterattack along the Marne River, throwing the Germans back toward their homeland. As German forces retreated, Americans continued to pour into France. Their total number passed the 1 million mark during the summer of 1918 and increased at a rate of some quarter million per month.

Crucial in allowing the Americans to cross the ocean in such numbers were developments in the battle of the Atlantic. During the first four months after the German announcement of unrestricted submarine warfare, the U-boats sank more than eleven hundred ships, a greater number than they had destroyed in all of 1916. This appalling toll caused the British admiralty to switch from a strategy of patrolling the sea lanes to one of convoying: gathering merchantmen into groups and escorting the groups with warships. This strategy prevented the U-boats from picking off lone freighters; as soon as a submarine fired a torpedo, it revealed its location to the warships guarding the convoy and immediately came under attack. Despite the fact that the change in strategy caused the German submariners to be more cautious, U-boat sinkings increased sharply. The entry of the United States into the fighting increased the pressure on the German submarine fleet, although the American navy began the fighting deficient in cruisers and other antisubmarine vessels. By the end of 1917, the German submarines were more an annoyance than a serious threat. Not a single American transport ship carrying troops to Europe was sunk by a German torpedo.

German reverses in France helped unravel the rest of the Central powers' position. In October 1918 Italians attacked Austria-Hungary from the south. The Austro-Hungarians were in even worse shape than the Germans after four years of war and blockade, and their armies soon disintegrated. The different national groups making up the Austrian imperial military forces abandoned the war effort and headed for their separate homes. At the beginning of November, Austria-Hungary took itself out of the war by signing an armistice. At about the same time, Ottoman Turkey, beset by Allied forces advancing through the Balkan peninsula, did likewise.

Germany, suddenly isolated and vulnerable to invasion from the west and south, began crumbling from within. Sailors mutinied at Kiel, seizing that city and other ports of northern Germany. A revolution broke out in Bavaria against the rule of the kaiser and his generals. The insurrectionary spirit took hold across the country, forcing Wilhelm's abdication and resulting in the proclamation of a German republic. Two days later, on November 11, 1918, German representatives accepted the Allies' offer of an armistice.

The Origins of the American National Security State

Although Americans played an important role in ending the fighting in Europe, the war had as great an impact on the United States as the United States had on the war. Economically, the war's impact came in two phases. The first phase preceded American entry: during this period, the purchases by the belligerents lifted American industry and American farms out of recession and reminded them of the invigorating effect of foreign wars on American profits and incomes. During this phase as well, Americans began lending heavily in Europe for the first time. About 1915 or 1916 the United States crossed the divide that separates debtor nations from creditors: prior to this time Americans had owed foreigners more than foreigners had owed Americans, while afterward the foreigners owed the Americans more. After American entry into the war, as the United States government began lending heavily to the governments of the Allies, the balance of credit shifted even more. In certain respects, the distinction between being a net creditor and a net debtor was mostly psychological: individuals and firms had to balance their own books regardless of the overall position of the United States relative to other countries. Yet as the debt the world owed America continued to grow, America's bargaining power with respect to other countries increased. And with the large bills owed by the Allied governments to the American government, Uncle Sam's voice carried more persuasive power than ever.

The second phase of the war's effect on the American economy followed American entry; during this phase, a modern and industrialized America fully mobilized for war for the first time. In the presidential campaign of 1912, progressives had split on the best method of keeping big business in line. Theodore Roosevelt advocated a policy of regulation: let big business stay big, but appoint government regulators to prevent it from trampling the little people. Woodrow Wilson had contended that big business would always defy regulation; government had to knock big business down to smaller size. Although Wilson won, he soon began rethinking his position. Partly because he came to see some wisdom in Roosevelt's arguments, and partly because he wanted to bring Roosevelt's followers into his reformist coalition, Wilson gradually moved in the direction of accepting big business as a necessary evil, or perhaps not even such an evil.

With the approach of war, Wilson started to see big business in a still more favorable light. Where the president formerly had stressed fairness in economic matters, now he concentrated on productivity. The country needed to churn out as many bullets, boots, bayonets, blankets, and bandages as possible in the shortest possible time. To achieve this output, Wilson turned to American business operating in alliance with government agencies of unprecedented powers. The most important of these agencies was the War Industries Board (WIB), headed by Bernard Baruch, a Wall Streeter whom Wilson would not have been caught dead with only a few years before. Working through a combination of statutory authority and moral suasion, Baruch and the WIB supervised all major aspects of American industrial production. The WIB apportioned raw materials, established quotas, and fixed prices. It effectively suspended the operation of the free market in large sectors of American industry, pushing America toward a corporatist economy in which big business, big government, and, to a lesser extent, big labor collaborated in making the country's big economic decisions.

For the first time, American business executives, American government officials, and American labor organizers came to realize the potential in close cooperation. American production boomed, profits soared, and wages increased, though not as rapidly as profits. Government protected business by suspending antitrust regulations, fostering cartel-like arrangements, and discouraging strikes. It protected labor by improving working conditions and hours and ensuring the right of collective bargaining. Labor leaders refrained from taking advantage of labor shortages to demand wages as high as they might otherwise have achieved. Business leaders refrained from pushing prices as high as they could have gone.

The social effects of the war were as great as the economic effects. The demands of wartime industry pulled hundreds of thousands of African Americans from the farms of the South to the cities of the North. Women entered the paid work force in greater numbers than before—giving impetus to demands for women's suffrage. The war also contributed to the drive for prohibition as temperance advocates persuaded the War Department to keep liquor out of the army's training camps lest the boys in uniform lose their bearings in stressful circumstances.

The war produced an atmosphere unconducive to dissent and nonconformity. Once American soldiers began dying in Europe, dissent began to look, to

Not many American women worked in weapons factories before the war, but by 1918 they were putting out bullets by the millions, along with countless other items of war. *U.S. Army*

many Americans, suspiciously like treason. Government officials and self-appointed vigilantes undertook to stifle all questioning of American war aims or motives. In 1917 Congress passed an Espionage Act specifying prison terms of up to twenty years for persons convicted of encouraging disloyalty to the United States. In 1918 the legislature approved a Sedition Act extending the ban to much run-of-the-mill criticism of the government. Private groups demanded "100 percent Americanism" and hounded German-Americans into renouncing their cultural heritage or at least renaming it: sauerkraut became "liberty cabbage," while hamburger became "Salisbury steak." Repression reached out to crush radical labor organizations like the Industrial Workers of the World and disable radical political parties like the American Socialists.

American involvement in the First World War also contributed to the concentration of power in the hands of the American president. During the war Wilson became more powerful than any president before him. As commander in chief he controlled an army of nearly 3 million and a large and rapidly growing navy; as head of the executive branch he directed the operation of the WIB and other boards, which in turn directed major sectors of the American economy. The Sedition Act allowed him to jail political opponents such as

Socialist leader Eugene Debs. Never in American history had one person so thoroughly directed the destiny of the nation. To many, the precedent seemed ominous.

Making Peace

Not surprisingly in light of his desire to have a strong hand in shaping the postwar peace settlement, Wilson started talking about peace arrangements well before the fighting ended. He received his best early opportunity at the beginning of 1918. In the several weeks since the Bolshevik takeover in Russia, Lenin and his accomplices had attempted to embarrass the capitalists of the world and promote world revolution by publishing various secret agreements among the governments of the Allied countries. These secret agreements described plans for apportioning the territories of the Central powers should they be defeated. Seasoned observers of international affairs found nothing especially shocking in the secret treaties, and Wilson himself had known of their existence, if perhaps not all of their details. Indeed, his suspicions about such pacts had been a major reason for his insistence that the United States be an associated, rather than an allied, power. But by publishing the treaties, Lenin cast the war aims of the Allies in a dubious light, and he forced Wilson to answer the obvious charge that there was little to distinguish the two sides in the war.

In January 1918 Wilson delivered his riposte. In his "Fourteen Points" speech, he outlined a vision of a world that in important respects paralleled the progressive America he had been attempting to create at home for five years. He called for "open covenants of peace openly arrived at," and he explicitly disavowed secret treaties. He specified freedom of the seas during peace and war. He affirmed the commercial principle of the Open Door (the removal of trade barriers, and equality of commercial opportunities), to be applied as widely as possible. He recommended a reduction of arsenals. He sought an adjustment of colonial claims and self-determination for the inhabitants of the Austro-Hungarian and Ottoman empires. As the capstone of this framework of international relations, Wilson advocated the establishment of a League of Nations, a prototype of world government designed to prevent future wars like the present one.

The Allied governments greeted Wilson's list with a scornful yawn. Clemenceau remarked that God had given man ten commandments and man had broken them all; now Wilson wanted to impose fourteen. After four years of an unimaginably horrible war, the Allies were not about to be cheated out of the fruits of victory. Let Wilson prattle about high ideals; the Americans, latecomers that they were, had not suffered the way the peoples of France and Britain had. Germany must pay for the destruction it had caused.

For the same reasons that London and Paris did not like the Fourteen Points, Berlin did. In October 1918 the Germans offered to lay down their weapons on the basis of Wilson's plan. Britain and France did not want to give any guarantees to Germany, but when Wilson hinted that British and French obstinacy might dispose him to consider a separate peace with the Germans, the British and French reluctantly accepted, subject to certain reservations on the details of some of Wilson's points. London and Paris calculated that if they could not get what they needed at this point, they might have better luck at the postwar peace conference.

Despite the Allied resistance, when Wilson traveled to Paris for the January 1919 opening of the peace conference he hoped to erect a peace treaty on the framework of his Fourteen Points. Though naive in certain respects, Wilson was perceptive enough to realize that getting the British and French to agree to the nonpunitive peace he had in mind would be a huge job. For this reason he had decided to go to Paris himself. The presence of the president, the only head of state at the conference (in contrast to mere heads of government such as Prime Ministers Lloyd George and Clemenceau), gave his views more weight than they would have had if forwarded by Secretary Lansing or some other underling. At the same time, however, his presence set him up for a greater fall. By devoting nearly half a year to writing a peace treaty in Paris, in a pre-airplane age when he could not readily hop back across the Atlantic and tend to American government business, the president placed enormous pressure on himself to come home with something worthwhile.

The task was not easy. The British and French had been willing to humor Wilson as long as they needed American supplies, money, and troops, but their good humor diminished drastically after the Allied victory, and America's political leverage decreased proportionately. (Nevertheless, Wilson, often thought a humorless prig, managed to find some levity for dealing with his fellow peacemakers. When Italian prime minister Vittorio Orlando laid claim to the Adriatic port city of Fiume on grounds that the language, population, and culture of the city were overwhelmingly Italian, Wilson put him off by saying, "I hope you won't press the point in respect to New York City, or you might feel like claiming a sizable piece of Manhattan Island." Orlando did not appreciate the joke, and he left the peace conference in a huff.) The British were not about to accept Wilson's demand for freedom of the seas; had the seas been free during this most recent conflict, the Germans might well have been the ones dictating terms to the British rather than the other way around. The British and French both were willing to help Wilson dismantle the Austro-Hungarian and Ottoman empires, but they looked decidedly askance at his call for a general adjustment of colonial boundaries and his embrace of the principle of self-determination. Equal commercial opportunity was easy for Wilson to advocate because America had the most powerful economy in the world; it was considerably less attractive to those in Britain and France who liked the coziness of protected markets. What good were empires if you could not close the door to outsiders?

At a deeper level, Lloyd George and Clemenceau perceived international relations quite differently from Wilson. As a progressive, Wilson believed that order was the natural state of world affairs, or could be made to be the natural state by the application of human intelligence. Humans might not be perfectible, but given the proper guidance they could get nearer to perfection. Wilson conceived of war as something akin to political corruption in the United States: an aberration rather than the norm. Just as curing American corruption required throwing out the bosses that thrived on it and establishing institutions, such as responsible city government and primary elections, designed to prevent the bosses' return, curing war required throwing out those governments that started it—the German people had already accomplished this for Germany— and establishing institutions, most importantly the League of Nations, designed to prevent its return.

Lloyd George and Clemenceau, perhaps because they had been closer to the war, held a much gloomier view of human nature. With most conservatives they felt the looming presence of violence at every turn. Anarchy, they believed, not order, was humanity's natural state. They rejected the possibility of an institutional solution to the problem of war, convinced that in the real world of tooth and claw each nation had to look out for itself. Against Wilson's untested internationalism, they preferred the tested nationalist approach to world politics.

While (left to right) Britain's Lloyd George and Italy's Orlando exchange thoughts about punishing Germany and its allies, France's Clemenceau and America's Wilson catch their breath from the Paris negotiations. *F.D.R. Library*

Wilson could often be righteously rigid, tending to give the impression that he had a direct line to God; but when forced, he knew how to cut a deal. Wilson's minimum position included the League of Nations. A bad treaty that contained a League, he judged, could be fixed—by the League. A good treaty that did not contain a League would not be good for long. Wise drafters might cope with the world as it was at this moment, but the world would change. The League was designed to deal with change, and to deal with it peacefully.

In the interest of the League of Nations, Wilson bargained away most of his Fourteen Points. The ones he held onto—the restoration of Belgian independence, the return of Alsace-Lorraine to France, the reestablishment of Poland—did not threaten either Britain or France. Lloyd George and Clemenceau deemed the League innocuous at worst and perhaps even helpful if it kept the Americans interested in preventing a resurgence of German militarism.

Besides giving away much of what he had brought to the table, Wilson accepted several items that arrived with the British and French. He acquiesced in a division of the German and Ottoman empires among Britain, France, and Japan. He agreed to an Allied occupation of the German Rhineland, whose resources were particularly coveted by the French. He approved saddling Germany with an open-ended bill for the costs the Allies had incurred fighting the war. And he let pass a clause laying full guilt for the war on German shoulders.

Wilson contended that the treaty that emerged from the Paris peace conference, and that was signed in June 1919 in the Paris suburb of Versailles, was the best that could be obtained under the circumstances, but his critics, then and for years later, disagreed. Conservatives held that while self-determination might be fine in principle, in practice it left much to be desired. The Allies broke up the Austro-Hungarian empire, but they created nothing to replace it. For all its flaws, that empire had ensured a certain measure of stability in central Europe. Who or what would keep the new successor states—Austria, Hungary, Czechoslovakia, Poland (largely taken from Germany and Russia as well), and Yugoslavia—from fighting among themselves, with repercussions that would spill over into the affairs of the rest of the Continent, just as the Balkan troubles had spilled over in 1914? Similar questions applied to the remains of the Ottoman empire, though the development of the system of "mandates" (territories administered by the great powers in the name of the League of Nations) mitigated to some extent the turbulence in the Middle East.

Critics also pointed to what they saw as the unrealistic economics of the Versailles treaty. Britain and France intended to force Germany to pay for the losses they had suffered; in theory this seemed fair enough, considering that the Germans had caused most of the damage and that Germany had survived the war uninvaded and with the physical structures of its industrial system essentially intact. But the unspecified terms and undoubtedly great magnitude of the reparations would stagger the German economy, perhaps for decades, and would thereby actually tend to prevent the Allies from receiving their money. The Germans could recognize that the harder they worked, the harder Paris and London were likely to squeeze them. What with the revolution in Germany and the other war-induced disruptions, getting the German economy

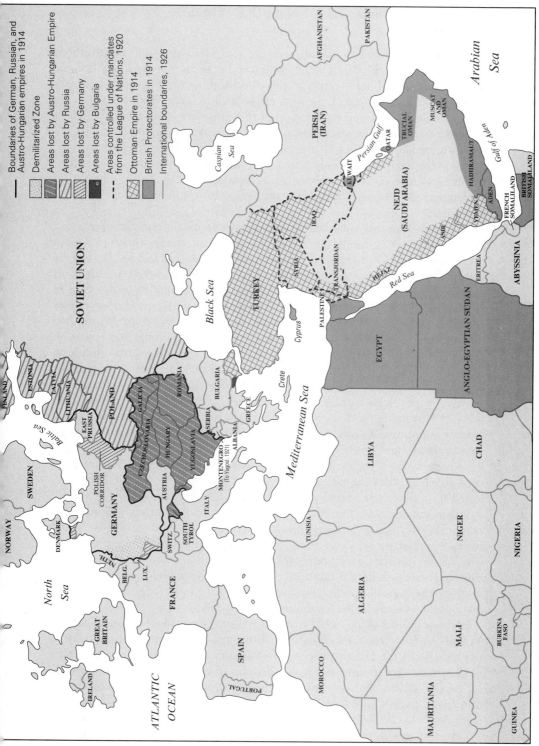

Europe and the Middle East in the 1920s

Boundaries of German, Russian, and Austro-Hungarian empires in 1914

Demilitarized Zone

Areas lost by Austro-Hungarian Empire

Areas lost by Russia

Areas lost by Germany

Areas lost by Bulgaria

Areas controlled under mandates from the League of Nations, 1920

Ottoman Empire in 1914

British Protectorates in 1914

International boundaries, 1926

NORWAY

SWEDEN

FINLAND

ESTONIA

LATVIA

LITHUANIA

SOVIET UNION

Baltic Sea

EAST PRUSSIA

POLAND

POLISH CORRIDOR

GERMANY

DENMARK

North Sea

GREAT BRITAIN

IRELAND

ATLANTIC OCEAN

NETH.

BELG.

LUX.

FRANCE

SWITZ.

SOUTH TYROL

ITALY

AUSTRIA

CZECHOSLOVAKIA

GALICIA

HUNGARY

ROMANIA

YUGOSLAVIA

SERBIA

MONTENEGRO (To Yugosl. 1921)

ALBANIA

GREECE

BULGARIA

Black Sea

TURKEY

Crete

Cyprus

Mediterranean Sea

SPAIN

PORTUGAL

MOROCCO

ALGERIA

TUNISIA

LIBYA

MAURITANIA

MALI

NIGER

CHAD

BURKINA FASO

NIGERIA

GUINEA

Caspian Sea

PERSIA (IRAN)

AFGHANISTAN

PAKISTAN

Persian Gulf

KUWAIT

QATAR

TRUCIAL OMAN

MUSCAT AND OMAN

Arabian Sea

Gulf of Aden

IRAQ

SYRIA

TRANSJORDAN

PALESTINE

HEJAZ

NEJD (SAUDI ARABIA)

HADHRAMAUT

ASIR

YEMEN

ADEN

Red Sea

EGYPT

ANGLO-EGYPTIAN SUDAN

ERITREA

FRENCH SOMALILAND

BRITISH SOMALILAND

ABYSSINIA

back on its feet would be a big job; with the added burden of uncertainty about how much money the Allies were going to take, the job could easily become overwhelming. And until Germany, the workshop of central Europe, got back on its feet, the rest of the Continent might well do little more than stumble along. The most scathing enunciation of this argument came from the pen of John Maynard Keynes, a member of the British peace delegation (and later the most influential economist of the twentieth century). When Keynes saw the direction the Paris negotiations were going, he stalked out of the conference in disgust and tore off *The Economic Consequences of the Peace,* which contended that the Versailles formula was a recipe for future war rather than future peace.

The Versailles treaty encountered additional, specifically American, criticism in the United States. By the time Wilson brought the treaty home to America in the summer of 1919, most of the enthusiasm Americans had felt toward the war had dissipated. The dissipation was partly the result of the typically short attention span of the American political system. The fighting had ceased in November 1918; nine months later the parades were over and people were getting back to their normal peacetime routines. More important, Wilson had oversold the treaty in advance—as indeed he had oversold the whole war effort. Wilson had convinced many Americans that the war was a crusade to make the world safe for democracy, but because he had never convinced the British and French, Americans were bound to be disappointed. Wilson exacerbated his problems by calling on Americans to treat the congressional elections of November 1918 as a referendum on his handling of the war. As a student of politics, Wilson should have recognized that congressional elections almost always turn on local, rather than global, issues. In addition, he should have been wary of the traditional sixth-year itch that often causes voters to seek a change from the policies of a second-term administration. Voters rejected Wilson's call and handed the president an embarrassing defeat.

Wilson's American critics included people with various motives. Some were honest skeptics; some were Republicans looking for a way to reclaim the White House for their party; some were people who simply could not stand Woodrow Wilson. Henry Cabot Lodge, the Republican chairman of the Senate Foreign Relations Committee, qualified on all three counts. Lodge was determined to block the Versailles treaty, and he employed the knowledge he had gained in a quarter century in the Senate toward that end.

Partisan politics aside, what worried Wilson's compatriots most about the Versailles treaty was the League of Nations and the foreign entanglements it implied. While the Europeans generally cared more about the concrete details of the treaty—location of borders, schedules of reparations, rules for demilitarization—than about the League, Americans, having little stake in the details, paid greatest attention to the League. They were especially concerned regarding what American membership in the League would commit them to. Wilson was fighting uphill trying to get them to join. A temporary entanglement in Europe's affairs, in response to direct German aggression against

Henry Cabot Lodge enthusiastically
promoted an ambitious American
foreign policy during the 1890s, but
two decades later he helped scuttle
Woodrow Wilson's ambitions for an
American role in the League of
Nations. *Brown Brothers*

Americans and American property, was one thing: the United States had to
defend itself. Yet the League of Nations was a permanent entanglement, what
Washington and Jefferson had warned about. Moreover, the League would
involve the United States in all manner of minor but dangerous quarrels bearing only in the most indirect fashion on American interests. What if Albania
and Yugoslavia got into a fight over Macedonia? The League might call on
American troops to intervene. Was this something Americans were prepared
to die over? Nor was the League the end of foreign entanglements: Wilson's
critics pointed with alarm to a separate agreement the president had negotiated
with Britain and France pledging Anglo-American assistance to France in the
event of future German aggression. The Europeans might be foolish enough to
refight the recent war, but there was no reason Americans had to be equally
foolish.

Despite the energetic efforts of Lodge and other opponents, Wilson almost
got his treaty. Had he shown even a moderate deference to senatorial sensitivities, he probably would have won Senate approval. But the president adopted
the stance that in Paris he had done all the compromising he was going to do.
A stroke he suffered in September 1919 while campaigning on behalf of the
treaty did not render him any more flexible. He resisted modifications put
forward to address the concerns of undecided senators, particularly with respect to League decisions involving war. His stubbornness, combined with that

of Lodge and other critics, killed the treaty. In November 1919 and again in March 1920, the Senate voted against acceptance. Although the final tally, on the treaty with certain reservations, including one that required the consent of Congress before the president put American troops into action overseas, showed a solid majority in favor, the ratifiers fell seven votes shy of the required two-thirds.

The Specter of Leninism

At the time the Senate rejected the notion that American soldiers ought to impose good behavior on unruly foreigners, American soldiers were trying to do something close to that in Russia. The Bolshevik coup of November 1917 had not only led to Russia's withdrawal from the world war; it had also signaled a challenge to the political and economic status quo in most of the great powers of the world.

The Russian Revolution followed the broad-gauged ideological tradition of the French Revolution rather than the narrower political tradition of the American Revolution. More precisely, while the first stage of the Russian Revolution—the stage that propelled Kerensky to the top of the Russian government—followed the moderate political lines congenial to most Americans, the second—communist—stage carried the revolution past politics into hardcore ideology. It was precisely the ideology of the Russian Revolution that the governments of other countries found so objectionable. Russia's was the first major revolution to be based explicitly on the teachings of Marx and the first to make socialism the guiding principle of political and economic life.

The success of Marxism in taking over Russia, however, owed less to Marx than to Lenin. Marx had contended that socialism would emerge as the outcome of a violent struggle between the class of propertyless industrial workers, or proletariat, and the class of property-owning capitalists. In Marx's conception, the contest between proletarians and capitalists would come to a head first in the most advanced industrial nations, where the growth and oppression of the proletariat had proceeded furthest. Marx looked to Britain, France, or Germany for the initial signs of the coming proletarian revolution. He expected nothing out of stagnant Russia. Lenin had a different idea. Like Marx, Lenin believed in the inevitability of socialism's triumph. But Lenin was more impatient than Marx and was unwilling to consign pride of precedence to a country other than his native Russia. Lenin acknowledged that the Russian proletariat possessed insufficient class consciousness to launch the revolution. The proletariat needed guidance. In offering his own guidance, Lenin made his great contribution to revolutionary theory and practice and put his name next to Marx's in the pantheon of Marxism-Leninism. Lenin conceived of the Communist party as the vanguard of the proletariat: a small, tightly knit cadre of dedicated revolutionaries who would lead the proletariat to the socialist promised land. In this conception the relative size and political maturity of the proletariat did not count for much; the thinkers and organizers who held the positions of power within the Communist party would provide whatever energy and insight the proletariat lacked. As a consequence, the revolutionary readiness of any particular country depended not on the slow development of a large class but on the talents and commitment of a small elite. By this reckoning, Russia was as ripe for revolution as any other country—perhaps riper, given Lenin's own unquestionable talents and ferocious commitment.

It was Leninism fully as much as Marxism that sent shudders through the ruling classes of the industrialized world, including the United States. Marxist socialism they despised as potentially dispossessing them of power, privilege, and property. Conservatives usually have good material reason for being conservative: well placed in the status quo, they have no burning desire to see the status quo shaken. But if socialism had to arrive by the slow method Marx described, they did not have to worry too much. The sun will run out of fuel someday, yet people do not lose sleep over it. Lenin's contention—the paradoxical argument that an elite could accomplish a revolution on behalf of the masses—threatened to move the termination date of the status quo considerably forward. Any country might contain such a revolutionary elite, either homegrown or imported. The small numbers required were what caused all the panic among capitalists. A scattering of domestic malcontents, it seemed, and perhaps a handful of foreign agents might suffice to overturn everything the capitalists held dear.

Marx had been a profound, if ponderous, theoretician, proceeding from premises to conclusions with Germanic resolve. But as a practicing revolutionary he was a flop. Lenin's theorizing was brilliant in its own way: a certain kind of genius was required to torture logic the way Lenin did in redefining as popular revolution what amounted to an elitist political coup. However, Lenin was even more brilliant as a practicing revolutionary, and it was his success at pulling off his coup that made him the model for scores of other revolutionary types in subsequent decades. Lenin followed Marx in describing revolution as an international phenomenon. For Marx, the internationalism of the socialist revolution was a theoretical corollary of the internationalism of capitalism, which produced an international proletariat. For Lenin, the internationalism of the revolution was, in addition, a practical political necessity. Lenin had no doubt that the capitalists would band together to crush the first socialist regime that came to power anywhere; without reinforcements, that regime would disappear under the onslaught. At the least, revolutions in other countries would distract the capitalist rulers of those countries and keep them from launching their assault on the pioneering socialist state.

Most of the capitalist governments in power at the time Lenin seized control in Russia in 1917 proved him right. Germany was something of an exception, but only because of the duress of war. Although the German government had no love for either Marxism or Leninism, it rightly recognized in Lenin an ally against the czar and against Kerensky, both of whom insisted on continuing the fight against Germany. The Germans went so far in assisting Lenin that they allowed him safe passage from exile in Switzerland through German lines into Russia shortly after the outbreak of the February revolution. Lenin returned the favor by pulling Russia out of the war.

As for the governments of Britain and France, Lenin's defection from the Allied coalition confirmed their distrust and dislike of him. Moreover, it provoked them to send troops to Russia in the summer of 1918. The immediate reason for the Allied intervention was to prevent military supplies cached in the Russian north from falling into German hands. With all the effort Britain had put into its blockade of Germany, the last thing the Allies wanted was for the kaiser's troops to come into a windfall of war materiel.

A related purpose of the Allied intervention was to see whether a viable alternative to the Bolsheviks still existed in Russia. Lenin's coup had not gone uncontested: a civil war—in fact several civil wars—raged throughout what had been the czar's domain. Any one of the generals and admirals who led these counterrevolutionary groups was ideologically preferable to the Bolsheviks in the eyes of the Allies, and several seemed more likely than the Bolsheviks to resume the fight against Germany. With a little foreign assistance, one of them might dislodge the Bolsheviks, to the relief of right-thinking governments everywhere and possibly to the benefit of the Allied war effort.

Japan also chose this moment of utmost confusion to invade Russia. The Japanese were the great opportunists of the First World War. They joined the Allies chiefly to pick off Germany's Pacific colonies; they took the opportunity of European and American preoccupation to harass China; and they assaulted Russia when the war and the revolution had knocked it to its knees. The Japanese endeavored to secure as solid a foothold on the Asian mainland as they could before the Western powers finished with their European fighting. Besides, with the other Allies invading Russia from the northwest, Japan believed it had every right to send troops into Russia from the east. In the summer of 1918, Tokyo dispatched seventy thousand soldiers to Siberia.

The United States participated in both interventions. Wilson ordered five thousand American troops to northwestern Russia and ten thousand to Siberia. The president did so reluctantly, aware of the bad company America was keeping in both instances. At a time when he was trying to convince the world of the merits of self-determination, meddling in Russian affairs cut against his grain. Yet if meddling would shorten the war against Germany and save American lives, he could not in good conscience oppose it. Besides, Lenin's regime hardly represented the Russian people in any democratic way; the Bolsheviks were no more legitimate than the revolutionary government of Mexico that Wilson had intervened against a few years earlier. The conservative "White" forces opposing the Bolshevik "Reds" had just as much claim to rule Russia as the Leninists did.

An additional consideration contributed to the American decision to enter Siberia. Since the closing of the eastern front in the world war, a group of Czechs fighting against the Central powers had been looking for a way to continue their struggle. No other avenue presented itself, so the Czechs headed

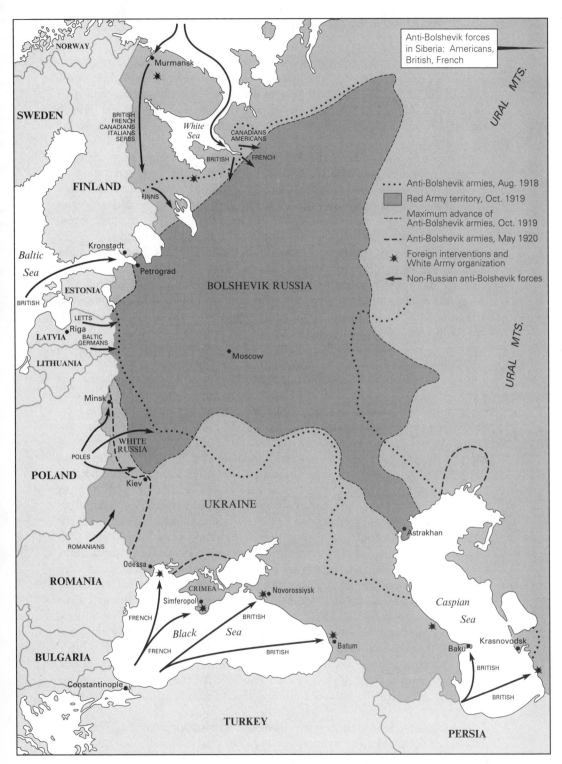

Allied Interventions in Russia and Siberia at the End of the First World War

east along the Trans-Siberian Railroad, figuring to reach the Pacific and board ship for western Europe. On the journey, however, they got tangled up in the Russian civil war. The Czechs had established an effective propaganda machine in the United States, and it did not seem outlandish for the Wilson administration to talk about sending troops to Siberia to help extricate the Czech legion.

A final reason for joining the Allied intervention may have been the most important. The British, French, and Japanese evidently were determined to invade Russia regardless of what the United States did. American troops could monitor the actions of the other countries' troops and perhaps moderate their behavior. The Japanese particularly required watching. Japan might claim some provocation and annex half of Siberia, just as it had annexed Korea. Ten thousand Americans would not eliminate the possibility, but they would make such a move more difficult.

Like many military adventures that lack clear objectives, the American intervention in Russia accomplished a minimum of good at a maximum cost. American troops found themselves caught up in the swirl of the Russian civil war, compounded by the designs and ambitions of the British, French, and Japanese. The Americans did no fighting to speak of, but they provided a small amount of logistical support to the anti-Bolshevik forces. For more than a year, it looked as though the major contingent of Whites, under Admiral Alexander Kolchak, had a chance of reversing the revolution. At one point Kolchak's army controlled most of the region east of the Ural Mountains. But the presence of the Allies and Americans corroded the credibility of the Whites. Although the Reds had given away hundreds of thousands of square miles of Russian territory to the Germans at Brest-Litovsk, Lenin and the Bolsheviks were able to portray themselves as the patriotic defenders of the motherland against foreign invaders, now in league with czarist reactionaries. Even more effective than Bolshevik propaganda was the Red army. After some initial ineptitude, the Bolshevik soldiers, led by Leon Trotsky, learned how to fight. The Reds scattered the Whites by the autumn of 1920 and won the civil war.

The Americans had departed by then. They left northwestern Russia in the summer of 1919 and Siberia the following spring. But the memory of their presence remained behind. For the next sixty years, whenever leaders of the Soviet Union (the new name for the empire the Bolsheviks inherited from the czar) wanted to make the case that the capitalist aggressors were bent on the destruction of socialism, they merely pointed to the fact that the great capitalist powers had done their best to strangle socialism at its Soviet birth. Soviet troops had never invaded Britain, France, Japan, or the United States, yet troops from each of those countries had invaded the Soviet Union. Moreover, they had actively collaborated with the traitorous enemies of the revolution.

From time immemorial, Russians have had an invasion complex. This complex is not without cause: living in a flat country, with almost no natural barriers against foreign armies, the Russians have seen their homeland ravaged time and again by Mongols, Tatars, French, Germans, and other intruders. With such a history, the Russians could hardly avoid developing a phobia regarding invasion. The Allied and American invasions at the end of the First World War reinforced this phobia. They tied the Russian people more closely than before to the Bolshevik government, and, as the invasions involved the United States, portrayed America as a den of vengeful capitalists. They definitely did not do any good for friendly Soviet-American relations.

The World War and Asia

Although by the time of the First World War the United States was arguably a global power, it still lacked the reach to fight major wars in Europe and the Pacific at the same time. Just as the conflict in Europe caused the Wilson administration to back away from its confrontation with Mexico, so the conflict caused the administration to tread lightly in East Asia.

The most significant event of the decade of the First World War in Asia was the final collapse of the Qing dynasty in China; and the fundamental significance of the Qing collapse was that it marked the political dissolution of China itself. Dynasties had come and gone in the past, more than a dozen in nearly four thousand years. In the Chinese view, rulers and ruling families retained the right to govern China so long as they enjoyed the "mandate of heaven," a loosely defined seal of providential approval. But once heaven rescinded the mandate—as evidenced by unusually severe or frequent calamities: floods, famines, civil unrest, foreign invasion—the Chinese people no longer owed the rulers their obedience. The idea was not too far from the social-contract notions of Enlightenment thinkers in the West, though it had mystical overtones that would have made Locke and Voltaire wince. The romantic Rousseau might have had an easier time with it.

The barbarian—that is, European and American—encroachments of the mid-nineteenth century had provided powerful testimony that the mandate of heaven was slipping from the grasp of the Qings. China's humiliation by Japan in the Sino-Japanese War at the end of the century added further testimony in the same vein. The foreign—including American—invasion to suppress the Boxer uprising in 1900, and first Russian and then Japanese meddling in Manchuria (the ancestral home of the Qings, of all places), appeared to clinch the argument.

The Qings made a final effort to save themselves. The empress dowager Cixi placed the Chinese army under the command of the capable and relatively forward-looking Yuan Shikai. Western topics were added to China's educational curriculum. Of greatest symbolic importance, the ancient system of examinations for public office, based on the Confucian classics, was abolished. But the reforms came too late—for the Qings, if not for China. Cixi died in 1908, and the old lady left the throne to a toddler. Bickering soon began over who should act as regent in the monarch's youth. The bickering provided the signal various revolutionary factions around the country had been waiting for.

The most important of the revolutionary factions was led by Sun Yatsen. Sun had received a Western education from American missionaries in Hawaii and from British colonialists in Hong Kong, and he had devised a political philosophy that put a Chinese twist on some of the basic ideas of the Enlightenment. He summarized his philosophy in a three-part slogan: Nationalism, Democracy, People's Livelihood. Although the third part was a bit obscure to many in the West, the first two seemed straightforward enough. That Sun was a Christian worked in his favor as well.

Sun had long looked to America for support in his revolutionary endeavors, partly because of America's revolutionary tradition and partly because the United States had expressed concern for China's welfare against pressure from the great powers—for instance by the McKinley administration's Open Door notes of 1899–1900. In fact, Sun was on a fund-raising tour in America in the

Sun Yatsen did not overthrow the Qing dynasty by himself, but he had more to do with the deed than anyone else. *The Bettman Archive*

autumn of 1911 when word arrived that a major part of the Chinese imperial army had abandoned the Qings. Within months much of southern and central China proclaimed itself free of Qing control. Sun returned to China and had himself named president of a freshly proclaimed Chinese republic.

Meanwhile Yuan Shikai was rallying loyalists in the army in the north. But rather than attack Sun, the general negotiated with him. The result was a bargain whereby Sun handed the presidency of the Chinese republic to Yuan in exchange for Yuan's agreement to engineer the peaceful abdication of the Qing emperor. No one asked the little boy's opinion; he was given the imperial palace to play in and promised all the toys he wanted.

Yuan was a strong president but not much of a revolutionary. He had no use for Sun's three principles and, after concluding his deal with Sun, no use for Sun either. Yuan attempted to monopolize power, to the extent of dreaming of restoring the monarchy with himself as emperor. Yet he failed to convince others of the worthiness of his dream, and though he held a firm grip on Beijing, the provinces increasingly slipped beyond the reach of the central government.

Americans watched the events in China with fascination often joined to puzzlement. They understood Sun, more or less, but Yuan was harder to fathom. At first his apparent embrace of the republic led the Wilson administration to extend diplomatic recognition to his government. His desire to make himself emperor, however, left Americans cold.

Besides recognizing Yuan, Wilson retreated from the Republican practice of dollar diplomacy in China. The Taft administration had twisted the arms of the European powers to let American bankers in on an international consortium for railroad construction in Manchuria. Although the Chinese government accepted the arrangement, many of the Chinese people did not, especially when Japan and Russia agitated to join the consortium. Popular disapproval of the concession was one of the contributing causes of the 1911 revolution. Wilson did not like acting as the agent of American capitalists, and he felt equally uncomfortable collaborating with the European imperialists and the Japanese against the Chinese. Not long after entering office, he withdrew the United States from the consortium.

In 1915 Wilson again came to the aid of the Chinese against foreign coercion. In that year the Japanese took advantage of Europe's distraction and China's disintegration to press Beijing for a special place in Chinese affairs. By the so-called Twenty-one Demands, Tokyo attempted to reduce China to a Japanese protectorate. Several of the demands—that Japan inherit Germany's sphere of influence in Shandong, for example, and that China not cede coastal areas to third powers without Japan's approval—were not entirely unreasonable in light of current international practices (including the American Monroe Doctrine, as the Japanese pointed out). But a final set of demands—that the Chinese government accept Japanese advisers in China's financial, police, and military ministries—would have made the Chinese government almost a puppet of Tokyo. Although this was essentially the arrangement the United States had established with Cuba (as the Japanese also pointed out), Wilson refused to accept Japan's argument or countenance its demands.

Not everyone in the Japanese government thought the Twenty-one Demands were a good idea. Most Japanese officials believed their country should have a large voice in what happened in Japan's neighborhood, just as the United States had a large voice in the Western Hemisphere; but many thought China was too big for Japan to handle. Japan trying to control China would be like a minnow trying to swallow a tuna.

Consequently, when the Wilson administration, after several months of hemming and hawing, protested the demands, and when Britain joined the protest, the Tokyo government backed off. Japanese expansionists did not drop the idea of puppetizing China, however; they simply deferred implementation of the idea until a more propitious moment.

To get the deferral on paper, the Wilson administration opened talks with Tokyo that led to the Lansing-Ishii agreement of 1917. By this accord the United States affirmed that Japan might expect to have "special relations" with China on account of the close quarters at which the two countries lived; in exchange Japan reiterated its support for the Open Door policy of Chinese territorial integrity. In addition, both parties consented to refrain from taking advantage of the world war to gain unusual privileges in China.

The Lansing-Ishii accord came amid another round of turbulence in American-Japanese relations. In the United States, Californians were up to their old anti-Japanese ways. In 1913 the state legislature in Sacramento had passed a law effectively barring Japanese from owning land in the state. The Japanese government, which really did not care all that much about expatriates who had abandoned Japan for America, used the measure to whip up anti-American sentiment in Japan and thereby create an incentive for Washington to do something nice to soothe Japanese feelings. Although the Twenty-one Demands turned out to be too much soothing for Washington's tastes, Japan's terms in the Lansing-Ishii pact proved acceptable.

Such modest good feeling as the Lansing-Ishii pact produced did not last beyond the end of the world war. At the Paris peace conference, the Japanese asked that a statement affirming racial equality be included in the charter of the League of Nations. Wilson opposed the inclusion, realizing that it would complicate approval of the peace treaty in the Senate since Californians and others in the United States feared that such a statement might lead to increased immigration from Asia. The British joined Wilson in opposition, due to similar resistance by Canada and Australia, for similar reasons. The Anglo-American veto killed the Japanese proposal and antagonized the Japanese.

*   *   *

The decade of the First World War introduced Americans to the blood-and-steel politics of international affairs in a way nothing before had. Americans were not alone in feeling they were experiencing something new: neither had anyone else encountered the collective insanity the war released across the Atlantic world. If the governments and people of the great powers had known in 1914 what the world war would demand of them, they almost certainly would not have let the minor altercation that started it get so far out of control. One German officer remarked, "No one would have dared at the beginning of the war to expect from the soldier what he afterward had to endure for years as a constant necessity." Much the same thing could have been said about the civilian populations involved. But wars develop a momentum of their own, and what staggered imaginations in 1914 scarcely raised eyebrows by 1916. The very horrendousness of the price the Europeans were paying for their folly made it all the more difficult for them to stop. No government could stand if it acknowledged that the losses its country had suffered had been in vain. Russia could not quit the war until two governments had fallen. Germany had to oust the kaiser and his generals before conceding that the cause was lost.

The one hope that remained to those who escaped the carnage was that it would not happen again. The world had barely survived this time; if another such war occurred, civilization would surely cease. The European victors had one answer to the question of how to prevent a repeat: crush Germany and keep it from rising again. Woodrow Wilson had another: create an international organization that could accommodate peaceful change and punish forcible change. Either solution—the nationalist or the internationalist—might have worked if implemented by itself and consistently. If Germany had been kept flat on its back, it would not have been able to cause the trouble it later did. If a League of Nations invested with effective enforcement powers and supported by all the biggest countries had come into existence, it might have provided enough room for states with grievances against their neighbors to complain and be heard, but not enough for them to batter their neighbors into submission.

The solution that emerged from the Paris peace conference, however, was neither one nor the other. Germany was burdened but not crushed, wounded but not killed. The Germans were made to confess to causing the war, yet they did not believe their own confession, and they left the conference feeling sinned against rather than sinful. Many people in the victorious countries saw reason in some of the German complaints, which only confirmed the sense of injustice the Germans felt and made it difficult for the victors to enforce the most punitive aspects of the treaty. Nor did the treaty suffice by internationalist criteria. Here the fault lay with the Americans, who refused to join the League of Nations. International law, which was what the League was designed to establish and uphold, is essentially an all-or-nothing affair: as soon as one major party to disputes opts out, the entire system tends to lose the respect of the rest. Before long, international law can become a dead letter.

Americans in 1920 had the luxury of opting out of the Versailles system. Those senators who rejected the treaty on behalf of the United States took the position that the American government could better protect Americans' interests by acting unilaterally. This had been the American position for the century and a half before the war; at war's end it again possessed great appeal. Considering what the war had cost and what had occurred at Paris to subvert the prospects of a lasting peace, this position was not at all unreasonable. A later generation would think it mistaken, but it was not unreasonable.

Sources and Suggestions for Further Reading

An exhaustive account of the origins of the First World War is Luigi Albertini's three-volume *The Origins of the War of 1914* (1952–57). Laurence Lafore, *The Long Fuse* (1965), is more concise. The best military history of the war is B. H. Liddell Hart, *History of the First World War* (1970). Barbara Tuchman, *The Guns of August* (1962), is an engrossing popular account of the beginning of the war.

The developments that led the United States into the war are treated in Ernest R. May, *The World War and American Isolation* (1959); Ross Gregory, *The Origins of American Intervention in the First World War* (1971); Patrick Devlin, *Too Proud to Fight* (1974); and John W. Coogan, *The End of Neutrality: The U.S., Britain, and Maritime Rights, 1899–1915* (1981). Daniel M. Smith, *The Great Departure* (1965), covers the period of American neutrality as well as America's participation in the war and the peace conference. Edward M. Coffman, *The War to End All Wars* (1968), concentrates on the military aspects of American involvement in the war, as does Laurence Stallings, *The Doughboys* (1963). The best description of American politics, economy, and society during the war is David M. Kennedy, *Over Here* (1980).

Numerous authors have studied Woodrow Wilson's diplomacy and leadership. Arthur S. Link is the most authoritatively sympathetic to Wilson, in several volumes, especially *Wilson: The Struggle for Neutrality, 1914–1915* (1960); *Wilson: Confusions and Crises, 1915–1916* (1964); and *Woodrow Wilson: War, Revolution, and Peace* (1979). N. Gordon Levin, Jr., *Woodrow Wilson and World Politics* (1968), is more critical of Wilson. Arno J. Mayer, *Wilson vs. Lenin* (1959), contrasts Wilson's approach to international affairs to Lenin's. Lloyd C. Gardner, *Safe for Democracy* (1984), sets Wilson's reactions to the turmoil of the decade of the war against the reactions of his British counterparts. George F. Kennan, *The Decision to Intervene* (1958), deals with the Allied and American interventions in the Soviet Union, as do Richard Goldhurst, *The Midnight War* (1978), and Betty Unterberger, *America's Siberian Expedition* (1956).

The Paris peace conference is well covered in Howard Elcock, *Portrait of a Decision* (1972), and Arno J. Mayer, *Politics and Diplomacy of Peacemaking* (1967). Thomas A. Bailey is critical in *Woodrow Wilson and the Lost Peace* (1944) and *Woodrow Wilson and the Great Betrayal* (1945). Herbert Hoover is more charitable in *The Ordeal of Woodrow Wilson* (1958). Seth P. Tillman, *Anglo-American Relations at the Paris Peace Conference* (1961), looks at one aspect of American peace diplomacy; Klaus Schwabe, *Woodrow Wilson, Revolutionary Germany, and Peacemaking, 1918–1919* (1985), looks at another. Robert J. Maddox, *William E. Borah and American Foreign Policy* (1969), and Ralph Stone, *The Irreconcilables* (1970), examine the opposition to the Versailles treaty in the United States, and with the books by Bailey and Hoover explain why the treaty failed in the Senate.

The policy of the Wilson administration toward East Asia is investigated in Burton F. Beers, *Vain Endeavor* (1962), on Robert Lansing's diplomacy toward Japan; and Daniel M. Crane and Thomas A. Breslin, *An Ordinary Relationship* (1986), on the American response to the Chinese revolution. Another angle is provided by James Reed, *The Missionary Mind and American East Asia Policy, 1911–1915* (1983).

Chapter 9

In the World But Not of the World, 1920–1937

Although some Americans would have been happy in 1920 for the United States to turn its back on the rest of the world, that was never a genuine option. America's stake in the world—in terms of economics, politics, and military security—was too great for Americans to retire into a shell. And no American administration from 1920 through the end of the 1930s attempted to do so. Yet each administration sought to control as closely as possible the terms on which the United States dealt with the world. Many Americans felt they had been suckered during the First World War into fighting for objectives determined by Britain and France rather than for objectives directly tied to American interests. During the 1920s and 1930s, American leaders took care to limit their commitments and thereby keep the initiative regarding American actions firmly in American hands. If three Republican presidents and one Democratic had not pursued such a policy on their own, they would have been nearly forced to it by a wary Congress and an equally skeptical American public.

Americans were not alone in their reluctance to go crusading abroad. The war had exhausted and disillusioned Europeans even more than Americans, and though the Europeans could not as easily avoid international commitments as the Americans, they often tried. The League of Nations, established to preserve international peace and order, failed to do so when its members could not bring themselves to take the strong actions necessary to make aggression unprofitable.

For a time, the international revulsion toward war had few ill effects, but the onset of a world depression at the beginning of the 1930s, which precipitated a trade war among the industrialized powers, together with the emergence of belligerently authoritarian governments in Italy, Japan, and Germany, produced an atmosphere in which the violence of the few proceeded unchecked by the hesitancy of the many. Americans managed to assert their interests in the Western Hemisphere without running what most of them considered to be undue risks. But in Europe and East Asia, the risks appeared larger and the interests less vital; consequently, Americans adopted a low profile, hoping the storm would blow over.

Chronology

1921	Washington Conference begins
1922	Fordney-McCumber tariff; Rapallo treaty between Germany and Soviet Union; Mussolini takes power in Italy
1923	German passive resistance to French occupation of Rhineland
1924	Dawes plan; Congress curbs immigration
1925	Locarno conference and treaties
1926	Army Air Corps established
1927	Oil dispute with Mexico settled; U.S. troops return to Nicaragua
1928	Kellogg-Briand pact; Clark memorandum on Roosevelt corollary
1929	Young plan; New York stock market crash
1930	Hawley-Smoot tariff; first cyclotron constructed, allowing nuclear fission; London naval conference extends limits on shipbuilding
1931	Credit-Anstalt bank fails in Austria; Hoover moratorium on reparations and debts; Japan seizes Manchuria
1932	Stimson doctrine of nonrecognition
1933	Japan abandons League of Nations; Franklin Roosevelt refuses important American role in London economic conference; Hitler becomes chancellor of Germany; Roosevelt recognizes Soviet Union
1934	Nye committee commences hearings; Moscow purges begin
1935	Italy attacks Ethiopia; Neutrality Act of 1935; Hitler repudiates Versailles treaty
1936	Neutrality Act of 1936; Spanish Civil War starts; German army reoccupies Rhineland; Anti-Comintern pact between Germany and Japan (Italy joins in 1937)
1937	Neutrality Act of 1937; Japan attacks China, brutalizes Nanjing; Roosevelt's "quarantine" speech

Running Like a Ford

The United States could not seriously consider retiring from world affairs because, for one thing, Americans were too dependent on the world economy. After the American international balance sheet broke even during the early years of the world war, with American debts to other countries matching other countries' debts to the United States, the ledger ran heavily into the black during the subsequent years. By the early 1920s the United States was the world's largest creditor, with substantial American claims, in the form of loans and investments, on Europe, Canada, and Latin America and smaller claims on East Asia. No American government, especially not the Republican administrations of the 1920s, could ignore these claims or the political concern they generated. Different factions in Washington and elsewhere in the country might differ over the most effective means for safeguarding American economic interests abroad, but few argued that the American government should not pay them careful attention.

In addition to investment and loans, Americans showed great concern for foreign export markets. The American prosperity of the war years had been generated in large part by foreign orders. Those orders diminished, as everyone expected they would, with the war's end. But neither the Wilson administration nor those of Warren Harding or Calvin Coolidge desired to see the prosperity end. Accordingly, they set out to promote American goods in foreign countries. Directives emanated from the State Department to American consuls abroad to report on promising opportunities for American products and firms and to strive to create such opportunities. The American Commerce Department, headed by the rising star of the Republican party, Herbert Hoover, was even more aggressive. Hoover organized what amounted to a second foreign service, one devoted exclusively to pushing American products in foreign

Herbert Hoover (right) was more loquacious than Calvin Coolidge but less lucky. The stock market is getting ready to crash. *Brown Brothers*

markets. The commerce agents' work was unspectacular, and most Americans were hardly aware of it. But America's economic competitors knew what these government-sponsored sales representatives were up to. They also knew of various other methods—favorable tax treatment, waivers of antitrust laws, diplomatic and economic pressure on foreign cartels, manipulation of American loans—Washington employed to open foreign markets and boost American sales and investment overseas. On the basis of this knowledge, America's competitors never took seriously the idea that Washington had somehow retired from international life.

In certain respects they wished Washington would have. During the 1920s America's economic strength became more obvious than ever, as American industry fully entered the age of mass production. Henry Ford's automobile factories epitomized the trend, spewing out vehicles by the millions and in the process driving prices down. At one time forecasters had predicted that the size of the automobile market would be limited by the number of persons who could act as chauffeurs; Ford's genius lay in conceiving of the automobile as a product for the common person and not just the wealthy. His genius also lay in the single-minded determination with which he put his conception into practice.

Ford benefited, as did other American manufacturers, from the huge size of the American market. Railroads linked every corner of the United States to every other, and not a tariff or a customs agent impeded passage of goods

America's not-so-secret weapon: New cars roll down the assembly line at Ford's latest plant. *Brown Brothers*

anywhere along the way. American industrialists could take maximum advantage of economies of scale—the lower unit costs that come from building the largest, most modern factories and running them at full production. A minor automobile producer might spread the cost of a new factory over ten thousand cars; Ford could spread the cost over 1 million cars. Ford's unit costs, needless to say, would be considerably lower than his lesser rival's.

No other market in the world came close to matching the American market in size, and no other country could make such use of the economies of scale. In Europe, where Britain, France, and Germany offered the United States the closest competition, markets were much smaller. The economies of the individual European countries were smaller than the American economy, and each was separated from its neighbors by tariffs and other trade restrictions. Free trade usually requires a generous and patient spirit among the countries trying to effect it, since the benefits of free trade are often distant, whereas those of protection are immediate. Generosity and patience were in short supply in Europe in the two decades after the First World War, and the protectionists got their way more often than the free traders.

The circle was a vicious one from the European perspective (a virtuous one from the American). Because the European markets were smaller than the American market, the Europeans could not take advantage of the innovations and long production runs that benefited the Americans. And because they could not take these advantages, their economies remained smaller than the American economy and in fact often lost ground. Though the Europeans might keep American products out of their own markets, they could not do so in third-country markets where the race increasingly went to the swifter Americans.

The American government helped keep the circle vicious for the Europeans and other foreign producers by keeping American tariffs high. Harding's election in 1920 added the White House to the Republicans' control of Congress; the GOP dominated both the legislature and the executive throughout the 1920s. As the party of protection, the Republicans took care to shield American producers from foreign competition. The Fordney-McCumber tariff of 1922 raised rates on a wide variety of foreign manufactured goods that competed with items produced in the United States, thereby guaranteeing their American makers increased market share and additional profits. The American high tariff policy also guaranteed foreign resentment, as the Europeans and others found themselves increasingly shut out of the largest market in the world—the one they needed to penetrate to earn dollars, pay back their debts, and decrease their economic dependence on the Americans.

The Globe Gets Smaller Than Ever

If American economic interests during the 1920s prevented the United States from retiring into an isolationist shell, continuing technological innovations in transportation and communication had a similar effect. At the cutting edge of transportation technology was air travel. Here the Europeans held a slight advantage over the Americans. In 1919 the British began flying regularly across the English Channel. In 1920 the Dutch commenced scheduled service between Amsterdam and London. During the following several years, air routes linked the other major cities of the Continent and the British Isles. In 1923 the Soviet airline, Aeroflot, inaugurated service, followed in 1924 by British Imperial Airways and in 1926 by Deutsche Lufthansa of Germany. By the end of the 1920s, European imperialists could journey to many of their remote African and Asian colonies by air. In 1932 British Imperial Airways flew nearly 2 million miles, carrying thirty-four thousand passengers to twenty-two countries.

Transoceanic aviation commenced in 1919 when a pair of British fliers crossed the Atlantic. In 1927 the American Charles Lindbergh made a solo nonstop flight from Long Island to Paris. Steadily, airplanes shrank the Atlantic world and tied its various parts more closely together. In 1931 a pair of Americans flew nonstop from Japan to Washington state. The Pacific world remained larger and less coherent than the Atlantic world, but it, too, was shrinking.

Air travel speeded delivery of the mails, yet electrical communications were still far faster. Notwithstanding improvements such as wireless transmission and the ability to send photographs over the wires, telegraphy increasingly gave way to direct voice communications. In 1915 Alexander Graham Bell and Thomas Watson repeated their historic telephone conversation, this time with Bell in New York and Watson in San Francisco. Long-distance phone lines soon spread across the United States and across other industrialized countries as well. By the late 1920s transatlantic telephone service was available, and in the early 1930s transpacific service began.

Even more revolutionary and world shrinking was the commencement of radio broadcasting. In 1900 the Canadian-born American scientist Reginald Fessenden had transmitted the human voice via radio waves. In 1904 radio broadcasting of music commenced in Austria. In 1906 Fessenden put together the first radio show including both voice and music. The commercial possibilities of the new medium grew apparent during the next decade. The Radio Corporation of America was established just after the end of the First World War, followed at the beginning of the 1920s by the British Broadcasting Company. By the end of the 1920s, millions of radios were playing to tens of millions of listeners in the United States, Britain, and other industrialized countries.

The advent of transoceanic telegraphy in the latter part of the nineteenth century had collapsed the time news needed to travel around the world, but the telegraph always placed a filter between news producers and news consumers. In this regard it served as a very fast newspaper. Radio, in contrast, allowed listeners to hear events as they happened: the crump of artillery, the whine of airplane engines, the voices of politicians explaining, exhorting, rationalizing.

On opposite sides of the Atlantic, radio contributed significantly to the rise of two national leaders who eventually held the fate of the world in their hands. Radio brought the reassuring voice of Franklin Roosevelt into American homes during the depression of the 1930s, explaining to a worried populace that although conditions currently were not very good the government in Washington was working hard to improve them. The American people responded to Roosevelt in a personal way they had never before responded to any of their leaders: at a time of great national crisis, he became a father figure, and tens of millions gathered around their radio sets regularly to hear his voice.

Adolf Hitler became another kind of father figure to Germans. Where Roosevelt soothed, Hitler stirred. German airwaves carried the speeches of the Führer to the German people, and though the radio voice of Hitler lacked some of the hypnotic appeal of Hitler in the flesh, the Nazi leader's message came across loud and clear. Germany had been wronged by foreign enemies and by the Jewish enemy within. Germany had been great; Germany would be great again. The National Socialists under Hitler's direction would lead Germany back to greatness. Whether or not listeners in German homes stood and raised their arms in the Nazi salute when Hitler concluded, or simply thrilled to the power of the German nation as "Sieg heil!" thundered over the airwaves, millions of them came to see Hitler as their salvation.

Money Talks

By the mid-1930s the Germans were certainly feeling that they had something to be saved from. The decade and a half since the war had been difficult for Germany. The biggest early problem involved war reparations. As expected, the French and British demanded a huge amount from the Germans; when the Germans resisted, Paris sent troops into a section of Germany's industrial Ruhr valley in the spring of 1921. The point of the occupation was both political, to force the German government to accept the Allied demands, and economic, to commandeer Ruhr production, particularly of coal, in lieu of monetary payment. Since the Ruhr would have to act as the engine for any German recovery, Germany had no choice but to acquiesce to the Allies' terms: the equivalent of $33 billion.

The reparations bill placed an unbearable strain on Germany's economy and people. In addition, because nearly all Germans rejected the war guilt clause that provided the ostensible justification for the reparations, neither the German government nor the German people had serious ethical qualms about seeking to avoid payment. For a year the Allies agreed to a moratorium on payments in the well-founded belief that dead cows give no milk. But at the end of 1922 the moratorium was allowed to expire. Germany responded by insisting that the moratorium continue; it refused to make the payments the Allies demanded. The French, this time assisted by the Belgians, resorted to force once again, occupying the entire Ruhr district.

Germans then adopted a campaign of passive resistance. The aim was to make the Ruhr unproductive for its occupiers. The campaign worked, but in the process it aggravated the distress of Germans themselves. Already Germany was rent by factional political fighting, with communists, reactionaries, and assorted secessionists pounding one another at every opportunity. The passive resistance campaign provided additional fighters by pulling hundreds of thousands of workers off their jobs. The German government inadvertently did its bit to promote chaos by running the printing presses at the mint overtime in an effort to pay its domestic bills and ease some of the country's economic pain. The effort only exacerbated the other troubles: newly issued marks swamped the German economy and pushed prices to undreamed of levels. In 1914 an American dollar had been equivalent to four marks; by the autumn of 1923 a dollar was worth 4 trillion marks. Germany's complete collapse appeared imminent.

Some of Germany's neighbors, having concluded that a healthy Germany was more than Europe could tolerate peacefully, would not have mourned a German collapse. Yet there were two good reasons for fearing such an outcome—or perhaps they were bad reasons, for neither had anything to do with concern for the well-being of the Germans. The first was that a civil war or another revolution in Germany might spill over into the countries next door. The second was that an utterly prostrate Germany would be unable to pay the reparations the Allies still hoped to collect. The governments of France and Britain had debts of their own, chiefly to the United States, and they looked covetously on whatever they could wring out of Germany.

The French and British debts to the Americans were what gave the United States a particular interest in Germany's troubles. American leaders did not relish the thought of a German collapse since anarchy in central Europe would hardly contribute to world peace and American prosperity. Far-sighted Americans recognized that the United States would be as hard pressed to stay out of another major European war as it had been to avoid the first. But in light of the once-burned-twice-shy attitude in the American Congress and among the American people, getting the United States involved in a European rescue effort required appeals to readily identifiable American material interests. The material interests most readily identifiable were the debts owed to the United States by the Europeans.

Calvin Coolidge was well known for his assertion that the business of America was business, and Coolidge's administration considered the collection of debts a major objective of American foreign policy. The Republican president (following Harding's untimely death in August 1923) steadfastly resisted the argument, predictably popular in Paris and London, that since France and Britain had sacrificed the flower of their youth to the cause of defeating Germany, the least the United States could do was forgive the debt the French and British owed the Americans. Coolidge retorted, "They hired the money, didn't they?" The Europeans knew the terms of the arrangement when they contracted the obligation, the president reasoned; the problem of repayment was theirs, not America's. It would be unfair, and bad business, to require American taxpayers to bail out improvident Europeans.

Yet when the German troubles threatened to produce a British and French default, the Republican administration moved quickly into action. With the encouragement of Secretary of State Charles Evans Hughes, American financier Charles Dawes headed an international commission established to restructure the cash flows of the Atlantic world. In April 1924 the Dawes commission presented its scheme for keeping the circulation of funds in western Europe and across the Atlantic from clotting to a halt. Although the Dawes plan dramatically reduced Germany's reparations payments, thereby easing the strain on the German people, humanitarianism had comparatively little to do with the matter. With American encouragement, the British and French had concluded that partial repayment was better than no repayment at all, and they decided to write down the reparations rather than have to write them off entirely. Under the Dawes plan, Germany would initially pay $250 million annually in reparations, with the annual payment to increase as Germany's ability to pay presumably increased. To jump-start the process, Germany would receive fresh foreign loans, with American financiers providing the largest contribution.

One consequence of the Dawes plan was to buy time for the economy of the Atlantic world to recover from the war and its aftermath; a second and related consequence was to tie the Atlantic economy more tightly together than ever and to tie the United States more firmly into it. Britain and France were already heavily in debt to the United States; now Germany would be, too. The arrangement was convenient and profitable for Americans: the Dawes plan ensured that American loans to Britain and France would be repaid, with interest, in large part by new American loans to Germany, which likewise would produce interest. There were risks involved, to be sure, but these were limited by capping the length of the new loans to Germany. Short-term money was easier to keep track of than long-term money, and if things got sticky, the loans could be called in. Of course, American financiers were factoring the risks into the interest rate they were charging, as prudent lenders always do. If all went well, the interconnections the Dawes plan produced would foster a greater sense of solidarity among the major powers of the Atlantic world. With the welfare of each country depending on the welfare of every country, each would want to promote the prosperity of the rest.

But nothing in life comes free, especially when money is at stake. And the same interdependence that afforded mutual support could also lead to mutual disaster. Mountain climbers rope themselves together for safety, yet sometimes the fall of one climber drags the others to death as well. Under the arrangement of the Dawes plan, a slip by one major country, especially the United States, could cause the entire scheme to slide over the edge.

Arms Limitation and Lesser Triumphs

The Dawes plan received only the informal backing of the American government. Coolidge and Hughes understood Americans' sensitivity regarding European entanglements, and they refused to stir up those many who would have attacked a formal American commitment across the Atlantic. But largely because Americans harbored fewer bad memories toward Asia—no great numbers of Americans having just died in battle there, to state the most obvious difference—Americans were willing to countenance greater involvement across the Pacific. Hughes chose to exploit his opportunity in that direction. During the winter of 1921–1922, the secretary of state engineered one of the most significant arms control accords of the modern era.

The Washington conference, the meeting that produced this accord, brought together the major naval powers of the world. The most important of these were the United States, Britain, and Japan. The Japanese had come out of the First World War strengthened, though not as greatly strengthened as they thought they deserved to be. While the peace settlement ratified Japan's control of Germany's North Pacific possessions, under the label of a League of Nations mandate, and legitimized the transfer of German rights in China's Shandong peninsula to Japan, these were mere scraps compared to what Britain and France were helping themselves to, particularly in the Middle East and Africa. The Japanese economy, like that of the United States, had boomed during the war. Japan's industries played much the same role as supplier in East Asia that American industries played in the Atlantic, and just as the war converted the United States from a foreign debtor to a foreign creditor, so it did to Japan, with Japan's billion yen deficit tipping over into a billion yen surplus. Feeling rich and full of themselves, the Japanese expected greater respect than they received. They had chafed when America objected to their Twenty-one Demands on China; they grumbled at the slim pickings they received at Paris and at the refusal there of the Western powers to accept a declaration affirming the principle of racial equality in international relations.

The Japanese were still grumbling when the American government invited the great powers to Washington in the autumn of 1921. The Harding administration, despite certain of its members' tendency to treat public resources as their own (the Harding era witnessed the worst federal corruption since Grant), hoped to cut back on government spending. In particular, the administration wanted to trim expenditures on the armed forces. But international tension, especially in East Asia, where the Chinese revolution had proceeded from the hopeful early stage of republicanism to a dismal and discouraging warlordism, appeared to require continued preparedness. The Harding administration felt obliged to maintain a navy strong enough to deal with threats to American interests in the Asia-Pacific area. Britain and Japan felt the same way about their own interests. The United States and Britain, in addition, having large interests in other parts of the world as well, had to prepare for trouble elsewhere. A costly naval arms race loomed.

To avert such a race, Charles Evans Hughes proposed that the great powers agree not to run. He recommended that the powers take a holiday from building new ships and that they scrap some vessels already afloat. Hughes's proposal caught many of the delegates at the Washington conference by surprise. In an era of endless and often meaningless conferences, they had expected nothing so startlingly substantive. But after they regained their composure, they decided that the American plan made sense. Within a few months the delegates worked out the details of the so-called Five Power treaty, which pledged the United States, Britain, and Japan, along with France and Italy, to suspend new construction of big ships for ten years and to reduce current fleets until their sizes were in the ratio of 5:5:3 for America, Britain, and Japan with France and Italy getting 1.75 each.

Tokyo complained about the Five Power treaty since it left the United States and Britain with more vessels and firepower than Japan got. But because Japan had no ambitions beyond East Asia and the Pacific, while the United States and Britain did, the discrepancy was effectively much less than it appeared on paper. Both Washington and London had to be ready to fight in the Atlantic as well as the Pacific; this meant that in practice Japan might well enjoy local superiority over the United States and Britain. The United States government knew that the Japanese complaints were partly for effect since American code breakers had cracked Japan's diplomatic code and were reading the messages between the Japanese delegation and Tokyo. In this case, modern technology—wireless telegraphy—allowed one side to take an advantage it would not have enjoyed in former days when diplomats sent messages by courier.

The Washington conference produced two other significant agreements. The Four Power treaty canceled Japan's 1902 treaty of alliance with Britain, which was somewhat anomalous after the defeat of Germany, the original primary target of the alliance; and it promised respect for the status quo in East Asia and the western Pacific. As an indication of this respect, America, Britain, Japan, and France promised not to fortify their possessions in the area. For the United States, this meant leaving the Philippines largely undefended. This was no great American sacrifice since Congress had never shown much interest in spending money defending the Philippines. The Nine Power treaty (adding China, Belgium, the Netherlands, and Portugal) committed the signatories to observe the Open Door principle in China. To the extent that they intended to honor their commitment, this pact represented something of a coup for the United States, for it now put the great powers officially on record as supporting the China policy America had been promoting for more than two decades.

The basic question regarding these treaties, as with all treaties, was how long the signers would stand by them. The answer, as always in a world where governments look after themselves first and last, was that they would do so just as long as it suited their interests.

As things happened, the system of the Washington conference held together fairly well throughout the rest of the 1920s. For Japan, the Washington system gave a great-power seal of approval to its leading influence in China. The Four

Power and Nine Power treaties were somewhat contradictory in that the status quo in East Asia did not quite accord with the spirit of the Open Door. But diplomats get paid to reconcile the irreconcilable, and the language of the two pacts was sufficiently stretchy to let Japan keep its sphere of influence in Manchuria while the other powers pretended such a sphere did not exist. For Britain, the Washington system helped stabilize East Asia at a time when Britain was hard pressed to hang on to what it controlled in South Asia, the Middle East, and Africa. For the United States, the Washington system allowed the American government and people to flatter themselves that they were living up to their obligations on behalf of China and the Philippines without in the process incurring unacceptable international commitments. American officials also breathed easier at the termination of the Anglo-Japanese alliance, which had always made them queasy. For all three countries, the ceilings on ships and fortifications saved money that became available for more productive use elsewhere.

The Washington system was the most important evidence that diplomats were earning their pay during the 1920s; but their efforts bore fruit in other areas as well. In Europe the big Western powers struggled with the twin problems of how to bring Germany and the Soviet Union back into the international political structure before those two outcasts got together to form a dangerous duo. In fact, the Western powers waited too long, and in 1922 Germany and the Soviet Union inked the Rapallo treaty of friendship and cooperation. For the revolutionary Bolshevik government in Moscow, the Rapallo accord was the first recognition by a major foreign government. For Germany, the Rapallo pact was a signal to Britain and France that if they pressed too hard on reparations and other matters, London and Paris might face a common front of the largest country in central Europe and the largest in eastern Europe.

To prevent such an occurrence, France, Britain, and Italy sponsored a meeting in Switzerland during the autumn of 1925. For ten days the diplomats conferred at Locarno and were treated to such sights as the French foreign minister rowing his German counterpart around in a small boat, both chatting amiably. The upshot of the Locarno conference was a series of agreements guaranteeing—on paper anyway—the long-disputed frontiers between France and Germany, promising arbitration of future disputes, and admitting Germany to the League of Nations. (This left only the pariah Soviet Union and the boycotting United States as the important nonmembers.)

Although the Americans had next to nothing to do with the Rapallo treaty, they had somewhat more to do with the Locarno accord. The Coolidge administration let the Europeans understand that it would have an easier time facilitating further transatlantic loans if they could arrange a peaceful resolution of their problems. They did, and it did; officially, however, the United States remained uninvolved.

Washington played a larger and publicly acknowledged role in an agreement of lesser importance but wider fame. Of course, it was precisely this unimportance that allowed the Pact of Paris of 1928, also called the Kellogg-Briand treaty, to slip past the guardians of American nonentanglement in the Senate. Foreign Minister Aristide Briand of France initially proposed a bilateral accord between his country and the United States. Briand hoped to pull France's former ally back into European affairs, the better to contain the Germans and, perhaps, the Soviets. But the American secretary of state, Frank Kellogg, refused to be drawn into any concrete commitments. Rather than turn Briand down flat, Kellogg proposed expanding the roster of signatories to include other nations, in accord with the oft-proved principle of international affairs that the greater the number of governments that agree to something, the less significant that something must be. In this instance what the signers, eventually including nearly all the governments of the world, agreed to was a pious pledge to outlaw war "as an instrument of national policy."

Because the Kellogg-Briand treaty included no enforcement provisions, it amounted to nothing more than an "international kiss," as its critics called it. The analogy may have been particularly apt in that just as kisses often fool those who engage in them into thinking they mean more than they do, so did the Kellogg pact. In theory, the treaty appeared a large step toward banning the curse of war from the face of the earth; in reality, it did no such thing. And those cads who, behind their noble promises, still considered war an effective instrument of national policy could take advantage of the romantics who did not recognize the discrepancy between theory and reality. The Senate approved the pact by a vote of 85 to 1, a margin that during this era of American skittishness about foreign entanglements amply demonstrated the treaty's innocuousness.

The Great Crash and Its Echoes

Nine months after the Senate vote, the American economy went into convulsions that would last for a decade. The economy had not been robust for the previous few years, although its frenetic activity masked the underlying weakness. The most frenetic activity took place on Wall Street, where stocks had been soaring since 1924. When the stock market shuddered in late 1929, then keeled over, it paralyzed the whole economy. Banks collapsed by the dozens, then by the hundreds, and eventually by the thousands; those that survived called in their loans, triggering the liquidation of tens of thousands of other businesses. Investment in new plant and equipment evaporated; unsold inventories clogged warehouses; unemployment soared to levels never imagined, let alone experienced. By the time the economy hit bottom, around 1933, between a quarter and a third of the American work force was jobless. The United States had suffered through other slumps before; most economists accepted them as inevitable side effects of the Industrial Revolution. But never had an economic downturn been so severe as the depression of the 1930s, and none had ever lasted as long as this one did.

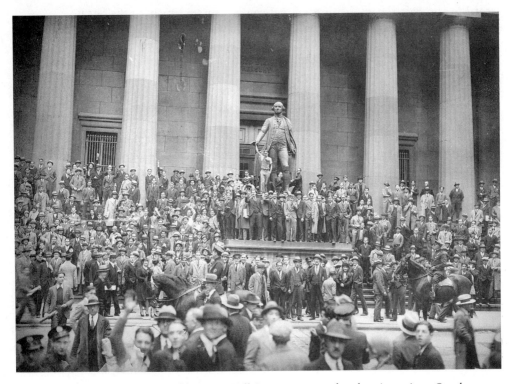

Chaos in the temple of finance: Wall Street reacts to the plunging prices, October 1929. *UPI/Bettman*

Neither had earlier slumps had such important international ramifications. The much increased size of the American economy relative to the rest of the world economy would by itself have dictated that the United States would export its troubles, at least in part. Americans' appetite for foreign goods had grown during the 1920s despite the high tariffs, and though the appetite did not diminish after the stock crash, Americans' wherewithal to pay for foreign goods did. As orders from America for those goods fell off, unemployment rose in the countries making those goods. With rising unemployment in other countries, American exports declined, diminishing American incomes further and reinforcing the cycle.

Besides its impact on trade, the onset of the Depression ripped the web of international finance developed during the 1920s. The web was none too strong when the Depression began: the speculative fever on Wall Street had diverted investment funds from Europe to the American stock market, crimping Germany's and the rest of Europe's growth. To address this and related problems, the Americans and Europeans agreed in early 1929 to a modification of the Dawes plan, designed to improve the efficiency of the system of loans and payments, to scale back payments again, and to establish a definitive timetable for the retirement of Germany's obligations to the world war's victors. But the Young plan, named for American financier Owen Young, barely had time to go into effect before the Depression began to render its provisions inoperable. The international financial markets stumbled through the first eighteen months after the American stock crash, but in the spring of 1931 the news that Austria's largest bank was on the verge of insolvency provoked a panic that cascaded across Europe, precipitating the crash of the Berlin stock market and forcing the British government to repudiate the gold standard. American president Herbert Hoover responded to the international panic with a call for a moratorium on the payment of debts and reparations. Hoover hoped that the moratorium would furnish a grace period that would foster a recovery and allow payments to resume. The measure proved insufficient, however, and before the crisis was over, nearly everyone stopped payments on nearly everything. Germany swore off reparations, and Britain and France walked away from their debts to the United States.

Contributing to both the evaporation of world trade and the international debt crisis were certain actions of the American Congress and the national assemblies of other countries. With American businesses closing their doors by the thousands, and with American workers losing their jobs by the millions,

This is why Americans had little attention to spare for international events during the 1930s. *UPI/Bettman*

protectionists in Congress gained influence, as protectionists almost always do during times of economic stress. In 1930 Congress passed the Hawley-Smoot tariff, which raised import duties to their highest levels ever. Hoover, facing a veto-proof majority, acquiesced in the measure. Notwithstanding the old saw that if all the economists in the world were laid end to end, they still would not be able to reach a conclusion, this time the economists overwhelmingly predicted dire consequences for protective measures; and this time they were right. The Hawley-Smoot tariff was interpreted abroad as hostile; an observer in France called it "a declaration of war, an economic blockade." As the economists predicted, it provoked retaliation by other governments. By 1931 European tariff rates were as much as two-thirds higher than they had been in 1927. World trade shrank accordingly, to less than half its predepression value.

The ill feelings produced by the debt and trade crises, together with the continuing protectionist sentiment in the United States, made it almost impossible for Hoover's successor, Franklin Roosevelt, to embark on any bold efforts toward international cooperation. Not that Roosevelt was initially disposed toward bold measures in foreign affairs, for when he took office in March 1933, a long list of domestic objectives headed his policy agenda. He refused to be diverted by the troubles abroad. Besides, he knew, as any student of American politics knows, that domestic matters are where the votes are. He could solve the world's problems, but unless he reassured voters that their domestic concerns were being addressed, he could forget about reelection. Conversely, if he solved America's domestic problems, the world could run to ruin for all most American voters would care.

Consequently, when the British hosted an international economic conference during the summer of 1933, with the purpose of ending the trade and financial warfare and seeking a cooperative solution to the world depression, Roosevelt declared forthrightly that the British and the others could count the United States out. Roosevelt took the understandable position that as American president his job was to look after American interests; the proposals being floated in London seemed to him more attuned to British and other foreign interests than to American. Besides, Roosevelt sincerely doubted that anything emanating from London would do much in the near term to alleviate the world depression, and he had no desire to burden his new administration with responsibility for the failure. Whether or not charity should begin at home, Roosevelt adopted the view that recovery ought to.

Roosevelt's scuttling of the London economic conference marked the culmination of a trend that since the beginning of the 1930s had been bringing America's foreign economic policy into line with America's foreign political policy. The 1920s had been a decade of American political nationalism, with the United States shying away from foreign political commitments, the most obvious being membership in the League of Nations. Yet the same decade had been a period of economic internationalism, as American merchants and investors, with the assistance of the American government, became more intensely involved than ever in foreign economic matters. The economic internationalism of the 1920s was not complete: the Republican tariff policy of the decade indicated a refusal to join the world economy without conditions. But the Dawes and Young plans, to cite the clearest examples, demonstrated an unprecedented American willingness to accept responsibility for the prosperity of a large and crucial part of the overseas world.

During the 1930s the United States remained politically nationalistic, but now its economic approach to the world became increasingly nationalistic as well. To some extent the retreat to economic nationalism was unintentional, the result of the contraction of world commercial and financial markets consequent to the onset of the Depression. Yet it was also deliberate, as demonstrated by the Hawley-Smoot tariff and Roosevelt's refusal to cooperate with other governments in economic affairs.

Not surprisingly, the political nationalism and the economic nationalism fed on each other. American politicians and pundits asserted that the United States government should not be doing any economic favors for foreigners, just as political nationalists had long claimed that the United States should not have to accept responsibility for the political welfare of other countries. By the same token, since economic commitments often produced pressure for political commitments, curtailing economic commitments lessened pressure for political commitments.

The Allure of Fascism

During the mid-1930s foreign political commitments looked like an ominously bad bet. Conditions were trying enough in the United States, but they were nothing compared to conditions in some foreign countries, and the inhabitants of those countries were responding in alarming ways. Germany and Japan provoked the greatest concern among Americans, though Italy and Spain also generated their share of worries. The most worrisome aspect in each case was the rise to power of a regime based on the principles of fascism: a reactionary philosophy of authoritarian government, state-protected capitalism, and often a fanatical zeal for racial or ethnic solidarity and exclusionism.

Italy had established the model of the fascist state and christened the fascist movement in the early 1920s. Many Italians had been disappointed with the outcome of the world war, thinking that the terms of the Versailles settlement had not adequately compensated their country for its sacrifices on behalf of the Allies. Italian dissatisfaction increased as the Italian economy misfired after the war. A variety of factions, of diverse political coloration, attempted to take advantage of the dissatisfaction; of these, the most successful was the Fascist party led by Benito Mussolini. Italian politics was a rough sport, and Mussolini and the Fascists played rougher than anyone else. They regularly beat up rival Socialists and trade unionists, resorting in more than a few cases to murder. At first the Fascists appeared barely better than thugs, but even as Mussolini unleashed his goons in the streets, he managed to persuade conservative property holders and clerics that he offered the best guarantee of their interests

Fascism with an Italian face: Mussolini announces the victory of Italy's forces in Ethiopia. *UPI/Bettman*

against the danger of leftist revolution. Many conservatives supported him, clandestinely at first, more openly as time passed. In 1922 Mussolini seized power in what amounted to a constitutionally sanctioned coup.

During the next several years, Mussolini consolidated his power in Italy. He overawed the Italian parliament and silenced critical voices in the Italian press. He joined forces with business leaders against labor unions and other complainers; in exchange the business leaders paid the bills of Mussolini's regime. He negotiated a landmark accord with the Roman pope, the Lateran treaty of 1929, by which Pius XI proclaimed the Catholic church's acceptance of Mussolini's program and Mussolini announced the Italian government's acceptance of the pope's sovereignty over the microstate of the Vatican. Although sniping between the papacy and the Fascists soon resumed, the Lateran treaty remained a feather in Mussolini's cap. To many American Catholics, it symbolized the approval of the church for what Mussolini was up to, and it facilitated support in the United States for the right-wing radicalism the Fascists preached.

As had some of his recent predecessors, Mussolini entertained grand ideas about reconstructing the Roman empire. Italians often suffered from an inferiority complex on the colonial issue; all they had to show for their part in the 1890s scramble for Africa were a couple of meager outposts on the Horn of East Africa and a desolate reach of shoreline in Libya. To this inferiority complex was added the indignation of seeing Britain and France get the choicest spoils of the world war. As a means of remedying the situation, Mussolini embarked on imperial adventures. Aside from American protégé Liberia and postcolonial South Africa, the only part of Africa that was not already claimed by a European power was Ethiopia; therefore Mussolini decided that Italy should have another try there. In October 1935 Italian forces invaded Ethiopia (or Abyssinia, as it was often still called). The fighting was brutally one-sided, matching Italian machine guns, airplanes, and poison gas against the pitifully equipped troops of Ethiopian emperor Haile Selassie. Even so, the conquest of the country required several months. Only in May 1936 did Mussolini's soldiers capture the capital, Addis Ababa.

Although the Italian invasion of Ethiopia disgusted most of the Western world, neither the Europeans nor the Americans did much more than shake their heads and cluck their tongues. The League of Nations verbally condemned the Italian action and voted certain economic sanctions; but the League's sanctions did not include an embargo of oil, which really would have curtailed the actions of Mussolini's military forces. Neither did the Roosevelt administration block oil exports to Italy; on the contrary, American oil sales rose significantly during the Ethiopian war. The hard fact was that no one else wanted to fight the Ethiopians' battles at a time when fighting the Depression was all the Western democracies could manage. The Ethiopians were left to fight and die on their own.

The lesson of the democracies' inaction was not lost on Mussolini's fellow fascists in Germany. The National Socialists, or Nazis, had been a fringe party in German politics during the 1920s. The party leadership included some frustrated pseudo-intellectuals, but the bulk of the rank and file was recruited from the same kinds of tough neighborhoods that spawned Mussolini's followers. At the top of the party structure was Adolf Hitler, an unbalanced but undeniably shrewd world war veteran who dreamed of greatness for himself and for the German people. That he was technically an Austrian, rather than a German, merely increased his desire to forge a union of all German-speakers. And that his own military career had been undistinguished simply enhanced his estimation of the martial virtues and of the character-molding influence of military practices.

The Nazis almost certainly would have remained a fringe party had life in Germany not been so disrupted by the Depression of the 1930s. The Depression hit Germany hardest of all the industrialized countries. While production plummeted by 40 percent, unemployment swelled to 6 million, meaning that two workers out of five were without jobs. Millions more had only part-time positions. Together with the disintegration of the banking system, which robbed even the thrifty of their savings, the nose dive in employment threw tens of millions of Germans into poverty and despair.

Communists in Germany took advantage of the dire conditions to preach radical revolution. Capitalism was showing its true nature, communists said, and its true nature was irredeemable. German communists pointed to the

Fascism with a German face (or Austrian, to be precise): Hitler acknowledges a crowd acknowledging him. *Brown Brothers*

Soviet Union, whose socialist economy appeared to be weathering the Depression quite well, and argued that there lay Germany's future. Many Germans thought the communists' arguments made sense.

But conservative business executives and property owners in Germany did not. The very thought of communism taking root in Germany spoiled their sleep, not to mention their property values. They found the specter of communism even more forbidding than the specter of Hitler and the Nazis, whom they recognized as lowlifes and social psychopaths. In the extremity of their fear, the conservatives threw their support to Hitler, believing that they could manipulate him once he suppressed the communists. Industrialists of the Rhine-Ruhr region held a crucial meeting in Cologne at the beginning of 1933, during which they promised to bankroll the Nazis in exchange for Hitler's promise to leave German big business alone. Four weeks later Hitler was named chancellor and commenced construction of the Nazi state.

Until the late 1930s it was hard for outsiders, including most Americans, to know how seriously to take Mussolini and Hitler. The fascists' pomposity, their endless strutting and saluting, and the interminable diatribes of their leaders were almost incomprehensible to those not caught in the fascists' spell. The American political tradition, with its inherent distrust of government, and the American cultural tradition, with its deep-rooted individualism, rendered most Americans not simply immune to the fascists' appeal but also unable to gauge the danger fascism posed to democratic institutions. Mussolini and Hitler were easy to ridicule, and many of those Americans who were paying attention to European affairs did precisely that. Only after the fascists, especially Hitler, created powerful military machines did Americans awake to fascism's true potential for havoc-wreaking.

Yet there was an additional reason for underestimating the fascists. Although fascism never came close to replacing democracy in the United States, many Americans found certain aspects of the fascists' program appealing. The Depression cast the same sorts of shadows across capitalism's future in America as it did in Europe, and though the shadows were not so dark as in Germany, some segments of the American population found the fascists' certitude comforting. At least the fascists knew what they stood for and where they were going. The fascists' staunch opposition to communism likewise counted in their favor. Business leaders in America were much taken by the fascists' evident ability to get things done; a spokesman for the American Chamber of Commerce described Mussolini as "a fine type of business executive," adding, "He cuts through. No idle words." Elbert Gary of United States Steel declared, "We, too, need a man like Mussolini."

Hitler was harder to admire. He was less personally attractive, and the racial intolerance he and the Nazis preached was disturbing to most Americans. When the preachment became practice with the promulgation of the Nuremberg decrees of 1935, which deprived Jews of citizenship and forbade their marriage to "Aryans," Americans found Hitler still harder to admire. But even Hitler had his defenders. Many American conservatives considered communism to be a greater danger than fascism, and Hitler's firm treatment of German leftists drew substantial, if often muted, applause.

American conservatives worried about communism for the same reasons German and Italian conservatives did: communism gained influence as capitalism staggered under the body blows of the Depression. The American Communist party has never been so popular or active as it was during the 1930s, enlisting intellectuals, students, and run-of-the-mill idealists by the tens of thousands. And while American conservatives tended to sympathize with European fascists, American leftists rallied to the aid of the fascists' opponents. The most noteworthy focus of the leftists' rallying, indeed the great cause of the international left during the 1930s, was the defense of the republican government of Spain during the civil war in that country.

On one side of the Spanish Civil War, which began in 1936, were the Nationalists, a coalition of rightist forces in league with the Spanish fascist party, the Falange. General Francisco Franco, the Nationalist leader, and his right-wing allies derived support from Spanish landlords, the Catholic church, and the military. On the other side were the Loyalists, a broad array of labor unionists, intellectuals, and other progressive-to-anarchist types who backed the constitutional government against the right-wing rebels. Each side drew heavy assistance from outside Spain. Germany initially sent transport planes to the Nationalists; Hitler later boasted, "Franco ought to erect a monument to the glory of the German transport aircraft." Later Hitler dispatched bombers and pilots of his so-called Condor Legion. Italy contributed bombers, tanks, and ground troops to Franco's side. The Loyalists received indirect and limited aid from France and more substantial help from the Soviet Union. Soviet premier Joseph Stalin sent aircraft and other weapons and military and political advisers. The political advisers, zealous communists all, lent leftist coherence to a movement that was already radical enough but often diffuse and disorganized. At the same time, Moscow's backing of the Loyalists elevated the reputation of Soviet communism in the eyes of much of the world; when almost no one else was standing up against fascism, the Soviets were.

The United States had recognized the communist government of the Soviet Union in late 1933 after sixteen years of wishing it would go away. One part of Roosevelt's reason for extending recognition was his desire to expand American exports to the Soviet Union during a period when the United States needed all the foreign markets it could find, but another major part was his hope that the communists would act to constrain the fascists. In Spain at least, the Soviets seemed to be living up to Roosevelt's hope, though obviously for their own purposes, not his.

Beyond such indirect diplomatic support, the American president declined to involve the United States in the Spanish Civil War. In 1935, at the time of the Italian invasion of Ethiopia, the American Congress had passed a neutrality act designed to keep the United States out of foreign wars by, among other devices, barring American arms shipments to belligerents. Although the measure contained a loophole—in certain instances the president could decide if a state of foreign war existed—the measure plainly signaled the intent of the legislature to steer America clear of overseas conflicts. The neutrality legislation, which Roosevelt signed without enthusiasm, reinforced his inclination to keep out of the Ethiopian conflict; on the issue of the Spanish Civil War, it helped him decide to follow the example of Britain, rather than of France, and stay out.

Yet the official American hands-off policy did not prevent hundreds of Americans from traveling to Spain and enlisting in an international brigade fighting alongside the Loyalists. The international contingent drew well-known intellectuals and activists from all over the Western world: André Malraux of France (who had fought with the communists in China's continuing civil war), Eric Blair (George Orwell) of Britain, Arthur Koestler of Hungary, Ernest Hemingway of the United States. The international brigade did not have much effect on the fighting in Spain, which gradually turned against the Loyalists. Confronting German air power and Italian armor, the Loyalists' efforts were doomed. At the beginning of 1939, Franco's troops captured Barcelona and Madrid, thereby entrenching fascism in control of the country. Yet the very losing nature of the Loyalist cause contributed to the legend of the Spanish Civil War, an exaggerated tale (as legends always are) of the valor of the popular antifascist forces that were drawn from all over the world to the defense of the Spanish republic. This legend lived for decades on the left in most Western countries, strengthened and elaborated by the work of the artists and writers involved. The Spanish artist Pablo Picasso captured the horror of the fascist offensives in his mural *Guernica,* which showed the destruction of a Basque village by German bombers and fighter planes. Ernest Hemingway's *For Whom the Bell Tolls* argued that those who thought they could turn away from evil in another country would find it following them home.

Thunder in Asia

The various manifestations of the fascist movement in Europe were united by proximity, mutual assistance, and common roots in continental politics, economics, and culture. Fascism in Japan shared some of the economic roots of European fascism, but its political and cultural antecedents were distinct. Since the early 1920s Japanese politics had been a stormy sea, with successive governments pitched high on one wave and then crashed down and swamped by the next. Factors external to Japanese politics contributed to the storminess. These included the Washington conference, which Japanese ultranationalists branded a sellout of Japan's honor; a 1923 earthquake, which razed Yokohama and flattened half of Tokyo; a 1924 American immigration reform law, which permanently barred the entry of Japanese and other Asians to the United States and which passed overwhelmingly despite the warning by the Japanese ambassador in Washington of "grave consequences"; the world depression, which started two years earlier in Japan than elsewhere, following a domestic fiscal crisis; a scanty rice crop in 1930, which produced widespread hunger in northern Japan; and the international trade war that followed the passage of the Hawley-Smoot tariff and ravaged resource-poor and trade-dependent Japan more than most countries.

Yet much of the Japanese turmoil resulted from an ongoing struggle between the relatively progressive forces that had ushered in the Meiji restoration of the nineteenth century and reactionary factions that longed for a return to the verities of authoritarianism and traditional Japanese values. With each jolt to the Japanese economy and Japanese society, the conservatives gained influence. A series of rightist-inspired assassinations and attempted assassinations of high government officials helped the conservative cause by removing or terrorizing opponents and by contributing to the general sense of anarchy that the conservatives battened on. Following the last murder, of Premier Inukai Tsuyoshi, the Japanese military seized effective control of the government in Tokyo.

The Japanese people acquiesced in the dominance by the military for two reasons. First, the soldiers had the guns to compel obedience if they had to. Second and more important, at a time when rampaging events were discrediting the regular politicians, the military seemed to offer a steady, if perhaps overly strong, hand at the helm. At least since the days when the Romans selected dictators to deal with emergencies, countries in crisis have taken refuge in strong leaders. In Italy it was Mussolini; in Germany, Hitler; in Spain,

Franco. In Japan it was not a single individual, partly because the Japanese tend to be less individualistic than Europeans; instead it was a tightly knit group of generals and admirals.

To a person with a hammer, everything looks like a nail; to soldiers, all problems tend to look like military problems. As the problems induced or exacerbated by the world depression persisted, the militarists in Tokyo sought military solutions to them. The militarists, along with many other Japanese, deemed resource-rich Manchuria vital to Japan's economic, and hence military, security. For most of the time since the collapse of the Chinese imperial government in 1911, the Japanese had been content to exercise what amounted to a protectorate over Manchuria. But in the late 1920s, the Chinese under Chiang Kaishek (Jiang Jieshi) began to pull their government together again. On current trends they might soon challenge Japan's position in Manchuria. To forestall such a challenge, the Japanese army in Manchuria faked an attack in September 1931 on an important railway line through the region. The Mukden incident, as the affair was called, provided the pretext for a full Japanese military occupation of Manchuria. The event was noteworthy not simply because it consolidated Japanese control over this critical province, which was soon converted into the nominally independent but thoroughly manipulated state of "Manchukuo," but because it further tightened the grip of the militarists on Japan's politics.

The Japanese seizure of Manchuria provided the sternest test of American foreign policy since the 1920 Senate vote on the Versailles treaty. With the move against China's northeastern province, Japan blatantly violated the Nine Power treaty of the Washington conference, not to mention the 1928 Pact of Paris. More generally, the militarists in charge of Japan's affairs indicated as clearly as could be imagined their entire disdain for world opinion. Until this point Tokyo had acted as though it valued the good will of the West, and much of Japan's foreign policy could be explained as an outgrowth of a desire on the part of the Japanese to be treated as equals by the great Western powers. The invasion of Manchuria told the West to save its good will for other countries; Japan did not need it. Japan was strong and would look out for Japanese interests itself. Many Japanese had long felt the world did not understand them; now Japan would force the world to understand, by means of the universal language of military might.

At the time of the invasion, Herbert Hoover was still president and Henry Stimson was secretary of state. In the early 1930s Stimson was midway through one of the most distinguished careers in the history of American public service. He had been secretary of war under Taft and would be again under Franklin Roosevelt and Harry Truman. He had helped arrange a settlement of a civil war in Nicaragua and been governor-general of the Philippines. Despite being a Republican, he served with equal distinction under Democrats. Stimson was a realist—though his decision to close the State Department's code-cracking division, which he explained with the comment "Gentlemen do not read each other's mail," might have suggested otherwise. While he understood the Japanese invasion of Manchuria to be a serious hazard to the security of

East Asia and the entire Pacific region, he likewise understood the limits of the Hoover administration's ability to reverse the Japanese action. To take vigorous measures against Japan would probably only reinforce Japan's militarists, who were contending that the West had always frustrated Japan's legitimate aspirations and always would. Besides, the American Congress and the American people were more inward looking than ever now that the economy was plumbing depths no one had conceived of three years earlier. Unlike Italy and to a lesser extent Germany, Japan had almost no apologists in the United States. The vast majority of Americans found Japan's treatment of China reprehensible. Even so, few wanted to do anything risky to stop it.

The other great powers were no help to Stimson or to China. The British felt vulnerable to Japanese pressure against Hong Kong and potentially Malaya, while the French felt exposed in Indochina. On balance, both European powers preferred that if the Japanese had to expand anywhere, they do so in Manchuria, which was of strategic importance only to the Soviet Union, among the European powers. If the Japanese and the Bolsheviks clashed, neither London nor Paris would much complain.

When the Chinese government appealed to the League of Nations, the League recommended that both China and Japan pull their troops back. Then it studied the matter for several weeks before appointing a commission to study the matter some more, which the commission proceeded to do at enormous length and in excruciating detail. Since none of the great powers had any more desire than the Americans to confront Japan, the commission provided them with a convenient excuse for doing nothing.

Meanwhile Stimson applied the Wilsonian treatment of nonrecognition to the puppet state of Manchukuo. In letters of January 1932 sent to the Chinese and Japanese governments, Stimson put forward what came to be known as the Stimson doctrine. He declared that the United States would not recognize any arrangement that violated the principle of the Open Door in China or that otherwise contravened treaty rights of the United States therein.

To this much the other great powers eventually decided they could agree. In February 1933, after the League of Nations commission finally delivered its report, the League approved a resolution pledging members not to recognize the state of Manchukuo.

The Japanese government responded to even this mild slap by a show of outrage. The Japanese delegate to the League of Nations called the territorial integrity of China a "fiction" that could no longer be sustained. Japan had dropped the charade even if no one else had. The delegate then gathered his papers, stood up, and walked out of the League chamber. He never returned, and neither did Japan. Manchuria, or Manchukuo, remained under Tokyo's thumb.

During the half decade after the Mukden incident, the Japanese continued to manhandle China—attacking Shanghai, encroaching toward Beijing—but Tokyo refrained from any single violation as outrageous as the hijacking of Manchuria. The Japanese hoped that the international furor, such as it was, would die down. It did. In the realm of international relations, memories are usually short: unless a country persists in offending international codes of conduct, or unless a particular affront serves a continuing political purpose in other countries, sins are usually forgotten, if not necessarily forgiven. Gradually the West began to treat the puppet state of Manchukuo as it did other countries. The fascist European countries—Italy, Germany, Spain—extended diplomatic recognition to Manchukuo. The Soviet Union stopped short of de jure recognition but otherwise dealt normally with Manchukuo. Britain dispatched a commercial delegation. Even the United States, while remaining on record as being opposed to recognition, allowed trade relations between Americans and firms and individuals in the puppet country.

Yet the easing of the international opposition to Japan's control of Manchukuo did little to mollify Tokyo. The main reason was that resistance to foreigners increasingly functioned as a motivating principle of Japanese policy. The Japanese convinced themselves that they had a right to do with China more or less as they desired. They saw mainland East Asia much as Americans viewed the Western Hemisphere and often spoke of an "Asiatic Monroe Doctrine." When Western governments, particularly Washington, complained of Japanese infringements on China's sovereignty, Tokyo treated the complaints as insolent meddling. That Japan depended on the United States for such critical imports as oil and scrap steel may have prevented the two countries from becoming totally alienated sooner than they did, but it did almost nothing to improve tempers in Tokyo. If anything, it made them worse. There are few things more galling than dependence on someone you despise.

Whether or not Japanese leaders had originally thought Manchuria would satisfy their hunger for expansion in Asia, it turned out to be merely an appetizer. By the mid-1930s they were ready for more. It piqued Japan's appetite that at just this time developments in China led Tokyo to believe that the next course of its meal might be snatched away if it did not act quickly. Manchuria had fallen to Japanese troops as quickly as it did because the Chinese were not sufficiently united to offer meaningful resistance. Until 1936 two factions waged a bitter struggle for control of the Chinese government and countryside. Chiang Kaishek and the Nationalist party, or Guomindang, were the incumbents; Mao Zedong's Communists were the challengers. With the Nationalists and Communists at each other's throats, the Japanese met only light resistance. But in 1936 some of Chiang's subordinates, impatient that he was treating the Communists as a greater threat than the Japanese, kidnapped him and held him hostage until he agreed, more or less, to call off the civil war and form a united Chinese front against Japan. When Tokyo learned of this occurrence, labeled the Xi'an incident, it decided that it should move before the united front firmed up.

In July 1937 Japanese troops on night patrol near the Marco Polo bridge north of Beijing lost track of one of their number. In their search for the missing soldier, the Japanese encountered Chinese troops, and the two sides exchanged fire. Although the lost man subsequently turned up, the Japanese exaggerated the confrontation into an excuse to flood the area with additional

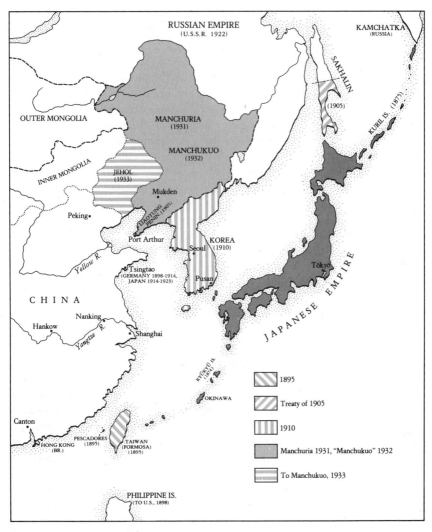

Japanese Expansion in China

units. In early August Japanese troops occupied Beijing. Shortly thereafter Japanese amphibious forces landed near the mouth of the Yangzi River. Although Japan did not bother to declare war, it acted as though it had. Japanese contingents invaded the coastal regions of northern and central China, seizing provincial capitals and later the national capital, Nanjing.

The conquest of Nanjing in December 1937 shocked a world that thought it had grown inured to brutality. For six weeks Japanese commanders encouraged their soldiers to rape, torture, and murder Chinese civilians, and the troops complied. Blood poured down the gutters, corpses were stacked in the streets, and the smoke of a hundred thousand houses deliberately set ablaze choked the city. The American vice consul in Nanjing likened the Japanese army sacking the city to a "barbarian horde."

China's overmatched government withdrew into the interior, where it established a temporary capital at Chongqing, far up the Yangzi. It called for international assistance against the Japanese aggression. Meanwhile guerrilla units of the Chinese Communist army harassed the Japanese and succeeded in denying them control of the countryside, even though the invaders occupied the coastal districts and most of the major cities. A stalemate ensued: the Japanese could not force the Chinese to surrender, but neither could the Chinese force the Japanese to leave.

The world reacted to the outbreak of war in China with revulsion against the Japanese; yet as in the case of the seizure of Manchuria, the revulsion was not enough to produce effective action against Japan. By this time the European powers were far more worried about Hitler, who was very close to their most vital interests, than about Japan, which was far away. The Soviet Union was the only partial exception to this rule, fearing Japanese expansion toward Siberia. The League of Nations declared Japan's actions unjustifiably aggressive and called on member nations to refrain from actions that might undermine China's power to resist the Japanese advance. But beyond this the League did nothing.

The United States did hardly more. In October 1937 Roosevelt decried the "present reign of terror and international lawlessness," and asserted that "innocent people, innocent nations are being cruelly sacrificed to a greed for power and supremacy which is devoid of all sense of justice and humane considerations." Likening the aggression of recent years to an epidemic, Roosevelt suggested that the international community band together to "quarantine" the aggressors. The deliberately unspecific nature of Roosevelt's remarks permitted the interpretation that he intended them to apply to other countries in addition to Japan, notably Italy and Germany; but the current crisis in China was what most of his listeners wanted to know about. Did the president's speech portend strong action against the Japanese invaders? It turned out not to. When American isolationists objected to getting involved in the affairs of Asia, and none of the other great powers except the Soviet Union picked up on Roosevelt's suggestion, Washington let the matter drop. Not even the Japanese machine-gunning and sinking of an American warship, the *Panay,* in Chinese waters provoked the Roosevelt administration to anything more than diplomatic protests. Tokyo, not wishing to press its luck at this stage, apologized, and the matter blew over.

The Culture of Appeasement

The American reluctance to oppose aggression in China was part of a broad international phenomenon. In nearly all the countries that had taken part in the First World War, the memories of that conflict remained raw and powerful. So horrible had the war been, and so far had its costs seemed to exceed its benefits, that popular opinion was overwhelmingly against almost anything that might result in a repetition of the agony. Curiously enough, the opposition to another war was strongest in those countries that had *won* the first war, in part because many persons in Britain and France had guilty consciences about the Versailles treaty, particularly about how it placed the whole blame for the war on Germany and made the German people liable for all the costs. Believing, with hindsight, that this was untrue and unfair, many in Britain and France were willing to overlook German violations of the treaty, especially when the alternatives entailed the risk of another war. Besides, even preparing for war cost money the depression-wracked governments did not have.

Hitler masterfully played on the gun-shyness of Germany's former enemies. Germany had quietly commenced rearming even before Hitler came to power in 1933; though this was a violation of the Versailles settlement, the other powers chose not to contest it, and Hitler concluded that they would not contest other violations. In 1935 he announced publicly that Germany would no longer be bound by the Versailles ban on arms. Conciliationists, later called "appeasers," in Britain and France contended that Hitler was claiming no more for Germany than any sovereign nation deserved, namely, the right of self-defense. In 1936 Hitler ordered German troops into the German Rhineland, which the Versailles treaty had ordered demilitarized. The French, who earlier had taken responsibility for policing the Rhine region, did nothing. France had suffered the most among the world war's victors, and the French people had no enthusiasm for fighting Germany again. After all, in stationing soldiers on Germany's own soil, Hitler was merely exercising a prerogative routinely exercised by all sovereign governments.

The failure of the Europeans to oppose Hitler's violations of the Versailles treaty exacerbated similar tendencies in the United States. Americans did not have the nagging consciences about the Versailles treaty the British and French did, since the United States had never ratified it. But many of those who cared about such things believed it was simply a victor's peace, one that treated Germany inequitably and unrealistically. This belief, of course, was an important reason many Americans had opposed the treaty in the first place. And though Americans had come away from the war with fewer losses than any of the other victors, American deaths and casualties had been quite high enough to convince most Americans that they should avoid another such fight if at all possible.

America's avoidance reflex gained strength from the revelations of a Senate committee investigating reports that certain American businesses had engaged in excessive profiteering during the war. The Nye committee, named for chairman Gerald Nye, began gathering evidence in 1934. During the next two years, the committee heard from hundreds of witnesses who showed unmistakably that major chemical and munitions makers had greatly increased their profit margins during the war and that the big financial institutions had done very well by the loans floated for the Allied governments. The revelations were educational, though they should not have been especially surprising to anyone familiar with the capitalist principle of profit maximizing and the law of supply and demand. Nonetheless, the Nye committee's investigations reinforced the feeling of many Americans that participation in the world war had not been in America's interests. During the depths of the Depression, American businesses were not held in particularly high esteem, and it was not hard to believe that the "merchants of death," as the arms manufacturers were often called, and the banking barons had dragged the United States into war for their own selfish purposes.

It was in the midst of the Nye investigations that congressional isolationists introduced the bill that became the Neutrality Act of 1935. That the experience of the world war was on the minds of the legislators, even as fresh war clouds gathered over East Asia and Europe, was evident from the law's ban on the export of American arms and ammunition to belligerents. The lawmakers appreciated the manner in which trade with the opposing sides in the world war had led to violations of American neutral rights and generated pressure to keep the trade going despite the dangers of American involvement. Had some ultraisolationists had their way, *all* trade with belligerents would have been barred; but during the Depression, when foreign sales were hard enough to come by, not many people wanted to try a repetition of Thomas Jefferson's disastrous 1807 embargo. The 1935 measure also warned Americans against traveling on vessels flying belligerent flags; the memory of the *Lusitania* still burned.

Subsequent modifications of the Neutrality Act extended the effort to prevent the United States from being pulled into present or future wars as it had been pulled into the world war. A 1936 update added a financial embargo to the stricture on arms sales; the ghost of William Jennings Bryan reminded legislators how American loans had given Americans a big monetary interest in the war's outcome. A 1937 amendment outlawed the sale of American weapons to the contestants in the Spanish Civil War. Another 1937 modification went beyond warning Americans about traveling on belligerent ships to forbidding them to. This last act also required that trade with belligerents in goods other than proscribed munitions be conducted on a cash-and-carry basis.

The Roosevelt administration was not particularly pleased with the neutrality legislation, though the president signed the measures. It was not that Roosevelt wanted to go to war; rather, he did not like having his freedom to conduct American foreign affairs diminished. Since 1789 the executive and legislative branches had struggled for control of American foreign policy. Generally the executive branch had held the upper hand, and the president had enjoyed the advantage over Congress in directing foreign affairs. Advantage did not imply complete control, however: Congress occasionally rebuffed presidential initiatives, as it did in rejecting Ulysses Grant's attempt to annex Santo Domingo. And sometimes it pushed presidents faster than they wished to go, as when the warhawks in the House of Representatives demanded war with Britain in 1812 and when anti-Spanish legislators called for thrashing Spain in

1898. But for the most part, the legislature had been content to leave the initiative in foreign affairs to the executive branch.

The period between the world wars was an exception to this general rule. In fact, the interwar years marked the high tide of congressional influence in foreign-policy making during the first two centuries of American history. When the Senate overturned Woodrow Wilson's foreign policy by rejecting the Versailles treaty, it demonstrated a legislative potency that continued through much of the next two decades. Sometimes this potency was largely unspoken, for example in limiting Stimson's and Hoover's options in response to the Japanese seizure of Manchuria and in disposing Roosevelt not to endanger his New Deal reforms by joining an international assault on the world depression. At other times Congress was more forthright. The neutrality laws of 1935, 1936, and 1937 were the clearest examples of congressional forthrightness.

Yet Roosevelt was not one to be corralled by Congress so easily. A slipperier president has never occupied the White House. This slipperiness was one of the character traits that caused Roosevelt's many enemies to hate him so—and it was a political trait he reveled in. Roosevelt liked to tell a story on himself about a staunch conservative who looked forward only to the day of the president's death. This man, a resident of New York's Westchester county, a bastion of Republicanism, every day purchased a copy of the *New York Herald Tribune* on the train platform on his way in to Manhattan to work. Every day he handed the newsboy a coin, glanced at the paper's front page, then gave the paper back to the boy. After some time the newsboy's curiosity got the better of him, and he asked the well-dressed gentleman why he looked only at the front page. "I'm interested in the obituary notices," the man replied. The boy, still puzzled, objected that the obituaries ran on an inside page. "The son of a bitch I'm interested in will be on page one," the man growled.

Although on the whole Roosevelt would have preferred not to have been constrained by the neutrality laws, he used them to suit his own purposes. Following the Japanese attack on China in 1937, the president took advantage of Japan's refusal to declare the war in China technically a war, and he declined to invoke the neutrality law. As a result, the Chinese were able to purchase American weapons. Sometimes Roosevelt employed the neutrality legislation as political cover. The 1937 congressional embargo of arms to the opposing factions in the Spanish Civil War relieved Roosevelt of much of the responsibility for the decision to stay out of that war—a decision that dismayed many of Roosevelt's liberal supporters. The cash-and-carry provision of the 1937 law promised the best of both worlds in noncontraband trade with belligerents. Purchasers had to pay for their purchases up front and take them away in their own ships. If the ships got sunk on the high seas, the losses were theirs. Meanwhile the United States did not sacrifice markets to economic competitors.

The result was that while Congress played a greater role in American foreign policy during the 1930s than either before or after, it did not play that role unaccompanied. Roosevelt was never far from center stage, even if he was not always in the spotlight.

Sprucing Up the Neighborhood: Latin America

In one area of American international relations, however, the executive branch continued to enjoy its traditional prerogatives. Since the early nineteenth century, when John Quincy Adams had defied congressional urgings that the Monroe administration recognize the new Latin American republics, and James Monroe had issued his eventually venerable doctrine without even consulting the legislature; through the early twentieth century, when Teddy Roosevelt had swung his Big Stick, when William Taft had conducted diplomacy with dollars, and when Woodrow Wilson had sent General Pershing after Pancho Villa, the region to the south of the United States had often been the playground of American presidents. The tradition continued into the 1920s and 1930s.

The first seventy years or so of the twentieth century were the great age of revolution in the nonindustrialized world. This revolution had two complementary elements: an attack on foreign influences that dominated local politics and local economies and an assault on indigenous structures of class and privilege that tended to deprive the ordinary people of wealth and power. In those parts of the world, particularly Asia and Africa, that had been colonized by the industrial states, the revolution typically took the form of a nationalist uprising against the colonial government and a simultaneous or subsequent civil war of radicals against conservative elites, the latter of which had often collaborated with the colonial power.

Although the revolution in the nonindustrialized world came to be associated most commonly with Asia and Africa, and flourished most visibly in the aftermath of the Second World War, it actually began in Latin America a generation earlier. Because most of Latin America had been independent since the 1820s, there was no formal colonial power to toss out; instead the revolutionaries focused on the United States, which was the next best thing. At the same time, they leveled their guns at the local elites that served as agents of American influence in the area.

In several countries of Latin America, the revolution was merely incipient, and the United States government worked hard to keep it that way. Haiti was one such country. For the nearly two decades from 1915 to 1934, American troops occupied Haiti and ran it almost as a military province. Woodrow Wilson had sent the troops to Haiti when assassins murdered the Haitian president shortly after the beginning of the First World War. German ships were lurking in the area, and the German government was known to have designs on the Caribbean. Although Wilson possessed no hard evidence that Berlin was about to move forcibly against Haiti, he preferred not to run any risks with a country that lay athwart the approaches to the just-opened Panama Canal and in which unrest had been chronic since the eighteenth century. Should a revolutionary or even independent-minded government gain power in Port-au-Prince, it might consider flirting with the Germans or other potentially unfriendly foreigners. American property holdings in Haiti were not extensive—the country was one of the poorest in the Western Hemisphere—but a radical takeover

U.S. Marines did not need tanks or airplanes to maintain order in Haiti; motorcycles and small arms sufficed. *AP/Wide World Photos*

would not do those any good either. The American marines were intended to make sure that such a takeover did not occur. They did. Several months after the troops arrived, and under their watchful gaze, the government of Haiti signed a treaty authorizing the American military presence. That presence persisted long past the time that the German threat, such as it was, disappeared. Not until 1934 did Washington pull the troops home.

The story in the Dominican Republic, formerly Santo Domingo, was similar. American soldiers had been in and out of the country during the days of Teddy Roosevelt, enforcing order and good behavior, as interpreted by Washington, under the "police power" provision of the Roosevelt corollary to the Monroe Doctrine. American soldiers returned in 1916 for the same general purpose as in Haiti: to guarantee stability during perilous times in a country strategically located with respect to the Panama Canal. The marines stayed in the Dominican Republic until 1924. While there, they did some commendable work building roads and sanitation facilities. They also did some less praiseworthy work, resorting to harsh tactics in dealing with dissidents and training a local police force, the Guardia Nacional (National Guard), to do likewise. Among the marines' prize pupils was Rafael Trujillo, a shrewd, tough, ambitious individual who rose from the ranks of the National Guard to the pinnacle of Dominican politics. In 1928, with American support, he made himself the ruler of the country. For thirty years Trujillo was the model of the Latin American military strongman. He brutally quashed dissent, which did not particularly please Washington, but he kept order in the Dominican Republic and preserved American investments, which did. On balance, until very near the end of his rule, when his repressiveness threatened to spark an explosion, the United States was happy to help him remain in power.

Nicaragua likewise had the misfortune of being too turbulent and too close to the Panama Canal for its own independence. The occupation that had begun under Taft continued until 1925. Although the personnel of the Nicaraguan government changed during this period, their deference to Washington's wishes varied only slightly and not enough to endanger American security or property interests. By the mid-1920s, with the world war safely over and with the Republican administration in the United States seeking ways to cut costs, Washington decided that the American troops in Nicaragua were no longer needed. In 1925 the troops were withdrawn. No sooner had they left, however, than the perennial dissatisfaction with the status quo of elite wealth and mass poverty bubbled over into armed revolt; the American marines quickly returned.

The moving spirit of the insurrection was Augusto Sandino, the son of a comfortable but nonetheless liberal landowner and one of his Indian servants. Sandino had been in Mexico when the latest fighting erupted; he immediately came home and joined the revolt. When the original leaders of the revolt accepted a 1927 peace accord mediated by Henry Stimson and heavily promoted by the American government, Sandino denounced the accord and refused to come down from the mountains. He would maintain the struggle, he said, until the Yankees had gone for good and the Nicaraguan people recaptured control of their destiny. "I was the one called to protest the betrayal of the Fatherland," he later explained.

From 1927 until the early 1930s, Sandino led a guerrilla insurgency against the Americans and the Nicaraguan government. He did not gain much ground against either, though he won a considerable following among the Nicaraguan peasantry. Yet neither were the American troops and the Nicaraguan government able to stamp out the insurgency. After the 1929 stock market crash and the onset of the Depression, the Hoover administration decided it had better things to spend American taxpayers' money on than chasing a rebel Robin Hood around the countryside of Nicaragua. Several months before the 1932 American elections, the administration announced the phased withdrawal of American forces. One thousand troops came out at once, and the rest followed by the beginning of 1934.

Shortly after the last American soldiers steamed away, Sandino accepted an offer by the Nicaraguan government to commence negotiations to end the civil war. Distrusting the government's good faith, and particularly distrusting the intentions of the head of the National Guard, Anastasio Somoza, Sandino nonetheless decided to take a chance. It turned out to be a bad gamble. As Sandino was leaving a dinner with the Nicaraguan president, Somoza's men arrested the rebel leader and three of his companions. They were driven to the outskirts of Managua and murdered.

Somoza then proceeded to muscle aside the president, getting himself elected chief executive in 1936 while continuing as commander of the National Guard. Between the two posts, he had no difficulty creating a political machine that dominated Nicaraguan politics for four decades.

By the second half of the 1930s, the German threat that had helped make Woodrow Wilson so touchy regarding unrest in the vicinity of the Panama Canal had resurfaced. While some other Latin American countries, such as Argentina, showed open affinities toward the European fascists, Nicaragua allied itself closely with the United States. In return, the Roosevelt administration overlooked Somoza's tendencies toward authoritarianism and assisted in the consolidation of his authority. American military advisers helped train officers of the Nicaraguan National Guard, and American loans helped finance American imports to Nicaragua. Roosevelt may or may not have said of Somoza (the president may have been speaking of Trujillo): "He's a son of a bitch, but at least he's our son of a bitch." Nevertheless, the comment captured the attitude of Washington toward Nicaragua (as well as toward the Dominican Republic).

Somoza's and Trujillo's Cuban counterpart was Fulgencio Batista, though it took longer for Batista's autocratic characteristics to develop. American troops, having initially left Cuba in 1902, had left again in 1909 following a three-year occupation. They returned in 1917, this time staying for six years. To the usual reasons for sending troops into Central America and the Caribbean, Wilson added, in the Cuban case, an insistance that turmoil in the island not interfere with sugar production during the world war. That such interference would also cut into the profits of the American owners of the sugar plantations provided a further incentive to reoccupy and a reason to remain after the war ended.

Cuban politics at the time produced corruption almost as readily as Cuban cane produced sugar; officeholders treated the treasury as their own and sold influence to the highest bidder. The corruption in high places engendered reform movements, some violent and some not. One of the nonviolent reformers, Gerardo Machado, won election as president in the first balloting held after the 1923 withdrawal of American troops. Machado started well: he built roads and bridges and instituted regulations designed to benefit small farmers rather than large landowners. He constructed new schools and even attempted, with less success than in the other areas, to encourage the prostitutes of Havana to retrain themselves for new jobs.

But Machado gradually fell into the self-serving pattern of his predecessors. When criticism arose, his police arrested and sometimes assassinated opposition leaders. They fired on striking workers and suppressed the dissemination of unflattering comments. A favorite tactic for disposing of the evidence of police brutality was to throw the bodies to the sharks in Havana harbor. As time went on, the sharks grew fatter.

Machado's repression merely put a stopper in the bottle of discontent without eliminating its sources. In 1933 the bottle exploded. A general strike paralyzed Havana and touched off mass violence. Machado, not the heroic type,

Fulgencio Batista examines a recent innovation in crowd control. *AP/Wide World Photos*

fled the country. After a few weeks of confusion, a group of noncommissioned army officers led by Fulgencio Batista seized the government. But not knowing quite what to do with it, or perhaps realizing that popular emotions still had some venting to do, the officers turned the reins over to Ramón Grau San Martín, a well-known civilian opponent of Machado.

Grau's government began by instituting a variety of social and political reforms. Among the first was the abrogation of the Platt amendment, which had authorized American intervention in Cuban affairs. Other reforms were along the lines of the New Deal that Franklin Roosevelt was pushing through the American Congress at this very time. Conservatives in the United States lacked the political power to block Roosevelt's reforms, but some of these same conservatives owned property in Cuba, and others held stock in banks that had issued loans to the Cuban government, and their complaints produced greater results in stopping Grau's reforms. The American conservatives predicted that Grau's initial moderate measures would give way to measures more radical; they urged the Roosevelt administration to withhold support from the new Cuban president. When experience bore out their predictions, with Grau halting payment on certain American loans and seizing some American-owned plantations, the Roosevelt administration threw its backing to Batista, who installed a president he could easily control.

For several years Batista governed Cuba through front men. Although something of a populist and leftist during this period, he stayed away from measures likely to alienate the United States. On the countrary, he made himself helpful, for example by allowing American warships and planes to use Cuban harbors and airfields. In exchange, the Roosevelt administration loaned Batista's government money toward the purchase of American goods. The administration also facilitated Cuban sugar sales in the United States and declared that it, too, considered the Platt amendment a dead letter. The arrangement with Batista was easier on American democratic scruples than those with Trujillo and Somoza; during this period Batista was quite popular with the Cuban masses.

Mexico never succumbed to long-term rule by a single person the way the Dominican Republic, Nicaragua, and Cuba did. Instead Mexico opted for long-term rule by a single party, eventually named the Partido Revolucionario Institucional (PRI). If the idea of an institutionalized revolution sounded paradoxical, it fairly reflected the contradictory character of Mexican politics. At least partly because of the opposition of the United States to the Mexican revolution during the 1910s, the idea of revolution became a shibboleth of Mexican politics. All but the most reactionary factions embraced revolution as a rhetorical device, however much some of them rejected the actual practice of revolution. Likewise, resistance to anything smacking of pressure from the yanquis animated nearly all political discussion in Mexico.

During the 1920s and early 1930s, the direction of Mexican politics fell to a pair of practical, business-minded men who spoke the language of revolution even as they undertook action to prevent a real revolution from occurring. Alvaro Obregón, inaugurated president in 1920, faced the task of restoring calm and normalcy (to borrow a term about to be coined by Warren Harding) after a decade of revolution and civil war. Not long after taking office, as peace was slowly returning to Mexico, Obregón asserted only half jokingly that he had solved the problem of banditry in the countryside by bringing all the bandits to Mexico City, where he could look after them. For four years Obregón did just that. In the process he forged a powerful coalition of capitalists, landlords, generals, and labor union leaders.

Obregón managed to avoid major problems with the United States despite his sworn obligation to uphold the Mexican constitution, which contained an article that almost guaranteed trouble with Washington. Article 27 of the 1917 constitution declared that all the land of Mexico as well as the minerals lying below the land belonged to the Mexican people. This article was aimed especially at American investors who held title to huge portions of Mexico's best land and most of Mexico's oil. The United States government took the position that Article 27 did not apply to titles acquired prior to the enactment of the 1917 constitution. For three years Washington withheld recognition from Obregón's government, hoping to pressure him into accepting the American interpretation of the land law. The pressure eventually worked. In 1923, at a moment when Obregón faced an imminent revolt by the Roman Catholic clergy and conservative landowners, both of which groups found even his moderate reforms threatening, the Mexican president struck a deal with Washington acknowledging that Article 27 was not retroactive. The Coolidge administration promptly extended recognition, thereby facilitating Obregón's purchase of American weapons, which he used to crush the revolt.

In 1924 Plutarco Calles succeeded Obregón. Calles was cut from the same cloth as Obregón, which was not surprising considering that Obregón had chosen him as successor. But Calles ran into greater difficulties with the United States as a result of a law passed by the Mexican legislature in 1925 limiting foreign oil concessions to fifty years, with the option of thirty-year renewal. Although this law promised to have little practical effect on working oil properties (most wells run dry in less than fifty years), it would prevent foreigners from buying oil rights and holding them for speculation. As Calles explained to the American ambassador, things might have been worse: radicals in his country were demanding nationalization of the oil industry, with expropriation of foreign holdings. Calles did not want this. The 1925 law was designed to steal the radicals' thunder.

Conservatives and oil industry lobbyists in Washington muttered darkly about Bolshevism in Mexico and asserted a need to stamp out revolution in the Western Hemisphere, by military force if necessary. Yet Coolidge was too cool a character to leap into war. With the help of other American business interests that feared expropriation, the Republican president resisted the warhawks. He also sent a new ambassador to Mexico City. Dwight Morrow, a Wall Street banker whose credentials reassured American corporate types, pointed out to Calles that American investors would naturally be reluctant to sink funds into a country where the rules changed after the fact. Calles recognized the role that American investment would probably have to play in the development of the Mexican economy, and he allowed himself to be persuaded. With encouragement from Calles, the Mexican supreme court overturned the 1925 law.

This solution settled the oil question for the next decade, through a couple more uprisings and the assassination of Obregón by a fanatical clericalist. In 1934 the election of Lázaro Cárdenas shifted Mexico's institutionalized revolution to the left, toward more revolution and less institutionalization. The new president sponsored a large-scale program of land reform; he began cleaning out the bureaucracy; he opened the doors of the National Palace to Indians, peasants, and others not usually heard from in Mexican politics. And in 1938, following a violent labor dispute in Mexico's oil fields, he decreed the nationalization of the oil industry. All foreign holdings in the oil business now became the property of the Mexican government. Compensation would be determined by Mexico.

Again hotheads in Washington spoke of military intervention to undo the dastardly deed. They received encouragement from reactionaries in Mexico, who concurred that Cárdenas was dangerously radical. The Roosevelt administration applied a modest amount of economic pressure against Mexico, curtailing American government purchases of Mexican silver. On their own hook, the oil companies that were losing control of Mexican properties organized a boycott of Mexican oil.

But international developments were on Cárdenas's side, as he doubtless recognized they would be. With Japan pillaging China, Italy brutalizing Ethiopia, and Hitler starting to get really ugly about what Germany had lost after the world war, Roosevelt wanted to avoid doing anything that might put the United States in such bad company. He immediately ruled out military action, determined to demonstrate that in the Western Hemisphere differences between countries could be settled amicably. Roosevelt accepted the principle of nationalization, which was (and is) nothing more than the right of a government to exercise sovereignty over its own territory. The only other issue was the appropriate amount of compensation. Negotiations on this question lasted until 1941, when the oil companies got less for their property than they thought they deserved but more than the Mexican government had originally wanted to pay.

Mexico's nationalization of American oil properties was the most direct test of what the Roosevelt administration called its "good neighbor" policy toward Latin America. Early in his first term, Roosevelt implicitly conceded that the United States had been something less than a good neighbor in the past; the most obvious indications of bad-neighborliness were the military interventions in the several countries of the Caribbean basin where American marines had made themselves at home. To improve the neighborhood, Roosevelt renounced further such interventions. Good neighbors did not storm into each other's houses brandishing guns.

Roosevelt did not go so far as to deny American interest in events in Latin America. The United States had large investments in the region; unrest and disorder threatened these investments. Unrest and disorder also threatened to bring to power regimes that might allow hostile states, especially Germany, to gain a foothold in the Western Hemisphere, perhaps dangerously close to the Panama Canal.

All the same, Roosevelt was insightful enough to recognize that heavy-handed military intervention would probably only exacerbate unrest. American soldiers in Nicaragua, for example, had simply spurred Sandino to greater efforts. It was not lost on American leaders that the American troops had hardly left before Sandino was captured and killed. Besides, American occupations cost money, which was in short supply during the Depression. And they eroded American moral credibility with other nations at a time when moral credibility was sorely needed.

Roosevelt's aims in Latin America were hardly less ambitious than those of his predecessors. He desired a stable region, secure from external threat and receptive to American investment and trade. To the extent that his policy toward Latin America differed from those of his predecessors, the difference was chiefly a matter of means. And even regarding means, the break was not abrupt. The Republicans had been moving toward a noninterventionist policy before Roosevelt arrived in the White House; in 1928 American undersecretary of state J. Reuben Clark drafted a memo asserting that the Roosevelt corollary's justification of American military intervention in Latin America rested on specious logic. Herbert Hoover subsequently accepted Clark's argument. Although this did not rule out military intervention, since Hoover was free to come up with his own corollary or doctrine justifying intervention, it did indicate growing disenchantment with the idea. Roosevelt crystallized the disenchantment into a stated policy. In the short term the new approach improved the atmosphere between the United States and its southern neighbors. In the slightly longer term it helped Washington line up Latin American support against Germany and Japan when a second world war came.

*   *   *

During the 1920s and 1930s, American policy toward Latin America was more consistent and self-confident than policy toward East Asia and Europe. This was true partly because the risks were smaller in dealing with Mexico, Cuba, and the other Latin American countries than in dealing with Japan or Germany and partly because Americans found it easier to define their interests close to home. Nearly all Americans agreed that the Panama Canal needed defending; most looked unfavorably on the possible emergence in the Western Hemisphere of regimes decidedly unfriendly to American economic or strategic interests. Whether these interests were described in terms of the Monroe Doctrine or merely simple common sense, they provoked little debate.

In Asia and Europe, by contrast, American interests were by no means so clear. The Washington conference treaties seemed sound both politically and economically, but on broader issues there was considerable room for debate. Did American physical or economic security require an independent and sovereign China? Put otherwise: Was the Open Door in China a necessity or a luxury? Few Americans were willing to call it a necessity, despite the efforts of leaders like Henry Stimson to explain where Japan's cavalier treatment of the concept might lead. As a result, ambivalence often characterized American actions toward Japan, which encouraged the Japanese to greater liberties in China.

In Europe, America's vital interests were even harder to discern. The Republican administrations of the 1920s judged it prudent to assist indirectly in the stabilization of the European economies, but the depression of the 1930s exploded their efforts. By the mid-1930s it appeared obvious that fascism as a general phenomenon was inimical to democracy, but the dangers posed by particular proponents of fascism were unclear. Was Mussolini a menace to the United States? It hardly seemed likely. Hitler was definitely a danger to some of Germany's own people, especially Jews, and possibly to Germany's weaker neighbors. But did he threaten the United States? Maybe someday, but not yet. Besides, if the British and the French were not doing anything about fascism in their own backyard, why should the United States? At the moment the length of the soup lines in Chicago seemed to most Americans a more pressing matter than Mussolini or Hitler.

As the 1930s wore on, though, the chances of another big war appeared to increase. Japan trampled the Chinese; Mussolini battered the Ethiopians; Hitler presumably had a purpose in rearming Germany. German and Italian participation in the Spanish Civil War was not for the health of the soldiers involved.

But a major war was no sure thing, and even if it came, there was no compelling reason the United States would have to get mixed up in it. Most Americans had trouble telling how their country, apart from big bankers and arms merchants, had benefited from participation in the first war. If another war did come, they would be happy to let other people fight it.

Sources and Suggestions for Further Reading

A brief introduction to American diplomacy between the world wars is Warren I. Cohen, *Empire Without Tears: America's Foreign Relations, 1921–1933* (1987). L. Ethan Ellis, *Republican Foreign Policy, 1921–1933* (1968), covers the same ground. Joseph Brandes, *Herbert Hoover and Economic Diplomacy* (1962), shows Hoover at work at the Commerce Department. Joan Hoff Wilson, *Herbert Hoover* (1975), shows him there and elsewhere. Mira Wilkins, *The Maturing of the Multinational Enterprise: American Business Abroad from 1914 to 1970* (1974), deals with one aspect of American international economic relations, while Joan Hoff Wilson, *American Business and Foreign Policy, 1920–1933* (1971); Michael Hogan, *Informal Entente: The Private Structure of Cooperation in Anglo-American Economic Diplomacy, 1918–1929* (1977); Carl Parrini, *Heir to Empire: United States Economic Diplomacy, 1916–1923* (1969); Herbert Feis, *The Diplomacy of the Dollar, 1919–1932* (1950); and Frank Costigliola, *Awkward Dominion: American Political, Economic, and Cultural Relations with Europe, 1919–1933* (1984), deal with others. Like Costigliola's book, Melvyn P. Leffler's *The Elusive Quest: America's Pursuit of European Stability and French Security, 1919–1933* (1979), covers much more than economic affairs. A wonderful introduction to the European (and some extra-European) diplomacy of the interwar period is the two-volume work edited by Gordon A. Craig and Felix Gilbert, *The Diplomats, 1919–1939* (1968–1974 ed.). On the Kellogg-Briand treaty, the best account is Robert H. Ferrell, *Peace in Their Time* (1952).

An illuminating account of the global depression of the 1930s is Charles Kindleberger, *The World in Depression* (1973). Lloyd C. Gardner looks at the Depression's influence on Roosevelt's foreign policy in *Economic Aspects of New Deal Diplomacy* (1964). Robert Dallek, *Franklin D. Roosevelt and American Foreign Policy, 1932–1945* (1979), is the best treatment of Roosevelt's foreign policies broadly. Robert A. Divine illuminates the efforts to prevent a repetition of the events leading to American involvement in the First World War in *The Illusion of Neutrality* (1962), while Wayne S. Cole, *Roosevelt and the Isolationists, 1932–1945* (1983), traces the president's struggles with congressional opponents of an active foreign policy. Edward Bennett portrays Roosevelt's opening to the Soviet Union in *Recognition of Russia* (1970). John L. Gaddis, *Russia, the Soviet Union and the United States* (1978), sets recognition in a longer context. Thomas R. Maddux, *Years of Estrangement* (1980), looks at what went on in Soviet-American relations before recognition. Joan Hoff Wilson, *Ideology and Economics* (1974) examines the same issues. Roosevelt's early policy toward Germany forms the subject matter of Arnold Offner, *American Appeasement* (1969). The question of what to do about Mussolini engages the attention of George W. Baer, *Test Case: Italy, Ethiopia, and the League of Nations* (1976). Douglas Little looks at the American position on the Spanish Civil War in *Malevolent Neutrality* (1985). Wolfgang

Mommsen and Lothar Kettenacher, eds., *The Fascist Challenge and the Policy of Appeasement* (1983), is more broadly constructed.

On the Washington Conference, the most valuable books are Roger Dingman, *Power in the Pacific: The Origins of Naval Arms Limitation, 1914–1922* (1974), and Thomas H. Buckley, *The United States and the Washington Conference* (1970). Other works discussing American relations with East Asia and the Pacific include Akira Iriye, *After Imperialism: The Search for a New Order in the Far East, 1921–1931* (1973); Charles E. Neu, *The Troubled Encounter: The United States and Japan* (1975); Michael Barnhart, *Japan Prepares for Total War: The Quest for Economic Security, 1919–1941* (1987); Warren I. Cohen, *The Chinese Connection* (1978); Dorothy Borg, *American Policy and the Chinese Revolution, 1925–1928* (1947), and *The United States and the Far Eastern Crisis of 1933–1938* (1964); Justus D. Doenecke, *When the Wicked Rise: American Opinion-Makers and the Manchurian Crisis of 1931–1933* (1984); and Armin Rappaport, *Henry L. Stimson and Japan, 1931–1933* (1963). Christopher Thorne, *The Limits of Foreign Policy: The West, the League and the Far Eastern Crisis of 1931–1933* (1972), treats much more than the American connection to the Manchurian crisis.

The evolution of U.S. policy toward Latin America is analyzed in Walter LaFeber, *Inevitable Revolutions: The United States in Central America* (1984); Kenneth J. Grieb, *The Latin American Policy of Warren G. Harding* (1977); Robert Freeman Smith, *The United States and Revolutionary Nationalism in Mexico, 1916–1932* (1972); Karl M. Schmitt, *Mexico and the United States, 1821–1973* (1974); Irwin F. Gellman, *Good Neighbor Diplomacy: United States Policies in Latin America, 1933–1945* (1979), and *Roosevelt and Batista: Good Neighbor Diplomacy in Cuba, 1933–1945* (1972); Alexander DeConde, *Herbert Hoover's Latin American Policy* (1951); William Kamman, *A Search for Stability: United States Diplomacy toward Nicaragua, 1925–1933* (1968); G. Pope Atkins and Larman C. Wilson, *The United States and the Trujillo Regime* (1972); and Bryce Wood, *The Making of the Good Neighbor Policy* (1961).

Chapter 10

Mugged by Reality, 1937–1945

As many predicted, the war came. And as wars so often do, it surprised people, in both the way it came and the way it turned out. After Japan's war against China stalled into a bloody stand-off, the militarists who had taken nearly complete control of Japanese affairs found other outlets for their aggression. They moved south and west into Indochina and toward the East Indies. In doing so, they provoked opposition from the United States, opposition with more punch than the wrist slaps that had gone before. American opposition produced greater Japanese belligerence, and in 1941 Tokyo decided on war against the United States. A sneak attack at Pearl Harbor in December 1941 announced the decision.

Almost as surprising as the Japanese attack on Pearl Harbor was the declaration of war against the United States by Germany that followed within days. But by then surprises were becoming almost a way of life with Hitler. Few people who had watched him assume the German chancellorship in 1933 thought he would last long. Few people had anticipated that he could flout international opinion as he subsequently did and get away with it. After a half decade of the most bitter German propaganda against the Soviet Union, a 1939 nonaggression pact between Berlin and Moscow overturned years of expectations regarding the giants of central and eastern Europe. The immediate result of the German-Soviet agreement was *not* especially surprising, though: a German invasion of Poland, which signaled the beginning of war in Europe. When Hitler later double-crossed Stalin by invading the Soviet Union in June 1941, he disrupted expectations once again. His declaration of war against the United States the following December seemed unnecessary and risky even for such a gambler as he had proved himself to be.

The twin surprises of December 1941—the Japanese attack on Pearl Harbor and the German declaration of war against the United States—converted the previously separate Asian and European wars into a full-blown world war, with America squarely in the middle. They also produced an unlikely coalition among the world's foremost capitalist power (the United States), the world's principal imperialist power (Britain), and the world's primary (and only) communist power (the Soviet Union).

The December surprises also led to a revolution in the international political order. With the United States, Britain, and the Soviet Union arrayed against them, the fascists had little chance of victory. They managed to postpone their

Chronology

1937   Neutrality Act of 1937; Japan attacks China, brutalizes Nanjing; Roosevelt's "quarantine" speech

1938   Mexico nationalizes American oil properties; *Anschluss* of Austria with Germany; Sudeten crisis and Munich conference

1939   Germany invades Czechoslovakia; German-Soviet nonaggression pact; German invasion of Poland starts Second World War; Roosevelt proclaims neutrality; Neutrality Act of 1939

1940   Fall of France; Japan invades Indochina; Battle of Britain; destroyers-for-bases deal with Britain; Selective Service Act; Tripartite pact among Germany, Italy, and Japan

1941   Lend-Lease program begins; Germany invades Soviet Union; Japan completes occupation of Indochina; Roosevelt freezes Japanese assets; Atlantic conference and Atlantic Charter; Japan attacks Pearl Harbor and Philippines; United States enters Second World War

1942   Battles of Coral Sea and Midway; Allied landings in North Africa

1943   Siege of Stalingrad broken; Allied invasion of Italy; Teheran conference of Roosevelt, Churchill, and Stalin

1944   Allied invasion of France, Bretton Woods conference; American invasion of the Philippines

1945   Yalta conference; German surrender; Potsdam conference; atomic bombing of Japan; Japanese surrender ends Second World War

defeat for three and a half ghastly years, but by the time the smoke lifted, Germany and Japan had been eliminated as major factors in world affairs. Britain had been exhausted, though this was less immediately obvious. Two powers, the United States and the Soviet Union, dominated the international landscape.

Pacific Rift

Understanding between Americans and Japanese has never been abundant. There are several reasons for this. The Japanese inhabit a few relatively small islands that are deficient in natural resources, whereas Americans occupy a continental domain that is among the most blessed on earth. The Japanese long existed in the shadow of China; the Americans were from the beginning of their national existence the big kids on their hemispheric block. Americans essentially invented the idea of individualism, with much emphasis on personal

The sailors in the foreground can only stare in shock as the U.S.S. *California* explodes during the Japanese attack at Pearl Harbor. *Harry S Truman Library*

liberty and relatively little on social obligation; the Japanese have tended to devalue personal autonomy in favor of social cohesion and responsibility to the community. Americans were in the second wave of the Industrial Revolution and quickly moved to the front ranks of the advanced economic powers; Japan struggled to catch up, never quite overcoming (at least until the last part of the twentieth century) its late start and dearth of resources. America was a heterogeneous nation from the beginning and only got more diverse with passing time; Japan was homogeneous to the point of being tribal and strove mightily to remain so. For much of American history, racial prejudice was an accepted, if not always admired, fact of social and political life, and the Japanese were frequently stereotyped in unflattering and pernicious ways; from the Japanese side, Americans were frequently stereotyped as well, sometimes in racial terms, yet equally often in cultural terms that were hardly less flattering than the views Americans held of the Japanese. Americans vented their expansionist energies during the nineteenth century when international standards of political acceptability still allowed the acquisition of new territory and of colonies and spheres of influence; the Japanese commenced major expansion only after the First World War when, thanks in no small part to Woodrow Wilson, self-determination became the standard of international affairs, required in rhetoric if not always practiced in fact. This last discrepancy appeared to the Japanese to be a double standard. The Americans had colonies, including the Philippines and Guam, right in Japan's backyard. They had the entire Western

Hemisphere as a sphere of influence. So how could they begrudge Japan, which needed growing room far more than they did, a sphere in Asia?

This question truly puzzled many Japanese during the 1930s. In prying Manchuria free from China and bringing it under Japan's protection, many Japanese thought they were doing very much what the Americans had done in springing Cuba, Puerto Rico, and the Philippines from Spain and pulling Panama from Colombia. To Japanese thinking, Manchuria was as important to Japan's security as Haiti, Nicaragua, and the Dominican Republic were to American security. Japan did not complain when the United States sent troops to maintain order in those countries; neither should Americans complain when Japan sent troops to Manchuria to restore order there. The Japanese protectorate over Manchukuo was hardly more onerous than the American protectorates over half the countries of Central America and the Caribbean. What were the Americans complaining about?

Whatever the original justification for the Japanese advance into Manchuria, expansion once under way acquired a momentum of its own, as expansion often does. To a large extent Japan's aggression in Manchuria and northern China was the product not of any grand design in Tokyo but of the headstrong determination of the officers commanding Japanese troops in the field. The leaders of Japan's Kwantung army, the force that invaded Manchuria, were the most successful at taking vigorous action and essentially daring Tokyo to disavow it. Each time the Kwantung officers made a bold move—as in the Mukden incident and its aftermath—and succeeded, the relative moderates in Tokyo grew politically and psychologically less able or willing to pull the generals back. The militarists became national heroes; the moderates were dubbed cowards or worse.

Economics figured centrally in Tokyo's calculations. An expansionist policy required a military build-up; the build-up injected new life into Japan's depressed economy, raising prices, employment levels, and hopes. Just as the Wilson administration had been reluctant in 1915 to take steps, such as barring American loans to belligerents, that might have strangled the war-induced American economic recovery, so the Japanese government in the 1930s was disinclined to endanger the recovery sparked by its military-expansionist policy. Furthermore, to a degree unusual among modern expeditionary armies, Japan's forces in Asia lived off the land, which was one reason for their rapacity. To withdraw the troops from China and Manchuria would require finding them an alternative source of support. With money tight, this would not be easy.

Japan was particularly sensitive on economic questions because of its vulnerable position with respect to the rest of the world economy. The trade war that had followed the onset of the Depression posed a graver threat to Japan than to most other countries. Foreign trade amounted to a much larger portion of national income in resource-poor Japan than trade did in a country such as the United States, which possessed within its borders most of what it needed. Britain and France, for their part, had empires to fall back on. If Japan was to survive the fragmentation of the world economy into competing trade blocs, the Japanese needed to carve out their own sphere. From this thinking arose the idea of a Greater East Asia Co-Prosperity Sphere, with Japan as leader.

Japan had another reason—namely, the Soviet Union—for believing it was justified in moving into Manchuria and from there into China proper. Following a period of quiescence, while first Lenin and then Stalin concentrated on consolidating the hold of the Communist party on the Soviet Union, the traditional rivalry between Russia and Japan for hegemony in northeastern Asia began to heat up again. After Japan occupied Manchuria, Stalin mobilized his Far Eastern forces and moved them to the Amur River, where only this narrow strip of water separated them from Japan's Kwantung army. Until 1937 the two sides glowered fiercely at each other but did little more. The outbreak of the second Sino-Japanese war, however, diverted Japanese troops to China and weakened those units left confronting the Soviets. Shooting started in the summer of 1938. It recurred in 1939. The latter fighting was particularly severe, with the Soviets inflicting some eighteen thousand casualties and a sharp defeat on the Japanese. Although the two sides eventually negotiated a cease-fire, Tokyo could not help drawing the conclusion that its hold on Manchuria was tenuous. And if Japan could not hold Manchuria, the future of its East Asian sphere seemed dim.

Worries about Manchuria aside, things were not going well for Japan. The Western democratic powers, including the United States, were increasingly treating Tokyo as a political pariah. This did not deter the hard-core ultranationalists in Japan from plotting additional expansion, but neither did it make other Japanese any more comfortable. If the West imposed trade sanctions against Japan—for example, by blocking the sale of oil and steel—life in Japan could become very difficult. More immediately ominous, the conflict with China was turning into a quagmire. As Japan moved farther into China, the Chinese Nationalist army retreated farther into the mountains. The Chinese Communists meanwhile sapped Japanese strength by a hit-and-run war of attrition. There appeared to be no end to the ordeal since the more territory and people Japan conquered, the more troops it needed to garrison that territory and control those people. China was a huge country, and Japan would run out of troops before China ran out of territory and people.

For a time the leadership in Tokyo considered a negotiated peace with the Chinese government. This would allow Japan to extricate some of the six hundred thousand troops that were tied down by the fighting in China. It would also ease the strain in relations with the Americans and other Westerners. The Chinese Nationalists gave indications of a reciprocal interest in peace. But the Chinese Communists adamantly resisted a settlement while Japanese troops occupied Chinese territory, and they forced the Nationalists to drop the idea. Meanwhile the Japanese government realized that it would have trouble explaining to the Japanese people why the great sacrifices already suffered in the war against China had failed to produce a victory. Japan lost seventy thousand killed and wounded in six weeks of fighting for Shanghai and Nanjing alone. (China lost five times as many.) In January 1938 Tokyo announced that it would not negotiate with Chiang Kaishek's government. In effect, it said that the Sino-Japanese war was a fight to the finish.

Yet Tokyo recognized that the war against China, if won at all, would be won elsewhere than in China. As long as Japan had to guard Manchuria against Soviet attack, it would have to keep a large army there. In fact, even the large army it already had in Manchuria would not suffice if full-fledged hostilities broke out with the Soviets. Soviet infantry and armored units vastly outnumbered the Japanese units arrayed against them. In addition, the Soviets had a fleet of three hundred heavy bombers that could cover the distance from Vladivostok to Tokyo and back. For Japan merely to consider a greater effort against China required neutralizing the Soviet threat.

The Japanese government sought to accomplish this by improving relations with Germany. In late 1936 Tokyo and Berlin signed the Anti-Comintern pact, an agreement designed to neutralize the activities of Moscow's political front organization and that included a secret protocol calling for mutual consultation and assistance in the event either side engaged in hostilities with the Soviet Union. Subsequently, Japanese diplomats worked toward still closer ties to Germany. By means of such actions, the Japanese government required the Kremlin to consider the danger that a war against Japan would lead to a two-front conflict, with the Soviet Union having to fight Germany as well. The Soviets would have to split their forces, lessening the pressure on Japan.

Yet the Japanese did not want Stalin to become *too* nervous about Japan lest the Soviet leader decide to preempt a possible Japanese attack and shoot first. Consequently, when in 1940 Tokyo signed the Tripartite pact with Germany and Italy, the agreement excluded the Soviet Union from the countries the signatories were required to help against in the event of war.

Neutralizing the Soviet military threat was one way for Japan to break the deadlock in China; another way, at least equally important, was to neutralize the economic threat of a Western embargo. The possibility of a cut-off of American oil kept Japan's military planners tossing in the night, for without oil Japan's military machine would sputter to a halt. The Japanese high command determined to strike south, toward the Dutch East Indies, which contained oil in abundance. By taking the Indies, Japan would go far toward ending its humiliating and debilitating dependence on the West. On the way Japanese forces would capture French Indochina, which had resources of its own and which was causing troubles in China by serving as an entry point for foreign supplies to the Chinese Nationalists.

A move into Southeast Asia might well provoke the Western powers, including the United States, into war. Japan's leaders were prepared for this eventuality. The government took the line, as aggressive regimes frequently do, that by attacking, it was merely defending itself. Tokyo contended that the Westerners, led by Americans, were attempting to encircle Japan to stifle Japan's rightful and necessary expansion. A Japanese government paper described America's policy: "To dominate the world and defend democracy, it aims to prevent our empire from rising and developing in East Asia." Although break-

Prime Minister Tojo explains to the Japanese parliament why peace requires war. *AP/Wide World Photos*

ing out of the encirclement was risky, to allow its completion was riskier still. General Tojo Hideki, the leader of the militarists, put the odds of defeat at fifty-fifty. But these odds, he asserted, were better than sitting idly by and letting Japan be "ground down without doing anything."

What Does Hitler Want?

Even as Japan's generals and admirals determined to attempt a breakout in Southeast Asia, they understood that their success or failure would largely be determined by the situation in Europe. At the time of the 1937 Marco Polo bridge incident, Britain, France, and the Soviet Union were trying to figure out what Hitler really intended and what they should do about it. Did the German dictator merely aim to rectify the anti-German excesses of the Versailles treaty? There was little strong sentiment in either Britain or France for chancing war to prevent that. The Soviets were more worried than the British or French, but Stalin was not prepared to act alone. Or did Hitler have larger plans? Was the Nazi ranting about expanding to the east something besides bluff? And if Germany did expand, who would suffer? In the mid-1930s the democratic capitalist powers were at least as alarmed by the communist Soviet Union as by fascist Germany. The best outcome, in the minds of many in Britain and France, and in the United States as well, might be a war between the Soviet Union and Germany. This thinking was precisely what had Moscow worried.

Moscow's worries put the Kremlin on relatively good behavior regarding the West. A 1935 meeting of the Communist International, or Comintern, the international revolutionary movement funded and controlled by the Kremlin, announced that the revolution was being put on hold for the time being. At the moment the danger to socialism from the fascists was greater than the danger from the capitalists. Therefore, communists around the world should link arms with liberals against the fascists.

The popular-front policy, as this approach was called, led to the domestication of communism, so to speak, in the West. Since the Bolshevik revolution of 1917, communists had placed themselves outside the realm of ordinary politics, in that they avowedly sought the overthrow not simply of parties in power but also of entire systems of government. Predictably, they were often treated by the governments they targeted as being beyond the pale. But with the formation of the popular front, the communists came in from the cold: they dropped their revolutionary rhetoric, accepted the legitimacy of elections and other democratic forms, and established coalitions with the respectable parties. In America the Communist party positioned itself just to the left of the New Deal Democrats, championing Roosevelt's reform program and working for its extension. In large measure because of this newly discovered moderation, which was almost entirely a response to the German threat to the Soviet Union, the American Communist party enjoyed the greatest growth and influence in its history. Being a Communist in the United States during the 1930s was scarcely more radical than being a Populist in the 1890s had been. This fact would go far toward explaining the ease with which Washington collaborated with Moscow at the end of 1941.

Disappointingly, however, the popular front did little to prevent Hitler from doing what the German leader wanted to do. In October 1937 he joined forces with Mussolini, announcing what came to be called the Rome-Berlin axis. The pact united the two major fascist powers of Europe and came near to creating a solid fascist bloc dividing western Europe from eastern.

In March 1938 Hitler moved to make the bloc even more solid. For years he had agitated about the necessity of uniting Germany with its southern neighbor Austria, which shared the German language and much of German culture. Many Austrians, too, had long held that union, or *Anschluss,* was desirable. At least they had before the rise of Hitler, who caused many of them, especially on the political left, to have second thoughts. But Hitler refused to be dissuaded by Austrian second thoughts. After a political war of nerves against the Austrian government, Hitler sent his tanks across the border. Austria surrendered without a struggle. Within hours, Hitler announced the annexation of Austria into the German reich.

Although Hitler's growing boldness furrowed brows and aggravated ulcers among government officials in Britain and France, in neither country was there

With a handshake, Mussolini and Hitler seal their alliance and the fate of millions in Europe. *Brown Brothers*

substantial support for calling Germany to account. Few French or British really cared about Austria. When a referendum in Austria ratified the German takeover by more than 99 percent, it was easy for Paris and London to say that the Austrians were only getting what they deserved. To be sure, Hitler's goons rigged the referendum. But quite plainly the Austrians were not fighting the union. So why should Britain or France?

Hitler's next move was harder to swallow. The creation of Czechoslovakia at the end of the First World War had placed about 3 million German-speakers in a Czechoslovak region known as the Sudetenland. The Sudeten Germans had never been especially happy living in Czechoslovakia, but amid all the other turmoil of the 1920s and early 1930s, they had found other grievances to focus on. Hitler chose to remind them of this grievance, and he sent Nazi agents across the border to inflame the situation. At first he declared that the Sudeten Germans must receive special status within Czechoslovakia. But not long after the takeover of Austria, he escalated his demands, insisting on the annexation of the Sudetenland to Germany.

The Sudeten issue troubled the West more than the Austrian question had. Whereas Austrians had acquiesced to Hitler's takeover, the Czechs resisted. Prague appealed to Britain and France to defend Czechoslovakia against German aggression. The appeal to the French was strengthened by the existence of a defensive alliance binding France to Czechoslovakia. Yet the French cared for the Czechs hardly more than for the Austrians, and, as in the case of Austria, it was not too difficult to argue that since the Sudeten Germans wanted to join their cousins across the border, they ought to be allowed to do so.

Too late, Britain's Chamberlain learned that Hitler's promise was worthless. *Owen from Black Star*

Perhaps the mapmakers who drew Czechoslovakia's boundaries, which were not even two decades old and lacked compelling historical validity, had made a mistake. In any event the dispute was not worth a war. Moreover, France lacked the military capacity to defend Czechoslovakia against German assault. France's military planning had been based almost entirely on a defensive strategy. France had invested its resources in building what was hoped to be an impregnable wall, the Maginot line, between Germany and itself. The French army was in no position to go marching off to Czechoslovakia.

French hesitation amplified an even greater reluctance in Britain. The British government of Neville Chamberlain distrusted Hitler and hoped to turn the German chancellor away from his expansionist designs; but more than anything else, Chamberlain hoped to prevent another European war. Chamberlain's policy of appeasement (not then a dirty word) had the objective of meeting Hitler halfway, giving Germany what it needed to feel once more an equal in the council of nations. Chamberlain's policy was based on two judgments, one accurate and the other not. The accurate judgment was that the British were not willing to fight Germany over what was, in the prime minister's words, "a quarrel in a faraway country between people of whom we know nothing." The inaccurate judgment was that a compromise would satisfy Hitler.

The inaccuracy showed in the wake of a September 1938 conference at Munich. Desperate to avert war, Chamberlain and French premier Edouard Daladier told Hitler he could have the Sudetenland. The Czechs felt betrayed, but the British and French people were greatly relieved at the prospect of securing what Chamberlain triumphantly called "peace for our time."

The Munich bargain survived only a few months. During the winter of 1938–1939, Hitler made clear that he wanted more of Czechoslovakia than the Sudetenland. In March 1939, in blatant violation of the promises he had given at Munich, he declared a protectorate over the Czech portion of the country. German tanks rolled into Czechoslovakia to enforce the declaration.

Hitler's betrayal on Czechoslovakia knocked the scales from the eyes of Western leaders. Until now they had been able to tell themselves that Hitler's expansionist aims extended only to territory occupied by German-speaking peoples. By seizing the land of the Czechs, Hitler gave the lie to this argument. And the lie revealed that he was not a man who could be dealt with peacefully. By the evidence of his own actions, Hitler respected only the language of force. If he was to be stopped, it would have to be by force.

Until the summer of 1939, the leaders of Britain, France, and the United States could hope that at least some of the force required to stop Hitler would

Joseph Stalin rallies the Russian people to the defense of the motherland. Soviet foreign minister V.M. Molotov watches. *UPI/Bettman*

come from the Soviet Union. Hitler's principal territorial objectives seemed to be in the east, and the Nazis' hostility toward communism sounded as bitter as ever. But the Western hope of an imminent clash between the totalitarians of the right and the totalitarians of the left displayed an underestimation of the ability of Hitler and Stalin to make tactical compromises. Stalin had no desire to fight Germany alone, and after the Western powers caved in to Hitler over Czechoslovakia, the Soviet dictator decided that wisdom lay in coming to terms with Berlin. In August 1939 Stalin sent a message to Hitler suggesting discussions.

These discussions quickly produced a treaty between Germany and the Soviet Union. The Molotov-Ribbentrop pact, named for the Soviet and German foreign ministers, pledged the two sides to nonaggression: neither one would attack the other. In addition, the Molotov-Ribbentrop talks yielded an agreement that Germany and the Soviet Union would divide Poland between them. Although this part of the pact was secret, its consequences grew painfully obvious within a week.

How a European War and an Asian War Became a World War

On September 1, 1939, German tank columns smashed into Poland. German fighter planes covered the advance, initiating a new style of warfare, the *blitzkrieg,* or "lightning war," that made the Second World War as different from the First World War as that war had been from the Napoleonic wars. Defenses had dominated the First World War, which soon settled into a nearly motionless war of attrition; during the Second World War Hitler's armies often moved farther in a day than anyone had moved in a year during the first war. During the first great war, politicians had been able to take their time making decisions, confident that nothing much would change from one week to the next; during the second great war, time was of the essence, and in a week an entire theater of battle could be turned almost upside down.

Britain and France, finally recognizing the nature of the German threat, responded within forty-eight hours to Hitler's invasion of Poland by declaring war on Germany. But by then it was already too late to save Poland. Germany's flying start allowed the Wehrmacht to slice through Polish defenses as though they did not exist. By the middle of September, German forces had seized half the country. They could easily have taken the rest, but Hitler's agreement with Stalin granted the eastern half of the country to the Soviet Union. The Red Army occupied its assigned zone, completing the destruction of Poland.

If the declarations of war by Britain and France had no measurable effect on the German campaign against Poland, neither did they have much effect on anything else for the next few months. The two Western democracies might have attacked Germany's rear while the Wehrmacht was engaged in Poland, but with the exception of a minor and brief French thrust against Germany's Saar region they did not. The war declarations signaled an understanding in the West that the policy of appeasement had failed, but they did not signify an enthusiasm for war. Since, in any case, efforts on Poland's behalf probably would have been unavailing, France and Britain chose to wait and see what Hitler would do next.

Through the late autumn and winter of 1939–1940, Hitler bided his time. The *sitzkrieg,* or "phony war," lasted until the spring of 1940, trying the patience of everyone except Hitler, who knew when the next blast would come and where. In the meantime the Soviets, who had occupied eastern Poland under the terms of the Molotov-Ribbentrop agreement, attacked Finland. With borders being relocated in eastern Europe, Stalin evidently decided the time was propitious for pushing the Finns away from the approaches to Leningrad. The ensuing "winter war" made the Soviets look doubly bad: first, for attacking little Finland without a declaration of war; second, for taking the whole winter to defeat the Finns. Americans, recalling that Finland alone of the European countries had continued to repay its loans throughout the Depression, cheered for the gutsy defenders and supplied a modest amount of aid, but not enough to avert a Finnish defeat.

Hitler again seized the headlines during the spring of 1940. In April, German forces slashed into Denmark and Norway. Denmark fell within hours; Norway held out for several weeks before the Norwegian king and government were forced to flee. In May 1940, Hitler unleashed his armor and aircraft against the Netherlands, Belgium, and, the real objective, France. While the French generals still thought in terms of the positional, ploddingly defensive tactics of the First World War, the German commanders attacked with speed and daring, concentrating their artillery, tanks, and planes to breach the French lines and pour their tanks through before the gap could be closed. Then the tanks, with close air support that overleaped the French lines, created havoc in the rear. They cut off large sections of the line, requiring the defenders to surrender or flee in disarray.

The German offensive succeeded brilliantly. It not only shattered French defenses—or circumvented them in the case of the Maginot line and in a daring thrust through the wooded Ardennes hills, which the French command had considered impassable. It also nearly annihilated the expeditionary force Britain had sent to the Continent. Only by the barest of margins, and by the luck of good weather, were the British troops and some one hundred thousand French soldiers able to evacuate from Dunkirk at the beginning of June. Two weeks later Paris fell to the Germans and France surrendered. With a swiftness that astonished almost everyone, probably including himself, Hitler had conquered an empire that stretched from the Pripet marshes of Poland to the English Channel. Only two countries remained to resist Germany's power: Britain and the Soviet Union.

Three, if one counted the United States. Whether to count the United States was the big question of world affairs in the summer of 1940. At that time it was a question not even Franklin Roosevelt could answer. Americans observed the rise of Hitler and the failure of appeasement with a mixture of alarm and gratitude at their forebears' wisdom in leaving such a deranged continent. At least until the Sudeten crisis of 1938, a solid majority of Americans who held an opinion on the matter believed that the United States should stay out of a European war, and that it could. After Hitler reneged on his Munich agreement and revealed the truly aggressive nature of Germany's foreign policy, nearly all Americans still desired to stay out of a European war; but somewhat fewer thought it would be possible to do so.

The increasingly tenuous character of European peace, combined with Japan's continuing depredations in China, sharpened the debate in the United States between those who argued that American interests required staying out of foreign conflicts and those who contended that American interests dictated getting in. The former group was often labeled isolationist, a pejorative but not entirely inaccurate tag. The isolationists preferred to think of themselves as American nationalists and realists; when they organized, they gathered under the name America First Committee. The thrust of their argument was that in a world so evidently bent on self-destruction, the American government had an obligation to the American people before any other people. One did not have to think Hitler was a nice man, or that the Japanese deserved an empire in Asia, to believe that the problems of Germany's Jews or of Czechs, Poles, or Chinese were not primarily America's problems. It was unfortunate, indeed a tragedy, that fascism was abroad in Europe and Asia. But earthquakes, hurricanes, and droughts were tragedies, too, and no one proposed that it was the duty of Americans to prevent those calamities. The United States government had plenty of work to do in America, if Washington was in the mood for rescue operations. Historian and political scientist Charles Beard, one of the most thoughtful of the isolationists, explained, "Anybody who feels hot with morals and is affected with delicate sensibilities can find enough to do at home, considering the misery of the 10,000,000 unemployed, the tramps, the beggars, the sharecroppers, tenants and field hands right here at our door." The world was a nasty place. The United States had tried to reform it during the First World War. The effort had been a disastrous failure. Only fools would wish to repeat the experiment.

The isolationists' opponents did not consider themselves deficient in nationalist feeling or lacking in realism. On the contrary, the interventionists held that their approach to the world crisis was quite as nationalistic as the isolationists', in the sense of looking out for American interests, and considerably more realistic. The interventionists were not always candid about their precise aims, however. Some expected to be able to keep the United States out of war by timely and judicious aid to the antifascist forces. Others thought American involvement in the war in Europe or the war in Asia, or both, was nearly inevitable and therefore the sooner the better; but such an attitude was not politic in the United States in the late 1930s, and so these hard-core dismalists kept their full agenda mostly to themselves. The two groups of interventionists agreed on a short-term policy of assisting the countries on the front lines of the fight against fascism. The most influential of the interventionist groups was the Committee to Defend America by Aiding the Allies, headed by journalist William Allen White. The very name of the organization indicated the nationalistic and realistic attitude interventionists wished to portray. Where the interventionists of Wilson's day had aimed to save the world, the interventionists of Roosevelt's day would be content to save the United States. If the world was saved in the process, good for the world. But the point was the defense of the United States.

The crux of the debate between the isolationists and the interventionists was the matter of just *which* American interests required defending. The isolationists, at least the honest among them, recognized that Americans might have to curtail their economic activities abroad if they wished to avoid war. Or at a minimum, American investors and merchants abroad would have to do business at their own risk. If their property got confiscated or they were forcibly evicted from foreign markets, that would be their tough luck; it would be no responsibility of the American government to bail them out. The brutally honest among the isolationists conceded that such a course might result in a lowering of the American standard of living since American national income would probably fall if American exports diminished. Yet some of the loss could be recouped from savings on the warships and other military paraphernalia currently devoted to keeping markets and shipping lanes open. The new, streamlined American army and navy would concentrate on a physical defense of the United States. And once the human savings of an avoided European or Asian war were factored in, the result of a narrowly focused policy would be a net gain to the American people.

The interventionists adopted a broader view of American interests. They considered access to foreign markets vital to future American prosperity, though they often downplayed this part of their argument. They recognized that it was a tough sell persuading mothers to send their sons to war to defend the right of Standard Oil, DuPont, and the Morgan bank to do business where they wished. Instead they spoke of democracy and human freedom and of the right of small nations to live in peace. They emphasized the ill treatment the fascists inflicted on defenseless peoples—the Nazis on Jews, Czechs, and Poles; the Japanese on Chinese and Koreans. If pressed, they had to admit that the opponents of fascism did not exactly come to the bar of world opinion with clean records. British imperialism in India and East Africa and French imperialism in Southeast Asia and West Africa might be different in degree from Japanese imperialism in Korea and Manchuria, Italian imperialism in Ethiopia, or even German imperialism in Czechoslovakia, but not in kind. Yet the interventionists argued that, whatever the deficiencies of the democracies, they did not possess the same all-consuming passion for expansion that drove Germany and Japan. And neither Britain nor France had any policies that approached Germany's maltreatment of the Jews. The United States could peaceably co-exist with Britain and France; it probably could not with Germany or Japan.

Through the middle 1930s, the isolationists held the advantage in the United States, with the neutrality legislation of 1935–1937 being the clearest expression of the isolationist view; but the outbreak of the Sino-Japanese war in late 1937, followed by Hitler's growing belligerence in Europe, shifted the balance of opinion in the direction of the interventionists. Franklin Roosevelt initially responded to the German invasion of Poland and to the British and French declarations of war against Germany by proclaiming American neutrality, as Woodrow Wilson had done on the outbreak of war in Europe twenty-five years before. Yet where Wilson had called on Americans to be neutral in thought as well as in deed, Roosevelt did not even try. The president and most Americans had no doubt where blame for the current European hostilities lay: the Germans were clearly the aggressors. The only question at issue was how far the United States should go to aid the victims of aggression.

The answer at first was not very far. A few weeks after the European war began, Roosevelt persuaded Congress to allow belligerents to purchase weapons in the United States on a cash-and-carry basis. Although ostensibly neutral, the cash-and-carry provision would benefit the British and French, who enjoyed naval superiority over the Germans. The isolationists complained that Roosevelt was taking the United States down the same slippery path that had led to American intervention in the First World War—which was true. But the Roosevelt administration and the interventionists succeeded in beating back the challenge. With the American economy still mired in depression, it did not hurt the administration's case that British and French purchases of American arms would put tens of thousands of Americans back to work.

The stunning German conquest of France in the spring of 1940 jolted Roosevelt into further action. Hitler followed his victory in France with an air campaign, known to history as the Battle of Britain, against England that lasted from August to November 1940. The German plan was to knock out British air power and then invade Britain across the English Channel. Considering the breathtaking speed with which Germany had crushed France, Britain's odds did not look very good. Yet the British refused to give in. Their attitude was captured in the comment of a probably apocryphal London Cockney, who told off a complainer, "Wot ye grousin' about? We're in the finals, ain't we? We're playin' at 'ome, ain't we?"

Roosevelt attempted to improve Britain's odds at the beginning of September by transferring fifty American destroyers to the British while the air battle over Britain raged. The president presented the deal as a sharp bargain for the United States. The vessels were old and worn, and in exchange the British granted the American navy basing rights in several Western Hemisphere locations from the Caribbean to Canada. But the fundamental purpose of the transfer was to bolster Britain's defensive capacity at a critical moment in the fight against Germany. Roosevelt in effect admitted as much by arranging the deal as an executive agreement, which did not require legislative concurrence, rather than a treaty, which would have.

At the same time, Roosevelt persuaded Congress to approve a law establishing the first peacetime military draft in American history. Although the Selec-

German bombs missed the dome of St. Paul's Cathedral in the most recent air raid but hit much else in London. *Bettman/Hulton*

tive Service Act of September 1940 had no immediate effect on the course of the fighting in either Europe or Asia, it demonstrated that the interventionists were continuing to gain ground in American politics. The United States might or might not ultimately go to war, but it was preparing for war, which was the necessary first step.

Roosevelt was as shrewd a politician as ever inhabited the White House. He carefully gauged how much change American public opinion would bear at any given time; he constantly assessed when the American people could be prodded and when they had to be let alone. He realized that it would do no good, and likely much harm, to enter the war prematurely. With public opinion behind an American war effort, no power could stand against the United States; with public opinion divided, disaster might well result.

Roosevelt had particular reason to weigh public opinion carefully in the summer and early autumn of 1940. The president was attempting to do something no American president had ever done: get reelected for a third term. Isolationists already charged Roosevelt with ignoring George Washington's advice about foreign entanglements; now others among Roosevelt's critics blasted him for defying the first president's two-term example.

But Roosevelt knew his electorate. With well-timed statements reflecting a sober assessment of American interests and a campaign platform pledging non-involvement in conflicts abroad—reinforced by his own personal promise to America's mothers and fathers: "Your boys are not going to be sent into any foreign wars"—Roosevelt convinced voters not to switch horses in midstream, especially when the stream was flowing as swift and high as the current stream of international affairs.

After he was safely reelected, Roosevelt took additional steps to bolster the British. By the middle of October, Hitler had abandoned plans to invade England, at least before the next summer. The Royal Air Force (R.A.F.) had proved too competent and the British people too determined to allow his Luftwaffe the victory in the fight for control of the skies. Britain's security benefited as well from one of the most important technological developments of the 1930s, radio detecting and ranging, or radar, which allowed the R.A.F.'s fighter control to spot Hitler's bombers approaching at a distance of as much as seventy-five miles. So Hitler called off the air offensive and plotted other means to subjugate Europe. While he was plotting, Roosevelt persuaded Congress to commence a major program of assistance to Britain. Roosevelt likened the idea of Lend-Lease, as the program was called, to the response of any ordinary person at seeing a friend's house on fire. You offer your friend a hose to put out the flames, and after the fire is out, you get it back. Critics countered by saying that the hose analogy was misleading, given that the president was talking about weapons, ammunition, and other consumables. A closer parallel, they said, was chewing gum: after somebody else uses it you don't want it back.

The Lend-Lease Law of March 1941 carried the United States to within a half step of war, as Congress understood in approving the measure. It also marked a complete reversal of the neutrality legislation of just a few years earlier. The new law allowed the president to provide weapons and other supplies to any country whose defense he considered vital to the defense of the United States. Terms of transfer would be worked out later.

The Roosevelt administration's bill drafters prudently declined to specify just which countries would get American Lend-Lease aid. The obvious candidates were Britain and China, and most of the testimony on the bill concentrated on these unquestionably worthy recipients. A few prescient individuals wondered whether by any chance the Soviet Union might qualify, should Moscow and Berlin have a falling out. The administration changed the subject as quickly as possible. In fact, Roosevelt and his advisers thought the Soviet Union might indeed qualify; moreover, such a falling out seemed increasingly possible during the spring of 1941.

After Germany's defeat in the Battle of Britain, Hitler turned his attention to the east. In December 1940 the German leader decided on an invasion of the Soviet Union. Hitler had never considered his treaty with Stalin anything more than a temporary expedient to safeguard his rear while he defeated Britain and France; Hitler was not a very good student of history, but he learned enough from his reading to realize that a war on two fronts would probably bring the end of his dreams. A two-front war had ruined Napoleon, and another two-front war had exhausted Germany during the First World War. Hitler had expected to knock out France and Britain before taking on the Soviets; Britain's stubborn resistance, inspired by the new British prime minister, Winston Churchill, upset his timetable. Yet Hitler believed that the British, though undefeated, were sufficiently exhausted that they would pose no serious threat while he dealt with the Bolsheviks.

Hitler's double-cross of Stalin was one of the worst-kept secrets in modern European history. During the first six months of 1941, the foreign ministries of the major powers buzzed with rumors that Germany would attack the Soviet Union. British electronic eavesdroppers picked up orders from Hitler's headquarters directing preparations for the attack. Stalin chose to ignore the rumors, and when the British passed along their intelligence intercepts, he denounced them as a device to instigate a war between Germany and the Soviet Union. Still not wishing to fight Germany, Stalin sought to avoid giving Hitler any pretext for claiming a violation of the nonaggression pact between the two countries. Even as German troops massed along the Soviet border in early June 1941, Stalin refused to order full mobilization.

Stalin's paralysis led to disaster for the Soviet Union and nearly to defeat. On June 22 German forces launched the largest attack in world history. Along a front that ultimately spanned two thousand miles, German tanks and motorized infantry swept across the western reaches of the Soviet Union. They

In private, Winston Churchill was often dogged by depression, but in public he put on a show that kept British spirits up at a time when the British had much to be depressed about. *Brown Brothers*

met little effective resistance. During the 1930s Stalin had engaged in a systematic purge of anyone in the Soviet Union who might challenge his authority. The Terror, as the purge was called, led to the execution of tens of thousands of government officials and Communist party members and to the death or exile (to the infamous Siberian labor camps) of millions of others. Among those purged were many of the best officers of the Red Army, in particular almost everyone who showed any spark of initiative or independent thinking. The result of the Terror was a thoroughly intimidated population; the effect on the army was a docile, inexperienced, and largely inept officer corps unable to deal with the German attack. Soviet units reeled under the German blows: by the end of the summer of 1941, the Germans had reached Leningrad in the north, had taken Kiev in the south, and were threatening Moscow in the middle.

Hitler's invasion of the Soviet Union was his greatest gamble. It might have paid off but for two factors the German leader did not sufficiently appreciate. The first was the ability of the Soviets to absorb punishment. Soviet losses in the initial German onslaught were staggering, and the casualties only escalated as Germans settled down to besiege Leningrad, Stalingrad, and various other centers of resistance. Yet the Soviet will to fight never collapsed—as it had collapsed during the First World War. Against all odds, given his brutalization of the Soviet people during the 1930s, Stalin succeeded in rallying the people around his regime. He shrewdly deemphasized the symbols and language of the Bolshevik revolution, in favor of those of the Russian motherland. His success was not complete, and at first some of the survivors of Stalin's Terror welcomed the Germans as liberators. But the Germans soon demonstrated that they were hardly an improvement, and for most Russians the war against Germany became the Great Patriotic War. For decades afterward people in Russia grew misty-eyed as they remembered Stalin's role in defending the country.

The second factor Hitler underestimated was the ability of the United States to get large amounts of aid to the Soviet Union. Despite the opinion of influential legislators such as Senator Harry Truman of Missouri, who argued that Washington ought to let the Germans and the Soviets kill off as many of each other as possible, Roosevelt ordered Lend-Lease supplies to the Soviet Union. The president by this time was convinced that the United States would be fighting Germany before long, and he took the view that every German soldier laid low in the Soviet Union was one fewer German that American troops would have to worry about.

Hitler and his colleagues knew full well of the American aid to the Soviet Union as well as to Britain—there was no attempt to keep it secret—and, just as German leaders had done regarding American supplies to the Allies during the First World War, they attempted to cut it off. During the autumn of 1941, an undeclared naval war broke out in the Atlantic. Roosevelt ordered American warships to escort merchant vessels, and when the convoys began encountering German submarines, he allowed the American vessels to shoot the German submarines on sight. Had Hitler desired to press the issue, full-scale war probably would have begun at this point. Roosevelt was looking for an incident that would release him from his repeated pledges to avoid foreign wars; the president called the German submarines "the rattlesnakes of the Atlantic," and after a German submarine fired on an American warship, he declared, "This was one determined step towards creating a permanent world system based on force, terror and murder." But Hitler was concentrating on the Soviet Union, where his offensive was slowing down. For the moment undeclared and irregular hostilities with the Americans, sufficient to harass shipping without provoking an all-out war, suited his purposes.

At the same time, halfway around the world, the Japanese were taking advantage of the distraction of the Europeans and the Americans. During the summer of 1940, after France's surrender to Germany, Japanese forces moved into the northern part of Indochina, assuming control of Hanoi and Haiphong in September. Meanwhile Japanese diplomats completed negotiations with Germany and Italy on the Tripartite (or Axis) pact. By this document the three countries agreed to come to the assistance of each other in case any one suffered attack from a country not currently involved in the fighting in Europe or Asia, not counting the Soviet Union. The principal target of the agreement was the United States: all three parties hoped the pact would give Washington additional pause in declaring war on any of them; the Americans presumably would find the prospect of a two-theater war daunting, perhaps daunting enough to make America stay out altogether.

The Japanese still worried about the Soviet presence on the border with Manchuria, but the German invasion of the Soviet Union in the summer of 1941 considerably diminished Tokyo's concerns on this score. The Japanese took advantage of their new carefreeness by seizing southern Indochina, which gave them an advanced launching platform for any thrust toward the East Indies.

To prevent such a thrust, the Roosevelt administration adopted a stringent economic policy toward Japan. The previous summer, after the first Japanese move into Indochina, the administration had imposed a ban on sales to Japan of scrap steel and aviation fuel; now in July 1941 the president froze Japanese assets in the United States. Without money to pay for purchases, Japan saw its trade with America virtually cease. To emphasize America's dissatisfaction, Washington embargoed oil bound for Japan.

The embargo and the freeze convinced the hard-liners who controlled Japanese policy that they had no choice but to strike out boldly to end their dependence on Americans. Even while negotiations with Washington took place, ostensibly toward the goal of a diplomatic solution to the current crisis, the Japanese government approved a plan for an attack against the American territory of Hawaii. The plan was the brainchild of Admiral Yamamoto Isoroku, though it had a number of godfathers. The basic idea was to smash the American Pacific fleet at Pearl Harbor; the blow would cripple the Americans' ability to oppose Japanese advances toward the East Indies, and by the time the Americans rebuilt their fleet, Japan would have captured what it needed. The

Americans then would be confronted with a choice between waging a long and costly war and accepting Japan's fait accompli. Selfish materialists that they were, they would choose the latter.

Speed was vital in assuring the success of this plan. With each week that the embargo of American oil persisted, Japan's petroleum reserves dwindled. Japanese analysts predicted that a war against the Americans would burn oil at a rate that would empty the country's tanks within a year.

Positions were hardening on both sides of the Pacific. The Roosevelt administration insisted that Japan withdraw not only from Indochina but also from China. From the Japanese perspective, leaving Indochina was conceivable although not acceptable; evacuating China, after all the blood and treasure Japan had poured into that country, was totally out of the question. Better to die with honor than live with such humiliation.

Attitudes like this make for bitter wars, especially when the other side is equally determined. By November 1941 Roosevelt had accepted the inevitability of war. The president was not anywhere near as fanatical in his feelings as the Japanese militarists, but he believed that the time had come to draw the line against aggression. He was still cautious regarding American public opinion, and though he thought the case for war was morally and strategically sound, he preferred to place the onus on the Axis. His insistence that Japan relinquish its gains from the last decade represented not a serious effort to avert war but an attempt to paint Tokyo into a corner. Of course, Roosevelt would have been happy for the Japanese to accept his terms and back down; however, he hardly expected them to do so. Instead he expected that they would lash out.

His conclusion on this point reflected more than the logic of the moment. Since the Russo-Japanese War of 1905, which had begun with a Japanese sneak attack, American military planners had anticipated that a war against Japan would commence with another such unannounced assault. During the early part of 1941, Tokyo-watchers reported rumors of a surprise blow against the American fleet at Pearl Harbor, against American forces in the Philippines, or against British positions in Hong Kong or Malaya. During the autumn of 1941, American code breakers, who had been listening in on Japanese government messages intermittently since the negotiations for the 1905 treaty of Portsmouth, picked up indications that an attack was imminent. Unfortunately, in the code-cracking business you can never be sure that what you are overhearing is not what the enemy wants you to overhear. The Americans had to allow for the possibility that the Japanese were allowing for the possibility that the Americans had broken Tokyo's ciphers. The Japanese might simply be leaking disinformation, trying to trick the Americans into shooting first. For Japan this was an important matter in that the Tripartite Treaty required an automatic war declaration by Germany and Italy only in case the United States attacked Japan. If Japan shot first, the guarantee did not apply. Finally—and somewhat contradictorily, but such is human nature—the fact that the United States had solved the Japanese code tended to generate overconfidence in

Washington. Presumably, the indications of an attack would grow more specific; at that time specific countermeasures could be taken.

But the specific indications did not come, not in time to do the sailors and ships at Pearl Harbor any good. The Japanese attack fleet observed radio silence on its approach toward Hawaii, and when Japanese fighter planes flew out of the rising sun on the morning of Sunday, December 7, on their final approach to their targets anchored in Pearl Harbor, they caught the Americans unaware and utterly unready. In two hours Japanese bombs and air-launched torpedoes sank six American battleships and heavily damaged two others, as well as three destroyers and three cruisers. Three hundred American planes in the area were rendered useless. Almost thirty-six hundred sailors and soldiers were killed or wounded.

On the same day (although it was already December 8 west of the International Date Line), Japanese planes blasted American positions in the Philippines. The surprise they achieved there was nearly incomprehensible: General Douglas MacArthur, the American commander, had had several hours to absorb the news from Pearl Harbor before the Japanese arrived outside Manila. But most of the American planes were still on the ground, and most were shot up by the Japanese.

Also on the same day, Japanese forces struck against the British in Malaya. By way of explanation for all the attacks, Japanese emperor Hirohito released a statement written by Premier Tojo's government asserting that the Americans and British had brought the conflict upon themselves by their "inordinate ambition to dominate the Orient." The emperor asserted that Japan had "no other recourse but to appeal to arms."

Notwithstanding the human tragedy the attack on Pearl Harbor entailed, it instantly solved Roosevelt's problem of how to get into the war against Japan. Because it did, conspiracy theorists, unreconstructed isolationists, and assorted Roosevelt-haters were quick to charge that the president had deliberately allowed the attack to occur. Such charges were almost certainly false. Beyond the monstrousness of consigning thousands of American troops to undefended death, no president would have been foolish enough to let the heart of his Pacific battle fleet be destroyed. A much less severe provocation would have sufficed to convince Congress to declare war on Japan, which it did the day after the Pearl Harbor raid.

The Japanese attack did not at once solve Roosevelt's other problem: how to get into war against Germany. Hitler was not bound to join Japan in a war Japan started, and, besides, as had become clear by now, Hitler was not above breaking promises. But Hitler did Roosevelt a favor by declaring war anyway. Precisely why remains a subject for speculation. Most likely, he underestimated the ability of the United States to fight in the Pacific and in Europe simultaneously and expected to have his work in Europe wrapped up by the time the Americans really got into the battle. In the near term the Americans could hardly do Germany more harm than they were already doing in the Atlantic. War with the United States was almost certain to come sooner or later. Germany might as well win the glory of boldly throwing down the gauntlet. On December 11 Germany declared war on the United States. The American Congress reciprocated the next day.

The Grand Alliance and the War in Europe

"We had won after all," Winston Churchill remarked, referring to Pearl Harbor and the events immediately following. In the British prime minister's judgment, the American entry into the war sealed the fate of the Axis. Although the fighting might last for years more and would certainly claim many thousands of lives, the result was not in doubt.

Joseph Stalin did not record his thoughts for posterity the way the Nobel Prize–winning (for literature) Churchill did. The Soviet premier, however, presumably also was relieved to learn that Germany now had a new foe to confront. Like Hitler, Stalin probably recognized that the United States would have little immediate effect on the fighting in Europe. And since the Soviet Union and Japan were not at war, Stalin did not care much about the Pacific theater. By the end of 1941, the Red Army had blunted the German eastern offensive; the Soviet Union would not fall the way France had fallen. But in planning the counteroffensive that would be necessary to drive out the Wehrmacht, Stalin could not help appreciating the diversionary effects American soldiers would have once they opened a second anti-German front in Europe.

Pearl Harbor knitted together the Asian war and the European war into the Second World War, by bringing the decisively powerful country, the United States, into both conflicts. It also created the winning coalition of America, Britain, and the Soviet Union. A less likely partnership could have been imagined but never put together. The Soviet Union brought to the coalition the largest army in the world, a ruthless government willing to accept tremendous losses, and a long-suffering people willing to bear those losses—partly for lack of choice in the matter. Britain brought a very formidable navy, a world empire with almost limitless resources of human power, and, in Churchill, one of the most inspiring orators ever to speak the English language. The United States brought an economy with greater capacity than those of the Axis countries combined, an indignation born of having suffered a sneak attack, and a self-confidence resulting from a recognition of America's economic power and a belief in America's role as the exemplar of democracy to the world.

Under less dire circumstances, the three countries would never have joined forces. The Anglo-American side of the triangle was the least surprising, though hardly inevitable. Most Americans respected British cultural and political traditions as the progenitors of American practices, but there existed in the United States a strong suspicion of British imperialism. These suspicions had not been eased by the elevation of the archimperialist Churchill to the

British prime ministership in 1940. Throughout the war Americans watched closely for signs that they were being used to safeguard the British empire. By the nature of the war, quite often they were. Each time it rankled. Yet cultural and political affinities, and shared danger, kept British and Americans together.

The Soviet-American side of the triangle was always more tenuous. War makes strange bedfellows and none stranger than the Soviet communists and the American capitalists. After a brief honeymoon following the Roosevelt administration's extension of diplomatic recognition in 1933, relations between Washington and Moscow had headed downhill. The hopes both sides invested in normalization proved excessive. The anticipated Soviet market for American exports turned out to be almost as illusory as the Chinese market had long been. American companies complained of Soviet industrial espionage, unfair licensing arrangements, and harassment of personnel stationed in the Soviet Union; accordingly, they refused to deliver many of the high-technology products the Kremlin desired. The American government disappointed Moscow by not standing up to Japan; at the same time Moscow's failure to challenge Germany frustrated Washington. The Soviet-German rapprochement of 1939 seemed to many Americans to be the last straw: Stalin showed his true colors in this surrender to cynicism. For his part, the Soviet leader saw his truce with Hitler as a last resort, a justified response to efforts by the West to get Germany and the Soviet Union into a fight.

Consequently, no love was wasted between Washington and Moscow when necessity forced them together at the end of 1941. A common enemy was all that united them, and it would have been unreasonable to expect that once the enemy had been vanquished, the togetherness would continue to hold. Yet something approaching this expectation developed among a significant portion of the American populace. Its development was not accidental: as part of the effort to generate enthusiasm for the war, the American government churned out pro-Soviet propaganda. This propaganda depicted in heroic colors the courageous fight of the Soviet government and people against the unspeakable Nazis. Stalin, recently the hard-visaged mastermind of the great purges, and the driving force behind the collectivization of Soviet agriculture, which resulted in millions of deaths by famine and disease (though the scale of the latter disaster was not yet widely known in the West), was recast as friendly Uncle Joe. Stalin cooperated in the recasting. While the war continued, and he continued to need American supplies and cooperation, he dropped his communist rhetoric in favor of the language of Russian patriotism. In most respects he acted the part of the model partner.

In the short term the war aims of the United States, Britain, and the Soviet Union coincided. Before all else the three governments desired to defeat the Axis powers. Washington, London, and Moscow agreed that the most dangerous of the Axis powers was Germany. For Moscow this choice was obvious at a time when the Wehrmacht was almost within artillery distance of the Kremlin. The choice was only slightly harder for London. Although Japan was hammering Hong Kong and menacing Malaya, the threat to Britain from attacks on those far-off portions of the empire was minor compared to the looming presence of Nazi armies and airplanes just across the English Channel and of German ships and submarines in the waters around the British Isles.

It would not have been surprising if Washington had considered Japan the greater danger than Germany. Japan, after all, had attacked American soil and gravely damaged the American Pacific fleet. In the aftermath of Pearl Harbor, rumors flew of an impending Japanese assault on California. Meanwhile Japanese troops were in the process of overrunning the Philippines. By contrast, Germany had hit only a few American ships in the Atlantic, and, bogged down as it was in the Soviet Union, Germany appeared almost wholly unable to mount any serious assault on American territory.

Yet the Roosevelt administration, partly to please its British and Soviet partners and partly from its own assessment of the situation, adopted the position that Germany had to be defeated first. If Germany knocked the Soviet Union out of the war—a result that looked less than likely by December 1941 but could not be ignored—Hitler would gain access to the enormous Soviet resources of oil, metal ores, grain, timber, and other vital materials. The German dictator would be well placed to swoop down on the Middle East, cutting Allied access to that region's petroleum and severing Britain's most important ties to India. With his eastern front secure, he could turn again on Britain and complete the job he had started in 1940. By then he would be the master of the largest, wealthiest, most powerful empire the world had even seen. It was a chilling scenario.

By contrast, even if Japan succeeded in capturing the East Indies and making itself self-sufficient in oil and some other resources, it would still be far from a superpower. And if Germany was defeated, Japan would face the combined might of the United States, Britain, and probably the Soviet Union. Any one of these three countries would have given the Japanese a good fight. Together, and with the aid of China, they would ultimately grind Japan as in a stone crusher. Even the Japanese had to admit as much—which was why Tokyo was hoping for quick military successes followed by peace talks.

These considerations led the three leading members of the "Grand Alliance" (Churchill's label for the antifascist coalition, which eventually numbered more than forty nations) to agree on the first principle of a common wartime policy: that the defeat of Germany took precedence over the defeat of Japan. By comparison with Germany and Japan, the third Axis partner, Italy, hardly registered in Allied concerns. For the United States the Germany-first policy meant holding the line against Japan in the Pacific while devoting the bulk of American resources and energy to the European theater.

The second principle of the coalition related to the first; it also reflected the suspicions that persisted among Americans, British, and Soviets. The Allied governments agreed on a policy of unconditional surrender toward Germany and Japan. Americans and British recalled how Russia had dropped out of the First World War and signed a separate peace treaty with Germany, thereby lengthening the war in the west. Given Stalin's demonstrated facility at flip-flopping, Washington and London worried that he and Hitler would make up once more as they had done in 1939. Such a maneuver would free much of the two-thirds of the Wehrmacht currently fighting in the east and make it available for defensive or offensive operations in the west. Stalin had similar worries about the Americans and British. Many politicians in both America and Britain continued to assert that the best solution to current problems would be for Germany and the Soviet Union to batter each other, while the democracies of the West stood clear. Roosevelt and Churchill sought to reassure Stalin that they had no such plans—lest he defect first. He did the same regarding them and from the same cause. As reassurance all around, the three leaders agreed that there would be no peace with the Axis short of unconditional surrender.

There was another reason for the unconditional surrender policy as it related specifically to Germany. In Hitler's rise to power, the German dictator had resurrected the charge that Germany had not really lost the First World War but had been sold out by traitors within, including German Jews. This historical revisionism gained specious plausibility from the facts that the first war had ended with an armistice, rather than a surrender, and that it had ended while the fighting lines remained outside Germany's borders. The Allies in the Second World War wanted to ensure that future German revisionists would have to work harder to deny the truth. This time Germany would be pounded into submission.

Of the three major Allies, the Soviets faced the greatest immediate threat. For Moscow the value of the alliance lay in both the continuing flow of supplies from America and the prospect of a second front in Europe. After the conquest of France, German troops in the west had had relatively little to do. Many were available for transfer to the eastern front and had been so transferred. As Stalin repeatedly told Roosevelt and Churchill, the United States and Britain could do the Soviet Union the most good by landing troops in Europe and requiring Hitler to transfer some of his eastern units back to the west.

Opening a second front was easier promised, which Britain and the United States soon did, than accomplished. Large-scale amphibious operations are among the most hazardous of all military maneuvers, as Churchill had learned to his dismay during the First World War, when he ordered a disastrous landing at Gallipoli on the Turkish shore. Never in hundreds of years had there been a successful crossing of the English Channel under fire. With German troops thoroughly dug in on the French side, an Allied crossing of the channel would be very dangerous. For this reason, and also to safeguard British access to the Middle East and India, Churchill advocated opening the second European front in the south, in what he called the "soft underbelly" of Europe. Churchill had a third reason as well. Looking toward the war's end, he desired to have British troops close to the Balkans in case the Soviets entertained designs on that sensitive region.

American commanders, led by Chief of Staff George Marshall, opposed the southern approach. They wanted to fight the Germans, not Italians, and they desired to start as soon as possible. In addition, they argued that an attack in

France would afford the greatest relief to the Soviets, thereby confirming for Stalin the good intentions of the British and Americans.

But Churchill won this argument. Britain would have to be the springboard for any attack on France, and without Britain's full cooperation the attack could never succeed. Instead of going straight for southern Europe, the Americans and British laid plans for an invasion of North Africa, which commenced in November 1942. The initial part of the operation went smoothly and successfully, in large part because the attackers persuaded Admiral Jean Darlan, the commander of the French forces in the area, to keep his troops in their barracks and not oppose the landings. Since Darlan was nominally loyal to the pro-Nazi government of occupied France, the Darlan deal stirred a storm of protest in the United States and Britain. The Allied soldiers were supposed to be shooting the Nazis and their collaborators, not bargaining with them. Dwight Eisenhower, the American general in charge of the operation, almost lost his job. But all was forgiven following the assassination of Darlan a short while later and amid continuing successes in the field by the Allies.

After consolidating their position in North Africa, a process that included much heavy fighting, some close calls, and considerable experience-gaining by the green American troops, Allied forces hopped the Strait of Sicily to Italian territory. While American and British soldiers conquered the island of Sicily and prepared to cross to the mainland, Italian dissidents rose up against Mussolini. In July 1943 the Duce fell to a coalition of disaffected Fascists and old-line monarchists. He had not fallen far, however, before he was caught by German reinforcements sent across the Alps to block the Allied advance. The Germans grabbed the northern half of the peninsula, including Rome, while the Allies occupied the southern half.

The fighting in Italy eased the pressure on the Soviet Union somewhat. By this time the Soviets had their counteroffensive well under way. In February 1943 the Red Army broke the siege of Stalingrad, ending one of the largest single battles in history. The victory cost the Soviets severely, but the cost to the Germans—an entire army of more than a half million men killed or captured—mattered more. The Soviet victory at Stalingrad broke the back of the German occupation of the Soviet Union; during the following months, the Soviets pushed the Germans away from Leningrad and Moscow. Despite dogged German resistance, the Soviet forces gradually rolled the eastern front back toward the west.

Yet even though victory was in sight, it remained a long distance off. Stalin still wanted a western front, and each delay afforded him reason to question the good faith of his American and British partners. Finally, two and a half years after the American entry into the war, American and British troops crossed the English Channel to Normandy. The June 1944 landing was as costly as expected; the casualty rates among the first contingents ashore were frightfully high. But once the beachhead was established, reinforcements began to flood ashore. Within days more than three hundred thousand troops had landed. General Eisenhower and his subordinates secured their base of opera-

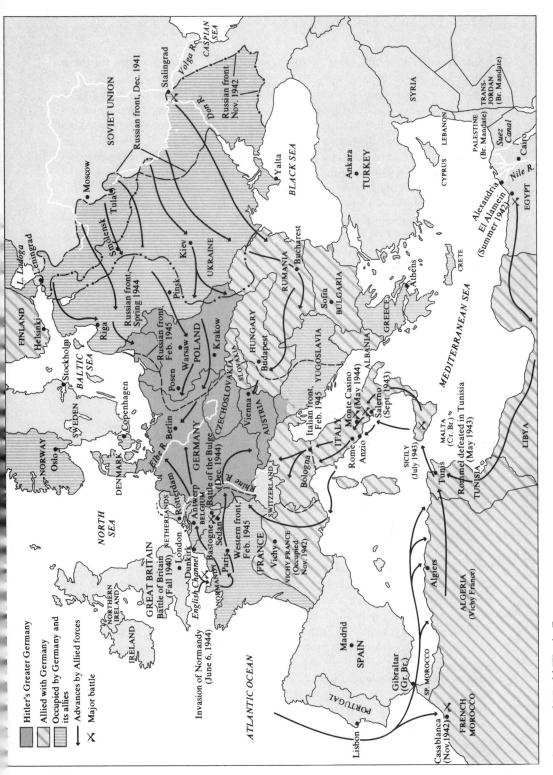

The Second World War in Europe

Legend:
- Hitler's Greater Germany
- Allied with Germany
- Occupied by Germany and its allies
- → Advances by Allied forces
- ✗ Major battle

Labels on map:

CASPIAN SEA

Stalingrad

Russian front, Dec. 1941

Russian front, Nov. 1942

Volga R.

Don R.

SOVIET UNION

Moscow

Tula

Smolensk

Kiev

UKRAINE

Russian front, Spring 1944

Pinsk

Riga

L. Ladoga

Leningrad

Helsinki

FINLAND

Stockholm

SWEDEN

NORWAY

Oslo

Copenhagen

DENMARK

BALTIC SEA

Russian front, Feb. 1945

Warsaw

Posen

POLAND

Krakow

Berlin

Elbe R.

GERMANY

CZECHOSLOVAKIA

SLOVAKIA

Vienna

AUSTRIA

HUNGARY

Budapest

Battle of the Bulge (Dec. 1944)

Rhine R.

Western front, Feb. 1945

NETHERLANDS

Rotterdam

Antwerp

BELGIUM

Bastogne

Sedan

Dunkirk

London

GREAT BRITAIN

Battle of Britain (Fall 1940)

NORTHERN IRELAND

IRELAND

NORTH SEA

English Channel

Paris

NORMANDY

Invasion of Normandy (June 6, 1944)

FRANCE

Vichy

VICHY FRANCE (Occupied Nov. 1942)

SWITZERLAND

ATLANTIC OCEAN

SPAIN

Madrid

PORTUGAL

Lisbon

Gibraltar (Gr. Br.)

SP. MOROCCO

FRENCH MOROCCO

Casablanca (Nov. 1942)

ALGERIA (Vichy France)

Algiers

TUNISIA

Tunis

Rommel defeated in Tunisia (May 1943)

LIBYA

MEDITERRANEAN SEA

MALTA (Gr. Br.)

SICILY (July 1943)

ITALY

Rome

Anzio

Monte Casino (May 1944)

Salerno (Sept. 1943)

Bologna

Italian front, Feb. 1945

CRETE

GREECE

Athens

ALBANIA

YUGOSLAVIA

RUMANIA

Bucharest

BULGARIA

Sofia

BLACK SEA

Yalta

TURKEY

Ankara

CYPRUS

SYRIA

LEBANON

PALESTINE (Br. Mandate)

TRANS-JORDAN (Br. Mandate)

Suez Canal

EGYPT

Cairo

Alexandria

Nile R.

El Alamein (Summer 1942)

tions through June and most of July; by August the march across northern France had commenced.

The Allies now had Germany in a vise. Following additional landings in southern France, the British and Americans, joined by French troops under Charles de Gaulle, liberated Paris at the end of August. In September Allied forces freed most of Belgium and part of the Netherlands. By the end of the month, Allied advance units had reached the Rhine. But then German defenses stiffened, and hopes for a quick conclusion to the war dissipated.

Meanwhile the Red Army was advancing on Germany from the east. In the spring of 1944, the Soviets threw the Germans out of the Ukraine and Crimea. In the summer Soviet units reached Poland and the German province of East Prussia. Soviet soldiers entered Romania and Bulgaria, forcing those countries to abandon the Nazis. But in Hungary the Germans dug in; and there the eastern front stabilized during the winter of 1944–1945.

The War in the Pacific

On the other side of the world, Japan's fortunes went from good to bad faster than Germany's. The simultaneous December 1941 attacks on the Americans at Pearl Harbor and the Philippines and on the British in Malaya provided the Japanese with a swift start toward the conquest of a larger portion of the globe than any country had ever controlled. The Japanese strategy for what they called the War of Greater East Asia was astonishingly ambitious but essentially simple: to complete the conquest of China and drive the Westerners out of East and Southeast Asia and the western Pacific. The Japanese high command allowed itself a half year to crush Chiang Kaishek and the Chinese, who would now be deprived of outside support. During the same period, the Americans would be ejected from the Philippines and Guam. The British would be thrown back from Malaya, Burma, and Hong Kong. The Dutch would be forced to give up the East Indies. While fortifying these territories against counterattack from the west, Japan would develop a line of island bases in the Pacific that would hold the Americans at bay in the east. At the same time, Japan's partner Germany would finish off the Soviet Union, thereby safeguarding the northwestern frontier of Japan's sphere.

Japan's strategy was premised on a fundamental misconception, one that continually bedevils international relations (not to mention interpersonal relations). The Tokyo leadership expected the Americans to react to Japan's actions as the Japanese would have reacted if they were in the Americans' place. In particular, the Japanese government believed that once Japan had established its largely self-sufficient, well-protected empire, the Americans would decide that attacking that empire would be excessively expensive. A large Japanese sphere in East Asia would not threaten vital American interests, as the Americans would come to understand. The Japanese strategy did not require destroying America's fighting capacity, which even the most bellicose fire-eaters in Japan recognized was beyond possibility. It merely required convincing the Americans that continuing the war would not be worth America's while.

Many years earlier, during the 1830s, the traveling French political scientist Alexis de Tocqueville had noted a tendency in Americans regarding war and peace. Tocqueville, the author of *Democracy in America*, thought the tendency was probably characteristic of democracies, but since there was only one large democracy at the time, he was really speaking about the United States. According to Tocqueville, democracies are slow to go to war but also slow to resume peace. The reason for this is that the rulers in a democracy, as opposed to rulers in monarchies and autocracies, are directly responsible to the people and therefore make decisions that closely reflect the people's will. Most people do not like war, which disrupts their lives and gets many of them killed. By contrast, monarchs and dictators can start wars lightly, knowing that *they* will not get shot at. Democracies consequently tend to fight wars only over very important issues—over matters of principle—and to defend themselves against external attack. For this reason, democracies are slow to go to war. For this same reason, they are slow to make peace because matters of principle are not easily compromised and because direct assaults on the homeland are not readily forgiven.

Japan's strategists apparently had not read Tocqueville. Or if they had, they did not believe that his comments applied to twentieth-century America. This was their big mistake. By attacking American territory at Pearl Harbor—without warning, no less—and killing more than three thousand Americans, Japan transformed a war in distant Asia fought over issues that most Americans did not care about into a conflict that directly touched the United States and that nearly all Americans cared a great deal about. Pearl Harbor changed the American mood completely. Americans were now angry and definitely not in a compromising mind. The Japanese had done a terrible thing to America; they must be punished.

In a sense the first bombs and torpedoes dropped at Pearl Harbor determined the outcome of the Pacific war. Japanese leaders understood that in a long conflict the United States would wear Japan down; what they did not understand, but eventually learned, was that Pearl Harbor guaranteed that the conflict in the Pacific would be a long one. It also guaranteed that the conflict would be a cruel one. For years many Americans had branded the Japanese as the "yellow peril," a race of treacherous schemers that would stop at nothing to achieve its malevolent aims. The sneak attack at Pearl Harbor appeared to confirm the stereotype. In doing so, it justified in most American minds a retributive war without mercy.

Yet during December 1941 and the first few months of 1942, Tokyo's strategy unfolded essentially according to plan. In daydreams Japan's admirals might have wished that the raid on Pearl Harbor had been even more successful: it worried some of them that American aircraft carriers had been at sea and therefore escaped the attack; and it would have been nice to knock out the support facilities at Pearl Harbor along with the American ships that went down. But otherwise they could hardly complain. In Southeast Asia, Japanese forces advanced from recently captured positions in Indochina toward Thailand. The Thais had been the only people in the area to avert colonization by Westerners, but they were not able to avert conquest by the Japanese. Within weeks Thailand capitulated. Within weeks more, at Tokyo's insistence, the Thai government declared war on the United States and Britain.

The conquest of Thailand allowed Japanese forces to attack British Malaya overland from the north. For years the British had built up the defenses of Singapore at Malaya's southern tip. But they had always expected an assault from the sea, and they arrayed their guns and fortifications with this in mind. When Japanese troops approached by land, much of the fortifying effort proved to have been wasted. In February 1942 the Japanese captured Singapore and completed the conquest of Malaya.

They then advanced into Burma, intending to close an important supply line to Chiang Kaishek's Chinese forces. This campaign was as successful as nearly everything else the Japanese attempted in the first months after Pearl Harbor. Rangoon surrendered in March; within six weeks more Japan dominated the country and closed the Burma road.

The Japanese subjugation of the Philippines required a little longer. After landing on the main island of Luzon in December 1941, Japanese troops invested Manila. The leadership of the commonwealth government of the Philippines fled to the island of Corregidor, along with the American high commissioner (President Roosevelt's representative) and the American military command headed by General MacArthur. American and Philippine troops fought a rear-guard action on the Bataan peninsula, with the last units evading capture until April 1942. Corregidor held out for a few weeks longer, minus MacArthur and the top American and Philippine civilian officials, who escaped by torpedo boat to the south and ultimately to Australia.

Other Japanese contingents simultaneously took the East Indies. The Dutch authorities had been planning to destroy the oil facilities in the Indies if Japan seemed about to seize them, but the rapidity of the Japanese advance caught the Dutch unready. By the middle of March, the central island of Java was in Japanese control, as were the most important oil fields.

In the majority of the Asian territories newly added to the Japanese sphere, as in China, resistance to the invaders continued long after Japan's military forces captured the major cities. For this reason Japan's control over its sphere was less impressive in practice than on paper. Yet given the modest size of Japan's population and resource base, that control was impressive enough.

In the Pacific Japanese expansion was even more impressive on maps but even less substantial in reality. By far most of what Japan nominally controlled was empty ocean. Japanese troops did land in the American Aleutian Islands; they captured Guam and American Wake Island. They took the Marshall and Gilbert island groups, thereby giving themselves a free hand in the central Pacific.

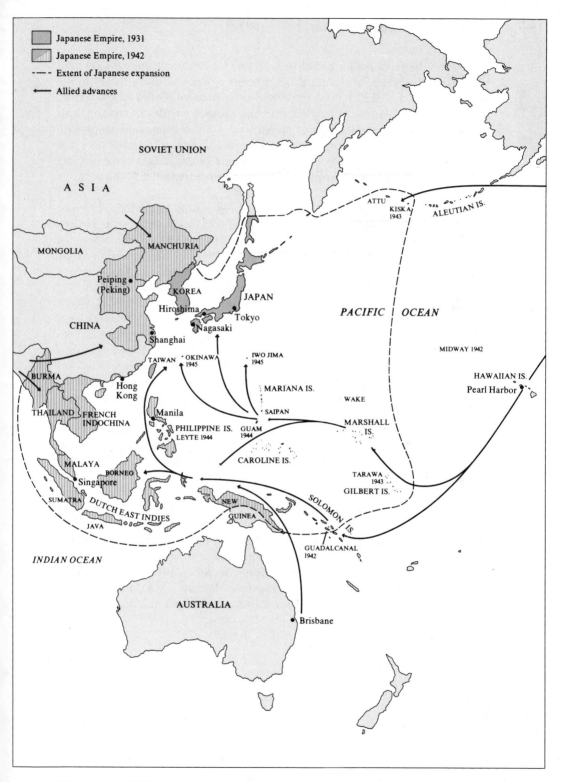

The Second World War in the Pacific and East Asia

But then the Japanese pushed their luck too far, and their bubble of expansion began to deflate. In the north an attempt to take Midway Island in the spring of 1942 failed in one of the single most decisive battles of the Pacific war. Planes from American carriers that had escaped the destruction at Pearl Harbor, and from American bases on Midway, pounded Japanese ships with thousands of bombs and torpedoes, heavily damaging the Japanese fleet and forcing it to turn back. At about the same time, a Japanese task force heading toward Port Moresby in Australian New Guinea was repulsed at the battle of the Coral Sea.

The failure of the Japanese to sustain their momentum during the spring and summer of 1942 marked the beginning of the end for Japan, just as Hitler's failure to force a Soviet surrender in the autumn of 1941 had marked the beginning of the end for Germany. Having arrested Japan's expansion in the Pacific, Allied forces led by the Americans began to reverse it. The reversing initially went slowly, in large part because the greater portion of American war supplies was being sent to Europe. Allied contingents gained a footing in the Solomon Islands at Guadalcanal; they fought north from Port Moresby across the backbone of New Guinea in mountain and jungle terrain and tropical climate as difficult as soldiers encountered anywhere in the war. They established beachheads in the Gilberts and the Marshalls. The Allied strategy was to capture a few positions in each island group but not waste time, lives, and materiel on every atoll and reef. Japanese units on the unreduced islands would be cut off from resupply and would eventually have to surrender or starve.

The island hopping continued past the Carolines into the Marianas in 1944. The securing of airfields in the Marianas, including Guam and Tinian, brought the home islands of Japan within reach of American B-29 bombers. It also brought the collapse of the Tojo government in Tokyo.

In October 1944 the liberation of the Philippines began. MacArthur's forces splashed ashore at Leyte and started pushing toward Luzon and Manila. The Japanese navy made a last stand off the Leyte coast but was shattered as an effective fighting force in the biggest sea battle in history. At the beginning of 1945, Manila was liberated, though it was almost completely leveled in the process. Iwo Jima and Okinawa in the Ryukyus fell in February 1945. With American bombers softening up the Japanese defenses, MacArthur and the other Allied commanders prepared for an assault on the home islands.

Diplomacy Under Fire

As the end neared for both Germany and Japan, the governments of the United States, Britain, and the Soviet Union discussed what would follow the military victory. American and British officials had been talking about this subject since before the United States entered the war. In August 1941 Roosevelt and Churchill met aboard ship off the coast of Newfoundland. The meeting itself was a closely guarded secret, for reasons of political and military security, but upon its conclusion the American president and the British prime minister released a statement of principles soon called the Atlantic Charter. They disclaimed territorial aggrandizement, affirmed self-determination of peoples, endorsed freer trade and freedom of the seas, and recommended economic cooperation, collective security, disarmament, and the settlement of disputes by peaceful means. The document was mostly vague and unspecific, though Churchill took pains on returning to England to reassure his conservative supporters that he did not mean for self-determination to apply within the British empire. Churchill's clarification helped provoke a major campaign of passive resistance to British rule in India. Hundreds of thousands of Indian nationalists demanded that the British leave the subcontinent at once. Churchill responded to the "Quit India" movement by slapping tens of thousands of its leaders in jail.

Although Stalin did not attend the Atlantic conference, Roosevelt and Churchill were thinking about the Soviet leader at the Newfoundland meeting. Four months still had to pass before the three big powers would be in the war together, but the president and the prime minister sent congratulations to Stalin on the Soviet Union's "brave and steadfast resistance" to Hitlerism and said they would like to dispatch representatives to Moscow to discuss the optimal apportionment of "our joint resources." In the meantime Britain and the United States—mostly the United States, under the Lend-Lease program—would continue shipping supplies to the Soviet Union as rapidly as possible.

Stalin accepted the Anglo-American suggestion, thus beginning close consultation among the three governments on matters of military planning. Consultation did not always imply friendly agreement, however. The long delay in opening the second front in western Europe rankled the Soviets and tended to make Americans and British somewhat defensive. Stalin was not above playing on his partners' sensitivities. Throughout the first two years of the combined war effort, he and other Soviet officials repeatedly reminded their American and British counterparts of the huge sacrifices the Soviet people were making, while the Americans and British had yet to really engage the common foe.

Notwithstanding the troublesome issue of the second front, military discussions among American, British, and Soviet leaders were straightforward and agreeable compared to their political discussions. There was a cause for this: although the three governments shared an overriding military goal—namely, Hitler's defeat—their political objectives diverged. In January 1942 Stalin's representative joined American and British delegates and officials from a score of other antifascist governments in signing the declaration of the United Nations. This statement of Allied war aims incorporated the Atlantic Charter, which the Soviets thereby ratified. However, the Kremlin appended a caveat explaining that the practical application of the general principles of the charter would have to take into account the historical peculiarities and particular circumstances of specific countries. In other words, Stalin did not intend to be held to the letter of the Atlantic Charter—just as Churchill did not.

As long as the end of the war remained far distant, the differences among the three major Allies on political questions remained muted. Much of the point of the unconditional surrender policy was to keep them muted by keeping the alliance focused on the military task at hand. But because war is fundamentally a political act designed to preserve or extend political power, discussions of the political questions could not be avoided completely.

These discussions brought out two essentially different approaches to creating a postwar international order. In many respects the two approaches were the same two that had dominated discussions of a postwar settlement at the end of the First World War. The nationalist approach was based on the idea that the major powers would police separate spheres of influence. By mutual agreement, they would determine the extent and boundaries of their respective spheres and would leave peace keeping within any particular sphere to the power in charge. This approach appealed to those who considered themselves realists. It was based on the way the world had worked for millennia and required no changes in human nature.

Its principal drawbacks were, first, its cynicism and, second, possible difficulties in defining the spheres. Regarding the cynicism, the creation of spheres of influence was essentially what the Germans and Japanese were trying to do. By claiming a right to such spheres for themselves, the big three Allies wandered off the solid moral ground of self-determination as proclaimed in the Atlantic Charter into the oozing mud of might-makes-right. Had the Soviet Union been a democracy, Washington and London perhaps could have joined with Moscow in claiming that democratic spheres were somehow less objectionable than fascist spheres. But the antidemocratic character of Stalin's regime ruled out this kind of appeal. Americans, among others, like to believe that they are fighting for a worthy cause; a peace based on spheres of influence would have difficulty qualifying.

The second drawback, involving defining the spheres, was equally troublesome. In the minds of critics, the observation that international affairs had been based for centuries on spheres of influences was hardly a recommendation. Two world wars in a single generation seemed to indicate that traditional methods of ordering the world did not work very well. Perhaps in the flush of victory the triumphant great powers could agree on who should get what. But the world was constantly changing, and before long they would begin bickering. The bickering would be aggravated, perhaps intentionally, by the small countries caught in the great-power spheres. If Poland did not like being in the Soviet sphere, or Cuba in the American sphere, or Egypt in the British sphere, resourceful Poles, Cubans, or Egyptians would appeal to the other great powers for help. To resist such appeals, the leaders of the powers would have to demonstrate more self-restraint than leaders historically had.

The alternative to the nationalist, spheres-of-influence model of postwar relations was the internationalist, collective-security model. This was the Wilsonian approach that had been embodied, minus the United States, in the League of Nations. Proponents of collective security contended that the League's failures had not proven the model itself to be defective, merely the imperfect version incorporated in the League. Because the world's greatest power, the United States, had boycotted the League, collective security had never been given a fair trial. With American support, an updated League would work. Potential aggressors would be made to know that they would be punished. This knowledge would in most cases cause them to shelve their aggressive plans. Had the West reacted sharply to the Japanese occupation of Manchuria, East Asia would not have become the battleground it currently was. Had the antifascist powers showed determination during the Sudeten crisis of 1938, Hitler never would have gone on his current rampage.

Critics of collective security, however, pointed to what they deemed its fatal flaw. There was a reason, they said, why the other powers had failed to stand up to Japan and Germany. That reason was called self-interest or just plain human nature. Every government looks out for itself and its country's national interests before anyone or anything else. The United States and the League of Nations settled for a limp nonrecognition of Manchukuo because in the estimate of most Americans and Europeans, Manchuria did not warrant a war. The democracies did not call Hitler's bluff on Czechoslovakia because the rights of the Czechs were not worth a fight to most ordinary people of Britain, France, or the United States. Thus it would always be: countries would defend their own interests but would not do much for the interests of others. Collective security required a selflessness humans had never exhibited; until human nature changed, they never would.

For all the Marxian claims that human nature is changeable, that it reflects social and political circumstances rather than inherent and immutable character traits, Stalin and the Soviets rejected the collective security model of postwar relations in favor of spheres of influence. Stalin was a thorough skeptic when it came to international affairs. He distrusted people who professed high ideals, and he especially looked askance at claims of good will toward the Soviet Union emanating from the West. For centuries the West had viewed Russia as a backward territory to be subjugated. Three times in the previous six generations, huge Western armies—one French and two German—had thrust deep into Russia, wreaking havoc and death as they came. For much of the twenty-five years since the establishment of the Soviet government, the capitalist states had bitterly opposed it, sending troops to strangle it in its infancy and engaging in diplomatic and economic warfare against it afterward. During the present war, the American and British capitalists were letting the Soviet Union bleed while they took their time opening a second front. As soon as the capitalists got what they wanted out of the Soviet Union, they could be counted on to revert to anti-Soviet form. Any Soviet leader would be a fool to rely on the good will of the capitalists; far better to look to the strength of the Red Army. Besides, the peaceful coexistence that collective security required contradicted the revolutionary principles of Marxism-Leninism. It was the historical duty of the Soviet government to work toward the triumph of world socialism.

The British were not much more enamored of collective security than the Soviets. Like the Soviets, the British could proclaim adherence to the ideals of the United Nations, but again like the Soviets they preferred to keep their powder dry. For one thing, Churchill was a conservative of the old school. Like most conservatives, he believed that human nature was fundamentally flawed and that self-interest was a more reliable motivator than altruism. In relations among states, the strong did what they could, the weak what they had to. Further, a spheres-of-influence approach came naturally to an imperialist power such as Britain since an empire was nothing more than a formalized sphere of influence. Too much idealistic talk inevitably led to attacks on imperialism. Churchill was not about to give up Britain's empire.

Of the big three members of the antifascist coalition, the United States showed the greatest interest in collective security, though Roosevelt often demonstrated a strong inclination toward a spheres-of-influence postwar settlement as well. After the outbreak of war in Asia and Europe, many Americans felt pangs of conscience at America's refusal to join the League of Nations. Had the United States not abdicated its responsibility for world peace, these people thought, the war might never have started, and all the horrors the war was visiting on humanity might never have occurred. Pearl Harbor caused a flood of conversions from isolationism to internationalism. In their desire to make amends for America's past mistakes, the converts enthusiastically embraced the idea of a revived League of Nations and the collective security ideal on which it rested.

Roosevelt recognized the appeal of collective security for Americans, and he was not immune to the appeal himself; yet at the same time, he was enough of a pragmatist to wonder whether the world was ready for the kind of responsibilities an effective system of collective security required. Americans might be hot for internationalism now, but how would they feel after the war was over? Would they be willing to go to war to protect the Czechoslovakias of the future? When the war ended, the United States would be the most powerful country on the planet. Would Americans consent to relinquish some of their power to an international organization? Would they be willing to accept decisions of the international organization when such decisions went against the United States? Would they approve the dismantling of America's sphere of influence in the Western Hemisphere?

Roosevelt had his doubts. As a consequence, he wavered between the collective–security and spheres-of-influence approaches during most of the war. As the end of the fighting neared, political issues relating to the postwar settlement increasingly occupied the leaders of the three great Allies. In November and December 1943, Roosevelt, Churchill, and Stalin gathered at Teheran. Roosevelt and Churchill knew each other well by this time, having met on several occasions. Churchill and Stalin had spoken in Moscow during the summer of 1942. But the conference in Iran was the first meeting of the three leaders together, and it was Roosevelt's first encounter with Stalin. The Soviet premier could be charming when he wanted to be, and he put on a good show for Roosevelt and Churchill. Roosevelt judged Stalin to be a person the United States could do business with. The president knew that Stalin suspected the British and Americans of conspiring against the Soviet Union, and Roosevelt went out of his way to offer reassurances. Although on a number of occasions at Teheran he met with Stalin separately from Churchill, Roosevelt avoided private meetings with Churchill.

The three leaders discussed several topics of substance at Teheran. Stalin suggested that Germany be partitioned after the war so that it would no longer possess the ability to molest its neighbors. Roosevelt indicated that partition might be acceptable but declined to commit himself. Stalin and Churchill discussed a revision of Poland's boundaries, but here again Roosevelt declined to be drawn out. Stalin reiterated a promise given earlier that after the defeat of Germany the Soviet Union would enter the war against Japan. This pledge was particularly good news for the United States, which was carrying most of the Allied burden in the Pacific war. Stalin sided with Roosevelt in arguing that the Americans and British should attack the Germans in France rather than in southeastern Europe.

On the subject of postwar security, Roosevelt broached a scheme that was something of a hybrid between collective security and spheres of influence. The president described an international body consisting of all or nearly all the countries of the world but controlled by four great powers: the United States, the Soviet Union, Britain, and China. Roosevelt included China partly for American sentimental reasons (American missionaries had had an effect on Washington if not so much of one on China), partly for domestic political reasons (Chiang Kaishek had powerful friends in America), and partly because Asia needed to be represented (Japan had obviously disqualified itself). Roosevelt spoke of these four countries as "policemen," though he did not specify just what their duties would be. Stalin expressed interest in the general idea but questioned that China qualified.

In the autumn of 1944, Churchill and Stalin met again. Roosevelt was busy at the time getting elected for a fourth term and did not join them. He was also quite sick, though this was not widely known. At their Moscow meeting, the British prime minister and the Soviet generalissimo demonstrated plainly their preference for a spheres-of-interest peace. Soviet troops were in control of most of Poland, but much of the rest of central Europe and the Balkans was still up for grabs. Churchill took out a sheet of paper and wrote down a formula for dividing up the region. The Soviet Union would have the largest say in Romania and Bulgaria, while Britain, perhaps in concert with the United States, would dominate Greece. Yugoslavia and Hungary would be divided evenly between the Soviets, on one hand, and the British and Americans, on the other. Churchill pushed the paper across the table to Stalin, who listened to the translation. As Churchill narrated later, "There was a slight pause. Then he took his blue pencil and made a large tick upon it, and passed it back to us. It was all settled in no more time than it takes to set down."

Actually, it was not all settled. The American government refused to be a party to any such blunt division of the spoils of war as this Moscow memo specified. Although Roosevelt did not reject spheres of influence in all cases, for public consumption he still promoted self-determination and collective security. In February 1945 the president met with Churchill and Stalin at the

Russian resort town of Yalta on the Black Sea. The strain of twelve years in office was telling on Roosevelt, who, after a serious earlier bout with polio, had not been especially robust to start with. Photographs of the Yalta meeting show him haggard and frail. Within two months he would be dead.

But though weak and worn, Roosevelt was mentally alert for what turned out to be the most important conference of the war. At the time of the Yalta conference, the outcome of the fighting was no longer in question. Germany would be defeated and soon; Japan would be defeated, though that victory would take longer. Until this point Roosevelt had postponed decisions regarding the postwar settlement; now postponement was no longer possible. Four issues dominated the discussions at Yalta. The first had to do with Soviet participation in the war against Japan. Confirming his earlier pledge, Stalin said the Soviet Union would join the fight against the Japanese within three months after the defeat of Hitler. Though expected, Stalin's restatement of his pledge was reassuring to American military planners at a time when the war against Japan was predicted to last for another year or eighteen months. The more help American forces could get in finishing off the Japanese, the fewer Americans would die. In exchange for Moscow's assistance, the Soviets would receive the Kurile Islands off Japan's northern coast and a return to the status quo in northeastern Asia as it existed before the Russo-Japanese War—a status quo markedly more favorable to Moscow than recent arrangements.

The second Yalta issue regarded the future of Germany. The three leaders agreed to partition Germany, at least for the purposes of occupation. The United States, Britain, and the Soviet Union each would take charge of one zone of Germany. France might also receive an occupation zone. Whether this initial partition would lead to permanent dismemberment would await further discussions. Stalin wanted a definite statement specifying dismemberment to ensure that Germany would not rise again. Roosevelt did not rule out a permanent division of Germany, but neither did he commit himself to it. The three leaders settled on a declaration specifying the need to destroy Nazism and German militarism and to take "such other measures in Germany as may be necessary to the future peace and safety of the world."

The third Yalta issue had to do with a successor to the League of Nations. Already the successor had a name: the United Nations Organization. Stalin did not conceal his disdain for the organization and for the collective security idea on which it rested. He contended that the three great Allies, which were carrying the weight of defeating the fascists, must have decisive power in preserving the peace after the war. To allow small countries that could not even defend themselves to have any significant influence on important matters of war and peace was ridiculous and unrealistic. Stalin said that he was willing to act in concert with the United States and Britain to protect the rights of the small powers but that he could never agree to let the small countries sit in judgment on the actions of the great powers. In other words, while the United Nations Organization might become a forum for talk, for real security the great powers must look to themselves and look after their spheres of influence, as great powers always had.

Of these three leaders at Yalta, only Stalin would still be in office six months later. Roosevelt would die and Churchill would be rejected by British voters. *F.D.R. Library*

Roosevelt conceded that the biggest powers should have the "greater re-sponsibility" for policing the world. And he did not deny the usefulness of spheres of influence. But he suggested that the American Congress and the American people would not go along with a permanent police role for the United States. He predicted that American troops might remain in Europe for perhaps two years after the war's end, but not much more. The American people would not stand for it. (At this, Stalin's aide, Andrei Vyshinski, told Roosevelt's interpreter, Charles Bohlen, that the American people should learn to obey their leaders. Bohlen responded that he would like to see Vyshinski try to teach this lesson to the American people. Vyshinski said he would be de-lighted to if given the opportunity—which he later was when appointed Stalin's representative at the United Nations during the most intense phase of Ameri-can postwar anticommunism. The pupils hated the teacher, and Vyshinski be-came one of America's favorite villains, decried by politicians and pundits of nearly all persuasions as the personification of evil.)

In the end Roosevelt and Stalin reached a compromise. Roosevelt split the difference between his own contradictory affinities for collective security and spheres of influence. In the United Nations Organization, all members would have a right to express their views, but on matters of substance the great powers would each possess a veto. This compromise preserved the appearance and some of the substance of collective security while leaving the door open for a spheres-of-influence peace. On issues on which the great powers agreed, the United Nations Organization could work the way the League of Nations had been supposed to. Where the great powers disagreed, the organization would be stymied, and the powers would fall back on their own resources.

The fourth Yalta issue was the future of Poland. This issue provided some insight into how widely the door to spheres of influence might be pushed open. In Britain and the United States, Poland possessed chiefly political and symbolic importance. Churchill reminded Stalin and Roosevelt that Poland's fate touched British honor: Britain had gone to war over Hitler's destruction of Polish freedom, and the British government wished to see that the war ended with Poland's freedom secured. For Roosevelt, Poland was a touchy domestic political issue. There were 6 or 7 million Polish-Americans in the United States, and the president had to take their feelings into account.

To the Soviet Union, by contrast, the issue of Poland was what Stalin called "a question of the security of the state," a matter "of life and death." Historically, Poland had served as a corridor for armies attacking Russia from the west. Twice in the previous thirty years alone, Germany had attacked Russian territory through Poland. The Soviet government had an obligation to the Soviet people to make certain that this did not happen again. Stalin said that the best guarantee of Soviet security on this point was a Poland that was "free, independent and powerful." What he meant was that Poland should be free and independent of influences hostile to the Soviet Union and powerful enough to repel any further attacks from the west. To this end he advocated turning control of the country over to a provisional regime established in Lublin—a group carefully vetted and guided by Moscow.

Roosevelt, backed by Churchill, preferred the Polish government-in-exile in London. The London group more accurately reflected Polish preferences than the Lublin regime did, and it was much more popular among Polish-Americans, most of whom hated Stalin passionately for partitioning their country with Hitler. Roosevelt thought that it might be possible to bridge the gap between the Lublin Poles and the London Poles by means of Polish elections soon after the war.

Stalin agreed to let the London Poles return to Poland and join a coalition government with the Lublin Poles. And he consented to "free and unfettered elections as soon as possible," in the words of the final Yalta communiqué. Yet despite this agreement, the difference in views regarding Poland between Washington and London, on one hand, and Moscow, on the other, was fundamental and deep. The United States and Britain wanted a democratic Poland, while the Soviet Union demanded a friendly Poland. Roosevelt told Stalin that the two objectives were "completely consistent," but in fact they were not. In light of long enmity between Poland and Russia, a genuinely democratic Poland would almost of necessity be *un*friendly to the Soviet Union. Stalin recognized this fact, and while he might soft-pedal it for the sake of wartime cooperation, he kept it squarely in mind for the future.

From Mass Production to Mass Destruction

By the time of the Yalta conference, the war against Germany and Japan had become chiefly a war of attrition. No one could doubt that the Allies would win; it only remained for them to destroy their enemies' capacity to continue fighting. The brutal character of the last phase of the war was partly the result of the fanatical nature of the ruling regimes in Berlin and Tokyo, where the leadership intended to go down fighting. Some anti-Hitler conspirators tried to assassinate the Führer with a bomb in July 1944, but by luck he escaped with modest injuries. The revenge he exacted on the would-be assassins, and on lots of other people besides, deterred others from trying the same thing. In Tokyo the fall of Tojo did not lessen the hold of the militarists on the Japanese government; and the sacrifices the militarists demanded only increased as Japan's fortunes faded. Japanese pilots undertook suicide kamikaze raids, and Japanese soldiers bade each other farewell with the sentiment "Until we meet in Yasukuni" (the shrine for the spirits of the fallen).

The bitter-end nature of the fighting was also the consequence of the Allies' policy of unconditional surrender. Although this policy made sense as a diplomatic cement to hold the Grand Alliance together, it held out little incentive to those in Germany or Japan who might want to overthrow the governments responsible for the war so as to terminate the fighting. The Germans would all have to go down together; likewise the Japanese.

The racial overtones of the war in the Pacific also contributed to the intensity of the conflict there. Propagandists on both sides described the enemy as racially inferior. Japanese publications spoke of Americans and British as "brutes," "wild beasts," and "devils." American newspapers and magazines commonly depicted Japanese as monkeys. Japanese troops inflicted atrocities on the prisoners they captured; accounts of the 1942 Bataan "death march" in the Philippines, as related by escaped survivors, curdled the blood of Americans. Many people in the United States took the attitude that the only good Jap was a dead Jap, though some doubted that this attitude went far enough. "Even a dead Jap isn't a good Jap," the *New York Times Magazine* asserted, explaining that Japanese troops booby-trapped the bodies of their fallen comrades to kill or maim unwary American soldiers.

Racism had different but still more appalling consequences in Europe. The onset of the war had broken what few shackles remained on the racist demonology of the Nazis; they carried the principles that had underlain the

Nuremberg decrees and subsequent additional discrimination and violence against the Jews to the logical but monstrous conclusion that the Jews should be eliminated as a people. The invasion of Poland increased the number of Jews under German control; the invasion of the Soviet Union added millions more to the total. At first the Nazis attempted to eliminate the Jews by mass shootings, but this proved inefficient and damaged the morale of the soldiers assigned to the firing squads. The Nazis then resorted to poison gas, first carbon monoxide from engine exhaust, later a special compound known as Zyklon-B. Squads of German soldiers, often assisted by local collaborators, rounded up Jews from the territories under German control and brought them to several killing centers, of which the largest was Auschwitz in Poland. The healthiest and strongest of the prisoners were forced to work in factories connected to the camps until the work wore them out; then they followed their weaker parents, children, and cousins to the gas chambers. By war's end more than 6 million Jews died in what came to be called the Holocaust. Smaller but still appallingly large numbers of Gypsies were put to death as well along with homosexuals, mentally retarded persons and others judged deviant or defective by the Nazis.

Although reports of the extermination camps surfaced in the Allied countries during the war, so terrible was the Nazi crime that the reports were nearly impossible to credit. In July 1943 a member of the Polish underground who had seen the death camp at Belsen for himself, and had additional information about Auschwitz and the camps at Dachau and Treblinka, brought the news to Washington. He told Felix Frankfurter, a Supreme Court justice and one of the most prominent Jews in America, that nearly 2 million Jews had been killed already and that the Nazis intended to kill all the rest they could lay their hands on. Frankfurter did not believe the report. "I do not have the strength to believe it," he said. Franklin Roosevelt, who listened closely to Frankfurter on matters involving Jewish interests, found the reports as hard to believe as Frankfurter did. The president recalled the exaggerated atrocity stories the British had put out during the First World War, and he had no desire for America to be played the fool again. Besides, he could reasonably contend that the best policy for saving the Jews was to defeat Germany as soon as possible. This was the position he adopted in response to the same report Frankfurter heard. "You tell your leaders in Poland they have a friend in the White House," the president said. "We shall win the war. The guilty will be punished."

The Nazi Holocaust was clearly the extreme case of civilians being victimized during the war, but it was by no means the only one. At the beginning of the fighting, the traditional distinction between combat personnel and non-combatants still existed. The distinction had been blurred in the First World War by German submarine attacks on ships like the *Lusitania*, which carried both civilian passengers and munitions, as well as by the British blockade of Germany, which in conjunction with the German government's apportioning policies starved the young, the old, and the infirm rather than soldiers. Yet most observers hoped that these actions were merely exceptions to the rule that people who could not defend themselves should not be attacked. The outrage, albeit ineffective, of the world community at Japan's abominable treatment of civilians in Nanjing in 1937 indicated that noncombatants might still expect to be treated differently from soldiers in a war between countries that considered themselves civilized.

The Second World War in Europe shattered this expectation. When the Germans took to the air over Britain, they discovered that hitting big, soft targets like London was much easier than hitting small, well-defended targets like naval yards and R.A.F. airfields. The blitz against London and other cities was designed to wreak maximum destruction on civilian life and thereby break British morale. As things turned out, regarding morale the bombing had just the opposite effect: with each night's air raids and every morning's casualty and damage reports, the British grew more determined to resist Hitler and eventually crush Nazism. When the opportunity arose, British and American airplanes adopted the approach of the German air force. Allied planes began flying missions across the English Channel in 1942; by the time of the 1944 invasion of Normandy, Allied aircraft had swept the Luftwaffe from the skies over France and were inflicting heavy damage on cities deep inside Germany. For public consumption, the Allied air raids were usually described as being aimed at targets of military importance: railyards, factories, refineries, warehouses, docks. In most cases they were, though stray bombs frequently found their way onto homes, schools, and other civilian structures. The longer the war lasted, however, and the higher the Allied death toll mounted, the greater the desire for vengeance became. Bomber crews got increasingly careless regarding what they hit, and their superiors looked the other way.

Eventually, hitting everything in sight became the basic purpose of the Allied air campaign. In February 1945, after the German counterattack at the battle of the Bulge revealed that the Germans had more fight left in them than the Allies thought (the Americans alone suffered more than one hundred thousand casualties), the Americans and British launched a new round of raids against German cities and other targets. The raid against Dresden surpassed in destructiveness anything yet seen in warfare. Hundreds of small fires caused by Allied incendiary bombs merged into a tremendous firestorm that converted the city into an inferno. Some thirty-five thousand Germans, mostly women, children, and old people, died from the bombs and the conflagration.

American air raids on Japan outdid even the attack on Dresden. Before the war Admiral Yamamoto had warned his colleagues of the danger to the home territory from aerial bombardment, especially by incendiary devices. "Japanese cities, being made of wood and paper, would burn very easily," Yamamoto predicted. "The Army talks big, but if war came and there were large-scale air raids, there's no telling what would happen." By the spring of 1945, the American air command had perfected its technique for setting cities aflame. American B-29s carried thousands of six-pound projectiles filled with a kind of jellied gasoline called napalm. On impact the napalm caught fire and spewed in all directions, creating a molten flame that stuck to roofs, walls, and people, igniting everything flammable.

In March 1945 more than three hundred American bombers staged a night-time assault on Tokyo. Armed entirely with incendiary bombs, the planes flew low over the city, spreading out to maximize the area of destruction. The fires started by the bombs were fanned by the wind, a large part of which the fires themselves created, until whole central part of Tokyo, one of the most densely populated cities in the world, was ablaze. More than eighty thousand people died, most of them burned to death; sixteen square miles of downtown Tokyo were gutted.

The American Pacific command considered the Tokyo raid a success and repeated the tactic many times during subsequent months. Five of Japan's most important industrial cities besides Tokyo received the fire-storm treatment. Dozens of smaller cities were bombed with both incendiaries and high explosives. Hundreds of thousands more civilians were killed or wounded. Millions lost their homes to the flames.

The strategic bombing campaign revolutionized the practice of warfare. For the first time in history, a country could be devastated in combat without enemy soldiers setting foot on its soil. Indeed, enemy soldiers did not even have to come close. Airplanes based many hundreds of miles distant could rain their destruction down and fly safely away. The people killed might never see their attackers, only the machines the attackers flew. And they might catch only glimpses of those machines if the planes loosed their bombs from high altitude or at night.

Ground zero: Hiroshima. *AP/Wide World Photos*

Even more revolutionary than the incendiary bombing raids was the new weapon introduced just at the Pacific war's end. Of course, it was not coincidence that the war ended just after the atomic bomb was used against Hiroshima and Nagasaki. The bomb was designed to crush the last of Japan's will to resist; and it worked.

Although the United States was the first country to develop an atomic bomb, Americans had plenty of help. The bomb marked the culmination of an international collaborative effort that included nearly all the technologically advanced nations, though most of the people involved did not know they were working toward a weapon of mass destruction. The collaboration stretched back to the 1890s, when the German physicist Wilhelm Roentgen discovered X-rays and the French scientists Antoine Henri Becquerel and Pierre Curie and Curie's Polish wife Marie Sklodowska Curie learned the properties of uranium and other radioactive elements. The English physicist Lord Rutherford provided an early explanation of radioactivity, showing it to be the result of the splitting of atomic nuclei. German-born Albert Einstein uncovered a crucial theoretical link between matter and energy: Einstein's famous formula (energy equals mass times the velocity of light squared) indicated the possibility of converting small amounts of matter into massive amounts of energy. Germany's Max Planck and Denmark's Neils Bohr provided a different perspective on many of the same phenomena with their development of quantum theory. James Chadwick of England identified the neutron, which turned out to be the key particle in producing atomic chain reactions.

By the late 1930s, the theoretical basis for the atomic bomb was fairly well laid. Until this stage American contributions to the field had been modest. What the United States contributed, starting about the time of the outbreak of war in Europe, was the technological know-how and the financial resources to transform theory into practice. America also provided a safe haven for such European refugee scientists as Einstein, Hungarian Leo Szilard, and Italian Enrico Fermi. In 1939 Einstein and Szilard wrote a letter to Franklin Roosevelt urging the president to give top priority to the development of atomic weapons. Roosevelt procrastinated until Pearl Harbor, but shortly thereafter he and Winston Churchill agreed to pool American and British expertise and push forward on the matter. Under the umbrella of the top-secret Manhattan Project, American and British scientists and engineers, along with the émigrés from the European continent, designed and built a prototype atomic bomb. The device was completed too late for use against Germany, a circumstance that was slightly ironic since fear that Germany would get the bomb first was a principal motivator of the Manhattan Project. In July 1945 the bomb was tested in New Mexico. Its explosive power stunned even many of those who were intimately involved in its creation.

So stunned, in fact, were the bomb's creators that some of them had second thoughts about its use in warfare. They suggested that instead of dropping the bomb on a Japanese city, it might be used against an unpopulated target as a demonstration of what would happen to Japan if the Japanese government continued to resist. A panel of American government officials and scientists considered the suggestion but ultimately rejected it. There was no guarantee that a demonstration would convince Japanese observers that their government must surrender, and there was still less guarantee that Japanese observers would be able to convince the militarists who determined Japanese policy. Besides, the American atomic arsenal at this point consisted of only two bombs; to risk one on a possibly fruitless demonstration would be foolish.

Other considerations entered the calculations of Harry Truman, president since Roosevelt's April death. The use of the bomb would probably hasten Japan's surrender, which would have two beneficial effects. The more important was the saving of many thousands of American lives that would be lost if an invasion of the Japanese home islands became necessary. Many Japanese lives would be saved, too. The less important was the termination of the war in the Pacific before the Soviets got in. Already some American officials were wishing Roosevelt had not promised the Soviets so much at Yalta regarding East Asia; if Japan surrendered before Stalin declared war, those promises might not have to be fulfilled.

In the end Truman decided in favor of the bomb's use. He would lose no sleep over the suffering the bomb caused Japan. The Japanese had started the war; they had committed countless atrocities against Americans and others. Truman and most other Americans believed that the Japanese deserved whatever they got. Truman did not wish to have to explain to the parents of American soldiers killed in a prolonged war how his tender-heartedness toward Tokyo had cost the lives of their sons.

The Second World War finally came to a close in mid-1945. The European phase of the fighting finished first when the Allied armies invaded Germany and converged on Berlin. Hitler, seeing his dream of a thousand-year German reich shattered after a scant dozen years, killed himself in his Berlin bunker while the battle still raged outside his door. Germany surrendered on May 7.

The war in Asia ended in August after the atomic bombing of Hiroshima and Nagasaki, which together killed more than 150,000 people. Almost until the very end, the American government had stuck to the unconditional surrender policy, but at the last minute it waffled. It tacitly accepted a surrender offer from the Japanese conditioned on the maintenance of the institution of the Japanese emperor. American officials believed that the emperor might be useful in persuading the Japanese to cease their resistance. This belief proved well founded. Many of Japan's military leaders wanted to fight to the death. Emperor Hirohito was forced to intervene personally, something he almost never did; he reasserted his authority and declared his desire to surrender. The emperor's action provoked a rebellion in the officer ranks, which was suppressed only with difficulty. On August 15 (Tokyo time; August 14 in the United States), Hirohito broadcast a message blaming America for employing a "new and most cruel bomb" against which Japan had no adequate defense. Because of this, Japanese resistance must cease, however humiliating surrender was.

It was historically fitting, though humanly tragic, that the Second World War should have concluded with the use of the atomic bomb. The bomb epitomized the industrial and technological supremacy of the United States, and it was this supremacy more than anything else that gave the victory to the Allies. American soldiers fought valiantly and intelligently, but it was the seemingly infinite supply of modern weapons they commanded—the thousands of ships, tens of thousands of airplanes and tanks, hundreds of thousands of artillery pieces, millions of rifles and other personal arms, and tens of millions of bombs, grenades, and bullets, not to mention the incessant stream of mundane but equally necessary trucks, jeeps, boots, field rations, bandages, and medicines—that gave the victory to the American side. A probably apocryphal story about a German antitank gunner summarized the Allied advantage. The gunner had taken up his position overlooking a key road. An American tank column was approaching up the road. Each time an American tank came into view, the gunner fired. He was a crack shot, and each round knocked out a tank. But the Americans eventually passed because, as he complained afterward, he ran out of rounds before the Americans ran out of tanks. Whether or not this specific story was true, the moral certainly was. In an all-out war in the industrial age, victory goes to the side with the most powerful industries.

*   *   *

The Second World War wrought an unfinished revolution in international affairs. It destroyed the balance of power that had existed in Europe since the unification of Germany in the 1870s and in Asia since the industrialization of Japan in the 1880s and 1890s. Germany and Japan disappeared as independent players in the game of nations. Who or what would replace them was the pressing question facing the winners at the fighting's end.

The war simultaneously wrought a revolution in Americans' perception of the role of the United States in world affairs. Americans had done their best to stay aloof from international commitments during the 1920s and 1930s, believing that such commitments would drag the United States into foreign wars. What most Americans discovered only after Pearl Harbor was that American interests—economic, political, military—were so globalized that for the United States there could be almost no such thing as a foreign war. What happened in Manchuria or Indochina or Poland or France or the Soviet Union had significant implications for the kinds of activities Americans wanted to undertake. Overseas markets might be shut to American exporters; hostile governments might endanger American lives, American property, American territory, or American trade routes; aggressive ideologies might jeopardize democracy.

After the fact, many Americans decided that they had been too late in recognizing the menace of foreign aggression. Like generals who prepare to fight the next war on the lessons of the last, Americans resolved to avoid their previous mistakes. This time they would not turn their backs on international commitments. Quite the contrary: they would embrace an ambitious interventionism. Where a vacuum of power existed, as in the vicinity of Germany or Japan, they would throw themselves into the breach. Only by preparing to fight, they believed, could they make further fighting unnecessary.

Sources and Suggestions for Further Reading

On Europe's descent into war for the second time in a generation, A. J. P. Taylor's *Origins of the Second World War* (1961) is controversial in portraying Hitler as basically just another German statesman. Less provocative are Joachim Remak, *The Origins of the Second World War* (1976), and Anthony Adamwaite, *The Making of the Second World War* (1979).

On how the war came to America, Robert A. Divine's *The Reluctant Belligerent* (1979 ed.) is clear and concise. Waldo Heinrichs's *Threshold of War* (1988) is more recent and detailed regarding the last months of American neutrality. Robert Dallek's *Franklin Roosevelt and American Foreign Policy* covers several years on either side of the declarations of war. David Reynolds, *The Creation of the Anglo-American Alliance, 1937–1941* (1982), details how the English-speaking powers became wartime allies. Dealing specifically with the approach of war in Asia are Akira Iriye, *The Origins of the Second World War in Asia and the Pacific* (1987), and Herbert Feis, *The Road to Pearl Harbor* (1962). The final phase of prewar relations between the United States and Japan, culminating in the attack at Pearl Harbor, has exercised the authors of numerous books, including Charles C. Tansill, *Back Door to War* (1952), which excoriates Roosevelt; Roberta Wohlstetter, *Pearl Harbor: Warning and Decision* (1962), which absolves Roosevelt of personal responsibility for the losses suffered in the attack by blaming the intelligence bureaucracy and bad luck; and Gordon Prang, *At Dawn We Slept* (1981), and John Toland, *Infamy: Pearl Harbor and Its Aftermath* (1982), which add new information but probably have not changed many minds.

A brief account of American wartime diplomacy is Gaddis Smith, *American Diplomacy during the Second World War* (1985 ed.). Winston Churchill's six-volume *The Second World War* (1948–53) is a compelling combination of memoir and history. Robert Divine, *Roosevelt and World War II* (1969), treats the conflict from the president's perspective. Herbert Feis, *Churchill, Roosevelt, Stalin* (1957), depicts the leaders of the three wartime partners. William H. McNeill, *America, Britain, and Russia* (1953), broadens the picture somewhat. These books all treat the important wartime diplomatic conferences, but also consult Diane S. Clemens, *Yalta* (1970), on that most controversial meeting.

On the war in the Pacific, the place to begin is Ronald H. Spector, *Eagle against the Sun* (1985). Christopher Thorne, *Allies of a Kind* (1977), describes the Anglo-American collaboration against Japan. Barbara Tuchman, *Stilwell and the American Experience in China, 1911–1945* (1971), portrays the frustrations of the Sino-American wartime collaboration, as encapsulated in the career of the acerbic Joseph Stilwell. John W. Dower, *War without Mercy* (1986), highlights cultural and racial issues in the Pacific war.

The development of the atomic bomb is most compellingly described in Richard Rhodes, *The Making of the Atomic Bomb* (1986). Other valuable studies of the production of the bomb and its use against Japan are Martin F. Sherwin, *A World Destroyed* (1975), and, more controversially, Gar Alperowitz, *Atomic Diplomacy* (1985 ed.), which suggests that Truman ordered the bomb used against Japan in order, at least in part, to impress the Russians. David MacIsaacs, *Strategic Bombing in World War II* (1976), looks beyond the atomic bomb to the other forms of aerial mass destruction.

Chapter 11

The Struggle for a New World Order, 1945–1950

For a quarter millennium before 1939, the great powers had been almost exclusively European, and the cockpit of international affairs had usually been Europe. The Second World War changed this situation in two ways. First, the war exhausted the three previously dominant European powers: Britain, France, and Germany. Second, the war catapulted one extra-European power, the United States, and another only partly European power, the Soviet Union, to primacy in global politics. After the war, as their erstwhile collaboration dissolved into confrontation, the two newly dominant powers effectively divided most of Europe between them, then extended their confrontation to other portions of the planet. A crisis in the Middle East, in Iran, marked the beginning of the overt phase of what was misleadingly labeled the Cold War (it was not a war but rather a protracted exercise in the avoidance of war, and it generated lots of heat). A second crisis, at the meeting of southeastern Europe and western Asia, involving Turkey and Greece, exacerbated the rivalry. The Chinese civil war intensified it still further, as did another civil war, in Korea.

That the most dramatic events in international affairs were taking place outside Europe demonstrated the success the superpowers enjoyed in imposing order on the Continent. Developments in Europe occasioned a good bit of nail biting over the years after 1945, but the most obvious feature of postwar European politics was its relative stability. Compared to the preceding generation, nothing much happened in Europe for four decades after the Second World War. The line of division that separated the Soviet army from the armies of the West at the war's end became the line separating the Soviet postwar sphere from the American sphere. Each superpower minded its own sphere, and that basically was that.

Establishing and policing spheres of influence in the world beyond Europe were considerably more difficult. In contrast to the situation in Europe, there was no obvious line of demarcation in the Middle East and Asia between the zones the two superpowers could claim without challenging each other. Moreover, the tumultuous developments triggered outside Europe by the war—especially several anticolonial revolutions—made the job of superimposing superpower spheres difficult and often dangerous. As a result, while Europe

Chronology

1945	Yalta conference; German surrender; Potsdam conference; atomic bombing of Japan; Japanese surrender ends Second World War
1946	Iran crisis; Churchill's "iron curtain" speech; Marshall mission to China
1947	Truman Doctrine; Marshall Plan proposed; National Security Act; GATT; United Nations votes to partition Palestine
1948	Creation of Israel sparks Palestine War; Berlin blockade and airlift
1949	North Atlantic treaty; Soviet atomic bomb tested; Communist victory in China
1950	McCarthy warns of communists in government; NSC 68; Soviet-Chinese alliance; outbreak of Korean War; China enters fighting

grew almost boringly predictable, the rest of the world provided plenty of unpredicability and excitement.

Europe's Troubles

When the war in Europe ended in May 1945, a large part of the Continent lay in ruins. The devastation in most places, excepting downtown Dresden and a few equally unfortunate neighborhoods, was not as complete as it had been in the moonscape of northern France after the First World War but it was far more widespread. As preparation for the Normandy invasion, Allied bombers had knocked out hundreds of key transportation facilities, including railyards, bridges, and docks, in France and the Netherlands. The Allied air campaign had blasted Germany's most important cities. The ground fighting ruined a great deal of what the bombers missed: the Allies did not skimp on firepower in chasing down the Germans, who in turn vented their frustration and attempted to slow their pursuers' progress by scorched-earth tactics. Britain, while spared ground battles, had been hit hard from the air early in the war and had scarcely begun to clean up and make repairs by the war's end. Italy and the countries of eastern Europe were similarly damaged, though being more rural than Britain, France, and Germany, their wounds were not so obvious. The Soviet Union had lost between 15 million and 20 million dead; the destruction of Soviet cities and countryside was commensurate to the destruction of life.

At the war's end the European continent was filled with millions of persons displaced in the fighting. The fortunate of these people had homes to return to, though often no way to get there except on foot and little or no money to

These people were among the lucky ones in Europe after the war: they were still alive.
Harry S Truman Library

support themselves on the road. The unfortunate had nothing awaiting them back home but ruined shells of houses and apartments and nightmarish memories. Yet they could not stay where they were since the regions of their temporary residence were hard pressed to feed and house their own inhabitants.

Emotional and psychological dislocations were for many of the war's survivors as severe as the physical uprootings. During the short life of Hitler's European empire, people in the conquered countries had had to choose between collaboration with the Nazis, or at least acquiescence, and resistance. The choice divided the populations during the war, and it continued to do so afterward. The archetype of the collaborators was Vidkun Quisling, a Norwegian official who cooperated outrageously with the German occupation forces and thereby gave his name to a whole class of Nazi sympathizers. The archetype of the resistance leaders was Josip Broz of Yugoslavia, commonly known as Tito. The Yugoslav resistance under Tito fought fiercely against German rule and against those who collaborated with the Germans. For years after the war, the political affairs of the European countries were colored by continued bad feelings between those who had followed the example of Tito (in spirit if not always in deed) and those who had patterned their actions after Quisling.

Because the collaborators had often come from the conservative part of the political spectrum—fascism being a kind of conservatism gone off the deep end—the war tended to tar conservatives with the brush of unpatriotic opportunism. Likewise, because leftists and, in particular, communists had been at the forefront of the resistance, the defeat of the Nazis enhanced the moral and political prestige of the left. Throughout Eastern Europe, with the help of the occupying Red Army, communists took control of the liberated governments. In some places the takeover required longer than in others. Czechoslovakia retained a pluralistic form of government until 1948, while in Poland, despite Stalin's Yalta promise to allow a coalition regime, the Moscow-backed Lublin communists squeezed out their noncommunist competitors almost from the start.

In Western Europe the leftward political shift did not overturn democracy, but it gave new respectability to radical parties. French and Italian communists emerged as serious challengers to the political status quo in their countries. In Britain the socialist Labor party ousted Winston Churchill and the Tories, dealing Churchill the personal embarrassment of defeat during a July 1945 summit conference at Potsdam, Germany, with Stalin and Truman. The situation in Britain was different from the situation elsewhere since Britain had not suffered the wrenchings of German occupation; even so the Labor victory indicated a belief on the part of millions that the capitalist system had failed, as evidenced by the Depression of the 1930s and the war. Socialism ought to be given a try.

It did not help the fortunes of European conservatives that the war had shattered what remained of the European economy after the Depression. For ten years of depression, businesses had deferred maintenance of buildings and equipment, trimming expenses wherever possible and hoping for an upturn that never arrived. During six years of war, maintenance had often been impossible, what with rationing and the war-induced shortages. Direct destruction from bombs, artillery, fire, and the like had further crippled industry and the transportation infrastructure on which industry depended. The trade wars of the Depression, followed by the blockading and embargoing of the world war, had thoroughly disrupted European commercial networks. In the best of times, the separate European national economies had not been self-sufficient; in the worst of times, including the early postwar period, the dearth of trade intensified the massive unemployment, homelessness, malnutrition, and overall discouragement.

The several months that followed the war's end only made matters worse, even among the victors. After a brief period of euphoria that greeted liberation and the Nazis' demise, the chill of reality set in. Estimates of the time needed to repair the damage done to factories, homes, schools, hospitals, and roads ranged upward from five years to a generation. Of course, much of the human damage, to the tens of millions dead and the additional millions physically and psychologically crippled, could never be repaired. The winter of 1945–1946 chattered teeth and shivered bones across the Continent. As cheap war-printed money chased scarce commodities, inflation soared. Only on the black market were many goods available and there only at prices beyond the reach of the people who needed them most.

The Triumph of the Free Traders

The scarcest commodity of all often was hope. Failing that, Europeans would settle for money, which they could use to regain their feet and thereby regain hope. As had been the case since the First World War, the obvious source of money was the United States.

In 1945 and for a short while afterward, the United States dominated the world economy as no country had before and none has since. The war tremendously enhanced America's economic power relative to the rest of the world in two ways. First, spending by the American government on war supplies, both for American troops and for those of the Allies, pulled the American economy out of its depression doldrums and propelled it on a course of unprecedented growth. American production soared, both of manufactured and agricultural commodities. Employment broke all records as those persons laid off during the Depression went back to work and as women and others not previously part of the work force took jobs on production lines and elsewhere. Personal income rose along with production and employment. Savings swelled, with more people than ever working, many of them overtime, and with consumer goods largely displaced by the needs of the troops.

Inadvertently, the American government validated the theories of John Maynard Keynes, the British economist who contended that governments might mitigate or eliminate depressions by heavy spending. In Keynes's view, put forth most directly in his 1936 *General Theory of Employment, Interest and Money,* the distinguishing feature of depressions was a shortfall of consumption: businesses and private individuals were unwilling or unable to spend enough money to keep the economy going. To remedy the shortfall, government ought to increase its own spending, borrowing against the future to finance the increase. Various governments, including that of the United States, had put their toes in the water of Keynesian theory, but none, with the partial exceptions of Japan and Germany, had gone in deep enough prior to the Second World War to test the theory rigorously. (This despite Keynes's warning that Western civilization was at grave peril as a result of the economic crackup of the 1930s. When asked whether anything comparable had ever happened before, Keynes replied, "Yes, it was called the Dark Ages, and it lasted four hundred years.") Washington's wartime spending spree obviously was not designed to confirm Keynes's ideas; it was designed to defend the United States. But it demonstrated that Keynes's ideas worked. During the next two generations, these ideas became a staple tool of governments combating economic downturns.

The second way the Second World War enhanced America's economic position was by debilitating the economies of America's competitors. Every other major power emerged from the war economically weaker than it had entered. Defeated Germany and Japan were in shambles. France and Britain, though on the winning side, were in serious straits. The Soviet Union, not an economic great power before the war, had been knocked to its knees in beating back the

German invasion. China had been poor before the war and was poorer afterward.

In 1945 American industrial output was roughly equal to that of the rest of the world combined. American factories were the most efficient in the world. The American work force was the most productive in the world. On a level playing field, American firms could outcompete the firms of any other country in almost every area of business enterprise. Available American financial resources relative to the rest of the world were even more impressive than American productive resources. What savings the British, French, Italians, Germans, and Japanese had managed to protect during the war would be sorely needed to rebuild those countries. And those savings would suffice only for a painfully slow rebuilding schedule. For anything faster the Europeans would have to look to the United States.

America's unequaled economic stature gave it tremendous leverage in designing a new world economic order for the postwar era. American officials had two objectives in their planning for the postwar world economy. First, they wanted to prevent a recurrence of the kind of destructive economic nationalism that had contributed to the outbreak of the war. It had long been a cardinal tenet of the free–trade school of international economics that where trade goods cross borders, soldiers do not. Put differently, countries that have extensive commercial ties with each other generally do not like to go to war against each other. War destroys all the work that has gone into forging the commercial ties and pummels the profits they produce. The American government aimed to foster a liberal free–trade atmosphere in which cross-border economic connections and the prosperity such connections contributed to would flourish. Some small steps had been taken in this direction by the Roosevelt administration even prior to the war. Secretary of State Cordell Hull, though ignored by Roosevelt in most matters, made the reduction of tariffs a primary objective, and during the 1930s he succeeded in negotiating reciprocal reductions with several countries. Hull and many others hoped to extend the principle significantly after the war.

A free–trade regime, or whatever approximation Washington could achieve in that direction, would do more than stabilize international relations; it would also help ensure against America's sliding back into depression. Although the war may have demonstrated the validity of Keynes's theories about the stimulative effects of government deficit spending, no one inside the American government, or outside, anticipated that the federal government would continue spending at its wartime rate. Production of airplanes, tanks, uniforms, boots, and the myriad miscellania of war would drop off drastically after the shooting stopped. Unless the workers engaged in producing these items quickly started producing something else, and unless American consumers soon commenced purchasing those other goods, the economy would start spinning downward in a depressive spiral. Workers would be laid off, incomes would plunge, and demand would drop off still further. Aggravating the situation would be the demobilization of more than 10 million soldiers and sailors currently under arms. Where would they find jobs in a contracting economy?

Dean Acheson, then assistant secretary of state, told a congressional committee in 1944 that the American economy had to look to markets other than America's to sustain itself. "Those markets are abroad," Acheson declared. "We cannot have full employment and prosperity in the United States without the foreign markets." American policy makers believed that freeing up world trade, in addition to creating cross-border links that would stabilize international relations, would go far toward enabling America to avoid another depression. They understood clearly that the American economy was the most efficient and powerful in the world and that under a free–trade regime American goods would find ready markets around the globe.

During the final year of the war, the Roosevelt administration undertook to create such a regime. In the summer of 1944, finance ministers and other top economic officials of the Allies met at Bretton Woods, New Hampshire, to discuss the structure of the postwar world economy. The American government, as host of the Bretton Woods conference and the presumptive bankroller of any agenda devised there, pressed successfully for measures to open foreign markets. The American delegation persuaded the other nations to accept a system of fixed exchange rates among their currencies. Because of the great size and strength of the American economy, this decision essentially pegged the other currencies to the dollar. The dollar in turn was pegged to gold at thirty-five dollars per ounce, effectively creating a single monetary system for much of the world economy. This result facilitated American investment overseas since it allowed potential investors to gauge investments' returns without having to gamble on fluctuations in exchange rates. The other governments accepted the Bretton Woods monetary scheme largely because they needed American money, even though the arrangement handed considerable control over their economies to the American government.

The Bretton Woods conferees additionally agreed on the establishment of two institutions designed to encourage international trade. The International Bank for Reconstruction and Development (commonly called the World Bank) would channel funds from the rich countries, chiefly the United States, to countries impoverished by the war or by lack of industrial development. As the principal underwriter of the World Bank, the American government was well positioned to impose its terms on countries receiving loans. American terms included the elimination or drastic reduction of trade-clogging tariffs, quotas, and other restrictions. They also included the dismantling of foreign cartels, the establishment of fair rules for doing business with state monopolies, and the easing of restraints on foreign investment. Many of the countries represented at Bretton Woods were not exactly thrilled at the likely consequences of such a program; they could perceive as well as the American leaders could that the open world economy Washington envisioned would be a world economy dominated by American firms. But under the dire circumstances these countries confronted at the end of the war, they could see no feasible

The American delegation to the Bretton Woods conference: Dean Acheson is standing third from left; Treasury Secretary Henry Morgenthau is seated second from right. *UPI/Bettman Newsphotos*

alternative to acquiescing to the American criteria. American money with strings was better than no money at all.

The second Bretton Woods institution was the International Monetary Fund (IMF). Roughly speaking, the IMF was intended to be to the world economy what the Federal Reserve Bank was to the American economy: the IMF would help stabilize the international currency system by making funds available to governments whose currencies were under pressure as a result of shifting trade balances. The availability of IMF money would encourage governments to refrain from competitive devaluations (whereby the British government, for example, might declare that the pound, previously worth perhaps four dollars, was now worth only three). Such devaluations acted as tariffs by raising the price of imports. (In the example cited, an imported item previously costing British consumers one pound, or four dollars, would now cost one and one-third pounds.) During the Depression countries had devalued their currencies as a means of keeping out imports. The IMF would remove some of the temptation to do so by providing assistance to strapped countries. As in the case of the World Bank, the United States put up most of the money for the IMF, and again as in the case of the World Bank, it was thereby able to stamp its free–market preferences on the policies of countries needing IMF assistance.

Another device of American economic diplomacy, the General Agreement on Tariffs and Trade (GATT), took longer to achieve definitive form. Negotiations on the GATT were laborious and slow (as GATT negotiations would continue to be for the next half century); not until 1947 did its twenty-three charter members put their signatures to the establishing document. The GATT pledged its members to the first major multilateral reduction in tariffs in history. The members, whose ranks were much enlarged during subsequent years, slashed tariffs on thousands of items involving tens of billions of dollars in trade.

These four instruments—the dollar-gold currency system, the World Bank, the IMF, and the GATT—established the closest thing to a system of global free trade in world history. To be sure, this closest thing was still relatively far from free–trade perfection. Much of the world, most notably that part dominated by the Soviet Union, opted out of the free–trade zone. And even among the avowed free traders, anomalies existed. Several countries protected their farmers by subsidizing production or by marketing exports below cost. Cartels or less formal arrangements persisted, allotting market shares and blocking entry by foreign firms. Governments adopted "buy domestic" policies. But even so the change from the belligerently protectionist days of the 1930s was striking.

The Bretton Woods–GATT system was a landmark accomplishment, and the American leaders who worked for its creation had reason to feel proud of their achievement; but it provided only a framework for global recovery. Injecting life into the framework called for additional measures. The American government approached the problem of reconstruction after the Second World War in a decidedly different fashion from the way it had approached reconstruction after the First World War. After the first war, Washington had relied on private American capital to fund the European recovery; after the second war, American public capital led the way. The difference reflected both the bad experience of the 1930s, when nearly everyone had defaulted on international debts, rendering private lenders wary of big overseas loans, and a greater willingness on the part of the American people to countenance active government involvement in European affairs. Besides, the big-government reforms of the New Deal had desensitized much of the American public to large government programs of a kind they would have found intolerable a generation before.

The first installment in the funding of European recovery was a government credit to Britain. In 1946 London sent a delegation to Washington to seek help with British reconstruction. John Maynard Keynes headed the delegation, whose members hoped to capitalize on the good feelings between the two countries left over from the war. American good feelings extended far enough for the American government to approve a $3.75 billion credit: a loan for goods purchased in the United States. The British delegation initially requested a loan without such conditions, but the Truman administration desired to guarantee that the American money contribute to the maintenance of American employment and incomes. Moreover, in approving the credit, the administration insisted that London begin to dismantle the system of imperial preference that protected trade within the British empire from outside competition. The British had been the original free traders during the nineteenth century, yet during the first part of the twentieth century, as competition from more recently industrialized countries such as the United States and Germany began pushing British goods aside, London retreated from free–trade principles. Now under pressure from the Americans, the British were returning to the faith.

The credit to Britain proved to be a false start. It was too small to give the British economy the jolt necessary to get going again, and it did not touch at all the larger problems faced by the countries on the European continent. Those countries had bigger problems than Britain and smaller prospects for repayment. In addition, by requiring Britain to repay the credit, Washington implied that relations with the Europeans were to be a business deal. A business deal they were, but not in the usual sense. If they had been, the British might have applied to American banks rather than the American government. Instead the British credit was as much a political deal as a business deal and was designed to bolster American exports and extend the principles of free trade. In exchange London got a better interest rate than private banks would have charged.

In 1947 the Truman administration went considerably beyond export credits in arranging reconstruction assistance for Europe. The administration announced a major program of grants: gifts that did not require repayment. Will Clayton, the American undersecretary of state for economic affairs, returned from an inspection of Europe in May 1947 with a recommendation for massive American aid. Clayton reported that the European economy was in worse shape than American officials had realized and was sinking fast. Without prompt American help, the economic, political, and social fabric of the continent would disintegrate. The impact of such disintegration would spread far beyond Europe. "Aside from the awful implications which this would have for the future peace and security of the world," Clayton said, "the immediate effects on our domestic economy would be disastrous: markets for our surplus production gone, unemployment, depression, a heavily unbalanced budget on the background of a mountainous war debt." He concluded, "These things must not happen."

The Truman administration did not propose to let them happen. In June 1947 Secretary of State George Marshall proffered a plan by which the American government would provide billions of dollars to the European countries for reconstruction. The money would take the form chiefly of grants toward the purchase of American products. In other words, the American government would pay American farmers, manufacturers, and shippers for goods and services to be delivered to Europe. By tying the grants to the purchase of American products, the administration would diminish somewhat their effectiveness in promoting European recovery: if the Europeans instead received carte blanche

Harry Truman (left) and George Marshall (next to Truman) confer with other administration officials regarding the reconstruction plan that bore Marshall's name. *Harry S Truman Library*

to spend the money where they chose, they could get more reconstruction bang for the American buck. But a large part of the purpose of the Marshall Plan, as the program soon came to be called, was to ensure prosperity in the United States.

Another large part was to promote the free–trading principles underlying the rest of the administration's economic program. The administration said it would leave much of the implementation of the Marshall Plan to the European governments, but it laid down some general principles that had to guide implementation. The most important of these involved measures designed to ensure the free flow of trade and capital into Europe and among the European countries themselves. American officials pressed for European integration: economic integration at first, leading perhaps to political integration.

To some degree the American insistence on steps toward economic integration—toward the removal of barriers to trade and investment—had the purpose of guaranteeing that American money not be wasted on needless red tape; but the desire for integration also reflected a belief that integration was the surest way to prevent another European war. By encouraging the Europeans to trade with each other, the United States would discourage them from fighting each other. If economic integration could lead to political integration—

toward a European federation or even something on the order of a United States of Europe—the discouragement of conflict would be all the greater.

The New Great Game: Containment and the Truman Doctrine

There was another reason for the American government's interest in European integration. By 1947 the differences between the United States and the Soviet Union regarding the postwar settlement had escalated into a serious confrontation. Stalin's refusal to allow free elections in Poland had convinced many in the West that the Soviet leader was no more to be trusted than Hitler, who likewise had refused to honor promises. The three big Western powers—the United States, Britain, and France—had been unable since the end of the European war to come to terms with the Soviet Union regarding the future of Germany. The Potsdam conference of July 1945 produced some interim agreements regarding rules of occupation and other matters but nothing in the way of a long-term settlement. The Soviets sought a harshly punitive answer to the German question, one that would ensure that Germany would not cause its neighbors problems for many years; the Western powers were more interested in resurrecting Germany as a responsible member of the international community. During the latter half of 1945, diplomats of the four governments repeatedly scuffled over the issue but reached no agreement. With the two sides at loggerheads, Germany remained divided among the four powers, each occupying a zone. The Red Army remained in control of much of Eastern Europe.

While the arguments over Germany, Poland, and other parts of Eastern Europe continued, the first major international crisis of the postwar period took place in the northern Middle East. Since the nineteenth century, the mountainous terrain of Iran and Afghanistan had been a battleground between the masters of two great Eurasian empires: the British, rulers of India, pushing into the region from the south, and the Russians, lords of the steppe country between the Black and Caspian seas, arriving from the north. The Russians hoped to find a warm water port on the Persian Gulf or the Indian Ocean, while the British attempted to keep them bottled up and largely landlocked. Britain's efforts to contain Russian expansion produced a series of bloody but inconclusive wars.

The twentieth century had brought a new competitor, Germany, to the area. And just as a shared fear of Germany had engendered an Anglo-Russian alliance in Europe, so that fear elicited Anglo-Soviet cooperation in the Middle East. During the Second World War this cooperation took the form of a joint occupation of Iran to keep the Germans away from the Persian Gulf and its oil. London's and Moscow's treatment of Iran was not entirely different from the German-Soviet division of Poland that touched off the war in Europe, but double standards are common in wartime. Besides, the two occupiers pledged that their presence in Iran was temporary and would cease within a half year after the war's end.

Yet promises elicited easily in war are often hard to enforce later. The termination of fighting produced not a quick pullout but rancorous wrangling over the terms of the withdrawal agreement. During the spring and summer of 1945, Stalin contended that the war the agreement referred to was the global war; therefore the clock calling for withdrawal from Iran would not start ticking until Japan and everyone else surrendered. The government of Iran protested that since the war against Germany was what had provided the ostensible excuse for the occupation of Iran, the war against Germany was the one that mattered. The British said they wished to honor their part of the agreement but would not pull out before the Soviets did.

The United States entered the picture as a friend of Iran and Britain and increasingly as a rival of the Soviet Union. Within the Truman administration, a group of midlevel officials who had studied Stalin's tyrannical behavior from the close range of the American embassy in Moscow during the 1930s grew convinced that the Soviet dictator was up to his old bad ways. Now that the threat from Germany had disappeared and he no longer needed the help of the West, Stalin was bent on expanding the Soviet empire. The entrenchment of the Red Army in Eastern Europe was one compelling item of evidence; the Soviet refusal to leave Iran was another. Led by George Kennan, currently stationed at the embassy in Moscow, and Loy Henderson, the head of the State Department's Middle Eastern division, the anti-Soviet faction in the Truman administration argued that the Kremlin's obstinancy regarding Iran portended an effort to detach at least the northern part of that country and add it to the Soviet sphere. When the Soviet occupation troops took the side of a secessionist movement in Iran's northern territory of Azerbaijan, and those troops failed to leave Iran even six months after the end of the Pacific war, the hard-liners' case against the Kremlin grew stronger. Henderson warned that a Soviet foothold in northern Iran might be the first step toward the oil fields of the Persian Gulf. For the Soviets to gain control of vital petroleum supplies would gravely endanger the economic health and hence the political independence of Western Europe.

From early in the twentieth century, when the great navies of the world had converted from coal to oil and automobiles and trucks had begun to displace railroads as the favored means of land transportation, oil had been one of the most sensitive issues in international affairs. The Allies of the First World War had defeated the Central powers partly because of the Allies' easier access to oil. In the words of British war secretary Lord Curzon, the Allies had "floated to victory on a sea of oil." The Second World War had been fought over oil as much as over any other single issue. Hitler's drive to the east, first against Poland and then against the Soviet Union, had as an ultimate objective the acquisition of the oil fields of the region near the Black and Caspian seas. Japan moved into Southeast Asia and the East Indies to secure a supply of oil independent of that of the United States. After the Second World War the recovery of western Europe hinged on access to oil. The Western Europeans possessed almost no oil of their own, relying instead on the oil pumped by European companies from wells in the Middle East. To lose this oil to the Soviets, or any other potentially unfriendly power, would be tantamount to falling hostage to that power. It was a thought that made the Europeans shudder; nor did it comfort the Americans, who increasingly saw the Europeans as allies against the Soviets.

To inform the Kremlin of the seriousness with which the American government viewed Soviet activities in Iran, Truman sent a stiff note of warning to Stalin in March 1946. The message fell short of the ultimatum Truman later claimed it to be, but it registered clearly Washington's displeasure at recent developments. More to the point, it indicated American support for the government of Iran against Soviet pressure.

At this stage of the sharpening Soviet-American confrontation, Moscow did not wish to make a big issue of Iran. Following some face-saving (for the Soviets) concessions by the Iranian government, which Teheran later squirmed out of, with America's blessing and support, Stalin ordered his troops to leave Iran.

The Iranian crisis intensified troubles on other issues that continued to develop between the Western countries and the Soviet Union. The two sides still discussed the German question, but the chances of agreeing on an answer appeared to diminish the longer they talked. The Kremlin's intention of dominating Eastern Europe grew more evident by the month; American officials complained about the Soviet Union's treatment of Poland and the other countries under the thumb of the Red Army, but they could not think of anything to do to change the situation short of threatening a war nobody wanted. In February 1946 Stalin delivered a speech proclaiming the fundamental incompatibility of capitalism and communism. The continued existence of the former, he declared, would make war inevitable. A few weeks later Winston Churchill, still very much in public view, gave a speech in Fulton, Missouri, in which he asserted that "from Stettin in the Baltic to Trieste in the Adriatic, an iron curtain has descended across the continent." The Kremlin's agents were hard at work around the world, Churchill said, and they constituted a growing peril to Christian civilization. Stalin read Churchill's speech and responded sharply; the Soviet leader charged that the former British prime minister's words were nothing less than "a call to war" against the Soviet Union.

This rhetorical rumbling lent credibility to the contentions of the hard-liners in the Truman administration. Also working in the hard-liners' favor was a facile identification in the minds of many Americans, and quite a few others in the West, of Stalin's style of governing with that of Hitler. As the United States fell out with the Soviet Union, there developed in America a popular theory of "Red fascism," which contended that there was little fundamental difference between Hitler and Stalin. Totalitarianism was totalitarianism, whether practiced by the fascists of the right or the communists of the left. And because totalitarian states conducted foreign relations in a characteristic manner, the United States could apply the lessons of past dealings with Hitler to current relations with Stalin. The democracies had failed to stop Hitler's aggression soon enough, for example at Munich in 1938, and thereby merely postponed the day of reckoning. Eventually Hitler grew so bold and powerful that he could be stopped only at the cost of a terrible war. American leaders determined not to repeat the mistake with Stalin. The Soviet dictator had seen how incremental aggression had succeeded in the 1930s, they said; now he was attempting to pursue his expansionist designs by like methods. To block his expansion and prevent another war, the United States and the other democracies must vigorously oppose even minor aggression. The fabric of peace was seamless; once it started to rip anywhere, its total destruction was imminent.

George Kennan did not accept the Red fascist argument in its entirety, noticing important differences between Stalin and Hitler; but Kennan did believe that America must oppose even minor aggression by the Soviet Union. In a lengthy telegram from the American embassy in Moscow to Washington in February 1946, and again in an article in the journal *Foreign Affairs* in the summer of 1947, Kennan advocated a policy of containment of the Soviet Union, by which he meant "the adroit and vigilant application of counter-force" in response to Soviet expansionist moves along the borders of Moscow's sphere. Kennan rejected the opinions of a militant few who advocated a war against the Soviet Union to push the Soviets out of Eastern Europe or even to topple the Stalinist regime in Moscow. This would be horribly costly, doubtless would trigger a third world war, and was probably unnecessary. If the United States and the other democratic countries maintained a continual guard against additional Soviet expansion, the communist despotism eventually would self-destruct.

Kennan's writings provided the catch-word—"containment"—and the rationale for a generation of American policy toward the Soviet Union. Not many Americans were eager for a fight with the Soviets, however evil communism appeared to be. On the other hand, neither did they want the Kremlin to extend its grip over the world's people. Containment offered a middle way. It did not appear too risky since if Washington clearly demonstrated America's resolve, the Soviets would shelve any expansion plans. After all, the United States possessed atomic weapons, and the Soviet Union did not. Nor did containment seem excessively expensive. To be sure, it would cost more than the narrowly nationalistic policies of the 1930s, but those policies had led to the Second World War, which had been astronomically expensive. If containment averted a third world war, it would be the bargain of the century.

A test of containment's appeal took place early in 1947. Since the end of the war, the Soviets had been pressuring the government of Turkey to allow Moscow more control over the straits leading from the Black Sea to the comparatively open waters of the Mediterranean. The Turkish straits had long been a sore spot for the Soviets since whoever held the straits could cork the Black Sea and severely impede Soviet communication with the outside world. The Soviets, feeling full of themselves after defeating the Germans, waged a campaign of political and psychological warfare against the Turks. Americans had no particular love for Turkey, which had sat out most of the war against the fascists. To the extent most Americans remembered anything about Turkey, it was that the Turks had been on the wrong side of the First World War and had been involved in the massacre of hundreds of thousands of Armenians during that period. Yet if the Truman administration was serious about containing the Soviets, Turkey was as good a place as any to start. To allow Moscow a foothold on the Turkish straits would be a strategic setback of the first order. In the event of war such a foothold would give the Soviets a running start toward the Mediterranean and such critical choke points as Gibraltar and the Suez Canal. Moreover, letting the Kremlin push the Turks around would deal a psychological blow to the West and to all countries looking to the United States for leadership. If Washington backed down in the face of Soviet pressure, then other countries would feel obliged to accommodate the Kremlin. By contrast, if Washington resisted Soviet encroachments against Turkey, then other countries would be encouraged to do so as well.

The situation next door to Turkey in Greece appeared equally dangerous. The world war had been horrendously hard on Greece, harder than on almost any other country. Almost one Greek in twelve had been killed between 1939 and 1945—a wartime death rate many times higher than that of the United States or Britain. The misery had not ended with the liberation of the country from Nazi occupation. Conservatives and radicals turned from fighting outsiders to fighting each other, producing a civil war of uncompromising ferocity. The conservatives who controlled the government received aid from Britain; the radicals, communists mostly, who challenged the government received help from communists across the border in Yugoslavia, Albania, and Bulgaria. It made sense to assume that the Soviets are also supporting the Greek communists, though firm evidence of material support was difficult to come by. (In actual fact, there was not much.) The Kremlin claimed that the uprising in Greece was an indigenous affair, but the Kremlin made similar claims about communist movements everywhere, even in circumstances that rendered these claims ludicrous. Hitler had said the same thing about agitation in Austria for *Anschluss* with Germany.

The Truman administration watched the civil war in Greece with concern until February 1947; at the end of that month, concern turned to alarm when the British government announced that financial exigencies were forcing it to cut off the support it had been supplying to the Greek government. The British said they would be cutting off support to Turkey as well. Officials in the Truman administration perceived the British withdrawal from Greece and Turkey as a major test of American determination to resist communist aggression. Turkey represented a straightforward case of external Soviet pressure on a small neighbor. In Greece the situation was somewhat more complicated in that the villains there were Greeks, even if they were communists and therefore co-ideologists of the Kremlin. But it was a fair guess that if the communists won in Greece, Moscow would gain influence in the Balkans and the Mediterranean. To prevent this and to demonstrate American resolve, the Truman administration asked Congress to approve an emergency package of $400 million in aid to Greece and Turkey. In the speech including his request and explaining the reasons for it, the president stated what quickly became known as the Truman Doctrine. "It must be the policy of the United States," Truman declared, "to support free peoples who are resisting attempted subjugation by armed minorities or by outside pressures."

The administration proceeded to launch an all-out campaign to convince senators and representatives of the necessity of the aid for Greece and Turkey. Administration officials had reason to believe that such a campaign was required, for not everyone in the United States accepted that the Soviet Union had become the moral heir to Nazi Germany. Henry Wallace, the former vice president and more recently Truman's secretary of commerce, loudly criticized the drift toward confrontation and blamed the Truman administration for bellicose policies that backed the Soviets into a corner. Walter Lippmann, perhaps the most distinguished journalist in America, likewise questioned whether a confrontational approach was the best way to handle the Soviets. Commenting on such criticism, Republican senator Arthur Vandenberg, who supported Truman's policies, warned the president that if he hoped to get Congress and the American people to go along with his plan, the administration would have to make its case clearly and starkly. It did, in testimony by administration officials before congressional committees, in speeches and in news conferences, and through the voices of friendly pundits. Again and again the administration described the situation in Greece and Turkey as a test of American resolve and leadership. The campaign succeeded smashingly; after quick debates both houses of Congress approved the measure by wide margins.

In doing so, they endorsed a position that marked a fundamental departure from previous American policies. Never before had the American government assumed such sweeping responsibility for the welfare of other countries. In certain unusual cases, such as the Spanish-American War, Washington had declared its intention to rescue foreign peoples from oppression. But those commitments had been confined to specific instances, and the targets of American interest had been immediately identifiable. The Truman Doctrine was open-ended and broad-gauged. Truman set no cutoff date for his promise of American support; for all anyone knew the president was committing the United States until the twenty-first century. Nor did he specify what he meant by "free peoples." The current context was not especially encouraging: the Greek government was hardly an exemplar of democratic ideals. It was notoriously corrupt, and its soldiers often conducted themselves in the take-no-prisoners fashion characteristic of many civil wars. About the only thing that could be said for the Greek government was that it was not communist. Interestingly, this was the one most important thing Truman did *not* say in his landmark speech. He carefully refrained from casting his doctrine in explicitly anticommunist language, though when he described two "alternative ways of life," one based on "the will of the majority," the other on "the will of a minority forcibly imposed upon the majority," he left his listeners in no doubt as to what he meant.

The open-ended nature of the Truman Doctrine bothered some American officials at the time of its formulation. They worried that the president was committing the United States to more than was necessary in the present or advisable for the future. But Truman, eager to impress Congress and the American people with the necessity for strong action, chose the kind of sweepingly principled language politicians in democracies frequently fall into. Worried about the emergency of the present, he was willing to let the future take care of itself.

Weakness at the Center: The Division of Europe

The Truman administration's 1947 decision to request aid for the governments of Greece and Turkey and Congress's approval of the request showed a willingness on the part of the United States to pick up where Britain was leaving off in the Mediterranean. It was not only in the Mediterranean that the British were leaving off during the years after the Second World War. And it was not only the British. The postwar decades were the twilight of the great European empires in Asia and Africa. Perhaps inevitably, the nationalistic spirit that had swept Europe during the nineteenth and early twentieth centuries, leading most conspicuously to the unification of Germany and Italy, and later to Irish independence from Britain and the breakup of the Austro-Hungarian empire, made its way to Asia and Africa. Vigorous nationalist movements developed in India, where the Indian National Congress agitated, for the most part peacefully, for an end to the British raj; in Kenya, where anti-British nationalism took a violent turn in the Mau Mau uprising of the 1950s; in Indochina, where nationalists such as Ho Chi Minh fought a war against the French colonialists and subsequently against the United States; and in Indonesia, where Sukarno and others demanded a termination of Dutch rule.

The nationalist movements succeeded with a swiftness few could have predicted before the Second World War. The war accelerated the trend toward decolonization in several ways. First, it exploded the myth of European invincibility. The collapse of France in the spring of 1940 gave heart to those who opposed French colonial rule in Asia and Africa and to the subjects of other European colonial powers as well. Similarly, the initial success of Japanese arms against American and British boosted the confidence of Asians and, by extension, Africans. Second, the war severely weakened the colonial powers. Britain and France had all they could do to keep body and soul together at home; they had little energy to spare for holding together fractious empires. Third, the rhetoric of the Allied war effort, especially the self-determination clause of the Atlantic Charter, echoed throughout the colonial world and generated pressure on the colonialists to live up to their fine words. Finally, partly as a result of their economic exhaustion, and partly as a result of the shift toward self-determination in world opinion, many people in the colonialist countries lost confidence in the legitimacy of their colonial mission. As nationalist agitation mounted within the colonies, voters in the colonialist countries increasingly indicated a desire to drop the thankless burden and have done with empire.

The single most important act of decolonization occurred in 1947 when Britain granted independence to India. For nearly two hundred years, India had been the richest prize in the colonial world. Possession of India and of the human and natural resources that India contained had magnified Britain's power immensely. Now India was on its own (or rather accompanied by Pakistan, sheared off from India at the moment of independence), and the stature of Britain was considerably diminished.

While the British were losing India, the Dutch were losing Indonesia, and the French were losing Indochina. The British were the best losers of the three: they left India on good terms with most Indians (and Pakistanis). The Dutch were less respected by the Indonesians, who claimed independence and forced the Netherlands to accept it. The French were the least gracious, departing Indochina only after a bitter eight-year war.

Americans viewed the demise of the European empires with ambivalence. On the one hand, independence for the colonies was in keeping with the longstanding American tradition of anti-imperialism and support for self-determination. On the other hand, the nationalists, being boat-rocking types by nature, usually included groups of distinctly radical and often avowedly communist persuasion. As the chill descended on Soviet-American relations, Americans tended to distrust those whose ideological views placed them closer to Moscow than to Washington. In addition, the enervation of Europe that the dismantling of the empires revealed portended problems in maintaining the postwar balance of power on the Continent.

Maintaining the European balance appeared to American leaders to be their foremost task in the years immediately after the war. The destruction of Germany, and that country's continued division, created a power vacuum in the center of the Continent. The Red Army had rushed into the vacuum from the east, pushing all the way to the Elbe River in the heart of Germany. The American army, along with the armies of Britain and France, held down the western part of Germany and much of the rest of the western half of the Continent as well. But the American military presence in Europe was, in the minds of most Americans, a temporary arrangement. Never before had the United States positioned large numbers of troops outside the Western Hemisphere during peacetime, and the Truman administration was not eager to break this tradition.

American officials originally looked to economic and political means to offset the Soviet presence in eastern Europe. The British credit and the Marshall Plan were intended to bolster the democracies of Western Europe by lifting them out of their postwar slump and setting them on the road to prosperity. American leaders had little doubt that the most effective antidote to communism was prosperity; Marxism-Leninism, they believed, appealed only to those under the greatest economic duress.

But economic revival was a painstaking process, and certain groups in Western Europe seemed unwilling to wait. Especially in France and Italy, lingering discouragement after the war caused many to look to the Communist parties in those countries for solutions. The Kremlin capitalized on the discontent by means of a well-coordinated program of propaganda and political action. In the autumn of 1947, the Communist parties of the Soviet Union, the Soviet-dominated Eastern European states, and France and Italy resurrected the Communist International (the Kremlin-led interwar alliance of Communist parties) under the new name "Cominform." With the encouragement of the Cominform, French Communists called for class action by French workers to bring down the French government. Violence spread through French factories and mines. Although the government managed to bring the violence under control, the experience sent shivers down spines in Paris, Washington, and other Western capitals. It was not at all inconceivable that upcoming elections in France and Italy would return Communist majorities or at least allow the Communists to broker deals that would produce government majorities.

The communist political gains in Western Europe were accompanied by other events that caused American leaders to question whether their hope of relying on economic assistance to prevent the spread of communism was unrealistic. In February 1948 members of the Communist party of Czechoslovakia staged a bloodless coup in Prague, shoving aside their competitors and thereby liquidating the last salient of democracy in Eastern Europe. Four months later the Soviet government cut off rail and road access from western Germany to Berlin. The postwar partition of Germany into four zones had been mimicked by the division of Berlin into four zones, even though the German capital was entirely surrounded by the Soviet zone. Since 1945 the Soviets had abided by agreements with the other Allies to let ground traffic through the Soviet zone to Berlin. But Moscow changed its mind early in 1948 when the Americans, British, and French took steps to merge their three German zones into a single West Germany. The Soviets, fearing the reemergence of a strong German state, protested by blockading Western access to Berlin.

Some of Truman's more bellicose advisers contended that the time had come to call the Kremlin's bluff. The president should order a column of tanks to head down the autobahn toward Berlin. If the Soviets wanted war, better to fight now while the United States still enjoyed an atomic monopoly. Although the American atomic arsenal still consisted of only a handful of bombs, this was the most tightly guarded secret in the Western world. Anyway, even a few bombs could hurt the Soviets badly.

But Truman refused to follow this advice. The president thought he could make his point—that the United States would not be forced out of Berlin—by less provocative means. Besides, he faced elections within five months, and the American people were hardly agitating for war. Truman ordered an airlift of supplies to Berlin. Should the Soviets really be determined to throw the West out of Berlin, they would have to shoot down a plane. Such an action would be somewhat less than dramatic than Pearl Harbor, but it would still galvanize American opinion behind strong countermeasures.

Berlin children await an airdrop of candy from an American transport plane (really). The plane is also bringing other supplies to the blockaded city. *Associated Press Photo*

Stalin chose not to contest the airlift. During the summer and autumn of 1948, a round-the-clock stream of planes ferried food, medicine, and other necessities of life to the stranded West Berliners. Stalin evidently hoped that winter would bring the airlift to an end, what with bad weather and the additional burden of flying heating coal to the city. But the Americans and British simply intensified the pace of the airlift, and the pilots learned to fly in some hair-raising conditions. By the spring of 1949, Moscow had to admit that the Berlin blockade had failed. West Berlin survived, if it did not exactly thrive, and the Americans, British, and French were more determined that ever to go ahead with the unification of their portions of Germany. In May 1949 the three governments announced the establishment of the Federal Republic of Germany, commonly called West Germany. The Soviets lifted the blockade of Berlin and a short while later declared the founding of the German Democratic Republic (East Germany).

The war scare over Berlin, coming after the communist coup in Czechoslovakia, convinced the Truman administration that it had to be ready to fight to preserve the postwar balance in Europe. Taking its cue from the by-now-conventional wisdom regarding the Second World War—that if the democracies had demonstrated their determination to resist Nazi aggression and had done so early, they might have averted the war—Washington sought to prevent a third world war by preparing to fight it. Before both world wars, the United

States had given aggressors reason to think the Americans would sit the conflicts out; in the spring of 1949, the American government proclaimed in the most unmistakable language its intention to be involved in a third world war from the start. The Truman administration sponsored the creation of the North Atlantic alliance, which comprised the United States and Canada, from the North Atlantic's western shore, and Britain, France, Norway, Denmark, Belgium, the Netherlands, Luxembourg, Portugal, and Italy from the eastern side, as well as Iceland from midocean. (If Italy seemed a stretch for a North Atlantic pact, the alliance had to stretch even farther in 1952 to accommodate Greece and Turkey. West Germany joined in 1955.) By the terms of the North Atlantic Treaty, all members would come to the aid of each other in the event of outside attack. Although the treaty did not mention Stalin by name, the message was unmistakable: if he ordered the Red Army to attack Western Europe, he would face the armed might of the United States.

The North Atlantic Treaty elicited considerable soul-searching in America. Never in the previous century and a half had the United States committed itself so directly to the defense of foreign countries. The Atlantic treaty represented precisely the kind of entangling alliance George Washington and Thomas Jefferson had warned about. Critics, led by Republican senator Robert Taft, reiterated Washington's and Jefferson's warnings. "By executing a treaty of this kind," Taft said, "we put ourselves at the mercy of the foreign policies of eleven other nations." For now those policies and American policy ran parallel; but who knew how long the parallelism would persist? Taft and other critics added that the administration's logic in justifying the treaty would inevitably lead to America's undertaking to arm the Europeans. The administration might label this treaty, and subsequent arms aid, as defensive, but the Soviets would not perceive it so. They would consider it offensive and might attack rather than wait for the West to get stronger.

After Munich and Pearl Harbor, after the Iranian crisis of 1946, after the Czech coup and the Berlin blockade, critics of active American involvement overseas were fighting a losing battle. The Senate approved the North Atlantic treaty by an overwhelming margin. Having suffered the consequences of irresolution before the last war, the senators and most of the American people did not want to be caught again.

America's decision to make the defense of Western Europe its own basically completed the postwar settlement in Europe, though widespread recognition of this fact required a few more years and a couple of additional developments—in particular, the admission of West Germany to the Atlantic alliance and the consequent formation of the Soviet-sponsored Warsaw Pact. As had been the case since the German surrender in May 1945, the western half of the continent lay in an American sphere of influence; the eastern half lay in a Soviet sphere. This arrangement left lots of people dissatisfied. Many Germans longed to put their torn country back together, while most of the inhabitants of Eastern Europe wanted out from under the Soviet thumb. But the arrangement had the merits of stability and, as it turned out, relative permanence.

Both merits derived from three facts. First, there was almost no confusion regarding where the boundary between the two spheres ran or regarding who controlled what. East was east, and West was west, and ne'er did the twain meet. Second, each side considered the boundary worth defending, evidently even at the risk of general war. This was the message of the Atlantic alliance and of the Soviet touchiness regarding Germany, and it deterred both sides from trying to change the boundary. Third, the two sphere holders were very much more powerful than the countries within the spheres. Consequently, Washington and Moscow could largely determine what happened inside the spheres. If the Germans, Poles, Czechs, or even the French did not like the arrangement, there was not a great deal they could do about it. To be sure, Washington allowed greater leeway for differences of opinion within the American sphere than Moscow did in the Soviet zone; even so the nuclear umbrella America held over Western Europe's head served to keep the allies huddled fairly close to the umbrella holder.

The two spheres established during the late 1940s persisted for quite a while, as persistence is measured in the modern world. For forty years not much happened to change the fundamental balance of power in Europe. Berlin remained a touchy issue into the 1960s, provoking additional posturing from both sides. A certain loosening occurred in the West as the Europeans gained strength relative to the United States. On a couple of occasions, Moscow took military action to prevent similar loosening in its own sphere from getting out of control. Yet the essential structure of European affairs that developed shortly after the Second World War remained intact until the end of the 1980s. During that time Europe enjoyed a longer peace than it had known since the middle of the nineteenth century. European politics grew almost dull. The real excitement shifted elsewhere.

The Second Front in the Anticapitalist War: The Chinese Revolution (Part II)

Events in Europe formed the backdrop to the creation of the North Atlantic alliance, but thunder offstage was equally responsible for causing Americans to violate the admonitions of the founders of their republic against peacetime alliances. During the months prior to the signing of the Atlantic pact, the Chinese Communist forces led by Mao Zedong scored a string of stunning successes in their struggle against Chiang Kaishek's Nationalist troops. The truce between the Communists and the Nationalists during what the Chinese called the Anti-Japanese War had been uneasy at best: even as they fought the Japanese, the two sides maneuvered to place themselves in the most advantageous position for the time when the Japanese lost the war, as both sides, once the Americans entered, knew they surely would.

The Nationalists' strategy was to fight the Japanese where unavoidable but to concentrate on cultivating the Americans and conserving resources for the

Mao Zedong and driver lead Zhou Enlai and driver during the final approach to Beijing in 1949. The jeeps are of American origin, captured (or perhaps purchased) from the Nationalists. *AP/Wide World Photos*

postwar showdown with the Communists. Cultivating the Americans was not always an easy task since many of the American officers sent to assist the Nationalists thought they should be fighting the Japanese more energetically than they were. General Joseph Stilwell ("Vinegar Joe," for his acerbic personality) personally despised Chiang, whom he habitually called "the Peanut" on account of his lack of hair and of what Stilwell considered good sense. Relations got somewhat better after Franklin Roosevelt replaced Stilwell with the easier-going General Albert Wedemeyer. The Nationalists' performance against the Japanese did not improve significantly, but Washington reduced its expectations of their war-fighting capacity.

Many American officials had greater respect for the Communists than for the Nationalists, not least since Mao's cadres were less corrupt and more inclined to fight against the Japanese. In part the Communists' strategy of active resistance to the Japanese was motivated by genuine patriotism; in part it was designed to win the loyalty of the Chinese peasants, who composed the vast majority of China's population, and to gain territory in preparation for the day when the Anti-Japanese War ended and the Chinese civil war resumed. The Communists' strategy did not come close to ejecting the Japanese, but it did enlarge the Communists' base of operations and enhance their credibility in the eyes of the Chinese people.

Mao and his followers capitalized on their credibility after the Japanese defeat. Although the American government tried to prevent a break between the

Nationalists and the Communists at the world war's end, neither Chiang nor Mao was willing to make the necessary compromises. Truman sent George Marshall to China in late 1945 to attempt a compromise; Marshall stayed until January 1947. He made some temporary progress but nothing that lasted. As often as the two parties agreed to stop shooting at each other, they changed their minds. The Communists had been spoiling to settle scores with the Nationalists since the late 1920s, when Chiang had suddenly renounced his then-existing alliance with the Communists and massacred several thousand of them. Now that the field was swept clean of distracting elements, the Communists intended to do the Nationalists in. The Nationalists had the same intention toward the Communists. Chiang enjoyed the continued support of the United States government; though many officials of the Truman administration still harbored doubts about the efficiency, not to say honesty, of Chiang's regime, the mere fact of his opposition to communism, in the context of the deepening competition between the United States and the Soviet Union, qualified him for American support.

The Soviet position in the Chinese civil war was more complicated. Stalin had never trusted Mao, who gained control of the Chinese Communist party during the 1930s over the opposition of Moscow's protégés in the party. Stalin recognized in Mao a potential competitor for leadership of the world communist movement. In the early aftermath of the war, the Kremlin offered its support to Chiang's Nationalist government in exchange for concessions in Manchuria and Outer Mongolia. But Stalin hedged his bets by facilitating the movements of Communist forces in Manchuria at the expense of the Nationalists. On the whole Stalin probably would have been happiest seeing China remain in turmoil, the better for the Soviet Union to secure its Far Eastern frontier. As Chiang's position deteriorated, Moscow retreated from its support for the Nationalists without providing conspicuous assistance to the Chinese Communists. If the latter were going to win the Chinese civil war, they would have to do so through their own efforts.

They did. Or, perhaps more descriptively, the Nationalists lost it. While Chiang himself was brave enough, many of his officers were not willing to risk their lives or their fortunes against the Communists. They preferred to bargain with the enemy, sometimes to the point of selling American-supplied weapons to the Communists. By their corruption and overall incompetence, they managed to alienate ordinary Chinese by the tens of millions and to undermine the morale of their rank and file. The Nationalists' morale slumped further with each Communist battlefield victory.

The Nationalists' declining fortunes prompted the Truman administration to put some distance between itself and Chiang's government. At a time when the president was pushing for the largest foreign aid package in American history—the Marshall Plan for Europe—he was not eager to ask for large amounts for other projects, especially one of such questionable merit and staying power. It was not easy for Truman to cut back on aid to Chiang, who had powerful friends in influential places, including Henry Luce, the founder and publisher of *Time, Life,* and *Fortune* magazines. The China lobby pressed hard for continued support of the Nationalist regime. It succeeded in squeezing a modest amount of aid out of the administration and Congress, but increasingly the administration took the position that aid to Chiang was, in the words of administration ally Senator Tom Connally, "money down a rat hole."

The Communist victories grew more frequent during 1948 as the Communists moved south from their stronghold in the northern countryside and captured city after city. The disintegration of the Nationalist position in northern China encouraged Chiang to sue for peace, which he did at the beginning of 1949. But the Communists had the taste of victory on their lips, and they refused any terms short of complete surrender. So abject had the Nationalists' situation become that the government's negotiators defected to the Communists. By the summer of 1949, the Nationalist retreat had turned into a rout. Chiang and the rest of the top leadership fled the Chinese mainland to Taiwan, protected by one hundred miles of ocean. The Communists completed their conquest of the mainland, and in October 1949 Mao proclaimed the establishment of the People's Republic of China, with its capital at Beijing. From Taipei on Taiwan, the Nationalists persisted in claiming that they represented the sole legitimate government of the Republic of China.

The communist victory in the Chinese civil war was the second great victory for the world communist movement. After the Bolsheviks seized power in Russia in 1917, the followers of Marx had suffered through a long dry spell, though because they believed in the inevitability of communism's triumph over capitalism, devout communists could accept this barren stretch with a certain equanimity. For a decade beginning about 1935, merely holding the communist line against fascism had required all the energy the partisans of world revolution could muster. But the victory over fascism—which, the communists could credibly claim, had been more their doing than that of the capitalists, including the late-arriving Americans—had reinvigorated communism. In China the Communist party trounced its rival of a generation and seized control of the government. In Indochina Ho Chi Minh's communist forces were gaining ground against the French. In Korea the communist regime of Kim Il Sung ruled half that country. In Eastern Europe communist governments were becoming firmly entrenched; if their entrenching owed largely to the support of the Red Army, that could be explained simply as a mark of socialist solidarity.

The great significance of the communist victory in China was precisely that it had *not* arrived on the treads of Soviet tanks. Mao's triumph was a triumph for national communism, in particular the Chinese variety of communism. Mao knew this, as did Stalin, which was why the Soviet leader so distrusted Mao. Nor did it help Sino-Soviet relations that the Chinese Communist victory added a third element to the theory of communist revolutions. Marxism signified the class struggle approach to history, with its doctrine of the inevitability of the triumph of socialism; Leninism added the idea that the Communist party, as the "vanguard of the proletariat," could make a revolution in the name of the proletariat without being itself of the proletariat. Maoism took Marxism-Leninism a step further. Mao was a dedicated Marxist-Leninist in the sense that he believed socialist revolution to be the answer to China's worst ills and the Communist party to be the driving force of the revolution. Yet he recognized with dismay that China had hardly emerged from feudalism. Mao could see that he would be long dead before China even advanced to the stage where a Leninist revolution was possible. So Mao decided to build his revolution on the peasantry, a class Marx had despised as retrograde and irredeemable and Lenin had largely ignored. Mao devised an entire theory of guerrilla warfare based on mobilizing the peasantry. He described communist guerrillas as fish that swam in the sea of the peasantry. Mao's approach, as vindicated by the success of the Chinese revolution, nearly threw orthodox Marxism out the window. The industrial proletariat, the heroes of Marxism, played a distinctly subordinate role in Maoism. The peasantry, the last group Marx had looked to for revolution making, assumed the lead.

Maoism opened the door to a new wave of revolutions in the nonindustrialized countries of Asia and Africa. Traditional Marxism had had little to say to impatient advocates of change in the colonial world. They would simply have to wait for the slow transformations that would bring the development, and eventual overdevelopment, of capitalist industrialism in their countries. Leninism offered a bit more hope, with its demonstration that the entire proletariat did not have to be ready for revolution and that a determined minority of radicals might press history's fast-forward button. But only Maoism provided both the theoretical basis for a peasant-led revolution—Mao's "Red Book" and other writings became best sellers among anticolonial agitators around the world—and the practical example of how such a revolution could succeed.

Compared to China's cutting-edge experience, the stodgy Stalinism of the Kremlin often appeared decrepit and irrelevant. Stalin's chief contributions to the Marxist tradition were the idea of socialism in one country, which was to say an abandonment of world revolution in favor of strengthening the Soviet Union, and the perfection of the system of state terror. Neither of these contributions much enhanced the international appeal of the Soviet model of communism. The Soviet Union retained the advantage over China of being a great power; this conferred a certain prestige on the Soviet Union's allies as well as more concrete kinds of economic, political, and military aid. Communists in East Germany, Poland, Hungary, and the other Eastern European countries did not have to worry about their popularity as long as they had the Kremlin's blessing and therefore the backing of the Kremlin's troops.

Yet no self-respecting nationalist in Asia or Africa wanted to govern merely on the sufferance of Moscow. The nationalists did not intend to throw out one set of foreign masters, the colonialists, only to install another, the commissars. Most anticolonial revolutionaries were happy enough to accept Soviet aid when available; but nearly all insisted on retaining their freedom of action. The communist victory in China helped them do so in two ways. First, the Maoist example showed how to construct a revolution with the materials at hand, namely, the peasantry. Second, it provided an alternative source of economic and political support. China remained a poor country after the revolution; its resources were meager compared to those of the Soviet Union. Yet it was still a large country, the most populous in the world, and if its leaders placed a priority on promoting revolution in other countries, which they did, they could scrape together sufficient weapons and other supplies to have an impact abroad. Radical revolutionaries now enjoyed the luxury of being able to play one communist power against the other: the Soviet Union against China.

The communist victory in China seriously frightened many Americans; the fact that it injected new life into world communism was a primary reason why. Americans' original fears of communism in the immediate aftermath of the Bolshevik revolution had subsided during the 1920s and 1930s, as the communists failed to make headway elsewhere. But by successfully planting the red flag of revolution in Beijing's Tiananmen Square, and by declaring their dedication to the destruction of capitalism, Mao and the other Chinese Communists provoked a new wave of anxieties in America. Communists had always preached the inevitability of their revolution, but for the last twenty years it had been easy to laugh at their pretensions. After the communist conquest of China, which occurred despite many years and billions of dollars of American assistance to Chiang's government, the laughing came considerably harder.

The communist takeover of China had additional significance for Americans on account of America's long-standing paternal attitude toward China. Since American missionaries had arrived in China in the nineteenth century, Americans had often considered themselves guardians of the best interests of the Chinese people. This feeling had grown with the formulation of Washington's Open Door policy at the end of the 1890s. It continued to grow with America's resistance to Japan's Twenty-one Demands on China, and it grew still more as the United States aided China during the Second World War. As a result, many Americans took the communist victory in China as a slap in the face. Although there were plenty of Chinese who did not applaud the communist seizure of power—the 2 million Nationalists and family members who fled to Taiwan being the most visible—no one could reasonably deny Mao's tremendous popularity. This popularity, combined with the virulent anti-Americanism of the Chinese communist revolution, seemed a rejection of everything the United States stood for, not to mention the most galling ingratitude for everything America had tried to do for China.

Injured feelings aside, the United States government could not help looking on the emergence of a communist government in China as a strategic setback of the first order. There was considerable debate within the American government regarding the extent to which China should be considered a satellite of the Soviet Union. In the immediate aftermath of Mao's coming to power, the Chinese and the Soviets succeeded fairly well in glossing over their differences. Mao visited Moscow and returned with a treaty of alliance and promises of economic and military aid. Some historically minded analysts in the American State Department and elsewhere pointed out that the Chinese and the Russians had been rivals for centuries and that the Chinese looked down on the Russians as being even more barbaric than most of the other foreign devils. It was conceivable that China's leaders might accept Soviet advice, but they would never accept Soviet dictation.

This debate in America over the staying power of the Sino-Soviet alliance got swallowed up in another debate, one regarding responsibility for the communist victory in China. The American proprietary interest toward China had fostered an exaggerated notion of American influence there. After the Second World War, this notion dovetailed with a broader American feeling about the world that sometimes bordered on an illusion of omnipotence. America alone possessed nuclear weapons; the United States boasted by far the strongest economy in the world; Washington was organizing what by this time was regularly being called the Free World into a mighty alliance against aggression. Feeling as powerful as they did, many Americans found it hard to believe that their side in China had been beaten in a fair fight. Millions preferred to accept the explanation forwarded by archconservative critics of the Truman administration: that responsibility for the communist victory in China rested with communists and communist sympathizers within the American government.

Although charges of communists in government had been a hot political topic at least since 1947 when Truman ordered loyalty probes of government officials, the issue became an American obsession only after the communist victory in China. Senator Joseph McCarthy and others made it the centerpiece of a campaign that converted the obscure Wisconsin lawmaker into a national scourge capable of causing the highest officials in the country to tremble. "Who lost China?" rang through Congress, through the press, and across the land. Republicans used the question to hammer Democrats and particularly to batter the Truman administration. Against most expectations, Truman had won reelection in 1948 after the Republican challenger Thomas Dewey had diplomatically and overconfidently declined to attack the president's handling of foreign affairs. The Republicans subsequently determined not to repeat Dewey's mistake. On the contrary, they launched a scorched-earth assault on the administration's foreign policy. For a brief moment the administration had flirted with the idea of recognizing the new government of China, perhaps after passions cooled somewhat. The McCarthyites, however, ensured that passions would not cool for decades. The very suggestion that the United States should recognize Beijing became political suicide.

The anticommunist brigade had another issue that was almost as potent as the communist triumph in China. In September 1949 American monitors detected radioactive fallout in the atmosphere. The timing of the discovery and the nature of the fallout made it highly unlikely that American atom bomb tests were the source. The Truman administration could only infer that the Soviets had discovered how to build their own atomic bomb; the Kremlin soon confirmed the inference.

The knowledge that the Soviets now possessed atomic weapons sobered even the most nonchalant in the West. Until this point Americans and their allies had rested secure in the confidence that comes from having an unanswerable, war-winning weapon. The Soviets had many more soldiers under arms than the United States since the American army had demobilized faster and more

Joseph McCarthy produces a document that, he claims, corroborates his allegations of communist subversion in the American government. *Associated Press Photo*

thoroughly than the Red Army, which in any case had been larger to begin with. But the American technological advantage, especially America's lock on atomic weapons, compensated for the Soviets' numerical advantage. It did, that is, until the Kremlin got a bomb of its own. Now the Americans would have to be considerably more careful. They could not brandish atomic weapons against the Soviet Union without having the Soviets brandish them back.

Just as many Americans found it hard to believe that communism could have captured China without the assistance of subversives in the American State Department and elsewhere in the American government, so many Americans found it hard to believe that the Soviets could have succeeded in building an atomic bomb without the help of subversives in the American atomic energy community. Some optimistic and poorly informed spokespersons for the American government had predicted that the Soviets, unassisted, would need a generation to replicate the feat of building an atom bomb. Such persons, and the much larger number of Americans who believed them, took the early Soviet acquisition of the bomb to mean that the Soviets had stolen America's atomic secrets.

There was enough corroborating evidence to make the charge of an atomic sellout plausible. A few genuine spies actually did turn up. The most infamous of the atomic spies was Klaus Fuchs, though he was not an American. Fuchs had been born in Germany but had fled the Nazis during the 1930s, choosing

Britain as his safe haven. The Second World War brought him to the United States to work on the Manhattan Project; while on this job and later back in England, he passed technical secrets to the Soviet Union. Fuchs was an admitted Communist and may have convinced himself that he was doing the world a good turn by helping prevent an American (or Anglo-American) atomic monopoly. Besides, when his spying started, the Soviets, Americans, and British were allies. Following the discovery of Fuchs's espionage and his arrest in 1950, Fuchs was convicted and sentenced to a long term in an English prison. After his release he returned to (East) Germany, where his devotion to the communist cause and his expertise were rewarded with an appointment as director of the East German Institute for Nuclear Physics.

The Fuchs affair caused a scandal in the United States—"Tie on your hat," President Truman said when an aide brought him the news of Fuchs's confession—but not such an uproar as two other cases. The first involved Alger Hiss, a long-time American diplomat charged with spying for the Soviets. Actually, Hiss was charged only politically, not legally, with spying since the statute of limitations had run out on his alleged crime. So rather than being tried for espionage, he was tried for perjury in denying the crime under oath. The McCarthyites and others used the guilty verdict in the perjury trial as proof of the accuracy of their assertion that the communists had penetrated the very citadel of American foreign policy.

The case of Julius and Ethel Rosenberg was closer to the Fuchs case than to the Hiss case. Like Fuchs, the Rosenbergs were alleged to have passed atomic secrets to the Soviets, secrets that helped the Soviets close the atomic gap between themselves and the Americans. Many observers in America and elsewhere believed that the Rosenbergs, or at least Ethel, had been framed by an American Justice Department anxious to demonstrate its capacity to ferret out spies. The Rosenberg case provoked a particular stir when the prosecutor asked for and received a death sentence for the two. Serious questions surrounded the conduct of the trial, and for decades afterward the debate continued to rage among contemporaries and their children regarding the Rosenbergs' guilt and the appropriateness of their punishment.

Drawing the Line in East Asia

The anxiety in the United States produced by the Soviet atomic bomb, the communist victory in China, the spy scares, and the charges of communists in government predisposed the American government to respond decisively, not to say precipitately, to a new threat that suddenly arose in June 1950. Since the beginning of the twentieth century, the central objective of American policy in East Asia had been to prevent any single power or group of powers from dominating the region to the exclusion of the United States. At first Washington had worried about the European imperialists carving up China. Subsequently, American leaders had fretted about the growing ambitions of Japan.

It was to frustrate Japanese ambitions that the administration of Franklin Roosevelt had taken the steps that provoked Tokyo to attack at Pearl Harbor. After 1949 the Chinese-Soviet alliance threatened to dominate East Asia.

One school of American strategic thought contended that the United States should not worry too much about what happened on the East Asian mainland. The Japanese had discovered in China during the late 1930s how the mainland could swallow entire armies. American armies would suffer a similar fate against the uncounted millions of Asians, these strategists said; better for the United States to concentrate on securing its interests along the chain of offshore islands that girded the Asian coast, from the Aleutians in the north, through the Japanese home islands, the Ryukyus, Taiwan, and the Philippines (these last independent since 1946 but still closely associated with America), and on to Australia and New Zealand. The island strategy would play to America's strengths in naval and air power and would avoid wars of attrition America could only lose. The Truman administration found this argument persuasive. In January 1950 Secretary of State Dean Acheson delivered a well-publicized address (it could not help being well publicized since it was delivered to a national gathering of newspaper editors) in which he outlined American strategic policy in offshore island terms.

Yet even those officials who considered the Asian mainland strategically nonvital to the United States acknowledged that it possessed some importance, particularly in its relationship to Japan. After bombing most of urban Japan to ruins, the United States had assumed the postwar task of rehabilitating that country. In contrast to Germany, where American troops shared the postwar occupation with the British, French, and Soviets, Americans had the occupation of Japan essentially to themselves. The Kremlin grumbled a bit about not receiving a role in the occupation, but considering that the Soviet war declaration against Japan had come just days before the Japanese surrender, Moscow had a weak case and knew it. When the Truman administration insisted that the occupation of Japan be an American show, the Soviets did not press the issue.

Rarely, perhaps never, in history has an American national wielded such unchecked power as the commander of the American occupation force wielded in Japan. Rarely has an American been so well suited, in his own mind anyway, to the exercise of such power. Douglas MacArthur had spent half his life in Asia, much of it in the Philippines, and he had grown accustomed to the deference with which he was commonly treated. As commander of the American occupation in Japan, MacArthur became almost a surrogate emperor.

MacArthur and the Americans in Japan faced the problem that confronts nearly every occupying power: how to rule a foreign and unfamiliar country without having to do everything themselves. MacArthur solved it the same way the Western allies solved the problem of governing their portion of Germany: by punishing a few leaders of the defeated state and bringing most of the rest back into government under new management. In any country, even the most technologically advanced and best educated, there is a limited pool of individuals qualified to administer the affairs of the government and the economy. To bar very many of these individuals from holding positions of authority hamstrings a new government.

For a brief moment a desire to crush Japan and prevent it from ever rising again motivated American policy under the postwar occupation; but the moment passed for two reasons. First, the experience with Germany after the First World War had demonstrated the difficulty and danger of trying to keep a naturally energetic and capable people down. No matter how righteously angry the people of the occupying power may be, they eventually tire of policing the occupied country; in the meantime they create a reservoir of resentment ready to be tapped by an opportunistic demagogue like Hitler. The Americans decided not to make that mistake with Japan. Second, not long after the American troops arrived in Japan, the fortunes of the Nationalists in China began to slip. Washington had hoped to elevate China to the position of preeminence in Asia to fill the vacuum left by the defeat of Japan. But with China evidently going communist, this idea went out the window. Instead of China reinforced to watch over Japan, the Truman administration shifted to a policy of reinforcing Japan to watch over China.

The reinforced Japan, however, would look decidedly different from the Japan of the pre-1945 era. For one thing, it would be an essentially demilitarized society. To a large extent the Japanese accomplished the demilitarization of their society by themselves before the American occupation forces arrived; they did so by the simple but effective expedient of losing the war in demoralizing fashion. For two decades the military had promised the Japanese people prosperity and glory. But after some temporary successes, the military delivered only destruction, dishonor, and death—though many of the military leaders tried to avoid dishonor by committing ritual suicide, or hara-kiri. The Americans under MacArthur did not have to try very hard to persuade the Japanese to renounce military ambitions, and the Japanese accepted without conspicuous complaint an antimilitary clause in the 1947 constitution the Americans helped them write.

MacArthur initially sought to reorder Japanese society in another way as well. He began to break up the great industrial combines—the zaibatsu—that had dominated Japan's economy before the war. Much like the big trusts in America during the 1890s, the zaibatsu and the families who controlled them were in many respects a law unto themselves. In the thinking of MacArthur and the Americans, the zaibatsu had to be dismantled so that Japanese democracy could take root and grow. To this end the occupation government froze the assets of the zaibatsu, required members of several of the most powerful families to resign their positions with the conglomerates, forced the sale of many zaibatsu assets to smaller firms and individuals, and directed the passage of antitrust laws designed to prevent the kinds of monopolistic practices that had given the zaibatsu their overwhelming strength.

But as the emphasis in American policy shifted from controlling Japan to containing China and the Soviet Union, the occupation government backed away from its anti-zaibatsu program. Containing China called for a robust Japan, and whatever else the zaibatsu had done, they had helped make the

Japanese economy robust. The people who had run the zaibatsu possessed proven skills and expertise. If zaibatsu practices did not always accord with American preferences, they seemed to suit the Japanese well enough.

Another factor encouraged the American retreat from the original emphasis on economic restructuring. In 1946 an anti-Democratic backlash in the United States had delivered control of Congress to the Republicans. The party of Coolidge and Hoover had long detested the governmental activism of the New Deal but had been unable to block or undo it. Now the Republicans thought they saw their chance. They were wrong, as events proved; too many Americans had grown too fond of such New Deal reforms as social security and farm subsidies to let them go. Yet the Republicans did succeed in putting a damper on the drive for additional government intervention in the economy. They stymied Harry Truman's proposed Fair Deal and otherwise threw a more conservative cast over American politics than had obtained for a decade and a half. The conservative shift in America encouraged a retreat from the campaign against the zaibatsu in Japan. American officials of the Japanese occupation got the message to go lightly on Japanese business; at a time when the careers of many diplomats were being imperiled by charges of leftist tendencies, the occupation officials took the message to heart.

The successes of Mao Zedong and his Communist colleagues in China only strengthened the conservative shift in American policy toward Japan. With China evidently being added to the Soviet sphere, or the communist sphere at any rate, American leaders determined that if a choice had to be made between liberalizing Japanese society and strengthening Japan against communism, the latter had to take precedence. Above all, Japan must be kept on the American side of the superpower struggle. The war against Japan had been bloody enough, even with the United States enjoying the help of China and the benevolent neutrality and belated assistance of the Soviet Union. The thought of fighting a third world war against an alliance that included Japan, China, and the Soviet Union boggled American minds. And even if Japan did not take an active part in a major war, the loss of American air and naval bases there would gravely damage the American position in the western Pacific. The United States' only hope for victory in a war against China would be an air campaign against China's cities since a ground war against 600 million Chinese was out of the question. The loss of airfields in Japan would significantly diminish America's capacity for hitting Chinese targets.

The best way to keep Japan out of the communists' clutches, American leaders believed, was to restore the country to prosperity. As in Europe, radicalism in Japan appeared to be in direct proportion to economic distress. In the process of Americanizing Japan right after the war, and of countering the power of the zaibatsu, the occupation government had encouraged the growth of labor unions. But before long the unions became a breeding ground for leftist politics, and when labor leaders threatened a general strike in 1947, MacArthur cracked down. During the rest of the occupation, labor remained firmly under control. Yet the brief period of turbulence demonstrated that Japan, like western Europe, contained the seeds of radicalism. As in the case of western

Europe, the Truman administration adopted the view that preventing the seeds from sprouting called for cultivating conditions that would promote Japanese prosperity.

Chief among these conditions was access to the resources and markets of Asia. Interestingly, and unpresciently, few Americans at this time saw the United States as a major market for Japanese exports; consequently American leaders looked to Asia as a necessary outlet for Japanese economic energies. American officials came to appreciate what the Japanese had been saying all along: that Japan needed access to Asia's resources and markets if it was to thrive. Although the United States had gone to war in 1941 to prevent Japan from forcibly acquiring the economic sphere Tokyo desired, American leaders after the war found themselves promoting something ironically similar to the Greater East Asia Co-Prosperity Sphere—absent, however, the brutality the Japanese had employed to create it.

The American desire to guarantee Japan's access to Asia, combined with the Truman administration's insistence on showing American resolve against communist aggression, caused Washington to react sharply when North Korea suddenly attacked South Korea in June 1950. Although the attack itself came as a surprise, the tension that spawned it had been building since the end of the Second World War. At that time the Soviet Union and the United States had arranged a de facto division of Korea. The purpose of the presumably temporary division of Korea was to facilitate the surrender of Japanese troops in that country. The Soviets would deal with the Japanese forces in Korea's north, above the thirty-eighth parallel of latitude; Americans would accept the surrender of the Japanese in the southern part of the peninsula. The future of Korea, which had been under Japanese control for a half century, would be determined in a postwar peace conference of the great powers.

But the postwar peace conference never happened, on account of the falling out among the Allies. As in the case of Germany, the partition of Korea persisted, acquiring an initially unintended air of permanence. Again as in Germany, the Soviets helped install a regime to their liking in their zone, while Americans did analogously in the zone of American occupation. But neither the Soviet-backed government in northern Korea, headed by the communist Kim Il Sung, nor the American-supported government in southern Korea, under long-time nationalist Syngman Rhee, desired to rule only half a peninsula. Both Kim and Rhee claimed the right to lead all of Korea, and both made bellicose noises about vindicating their claims.

Kim moved first to put his claims into effect. On June 25, 1950, North Korean units stormed across the thirty-eighth parallel. Within days they captured the South Korean capital, Seoul, and put Rhee's government to flight. Their momentum threatened to carry them clear to the end of the peninsula and make Kim the undisputed ruler of Korea.

The Truman administration interpreted the North Korean invasion of South Korea as a threat to the peace of the world and the future of democracy—"an open, clear, direct challenge," in the words of Dean Acheson. The American president and his advisers waved aside complaints that Rhee's government fell short of democratic perfection; it did not really matter, they said, that the South Korean president was an autocrat. The issue was not Rhee, but Kim. The North Koreans had attacked South Korea, and regardless of Rhee's merits or demerits, the peace-loving peoples of the world must rally to South Korea's defense. The Truman administration similarly overruled objections that the conflict in Korea was a civil war. To be sure, the administration conceded, Koreans were fighting Koreans; but Kim could never have launched his attack without the connivance of the Kremlin. The Soviets and the Chinese were watching America very carefully to see how Washington would react. So were America's Atlantic allies. The Atlantic alliance, as everyone knew, was only as strong as America's word. Did the Americans really intend to honor their pledge to protect Europe against attack? South Korea was not a formal American ally, but its plight seemed to the Truman administration to be a test of American moral courage. Korea in 1950 looked a lot like the Sudetenland in 1938. If the United States sat on its hands, the communists would be emboldened and America's allies disheartened. Moscow might squeeze Berlin again, and the western Europeans might feel obliged to accommodate the Kremlin. Beijing might attack Taiwan. But a staunch American response in Korea would have just the opposite effect. It would give pause to the communists and courage to the allies. And it might well prevent a much larger war.

The Truman administration moved swiftly and vigorously against the North Korean attack. Within hours of the first wave of the invasion, Truman ordered American air and naval units to the area of the fighting. A short while later he dispatched American ground troops from Japan to South Korea. To underline his determination to thwart communist aggression in Asia, Truman directed American naval vessels to patrol the Taiwan Strait and prevent the Chinese from attacking Chiang's final redoubt. The administration also wanted to keep Chiang from attacking the mainland, perhaps to provoke a Sino-American war that would allow his return to the mainland, but it did not publicize this part of its reasoning. In addition, Truman ordered American supplies to be sent to French forces fighting the communist guerrillas in Indochina.

On the diplomatic front, the administration worked the channels at the United Nations. Until now the international organization had been a disappointment to many Americans and others who hoped that it would become an effective version of the League of Nations. The United Nations had run into the same problem that afflicted the League of Nations—and has crippled every attempt to create something approaching an international government. The essence of government is the demonstrable capacity to compel compliance with government decisions. For a government to compel compliance, it must have greater authority and power than the groups or individuals it comprises. Most national governments do, most of the time. When they do not, a revolution or coup usually rectifies the situation.

But the United Nations, like the League of Nations before it, lacked this essential capacity to compel compliance. The biggest member states were stronger than the United Nations and could resist the authority of the international body. The fact that the parts were stronger than the whole was the direct result of the refusal by the great powers, especially the United States and the Soviet Union, to relinquish any substantial sovereignty to the world organization. As a result of the Yalta compromise, fleshed out in subsequent conferences, the United Nations came to consist of two separate bodies, the General Assembly and the Security Council. All members belonged to the General Assembly, where each had a single vote. Some diplomatic horse trading granted Moscow two additional votes, in the names of the Soviet republics of Byelorussia and Ukraine, as recompense for Washington's expected ability to dictate the voting patterns of most of the Latin American republics. But the votes in the General Assembly did not bind anyone to anything important. For the most part, the General Assembly served as a forum for airing grievances, especially those of the lesser powers. The serious business of the United Nations took place in the Security Council. The five permanent members of the Security Council—the United States, the Soviet Union, Britain, France, and China—each possessed a veto. The United States, no less than the Soviet Union, had insisted on this veto as a means of safeguarding American interests against foreign meddling; the echoes of George Washington's warnings had not entirely faded away. The consequence of the veto arrangement was that any of the great powers could block substantive action by the United Nations.

If the United States and the Soviet Union had not switched from collaboration to confrontation almost as soon as the Second World War ended, the veto system might not have blocked action by the United Nations. As it was, the organization compiled a modest record of accomplishment over the following decades. In 1947–1948 it authorized the creation of Israel out of the British mandate in Palestine, and it subsequently assisted in the decolonization of various other territories. It sent cease-fire–monitoring forces to several regions of conflict, and its specialized agencies coordinated educational, public health, and technical assistance operations. But because of the competition between the United States and the Soviet Union, the United Nations for forty years failed almost entirely to fulfill the hopes of its many early supporters that it would serve as a powerful instrument of collective security in the postwar world.

The one major exception to this record of United Nations failure on collective security was Korea. At an emergency session immediately after the North Korean invasion of South Korea, the Security Council voted to call on United Nations members to help the South Koreans resist the aggression from the north. This exception was indeed exceptional, made possible only by the absence of the Soviet delegate, who was boycotting council meetings to protest the refusal of the other members to seat the Chinese representative in place of the representative from Taiwan. Absent, the Soviet delegate was unable to cast a veto. Moscow's man later returned, thereby restoring the deadlock in the Security Council.

The significance of the Security Council resolution on Korea was primarily political. The resolution provided political cover to the governments that joined Washington in aiding South Korea, several of which might otherwise have had difficulty justifying following so closely in the American wake. The commander of American forces in Korea, Douglas MacArthur, doubled as the commander of United Nations forces; the fifteen other countries that accepted the Security Council's call to aid South Korea were generally content to let MacArthur and the Americans lead the way. The arrangement satisfied the Truman administration as well: the American president liked the international seal of approval the United Nations supplied, yet he also liked the relative freedom from restraint the loose oversight allowed.

During the first several weeks of the war in Korea, there was not much else for Truman to like. The North Koreans capitalized on their flying start and swept irresistibly down the peninsula. The arrival of American units from Japan did little to slow the North Korean offensive, and for a brief but agonizing period it looked as though the defenders might be tossed into the Sea of Japan. Eventually, however, the South Koreans and Americans dug in outside the city of Pusan and stabilized the front.

In the late summer of 1950, MacArthur devised a daring plan for a counterattack. He would land an amphibious force far behind the North Korean lines, at Inchon, not far from Seoul. The landing involved grave danger, not least on account of the large difference between high and low tides at Inchon. If the operation was delayed just a few hours, the landing barges would stick in the mud far offshore, and the marines the barges carried would be easy targets for North Korean fire. Yet precisely because of its dangers, the Inchon plan might catch the North Koreans by surprise.

It did. At dawn on September 15, 1950, American troops splashed ashore at Inchon. They quickly secured a beachhead and then raced toward Seoul. They liberated the capital within days and began closing the noose about the North Korean armies nearly trapped behind the new front lines.

Only by a headlong retreat were most of the North Koreans able to evade capture. They streamed north back across the thirty-eighth parallel. Although the original United Nations directive—to repel the invasion—was thereby fulfilled, MacArthur and other American officials argued that allowing the North Koreans to escape would only permit them to attack again later. The aggressors must be punished and taught a lesson.

Truman and some of his advisers had reservations about carrying the war into North Korea. They feared that they might lose the support of some of the United Nations allies and that China might enter the fighting if American troops got too close to the North Korean–Chinese border. But the opportunity looked too tempting to pass up. Truman's critics had never stopped blaming him for losing China; here was a chance to win some ground back from the communists.

Accordingly, Truman gave the order for American units to advance into North Korea. For several weeks during the autumn of 1950, the invasion proceeded successfully. American troops marched clear to the Yalu River, where they could see Chinese troops on the far side. They inflicted stinging defeats on the North Koreans. MacArthur confidently predicted an imminent end to the war; American boys, he said, would be home by Christmas.

The Korean War

United States and United Nations forces

North Korean forces

Intervention by Chinese forces, Oct. 1950

CHINA

MANCHURIA

Yalu R.

Antung

Chosan

Chosan

Kanggye

Unsan

Hyesanjin

Tumen R.

Vladivostok

U.S.S.R.

Chongjin

Kilchu

Iwon

Farthest U.S. advance Oct.–Nov. 1950

Hungnam

Taedong R.

Pyongyang

Nan R.

Wonsan

SEA OF JAPAN

NORTH KOREA

Armistice Line July 7, 1953

Sariwon

Haeju   Kaesong   Chunchon

38th Parallel

Panmunjom   Samchok

Seoul

U.S. landing Sept. 1950

Inchon

Han R.

SOUTH KOREA

YELLOW SEA

Taejon

Naktong R.

Yongdok

Pohang

Kunsan

Taegu

Farthest North Korean advance Sept. 1950

Sunchon

Pusan

TSUSHIMA

But as the Americans drew near, the Chinese got increasingly nervous. Mao's government looked more stable from the West than it felt to Mao and his comrades in Beijing. They feared the unsettling effects of a large American force on China's border. Nor could they rule out an American attack on China. Loud voices in the United States spoke of the desirability of war against China, and, for all Mao and the rest of the Chinese government knew, Truman might feel obliged to heed those voices. To warn the Americans off, Beijing sent messages to Washington not to get too close. But such messages were tame compared to the regular propaganda emanating from China: virulent diatribes against the "paper tigers" of the West and their "running dogs" in Asia. The Truman administration scoffed at the warnings, judging them mere bluffs.

The Chinese soon revealed that they were not bluffing. Starting in October, Beijing infiltrated Chinese troops across the border into North Korea; by the last week of November, it had enough to launch a massive surprise assault against the forces at MacArthur's command. Just as the Inchon landing had dramatically reversed the course of the war in favor of the South Koreans and Americans, the Chinese intervention reversed the momentum again, this time in favor of the communists. The Chinese army, pouring down from North Korea's frozen mountains, threw the Americans and South Koreans into disarray. Thousands were killed and thousands forced to surrender, while the rest fled south. Truman put a scare into much of the world, including America's United Nations allies in Korea, by hinting at the use of atomic weapons against the Chinese. But he subsequently moved his finger away from the nuclear trigger, and after a fighting retreat of several harrowing weeks, which carried the American and South Korean forces back across the thirty-eighth parallel into South Korea, the South Koreans and their allies succeeded in establishing a defensible line.

The fighting was far from over. In fact, it would continue for two and a half years more, with the opposing sides bleeding each other badly while moving the front lines a little this way, then a little that. Yet the emergency had passed and with it the possibility that the war in Korea would touch off a third world war.

*   *   *

What the Second World War began, the first half decade after the war completed. The world war had discredited American isolationists, convincing the great majority of Americans that external aggression posed a grave danger to interests they considered vital to their well-being. Americans had been convinced of the same thing during the First World War but lost their conviction once the shooting stopped. After the first war, they retreated to the noncommittal, political standoffishness that had characterized their country's attitude for more than a century. After the second war, by contrast, they remained committed to close involvement in world affairs. Politically, by the Truman Doctrine, the United States pledged itself to the support of friendly governments threatened by subversion or aggression. Economically, by the Marshall Plan, Washington took responsibility for rebuilding Western Europe. Militarily, through the North Atlantic Treaty and participation in the defense of South Korea, the American government drew a clear line against communist expansion.

Americans had never committed themselves to anything as ambitious as all this. Indeed, no country in world history had ever defined its vital interests as broadly as the United States did during the half decade after 1945. Whether Americans could make good on their new commitments was the big question for the following decades.

Sources and Suggestions for Further Reading

The development of the international financial network at Bretton Woods and after is the subject of William M. Scammell, *International Monetary Policy* (1975); Alfred E. Eckes, *A Search for Solvency* (1975); Michael Moffitt, *The World's Money* (1983); and Michael D. Bordo, *The Bretton Woods International Monetary System* (1992). On the

GATT, see Robert E. Hudec, *The GATT Legal System and World Trade Diplomacy* (1990 ed.).

The disintegration of the wartime anti-fascist alliance into the confrontation of the Cold War has been the subject of a great deal of investigation and much controversy. Early studies by American authors, notably including participants in the events of the era, tended to stress the noble, not to say, heroic, side of the story. Joseph Jones, *The Fifteen Weeks* (1955), is almost breathless in its depiction of the courage and capacity of those individuals in the Truman administration who fashioned the Truman Doctrine and laid the basis for the Marshall Plan. Dean Acheson, *Present at the Creation* (1969), though published somewhat later, falls into this genre; at the same time, it is one of the finest memoirs ever written by an American diplomat. George Kennan, *Memoirs: 1925 to 1950* (1967), is of comparable distinction. Subsequent authors, often writing against the backdrop of the war in Vietnam, questioned both the motives and the accomplishments of the framers of American Cold War policies. David Horowitz, *Free World Colossus* (1965); Gabriel Kolko, *The Politics of War* (1968); Lloyd C. Gardner, *Architects of Illusion* (1970); and, to a lesser extent, Thomas G. Paterson, *On Every Front* (1979 ed.); are good examples of this revisionist scholarship. John L. Gaddis, *The United States and the Origins of the Cold War* (1972), and Daniel Yergin, *Shattered Peace* (1978), are in a category often labeled postrevisionist; this school attempts to strike a balance between the blame-the-Russians approach of the early writers and the blame-the-Americans approach of the revisionists. Other works on the subject, not all so easily pigeon-holed, include James L. Gormly, *The Collapse of the Grand Alliance* (1987); Walter Isaacson and Evan Thomas, *The Wise Men* (1986); Terry H. Anderson, *The United States, Great Britain and the Cold War, 1944–1947* (1981); Walter LaFeber, *America, Russia and the Cold War* (1993 ed.); and Robert A. Pollard, *Economic Security and the Origins of the Cold War* (1985).

On specific aspects of the superpower confrontation, John Gimbel, *The American Occupation of Germany* (1968); Bruce Kuklick, *American Policy and the Division of Germany* (1972); and John H. Backer, *Priming the German Economy* (1971), deal with the German question. Bruce R. Kuniholm, *The Origins of the Cold War in the Near East* (1980), and Lawrence S. Wittner, *American Intervention in Greece* (1982), deal with the events in the region stretching from the Balkans to Iran. Wm. Roger Louis, *The British Empire in the Middle East, 1945–1951* (1984), has a large amount of information on American policies regarding the same region. Richard Freeland, *The Truman Doctrine and the Origins of McCarthyism* (1977), connects the Truman Doctrine to the postwar anticommunist backlash in American politics. Gregg Herken, *The Winning Weapon* (1980), examines atomic diplomacy and the development of the first generation of atomic weapons. Michael Hogan, *The Marshall Plan* (1987), is the authority on American reconstruction aid for Europe, while Timothy P. Ireland, *Creating the Entangling Alliance* (1981), and Lawrence S. Kaplan, *The United States and NATO* (1984), deal with America's first peacetime alliance in a century and a half.

On events in East Asia, see Marc Gallicchio, *The Cold War Begins in Asia* (1988); Dorothy Borg and Waldo Heinrichs, eds., *Uncertain Years: Chinese-American Relations, 1947–1950* (1980); Nancy Bernkopf Tucker, *Patterns in the Dust: Chinese-American Relations and the Recognition Controversy, 1949–1951* (1983); Robert M. Blum, *Drawing the Line: The Origins of the American Containment Policy in East Asia* (1982); William Stueck, *The Road to Confrontation: American Policy toward Korea and China* (1982); and Bruce Cumings, *The Origins of the Korean War*, 2 vols. (1981–90). Michael Schaller, *The American Occupation of Japan* (1985), looks at American efforts to remake Japan.

European perspectives on what the Cold War was all about inform A. W. DePorte, *Europe between the Superpowers* (1979); Vojtech Mastny, *Russia's Road to the Cold War* (1979); Alvin Z. Rubenstein, *Soviet Foreign Policy since World War II* (1981); and Hugh Thomas, *Armed Truce* (1987).

Chapter 12

The Rise of the Third World, 1950–1962

During the 1950s and early 1960s, the drama in world affairs shifted still farther away from Europe and toward regions that previously had been marginal in international relations. This was partly because the superpowers continued to solidify their positions in Europe. The United States decided in 1951 to station troops indefinitely in West Germany; a corollary to this decision was the evolution of the North Atlantic alliance into the North Atlantic Treaty Organization (NATO), which included a joint military command and a tighter decision-making apparatus. In 1955 the NATO allies brought West Germany into their group. Moscow responded by the creation of the Warsaw Pact, the Eastern European analogue to NATO. This completed the formalization of the spheres of influence that had developed on a de facto basis at the end of the Second World War. But none of this was really new; it was basically more of what had gone before.

The regions beyond Europe were where the greatest changes were occurring. As the European empires divested themselves of colonies, they created successor states that assumed an ever-larger role in global affairs. The countries of this "Third World"—in contrast to the two worlds of the American and Soviet alliance systems—self-consciously placed themselves beyond the confines of the superpower rivalry. At any rate they tried to. Yet the competition between the United States and the Soviet Union spilled over into this new arena, providing Washington and Moscow with more opportunities than ever to annoy and threaten each other.

For most of the 1950s, the United States and the Soviet Union managed to avoid direct confrontation. Indeed, fractiousness within the two alliance systems sometimes caused as much trouble as tension between the systems. The United States and Britain suffered an acrimonious quarrel in 1956 when the British invaded Egypt. At just the same time, the Soviet Union felt obliged to send troops into Hungary to keep restive Hungarians from pulling their country out of the Warsaw Pact.

It was especially fortunate that the superpowers stayed off each other's toes during this period, for these same years witnessed the rapid development of the nuclear arsenals of both sides. With ever-growing numbers of ever-more-powerful weapons at their disposal, American and Soviet leaders possessed a capacity for destruction undreamed of by earlier generations. A slip during a

Meetings of the NATO foreign ministers were never very cozy affairs, but this session in Bonn was even more formal than most. *UPI/Bettman*

superpower crisis now could mean deaths mounting to the hundreds of millions. Wars had often been disasters for humanity before, but no disaster had ever approached the scale nuclear weapons made possible.

Yet the good luck, such as it was, that kept the superpowers apart could not last forever. In the early 1960s, Washington and Moscow locked up in the most frightening crisis of the nuclear era. It was not coincidental that the crisis centered on Cuba, which recently had broken from the American sphere. While the lines of demarcation between the American and Soviet zones were clear in Europe, elsewhere there remained much disputed territory. The October 1962 dispute almost cost the world a nuclear war.

Nationalism and Neutralism

During the 1950s and early 1960s, anticolonial nationalism continued to spread throughout the colonial regions, from coastal West Africa to the highlands of East Africa and from the deserts of the Middle East to the jungles of Southeast Asia. Colonialism as a political institution lost its legitimacy almost entirely. Twenty years earlier colonialists had stoutly defended their actions as being in the best interests of the colonized peoples fully as much as in the

Chronology

1950   McCarthy warns of communists in government; NSC 68; Soviet-Chinese alliance; outbreak of Korean War; China enters fighting

1951   Senate votes to station troops in Europe; American occupation of Japan ends; Mossadeq orchestrates nationalization of British oil properties in Iran

1952   American hydrogen bomb tested; Egyptian revolution

1953   Stalin dies; Korean truce; Soviet hydrogen bomb; Mossadeq ousted in Iran

1954   Geneva conference ends Indochina war; Arbenz overthrown in Guatemala; confrontation in Taiwan strait; SEATO established

1955   Geneva summit conference; West Germany joins NATO; Austria neutralized

1956   Warsaw Pact; Khrushchev denounces Stalin's policies; Suez crisis and war; Soviet troops crush reform movement in Hungary

1957   Eisenhower Doctrine; Treaty of Rome establishes European Economic Community; British hydrogen bomb; *Sputnik*

1958   Revolution in Iraq; American troops to Lebanon; another Berlin crisis

1959   Castro takes power in Cuba; Khrúshchev visits America

1960   U-2 incident with Soviet Union; abortive Paris summit conference; NLF founded in Vietnam

1961   Bay of Pigs affair; Geneva conference on Laos; Kennedy meets Khrushchev in Vienna; Berlin wall erected; Alliance for Progress established

1962   American military advisers to Vietnam; Cuban missile crisis

interests of the colonizers. Colonialism, the colonizers said, brought good government and modern technology to peoples lacking both. The apologists for imperialism were not entirely wrong, but after the publication of the Atlantic Charter and the establishment of the United Nations, these arguments were swept away in the rush to embrace self-determination. As Manuel Quezon, first president of the Philippines said, it was better to be governed like hell by one's compatriots than like heaven by somebody else. Other-determination had not quite disappeared; the European colonialists still hung on to parts of their empires; the Soviets suppressed anything approaching independence in their Eastern European empire; and the United States found various means of imposing its wishes in Central America. But the Europeans, the Soviets, and the Americans felt obliged to rationalize or disguise their actions so as to minimize the affront to self-determination. The Europeans generally conceded that independence would have to come to the colonies someday, though they quibbled over the timetable for granting it. The Soviets explained away their denial of self-determination in Poland, Hungary, and the other countries of the satellite belt as necessary for the prevention of counterrevolution. The Americans resorted to covert methods and proxy pressure to keep dissatisfied Guatemalans and other Central Americans in line.

As the colonies won their independence—by ones, twos, and handfuls during the 1950s, then in a big rush during the early 1960s—many of them discovered that political independence fell short of genuine independence. Former colonials remained economically tied to their former masters, who continued to provide investment capital, technical expertise, export markets, and in some cases military protection. Beyond this the newly independent countries found themselves caught in the crossfire between the United States and the Soviet Union, having to duck the ideological and political bullets the two superpowers were zinging at each other. The majority of the new states learned how to avoid serious hits, but the experience was far from comfortable.

The largest and most influential of the postcolonial countries during the 1950s was India. Since independence in 1947, India had steered a course that kept it free of commitments to either superpower. India's prime minister, Jawaharlal Nehru, espoused a foreign policy of nonalignment, also called neutralism. Nehru had two objectives in his approach. The first was the negative one of keeping India out of war. During the period following India's achievement of independence, war between the superpowers often appeared imminent. Such a war could be expected to spread to the allies of each superpower but perhaps not much farther. By eschewing alliance with either side, India could hope to stay out of the war. Nehru's second aim was to maximize India's influence in the world by making the two superpowers compete for India's favor. If India aligned openly with either Washington or Moscow, it could expect to be taken for granted before long. Better to play the field and make the superpowers bid for India's support. India was a poor country; the higher the bidding went, the better for India's people—and the better for Nehru, who had ambitions to be one of the great leaders of the world.

Nehru pursued his neutralist goals throughout the 1950s. India was among the earliest countries to recognize Mao Zedong's government as the legitimate government for China. India sought to mediate between the Chinese and the West, for instance during the Korean War. It was through the Indian ambassador in Beijing that China passed its warning to the United States not to invade North Korea. The Truman administration considered the Indian ambassador an unreliable source, a judgment that contributed to Washington's decision not to heed the warning. In 1955 India was a principal sponsor of a conference of nonaligned Asian and African countries at Bandung, Indonesia.

Meanwhile India encouraged overtures from both the United States and the Soviet Union. In terms of political economy, Nehru found the Soviet Union a

India's prime minister Nehru embraces his daughter, Indira Gandhi, later prime minister herself. © *Mrs. Homai Vyarawalla, Black Star*

more compelling model for Indian development than the United States. He saw Americans as crass and shallow and concluded that these deficiencies followed from Americans' worship of the dollar. Besides, economic development along the capitalist lines followed by the United States and the other Western industrial powers had taken centuries. India's hundreds of millions of poor people, growing in numbers all the time, could not wait that long. The centralized planning practiced by the Soviet Union had, within a few decades, vaulted that country to the forefront of world powers, as evidenced by the Soviet defeat of Germany in the Second World War. Nehru decided to emulate the Soviets in this regard. He and India's government, which until his 1964 death he thoroughly dominated, inaugurated a series of five-year plans. Like the Soviet plans, these called for a major role for government in directing the economy, though they allowed more room for individual initiative and enterprise than the Soviet plans did. Indian planning also counted on Soviet economic aid, which Moscow, thrilled at the thought of capturing the heart of the leader of the world's second most populous nation, gladly provided.

Although India followed the Soviet example in important matters of economics, it followed the American example in matters of politics. More exactly, India followed the British political example, which had similarly provided the original model for American politics in the eighteenth century. India exhibited a vigorous, raucous democracy, and the Indian people enjoyed a broad array of civil liberties. The masses of people voted regularly and enthusiastically, and if they always returned Nehru's Congress party to office, that was their democratic prerogative. This prerogative was reinforced by the Congress party's shrewd exercise of the advantages of incumbency.

Indian political practices reflected the genuine conviction of Nehru and most other members of the Indian elite that democracy was necessary and desirable; at the same time Indian democracy recommended India to American public opinion, which Nehru aimed to cultivate so as to receive American aid and prevent India from slipping into dependence on the Soviet Union. This attempted balancing act was typical of Third World leaders, but it was not easy. As in most countries that had once been colonies of Western powers, India contained a vocal anti-Western element. While India had remained a British colony, this element concentrated its criticism on Britain, but with the end of the British raj, the anti-Western criticism focused on the United States, the most powerful of the Western countries. Among some factions in India, the anti-Westernism reflected a sincere commitment to communist ideology; for a larger number, it was a historical hangover. Indians liked to say that the East had not invaded and conquered India, at least not since Babur and the Moguls swept down from Central Asia in the early sixteenth century; but the West had. The Soviets now represented the East; the United States, the West. Under the circumstances it was easier to be suspicious of the Americans than of the Soviets.

Suspicions or no suspicions, India soon found itself in need of American economic aid. This need showed most graphically at the beginning of the 1950s when a succession of natural calamities, culminating in the failure of the monsoon, cut deeply into India's grain supply and threatened a famine. India requested emergency relief from the United States. The Truman administration approved the request, as did the American Congress, and millions of tons of American wheat flowed to India.

The shipments helped avert widespread hunger, though they did not strengthen relations between India and the United States as much as well-wishers on both sides hoped. Many Americans thought Nehru should express gratitude for America's help by joining the American-led fight against communism, at least rhetorically; they were disappointed and upset when he did not. Indians resented the very thought that Washington might consider conditioning aid to starving children on India's succumbing to American political dictates. In fact, the Truman administration attempted no such pressure, knowing it would backfire; but conservatives in Congress tried to attach a quid pro quo to the grain shipments. From ten thousand miles away, it was easy for Indians to confuse the American executive with the American Congress, especially as in India's parliamentary system, the executive *was* the Congress (party).

If American relations with India were often testy, they were not any better with Egypt, another leader of the nonaligned movement. In 1952 a group of military officers inspired by Colonel Gamal Abdel Nasser overthrew the Egyptian monarchy of King Farouk. Nasser and his fellow conspirators had a number of grievances against Farouk, including widespread corruption and the humiliation of Egypt's defeat in the 1948–1949 Palestine War. But the most pressing immediate issue was Britain's continued occupation of Egypt, which Farouk was failing to end. The British had arrived in the 1880s, coming to protect the Suez Canal and guarantee payments of debts to British bondholders. They stayed for the next seventy years despite the complaints, sometimes violently expressed, of Egyptian nationalists. During most of that time, the British justified their presence as necessary to guard the short route to India. London's withdrawal from India in 1947 demolished this argument, yet the British still had important interests in the Middle East, especially in the Persian Gulf, and they wanted to hold onto a large military base in Egypt's Suez district as a potential staging ground for operations farther east. The Egyptian nationalists led by Nasser could not have cared less about Britain's interests in the Persian Gulf or elsewhere; they wanted the British out of Egypt.

The Egyptians were not strong enough to throw the British out bodily, at least not in a frontal assault. Instead they engaged in political demonstrations, sabotage, and guerrilla warfare. They also sought to enlist the support of world opinion against this manifestation of continuing Western imperialism. Shortly after seizing power in 1952, Nasser and his associates approached the United States for help. They urged the Truman administration, and subsequently the Eisenhower administration, to apply pressure against Britain. Washington hesitated to do so, partly because it feared undermining the "special relationship" that had developed between the two English-speaking allies during the course of the twentieth century, partly because it liked the idea of a British military presence in the Middle East, and partly because it distrusted Nasser.

The Egyptian leader was not difficult for Americans to distrust. Like many charismatic figures, he had a mercurial personality. He could be disarmingly frank and good-humored in private conversations, but in front of crowds he often launched into emotional flights that carried both himself and his audiences to unpredictable destinations. Many Americans and other Western observers who watched him in action caught disturbing reminders of that other spellbinder: Adolf Hitler.

Nasser's politics were as worrisome as his personality. He preached a message of an Arab nationalism that transcended the borders of all existing Arab states. Nasser's pan-Arabism envisaged a single unified Arab state, something on the order of the Arab empire of the seventh and eighth centuries, with Nasser evidently the leader of this great modern state. Western officials simply did not take Nasser's idea seriously. Bitter, ancient rivalries among the different Arab groups, especially between Iraqis and Egyptians, had long ago rendered such an empire impossible, and few students of Arab politics expected such conflicts to end in the foreseeable future. Yet even if Nasser never succeeded in welding all the Arabs together, his efforts to achieve even a partial welding might throw the Middle East into confusion. The last thing the Western countries, including the United States, wanted in the Middle East was more confusion than already existed there. The status quo in the Middle East in the early 1950s favored the West. Middle Eastern oil and very large profits therefrom flowed to the West; the strategic passageways of the region—the Turkish straits, the Suez Canal, the Strait of Hormuz at the entrance to the Persian Gulf—were firmly in Western control. Any change was bound to be for the worse. Nasser wanted change; therefore he spelled trouble.

If Nasser spelled trouble for the West, he spelled real danger for Israel and therefore potentially more trouble for the United States. The American government and the American people had taken a close interest in Israel's predicament since even before the 1948 founding of the Jewish state. From 1945 until 1947, Britain tried to get the Americans to share responsibility for finding a solution to the vexing question of how to split its Palestine mandate between the Arabs and Jews who lived there (with the latter looking forward to the immigration of many more Jews from outside). The Truman administration rejected Britain's solicitations, not least because of a rancorous dispute between the State Department, which sympathized with the Arabs and contended that backing the Zionists would open the region to Soviet adventurism, and White House staffers, who felt a moral obligation to the Jews, especially in the wake of the Nazi destruction of most of European Jewry. But when the British grew exasperated at escalating violence between Arabs and Jews in Palestine and turned the issue over to the United Nations, the Truman administration lobbied heavily in favor of a declaration partitioning Palestine and thereby granting the Zionists their state. The American lobbying was successful and opened the way to the creation of Israel in May 1948.

This outcome pleased the Jews immensely; at the same time it greatly antagonized the Palestinian Arabs. The Palestinians contended that the creation of Israel amounted to the theft of half their homeland, and they refused to accept the United Nations' offer of the other half: the state of Palestine that was to be Israel's twin. This refusal triggered the first Arab–Israeli war, the Palestine War of 1948–1949. The armies of several Arab states took the Palestinians' side and invaded Israel, but the Israelis fought them off and even seized some of the territory assigned to Palestine.

After the fighting stopped, the Arabs refused to negotiate a peace treaty with the Israelis. Not only that, they refused to recognize Israel's right to exist. And the state that was to have been Palestine disappeared in three directions: to Israel, which annexed various portions it had seized during the war; to Jordan, which assumed administration of the Jordan River's western bank (called simply the West Bank); and to Egypt, which assumed control of a strip of land near Gaza on the Mediterranean (the Gaza Strip). It was a settlement that pleased no one, though Arabs were more displeased than the Israelis. Among the Arabs, the Palestinians, hundreds of thousands of whom had fled what now was Israel and currently lived in refugee camps, were the most displeased of all.

But peace, even if uneasy, was better than war, especially in a region as volatile and important to the West as the Middle East. So, at any rate, judged the governments of the United States, Britain, and France. And lest anyone get any ideas about challenging this judgment, Washington, London, and Paris in May 1950 issued a statement known as the Tripartite Declaration saying that they would resist forcible efforts to change the status quo in the vicinity of Israel. Moreover, the three governments pledged to refrain from selling weapons to the participants in the Arab-Israeli dispute. Since Britain and France were the principal arms suppliers to the Middle East, this joint policy effectively averted an arms race.

It did until 1955, that is. In that year Egypt's Nasser announced an agreement between Egypt and the Soviet Union whereby Nasser's government would receive weapons from Czechoslovakia in exchange for Egyptian cotton. The Cairo-Kremlin deal broke the embargo on weapons to the Middle East and threatened to produce one of two evil consequences. Either the Arabs would feel strong enough to attack Israel, or the Israelis would feel frightened enough to attack the Arabs before the Arabs got too strong. Neither alternative afforded any comfort to the Americans or other Westerners.

The Egyptian arms deal set alarm bells ringing in the West for another reason, too. Until now the United States and its allies had been able to prevent the Soviet Union from getting a foot in the Middle Eastern door. By negotiating his deal with Moscow, Nasser kicked the door wide open for the communists. Soviet advisers would accompany the weapons; Egypt would come to depend on the Soviet bloc for ammunition and spare parts. This dependence would foster additional ties between the Kremlin and Cairo. Had Egypt been merely another nonaligned country, such a prospect might not have mattered much; but Egypt was the largest of the Arab states, and it controlled the Suez Canal. Nasser's capacity for mischief was very great. He bore watching with extreme care.

India and Egypt were the most important of the nonaligned countries, but other neutralists also made their presence known. Indonesia's Sukarno promoted his country as a bridge between the Middle East and East Asia: though Indonesia was located off the Southeast Asian coast, it contained more Muslims than any other nation in the world. In addition, Sukarno touted his "New Order" as a blend of the best of East and West: state-directed economic development along socialist lines, married to the political tolerance characteristic of the democratic countries of Europe and North America. Critics thought Sukarno's New Order was merely a ruse for gathering power to himself and distracting Indonesians from their persistent poverty. But whatever Sukarno's deficiencies, he enjoyed enormous popularity among the Indonesian people, who liked him well enough to keep him in power until the mid-1960s, when a military coup pushed him out.

Yugoslavia was something of the oddball in the nonaligned movement, being European rather than Asian or African. Yugoslavia was also eccentric in having arrived at nonalignment by defection from the Soviet bloc rather than by decolonization from a European empire. Yugoslavia's 1948 break with Moscow was chiefly the consequence of an acrimonious feud between Tito and Stalin; Tito, having climbed the greasy pole to power by fighting off the Nazis during the Second World War and fighting off Balkan rivals then and later, did not take orders from other people. Stalin was as uncomfortable with Tito as with China's Mao and for the same reason: neither Tito nor Mao owed his

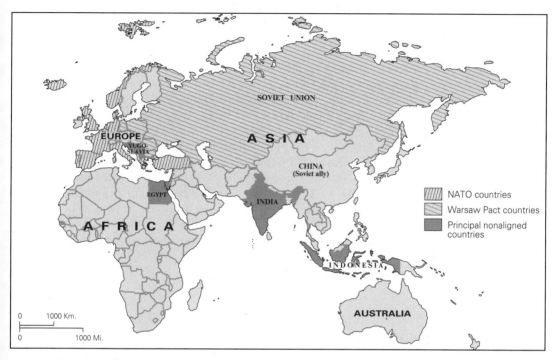

Eurasia in the Late 1950s

power to Stalin, and everyone knew it. Stalin tried to force Tito to recognize Moscow's right to dictate to the world communist movement, but Tito refused, and in the summer of 1948 the Kremlin excommunicated the recalcitrant Yugoslavian leader.

Fearing stronger action, such as a Soviet invasion, Tito turned to the United States for support. During one of the tensest stretches of the postwar era—these summer months of 1948 were the period of the Berlin blockade and airlift—this was a novel idea: American aid for a communist country. But Washington choked back its anticommunist scruples and sent economic aid, followed by military aid. American reasoning was twofold. First, should war break out between East and West, the United States would benefit from not having Yugoslavia's thirty divisions fighting on the side of the East. If Tito could be persuaded to enlist these divisions in the ranks of the West, all the better; but even a neutral Yugoslavia was preferable to one attached to the East. Second, Yugoslavia could serve as an example of a country that had broken free from the Soviet sphere. What Tito had done leaders of other communist countries might be inspired to do. American officials did not hold out much hope for the states of Eastern Europe: the Red Army was too firmly entrenched there—as it had not been in Yugoslavia—and the ruling regimes of those countries leaned too heavily on Moscow. But China was another story. American officials appreciated the parallels between Tito and Mao, and they looked forward to the day when Mao would get as fed up with Soviet over-bearingness as Tito had. In this respect American officials did not begrudge Tito his continuing devotion to communism; indeed, they were just as happy that he stayed communist. A neutral but still communist Yugoslavia would have more pulling power with China, whose leaders were sincere disciples of Marx and Lenin, if not Stalin, than a Yugoslavia gone over to capitalism.

American relations with Yugoslavia summarized the difficulties American leaders faced in dealing with the nonaligned countries generally. At a time of reflexive hostility in America to all things communist, and to many things not fervently anticommunist, American policy makers had to exercise great care regarding the neutralists. To appear too friendly might set off an uproar among the McCarthyites and their fellow-travelers in Congress and in the public at large. Beyond the political damage this could do to a president's adminis-tration, such an uproar might well trigger a backlash that would ruin rela-tions with the nonaligned country in question. On the other hand, to appear hostile risked driving the neutralists toward Moscow, with equally unfortu-nate results.

Covering the Earth: The Thermonuclear Age

Relations with the nonaligned countries illuminated the dual nature of the su-perpower rivalry. The competition between the United States and the Soviet Union was a matter of both ideology and geopolitics. Americans opposed the Soviet Union because its government was communist, and communism threat-ened much that Americans held dear, especially private property and political liberty. Soviets opposed the United States because it was a capitalist country, and capitalism threatened much that Soviets held dear, especially economic equality and social responsibility. At the same time, Americans opposed the Soviet Union because it was a great power and, as a great power, possessed the capability to do the United States great harm. In this respect the fact that the Soviet Union was communist was merely incidental. Only a few years ear-lier, the Americans had joined hands with the communists of the Kremlin against Germany and been grateful for the help. Analogously the Soviets feared the United States because as a great power the United States was capable of doing the Soviet Union great harm. In this regard the fact that the Americans were capitalists was beside the point. The Soviets had been just as happy as the Americans to participate in the grand capitalist-communist coalition against the fascists.

Throughout the postwar period, the relative importance of these two aspects of the superpower rivalry varied. At times the ideological aspect predominated; at other times geopolitics took precedence. The ideological phases tended to witness a heightening of tension between the two sides. Americans looked on the Soviets as communists bent on world revolution, conspiring to extend their godless and totalitarian ways across the face of the globe. Soviets viewed the

Americans as voracious capitalists eager to get their greedy hands on the resources and markets of the entire planet. Between two parties holding such loaded judgments of each other, compromise was difficult. The geopolitical phases, in contrast, often produced improvements in relations. If a principal obligation of ideologues is to resist evil, the primary chore of geopoliticians is to protect their countries' interests. When two great powers possess the capability to do each other serious damage, the foremost responsibility of the geopoliticians is to reduce the risks of incurring that damage.

A variety of factors induced transitions from one phase to another. These included domestic politics within each superpower and politics within each alliance system. They also included technological changes, in particular the development of new weapons systems that scared the daylights out of both sides and prompted them to set aside ideological differences in the common interest of mutual survival. Put simply, when the technological possibilities of the United States and the Soviet Union blowing each other to radioactive smithereens increased, so did the incentive to reduce the likelihood of doing so. During the geopolitical phases of the superpower competition, Americans and Soviets did not necessarily view each other as less evil than during the ideological phases; but they did view each other as more dangerous. Unnecessary provocation under such conditions seemed unwise.

The first phase of the superpower rivalry, from the late 1940s to the early 1950s, was marked by ideology on both sides, with Stalin thundering about the incompatibility of capitalism and communism, and America consumed by the passions of the second "Red scare." This phase gave way to a more geopolitical approach during the mid-1950s, as exemplified by a 1955 summit conference at Geneva between American and Soviet leaders, the first such meeting since the Potsdam conference of 1945. A phrase, the "spirit of Geneva," was coined to represent this thaw in the Cold War and the lessening of tensions it produced.

A number of influences contributed to this shift from ideology to geopolitics, including the death of Stalin in March 1953 and the inauguration of a new American administration shortly before. But more than anything else, the thaw reflected an acceleration in the weapons race between the superpowers. For a brief moment after the Second World War, at the dawn of the atomic age, some people hoped that an all-out arms race might be averted. In 1946 the Truman administration proposed a plan for atomic arms control, with the stated goal of internationalizing atomic-energy knowledge and technology. But the Baruch plan (named after Bernard Baruch, the financier who had overseen American war production during the First World War) was so hedged about with guarantees for the United States as to ensure a Soviet veto. The plan died a diplomatic death, and the two sides went their separate atomic ways.

Until 1949 the American way was demonstrably superior to the Soviet way, and American leaders rested confident that if war broke out against the Soviet Union, for example during the Berlin crisis of 1948, they could counter the Soviet conventional (that is, nonnuclear) advantage with American atomic bombs. Although the American atomic arsenal was still fairly small, the Soviets presumably did not know how small it was; besides, even a few well-placed atomic bombs could do sufficient damage to the Soviet Union to make the cost of war unacceptably high.

The Soviet atomic test of September 1949 changed this calculation considerably. To be sure, the United States retained a big advantage over the Soviet Union in the number and sophistication of weapons as well as in the likelihood of delivering the atomic bombs on targets of high value. The Americans, with air bases on the territory of their North Atlantic allies, could reach Moscow, Leningrad, and other major Soviet cities with long-range bombers, whereas the Soviets, lacking bases in the Western Hemisphere, had no comparable access to targets in the United States. Yet the Soviets *could* reach targets in Europe, such as London and Paris, and though the prospective annihilation of the capital of an American ally lacked the emotional impact for Americans of the leveling of Washington or New York, the possibility gave American leaders second thoughts about using atomic weapons against the Soviet Union. Needless to say, the leaders of America's allies encouraged these second thoughts. The result was that the American atomic advantage was largely neutralized.

Everyone had known that the Soviets would be able to build an atomic bomb sooner or later; the only question had been whether it would be sooner or later. Now that Moscow had succeeded in building a bomb, some Americans, including many American scientists, were willing to call the arms race a tie and call it off. But others were intrigued by the prospect of a much bigger bomb, the theoretical basis for which had been developed even before the first atomic test in New Mexico in 1945. The atomic bombs derived their explosive force from the breakup, or fission, of the nuclei of heavy elements such as uranium and plutonium into lighter elements. The bigger bombs would derive their energy from the coalescing, or fusion, of several nuclei of the lightest element, hydrogen, into heavier helium. By the physics of the matter, a fusion bomb (also called a hydrogen bomb or thermonuclear bomb or at first simply "the super") could be made thousands of times more powerful than any fission bomb. A hydrogen bomb would be to the bomb that devastated Hiroshima as a stick of dynamite was to a firecracker.

Interest in the hydrogen bomb waned somewhat during the years of the American atomic monopoly but picked up considerably after the Soviet atomic test of September 1949. The new interest was as much political as scientific: with the Truman administration under Republican fire for alleged laxness in confronting the communists, a decision in favor of the hydrogen bomb assumed symbolic importance as an indication of the administration's resolve. Edward Teller, an émigré from Hungary who had worked on the Manhattan Project and an ardent proponent of the hydrogen bomb, lobbied friends and public officials for support. Teller argued that the Soviets were probably busy working on the hydrogen bomb and that the United States could not afford to let the perception develop around the world that the Soviets could do something Americans could not. America's allies would be demoralized, and America's enemies would be encouraged. Teller easily elicited the support of the

American Defense Department, which had bureaucratic reasons—more weapons meant more money and more jobs for defense officials—in addition to the military rationale for pursuing cutting-edge technology. Influential senators and representatives fell into step as well. The campaign for developing the hydrogen bomb reached a climax just as China was passing into the hands of Mao and the Chinese Communists. Battered by the right on the China issue, Truman chose not to give his critics any more ammunition. He overruled such opponents of the hydrogen bomb as Albert Einstein and early in 1950 ordered development to proceed with all swiftness.

Truman's decision in favor of the hydrogen bomb dovetailed with a more comprehensive bolstering of the American military. After the Soviet atomic bomb test and the communist victory in China, Truman ordered his administration's thinkers to review American foreign policy. The review filled the first months of 1950, and in April the reviewers delivered their report to Truman's National Security Council. This report, labeled NSC-68, described the struggle between the United States and the Soviet Union in extremely ideological, almost apocalyptic, language. The world was experiencing "a basic conflict between the idea of freedom under a government of laws and the idea of slavery under the grim oligarchy of the Kremlin." Communism was bent on global conquest, and the Soviet practitioners of this "fanatic faith" would not rest until they had accomplished their goal. Moral arguments were useless in the contest, for the communists responded only to arguments backed by military force. The United States had no choice but to gird for the battle. War was not the necessary outcome of a vigorous American policy; in fact, war was more likely to result from an insufficiency of American vigor, which the Kremlin would take for weakness. But only by preparing for war might the United States avoid it. NSC-68 called for a major increase in American spending on the military. Although the American government in the past had often hesitated to approve large defense budgets for fear of overburdening the American economy, the authors of this report asserted that the economy could sustain a much larger defense effort than it was supporting at present. Americans had to recognize that there was a war going on, albeit not a shooting war, and act accordingly. If they did, they could win the war; if they did not, they would surely lose.

Truman approved NSC-68 in principle in April 1950. With the president's approval, the report became a basic blueprint for American foreign policy. But blueprints, especially those requiring big government expenditures, have a habit of getting misplaced in Washington and never being heard of again. Not so, however, with NSC-68. Its staying power resulted partly from the support of influential sponsors like Dean Acheson, who understood that its overheated language represented what he called an attempt to "bludgeon the mass mind of 'top government'" but who nonetheless supported its objectives. Even more important, the success of NSC-68 resulted from the fact that President Truman had scarcely finished reading it when the North Koreans invaded South Korea. The North Korean invasion appeared to be just the sort of thing NSC-68 had warned of, and the invasion provided crucial momentum to Truman's decision in principle to strengthen the American military. In wartime Congress has usually given the president whatever he says he needs for the military; Congress did so during the Korean War. American spending on defense jumped from $13 billion in 1950 to more than $50 billion three years later.

Most of the money went into the mundane materials that always absorb most of the expenditures devoted to the military: boots, bullets, beefsteak, bandages. But a substantial portion also went to research and development of the hydrogen bomb and the means for its delivery. By late 1952 America's bomb builders were ready to test their new baby. In November of that year, the first hydrogen bomb ever detonated sent an enormous mushroom cloud of water vapor and radioactive debris into the stratosphere above Eniwetok in the American Marshall Islands.

Americans congratulated themselves on beating the Soviets to the thermonuclear punch, but their self-satisfaction did not last long. In the summer of 1953, the Soviet government announced that it, too, had successfully tested a hydrogen device. American scientists, sampling the atmosphere downwind of the Soviet test site, confirmed the announcement. The American lead in the arms race, which had been four years in the case of the fission bomb, had shrunk to less than a year. At the rate the Soviets were catching up, one did not have to be an alarmist to predict that they might overtake the Americans before long.

The first hydrogen devices were not really weapons in any useful sense. They weighed many tons, occupied thousands of cubic feet, and required the most painstaking and delicate treatment prior to detonation. Yet once each side was satisfied that it understood the basic principles involved, its scientists and engineers moved rapidly to miniaturize the hydrogen devices so that they would be useful in battle conditions.

Before long the hydrogen explosives had shrunk sufficiently to fit into the bomb bay of a large airplane. By the mid-1950s the acme of the rapidly evolving art of strategic air power was the extended-range jet bomber (in the American case, the B-52), which could fly thousands of miles from base to targets in the enemy homeland. These targets usually included the enemy's major cities. The targeting of cities was partly a consequence of the erosion of the distinction between combatants and noncombatants that the bombing campaigns of the Second World War had revealed; it was also a consequence of the relative dearth of nuclear weapons in these early days. With few bombs on hand, each side wanted to use them where they would have the greatest effect. The enemy's capital and largest cities were obvious places to start. Moreover, targeting cities and civilians was a consequence of the logic of nuclear deterrence. To prevent the other side from using nuclear weapons, each side had to threaten the most dire consequences in retaliation. Deaths by the millions did not seem excessively dire given that the physical security of the nation was at stake.

Yet even as American and Soviet aircraft designers and builders produced more powerful bombers, scientists on both sides pressed forward with a still more threatening technology. In the final stages of the Second World War, Germany had employed a revolutionary new weapon against British cities: the ballistic missile. Although the German V-2 lacked accuracy and could carry only a small warhead, it was unstoppable by current countermeasures. The missiles were launched from bases in Germany, then ascended high into the atmosphere on their way to their targets; they came streaking down at many times the speed of sound, like thunderbolts from a clear blue (or, in the customary case of Britain, overcast) sky. After the war American and Soviet scientists, both assisted by Germans spirited away from the wreckage of Hitler's reich, launched their own rocket programs. During the early 1950s, the rockets were still too small and the nuclear weapons too large for the former to carry the latter very far. But improvements in rocket motors and downsizing of hydrogen warheads narrowed the gap; by the late 1950s, each side was testing intermediate-range missiles capable of carrying nuclear warheads several hundred miles. American versions of such missiles could strike targets far inside the Soviet Union from American bases in Turkey. The Soviet Union was handicapped in this regard by its lack of allies close to the United States—which was one reason for Moscow's intense interest in any stirrings of revolution in such Western Hemisphere countries as Cuba.

From intermediate missiles to intercontinental missiles was but a step, though one fraught with technological difficulties. The Soviets demonstrated in spectacular fashion that they had overcome most of these technological difficulties when they put the first artificial earth satellite, *Sputnik*, into orbit in 1957. *Sputnik* was a scientific instrument rather than a warhead, but it did not take much physics to infer that a Soviet rocket big enough to blast a satellite clear around the earth could probably shoot a warhead a quarter of the way around, for instance from the Soviet Union to the United States. As matters turned out, however, the Americans were the first to deploy large numbers of intercontinental missiles; the Soviets followed at a slower pace.

The introduction of intercontinental nuclear-tipped missiles marked a new stage in the shrinking of the earth that had been going on for centuries. Columbus had brought the Old World (back) into contact with the New at the end of the fifteenth century. Advances in sailing technology during the next three hundred years diminished the time required to reach the New World from the Old and to get from place to place within each. Steamships diminished the time still further during the nineteenth century. Railroads brought cities and towns closer together by land. The telegraph, then telephone, then radio, had reduced the time required for people far apart to speak to one another. In the twentieth century, airplanes allowed passengers to cover in hours distances that formerly had taken days or weeks or months. As instruments of military might, airplanes allowed the great powers to deliver destruction upon each other with a speed and efficiency previously unknown. Intercontinental nuclear missiles carried the trend almost to its ultimate conclusion. Now the destruction of large cities could be accomplished in minutes and the destruction of countries in hours.

In the pre-industrial era, the earth had been a very large place relative to humanity's power to affect it. The consequences of human actions rarely showed on more than a local, or at most regional, scale and then only slowly. A tribe might migrate from one territory to another next door, or a road might be built to connect this town to that. Changes occurred in the face of the planet, but the changes were gradual. Had observers from outer space been watching, they would have noticed almost nothing new from one day to the next.

By the early 1960s, humanity's ability to change the face of the earth had grown enormously. Before-and-after pictures from space (which now were possible by means of reconnaissance satellites) taken twenty-four hours apart would show dramatic changes if a nuclear war intervened (and if there were technicians still alive to receive the pictures from space). Whole cities would have been reduced to rubble, with their ruins flaming and most of their populations eliminated. Smoke and dust would fill the atmosphere, spreading downwind to countries not directly hit by warheads. For the first time, the effects of human actions could rapidly become global.

In fact, some of the effects of the nuclear revolution already were global, though such effects were not obvious from a distance. Since the beginning of the nuclear era in 1945, the detonation of fission and then hydrogen bombs (all but two as tests) had been producing large amounts of radioactive fallout. This was something new in terms both of science and medicine and of international relations. Prior to 1945 the effects of radioactivity on humans and other inhabitants of the earth were mostly unknown. Radiation was understood to be dangerous in large doses; it had killed Marie Curie and many of the victims of the bombings of Hiroshima and Nagasaki. But what effects modestly radioactive materials broadcast over wide portions of the globe would have on people, animals, and plants was something nobody could tell. Complicating the confusion regarding the scientific and medical effects was the matter of international law and liability. If the United States conducted hydrogen bomb tests in the Marshall Islands and the fallout drifted over other island groups or across the Americas and the other continents, was the United States government responsible for injuries to people, livestock, and crops? If Soviet tests in Central Asia spread radioactive materials across India, China, and Japan, what recourse did the Indians, Chinese, and Japanese have?

These questions were far from academic. In 1954 an American bomb test in the Marshalls blanketed a Japanese fishing vessel—ironically named the *Lucky Dragon*—with radioactive fallout. The crew became sick, and one man died. The Japanese government complained to Washington, which responded with an apology and payments to the injured men and the family of the deceased.

The incident provoked protests in many countries against the contamination of the atmosphere by nuclear testing. Radioactivity began appearing in drinking water, in food grown on contaminated land, in mothers' milk, and in the bones of young children. The people of the nuclear powers—since 1952 including Britain as well as the United States and the Soviet Union—had only themselves or their governments to blame; but the people of other countries reasonably felt victimized. Taking a cue from the American radicals of the 1760s, they declared, "No radiation without representation." For the first time, an issue involving the global environment mobilized individuals all over the planet. They demanded an end to nuclear testing, with many calling for nuclear disarmament as well.

For several years Washington, Moscow, and London resisted the demands. The United States government declared that continued testing was necessary to maintain and improve the American arsenal lest the Soviets think they could get away with something. The Soviets, who had many fewer nuclear weapons than the Americans, argued that they needed to catch up, in order to be able to defend themselves against the Americans. The British saw no reason to stop testing until the Americans and Soviets did. All three governments admitted that there were certain risks to human health and the environment from continued testing, but they argued that these risks paled in comparison to the risks of a failure of deterrence—that is, of nuclear war.

Yet eventually the complaints of the world community created political problems for the superpowers. Hoping to keep the support of their allies and win the support of the newly emerging countries of Asia and Africa, the United States and the Soviet Union realized they had to pay attention to the objections regarding the contamination of the earth's biosphere. Each superpower liked to portray itself as an exemplary world citizen. Although the American and Soviet defense establishments resisted calls for an end to testing, the civilian leaders in Washington and Moscow decided to take action. In early 1958 Soviet leader Nikita Khrushchev announced (conveniently right after the completion of a series of Soviet tests) that the Soviet Union would suspend testing, in hopes that the United States would join in the moratorium. Eisenhower initially dismissed the move as a public relations ploy, but the strongly favorable response from around the world soon forced him to follow suit (conveniently right after the completion of the most extensive series of American tests to date).

The two sides then began trading proposals for test bans, sometimes via the news media, sometimes via more serious diplomatic methods. Each side was hampered by the refusal of its generals to accept a total ban on testing, but eventually Moscow and Washington began talking about an end to testing in the atmosphere. Scientists had discovered that they could test their bombs in mineshafts far underground, thereby eliminating almost entirely the problem of nuclear fallout. The generals demanded to be convinced that they could learn what they needed to know from underground tests; they never were, completely. But despite the generals' skepticism, the political leaders decided they could not continue to suffer the moral and ecological opprobrium attached to atmospheric testing. In the summer of 1963—after the Cuban missile crisis reinforced everyone's fear of a nuclear blowup—the four nuclear powers, now including France, signed a treaty banning nuclear testing in the atmosphere, as well as in space and in the ocean. The American Senate quickly ratified the test ban treaty, as did the appropriate bodies in the Soviet Union, Britain, and France.

Exit, Europe; Enter, America

Although the British and French joined the Americans and Soviets in the highly exclusive nuclear club, in other respects Britain and France continued to fade as world powers. Nationalism had European colonialism on the run throughout Asia and Africa. Opposition to French rule was especially conspicuous in Indochina during the early 1950s. Ho Chi Minh, the most prominent nationalist in Vietnam (one of the three countries constituting French Indochina, the others being Laos and Cambodia) had been conspiring and fighting against the French for three decades. The Japanese occupation of Indochina during the Second World War had promised an end to French colonial rule, but after the Japanese defeat in 1945 the French had returned. In 1946 Ho declared a war of liberation against the French. Ho and his party of Vietnamese nationalists, called the Vietminh, made modest progress during the late 1940s. They lacked the equipment and numbers to confront the French head-on and so adopted the guerrilla tactics traditionally beloved of revolutionaries. The French retained control of the cities of Vietnam and the support of much of the French-educated elite, but the Vietminh made deep inroads in the countryside and among the peasantry.

Nationalist revolts are rarely straightforward affairs. Both sides in such conflicts, but especially the outgunned nationalists, look high and low for allies, taking assistance wherever they can find it. The nationalist revolt in Vietnam was complicated by the concurrent global competition between the communist and capitalist camps. Ho and the top leadership of the Vietminh were communists, partly from socialist conviction and partly from a belief that communism provided the sharpest knife for cutting Vietnam loose from the capitalist imperialism of France. As communists they looked to their co-ideologists in the Soviet Union and China for help. The Chinese traditionally had little love for the Vietnamese; they had long sought, with frequent success, to dominate Vietnam's territory and affairs. The Vietnamese, being on the receiving end of China's impositions, had even less love for the Chinese. Yet the needs of the Vietminh revolt against France and the shared adherence of Vietnamese communists and Chinese communists to the teachings of Marx and Lenin caused Ho to ask Mao for support, which Mao provided. Stalin also sent help, partly to vex the French and partly to prevent Vietnam from falling back into China's sphere.

The French similarly sought outside assistance. The obvious place for Paris to look was the United States, the source of Marshall Plan money and, as of the 1949 ratification of the North Atlantic Treaty, France's avowed protector against communist aggression. Initially the French had trouble selling the Americans on the idea of helping to suppress an anticolonial revolution in

Ho Chi Minh (left) enjoys a dinner put on by Zhou Enlai in Beijing. Besides the egg rolls, Zhou provided his guest with weapons and ammunition. *Wide World Photos*

Indochina. Americans remembered their own anticolonial national origins, and they resented any thought that they might be making the world safe for French imperialism. But the French promised (eventual) Vietnamese independence and stressed Ho's ties to the world communist movement. In addition, Paris indicated that France would experience great difficulty helping the Atlantic alliance in Europe if the leading member of the Atlantic alliance did not help France in Vietnam.

The Truman administration, currently taking a beating for the "loss" of China to communism, preferred not to be blamed for losing Vietnam to a communist regime; and desiring France's active involvement in European security affairs, the administration chose not to test Paris's resolve. Initially, the administration quietly allowed the French to use Marshall Plan money to free up resources for employment against the rebels in Indochina. On the outbreak of the Korean War in June 1950, Washington began sending American aid directly to the French in Vietnam.

Paris hoped the latter action would be a turning point in the fight against the Vietminh; but these hopes proved illusory. Ho and the nationalists continued to eat away at French control in Vietnam. The French were trying to wear down the rebels, to convince them that however long they might be able to fight, France would fight longer. Just the opposite happened. The French people had not recovered from the Second World War when the Indochina war

 any of them were thoroughly weary of the
. Although the Americans by now were foot-
French sons, husbands, and fathers continued
o have no end. A growing portion of the French
ment to wash its hands of the whole business and

mmand, caught between the increasing strength of
na and the diminishing support in France for the war,
war-ending operation. France's generals laid a trap for
ienphu in the mountainous northern reaches of Vietnam.
e within apparently easy reach of the rebels, the French
inten. em out into the open. There the French forces would smash
the Vietm. ops.

The operation ended the war all right, but not as the French anticipated. The Vietminh defied French expectations and managed to haul heavy artillery to ridgetops surrounding the French fortress. They pounded the French position and cut off ground access from the outside. Gradually they reduced the perimeter of the French position until they were able to prevent airplanes from landing. French aircraft managed to drop supplies in by parachute, but even this grew dangerous.

As the French situation at Dienbienphu deteriorated, Paris hoped to find one last trump card up its sleeve. The French government sent an emergency mission to Washington requesting American relief for the beleaguered garrison. An American air strike, the French said, perhaps using small nuclear bombs, would shatter the Vietminh and reverse the fortunes of the war.

President Eisenhower and his chief advisers considered the French plan carefully. Eisenhower was no more pleased at the thought of Vietnam going communist than Truman had been. But the Republican president was reluctant to get the United States involved in another Asian war. Only the previous summer, he and Secretary of State John Foster Dulles had succeeded in negotiating an end to the Korean War. The diplomacy leading to the Korean armistice was exhausting and exasperating, at one point provoking Washington to hints of using nuclear weapons unless the North Koreans and Chinese accepted reasonable terms. By the time the shooting finally stopped in July 1953, after claiming more than fifty thousand American lives and leaving Korea as divided as before along almost the same boundary, most Americans were thoroughly sick of Asian wars. There was almost no public support for joining another such conflict. Eisenhower's personal military experience as, among other things, the commander of Allied forces in Europe during the Second World War, cautioned him against placing too much credence in optimistic forecasts by beset generals; and his political sensitivities told him not to go to war without public support. So he decided to pass the buck on the French request for help. He insisted that Britain join the United States in any military intervention in Vietnam, and he added that the American Congress should vote approval of such intervention. Only then would he give the order.

The British did not want to entangle themselves in a war in Indochina, as Eisenhower knew. They had troubles enough of their own elsewhere. Nor did Congress like the idea, as Eisenhower also knew. The result was that American planes and troops stayed out of the war in Vietnam—for the time being. The French garrison at Dienbienphu capitulated to the Vietminh in May 1954. The following summer an international conference at Geneva devised an arrangement for ending the fighting and creating an independent Vietnam. The French would pull all their forces from northern Vietnam back to below the seventeenth parallel, while the Vietminh would withdraw from southern Vietnam to north of the parallel. This division of the country would be only temporary. Within two years countrywide elections would be held to form a government of a unified and independent Vietnam.

Things did not work out as specified by the Geneva accords. The French pulled south of the seventeenth parallel and eventually withdrew from Vietnam altogether, but the scheduled elections never took place, largely because the government that took over from France in southern Vietnam feared it would lose. As a result, two governments developed in Vietnam. In the north Ho's communists ruled. In the south a regime headed by Ngo Dinh Diem directed affairs. Ho continued to look to the Chinese and Soviets for support, while Diem turned to Americans. Washington provided Diem with financial and military aid and the reassurance of a 1954 treaty establishing the Southeast Asia Treaty Organization (SEATO), pledged to the defense of South Vietnam against communist aggression. Yet despite the deepening division of the country, both Ho and Diem claimed the right to govern the whole country. Of the two Ho appeared the more likely to attempt to vindicate his claim; it seemed that Diem would have his hands full merely hanging onto South Vietnam.

France's ignominious departure from Indochina (the French pulled out of Laos and Cambodia, too) did not do much for the prestige of European imperialism; neither did a series of setbacks suffered by Britain in the Middle East. Britain's difficulties started in Iran, which many British imperialists insisting on calling by the old name of Persia. In 1951 an ardently nationalist government came to power in Teheran, pledged to a policy of breaking Britain's hammerlock on the Iranian economy. Britain's hold on Iran resulted chiefly from British control of Iranian oil; consequently, the government of Iranian prime minister Mohammed Mossadeq attempted to loosen the British grip by nationalizing Britain's oil properties in Iran, including the world's largest refinery at Abadan.

London cried foul. Although the British did not deny the right of a foreign government to assert sovereignty over external holdings within its territory, they claimed that a previously negotiated agreement granting Britain concessionary petroleum privileges in Iran expressly prohibited nationalization. The British government organized a boycott of Iranian oil, threatening to sue any company that handled the oil the British claimed was justly theirs. The major international oil companies were happy enough to cooperate in the boycott: they did not want to encourage Middle Eastern governments to nationalize other oil properties, including the companies' own. Besides, a shortfall of oil on the world market resulting from the boycott of Iran would tend to drive up prices and pad the companies' profits.

Simultaneously, the British government plotted stronger measures against Iran. Convinced that if Mossadeq got away with what London was labeling "piracy," then neither Western property nor Western rights would be safe in the Middle East, the British laid plans for an invasion of Iran. British troops would seize back the oil fields and the Abadan refinery. If Mossadeq was over-thrown as a result, too bad for him.

The British scheme ran into one crucial hitch, however: American opposi-tion to the plan. The Truman administration made clear that it would not tolerate a British attack against Iran. The administration reminded London that the United States had defended Iran against Soviet pressure in 1946 and that it could not tolerate from a friend behavior it would not allow an enemy. For other countries to get the impression that the United States applied a dou-ble standard in international relations would irreparably harm American pres-tige. Truman did not specify what measures he would take if the British refused to drop their invasion plans, but Clement Attlee, the British prime minister, decided not to find out.

This was one of Attlee's last decisions in office. Soon afterward he gave way to Winston Churchill, who returned to the prime ministership following six years of Labor party rule. Churchill was more determined than Attlee to de-fend the British empire against what he took to be the unconscionable assaults of irresponsible demagogues like Mossadeq. Yet Churchill was also the chief cheerleader for the Anglo-American "special relationship," and so he hesitated to defy plainly stated American wishes. He settled instead for negotiations with the Iranian government mediated by the Americans. Whether the negotiations would produce an agreement with Teheran, Churchill could not say. If they did not, they might well persuade the Americans of the impossibility of dealing with Mossadeq. So persuaded, the Americans might reconsider their veto of stronger action.

The stand-off between Britain and Iran dragged into 1953 and into the administration of Dwight Eisenhower. Like Truman, Eisenhower frowned on using force to settle the Anglo-Iranian dispute. Notwithstanding British com-plaints about Mossadeq's highhanded behavior, Eisenhower saw the dispute as essentially a business squabble. The question of oil rights in Iran was a matter for lawyers, not soldiers. Moreover, if Britain used force against Iran, the United States would surely share in the blame. Iranians, other Middle East-erners, and much of the rest of the world often saw Westerners as all alike. Britain's sins would be charged to America's account hardly less than to Brit-ain's. Therefore, it behooved Washington to keep London from sinning.

Yet if Eisenhower refused to countenance the use of military force against Iran, he was definitely not unconcerned at the trend of events in that country. Since Mossadeq had taken office in 1951, the Iranian prime minister's political power had rested on an unstable coalition of often competing groups. On the left wing of Iranian politics was the pro-Soviet Tudeh party. The Tudeh consid-

Dwight Eisenhower, who was more often photographed grinning, makes a serious point. *Dwight D. Eisenhower Library*

ered Mossadeq preferable to the prime minister's principal rival, the monarch Mohammed Reza Shah Pahlavi, but Mossadeq could hardly count on the Tudeh's support. On the right wing, more or less, of Iranian politics were the Islamic fundamentalists, led by Ayatollah Abol-Qasem Kashani. The Islamic fundamentalists did not like Mossadeq any more than the Tudeh did, but they were willing to go along with him, as the Tudeh was, until they saw a chance to strike for power on their own. Somewhere between the Tudeh and the Islamists was the Iranian military. The generals appeared to be loyal to Shah Pahlavi, but they were not sticking their necks out.

The chief worry of the Eisenhower administration was that Mossadeq would fall from power and be replaced by Kashani or one of his followers or by the Tudeh. Neither prospect boded well for Western interests in Iran and in the region of the Persian Gulf. A Tudeh government would look to Moscow for assistance and presumably would grant favors in return. Such favors might include a Soviet base in the gulf, which was the kind of thing Britain, and more recently the United States, had been trying to prevent for more than a century. If nothing else, the Soviets would gain the opportunity to make much mischief in the region that produced the oil Western Europe depended on. A government led by the Islamists would be almost as bad as one headed by the Tudeh, in Washington's view. Not only were the religious fundamentalists bitterly anti-Western, but they were also probably incapable of holding power for long.

that an Islamist regime would fall to the Tudeh
e same unfortunate results as a direct Tudeh take-

Mossadeq's never-sturdy coalition began creak-
ımpted the Eisenhower administration, with the
ill government in London, to consider nudging
leh or the fundamentalists did and replacing him
The American ambassador in Teheran encour-
deq and even suggested a successor. The Amer-
y (CIA) in conjunction with the British intelli-
uevised a scheme to assist in the substitution.

The plan succeeded in August 1953, but only barely. When the shah tried to
fire Mossadeq, the prime minister arrested the messenger bearing the news and
refused to be fired. Mobs supporting Mossadeq took to the streets of Teheran,
and the shah fled the country in fright. But then counter-mobs hired by the
CIA and including a frightening bunch of weighlifters from the gyms of South
Teheran appeared. They roughly handled Mossadeq's supporters and clamored
for the return of the shah. Meanwhile the successor prime minister designated
by the American ambassador declared his intention to assume his new post
forthwith. It helped matters that he was an army general, for the tanks he
dispatched to the center of the city soon sealed Mossadeq's fate and guaranteed
the transfer of power. The shah returned in triumph from his brief exile.

The short-term consequence of the 1953 coup (or countercoup, as its supporters described it: they claimed that Mossadeq had acted illegally in not
acceding to his dismissal by the shah) was the shoring up of the Western position in Iran. The pro-American Pahlavi replaced the questionable Mossadeq,
and the threat of a Soviet presence in the Persian Gulf diminished greatly. Iranian oil began flowing again after the shah concluded a deal with Britain. As
a bonus to the Americans, the oil deal included a provision that broke Britain's
domination of the Iranian oil industry and allowed American and a few other
foreign companies to participate.

The long-term results of Mossadeq's overthrow were less positive. The coup
confirmed a popular Iranian perception of the Western powers as being irrevocably manipulative of Iran's affairs. This perception played into the hands of
the Islamic fundamentalists, who castigated the West for all manner of crimes
of omission and commission. The American aid that flowed to Pahlavi in the
aftermath of the coup went to the shah's head. He suppressed civil liberties
and created a secret police force that habitually tortured and otherwise silenced
many of those who disagreed with his methods of ruling the country. This, too,
played into the hands of the fundamentalists, who lambasted the shah as an
apostate to Islam and a lackey of the American imperialists.

There was another consequence of Mossadeq's overthrow that seemed positive at the time but later would appear less so. The Iranian operation was the
first important success of the CIA in covert operations. The intelligence agency
had been created in 1947 as part of a reorganization of the American defense
establishment, a reshuffling that also created a single defense department out

of the War and Navy departments and founded the National Security Council as an advisory board to the president. But because Truman disliked the idea of allowing the development of what he called an American "Gestapo," the CIA had operated on a short leash during its initial years of existence. Eisenhower, however, had fewer qualms about covert operations, and during the Republican president's two terms in the White House, the CIA expanded its activities greatly. The successful Iranian operation encouraged the agency to attempt a similar offensive against the government of Guatemala in 1954. American agents tampered with elections in the Philippines and Syria and flew secret bombing missions in support of rebels against the government of Indonesia. By the end of the decade, American clandestine warriors were actively plotting the assassination of foreign leaders, including Fidel Castro of Cuba and Patrice Lumumba of the Congo (Zaire).

Eisenhower appreciated the freedom the CIA allowed him in conducting foreign policy. Covert operations fell into a gray area between war and peace and accordingly seemed admirably suited to the Cold War, which likewise was something between war and peace. If the covert warriors achieved the administration's objectives, the administration could quietly congratulate itself; if they failed, who would know?

The problem with the arrangement was the same problem that chronically afflicts those who exercise power without accepting responsibility. Absent outside controls or oversight, the people directing the covert operations eventually got carried away with themselves. In arranging assassination attempts against leaders of countries not at war with the United States, they went beyond the bounds of what most Americans would have countenanced. And ultimately they would get themselves into situations that gravely embarrassed American leaders and seriously compromised America's reputation.

The Lion's Last Roar: The Suez War of 1956

Although the British were moderately pleased at the outcome of their struggle with Mossadeq—he wound up in jail, and they got back their oil wells and refinery—they could not help recognizing that the Iran affair signaled another step in the process by which the United States was supplanting Britain as the predominant Western power in the Middle East. The process reflected the dual facts of America's tremendous strength and Britain's growing weakness. Britain had probably reached the peak of its power relative to the rest of the world sometime before the First World War. Between the wars it coasted on previously acquired momentum, but after 1945 it began slipping noticeably. Britain's domestic economy could not support the activities of a great power, and as Britain's colonies peeled off one by one, they were no longer available to make up the shortfall in British strength. Yet the British found it hard to readjust their perceptions and expectations of the world downward to match their diminished status. The Labor party, which governed from 1945 to 1951, being the more anti-imperialist of Britain's two major parties, started the process of decolonization with decorum, notably in India. But though the return of the Conservatives in late 1951 did not slow Britain's decline significantly, it did lessen the decorum with which it was accomplished.

The most indecorous maneuver of Britain's postwar downhill run occurred in the autumn of 1956. After protracted and bitter haggling punctuated by violence against and by British soldiers, the British government in 1954 had come to terms with the Egyptian government regarding Britain's withdrawal from Egypt. The negotiations left a bad taste in British mouths and left London deeply suspicious of Nasser. Because the American government had been less helpful in the negotiations than London had desired, a residue of resentment toward Washington also existed in some British circles.

This was a bit ironic, in that the Eisenhower administration was almost as suspicious of Nasser as Churchill and British foreign secretary Anthony Eden were. Nasser's neutralism did not sit well with the Republican administration, and when Nasser announced his 1955 weapons deal with the Soviets, Eisenhower and John Foster Dulles grew more irritated still. Even so Eisenhower and Dulles were not ready to write Nasser off. For several years Egyptian engineers and government officials had been drafting plans for a large dam on the Nile River at Aswan. The Aswan Dam would harness the power of the Nile, helping bring the Egyptian people into the electrical age. More important, it would control the floods of the Nile and provide year-round irrigation that would greatly increase crop yields. But the dam would cost far more money than Egypt had available, and the Egyptians were looking abroad for support. The United States was the likeliest source of funding. Nasser might have taken a more anti-Western line in international affairs than he did but for his desire to have Washington underwrite the Aswan project.

The Eisenhower administration initially expressed interest in the project. Eisenhower and Dulles appreciated the positive publicity the Aswan Dam would produce for the United States. Critics of America in Asia and Africa typically accused Washington of spending billions on weapons and on aid to America's relatively rich European allies but precious little on humanitarian projects for the world's really needy. The Aswan Dam would go far to counter these criticisms. What could be more humanitarian than a dam to provide irrigation and hydropower for the Egyptian fellahin? And Nasser certainly could not be considered an American stooge, as his weapons deal with the Eastern bloc demonstrated. By underwriting the Aswan Dam, the United States would show its tolerance for international diversity.

There were other considerations behind the Eisenhower administration's backing for the dam. The Soviets were talking about providing money to build it if the United States did not. Eisenhower and Dulles thought the Soviets might be bluffing: the president and secretary of state questioned whether the Kremlin could pony up the $100 million or so the dam would require. But in any case, they wanted the credit for such a worthy project to go to America. In addition, they believed that keeping Nasser focused on the Aswan Dam, in which he had taken an intense personal interest—some people were calling it

Nasser's answer to the Pyramids—would keep him out of trouble. Nasser periodically agitated the Arab-Israeli dispute and threatened to smite the Zionists. To some degree his threats reflected his genuine umbrage at the existence of Israel and at Israel's policies. To some degree as well, however, they were a manifestation of the age-old habit of national leaders of finding foreign devils to distract the masses from their problems at home. If Nasser could point to the Aswan Dam as a concrete measure of his concern for the Egyptian people, he would feel less need to take actions that might push Israel toward war. At a minimum, lending Egypt a lot of low-interest money to build the dam would sop up, as repayment, Egyptian funds that Nasser might otherwise spend on weapons.

Yet Nasser was a prickly character, and the Eisenhower administration encountered serious political problems getting the American Congress to approve the money for the Aswan Dam. Anticommunist conservatives complained that the administration seemed to be rewarding Nasser's neutralism; the United States ought to concentrate on its friends: on those countries that were willing to stand up and be counted in the battle against communism. Fiscal watchdogs complained that the administration was wasting the taxpayers' money; if money needed to be spent alleviating poverty, let the administration spend it at home. Southern cotton growers objected to what amounted to an American subsidy for their Egyptian competitors. American friends of Israel questioned anything that strengthened Israel's most powerful foe.

During the first half of 1956, Nasser raised the political cost to the Eisenhower administration of funding the dam. He extended diplomatic recognition to China at a time when the United States was trying to isolate Beijing. And he rejected an American-sponsored effort to find a settlement of the Arab-Israeli conflict. By the summer of 1956, Eisenhower and Dulles had decided that they just could not do business with Nasser. In July the administration withdrew its offer of financing for the Aswan Dam.

Nasser took the withdrawal hard. "This is not a withdrawal," he declared. "It is an attack on the regime." To emphasize his anger, he told the American government, "Drop dead of your fury! For you will never be able to dictate to Egypt." He then delivered his substantive riposte: he announced that Egypt would nationalize the Suez Canal Company, thereby seizing control of the canal. The tolls from the canal would go toward building the Aswan Dam.

Although it was an American action that was primarily responsible for his reaction (but not entirely responsible: Britain simultaneously withdrew a much smaller aid package), Nasser's retaliatory strike hit the British hardest. The British government held the largest stake in the Suez Canal Company and found itself suddenly deprived of an important source of revenue. More fundamentally, for London to lose control of the Suez Canal would demonstrate that Britain really had sunk to the level of an international also-ran. The canal was an important passageway on the route to Britain's holdings in the Persian Gulf, to British Malaya, and to British Hong Kong. It also afforded communication with India, Pakistan, Australia, and New Zealand, which, though no longer colonies, were members of the British Commonwealth, the successor to the British empire. And beyond this the Suez Canal had tremendous significance as a symbol of British prestige. Nasser's grab of the canal was an insufferable insult.

Almost at once the British government prepared to reverse the seizure. Anthony Eden, who had taken over as prime minister upon Churchill's long-delayed retirement, cabled Eisenhower, "My colleagues and I are convinced that we must be ready, in the last resort, to use force to bring Nasser to his senses." Eisenhower attempted to calm Eden down. The president argued that the diplomats must be given first chance to solve the Suez dispute. Eisenhower held no brief for Nasser, but the president judged that military action would probably prove counterproductive. The West was competing with the Soviets for the affections of the peoples of Asia and Africa, most of whom already distrusted the Western Europeans, and to some extent the Americans, as inveterate imperialists who desired to crush any indication of independence on the part of the lesser powers. For the British to attack Egypt on account of a dispute over property rights would tend to corroborate these negative opinions. And for the United States to back the British in such an attack, which was Eden's wish, would be even worse for American interests. The likely result, Eisenhower predicted, would be to "array the world from Dakar to the Philippines against us."

Through diplomatic delaying tactics, Eisenhower and Dulles managed to postpone military action by the British; but Eden was determined. During the early autumn of 1956, Eden secretly communicated with the governments of France and Israel and prepared a plan to pry the Suez Canal loose from Nasser's grasp and probably topple the Egyptian leader. Both France and Israel had reason to wish Nasser ill. Nasser was encouraging rebels against French rule in Algeria; Paris wanted to stop the encouragement and signal other Arab leaders to stay out of France's affairs. Israel feared that Egypt was getting too strong, especially now that Nasser was receiving Soviet bloc weapons. Moreover, Nasser was abetting guerrilla attacks on Israel from bases in the Gaza Strip. And finally, his pan-Arab rhetoric rendered improved relations between Israel and its neighbors nearly impossible. Someone needed to teach that loudmouthed provocateur a lesson.

According to the plan the three governments agreed on, Israel would attack Egypt, slicing across the Sinai Peninsula toward the Suez Canal. Britain and France, ostensibly in the interests of protecting the canal from damage or blockage, would deliver an ultimatum to the opposing sides to pull their forces back from the canal. The Israelis would comply, while the Egyptians presumably would not. Nasser could hardly accept dictation from London and Paris about how to repel an Israeli invasion or where to position Egyptian troops within Egypt. When Nasser refused to comply, Britain and France would invade Egypt. At the least the British and French forces would seize control of the canal; with luck Nasser would go down politically, if not physically, in the fighting and confusion.

Eden exerted great pains to conceal his plan from Americans. The British prime minister evidently thought Washington might accept a swift stroke that restored the canal to Western control, and perhaps ousted Nasser, so long as Americans did not have to get their hands dirty. But he suspected, quite rightly as matters proved, that Eisenhower would never agree to such an operation in advance.

At the end of October, Israeli troops attacked Egypt as planned. Within hours they closed in on the canal, and London and Paris issued their ultimatum. The Israelis backed off as planned; the Egyptians, also as planned, did not. British and French forces thereupon joined the battle, bombing Egyptian positions and landing at the northern end of the canal.

At this stage the operation began to fall apart. Eisenhower realized by now that Eden had tried to pull a fast one, and the American president was furious. Eisenhower publicly condemned the British-French-Israeli action and took steps that forced Eden to call off the invasion. The outbreak of fighting had provoked a run on the British currency, which put a severe strain not only on the pound but also on the British government's entire fiscal situation. London tried to alleviate the strain by means of an emergency loan from the International Monetary Fund. Eisenhower blocked the loan, directing the American representative to the IMF to veto it until the British dropped their insane action in Egypt. At the same time that the British currency was nosediving, Britain was running short of oil. The fighting in the Middle East had disrupted shipments from the Persian Gulf, and the British wanted Eisenhower to arrange rerouting of shipments from the Western Hemisphere to Britain. Eisenhower refused.

Eisenhower's anger at what he perceived to be Britain's outrageous behavior was compounded by the concurrence of similarly bad conduct on the part of the Soviet Union in Eastern Europe. In October 1956 popular dissatisfaction with the communist regime that had been imposed on Hungary by the Kremlin burst into revolution. Rioters in Budapest, encouraged in part by loose talk among individuals linked to the Eisenhower administration of an American intention to "roll back" communism and "liberate" Eastern Europe, drove Moscow's men from power and pushed Hungary rapidly toward the restoration of democracy and withdrawal from the Warsaw Pact. The Kremlin responded with a massive display of force. Tanks of the Red Army crushed the rebellion and attached Hungary more firmly than ever to the Soviet bloc. The Western governments stood by helplessly. Despite the Republican rhetoric of "rollback," Eisenhower recognized that he could do little for the Hungarians without running an unacceptable risk of war against the Soviet Union. Washington might have been able to make a good diplomatic and political case against this latest example of Soviet imperialism—except that the British and French were engaged in exactly the same sort of thing at precisely the same time. The thought of the squandered opportunity sent Eisenhower's already high blood pressure many points higher.

Eisenhower's sanctions against Britain stopped the Suez invasion in its tracks. The British had no choice but to go along with Washington's demands that they cease fire and withdraw. The French, not wishing to be exposed to international obloquy without the company of the British, chose to follow the British lead. The Israelis were slower to give in but did so eventually.

The immediate result of the Suez invasion was the humiliation of the British. Eden had to resign from office, and Britain's status as a world power crumpled overnight. The British had shown themselves to be not merely duplicitous and arrogant but also ineffectual. It was a bitter pill for Britain, once the master of the greatest empire on earth, to have to take orders from the United States.

The more lasting result was deeper American involvement in the affairs of the Middle East. Until this point American leaders had had no particular desire to elbow the British aside; they understood that American interests in the Middle East generally paralleled those of Britain. American officials had been glad for the opportunity to cut American companies in on the action in places like Iran, but otherwise they saw that it was to America's benefit, as much as to Britain's, to let the British keep the lead in guaranteeing the status quo in the area. Only when the British proved incapable of maintaining the status quo, and when they compounded their incapacity by such bungling as the Suez fiasco, did American leaders decide that they would have to do the job themselves.

The Eisenhower administration set about replacing the British just several weeks after the debacle of the autumn of 1956. Early the following year, the president announced, and Congress approved, what came to be called the Eisenhower Doctrine: a policy of willingness to employ American military forces in the defense of friendly governments in the Middle East threatened by communism. This policy was a sharpened version of the Truman Doctrine of a decade before. Where Truman's doctrine had been very broad, applying potentially to countries anywhere on the planet, Eisenhower's dealt only with the Middle East. And where Truman's doctrine had been unspecific about the nature of American support and had in fact delivered, in the cases of Greece and Turkey, only dollars and advice, Eisenhower's specified military force.

What Eisenhower specified, he delivered. In the aftermath of the Suez War, Nasser's prestige had soared in the Arab world. The Egyptian president had stood up to the imperialists and the Zionists and had forced them, albeit with American help, to retreat. Nasser's enhanced stature gave encouragement to other radical Arab nationalists, who worked more energetically than ever to topple the conservative pro-Western regimes in the area. The Jordanian monarchy of King Hussein found itself besieged, as did the Lebanese government of President Camille Chamoun. The position of Chamoun was especially uncertain, in that Chamoun, a Maronite Christian, headed a country that was predominantly Muslim. The Muslims were demanding a larger share of political and economic power, which Chamoun and the Christians were resisting relinquishing. Radicals among the Muslims looked to Nasser for inspiration and backing, while Chamoun looked to the West. In particular, after the announcement of the Eisenhower Doctrine, Chamoun looked to Washington. The terms of the Eisenhower Doctrine stated that it applied to situations where friendly governments came under attack from communists or communist sympathizers, but Chamoun hoped to persuade the Eisenhower administration to stretch the notion of communist sympathizers to include his enemies. It would require a sizable stretch since the insurgents in Lebanon had almost no affinity for communism.

The Lebanese insurgency sputtered along sporadically until the summer of 1958, when it suddenly threatened to explode. The event that appeared about to trigger the explosion was a revolution in Baghdad. Some radical Iraqi military officers overthrew the Hashemite monarchy of King Faisal, assassinating all the members of the royal family they could lay hands on, as well as the pro-Western prime minister. This brutal action sent shock waves across the Middle East. Conservative regimes throughout the region reinforced their palace guards and turned toward the West for assistance. Lebanon's Chamoun demanded that Eisenhower back up his brave words with action and send troops to Lebanon.

Eisenhower hesitated briefly, aware that the trouble in Lebanon had almost nothing to do with communism. Yet the president decided that, communism or no communism, the United States could not afford to let down a regime that was counting on it for support. If Chamoun did not get the troops he was requesting, he assuredly would blame the Americans for irresolution, even cowardice. Regardless of whether his finger pointing was justified, it would damage American prestige in the Middle East and elsewhere. Besides, the administration could contend, and did, that even if communism per se was not a threat in Lebanon, the overthrow of the conservative government in that country would weaken Lebanon's resistance to future communist encroachment.

Eisenhower went ahead and approved Chamoun's request. Some fourteen thousand American marines hit the beach at Beirut, surprising many of the bathers there, who were treating the insurgency far more casually than either the Lebanese or American governments. As matters happened, the mere arrival of the American troops sufficed to quell whatever ambitions the insurgents had entertained of repeating the Iraqi experience in Lebanon. These ambitions may have been quite modest to begin with, as the outcome of the affair suggested. With the American soldiers standing by, American diplomats helped negotiate a settlement of the conflict that was essentially the same as one suggested months earlier by, of all people, Nasser. The settlement, which included a Christian replacement for Chamoun as president and a prominent Muslim as prime minister, satisfied the various parties to the conflict sufficiently that they put down their weapons and went back to what they had been doing before. The American troops left the country within a few months of their arrival.

The Eisenhower administration claimed victory for its policy of supporting friendly conservatives in the Middle East. The claim was exaggerated. Although conservatives held on in Jordan (with the help of British paratroops, which had gone to King Hussein's aid at the same time that the American marines moved into Lebanon) and Saudi Arabia, the revolution in Iraq had seriously frightened them. The two most populous and politically important Arab countries, Egypt and Iraq, were both now controlled by radical regimes.

This might have produced a tilt toward the Soviet Union in Middle Eastern politics, except for a resumption of the long-running conflict between Iraq and Egypt. Baghdad turned to Moscow for aid, causing Nasser to begin turning toward the West. A regional competition developed between Iraq and Egypt, with the result that neither side in the superpower competition came out much ahead.

Rekindling the Revolution: Latin America

The radicalism that was gaining ground in the Middle East had its counterpart in Latin America. After the Mexican revolution of the 1910s, the demands for fundamental change quieted for a time, hushed by the emergence of strong men—Somoza in Nicaragua, Batista in Cuba, Trujillo in the Dominican Republic—who browbeat those who would have complained and bought off those they could not browbeat. The depression of the 1930s also helped stifle demands for change. Preoccupied with holding body and soul together, most people in Latin America did not have time for the luxury of revolution. Desperately poor people rarely revolt; revolutions are almost always the work of folks with food in their stomachs. The Second World War similarly blunted revolutionary agitation in many countries but for a different reason. The war boosted the prices of commodities on which various Latin American economies depended; at the same time, the war diverted most of the manufactured goods the Latin American countries had imported from the United States and Europe, encouraging the development of manufacturing within the Latin American countries themselves. Both developments stimulated the Latin American economies. The stimulation brought the promise of prosperity, which made revolution appear unnecessary to the middle classes that often had been its instigators.

There were exceptions to this pattern. Guatemala, for example, felt the war as a second powerful blow. The Depression had halved the world prices of coffee and bananas, knocking the Guatemalan economy to its knees. The war prevented Guatemala from getting up by cutting it off from European markets. Where entrepreneurs in other Latin American countries branched out during the war into new activities, Guatemalans failed to do so, in part because of the long tradition of dominance by an aristocracy of planters. Economic discontent in the small urban middle class joined with political annoyance at the profascist sympathies of the dictator Jorge Ubico to produce a 1944 general strike and a series of additional antigovernment demonstrations. When a key group of army officers abandoned Ubico for the protesters, the government fell. Elections in December 1944 placed the reformer Juan José Arévalo in office.

The Arévalo government was revolutionary only by comparison to the Ubico regime. The government instituted a number of social reforms, building schools and hospitals, banning forced labor, and creating a social security system. It guaranteed the right of workers to organize into unions and to bargain collectively with employers. It regulated the activities of major foreign-controlled businesses, such as the American-based United Fruit Company. But on the whole, the Arévalo program was no more radical than the New Deal in the United States.

With the election of Jacobo Arbenz to Guatemala's presidency in 1950, the Guatemalan revolution took a left turn. Arbenz inaugurated a sweeping reform of land ownership, the centerpiece of which was a 1952 law nationalizing large plots of idle land, which would be transferred to landless peasants. The primary target of this reform was the United Fruit Company, the owner of thousands of acres of unused land. The company had purchased the land for future development but in the meantime kept farmers and others off it. Arbenz's nationalization law specified that United Fruit would be compensated for the land at the value assessed for tax purposes. This seemed fair enough to many Guatemalans since the assessed value reflected the degree to which the company had been pulling its weight in paying for Guatemalan public services. But the company complained that the assessed value was far below the market value, which was true. Over the previous years, company executives had persuaded friendly Guatemalan officials to keep the assessed value, and therefore the company's taxes, artificially low.

The United States government observed the changes in Guatemala with growing concern. The Truman administration had had little difficulty accepting Arévalo's moderate reforms; Truman probably wished he could have enjoyed as much luck getting his own Fair Deal program through the American legislature. But Arbenz's 1952 land reform law, followed by the 1953 installation of the more conservative Republican administration in Washington, increased the tension between the American and Guatemalan governments. The United Fruit Company had close connections to the Eisenhower administration: several Eisenhower appointees had ties of ownership or professional service to the company. But the personal connections mattered less than the administration's fear that Arbenz's land reform policies indicated an unacceptable degree of independence on his part.

The complaints of United Fruit notwithstanding, the Eisenhower administration did not care much one way or the other what kinds of policies Arbenz instituted within Guatemala. Washington had made its peace with the principle of nationalization in 1938 when Mexico seized American oil holdings there. Yet the administration cared very much what kinds of policies Guatemala pursued with respect to the rest of the world. And Arbenz's radical land policies suggested a potentially radical approach to foreign affairs—an approach that might well involve cultivating closer relations with the Soviet Union. Ever since the 1823 promulgation of the Monroe Doctrine, the United States had sought to minimize the influence of extrahemispheric powers in Latin America. In the post–Second World War period, the extrahemispheric influence Washington most wanted to minimize was that of the Soviet Union.

When Arbenz took delivery of a shipload of Czech weapons, Washington's suspicions of him grew stronger than ever. The United States embassy in Guatemala City began looking for a replacement, and the CIA started training disaffected Guatemalan émigrés for a coup against Arbenz. In June 1954 a rebel force under the leadership of Carlos Castillo Armas entered Guatemala from Honduras. With the assistance of CIA-piloted airplanes, which dropped anti-Arbenz literature on the capital, along with some light explosives that did more psychological damage to the government than physical harm, the rebels forced Arbenz from power.

Castillo Armas assumed the presidency and inaugurated a counterrevolution. The 1952 land reform law was repealed, and Arbenz's supporters were killed en masse. The Eisenhower administration applauded the overall result of the coup, if not all its details. Guatemala no longer threatened to be the door by which Soviet influence might enter the Western Hemisphere.

For a time Bolivia looked as though it might take on that role. In 1952 a leftist government spearheaded by Victor Paz Estenssoro gained power and instituted a broad agenda of reforms. The new government nationalized Bolivia's tin mines, broke up large farms, and converted the army to a workers' and peasants' militia. Washington wondered how far to the left it could allow Bolivia to go.

But Paz Estenssoro shrewdly steered away from anything that could be interpreted as an overture to the Soviet Union, and eventually he convinced the Eisenhower administration that he was not leading Bolivia down the communist path. Washington encouraged good behavior in La Paz with a succession of packages of economic and military aid.

Cuba, not Bolivia or Guatemala, turned out to be the entryway for Soviet influence into the Western Hemisphere. After six years of controlling Cuban politics through pliable presidents, Fulgencio Batista in 1940 had had himself elected to the top job. He served until 1944, then stepped down as mandated by the Cuban constitution. Batista retired from active politics for several years but watched unhappily as corruption and political confusion spread across the country. The confusion only increased when one of the leading candidates in the 1952 election campaign committed suicide while in the middle of a radio broadcast, evidently as a protest against the thuggery and graft that were becoming common in Cuban politics. Batista decided to take control of the situation once more. The former president led a group of midlevel army officers who ousted the current president and canceled the 1952 elections. Dispensing with the trappings of democracy, Batista set himself up as dictator.

Batista's return sparked a new outburst of disaffection among Cubans. In Florida middle-class Cuban exiles devised plans for returning to Cuba and tossing out the despot. In Havana student activists hatched plots in their dormitories and coffeehouses. One graduate of the student cabals, Fidel Castro, led a small group of militants on a raid against an army barracks at Moncada, near Santiago de Cuba. The attack failed miserably, and nearly all involved were captured or killed. Castro was imprisoned on the Isle of Pines, just off Cuba's southern coast, after a trial in which he delivered an impassioned ora-

Fidel Castro gives a victory wave upon entering Havana in January 1959. Fulgencio Batista is not around to wave back, having fled the city for Miami. *UPI/Bettman*

tion that justified revolt against Batista in the same Enlightenment social–contract terms that Thomas Jefferson had used to justify the American Revolution 180 years before. Regarding Batista's future, Castro commented, "Dante divided his hell into nine circles; he put the criminals in the seventh, the thieves in the eighth and the traitors in the ninth. What a hard dilemma the devil will face when he must choose the circle adequate for the soul of Batista."

Castro served a term of nearly two years before a general amnesty in 1955 sprung him loose. He left Cuba for Mexico, where he continued scheming against Batista. In 1956 Castro and a band of some eighty other rebels crammed aboard a small sailing vessel and left Mexico for their homeland. The invasion proved almost as thorough a fiasco as the Moncada raid. Castro and a handful of followers were lucky to survive the landing and escape to the mountains of Cuba's Sierra Maestra.

Although Cuba was not quite the issue in American politics it had been in the 1890s during the runup to the Spanish-American War, Americans were still paying attention. The *New York Times* sent reporter Herbert Matthews into the mountains to confirm or disprove Cuban government claims that Castro had been killed and the insurgency all but destroyed. Matthews found Castro, who gave the reporter an interview in which the rebel leader portrayed his aims as moderate and thoroughly democratic. The articles Matthews wrote for the *Times* made Castro an international figure. They also helped enormously in Castro's efforts to generate support among the Cuban people. During the next year and a half, Castro's insurgency gained momentum and adherents.

Castro's success in the mountains elicited imitation elsewhere in Cuba. In the autumn of 1957, a group of naval officers at Cienfuegos mutinied. Batista responded with heavy-handed force, which included the use of American-supplied military equipment. Partly because Batista's aid agreement with Washington prohibited such domestic use of the American weapons, and partly because the Eisenhower administration was beginning to wonder whether Batista was still a good bet, the United States cut off arms shipments to Cuba. In a final effort to suppress the rebellion, Batista launched a major offensive against Castro in the spring of 1958. The offensive failed. During the final months of 1958, Castro's guerrillas moved down from the mountains and pushed toward Havana. At the beginning of 1959, Batista fled the country for Miami. A week later Castro arrived in the capital.

It did not take Castro long in power to decide that the democracy he had been speaking of needed to be deferred. He gathered both legislative and executive control to himself and suppressed free speech and opposition parties. This concentration of control dismayed many of Castro's Sierra Maestra comrades, who had taken his talk of democracy and personal freedom seriously. A falling out ensued, with some of the disaffected heading for Florida and others winding up in Cuban prisons or before firing squads. To solidify his regime against such dissent, Castro turned toward the Cuban Communist party.

At the same time, Castro undertook to socialize the Cuban economy and diminish its dependence on the United States. Land reform topped his agenda, followed by the negotiation of a sugar-for-oil deal with the Soviet Union. The Soviet deal predictably provoked a reaction in Washington: the Eisenhower administration pressured American oil companies operating refineries in Cuba to refuse Castro's demand that they refine the Soviet crude. Castro responded by nationalizing the refineries. Eisenhower retaliated by canceling Cuba's sugar quota, effectively cutting Cuba off from the largest market for its most important export. Castro countered by seizing more American property in Cuba. Eisenhower suspended nearly all American trade with Cuba. Castro expropriated more American holdings.

The result was a thorough alienation of Cuba from the United States. Castro did not complain at this outcome, though he might have wished it had not happened so fast. For Castro, the United States served as a convenient scapegoat, and the nastier Washington acted, the more credible a scapegoat it was. With American distrust escalating to the level of political and economic warfare, Castro could justify his suppression of democracy and civil liberties as necessary war measures. He might have found other justifications in the absence of American hostility, but they would not have been so easy to sell to the Cuban people.

While the rupture of relations with the United States probably pushed Castro toward the Soviet Union more swiftly than he might otherwise have chosen to go, it almost certainly did not force him into anything he really did not want to do. Like Nehru of India and Nasser of Egypt, Castro appreciated the benefits of playing one superpower against the other. If Castro stood for anything, it was for Cuban nationalism and independence. For decades Cuba had struggled along in America's shadow; by one means or other Castro intended to pull Cuba out of that shadow. The Soviet Union, always eager to discomfit Washington, was happy to help.

Castro's courting of the Kremlin, a process that included his announcement that he was an ardent Marxist-Leninist and had been for years—a fact, if fact it was, he had neglected to share with anyone else before he got to Havana in January 1959—merely intensified American suspicions of Cuba's new leader. Several months prior to departing office at the beginning of 1961, Eisenhower approved a CIA plan for training Cuban exiles who desired to overthrow Castro. The secret planning and training continued through the transition to the Kennedy administration and into the first months of John Kennedy's presidency.

The planning was seriously flawed, based, as events proved, on wishful thinking rather than hard intelligence. According to the CIA's scenario, the exile army, with American assistance, would land on Cuban shores and establish a beachhead. This would trigger an uprising within Cuba itself, which would lead to Castro's ouster. Although some members of the Kennedy administration wondered about the odds of a popular anti-Castro uprising, the president and most of his closest advisers were brand new at their jobs, and as a group they lacked the experience and self-confidence to grill CIA officials closely. Kennedy knew about the agency's successful roles in the overthrow of Mossadeq in Iran and Arbenz in Guatemala; he probably did not know about the unsuccessful CIA effort to overthrow Indonesia's Sukarno in 1958. Consequently, it was difficult for him to argue with Allen Dulles, the legendary CIA director, who had been involved in espionage almost since before Kennedy was born.

Moreover, as a candidate for the presidency in 1960, Kennedy had criticized Eisenhower for not doing enough to stop the spread of communism. As a result, the president was politically disinclined to nix a project that offered a chance to rescue Cuba from communism and prevent the Soviets from penetrating the Western Hemisphere and subverting the Monroe Doctrine. For Kennedy to veto the project would have opened him to damaging news leaks suggesting that he was as irresolute as he had charged Eisenhower with being. When Kennedy received the personal assurances of Allen Dulles that the anti-Castro operation was sound, the president gave his approval.

The April 1961 invasion, which took its name from the Bay of Pigs where the invaders landed, was a disaster. The invading force barely made it to shore after hitting unexpected shoals; they were immediately discovered by Castro's soldiers and repeatedly strafed by the small Cuban air force. The invaders were quickly rounded up and imprisoned.

The Bay of Pigs disaster greatly embarrassed the Kennedy administration. Not only had the United States been caught engaging in armed hostilities against a neighbor with which it was not at war, but it had also failed in the attempt. A tiny country had defeated the United States. The Cuban revolution had withstood American imperialism. Castro became an instant hero in Cuba and throughout the nonaligned world.

October Surprise: Missiles in Cuba

Kennedy's embarrassment over the Bay of Pigs bungle was by no means the last word in the president's dealings with Castro. Kennedy considered Castro as much of a threat as ever to American interests in the Western Hemisphere— more of a threat, in fact, with his enhanced prestige and his strengthening relations with Moscow. The president directed the CIA to conduct a campaign to undermine Castro. The intelligence agency sponsored raids by Cuban exiles against Cuban territory and attempted to disrupt Cuban trade with other countries. The agency went so far as to plot assassination attempts against Castro, evidently some in conjunction with representatives of the Mafia crime syndicate, whose leaders disliked Castro for closing down the Havana casinos and nightclubs that had been big moneymakers for the mob. Some of the CIA plans were bizarre. One aimed to use an exploding seashell as the murder weapon, planted in a place where Castro was known to enjoy diving. Another plan involved the use of a depilatory powder that would cause his beard to fall out. During the Sierra Maestra days, Castro and his followers had been known as the *barbudos,* or "bearded ones"; someone in the CIA apparently thought that a smooth-chinned Castro would lose his appeal for the Cuban people.

None of the assassination plans succeeded. Perhaps the point was less to kill Castro than to harass him and remind him that Washington was watching his every move. Castro was aware that the American government was trying to do him in, though he probably blamed the United States for more than it deserved. Not surprisingly, Castro tried to protect himself and defend the Cuban revolution by still closer ties to the Soviet Union. Equally unsurprisingly, the closer he got to Moscow, the more he antagonized the United States.

Washington was especially sensitive on the Soviet issue during the early 1960s. In the previous few years, relations between the superpowers had grown more ideological again after the predominantly geopolitical phase of the middle 1950s. The shift reflected political conditions in the United States, where Democrats like Kennedy lambasted Eisenhower's moderation as a means of reclaiming the White House; the shift also reflected a parting of the ways between the Soviet Union and China, which left both former allies claiming to be the true disciples of Marx and Lenin. To stay one socialist jump ahead of Mao Zedong, Nikita Khrushchev felt obliged to berate and threaten Americans at every opportunity.

He encountered an irresistible opportunity in May 1960 when Soviet air defense shot down an American U-2 spy plane—another of the CIA's projects. Eisenhower tried to cover up this invasion of Soviet airspace by claiming that the downed craft was a weather research plane blown off course, but Khrushchev trapped Eisenhower in his lie by producing both the wrecked plane, which obviously was more than a weather craft, and the pilot, who confessed to being a spy. Eisenhower was forced to admit the truth. Although he did his best to shift the blame to the Soviets for engaging in excessive secrecy, the net result was a black eye for Eisenhower and the United States. Khrushchev brandished righteous indignation with relish. He consented to attend a previously scheduled summit conference at Paris just days later, only to turn the conference into a forum for denouncing what he called "the reactionary circles of the United States" and the "small, frantic group in the Pentagon and militarist circles who benefit from the arms race and reap huge profits." For good measure, Khrushchev also blasted America's allies, including the government of West Germany, which he accused of sending to Paris "some of these fascist bastards we did not finish off at Stalingrad." Khrushchev demanded an apology from Eisenhower; when the apology was not forthcoming, the Soviet premier stalked out.

Khrushchev was still waxing indignant when he and Kennedy met for another try at a summit conference in Vienna in June 1961. Khrushchev took the opportunity to press Kennedy on Berlin. Ever since the Soviets had dropped their blockade of West Berlin in 1949, that half city had continued to serve as a pressure point in relations between the American alliance system and the Soviets. In 1958 Khrushchev tried to loosen ties within NATO by demanding that the American, British, and French troops garrisoning West Berlin evacuate the city. Because the garrison forces were too small to defend themselves, the demand carried a considerable threat: if trouble broke out, the Western allies might feel obliged to reinforce these troops across East German territory, leading to a confrontation with the Soviets. Khrushchev evidently hoped that the ultimatum would frighten America's European partners into reconsidering whether they wanted to run the risks inherent in tying their fate to Washington's policies. The Europeans decided they did, and they stood firm.

Khrushchev let his ultimatum slide, only to revive it in 1961. West Berlin did not gall the East Germans and Soviets simply on account of the presence of NATO troops deep inside East Germany; it also disturbed the Soviet side as an escape hatch for East Germans unhappy with their prospects in the communist half of the country. When the two half Germanys had been equally hard up just after the Second World War, the attractions of the western half had not been overwhelming, but as the West German economy revived during the 1950s, more and more people began ducking under the Iron Curtain by way of Berlin. In 1960 the defections totaled more than 2 million, with many of those fleeing possessing advanced educational degrees and scarce skills. The massive departures were both a political black eye and a threat to East Germany's economic development.

Nikita Khrushchev and John Kennedy exchange smiles at Vienna in 1961. Frowns and growls were more common between Khrushchev and Kennedy during this period. *Associated Press Photo*

To close the escape hatch, Khrushchev reiterated his demand for Western withdrawal from Berlin. At his Vienna meeting with Kennedy, he blusteringly insisted that the anomalous position of Berlin must end. The Allied occupation had long outlived its usefulness. The Soviet Union would sign a peace treaty with East Germany and turn East Berlin over to the East Germans. The Americans, British, and French must do likewise with the West Germans. West Berlin should be transformed into a free city.

Kennedy did not like Khrushchev's abusive tone—though the president had to smile at Khrushchev's sense of humor. When he asked whether the Soviet leader ever admitted mistakes, Khrushchev answered, "Certainly I do. In a speech before the twentieth party congress, I admitted all of Stalin's mistakes." Kennedy refused Khrushchev's demands regarding Berlin, and he continued to refuse even after the Soviet leader threateningly announced a large increase in the Soviet military budget. Kennedy reaffirmed America's promise to defend West Berlin and matched Khrushchev's budgetary ante upping with a request to the American Congress for a big increase in American defense spending.

With the international tension growing by the week, the Soviets suddenly made a sneak end run around the Western diplomatic position. In August 1961 the East Germans, with obvious Kremlin approval, built a wall cutting East Berlin off from West Berlin. Almost overnight the wall shut off the flow of East Germans into West Berlin. So well did it work that Khrushchev subsequently withdrew his demand that the West get out of West Berlin.

Viewed from one angle, the Berlin Wall was an abject admission of the bankruptcy of life under communism. What kind of country and what kind of system had to fence people in? Viewed from another direction, however, it showed the impotence of the United States and the West. Even though the NATO powers might denounce the wall as barbaric, there was nothing they could reasonably do about it. The wall was on East Berlin's side of the dividing line and was not worth risking a war to bring down. Although Kennedy tried to play up the first angle, politically the second often seemed more important. The Kremlin had slammed shut the jail door on yet another country, and the American president had been unable to prevent the slamming. Kennedy decried the construction of the wall as fresh evidence of the oppressiveness of communism, and on a subsequent visit to West Berlin, he dramatically declared America's solidarity with the people of the city. "As a free man," he said, "I take pride in the words, *'Ich bin ein Berliner!'*" (I am a Berliner). But Kennedy's bold words did not dismantle the wall, and they afforded scant comfort to those who got shot by East German guards while trying to scale it.

East German construction crews erecting the infamous wall in Berlin during the summer of 1961. It would become much more formidable before they finished. *AP/ Wide World Photos*

Kennedy's troubles with Khrushchev regarding Berlin, combined with his continuing annoyance at Castro, disposed the president to react sharply to any tightening of ties between Cuba and the Soviet Union. Just such a tightening occurred during the summer of 1962 when the Soviets secretly began work on the installation of nuclear-tipped missiles in Cuba. Castro feared an American invasion; even more effectively than the Soviet troops Khrushchev had sent to the island, the missiles would cause the Americans to think twice about doing so. Khrushchev, for his part, hoped to steal a march on the Americans by planting a few dozen missiles uncomfortably close to their border and thereby demonstrating the Soviet Union's readiness and capacity to defend its interests and allies. This would enhance the Kremlin's prestige abroad and Khrushchev's prestige at home.

American intelligence monitors learned about the missiles only in October 1962. When American aerial reconnaissance planes brought back photographs of the missile launch sites under construction, Kennedy found himself in a tight spot. To allow the missiles to go in might or might not materially alter the strategic balance between the United States and the Soviet Union: Kennedy's defense secretary, Robert McNamara, pointed out that the missiles in Cuba would not be able to hit any targets that missiles in the Soviet Union could not already hit. Others in the Kennedy administration agreed but added that Cuban missiles could hit Washington and New York far faster than Soviet Union-based missiles could and that in a nuclear exchange a difference of a few minutes might be very important. Besides, even one more missile capable of reaching American soil was one more to worry about.

Whatever the strategic implications of missiles in Cuba, Kennedy could not afford politically to act other than decisively. The Democrats were the ones who had complained that the Eisenhower administration had allowed a "missile gap" to develop between the Soviet Union and the United States. After winning the presidency, Kennedy had learned that a missile gap existed all right but that it was greatly in America's favor. Although Khrushchev knew the score as well as Kennedy did, Khrushchev was not admitting it; he preferred to rattle rockets he did not possess, confident Kennedy could not prove him wrong without compromising American intelligence sources. The Soviet leader's confidence was well placed. Even so, after the Democrats had stirred up such a storm over Soviet missiles that did not exist, Kennedy felt obliged to take strong action when confronted with Soviet missiles that undeniably did—and that undeniably would help close the real missile gap.

On October 22, 1962, Kennedy went on television to announce the discovery of the Cuban missiles. He demanded that the Soviets remove the missiles, and he announced an American naval blockade of Cuba—though he called it a "quarantine"—to ensure that no more missiles or related paraphernalia arrive on the island. At the time American officials did not know whether the warheads for the missiles were in Cuba or on their way. (Long after the event, Cuban and Soviet sources said that the warheads were indeed in Cuba at the time of Kennedy's speech.) To underline his seriousness, Kennedy added that he would consider a missile attack launched from Cuba against the United

MISSILE EQUIPMENT
MARIEL PORT FACILITY

4 MISSILE TRANSPORTERS

OXIDIZER TRAILERS

FUEL TRAILERS

LAUNCH STANDS

17 MISSILE ERECTORS

2

(APPROX. 3.5 NM NORTH OF MAIN PORT FACILITY)

The pictures that almost started a war: Aerial photos show the signs of missiles being installed in Cuba. *AP/Wide World Photos*

States to be an attack by the Soviet Union. The United States would retaliate against the Soviet Union.

Kennedy's message was accompanied by a great deal of activity on American military bases around the world, which the administration made little effort to conceal. The navy rushed to implement the blockade order; bombers scrambled; marines prepared for an invasion of Cuba.

Kennedy had considered the option of an air strike directly against the Cuban missile sites. A number of his advisers urged precisely such an action. Kennedy did not rule out this option and was prepared to give the order in the event Khrushchev failed to respond to the blockade. But the president did not want to fire the first shot, especially when that shot would probably kill Soviet soldiers or technicians and would thereby put tremendous pressure on Khrushchev to respond with similar energy. Besides, at a time when the United States had nuclear missiles in Turkey, right next door to the Soviet Union, Kennedy was not sure the rest of the world would consider Soviet missiles in Cuba an adequate cause for a major war.

For the next few days, nail biters around the world nibbled furiously. The first question was whether the Soviet ships heading for Cuba would challenge the American blockade. They did not. They stopped in midocean. The next question was whether Khrushchev would comply with Kennedy's demand to pull the missiles out of Cuba. The Soviet leader did his best to obscure the issue. He offered to meet with Kennedy and discuss the matter face to face. Kennedy told him to get the missiles out of Cuba; then they could talk.

On the fourth day after Kennedy's address, Khrushchev indicated by letter to Washington that he would be willing to withdraw the Cuban missiles in exchange for an American promise not to invade Cuba. The Soviet leader fudged this offer the next day by requiring, as a condition of removing the Cuban missiles, an American commitment to pull the American missiles out of Turkey.

Objectively, Khrushchev's offer was hard for Kennedy to refuse. Kennedy had no particular desire to invade Cuba. Besides, it flew against avowed American policy to invade countries that had not attacked the United States. As for the American missiles in Turkey, they had been made obsolescent by recent developments in American missiles technology and had been scheduled for mothballing anyway.

Yet while Kennedy was willing to promise not to invade Cuba, he did not want to be seen bargaining away part of America's nuclear deterrent, especially without the concurrence of the Turks. America's smaller allies lived in constant fear of being considered pawns by Washington; in fact, this was how American leaders often did consider them, but there was nothing to be gained by broadcasting the fact. Moreover, to negotiate away the missiles in Turkey would give the appearance of rewarding Khrushchev for his gamble.

Kennedy solved this puzzle by publicly accepting Khrushchev's condition about pledging not to invade Cuba and only privately consenting to withdraw the American missiles from Turkey. Khrushchev agreed to this deal on October 28. His agreement ended the crisis.

It was a close call—the world's closest call to nuclear war during the first five decades of the nuclear age. Just how close was unclear at the time. Not knowing whether the missiles had their warheads nearby, Kennedy and his advisers did not know whether their blockade could prevent the missiles from becoming operational. They did not know whether an air strike was necessary. They assumed the worst: that the warheads already *were* in Cuba, which turned out to be correct. They did not know how the Soviets would react to an air strike or an invasion if the situation came to either of those. They did not even guess something suggested by much later reports: that the Soviet army commander in Cuba possessed tactical nuclear weapons and was authorized to use them against an American invasion force if necessary.

Khrushchev did not know how serious Kennedy was about his ultimatum. Would he really attack Cuba and risk nuclear war over the distinction between a public promise to pull American missiles out of Turkey and a private pledge to do so? Hindsight later indicated that Kennedy was not going to start a war over such a quibble. Dean Rusk, Kennedy's secretary of state, explained many years afterward that the president had told United Nations Secretary General U Thant that he would order the missiles out of Turkey; if Khrushchev refused

Kennedy's private assurances about the missiles, Thant could make Kennedy's statement public.

It was the unknown parts of the equation that made the Cuban missile crisis of 1962 so frightening. Human decisions had always been fraught with miscalculations and presumably always would be. But never before had the stakes been so high and the price of error so staggering.

In the short term, the Cuban crisis seemed a victory for Kennedy and the United States. The American president had boldly demanded that the Soviets clear their missiles out of the Western Hemisphere, and Khrushchev had yielded. After a series of episodes in which the United States had appeared unable to deal effectively with Soviet actions, Kennedy decisively demonstrated American resolve and American power.

The long-term consequences were less favorable to the American side. By making a public issue of the Cuban missiles, rather than dealing with the matter privately, Kennedy had forced Khrushchev into a position where his only choices were war and humiliation. Fortunately for the world, Khrushchev chose humiliation. The experience contributed materially to Khrushchev's fall from power a year and a half later. It also contributed to a decision by the Soviet leadership not to be caught again in a position of nuclear inferiority. During the middle and late 1960s, the Kremlin rapidly accelerated its nuclear program, pushing the superpower arms race to new levels of expense and potential destructiveness.

* * *

To a certain extent the Cuban missile crisis closed a circle of international affairs. After facing off against each other in Europe in the late 1940s, the United States and the Soviet Union had spent much of the next decade conducting their rivalry by proxy in other parts of the world, in such places as Korea, Indochina, and the Middle East. The proxy approach to superpower competition produced some bloody conflicts, but it had the merit of keeping the Americans and Soviets from banging directly against each other. While such a separating effect would have been a good thing at any time in history, it was particularly positive now that the two superpowers were acquiring the capacity to annihilate each other and a substantial portion of the rest of the world besides.

Yet the proxies had minds of their own, and the leaders of the superpowers, being human, were bound to make mistakes. The mistakes were nowhere more likely than in the Third World, where the boundaries between the superpower spheres, and between the acceptable and unacceptable in superpower behavior, were often indistinct. The Soviets misjudged what they could get away with in Cuba in 1962, and their misjudgment brought them squarely up against the Americans.

But if the crisis had not happened in Cuba, it probably would have happened somewhere else sooner or later. If missiles had not started it, the cause could have been oil wells or submarine bases. The basic reality of the matter was that the world had become a far more complicated place by the early 1960s than it had been fifteen years before. As the European empires crumbled, they created scores of new countries. These new countries, together with some that had been at least nominally independent all along, demanded control over their own destinies. Through experience, and by watching others, several of these countries learned how to play the superpowers off against each other to their own benefit. American leaders often resisted such playing-off efforts: by Mossadeq in Iran, by Arbenz in Guatemala, by Ho Chi Minh in Vietnam, by Nasser in Egypt, by Castro in Cuba. Sometimes the American resistance stymied the efforts; sometimes it did not.

But both the playing and the resisting could be dangerous. And it grew more dangerous as the superpowers enlarged their capacity to wreak wholesale havoc on the earth. The game would not grow any less dangerous for many years. The players would simply have to be more careful.

Sources and Suggestions for Further Reading

Questions of nationalism and neutralism are examined in H. W. Brands, *The Specter of Neutralism: The United States and the Emergence of the Third World* (1989); S. Neil MacFarlane, *Superpower Rivalry and Third World Nationalism* (1985); L. S. Stavrionos, *The Third World Comes of Age* (1981); Gabriel Kolko, *Confronting the Third World: United States Foreign Policy, 1945–1980* (1988); Rupert Emerson, *From Empire to Nation: The Rise to Self-Assertion of Asian and African Peoples* (1962); Paul Bairoch, *The Economic Development of the Third World since 1900* (1975); Melvin Gurtov, *The United States against the Third World* (1974); Roger Kanet, ed., *The Soviet Union and the Developing Nations* (1974); Geoffrey Jukes, *The Soviet Union in Asia* (1973); and John D. Hargreaves, *The End of Colonial Rule in West Africa* (1979). On this general topic, but relating more directly to the Middle East, are Howard M. Sachar, *Europe Leaves the Middle East, 1936–1954* (1972); John Talbott, *The War Without a Name: The French in Algeria, 1954–1962* (1980); Robert W. Stookey, *America and the Arab States* (1975); and Oles Smolansky, *The Soviet Union and the Arab World under Khrushchev* (1974).

A good survey of the nuclear arms race is Charles R. Morris, *Iron Destinies, Lost Opportunities* (1988). Other valuable references are Lawrence Freedman, *The Evolution of Nuclear Strategy* (1981); Ronald E. Powaski, *March to Armageddon* (1987); Michael Mandelbaum, *The Nuclear Revolution* (1981); David R. Holloway, *The Soviet Union and the Arms Race* (1984 ed.); and, on the 1950s, Werner Schilling, Paul Y. Hammond, and Glenn Snyder, eds., *Strategy, Politics and Defense Budgets* (1962). On the question of nuclear testing, the best study is Robert Divine, *Blowing on the Wind* (1978). On the test ban treaty, see Glenn T. Seaborg, *Kennedy, Khrushchev and the Test Ban* (1981). The impact of Sputnik on American thinking and policy is delineated in Robert Divine, *The Sputnik Challenge* (1993).

On Eisenhower's foreign policy in general, see H. W. Brands, *Cold Warriors: Eisenhower's Generation and American Foreign Policy* (1988); Stephen E. Ambrose, *Eisenhower,* vol. 2 (1984); and Robert Divine, *Eisenhower and the Cold War* (1981). Richard Immerman, *The CIA in Guatemala* (1982), and Stephen Schlesinger and Stephen Kinzer, *Bitter Fruit* (1983), reveal American covert activities in the overthrow of Arbenz; Barry Rubin, *Paved with Good Intentions* (1980), and James A. Bill, *The Eagle and the Lion* (1988), show what American clandestine operators were up to in Iran. Lloyd C. Gardner, *Approaching Vietnam* (1988), traces early American involvement in Southeast Asia. An eminently readable account of the Suez affair is Donald Neff, *War-

riors at Suez (1981), which can also serve as a guide to other works on the subject. The most thorough rendering of the U-2 imbroglio is Michael Beschloss, *Mayday* (1986).

For other aspects of the Soviet-American contest during this period, two overviews are Adam B. Ulam, *The Rivals* (1971), and LaFeber, *America, Russia and the Cold War* (1993 ed.). Honore M. Catudal, Jr., *The Diplomacy of the Quadripartite Agreement on Berlin* (1977), and Jack M. Schick, *The Berlin Crisis* (1971), deal with troubles over the divided city.

Kennedy's approach to foreign affairs is the subject of Richard J. Walton, *Cold War and Counterrevolution* (1972). Richard D. Mahoney, *JFK: Ordeal in Africa* (1983); Madeleine G. Kalb, *The Congo Cables* (1982); and Stephen Weissman, *American Foreign Policy in the Congo* (1974), treat American policy toward Africa. On American relations with Cuba, see Langley, *The United States and the Caribbean in the Twentieth Century*; Morris Morley, *Imperial State and Revolution: The United States and Cuba, 1952–1986* (1988); and Richard E. Welch, *Response to Revolution: The United States and the Cuban Revolution, 1959–1961* (1985). On the Bay of Pigs affair specifically, consult Peter Wyden, *Bay of Pigs* (1979); and Trumbull Higgins, *The Perfect Failure* (1987).

The Cuban missile crisis is dissected in numerous works. Robert F. Kennedy, *The Thirteen Days* (1969), is a memoir. Raymond Garthoff, *Reflections on the Cuban Missile Crisis* (1987), possesses the insights of a former policymaker. Michael Beschloss, *The Crisis Years* (1991), places the missile crisis in the context of Kennedy's tense overall relationship with Khrushchev.

Chapter 13

The Postwar Order Fractures, 1962–1968

During the 1960s the shift of emphasis in international affairs from Europe toward the nonaligned world continued. The most noticeable manifestation of this shift was the increasing inability of the superpowers to dominate global affairs. The nonaligned countries were more independent-minded than ever, paying attention to Washington and Moscow only when it suited their own interests. After the close call of the Cuban missile crisis, the superpowers stayed well away from war against each other, but minor powers found plenty to fight about. India and Pakistan leaped on each other in August 1965 after years of threatening to do so. Israel attacked Egypt after Cairo acted in too menacing a manner for its own good; this third round of the Arab-Israeli war quickly spread into Jordan and Syria. In Vietnam the efforts by Ho Chi Minh and the communists to reunify the country under their control escalated to new levels of violence.

Even within the two major alliance systems, rifts developed. The relationship between the Soviet Union and China, always under strain, broke down completely. By the mid-1960s the Soviets and Chinese were firing ideological bullets at each other; by the end of the decade, they were firing real bullets across their common border. In Europe Czechoslovakia challenged the Kremlin's right to dictate to the smaller communist countries. Moscow managed to quell the challenge, but the fact that it had to resort to military violence to do so did not speak well for socialist solidarity.

The American alliance system witnessed no breakdown so spectacular as the Soviet-Chinese divorce and no demonstration of superpower control so heavy-handed as the Soviet invasion of Czechoslovakia. Yet France walked out of NATO, requiring American strategists to modify their contingency planning for the defense of Europe. And in the Western Hemisphere, an incipient revolution in the Dominican Republic provoked Washington to dispatch an occupation army to ensure that the country did not go the way of Cuba.

America's big problem of the decade, however, was Vietnam. The conflict there grew into a full-blown war, and American participation increased commensurately. The war turned out to be much more than American leaders or the American people had bargained for, and it forced Americans to confront the possibility that the task they had set for themselves at the beginning of the postwar period—to contain communism wherever it appeared—was beyond their capacity.

The Communist Crackup

As long as Stalin had lived, the alliance between China and the Soviet Union remained firm. This owed nothing to Stalin's love for Mao, which was nonexistent; it followed rather from the respect in which the leaders of China held the Soviet dictator. Stalin was Lenin's heir; Stalin had directed the industrialization of the Soviet Union, transforming it within one generation into a superpower; Stalin guided the Soviet Union to victory over Germany; Stalin waged ideological war against the imperialists and insisted on the abiding conflict between communism and capitalism; Stalin provided aid to China against the United States in Korea. Stalin was strong, a giant among world leaders. China's leaders respected strength, and they respected Stalin.

Of Stalin's successor, the Chinese had a much lower opinion. That Khrushchev required several years after Stalin's 1953 death to establish primacy in the Kremlin did not say much for his forcefulness as a leader. Khrushchev's repudiation of Stalin's legacy in a widely noted speech before a 1956 congress of the Soviet Communist party, and his attacks on the "cult of personality" in Soviet society, struck Mao in particular as a blow against the legitimacy of one-person rule. This did not sit very well with the Chinese leader, for Mao was attempting to create just such a cult of personality for himself in China. Khrushchev's backing away from confrontation with the capitalists, demonstrated by his summit conferencing with Eisenhower and Kennedy, indicated a retreat from the fundamentals of Marxism-Leninism. If Marxism-Leninism stood for anything, it stood for struggle: of workers against capitalists and of the socialist countries against the imperialists of the West. The Chinese suspected, and then accused, Khrushchev of betraying the communist revolution.

Khrushchev naturally saw things differently. Having lived through the terrors Stalin imposed on the peoples of the Soviet Union, Khrushchev considered those actions an evil to be unmasked and expunged. His reaction to a question regarding his own role during the Stalinist era said much. "You were one of Stalin's colleagues," a voice from a crowd at a public meeting shouted. "Why did not you stop him?" Khrushchev glared at the group. "Who said that?" he demanded menacingly. No one spoke; no one in the room even breathed. "Now you know why," he said softly. Khrushchev understood that his country was targeted by ever-larger numbers of American nuclear bombs, and he believed that the Soviet Union had no choice but to seek coexistence with the United States. Competition between the capitalist and communist camps would continue, but it had to be ideological competition, rather than military. To argue, as Stalin had and as the Chinese still did, that war was inevitable was tantamount to arguing that the world had to destroy itself. It was easy for

Chronology

1962   American military advisers to Vietnam; Cuban missile crisis

1963   Partial test ban treaty with Soviet Union and Britain; Diem overthrown in Vietnam; Kennedy assassinated

1964   Gulf of Tonkin incident and resolution; Cyprus crisis; Johnson defeats Goldwater for presidency

1965   Bombing of North Vietnam commences; Johnson orders major increase of troops in Vietnam; American marines to Dominican Republic

1966   De Gaulle ejects NATO from France; Cultural Revolution in China

1967   June (Six Day) War in Middle East; big antiwar demonstrations in United States

1968   Tet offensive in Vietnam; Johnson suspends most bombing; peace talks begin; nuclear nonproliferation treaty signed; Warsaw Pact troops smash reform in Czechoslovakia; Nixon elected on promise to end Vietnam War

Mao to assert that the United States was a "paper tiger," but this tiger, as Khrushchev reminded Mao, had atomic teeth. Only an idiot would not be careful around such a beast.

During the late 1950s and early 1960s, the Soviets and Chinese contented themselves with insults at Communist party congresses and in the controlled media of each country. Beijing blasted Moscow for "revisionism," meaning appeasement of the class enemy, capitalists. The Kremlin castigated China for "adventurism": reckless risk taking to no good purpose.

Behind the insults was a bitter struggle for leadership of the world communist movement. Khrushchev and the Soviets felt that the Communist parties of other countries should follow Moscow's example and directions. The Soviet Union was by far the strongest socialist country; it had been the first, and remained the oldest, socialist country. For two generations and through two world wars, the Soviet Union had weathered the assaults of imperialists. Beijing heatedly disputed Moscow's claim to preeminence. The Soviets had lost their revolutionary edge after forty years, the Chinese asserted. And besides, the revolution of the 1960s was principally a Third World affair. China had a great deal more to say to the peasants of Asia, Africa, and Latin America than the Soviet Union did.

Although Khrushchev did not agree with the Chinese criticisms of Soviet policy, he could not simply ignore them. Soviet pride was on the line. Was the Soviet Union the country of the future, or had that title passed to China? Soviet security was at risk as well. The Kremlin hoped to gain tangible benefits from the nonaligned countries it befriended—benefits such as naval bases, airfields, and communication posts that would be of value in the Soviet Union's competition with the United States. If China horned in, the Soviet Union would lose some of these benefits.

The two communist governments projected their competition all around the world. In Latin America, Beijing tried to convince indigenous radicals that Mao's way had more to offer than Khrushchev's. The Chinese brought hundreds of Latin American students and intellectuals to China to demonstrate the virtues of the Chinese route to communism. Moscow responded in kind, preaching the message of Soviet superiority. Most Latin American countries that had a Communist party in fact had two: one oriented toward the Soviet Union, the other toward China. To some degree Khrushchev's attempt to slip Soviet missiles into Cuba reflected a desire on his part to demonstrate what the Soviets had to offer allies: in this case, protection against American aggression. Although the Chinese voiced support for the Soviet Union during the phase of the crisis in which world war seemed worrisomely likely, Khrushchev's comeuppance doubtless elicited chuckles of self-satisfaction in Beijing. That Khrushchev's fumble allowed China to gain ground in the ideological competition between the two countries contributed to his subsequent demise at the hands of his Kremlin colleagues.

Soviet and Chinese diplomats chased each other around Africa as well. Beginning in the late 1950s and continuing for a decade thereafter, new countries appeared in the second-largest continent on an accelerating basis. The most important of the European imperialists had concluded that the game of colonialism was not worth the candle of prestige and power anymore and decided to pull out. The French left Algeria in 1962 after a cruel war of several years that not only ravaged Algeria but also tore French politics and society nearly apart. France withdrew more peacefully from its West African colonies. The British delivered independence to Britain's colonies in East and Central Africa, retaining only Rhodesia (Zimbabwe) on account of the comparatively large number (but still a minority within the country) of British colonists who liked the security of the British empire. Belgium departed from the Congo (Zaire).

As independence swept across Africa, Moscow and Beijing competed with each other to be the first to recognize the new regimes and to extend friendly socialist greetings. The Soviet Union had more aid to dispense, but the Chinese contended that as fellow nonwhites long pushed around by the Europeans they could more readily identify with black Africans. In 1964 Chinese prime minister Zhou Enlai made a highly publicized tour of Africa. Western diplomats, including some Americans, watched Zhou's progress with concern; American secretary of state Dean Rusk called it "a major political offensive in Africa." Exactly how Moscow read the event is unclear, but Soviet leaders could not have been pleased by the enthusiastic reception the Chinese premier received.

Africa became an arena for more than intercommunist rivalries during this period. As the European colonialists exited the continent, American officials worried that the communists—either Zhou and the Chinese or, more troublingly, the Soviets—would move in. Washington hoped to preempt such a development. The problem appeared particularly acute in the early 1960s in the Congo. The Belgian colony gained self-government in the summer of 1960 woefully unprepared to look after its own affairs: after eighty years of colonial rule, the Congolese were impoverished, uneducated, and riven by tribal factionalism. The various individuals and groups that attempted to fill the void created by Belgium's withdrawal looked to outside sponsors for help. Patrice Lumumba, the prime minister and leader of a radical faction, called on the Soviet Union for help. Lumumba's rivals, led by Joseph Mobutu (Mobutu Sese Seko) got on the line to the United States.

Although the anti-Lumumba group soon succeeded in forcing the prime minister out of office, the Eisenhower administration still considered him very dangerous. The CIA began conspiring with Lumumba's rivals, concocting plans to kill the charming (too charming, in the American view) revolutionary. American biological warfare experts sent a lethal pathogen to the Congo in preparation for an attempt to inject it into his food or onto his toothbrush. Lumumba lay low for several weeks, aware that he was a marked man. Finally, he made a break for what he thought would be friendly territory in the Congo backcountry. He never reached his safe haven: his Congolese enemies captured and killed him. The CIA evidently had nothing to do with the final deed, though the agency applauded the result. The CIA station chief on the spot wrote to Washington, "Thanks for Patrice. If we had known he was coming we would have baked a snake."

America's troubles in the Congo did not end with the death of Lumumba. The civil war there persisted through the Kennedy years into the administration of Lyndon Johnson. In 1964 leftist rebels seized hundreds of foreign hostages, including several American consular officials. Recently, Washington had supplied airplanes to the Congolese government, which it considered preferable to the available alternatives; now the rebels threatened to kill the hostages if the government did not cease its attacks against rebel positions. After negotiations failed to gain the hostages' release, Johnson ordered American transport planes to ferry Belgian paratroops on a rescue operation. This operation, and subsequent ones in which American aircraft also participated, dispersed the rebels but did not save the hostages. The rebels killed more than three hundred foreigners, including eight Americans. In the meantime the governments of several African countries blasted the United States for neocolonial collaboration with the Belgians and the reactionary Congolese regime.

American interest in the Congo and other parts of Africa had been piqued by the attention the Soviet Union and China were showering on that continent; given the unfortunate outcome of the intervention in the Congo, it was just as well for America that the focus of rivalry between the two great communist powers shifted geographic focus during the second half of the 1960s. In 1965 Mao unleashed the "Great Proletarian Cultural Revolution" in China. This astonishing campaign against the status quo began as an effort by Mao to reassert his control over Chinese politics, against the congealing influences of bureaucrats and leftover elitists. But the Cultural Revolution grew into a social hurricane that turned Chinese society upside down. Mobs of ultraradical students terrorized campuses, forcing professors to recant allegedly incorrect teachings. Intellectuals were banished from jobs and cities and were sent to work on farms. All traces of "rightist" thought were suppressed.

This atmosphere of intolerance toward any deviation from the most rigorous Maoism exacerbated tension with the Soviet Union, which was reviled more than ever as a nest of revisionism. The tension produced an armed face-off along the border between China and the Soviet Union, where eventually more than 1 million Soviet Red Army troops glared at an even larger number of Chinese People's Liberation Army Soldiers. The nadir of relations between the two communist powers came when the opposing armies exchanged fire in 1969. For a moment the thought of war between the two great communist powers crossed the minds of many observers. Some in the West gained a certain satisfaction from such a prospect; but others, remembering that China possessed (since 1964) nuclear weapons, shuddered at the idea. The dangers involved caused the Soviets and Chinese to pull back from war, though tension on their border remained high.

Preparing a Quagmire: Vietnam Gets Sticky

A different, more subtle form of Sino-Soviet competition took place in Southeast Asia. Since the early 1950s, both Moscow and Beijing had supported Ho Chi Minh's communists in Vietnam. The Soviets and the Chinese agreed on the broad desirability of throwing the Americans out of South Vietnam and of reunifying the country under communist control. Yet within this agreement there existed differences. Mao's Chinese government did not like the idea of a strong Vietnam on China's southern border any more than other Chinese governments had for centuries. The Chinese feared the Americans considerably more than they feared Ho, which was why they were willing to cooperate in throwing the Americans out; but they desired to create a communist Vietnam dependent on China rather than one that was truly independent. The Soviets, in contrast, were quite happy to see Ho grow strong. Moscow had no particular love for the Vietnamese, but anything that would keep the Chinese off balance looked good to the Kremlin. For his part, Ho aimed to work both sides of the communist street. Winning the war against South Vietnam and the Americans would take all of North Vietnam's resources and everything Hanoi could muster from its friends and allies; if China and the Soviet Union vied for Hanoi's favor, and if this increased the support they were willing to give to the cause of Vietnamese unification, that was all to the good.

That both the Soviet Union and China supported the communists in Vietnam doubled the determination of the American government that Ho and his cadres not be allowed to win. Until the early 1960s, this possibility appeared relatively remote. Ho concentrated on building socialism in the north, by measures such as land reform, and on tightening the grip of the Communist party on his half of Vietnam. These efforts absorbed most of his government's energy—to some extent because of a campaign of sabotage and obstruction conducted in North Vietnam by the American CIA and its South Vietnamese protégés.

Beginning in 1960, however, the drive for Vietnamese unification under communist control began anew. Former Vietminh guerrillas living in the south had been pressing Hanoi for some time for support against Ngo Dinh Diem's government in Saigon. Hanoi had hesitated to supply substantial support, partly from a belief that Diem would hang himself if given enough rope and partly from a desire to avoid provoking the Americans. But as the agitation in the south for Diem's ouster increased, coming from many people besides the communists, Hanoi decided that it had better back the uprising or it would risk losing control of it. Hanoi directed communists in the south to join hands with other insurgents in a joint attempt to topple Diem. In December 1960 the communists and other anti-Diem groups formed the National Liberation Front for this purpose. The Saigon government branded the insurgents "Vietcong," an unflattering shorthand for "Vietnamese communists." Although the label was deliberately misleading, it stuck.

The Vietcong harassed Diem and the South Vietnamese government, waging a guerrilla war in the provinces and sapping the strength of the regime. The insurgents' successes swelled their ranks. They recruited both from within the south and from the north; by 1963 there may have been as many as one hundred thousand persons in arms against Diem's government.

The United States responded to the increasing pressure on Saigon by increasing the level of American economic and military aid and by instituting specific counterinsurgency measures. The most conspicuous of the latter was the "strategic hamlet" program, which was essentially an updated version of the *reconcentrado* policy adopted by the Spanish in Cuba in the 1890s (and condemned by Americans at the time) and employed by the United States in the Philippines a couple of years later. Government soldiers assisted by American advisers uprooted villagers from their homes and forcibly transplanted them to new villages. Those who chose not to move, or who wandered away from their new homes without permission, were presumed to be Vietcong. Although conditions in the hamlets were better than the analogous conditions in Cuba and the Philippines had been, the policy was equally detested by the peasants. Rather than strengthen Diem's rule in the countryside, the strategic hamlet policy undermined it further.

The prospects for South Vietnam did not appear to be enhanced by a simultaneous insurgency across the border in Laos. The guiding elements in the Laotian insurgency were the Laotian communists, the Pathet Lao; and just as the American government was resisting the conquest of South Vietnam by Ho's communists, so it opposed a takeover of Laos by the Pathet Lao. During the 1950s and early 1960s, Washington pumped tens of millions of dollars in aid to the government in Vientiane. But as was the case in South Vietnam, much of the aid was wasted, lining the pockets of government officials and filling their foreign bank accounts. Conditions declined to a point in late 1960 where Dwight Eisenhower strongly considered American military intervention.

Lyndon Johnson grapples with Vietnam. Dean Rusk is seated next to the president.
Lyndon B. Johnson Library

Eisenhower retired to his farm at Gettysburg before events in Laos required a decision on military intervention; John Kennedy, reasoning that Laos was not an especially critical topic with the American electorate, chose the path of compromise. Kennedy accepted an invitation by Britain, the Soviet Union, and Cambodia to help negotiate a solution to the Laos problem. The negotiations commenced in the spring of 1961 and continued until the following year. The talks ultimately specified a coalition government for Laos, one in which the Pathet Lao would share power with right wingers and centrists. From Kennedy's perspective, this solution was not as good as a forthright defeat of the Pathet Lao would have been, but it was better than a Pathet Lao victory. No one could say John Kennedy had lost Laos to the communists.

But people might soon be able to say that about South Vietnam if trends there persisted. Despite steady increases in American aid and military personnel, the latter totaling some eleven thousand troops by the beginning of 1963, the Diem regime continued to stagger. In January 1963 a South Vietnamese unit of roughly two thousand cornered a far smaller contingent of Vietcong near the village of Ap Bac; the South Vietnamese enjoyed large advantages in firepower and mobility, the latter courtesy of American-piloted helicopters, as well as in numbers. (Vietnam was the first war in which helicopters played a central role.) For all their advantages, however, the South Vietnamese suffered a sharp defeat at the hands of the more determined Vietcong. The portents were ominous.

The portents grew more ominous during the next several months. Until this point opposition to Diem had been concentrated in the rural parts of South Vietnam; now it moved to the cities. In Saigon, Buddhist monks protested government actions favoring Roman Catholics, a minority in the predominantly Buddhist country but one that included Diem and his family. After government troops fired on the demonstrators, a Buddhist monk deliberately burned himself to death on a busy Saigon street corner as a way of registering his outrage. Others followed his example. The government only aggravated the unrest by attacking Buddhist pagodas and arresting more than a thousand monks. Diem's influential sister-in-law derided the self-immolations as "barbecues." She added, "Let them burn, and we shall clap our hands."

Officials in the Kennedy administration realized that with friends like these in Saigon, the United States hardly needed enemies. Consequently, when a clique of South Vietnamese generals began plotting the overthrow of Diem, the administration encouraged them. At the beginning of November 1963, the generals moved. They drove Diem from the presidential palace and murdered him.

Before the Kennedy administration had time to size up Diem's replacements, Kennedy himself fell to an assassin's bullet. Lyndon Johnson, Kennedy's vice president and successor, reportedly told a friend that Kennedy's killing was divine retribution for his role in Diem's assassination. All the same, the new president committed himself to pursuing the policies Kennedy had mapped out in Vietnam.

Johnson might have decided differently. Every president who enters office—for that matter, every king, prime minister, general secretary, or other political leader—has the option of disavowing the policies of those who have gone before. All you have to do is blame the previous rascals for the current mess, and proceed to do what you want. In practice, however, the dead hand of the past often weighs heavily on the present and future. The past weighed especially heavily on Johnson. Unelected to the White House, Johnson had no popular mandate for policies of his own. Perhaps he would gain a mandate in the election of 1964, but until then such legitimacy as he possessed came from Kennedy. That Kennedy's assassination made the late president a martyr in many minds rendered his posthumous influence all the greater.

There was another consideration, more important than the memory of the fallen president, that militated against any decision by Johnson to change course in Vietnam. Since China had gone communist in the late 1940s during Harry Truman's presidency, the Democratic party had labored under the stigma of being suspiciously soft on communism. The Republicans, the party of McCarthy, generally did not have to worry about attacks from the right, but the Democrats did. Johnson had big plans for domestic legislation to create what he called a "Great Society" in America; the Republicans and other conservatives would try to frustrate Johnson's plans, as he knew full well. And if his critics could damage his credibility by attacking his foreign policy, they would injure his credibility in domestic matters as well. Johnson, formerly the

Saigon, 1963. *AP/Wide World Photos*

Senate majority leader, was a veteran of many tough fights on Capitol Hill, and he understood how politics in Washington worked. To safeguard his domestic measures, he tended to choose the path of least resistance overseas. Regarding Vietnam, this meant keeping on the course charted by Truman, Eisenhower, and Kennedy. Not long before he died, Kennedy had rejected calls for an American pullout from Vietnam. The United States must maintain its effort to preserve a noncommunist government in South Vietnam, he said. "For us to withdraw from that effort would mean a collapse not only of South Vietnam but Southeast Asia. So we are going to stay there."

At the end of 1963, however, there was some question whether the government of South Vietnam was quite as determined as Washington was. The first post-Diem regime in Saigon flirted briefly with a neutralist, Laos-like solution to Vietnam's troubles. Many in South Vietnam had no particular difficulty accepting a role for communists in government; their big objection had been to Diem, and now he was gone. The idea of neutralization also had attractions for Hanoi, which feared the strain a major military effort in the south would place on the north. At the least, a war in the south would divert resources badly required for the north's economic development; at the worst, it would lead to an American bombing campaign against the north or even an American invasion. In either of these cases, the costs to the people and government of North Vietnam would be very great. If these costs were avoidable, maybe they should be avoided. Among the outside powers, France was pushing hard for a neutralist solution. The French missed the influence in Indochina they had lost by their withdrawal a decade before; Paris thought that brokering a settlement to the Vietnam War would restore some of that influence, besides being a boon to the suffering people of Vietnam.

But Washington did not want a neutralist settlement. American prestige was on the line in Vietnam, and a compromise would diminish that prestige. Superpowers are supposed to *defeat* minor countries like North Vietnam. The United States had fought to a tie in Korea, and the memories of that war still burned in American minds. Fifty thousand Americans had died in Korea—for what? Simply to restore the status quo, with communists laughing from behind the thirty-eighth parallel. Besides, the Johnson administration placed no confidence in North Vietnam's willingness to abide by the terms of a compromise settlement. Once Hanoi got its nose under the flap of the tent, the rest of the camel would be inside before long; there would not be any room for anyone else then.

To underscore its opposition to a compromise peace, Washington once more gave its encouragement to plotters against the South Vietnamese government. What became known as the "Pentagon's coup" installed a second group of generals in Saigon in January 1964, a group firmly committed to fighting it out against the communists.

But the fighting required more American help. The Johnson administration, desiring to show approval of the new leadership, sent thousands more American troops to Vietnam and again boosted American military aid to the South Vietnamese army. American airplanes and warships increased their activities on behalf of the South Vietnamese, providing logistical and intelligence support.

It was during such activities that an incident occurred that proved to be a turning point in the war. In August 1964 an American destroyer in the Tonkin Gulf was fired on by North Vietnamese patrol boats. The American ship had been engaged in electronic monitoring of North Vietnamese coastal defenses during a raid by South Vietnamese forces. This part of the story was supposed to be secret, however, and the Johnson administration chose to portray the North Vietnamese attack as an unprovoked assault on American lives and property by the aggressor Hanoi regime. Johnson warned the North Vietnamese against repeating it. Under confusing circumstances a second attack on an American vessel in the same vicinity was reported two days later, but almost immediately the reporting officer indicated that he might have been mistaken. Nonetheless, the Johnson administration seized on the affair as just cause for striking back directly at North Vietnam. The president ordered retaliatory air raids against North Vietnamese positions and requested congressional approval for further action. The House of Representatives and the Senate considered the administration's request only briefly, then passed it with but two dissenting votes. As approved, the Tonkin Gulf resolution authorized the president to employ in the vicinity of Vietnam "all necessary measures to repel any armed attack against the forces of the United States and to prevent further aggression."

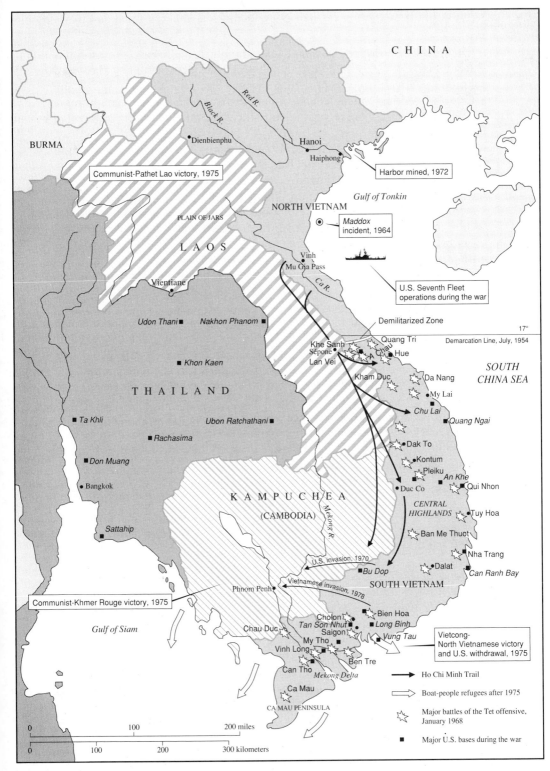

CHINA

Black R.

Red R.

Dienbienphu

Hanoi

Haiphong

Harbor mined, 1972

BURMA

PLAIN OF JARS

Communist-Pathet Lao victory, 1975

NORTH VIETNAM

Gulf of Tonkin

Maddox
incident, 1964

LAOS

Vinh
Mu Gia Pass

Vientiane

Ca R.

U.S. Seventh Fleet
operations during the war

Udon Thani ■   ■ Nakhon Phanom

Demilitarized Zone

17°

■ Khon Kaen

Khe Sanh
Sépone
Lan Vei

Quang Tri

A Chau Hue

Demarcation Line, July, 1954

THAILAND

Kham Duc

Da Nang

My Lai

SOUTH
CHINA SEA

■ Ta Khli

Ubon Ratchathani ■

Chu Lai

Quang Ngai

■ Rachasima

Dak To

■ Don Muang

Kontum
Pleiku

An Khe

Qui Nhon

• Bangkok

KAMPUCHEA

(CAMBODIA)

Mekong R.

Duc Co

CENTRAL
HIGHLANDS

Tuy Hoa

Ban Me Thuot

■ Sattahip

U.S. invasion, 1970

Nha Trang

Bu Dop

Dalat

Can Ranh Bay

Vietnamese invasion, 1978

Communist-Khmer Rouge victory, 1975

Phnom Penh

SOUTH VIETNAM

Gulf of Siam

Chau Duc

Cholon
Tan Son Nhut
Saigon

Bien Hoa

Long Binh

My Tho

Vung Tau

Vinh Long

Ben Tre

Vietcong-
North Vietnamese victory
and U.S. withdrawal, 1975

Can Tho   Mekong Delta

Ho Chi Minh Trail

Ca Mau

Boat-people refugees after 1975

CA MAU PENINSULA

0   100   200 miles

Major battles of the Tet offensive,
January 1968

0   100   200   300 kilometers

■ Major U.S. bases during the war

The Vietnam War

The loosely worded resolution—"Like grandma's nightshirt," Johnson privately remarked, "it covered everything"—had two purposes. First, it covered Johnson's political flanks against congressional criticism. With the House and Senate on his side, Johnson could escalate the war with relative impunity. He did not want to ask Congress for an outright declaration of war, which would make the troubles in Vietnam appear to be bigger than they were, or at least than they seemed to be in August 1964, and which doubtless would derail Johnson's domestic reforms. The Tonkin resolution was the next best thing. Second, the resolution was intended to impress Hanoi with America's determination to defend South Vietnam. In conjunction with the air raids against North Vietnamese targets, the resolution would show that Washington was willing to match North Vietnam tit for tat. North Vietnam, appreciating the overwhelming advantage the United States had in military power, would realize the futility of trying to conquer South Vietnam and would give up.

The first purpose of the Tonkin resolution—coopting Congress and thereby blunting criticism—was the more immediately important. During the summer and early autumn of 1964, Johnson had his eye on one goal above all: getting elected in his own right. In the 1964 election campaign, Johnson positioned himself as the peace candidate, which was not especially difficult given Republican challenger Barry Goldwater's penchant for careless talk about war against China and the Soviet Union. Like most professional politicians in democratic countries, Johnson subscribed to the view that a political leader cannot lead without getting elected. Developments in Vietnam strongly suggested to Johnson that a larger American role would be necessary before long: in the autumn of 1964, Hanoi sent the first contingent of regular North Vietnamese troops into South Vietnam. Yet Johnson chose to downplay the possibility of American escalation. First he would get elected; then he would worry about escalation.

No More Cubas

Through the early 1960s, American leaders worried more about the activities of Fidel Castro in the Caribbean basin than about Ho Chi Minh in Southeast Asia. The Cuban missile crisis did not quite cure Washington of its desire to overthrow Castro. For several months after the October 1962 showdown, the CIA's anti-Castro Operation Mongoose continued. But what the near brush with nuclear war did not accomplish, Kennedy's assassination did. Johnson, noting the Cuban connections of Kennedy assassin Lee Harvey Oswald, decided that the campaign against Castro was getting too close to home and canceled the covert operation against him.

The cancellation hardly reflected an end to American concern about Castro, however; American fears of a replay of the Cuban revolution only increased. It was bad enough having one Soviet client in the neighborhood; having two would be disastrous in terms both of domestic politics and of international affairs. The Eisenhower administration, being Republican and the more reassuringly conservative of the two major parties, had weathered with comparative equanimity the fallout from the rise of Castro in Cuba; in addition, it helped matters, from Eisenhower's perspective, that Castro's unequivocal embrace of Marxism-Leninism had not happened until after Kennedy's election. If Castro's example spread to other parts of the hemisphere while a Democratic president occupied the White House, the Democrats could count on receiving another beating like that which had followed the communist victory in China.

Internationally, another successful communist revolution would lend credence to the communists' claims that Marxism-Leninism was the wave of the future. In ideological matters more than most areas, nothing succeeds like success. During the two decades starting in the early 1940s, communism had been very successful. The Soviet Union beat Germany in the Second World War; Eastern Europe went communist at the end of the war and in the three years shortly after; China chose communism in 1949; North Korea's communists would have defeated South Korea's anticommunists if the United States had not intervened; Vietnam's communists drove the French out of their country in the mid-1950s; Castro took Cuba communist after his 1959 victory there. When Khrushchev boasted at the United Nations in 1960 that communism would "bury" capitalism, his words carried an undeniable ring of truth. Communism controlled the bulk of the vast Eurasian landmass from the Elbe River in Germany to the Pacific Ocean. Communism governed the lives of a third of the earth's population. Its agents were busy fomenting revolution around the globe. Its propagandists were spreading the news of the inevitability of socialism, and people were listening.

This was what made Castro seem so threatening to American leaders. A Cuba allied to the Soviet Union caused American strategists headaches, but what really gave them nightmares was the thought of Castro exporting his revolution to other countries of the hemisphere. Latin America, where poverty and inequality were rife, was fertile soil for revolutionary ideas. Washington determined to keep the weeds down by whatever means were necessary.

Kennedy tried economic aid. Building on promises by the Eisenhower administration, Kennedy inaugurated the Alliance for Progress, an aid program for Latin America designed to forestall revolution by raising the living standards of ordinary people throughout the southern two-thirds of the Western Hemisphere. The Alliance for Progress formally commenced its existence in 1961, to great fanfare and high expectations, and within a short time the Kennedy administration pumped some $2 billion in assistance to Latin America.

But the Alliance failed to meet its goals. Part of the problem was that the American Congress got distracted by other expensive programs, notably Johnson's Great Society and the war in Vietnam. A larger part of the problem was that the conservative elites that governed most of the Latin American countries resisted the sorts of changes—land reform, for instance—that the United States government hoped would ensure that American aid money reached those people who really needed it. As a result, the Alliance did little to defuse popular demands for a radical overhaul of the Latin American status quo.

The demands grew most insistent during the mid-1960s in the Dominican Republic. In 1961 an assassin ended the reign of long-time dictator Rafael Trujillo. Washington had soured on Trujillo during the late 1950s, by which time he was carrying his brutal methods to such extremes as to embarrass his American sponsors. Moreover, in light of Castro's rise in Cuba, it appeared to American leaders that the longer Trujillo remained in power in Santo Domingo, the more likely a Cuban-style revolution in the Dominican Republic would be. The American government discreetly encouraged Trujillo's opponents in the Dominican military; when the generals had Trujillo killed, many observers thought Washington bore part of the blame—or credit, depending on one's point of view.

After some delay the generals allowed the Dominican people to vote for a president. The person the people chose turned out to be a distinct disappointment to the generals and to Washington as well. Undersecretary of State George Ball offered one of the kinder criticisms of Juan Bosch when he called him a "muddle-headed, anti-American pedant," and said he had rarely met a man "so unrealistic, arrogant and erratic." Consequently, American leaders shed no tears when the Dominican military shoved Bosch aside in 1963.

But the military did no better running the country than Bosch had, and within several months after the Dominican president's ouster, agitation developed for his reinstatement. Radicals, including a number of avowed Castroites, hoped to accomplish greater change than merely restoring Bosch to the presidency, but for the moment the deposed leader seemed a handy instrument for prying the military loose from power. In April 1965 a group of disgruntled officers defected from the ruling junta, precipitating a crisis in the country's politics. The junta, claiming that the Castroites were about to take over, appealed to Washington for help.

The Johnson administration initially hesitated; Johnson wanted to see whether the danger was as great as the Dominican junta alleged. But within days the president decided to send troops to Santo Domingo. Johnson justified the American intervention as necessary to safeguard American lives. He paraphrased (exaggeratedly) the American ambassador in the Dominican Republic as saying that Washington must dispatch troops or "American blood will run in the streets." For a brief moment some Americans may have been in danger, but the the danger soon passed. Johnson, however, was determined not to risk letting the Dominican Republic go the way of Cuba, and he continued sending troops into the country until their number topped twenty thousand.

The American occupation of the Dominican Republic reversed thirty years of American nonintervention (*military* nonintervention, that is) in Latin American affairs. Johnson knew the reversal would stir howls of protest; other nations of the hemisphere could be counted on to denounce this new manifestation of *yanqui* imperialism. Many liberals in the United States would find Washington's heavy-handedness equally distasteful. But Johnson decided that the dangers of intervening were less than the dangers of not intervening. If there was the slightest chance that pro-Castro forces might seize power in Santo Domingo, the American president wanted to snuff it out.

The American intervention produced the expected protests and more. Most of the Latin American governments, after some strenuous lobbying by the Johnson administration, supported the American intervention, to the point where several members of the Organization of American States sent small peace-keeping contingents themselves. But as was often the case in Latin American politics, the actions of some of the governments did not reflect the feelings of the masses of people in those countries. The American intervention in the Dominican Republic appeared to perhaps a majority of Latin Americans to be another example of Washington's hypocrisy: rhetorical support for self-determination but suppression of self-determination that threatened Washington's vested interests.

Johnson shrugged off the protests of the Latin American leftists and moderates, especially after the situation in Santo Domingo calmed down. Within months most of the American troops went home, and in the spring of 1966 the Dominican people elected a president of safely conservative opinions. From Johnson's vantage point, and arguably from the vantage point of the Dominicans, at least those who voted for the new president, the affair had a reasonably happy ending.

But though Johnson could ignore the Latin American protests, he had a harder time shrugging off the complaints of critics in the United States. Johnson's critics thought his handling of the Dominican affair was slippery and even downright dishonest. To justify the landing of the marines, the Johnson administration had put out a list of alleged communists leading the attack on the government. The list was sloppily compiled, showing a greater concern for inflating the communist threat than for strict accuracy. Reporters soon began picking holes in the list. They demonstrated that several people on the list had been out of the country at the time of the revolt; others had been in prison. One individual on the list had served on the Dominican supreme court for more than two decades. As the nature and extent of the exaggeration came to light, a number of important American legislators began to believe that Johnson had played them for fools. The most important of the resentful lawmakers was J. William Fulbright, the Democratic senator who headed the Senate Foreign Relations Committee. Fulbright should have been Johnson's strong right arm on Capitol Hill; instead he became a critic of Johnson's foreign policy and not just regarding Latin America.

A Third–World War

Those critics of Johnson who complained of a "credibility gap" in the president's handling of the Dominican affair felt he was overreacting to what was really a very modest threat to American security. Overreaction was not usually a problem with Johnson; in most other areas of international affairs, restraint marked his administration's approach. Restraint especially characterized Johnson's reaction to the 1965 India-Pakistan war—with the result that his administration was criticized for not acting vigorously enough.

The India-Pakistan war was another indication of the obsolescence of the bipolar conceptual framework for international relations. During the early 1950s, the United States had signed several defense pacts with countries of Asia and the Pacific: Japan, Taiwan (the Republic of China, in its own and the American interpretation), the Philippines, Australia, New Zealand, Thailand, Pakistan. In some cases the treaties were bilateral (just the United States and the country in question), while in others the signatories were grouped in bunches. Thus, Australia and New Zealand joined the United States in the ANZUS (an acronym for the three countries) pact, while Australia, New Zealand, Pakistan, Thailand, and the Philippines linked arms with the United States (as well as with Britain and France) in SEATO. The United States supported the Baghdad Pact—comprising Iraq, Pakistan, Iran, Turkey, and Britain—informally until 1959. After Iraq's revolution and withdrawal, the organization changed its name to the Central Treaty Organization (CENTO), and the United States joined formally.

Opponents of this "pactomania" (their term for it) contended that America's allies in these ventures had considerably less enthusiasm for American values than for the American money and weapons that usually accompanied the treaties. The opponents were right, though the truth of their assertions was hardly news to American officials. For purposes of public consumption, Washington praised its allies' devotion to democracy, but within the conference rooms of the State Department and the Pentagon, quid pro quo was the language most often spoken. The United States sent aid to the Philippines in exchange for access to Clark air base and the Subic Bay naval facility. Australia and New Zealand pledged troops to help defend the Middle East. Turkey provided electronic listening posts, air bases, and missile sites. Pakistan served as a takeoff point for American U-2 missions across the Soviet Union. Japan agreed not to rebuild its army and navy and not to develop nuclear weapons. In sum, the American alliance system was grounded, as all successful alliance systems throughout history have been grounded, in complementary self-interest.

But self-interests change, and unless alliances make accommodations for the changes, the alliances get brittle. America's alliance with Pakistan illustrated this principle. The United States committed itself to sending weapons to Pakistan in February 1954 primarily as a means of encouraging Pakistan to join what would become the Baghdad Pact. Several months later Pakistan also joined SEATO. (At that time Pakistan included the territory that would break away in 1971 and become Bangladesh; consequently, Pakistan's adherence to an organization for the defense of Southeast Asia was not completely implausible geographically.)

India, Pakistan's much larger neighbor in South Asia, complained at Washington's decision to supply arms to Pakistan. Prime Minister Nehru worried that the Pakistanis aimed to use the weapons against India rather than against communists. At the least, Nehru said, the American shipments would spark an arms race in South Asia and suck the region into the maelstrom of the super-power rivalry. Nehru, as a leader of the nonaligned movement, could only decry such a development. For their part the Pakistanis promised not to use the American weapons for unsanctioned purposes, such as against India; but in moments of candor, Pakistani officials argued that if they did use the weapons against India, it would only be in self-defense. India overmatched Pakistan in nearly all measures of national strength: area, population, resources, economic prowess. Furthermore, though Nehru and the Indian government publicly shunned designs on Pakistan's territory, India contained plenty of irredentists who still resented Britain's decision to divide the subcontinent in 1947. These individuals dreamed of restoring India to its full size, and if they ever came to power, Pakistan would have to look out.

Being so suspicious of India, the Pakistanis could not help getting annoyed when Washington sought friendlier relations with India during the middle and late 1950s. Although John Foster Dulles publicly denounced neutralism as "immoral," claiming that the countries of the world ought to stand up and be counted in the great fight against totalitarianism, in practice the Eisenhower administration got along well enough with neutralist India. Eisenhower established a warm personal relationship with Nehru and approved large packages of American aid for India. The Pakistanis felt two-timed.

For reinsurance, Pakistan looked across the Himalayas to China. For a few years after the communist victory in China, Pakistan had worried about the budding friendship between India and China. But the buds never opened. Nehru and the Chinese leadership did not get along at all. "I have met American generals," Chinese premier Zhou Enlai said. "I have met Chiang Kaishek. But I have never met a more arrogant man than Mr. Nehru." In addition, as the latent competition between China and the Soviet Union became less latent, the Chinese chilled toward India, Moscow's principal project in the Third World. Finally, beneath everything else the Chinese and the Indians were contesting for dominance of Asian affairs, as they had for millennia. For most of those millennia, the Himalayas had sufficed to keep the contestants militarily apart; but the Sino-Indian rivalry transcended military matters, touching deeper issues of religion, cultural mores, and social organization. If Chinese like Zhou thought Nehru and the Indians were arrogant, many Indians thought the Chinese were insufferable.

The friction between China and India produced jostling between border patrols in the high valleys of the Himalayas during the middle 1950s; the friction intensified when an anti-Chinese revolt broke out in Chinese-occupied Tibet in 1959 and the Dalai Lama (the religious and political leader of Tibet) and several thousand of his followers fled into India. Beijing blasted New Delhi for meddling by letting the refugees enter. To emphasize its annoyance, China laid claim to forty thousand square miles of territory long controlled by India. Finally, in the autumn of 1962 the Chinese army attacked the Indian frontier in several places, routing Indian troops, taking thousands of prisoners, and threatening to pour down from the mountains onto the Indian plain.

The Chinese chose a convenient time for moving against India: the middle of the Cuban missile crisis. Beijing doubtless calculated that the Soviets would be too busy trying to figure out what to do with Kennedy's ultimatum to come to India's rescue. The Chinese calculated correctly. To cover the shortfall in Soviet support, India appealed to the United States.

John Kennedy had been a fan of India for some time. He had backed increased aid to India while a senator during the 1950s; since becoming president, he had made good relations with India a priority, in keeping with a broader Third World initiative that included the Alliance for Progress and the Peace Corps, a civilian army of American volunteers dispatched to poor nations to provide technical training and assistance. Kennedy approved the Indian request for weapons and advisers. Within months there were more American military advisers in India, ostensibly a nonaligned nation, than there were in Pakistan, a pledged American ally.

The Pakistanis took this latest development as further evidence of American favoritism toward India; they responded by additional moves of their own in the direction of China. These were designed chiefly to deter the Indian government from striking against Pakistan, perhaps to assuage New Delhi's humiliation at Beijing's hands. But the Pakistani moves had the added objective of reminding Washington that Pakistan could not be taken for granted. At the same time and for the same purposes, Pakistan cultivated friendly relations with the Soviet Union. Although Pakistan did not withdraw from its two alliances with the United States—SEATO and CENTO—it might as well have for all the good its participation did the United States.

While maneuvering between the great powers, Pakistan kept its eye on India, especially on the disputed territory of Kashmir. When Britain had partitioned the subcontinent into India and Pakistan in 1947, the British had given the several princedoms in the subcontinent the option of joining either India or Pakistan. The Hindu maharajah of Kashmir had chosen India, which was largely Hindu. But the Muslim majority of his people preferred Muslim Pakistan. Fighting quickly broke out, and Pakistan supported the anti-Indian group. The fighting soon involved the armies of Pakistan and India in a regular war. Before the firing ceased, encouraged by an American embargo of weapons to both sides, Kashmir had been partitioned by the two armies, with Pakistan occupying the northern portion of the territory and India the southern part. Kashmir remained a sore spot in dealings between India and Pakistan during the mid-1960s. Each side accused the other of aggression and duplicity on the Kashmir issue. The rumblings that often developed between Hindus and Muslims within India echoed across Kashmir to Pakistan. From the other direction, the military character of the Pakistani government caused the Indians to view the Kashmir question as a test of India's ability to defend itself against attack.

In 1965 the trouble came to a head. Initially, the 1965 clash did not have anything directly to do with Kashmir. The border between India and Pakistan in the Rann of Kutch in India's far west and West Pakistan's south had never been definitively determined, for the good reason that neither side had been able to figure out what to do with this sub-sea-level salt marsh even during that part of the year when it was not under water. In the spring of 1965, Indian and Pakistani troops, each sporting American weaponry and other equipment, decided to test each other's strength in the area. The Pakistanis proved stronger in the encounter, pushing several miles into Indian territory. Although a cease-fire soon restored a surface tranquillity, Pakistan was eager to exploit its demonstrated advantage, while India itched for revenge. Incidents along the partition line in Kashmir ratcheted up the tension during the summer of 1965 until at the beginning of September, Pakistan launched a major tank assault against Indian positions.

The fighting in South Asia raged furiously for three weeks. Although the Johnson administration scrupulously avoided overt involvement, the fact that the two sides were using American weapons meant that Washington could not wash its hands entirely of the affair. At first the Pakistanis seemed to be winning; then the Indians counterattacked and reversed the momentum. The fighting expanded beyond Kashmir into the territory proper of each country. It threatened to expand further after India mounted a drive toward Lahore in West Pakistan, which prompted China to threaten to enter the war on Pakistan's side. It was difficult to tell whether the Chinese were bluffing, but electronic intelligence gathered by American eavesdroppers did indicate heightened military activity in the regions of China close to the Indian border.

The Johnson administration maintained strict neutrality, favoring neither India nor Pakistan and urging the belligerents to stop fighting. Already, both sides were lambasting Washington for killing their sons by having supplied arms to the enemy; lest it incur additional blame, the administration suspended shipments of weapons, spare parts, and ammunition to both sides. The embargo on spare parts and ammunition had the greatest effect. Modern tanks and aircraft require a steady stream of spare parts to keep going; without the parts, they quickly clank to a halt. The same is true with respect to ammunition, which shrewd donors dole out cautiously. In the case of India and Pakistan, the Pentagon had designed its aid programs in such a way that neither country was able to stockpile more than a few weeks' worth of shells and bullets.

Partly as a result of their shortness of American supplies, and partly from a shared belief that the war had accomplished all the good it was going to accomplish, India and Pakistan agreed in late September to a cease-fire. Subsequent negotiations disentangled the armed forces of the two parties and arranged a return of prisoners. The underlying source of conflict—the uncertain state of Kashmir—remained unresolved.

For its neutrality in the India-Pakistan war, the United States won nothing but abuse from the two combatants. The Indians pointed I-told-you-so fingers at Washington, reminding the American government that they had predicted all along that Pakistan would use its American weapons against India. The Pakistanis complained that the Americans had proved false friends and agents of Hindu imperialism. If this was what an alliance with the United States brought, who needed it? Significantly, it was the Soviet Union, not the United States, that mediated the postwar peace negotiations, in the Soviet Central Asian city of Tashkent.

The India-Pakistan war of 1965 demonstrated, among other things, that beneath the nuclear-enforced stand-off between the superpowers, regional rivalries remained as virulent as ever. The half century after the Second World War was an era of relative peace among the greatest powers; war had become so dangerous that the most powerful countries would not risk fighting each other. But while making the world too dangerous for war between the superpowers, nuclear weapons left the world safe for wars between lesser countries, especially those outside the superpower spheres. The United States repeatedly vowed to go to war to defend West Germany against the Soviet Union or its allies, and the vow seemed credible enough that the Kremlin was not willing to test it. Analogously, the United States refused to aid the Hungarian rebels of 1956 for fear of provoking the Soviets. But the United States gave no guarantee to Pakistan regarding an attack by India, and the Soviet Union gave no promise to India regarding an attack by Pakistan. Consequently, the two South Asian countries could pound away at each other more or less unconcerned about interference from Washington or Moscow. While the period after 1945 witnessed no third world war, it saw more than its share of Third World wars.

On the Seventh Day They Rested (But Not Until Then): The June War of 1967

Of those Third World wars, several occurred in the Middle East. The recurrence of war in the Middle East resulted from the fact that the wars there, like the India-Pakistan wars of 1947–1949 and 1965, did not resolve the fundamental causes of the conflicts. The Palestine War of 1948–1949 and the Suez War of 1956 left the heart of the Arab-Israeli dispute untouched. Israel still occupied territory the Palestinians thought belonged to them, and the Arabs still refused to recognize Israel's right to exist. Until these two disputes were settled, there would not be any real peace in the area.

But the absence of real peace is not the same as open war, and for more than a decade after the Suez War, a comparative calm hovered fitfully over the region. The Arabs found more to fight about among themselves than with the Israelis. The chronic competition between Egypt and Iraq grew increasingly contentious. Egypt's Nasser exercised his pan-Arabist ambitions in a short-lived merger with Syria, a union that produced the United Arab Republic. Nasser continued to challenge the conservative regimes in the Arab world. When a civil war broke out in Yemen in 1962 and Saudi Arabia took the side of Yemeni royalists, Nasser sent Egyptian troops to fight on behalf of Yemeni republicans.

The Yemen war disrupted American relations with the Arabs. The United States had cultivated Saudi Arabia since before the Second World War. A consortium of American oil companies, operating as the Arabian-American Oil Company (Aramco) established a cozy relationship with the Saudi government and acted as a de facto agent of American diplomacy. From the Saudis, Aramco received concessionary rights to oil that produced profits by the gusherful; from the American government, the company received favored tax treatment. The arrangement suited both the Saudis and the American government, for though Riyadh appreciated kindly attention from Washington and Washington was willing to supply it, both sides were happy to keep the attention low key and informal. A formal alliance would have stirred trouble in the United States among American advocates of Israel; it would also have provoked the Arab radicals whom the conservative Saudi regime hoped to mollify. Between Riyadh and Washington, the more that was left unsaid the better.

Nasser of Egypt was one of the Arab radicals who did not appreciate close ties between Saudi Arabia and the United States. During the late 1950s and early 1960s, however, Nasser was willing to overlook Washington's sins in this regard in return for American support against even more radical Iraq, which was fast becoming a Soviet client. An Egyptian-American rapprochement commenced during Eisenhower's last two years in office and accelerated during the first two years of Kennedy's administration. Kennedy made good relations with Egypt part of his pro–Third World campaign.

There were limits to how far the Egyptian-American rapprochement could go, however. One limit was America's close connection to Saudi Arabia. When the Yemen civil war provoked clashes between Saudi forces and Egyptian units, the American government found itself caught in the middle. Kennedy did his best to maintain that middle ground, guessing that both parties might eventually forgive neutrality in the war but that neither would find it easy to forgive favoritism toward the other. Kennedy ordered the State Department to extend diplomatic recognition to the Yemeni republicans, thereby pleasing Nasser and annoying the Saudis; to offset this action, the president sent eight American airplanes to Saudi Arabia for use in defending Saudi border towns against Yemeni republican and Egyptian attack.

American intelligence analysts had predicted that the war in Yemen would not last long and that the royalists would collapse soon. But the analysts were operating largely in the dark: Yemen was very far off the beaten track, and the Americans who qualified as experts on the country could be counted on one hand and did not work for the American government. In fact, the royalists confounded the predictions, fighting doggedly on. Had the war ended quickly, Kennedy's fence straddling might have succeeded, but as matters turned out, it served only to antagonize both Nasser and the Saudis.

Even so, it did not antagonize Nasser as much as another aspect of American policy toward the Middle East. During the 1960s a fundamental shift in American relations with Israel occurred. The Truman administration had strongly supported the creation of Israel in 1947 and 1948, applying intimidating pressure on American friends and clients at the United Nations to secure a favorable vote on the resolution calling for the creation of Israel. Subsequently, however, the Truman administration had taken a relatively neutral position between Israel and the Arabs. The Eisenhower administration had extended this neutral policy, upsetting first the Arabs by backing out of the Aswan deal and then the Israelis by forcing them to give up the territory they occupied at the end of the Suez War.

Kennedy talked about a balanced approach to Arab-Israeli issues, and his efforts to woo Nasser indicated that his approach was not entirely talk; but the Democratic president staffed his administration with determined and bureaucratically effective supporters of Israel, who succeeded in pushing American policy gradually but decidedly in Israel's favor. During the Kennedy years, the Israelis requested permission to purchase American-built Hawk antiaircraft missiles. They had previously made the request of Eisenhower and been turned down. The State Department had explained that the United States did not want to contribute to a Middle Eastern arms race. The Eisenhower White House, annoyed at the Israelis for their part in the Suez conspiracy, agreed with the State Department.

Israeli officials tried again after Kennedy's election. They argued that while an American policy of abstention from a Middle Eastern weapons race made sense in theory, it did not in practice. The Soviets had been arming the Arabs since the Czech deal of 1955, creating the kind of imbalance that could easily lead to war. American approval of the Hawk sale, rather than destabilize the situation, would tend to *re*stabilize it.

Although the State Department still opposed the sale, the Kennedy White House was friendlier territory than the Eisenhower White House had been. The president decided in favor of the Hawk request just in time for the 1962 congressional elections.

Kennedy's decision marked a turning point in American relations with the Middle East. By allowing the United States to become Israel's armorer, the Kennedy administration fostered what the president described to Israeli prime minister Golda Meir as a "special relationship" between their two countries. Washington never formalized an alliance with Israel; to do so would have unnecessarily antagonized Arabs. But Kennedy assured Meir that Israel could count on the United States for protection if Israel was invaded. Subsequent administrations repeated the assurance. Israel became an informal American ally, often receiving better treatment than some formal American allies.

The "special relationship" grew stronger under Lyndon Johnson. No American president ever took a more personal interest in Israel than Johnson, who had many close Jewish friends, who recognized the domestic political advantages of being nice to Israel, and who sympathized with Israel's status as a beleaguered outpost surrounded by enemies—something like the Alamo in Texas history, as Texan Johnson could appreciate. Shortly after Johnson assumed the presidency, he received a request for Israeli purchase of several hundred American tanks. As in the case of Hawk missiles, the Israelis contended that approval of the request would merely restore balance to the weapons situation in the Middle East. The State Department opposed the request, as did the CIA, both agencies arguing that the tanks would cause more prob-

The face that launched three hundred planes: Golda Meir attends a meeting of the United Nations. *Brown Brothers*

lems for the United States with the Arabs than benefits with the Israelis. The tanks were a considerably touchier subject than the Hawk antiaircraft missiles: the latter were strictly defensive, whereas the former could be used for attack.

Johnson overruled the objectors in his administration. The president told the Israelis they would get their tanks. He encouraged Israelis to look elsewhere first and specifically suggested West Germany; but he said that if all else failed, they could buy the tanks in the United States. All else did fail: Bonn declined to run the diplomatic risks with the Arabs of selling shiploads of tanks to Israel. Johnson accordingly approved the sale of the American tanks. Not long after, the president allowed the Israelis to purchase several dozen advanced American warplanes.

The American weapons sales to Israel significantly enhanced the Israelis' fighting capacity; the sales also bolstered the Israelis' confidence that the Johnson administration would not pull the rug out from under them in a tight spot, the way Eisenhower had in 1956. During the mid-1960s the Arab-Israeli dispute was again working its way into a tight spot. The essential cause of the dispute remained as before: Israelis and Palestinians claimed the same land. But Arab politics added some new twists to the tangle. In February 1966 a coup in Syria led to the emergence of the ardently anti-Israel Baath party. The Baathists supported a guerrilla offensive against Israel from Palestinian bases in the West Bank and the Gaza Strip as well as from Syria itself. At the same time, Damascus established warmer relations with the Soviet Union; Moscow responded with deliveries of economic and military aid.

The Israelis answered Syria's actions by means of reprisals against the guerrilla bases. An eye-for-an-eye contest developed, and by the beginning of 1967, the artillery exchanges across the Israel-Syria border along the Golan Heights hardly made the nightly news. In April 1967 the Israelis launched an especially vigorous air raid over the frontier, causing the Syrian air force to scramble and challenge the attackers. The Israelis rocketed the Syrians out of the sky and screamed low over Damascus to warn the Syrian government what Israel could do if it got really mad.

Although Syria had seceded from its union with Egypt in 1961, Nasser still aspired to leadership among the Arabs, and he could not accept this affront to Arab pride without a protest. Nasser had fought the Israelis twice already and had gained a healthy respect for their military prowess. But because opposition to the Zionists was almost the only issue holding the Arab nationalist movement together, he could not afford to be seen as less anti-Israel than the Syrians. In November 1966 he signed a mutual defense treaty with Damascus; after the Israeli air attack of April 1967, the Syrians demanded that he honor his commitment and come to their aid.

At the same time, Nasser faced pressure on another front. Since the Suez War of 1956, a United Nations Emergency Force (UNEF) had stood between the armies of Israel and Egypt in the Sinai Peninsula. Arab radicals castigated Nasser for cowering behind the skirts of UNEF. Hard-liners in Syria, Iraq, and elsewhere complained that the Egyptian president knew only how to talk; if he was serious about Arab unity and the struggle for Palestine, he would order UNEF out and punish the Zionist aggressors.

Nasser worried about what such a move might lead to, but he bowed to the criticism and told the United Nations to withdraw its forces from Egyptian territory. Secretary General U Thant directed the international organization's blue-helmeted troops to comply with the Egyptian demand.

Nasser went two steps further a week later. He reinforced Egyptian army divisions along Israel's southwestern border, and just as the last UNEF units were leaving Sharm el Sheikh, on the Strait of Tiran at the entrance to the Gulf of Aqaba, Nasser announced that Egypt would close the strait, and thereby the gulf, to Israeli ship traffic.

Nasser's moves were motivated principally by his concerns regarding Arab politics. He wished to demonstrate that he could be as tough on Israel as anyone else. Moreover, all his actions were within his rights as he interpreted them. Egypt had invited UNEF to come; it could ask UNEF to go. Whether and how to strengthen Egypt's defenses were matters for Egypt alone to decide. As for the Tiran strait, Egypt had long maintained that this lay within Egyptian territorial waters. Cairo had allowed the Israelis to pass through the strait as a matter of privilege, not as a matter of right.

The Israelis, unsurprisingly, perceived Egypt's actions differently. Given that Egypt and the other Arab states remained technically at war with Israel and that Israel was so small as to allow almost no room for retreat, the Israeli government could only look on the massing of Egyptian troops as a threat to Israel's existence. The same applied to the closing of Tiran and the Aqaba gulf, which deprived Israel of reasonable access to countries to its east and foreshadowed a trampling of Israel's rights. With greater cause—namely, the Nazi death camps—than any other people, the Israelis remembered German tactics under Hitler: how Berlin had bullied and threatened and then watched to see how the world would react. The Israelis classed Nasser in the same category as Hitler, and they determined to do to Nasser what the great powers had failed to do to Hitler. They would call Nasser's bluff, hit him hard, and force him to retreat.

The United States government appreciated Israel's determination, and Washington spent the last two weeks of May and the first week of June 1967 trying to get the Israelis to reconsider. American intelligence analysts did not think Nasser would really order an attack against Israel. Nasser had to know that Egypt, even with the help of the other Arabs, was no match for Israel. American analysts believed that Nasser was posturing for the benefit of Arab radicals. If the Israelis sat tight, there would not be a war.

Convincing the Israelis of this was another matter. Johnson tried. The president communicated with Israeli prime minister Levi Eshkol and urged forbearance. He spoke with the Israeli ambassador, saying that the United States was doing all it could through the United Nations to end the blockade of Tiran and Aqaba. The least Israel could do in return was hold its fire until the diplomatic initiatives had been exhausted. Johnson told the ambassador that Israel would not be left alone in its hour of trial—unless, he added significantly, "it decides to go alone."

Despite Johnson's reassurance and veiled warning, Israel chose not to wait for the diplomats to finish talking. At dawn on June 5, Israeli jets struck Egypt by surprise. The Israeli planes destroyed more than three hundred Egyptian aircraft in the first few hours of fighting while losing less than a score of their own. After blasting the Egyptians, the Israelis turned against Jordan, eliminating that country's air force in a matter of minutes. Syria received similar treatment in the early afternoon of the same day.

Israel's domination of the air guaranteed victory on the ground. Israeli armor, supported by Israeli fighter planes, invaded the Gaza Strip and the Sinai, slicing through Egyptian lines and racing toward the Suez Canal. Other Israeli columns invaded the West Bank and the Old City of Jerusalem. Within three days the Israelis suppressed most resistance in these areas.

The Israeli attack placed the United States in a ticklish position. The Israeli government put out a cover story contending that Egypt had moved first, but the story quickly fell apart. The fact that Egypt's air force had been massacred on the ground was telling evidence against the Israeli story. For Washington to do nothing invited charges of complicity in the sneak attack, especially since American-supplied weapons were responsible for much of the damage to the Arabs. But because the Israelis considered preemption their prerogative, given their exposed position, for the Johnson administration to criticize Israel would

The wages of war in the Middle East: Jordanian women consider what to do about their home, destroyed in fighting with Israel. *Associated Press Photo*

probably provoke claims of betrayal of the American-Israeli "special relationship." Early in the war, a State Department spokesman described the American stance as one of neutrality between the combatants. Immediately the many friends of Israel in the United States put up a hue and cry. How could the American government be neutral at this moment of truth? Israel had merely defended itself against intolerable threats. Johnson quickly acted to soothe the situation. He got on the telephone to his numerous contacts within the American Jewish community and declared that Israel could count on Lyndon Johnson, just as it always had.

Despite his efforts at soothing, Johnson was not pleased that the Israelis had defied his warning about not firing first. The president grew even more upset, indeed nearly apoplectic, on the fourth day of the war when Israeli warplanes attacked an American intelligence ship, the *Liberty,* off the Egyptian coast. From all evidence the attack, which wounded more than two hundred American sailors and killed thirty-four, was not accidental. The sky was clear, visibility was excellent, and the ship was well marked. Israeli reconnaissance planes repeatedly flew close overhead prior to the attack. Although the Israelis never admitted as much, the most likely explanation for the attack was that Israel's commanders wanted to keep the Americans from learning of an Israeli plan to widen the war. Jordan had quit the day before, accepting a United

Nations cease-fire proposal; Egypt was on the ropes and would give up within hours. Israeli forces had seized the West Bank from Jordan and the Gaza Strip from Egypt, both of which served as staging grounds for Palestinian raids against Israel. The Israelis also controlled the Sinai, the large buffer zone between the rest of Egypt and Israel's southwestern flank. The only part of the Israeli military's agenda that remained unaccomplished was the capture of Syria's Golan Heights, from which Syrian gunners looked down on Israel's northeast. Control of the Golan would also help secure Israel's water supply. Washington was pressing Israel to halt the fighting, but the Israeli military did not want to stop before gaining the Golan. If the Americans gained incontrovertible proof of an impending attack on Syria, such as military messages of the kind the *Liberty* was designed to intercept, they might object publicly and try diplomatically to block the attack. Better that they find out only after the fact. If this required taking out the *Liberty,* such a move could be explained away as an accident—which is just what the Israelis did.

Johnson administration officials did not believe the accident story for a minute. Even Clark Clifford, one of the oldest and most influential friends of Israel in American politics and a close adviser to Johnson, told the president it was "inconceivable" that the attack had been an accident. But Johnson decided, as the Israelis doubtless believed he would, that the middle of a war was not a good time for a spat between the United States and Israel. Although he cursed the Israelis under his breath, he accepted Israel's apology and ordered the incident hushed up.

One big reason for Johnson's refusal to take stronger action against Israel was the looming presence of the Soviet Union behind Egypt and Syria. The Soviets had been deeply embarrassed by the poor showing of their Arab clients against America's Israeli protégés; if nothing else, the ease with which the Israelis had blasted the Arabs' Soviet weapons would diminish demand for Eastern bloc hardware in the Third World. Worse, it would cause allies and prospective allies to doubt Moscow's ability to protect those it said it would.

The first stage of the fighting—Israel's attacks against Egypt and Jordan—had effectively ended before the Soviet Union could do anything worthwhile about it; but the Israeli invasion of Syria, which began on schedule just hours after the crippling of the *Liberty,* provoked the Kremlin beyond endurance. Moscow broke diplomatic relations with Israel, and Soviet premier Aleksei Kosygin phoned Johnson to warn that the situation in the Middle East had reached a "very crucial moment." A "grave catastrophe" was about to happen. Kosygin declared that unless the Israelis suspended operations at once, the Soviet Union would take "necessary actions, including military."

Johnson was not sure how serious the Soviets were. The CIA had discounted the possibility of Soviet intervention as minimal, arguing that the benefits Moscow might gain by jumping into the war on the Arabs' side were much smaller than the likely costs of a consequent confrontation with the United States. To cover himself both ways, Johnson replied to the Soviet action with a combination of firmness and conciliation. He ordered the American Sixth Fleet, on patrol in the Mediterranean, to head toward the scene of the fighting. And he told Kosygin that the American government was doing all it could to end the bloodshed.

It was unlikely that the superpowers would actually have committed troops, ships, or planes to battle in the Middle East at this time. For both sides the risks were too great compared to the potential gains. Yet each side had to give the appearance of looking out for its friends in the conflict. Prestige was as important as ever.

Before either Washington or Moscow had to decide on the direct use of force, the fighting stopped. The Israelis by now had seized the Golan Heights, their final objective, and on the sixth day of the fighting they agreed to a cease-fire with Syria. This closed the conflict on the war's third and final front.

The June War of 1967 (often called the Six Day War), despite its brevity had consequences of the utmost significance. One consequence was the creation of a myth of Israeli invincibility. The Israelis had acquitted themselves well in the two previous wars but had shown nothing like the overwhelming superiority they demonstrated in the 1967 war. The Israelis learned to scorn Arab military capacity—to Israel's cost later. The Arabs burned to vindicate their honor.

As a second consequence, the Middle East grew more polarized than before. The United States became more closely associated than ever with Israel in the eyes of the Arabs and most of the rest of the world, while Egypt and Syria, which had broken diplomatic relations with the United States during the fighting, gravitated toward Moscow. The Johnson administration restocked Israel's arsenal, delivering some of the most potent American warplanes along with items less glamorous but equally essential. The Soviets set to rebuilding the military forces of Egypt and Syria.

The third and most lasting consequence of the 1967 war was Israel's seizure of territory from its neighbors: the Sinai and Gaza Strip from Egypt, the West Bank and East Jerusalem from Jordan, and the Golan Heights from Syria. Israel's occupation of the Sinai aggravated the situation least, in that relatively few people lived there and the Israelis had no special attachment to it. The Golan constituted a harder problem because Israel deemed it to be of considerable military value and of economic consequence for its function in the water supply of the area. Gaza was harder still, being the ancestral home of some sixty thousand Palestinians and the more recent refuge of a quarter million Palestinian refugees from the 1948 war. All of a sudden Israel found itself governing a large population of people there who longed for nothing more than to see Israel destroyed. The West Bank and East Jerusalem posed the hardest problem of all. East Jerusalem included the Old City, which contained some of the holiest shrines in Jewish history and religion. No conceivable Israeli government would even consider relinquishing the Old City. The rest of the West Bank was the original home of hundreds of thousands of Palestinians and the current abode of additional hundreds of thousands of refugees. The problems of governing a resentful population were compounded by the fact that to a large and influential portion of the Israeli populace, the West Bank was really a part of Israel—the Judea and Samaria of biblical times. For nearly

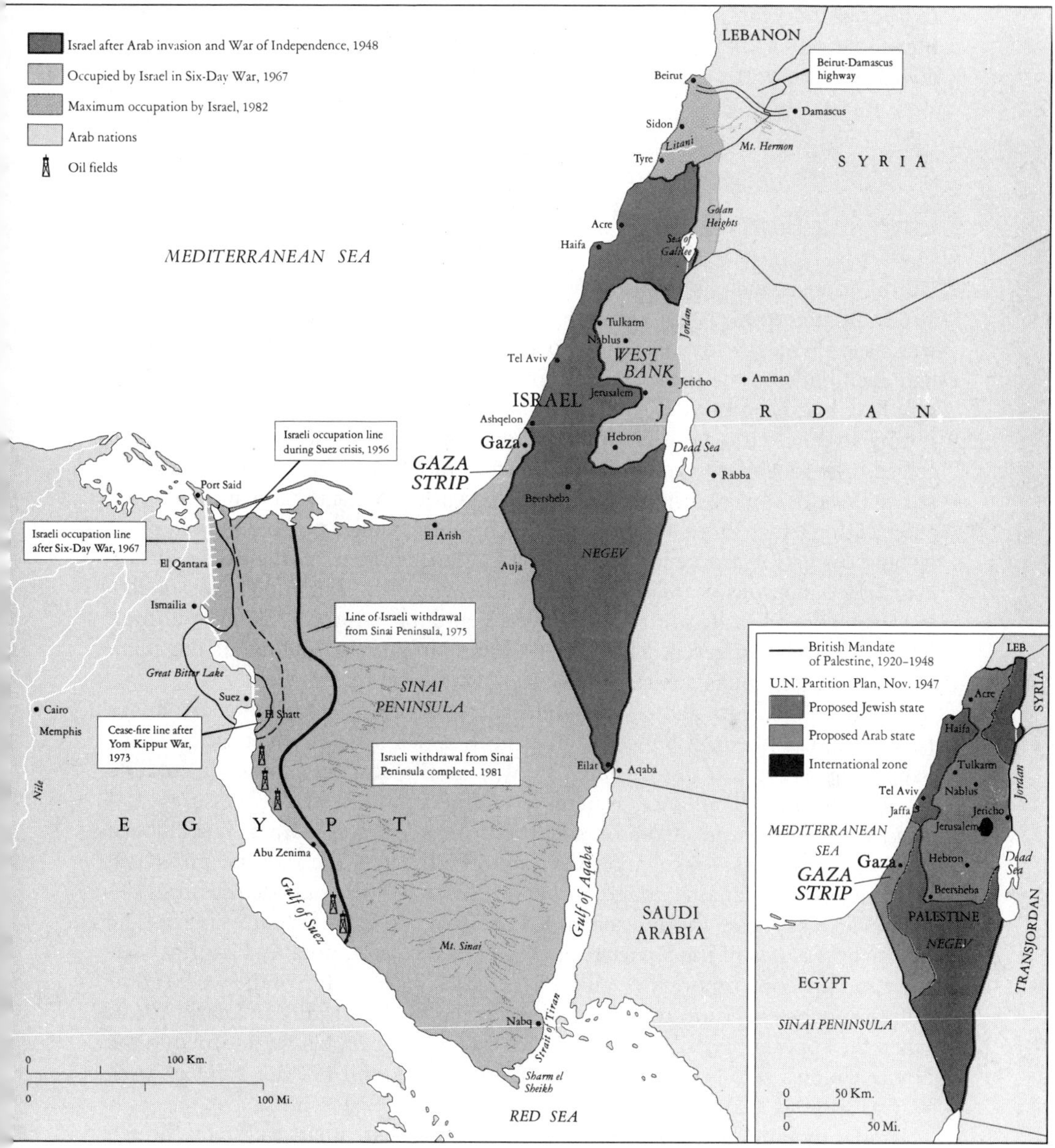
Israel after Arab invasion and War of Independence, 1948
Occupied by Israel in Six-Day War, 1967
Maximum occupation by Israel, 1982
Arab nations
Oil fields
LEBANON
Beirut
Beirut-Damascus highway
Damascus
Sidon
Litani
Mt. Hermon
Tyre
SYRIA
Golan Heights
Acre
Haifa
Sea of Galilee
MEDITERRANEAN SEA
Jordan
Tulkarm
Nablus
Tel Aviv
WEST BANK
Jericho
Amman
ISRAEL
Jerusalem
JORDAN
Ashqelon
Gaza
Hebron
Dead Sea
Israeli occupation line during Suez crisis, 1956
GAZA STRIP
Rabba
Port Said
Beersheba
El Arish
Israeli occupation line after Six-Day War, 1967
El Qantara
NEGEV
Auja
Ismailia
Line of Israeli withdrawal from Sinai Peninsula, 1975
Great Bitter Lake
SINAI PENINSULA
Suez
El Shatt
Cairo
Memphis
Cease-fire line after Yom Kippur War, 1973
Israeli withdrawal from Sinai Peninsula completed, 1981
Eilat
Aqaba
Nile
EGYPT
Abu Zenima
Gulf of Suez
Gulf of Aqaba
SAUDI ARABIA
Mt. Sinai
Nabq
Strait of Tiran
Sharm el Sheikh
RED SEA
0 100 Km.
0 100 Mi.
British Mandate of Palestine, 1920–1948
U.N. Partition Plan, Nov. 1947
Proposed Jewish state
Proposed Arab state
International zone
LEB.
SYRIA
Acre
Haifa
Tulkarm
Tel Aviv
Nablus
Jaffa
Jericho
Jerusalem
MEDITERRANEAN SEA
Gaza
Hebron
Dead Sea
GAZA STRIP
Beersheba
PALESTINE
NEGEV
TRANSJORDAN
EGYPT
SINAI PENINSULA
0 50 Km.
0 50 Mi.

Israel and Surrounding Countries in 1967

two thousand years, Jews had hoped and prayed and fought to reclaim their homeland. Now they had succeeded. For any Israeli government to propose giving up even part of it would touch off a political firestorm in Israel.

Growing Pains in the Alliances

During a crisis such as the June War of 1967 or the Cuban missile affair of 1962, the superpowers could usually rely on their allies to rally around. There was a simple reason for this. The two alliance systems, like all alliance systems, had been built on the perceived self-interest of the parties involved. The Warsaw Pact had been built on force, but at least the governments of the Eastern European countries, as often opposed to the peoples of those countries, perceived their self-interest to lie in the direction of Moscow. The most important self-interest of any government is self-preservation, which seems most threatened during times of great danger. At such times smaller powers huddle close to big powers for protection. The NATO alliance system had its origin in the evidently dangerous years of the late 1940s, when the communists were making tremendous headway around the world, and the nations of Western Europe felt seriously endangered. The Soviet-Chinese alliance grew out of the same period; the communists felt analogously endangered by the West.

If danger tends to tighten the bonds of alliances, the lessening of danger tends to loosen them. Alliances can be the victims of their own success: established to prevent war, they usually weaken in the absence of war or credible threat of war. All alliance systems contain certain internal pressures and strains. When pressures from outside the system—threats from a rival alliance system, for instance—are large, they can overbalance the internal pressures, and the alliance remains united and coherent. When the outside pressures decrease or disappear, the internal pressures can blow the alliance apart. The internal pressures of the Soviet-Chinese alliance system, notably historical distrust and the contemporary rivalry for ideological leadership of the world communist movement, ruptured that system during the late 1950s and early 1960s when the apparent possibility of Western attack receded. China returned to the Soviet Union's side briefly during the Cuban crisis of 1962 but went its own way as soon as the danger passed.

Similar dynamics were at work within the American alliance system, though the damage they did to the alliance was not so striking as in the Soviet-Chinese case. At the time of NATO's founding, the three pillars of the Atlantic alliance were the United States, Britain, and France. There were few big obstacles to bringing these three countries together: they had been partners during two world wars, and not in living memory had any one of the three fought against any of the others. West Germany was a different matter. The Americans, British, and French allowed the Germans living in the Western occupation zones to form a government in 1949 partly because Washington, London, and Paris realized they could not occupy and run western Germany forever and partly because they wanted the Germans to assume some of the responsibility for defending themselves against the Soviets. Yet encouraging the Germans to govern and defend themselves entailed risks, specifically the risk that Germany would do a third time what it had done in 1914 and 1939. West Germany was brought into NATO in 1955 to strengthen the Atlantic alliance against the Soviet system but also in order that the Americans, British, and French could keep an eye on the Germans. American troops, British troops, and French troops were stationed in West Germany for the acknowledged purpose of deterring an attack from the east; the unstated purpose was to prevent West Germany from getting too strong. With the three allies defending them, the West Germans did not have to create a threateningly large army. Nor did they have to build nuclear weapons since the American nuclear arsenal would deter a Soviet attack.

For about a decade, this tacit agreement worked reasonably well; and to a lesser extent something similar applied to American relations with France and Britain. The United States consented to shoulder most of the burden of the defense of the Atlantic alliance against attack, and Britain, France, and West Germany agreed to accept the secondary role that dependence on another power for military security implies. The advantage for the United States was the predominant voice in Atlantic alliance affairs. The advantage for America's allies was freedom from the expense of having to construct self-sufficient military defenses.

When Britain, France, and West Germany were very poor compared to the United States, most conspicuously during the years of the Marshall Plan, none of the parties to this arrangement complained much; but as the Western Europeans regained strength and self-confidence during the 1950s, their secondary status within the alliance began to rankle. Britain, France, and Germany had been proud countries; their people were still proud. Many of them did not like having to defer to the wishes of the Americans.

The rankling affected Britain less than France or Germany. The ties of culture that had long caused Americans to look on the British with comparative fondness worked the other way as well. Although many British found Americans unsophisticated and materialistic, many others regarded them with some of the pride older cousins feel for successful younger cousins. Winston Churchill waxed enthusiastic about the "special relationship" between Americans and British and about the glorious future of the "English-speaking peoples." A common metaphor decreed that Britain should be to America as Greece had been to Rome—less elegantly, that Britain should supply the brains of the partnership and America the muscle. The British insisted on developing nuclear weapons of their own, in part to remind the Americans of Britain's key contributions to the Manhattan Project. But otherwise, and with a few exceptions such as the Suez affair of 1956 and the Skybolt contretemps of 1962, in which Kennedy abruptly canceled development of a missile Britain had been relying on for delivery of nuclear warheads, the British accepted their status as junior partners with relative good humor and good grace.

The West Germans felt no such close ties of kinship to America as the British did, yet the West Germans had their own reasons for accepting a subordinate status for their country. In the first place, of all the NATO countries West Germany was the most vulnerable to attack. The Warsaw Pact states massed large military forces just across the border in East Germany; against these, the West Germans were happy for all the help they could get. Second, many Germans had guilty consciences about their past. With good reason: the crimes the Nazis had inflicted on neighboring countries, on Jews, and on many others was enough to make anyone feel guilty. The guilt gradually wore off as the generation of the Nazi reich and the Second World War died, but while that guilt lingered, it discouraged Germans from demanding an equal place with the greatest powers. Third, Germany remained divided. Some Germans were willing to accept division as their fate, but many others dreamed of the day when their country would be whole again. If nothing else, reuniting West Germany with East Germany would facilitate visits to relatives caught on the wrong side of the split. Unification would come most likely, if at all, as a result of relaxation between the superpowers. The interest of the unifiers therefore consisted in reducing tensions, not in enlarging them. And the best way for Germans to reduce tensions was to lie low.

The French had the greatest difficulty living in the American shadow. The French had few cousinly feelings toward the Americans and experienced no warmth from America's reflected glory. Neither did the French harbor the guilt the Germans did about the Second World War. Doubtless some of the Nazis' French collaborators had trouble sleeping nights, but the great majority of the French considered themselves victims of the Germans rather than accomplices. And ultimately they had been victors over the Germans. Nor did the French have the incentive to placate the Americans that motivated the German unifiers.

What the French *did* have was Charles de Gaulle. The French general emerged from retirement in 1958 at the moment of dissolution of France's Fourth Republic. Disgruntled French conservatives in Algeria, frustrated at the French government's handling of the Algerian war, had revolted in May of that year against the authority of Paris. Most of the French army in North Africa sided with the rebels. Unable to deal with the insurrection, the Paris government collapsed, giving way to a new government headed by de Gaulle. With parliamentary approval, de Gaulle presided over the demise of the Fourth Republic and the drafting of a new constitution to establish a Fifth. The new charter, approved by referendum in September 1958, shifted the balance of political power within the French government from the legislature to the executive and within the executive to the president. On his election as president in December, de Gaulle gained authority unprecedented in recent French history.

The general knew what to do with it. He quelled the insurrection in Algeria by stern action against the insurrectionists, but at the same time he prepared the way for Algerian independence, which eventually arrived in 1962. He simultaneously charted a more autonomous course for France in international

Charles de Gaulle ends a speech in characteristic fashion. *Associated Press Photo*

affairs. He believed implicitly in French greatness. He once said he considered himself something of a cross between Joan of Arc and Napoleon. He was convinced that France's destiny included a leading role among the world's nations. He challenged what he perceived to be American favoritism toward Britain within the Atlantic alliance. This perception was not entirely inaccurate. The United States did indeed favor Britain, partly because of cultural compatibility but also because the procession of unstable governments in France since the Second World War had made reliance on France difficult. By comparison with the French, the British were reassuringly predictable. Although de Gaulle refused to accept the American reasoning, he understood the problems of French volatility. "How can one govern a country that has three hundred and fifty kinds of cheese?" he once asked.

To increase France's weight in European and world affairs, de Gaulle insisted that France develop its own nuclear weapons. This decision dismayed the Americans, who adopted the view that the fewer countries that possessed these ultimate weapons, the safer the world would be. But de Gaulle was determined to press ahead. He did, and in 1960 French scientists successfully detonated a fission bomb in the French Sahara. For the moment the significance of France's atomic arsenal was mostly symbolic. In reality de Gaulle may actually have lessened French security: the French had enough bombs to cause the Soviets to aim some of their own nuclear warheads at France but not enough to prevent the Soviets from firing.

Beyond developing nuclear weapons, de Gaulle tried to establish closer ties with West Germany. Such ties, he believed, would help offset the Anglo-American tilt in the Atlantic alliance. In West German chancellor Konrad Adenauer, de Gaulle found a kindred spirit: a domineering individual who, while not disrespecting democracy, considered that his own voice counted for more than his compatriots'. But though France and West Germany signed a mutual security treaty in 1963, the Paris-Berlin axis never really firmed up. Too many French people still distrusted the Germans, and Bonn was not as willing to challenge American primacy as de Gaulle was.

De Gaulle positively reveled in challenging the United States. Indeed, as his countryman Voltaire said of God, if America had not existed, the general would have had to invent it. The United States served as de Gaulle's foil. Many of his supporters in France resented America, both for America's wealth, which was made the more annoying by France's acceptance of American charity after the war, and America's pretensions. American officials often acted, as representatives of powerful countries tend to do, as if they knew best. Sometimes they were right; sometimes not. But no one likes to have to deal with such people. The French, painfully aware of how far they had fallen in the ranks of world power, liked it less than most. De Gaulle took almost every opportunity to affirm French independence by striking a different course from that indicated by Washington. He continued to develop France's independent nuclear deterrent, the *force de frappe*. He vetoed British membership in the European Economic Community (EEC), or Common Market, which membership Washington had supported. He extended diplomatic recognition to Communist China, which the United States was still trying to isolate. He loudly advocated a neutralization scheme to end the war in Vietnam. He launched a diplomatic initiative designed to improve French relations with the Soviet Union.

De Gaulle also challenged the integrity of NATO. His insistence on an independent French nuclear force was part of his challenge since it implied skepticism that the United States would really risk nuclear war to defend France. His separate initiative toward West Germany was another part since it suggested that the NATO ties binding France and West Germany were insufficient to French needs. His initiatives toward Moscow suggested a weakening of French ties to the West.

But de Gaulle's most direct challenge to NATO came in February 1966 when he ordered the evacuation of American and other foreign forces from France and announced that France was leaving NATO. In explaining his move, the general asserted that France had to reassume on its own territory "the full exercise of her sovereignty, which is at present impaired by the permanent presence of allied military elements." France remained committed to the Atlantic alliance, de Gaulle added, and would come to the assistance of its allies in the event of war. But the unified command of the NATO military structure compromised French independence; therefore France had to withdraw.

De Gaulle's demarche did not surprise Washington. Rumors of a French withdrawal from NATO had been floating around the American embassy in Paris for some time. Johnson recognized that there was little he could do about the situation. From the time of Johnson's accession to the American presidency, he had deliberately adopted a low profile with respect to de Gaulle. He refused to get into what he privately called a "pissing match" with the general. "I keep mum," Johnson told a group of French reporters. "If you hear something nasty about de Gaulle, it has not come from me or anybody in the White House. I told everybody in the government to be polite to President de Gaulle. Just tip your hat and say, 'Thank you, General.'" Nor did Johnson contest de Gaulle's eviction notice. "When a man asks you to leave his house," the president said, "you do not argue. You get your hat and go."

Johnson's refusal to challenge de Gaulle reflected a judgment that disputing the general's action would merely exacerbate tension between America and France. It also reflected a belief that there was less to the French withdrawal from NATO than met the eye. France's absence from the NATO command would complicate joint planning, but because France remained within the Atlantic alliance and was pledged to collective defense against the Soviet Union, the balance of power in Europe had not changed much. Moreover, American officials anticipated that many of the current problems of the Franco-American relationship would diminish upon de Gaulle's passing from power. That relationship was based on abiding national interests, which in turn were shaped by geography, economics, and shared political values. De Gaulle could influence those interests, but he could not eliminate them or revise them single-handedly. He would leave; they would last.

Another reason for Johnson's refusal to react strongly to de Gaulle's challenge to NATO was that the American president was distracted by troubles elsewhere in the Atlantic alliance. In 1964 and again in 1967, Greece and Turkey almost went to war with each other over Cyprus. At the time that the two southeastern European nations had joined the Atlantic alliance, some observers predicted trouble. For millennia—at least since the Trojan War of Homer's era—Greece and Turkey had been rivals. At present they might be more scared of the Soviet Union than of each other, but eventually their rivalry would resurface.

It did, most noticeably on Cyprus, where Greeks and Turks had long lived uneasily together. The uneasiness increased in 1960 when Cyprus gained independence from Britain. The constitution of the new island-state was supposed to guarantee the rights of the minority Turkish Cypriots, but it did so only by circumscribing what the majority Greek Cypriots took to be *their* rights. Cyprus became a passion-producing issue in the politics of both Greece and Turkey, with each government feeling obliged to promise protection to its people's cousins on Cyprus.

Between 1960 and 1963, incidents of violence occurred sporadically, but near the end of 1963, as the government headed by (Greek) Cypriot president Archbishop Makarios III sought changes in the constitution, changes the

Turkish Cypriots found threatening, violence intensified. Britain attempted a negotiated settlement among Greece and Turkey and the two communities on Cyprus. The negotiations failed, and during the first part of 1964 the violence on the island got still worse. In June 1964 the Turkish government mobilized its military forces for an invasion of the island.

Washington did not care much about Cyprus as Cyprus. American officials found Makarios to be politically unreliable and personally obnoxious. "I have sat across the table from that pious-looking replica of Jesus Christ," remarked Adlai Stevenson, the American representative at the United Nations, "and if you saw him with his beard shaved and a pushcart, you would recall the old saying that there hasn't been an honest thief since Barabbas." But Washington desired greatly to avert a war between two members of the NATO alliance. At the least such a war would undermine NATO's southeastern flank; worse, it might open a route for more extensive Soviet penetration of the eastern Mediterranean and the Middle East.

Lyndon Johnson knew how to be subtle and deceptive when circumstances required, but he also knew how to be brutally blunt. He chose the blunt approach in telling the Turks they had better not move against Cyprus or Greece. The president wrote a letter to the Turkish prime minister that Dean Rusk described as "the diplomatic equivalent of an atomic bomb." Johnson declared that if Turkey invaded Cyprus, it would be reneging on its commitments to NATO, to the United Nations, and to the United States. This being the case, the United States would have to reconsider its position with respect to Turkey. Very pointedly, Johnson said that should the Soviet Union take advantage of Ankara's preoccupation with Cyprus to attack Turkey, the Turks had better look to their own devices.

Johnson's ultimatum kept the Turkish troops in their barracks and Turkish planes on the ground. It probably prevented a war over Cyprus. But it embittered many Turks against the United States. And it left the source of the problem, the hostile feelings between Greeks and Turks on Cyprus, unresolved. Subsequent American-sponsored negotiations came no closer to settling the issue, which continued to vex NATO relations for the next generation.

On another NATO front, Washington had better luck. Since the 1950s the stationing of American troops in Germany had caused balance-of-payments difficulties between the United States and West Germany. Money spent by the American government on supplies for troops and dependents and money spent by those troops and dependents on various necessities and luxuries of life caused a large outflow of dollars from the United States to West Germany. As the West German economy revived and grew in the 1950s and early 1960s and German exports to the United States expanded, the deficit ballooned. During the Kennedy years, the American and West German governments papered the problem over by a series of ad hoc arrangements whereby Bonn pledged to offset American expenditures in Germany by purchases of American military equipment.

These offset agreements worked reasonably well for a time, but by 1964 they had begun to groan under the strain of West German budget deficits. Since the hyperinflation of the post–First World War era, German governments had been deathly afraid of anything that caused inflationary pressure on the German currency. Among the principal potential culprits were government deficits, and Bonn felt obliged to keep its deficits low. Because the offset payments to America were a highly visible contributor to the West German budget deficits, the government of Chancellor Ludwig Erhard desired to reduce those payments. In addition, German arms manufacturers wanted the business that was going to American producers. They claimed that something as vital to German welfare as the instruments of national defense should not be contracted out to foreigners; they also thought they ought to be making the profits from the arms sales.

Britain faced a balance-of-payments shortfall with Germany that was similar to that between the United States and Germany, though smaller. Yet while Britain's shortfall was smaller, the smaller size and weaker condition of the British economy compared with the American economy magnified the shortfall's ill effects.

In both the United States and Britain, the balance-of-payments problems exacerbated a feeling that maybe the time had come to bring the troops home from Germany and let the Germans defend themselves. In Britain the feeling became such a political factor that the government of Prime Minister Harold Wilson announced in July 1966 that it would withdraw many of Britain's troops unless Bonn consented to offset completely the cost to Britain of maintaining them in Germany.

Only occasionally have the political difficulties of British governments become political difficulties in Washington; this threatened to be one of those occasions. Wilson's announcement shortly followed de Gaulle's decision to throw American troops out of France, and it contributed to a general impression in the United States that the Europeans were an ungrateful bunch who were happy to accept American dollars but were unwilling to offer much in return. A movement developed in the American Congress to bring American soldiers home from the Continent. The movement only gained impetus from the fact that Britain and France, despite being charter members of SEATO, were conspicuous by their absence from the effort to defend South Vietnam against the communists. Adding insult to injury, de Gaulle publicly criticized American policies in Southeast Asia.

Johnson remembered the American isolationism of the 1930s, and he had no wish to see America and the world travel that road again. He placed the highest importance on solving the NATO offset problem before it triggered an unraveling of the Atlantic alliance. He appointed as his personal representative to Bonn and London the former American high commissioner to Germany after the war, John McCloy.

Three-way talks among the United States, West Germany, and Britain commenced in the fall of 1966. They went slowly, as economic negotiations generally do. The fall of Erhard's government in Bonn slowed the pace still further. But gradually McCloy and his German and British counterparts narrowed the gap between them, and finally they arrived at a deal. The key to the bargain was an American decision to let the Germans offset the American troop expenses by purchasing American government bonds rather than American military hardware. This yielded the immediate return flow of dollars Johnson needed politically, but because the bonds would have to be repurchased with interest by the United States it proved acceptable to the Germans. The British, receiving a pledge of higher payments from Bonn, agreed to keep all but a token number of their troops in Germany. The Johnson administration defused the demands for bringing American troops home by what amounted to a shell game. Some American troops would be rotated between bases in the United States and bases in Germany. While the administration could claim, and did, that these troops remained "fully committed to NATO," it could simultaneously appease American neoisolationists by holding photo sessions showing Pentagon officials greeting the returning soldiers as they rotated home.

The various problems within the Atlantic alliance occasioned considerable worry in Washington, as in other NATO capitals; but these problems also provided a certain reassurance. For it was precisely because NATO was working so well at its primary task of providing security against Soviet attack that the members of the alliance felt comparatively free to bicker among themselves. Governments, like people, tend to deal with their most pressing concerns before proceeding to worry about lesser matters. The fact that these intramural problems had risen to the top of the worry list indicated that the problem of the Soviet Union had fallen considerably.

But it had not disappeared. During the first half of 1968, reformers in Czechoslovakia attempted to loosen the iron grip of communism on their country. For a few months, the air seemed softer, and people breathed more freely during this "Prague spring." But the fine weather did not last. The Soviet Union, having watched Yugoslavia spin out of Moscow's orbit in 1948 and China go its own way a little more than a decade later, did not intend for the same thing to happen in the heart of the satellite belt. Soviet leader Leonid Brezhnev unveiled what was quickly dubbed the Brezhnev Doctrine, the shorthand for which was "Once socialist, always socialist." What Brezhnev meant was that any country under Soviet control would stay under Soviet control. Brezhnev ordered Soviet tanks into Czechoslovakia and crushed the reform.

The 1968 Soviet invasion of Czechoslovakia reminded NATO members that their alliance was not yet obsolete. The Russian bear still had sharp claws and a nasty disposition. At the same time, however, the invasion demonstrated that some of the divisive forces that were at work among America's Western European allies were also at work among the Soviet Union's Eastern European allies. These forces had to work harder in Eastern Europe to accomplish much; Moscow refused to let Czechoslovakia get away with considerably less than what Washington tolerated from France.

The difference in the superpower reactions to demands for change underscored a fundamental difference in the nature of the alliance systems, at least as they involved Europe (the difference was fuzzier elsewhere). The American system had been created by the free choice of its members, whereas the Soviet

Brezhnev answers Czech calls for liberalization. *Photo—Orbis Ent., Ltd. from Black Star*

system had been largely imposed by the Red Army and continued to be. Chiefly for this reason, the American system turned out to be more durable in the long run, besides being more humane in the short.

Throwing Good Money After Bad: Vietnam Again

Great powers are known by their ability to persist in mistakes. Small countries have to be smart to survive, but big countries can often get away with being merely strong. Britain and France knew they were over the hill in 1956 when their conspiracy against Egypt was curtly canceled within days by the United States. In 1965 America's Vietnam venture was a decade and a half old. Already some Americans were calling it a mistake. Lyndon Johnson did not agree, and he was determined to prove the naysayers wrong.

Until the 1964 Tonkin Gulf incident, the United States had defended South Vietnam almost exclusively in South Vietnam; American actions north of the seventeenth parallel had been inconsequential. The reprisals after the Tonkin

Gulf affair changed the situation and portended a major expansion in the theater of American operations. Johnson delayed the expansion long enough to
get elected in November 1964, but several weeks into the following year, following a sharp Vietcong attack on American marines stationed at Pleiku, he
gave the order.

Operation Rolling Thunder, an American air offensive against North Vietnam, was designed to convince Hanoi that the war was unwinnable. The
United States would show that it could inflict heavy damage on North Vietnam
at relatively little cost to itself. The North Vietnamese rightly doubted America's willingness to lose lots of lives on behalf of South Vietnam, but waging
war by air would not require many American lives. An air war would rely
chiefly on American technology and American economic might—the latter to
pay for the expensive technology.

This reasoning was logical but suspect. It assumed that the damage from
bombing would materially lessen Hanoi's ability to carry on the war against
Saigon. This was a dubious assumption at best. Studies conducted after the
Second World War had demonstrated that the Allied bombing campaign
against Germany had *not* crippled Germany's war industries or otherwise
strangled the German war effort. The Germans had lost the war to Allied tanks
and infantry, not to Allied bombers. By all odds a bombing campaign against
North Vietnam would be even less effective than against Germany because
North Vietnam was a largely agricultural country with few high-value targets
for American bombs. If the war against Germany had been won on the ground,
all the more would the war against North Vietnam have to be won on the
ground.

Another American assumption was equally dubious. Washington and most
Americans accepted the premise that South Vietnam was a separate country
from North Vietnam. This premise had a shaky legal foundation: the Geneva
accords of 1954 stated explicitly that the division of Vietnam was to be only
temporary. But whatever its legal basis, the communists of North Vietnam
rejected it. To Ho and his followers, South Vietnam was simply southern Vietnam, and the war against Saigon was a civil war. The Americans considered
themselves defenders of an independent country beset by external aggression,
but to the communists the Americans were the invaders, meddlers trying to
prop up a puppet regime that had no firm base among the Vietnamese people.
The Americans assumed that at some point Hanoi would accept the division
of Vietnam and reconcile itself to governing the northern half. The communists, however, considered the fight against the Americans merely a continua-
tion of the fight against the previous occupiers, the French and Japanese. The
most committed of the nationalists, such as Ho, had been fighting for what
they conceived to be Vietnamese independence for forty years. They had out-
lasted the French and Japanese and were determined to outlast Americans.

What the war in Vietnam ultimately reduced to was a test of wills. Which
side—American or communist—was more determined to win? Had the stakes
been the same for both sides, there would have been no doubt regarding the
answer. American resources far outstripped anything the North Vietnamese

could muster. But the stakes were not the same. No matter how much political capital successive American administrations invested in Vietnam, that country remained far away and not intrinsically very interesting or valuable to most Americans. For the United States, packing up and going home was always a viable option and often a tempting one. The Vietnamese, by contrast, had nowhere else to go. This *was* their home. Vietnam always meant far more to the Vietnamese than it did to the Americans. Whether something that mattered a little to a very powerful people would count for more than something that mattered a lot to a comparatively weak people was the essential question of the Vietnam War.

If a stable and self-sustaining government had developed in Saigon, the calculations would have been different. In that case the desires of the Vietnamese anticommunists might have offset the determination of the Vietnamese communists, and the United States could have tipped a close balance in favor of the former. But no such government ever emerged. That it did not owed partly to the corruption and ineptness of the successive factions that ruled in Saigon. It owed partly to the pressures of the war. Democracy has difficulty taking root in the best-prepared soil; it has a much harder time in soil pounded and poisoned by civil war. And it owed partly to the very efforts of the United States to create such a government. Of all the regimes that governed in Saigon from 1954 to the end of the war in 1975, none ever escaped the charge of being a creature of the Americans. This burden added immensely to the credibility problems each regime faced.

Saigon's credibility did not increase with the onset of the American bombing campaign against North Vietnam, despite American hopes that it would. If anything, it decreased. While the United States had merely been providing support to South Vietnam's military forces, Saigon could claim that it was carrying most of the weight of the burden of defending the South Vietnamese people from communism. But once the United States began bombing North Vietnam, the war increasingly became an American war. This allowed the communists to portray the war more convincingly than ever as a classic nationalist struggle against imperialist oppression.

Several months of bombing North Vietnam did almost nothing to diminish the pressure on Saigon, and this failure led Johnson's military advisers to contend that unless Washington committed major American combat forces directly to the fighting, South Vietnam would fall. In March 1965 the president had authorized the commitment of American units, which previously had served chiefly in advisory and logistical capacities, directly to the fighting; now the American commander in Vietnam, General William Westmoreland, wanted 150,000 more troops. Johnson had just launched his campaign for the Great Society and was in no mood to let Saigon collapse and thereby provide the Republicans with ammunition to attack him. Yet neither was he willing to make such a major effort in Vietnam as his generals wanted. It is a commonplace of military planning that the larger the disparity in forces favoring one side in battle, the fewer casualties the favored side will suffer. British field marshal Bernard Montgomery of Second World War fame usually tried for a

A U.S. plane drops napalm on a position held by North Vietnamese forces.
UPI/Bettman

numerical advantage of fifteen to one—prompting Ernest Hemingway, who liked his martinis mixed in that ratio, to call his favorite drink a "Monty." Johnson's generals wanted to apply this principle to Vietnam. But the president desired to keep the conflict there as quiet as possible, short of pulling out. Throughout his time in office, he regularly refused the full deployments the generals requested. In July 1965 Johnson approved fifty thousand troops to be sent at once and fifty thousand for later in the year. Hoping to ease Americans into the idea of a larger war, Johnson withheld the announcement of the second fifty thousand until closer to their departure.

The entry of large numbers of American combat troops into the war continued the trend toward the Americanization of the anticommunist side of the conflict. It further eroded the credibility of the Saigon government, which was suffering on its own from a rapid turnover of leadership. Every few months a new group grabbed control. Nor did the American escalation do much to stem the communist advances. By now large numbers of regular North Vietnamese soldiers were fighting in the south along with the local Vietcong. Like other guerrilla wars, this was a conflict without front lines. Communist strongholds were scattered among positions held by South Vietnamese and American units. Because geography offered no solid guide to progress, American commanders waged a war of attrition, relying on the "body count" to measure how well they were doing. But counting bodies was deceptive even when the numbers were not deliberately inflated by field officers or higher-ups intent on making themselves look good—which they often were. American and South Vietnamese soldiers killed North Vietnamese and Vietcong troops at a rate perhaps three times that at which they themselves were being killed. Yet the ranks of the communist side continued to increase, swollen both by recruitment from within South Vietnam and by infiltration from the north. Moreover, Hanoi was willing to accept the higher toll. Ho Chi Minh had warned the French in 1946 that even if they killed ten of his men for every one French soldier the communists killed, his forces would win; France would tire of the fight before his side would. France had indeed tired of the fight first, and Ho fully expected that the United States would, too.

Johnson tried to put a brave aspect on the situation. Where so much about the war was unknowable, administration officials could convince themselves, or at least try to, that the situation was improving. They told themselves and the American people that America had turned a corner in the battle for South Vietnam, that they could see the light at the end of the tunnel. This proved to be wishful thinking. Despite a continued and massive buildup of American forces in Vietnam, to nearly five hundred thousand troops at the end of 1967, and despite a comparable increase in the intensity of the air war, to more than one hundred thousand missions flown against North Vietnam in 1967 in addition to a heavy air campaign in support of operations within South Vietnam, the capacity of the communist side to carry on the war remained intact.

The communists demonstrated this dramatically at the beginning of 1968. The commander of North Vietnam's forces, General Vo Nguyen Giap, proposed to Hanoi's political leadership a series of simultaneous assaults on South Vietnamese and American positions throughout the length of South Vietnam. The purpose of the offensive was chiefly political: to demonstrate to the Americans that they were farther from victory than ever and to demonstrate to the South Vietnamese that the Americans were unable to protect them. Both Americans and South Vietnamese would be demoralized by the demonstration. With luck, the Americans would decide to quit the war, while large numbers of the South Vietnamese would join the insurrection against the Saigon government.

The North Vietnamese leadership approved Giap's proposal, and the offensive began at the end of January 1968, at the time of the Tet lunar new year. The Tet offensive was the biggest operation the communists had attempted during the war. North Vietnamese and Vietcong units assaulted the six largest cities, thirty-six of forty-four provincial capitals, and scores of smaller towns and villages. For hours in some cases and for days in others, the communists held the initiative. One commando unit even managed to penetrate the American embassy compound in the heart of Saigon.

Eventually the South Vietnamese and Americans regained control of the situation and in fact inflicted heavy losses on the communists; but Hanoi had made its point. The war was nowhere near over. There was no light at the end of the tunnel, at least not for the Americans. So profound was the political shock value of the Tet offensive that Johnson felt obliged to change course dramatically. Increasingly since the 1965 American escalation, critics of Johnson's Vietnam policy had protested American activities in Vietnam, contending, depending on the critics, that American actions in Vietnam ranged from foolish to criminal. Contributing to the complaints was graphic television coverage of the fighting. For the first time in history, voters could witness war in a far-off land as it happened. Wars are never pleasant affairs to watch, and every evening on the news Americans had to confront the particular unpleasantness of this one. As victory continued to elude the American side, many asked whether it was all worthwhile. Yet until the Tet offensive, Johnson could ignore much of the criticism as coming from beyond the mainstream of American political life—from student radicals, out-of-touch intellectuals, and others with no firm grasp on how the real world worked.

The Tet offensive altered the situation significantly. The military balance in Vietnam remained much as before, but the political balance in the United States was reversed. Now the criticism of Johnson's policy came from across the spectrum of American politics. Influential public figures from all areas of national life decided that the bloodshed had to end. Johnson could no longer claim the support of even the so-called Wise Men, a panel of former high officials, including Dean Acheson, to whom the president turned for counsel on major policy decisions. Until Tet, Acheson and a majority of his colleagues on the panel had urged Johnson to stay the course in Vietnam; after Tet they told him to cut America's losses and seek a negotiated settlement. Johnson's near loss in the New Hampshire Democratic primary in March 1968 to peace advocate Eugene McCarthy reinforced the advice of the senior sages.

Bowing to the demands for change, Johnson at the end of March announced suspension of most bombing of North Vietnam as preparation for cease-fire talks. In addition, he said he would not seek reelection but would retire from public service at the end of his current term, ten months hence.

*   *   *

The Tet offensive did not end the war in Vietnam. Far from it: five years remained before the Paris peace accords of 1973 terminated direct American involvement in the fighting in Vietnam, and more than seven years elapsed before the North Vietnamese conquered Saigon and completed the reunification of the country.

The significance of Tet was principally symbolic, and the symbolism went beyond convincing Americans that Vietnam was a losing proposition. In certain important respects, Tet and the events surrounding it signaled the close of a phase of world history that had begun in 1945. At the end of the Second World War, the United States was so much stronger than all other countries militarily and economically that Americans could entertain the idea of policing almost the whole globe against communist expansion. The Truman Doctrine of 1947 announced America's intention to do this. The North Atlantic Treaty of 1949 and the various treaties of the 1950s filled in details of the commitment. The Marshall Plan of 1948–1952 and other foreign aid programs funded the economic development of American allies and friends, as well as of a few nonaligned countries that were neither allies nor friends but that Washington did not want to see grow too dependent on Soviet help.

The expansion of American commitments followed from the primary premise that communism was out to conquer the world and from the secondary assumption that America's rivalry with the Soviet Union was a zero-sum contest in which a gain for one side was necessarily a loss for the other. By the evidence of the Kremlin's actions, the Soviets viewed the superpower competition in much the same way. As a result, neither side willingly conceded territory to the other. The confrontation that had begun in Europe expanded to much of the rest of the globe, and America's self-imposed obligations expanded with it.

American resources also expanded during this period, but not as fast as American commitments. A gap developed between commitments and resources. For a time Washington was able to finesse the discrepancy, yet by the end of the 1960s the finesse was running out. The Tet offensive, coming after the various troubles with the Atlantic allies, in the Middle East and South Asia, and in the Caribbean, strongly suggested that the United States lacked the resources to cover all its commitments, at least at the level of effort Americans were willing to expend. Johnson could have taken the Tet affair as evidence of a need to redouble American efforts in Vietnam; some of his advisers suggested precisely such a course. But more and more Americans were demonstrating that they had had enough of Vietnam and wanted out.

This did not mean American power had vanished. The United States still remained by far the most powerful country in the world. Had American leaders brought the full weight of American power to bear against North Vietnam, they could have crushed that country just as the United States had crushed Japan in the Second World War. Yet to American leaders and most Americans, Vietnam was not worth the effort. More important, it was not worth the danger of confrontation with China or the Soviet Union that an invasion of North Vietnam, for example, would have entailed. In the age of nuclear weapons, there were severe constraints on the actions even of superpowers.

What the apparent failure of American policy in Vietnam *did* mean was that Americans would have to reconsider the task they had set for themselves in the late 1940s. Policing the planet was an awfully big job. Maybe it could not be done.

In reconsidering, Americans could draw some comfort from the fact that the Soviet side was also encountering problems during this period. If American commitments were coming due faster than Americans could redeem them, and if the American alliance system was showing strains, the Soviet system had been cleavered in two by the defection of China. South Vietnam might be a disappointment and France a trial, but at least the United States was not having to worry, as the Soviet Union was, about a possible war against its recent most important ally.

Taken together, the troubles of the superpowers indicated that the postwar order was in serious trouble. Some major changes in international alignments were due and soon.

Sources and Suggestions for Further Reading

The breakup between the Soviet Union and China is well delineated in Alfred D. Low, *The Sino-Soviet Dispute* (1978). Other facets of the changing alignment in world affairs are examined in W. W. Rostow, *The Diffusion of Power* (1972); F. Roy Willis, *France, Germany and the New Europe, 1945–1967* (1968); Karl Kaiser, *German Foreign Policy in Transition* (1968); Hans W. Gatzke, *Germany and the United States* (1980); Frank Costigliola, *France and the United States* (1992); and Robert M. Hathaway, *Great Britain and the United States* (1990).

Johnson's foreign policy has produced relatively few book-length studies. H. W. Brands, *Hegemony's End: Lyndon Johnson and American Foreign Policy* (1994), is the place to begin. Another broad-gauged view is Vaughn D. Bornet, *The Presidency of Lyndon B. Johnson* (1983). Thomas Schoenbaum, *Waging Peace and War* (1988), is about Dean Rusk. Rusk tells his own story in *As I Saw It* (1990). Warren I. Cohen, *Dean Rusk* (1980), gives an earlier and less complete picture. Abraham Lowenthal, *The Dominican Intervention* (1972); and Piero Gleijeses, *The Dominican Crisis* (1978), cover the Dominican affair. Jerome Levinson and Juan de Onis, *The Alliance That Lost Its Way* (1970), chart the checkered course of the Alliance for Progress. On the affairs of the Middle East, Nadav Safran, *From War to War* (1969), leads up to the June War of 1967. Donald Neff, *Warriors for Jerusalem* (1984), covers the conflict in detail.

There is no end to the literature on Vietnam. Start with Stanley Karnow, *Vietnam* (1983); then proceed to Gary Hess, *Vietnam and the United States* (1990); James P. Harrison, *The Endless War* (1989 ed.); George C. Herring, Jr., *America's Longest War* (1986 ed.); George McT. Kahin, *Intervention* (1986) and Marilyn B. Young, *The Vietnam Wars, 1945–1990* (1991). Melvin Small, *Johnson, Nixon and the Doves* (1988), examines the antiwar movement.

The student should be aware of changing interpretations over time of the American involvement in Vietnam. Early works tended to be critical, written as the war was going sour. A good example is David Halberstam, *The Making of a Quagmire* (1965), by a *New York Times* reporter. Halberstam's *The Best and Brightest* (1972) extends the argument. Other early critical studies include Joseph C. Goulden, *Truth is the First Casualty* (1969), on the Tonkin Gulf affair; and Chester L. Cooper, *The Lost Crusade* (1970). Although there were some early defenders of the war, the pendulum in the literature on the subject did not really swing in their direction until after the dust of defeat had settled. Two good examples of Vietnam revisionism are the scholarly Guenter Lewy, *America in Vietnam* (1978), and the polemical Norman Podhoretz, *Why We Were in Vietnam* (1982).

Chapter 14

The New World Disorder, 1969–1979

he changes in international alignments commenced with the beginning of the 1970s. As with most big changes in human affairs, these did not come easily or all at once, and the demolishing of the old order continued even while construction was under way on its replacement. In fact, during much of the 1970s, the demolition was considerably more obvious than the construction. The Bretton Woods system of international finance crashed to the ground early in the decade, a casualty of the decline of the American economy relative to the economies of America's trading partners. Then, while the industrialized countries were trying to adjust to the downfall of Bretton Woods, a third Arab-Israeli war touched off a succession of staggering increases in the price of petroleum, transferring enormous quantities of wealth from the oil-consuming countries to the oil-producing countries, mostly of the Middle East. Small, previously obscure nations now wielded power they could only have dreamed of a few years before. The shift of wealth and power to the oil producers of the Middle East delighted the leaders of those countries, but some of the consequences of the shift antagonized groups that considered themselves keepers of traditional values. Militant Islamic fundamentalists attacked the ruling regimes in several Middle Eastern states, most successfully in Iran, where the Islamic militants toppled the Pahlavi dynasty. The tremors triggered by the Iranian revolution soon spread throughout the region. Among the countries rocked was Afghanistan, where a bitter revolution-cum-civil-war rent the status quo to the point where the neighboring Soviet Union felt compelled to intervene. Essentially unrelated to the oil shocks of the 1970s but similarly indicative of the collapse of the old order was a revolution that broke out in Nicaragua and swept long-time American protégé Somoza from power.

Amid all this evidence of demolition, the most obvious sign of the new construction was the emergence of détente: a more cooperative relationship between America and the Soviet Union. For both superpowers, détente signaled a recognition that they had much to worry about besides each other. For the Soviet Union, China continued to be the biggest worry, especially after the Americans reversed their twenty-year-old policy of trying to ostracize the Chinese. For the United States, Vietnam remained the chief source of concern.

317

Chronology

1968   American spy ship *Pueblo* seized by North Koreans; Tet offensive in Vietnam; Johnson suspends most bombing; peace talks begin; nuclear nonproliferation treaty signed; Warsaw Pact troops smash reform in Czechoslovakia; Nixon elected on promise to end Vietnam War

1969   "Vietnamization" commences; secret American bombing of Cambodia; Americans walk on the moon; border fighting between China and Soviet Union

1970   American troops invade Cambodia; major demonstrations in United States; civil war in Jordan

1971   Nixon's opening to China announced; Bangladesh secedes from Pakistan despite U.S. opposition; Bretton Woods financial system totters

1972   Nixon visits China; Nixon and Brezhnev codify detente at Moscow, sign SALT I accords; Watergate break-in; Christmas bombing of Vietnam

1973   Paris accords end American fighting in Vietnam; October (Yom Kippur) War in Middle East; first oil shock; Arab OPEC embargo

1974   Turkey partitions Cyprus; Nixon resigns

1975   Saigon falls, completing reunification of Vietnam; congressional investigations unearth dirty tricks of CIA; civil war in Angola; civil war in Lebanon

1976   Congress bars aid to Angolan rebels; Carter elected

1978   Camp David accord between Egypt and Israel, leads to 1979 peace treaty

1979   Nicaraguan revolution; Iranian revolution; American hostages seized in Teheran; Soviet invasion of Afghanistan

It was Vietnam that provoked the Nixon administration to reverse America's policy regarding China and laid the basis for the American side of détente.

Détente promised to produce a transformation in dealings between the Americans and the Soviets. Some observers predicted that this transformation would yield a more peaceful and stable world. They missed the point. Détente was, in a fundamental sense, an admission by the superpowers of the degree to which world events had spun out of their control. The bipolar order that had evolved from the Second World War was being supplanted by something else; but that something else was far from stable, and it did not promise to be very peaceful.

Bretton Woods Goes Bust

The two decades after 1945 witnessed some of the most remarkable economic growth in modern world history. America led the way toward greater prosperity, but after injections of American aid and investment, the Western European countries and Japan hopped aboard the economic elevator and rode to levels of production and consumption they had never achieved before. In no small part this growth was what caused the loosening of the bonds of the American alliance system: as countries such as West Germany, France, and Japan became increasingly independent of America economically, they also tended to become independent politically.

Much of the growth of the Western economies—customarily defined as including Japan—owed to the stability and strength of the system of international finance established at Bretton Woods in 1944. By pegging other currencies to the American dollar and pegging the dollar to gold at thirty-five dollars per ounce, the Bretton Woods system effectively dealt with the dual difficulty of maintaining both confidence and flexibility in the international currency system. Maintaining confidence requires assuring creditors that the currency will not be debased by the issuance of lots of new money. The link to gold guaranteed this. Maintaining flexibility requires that the money supply be able to grow along with a growing world economy. That the American economy was so large relative to the economies of the other countries allowed America's central bankers, in effect, to manage the world money supply by managing the dollar. They could increase the money supply to accommodate economic growth, thereby helping avert the kind of panics and depressions that had repeatedly plagued the world economy during the nineteenth century and the first half of the twentieth.

But there is a built-in tension in any international financial system. Since the financial revolution of the eighteenth and nineteenth centuries, when governments began printing paper money, governments had been tempted to spend themselves out of debt by the expedient of issuing more money. The temptation was greatest when the debt was owed to foreigners since inflation robs one group of people (creditors, who get paid back in depreciated money) to the unearned advantage of others (debtors), and if the creditors are foreigners, their complaints usually carry less weight than those of people within the country. In countries such as Britain and the United States, control of government, and therefore of the currency, long remained largely in the hands of the creditor class. For this reason, and because the government of neither country owed a lot of money to foreigners, there was little incentive for government to expand the currency much. But as the politics of America and Britain, along with many other countries, grew more democratic, with debtors gaining increasing influence, the temptation toward depreciation became harder to resist.

The Keynesian revolution of the mid-twentieth century additionally weakened governments' resistance to currency expansion. As governments learned how to stimulate economic growth by deficit spending, with the Second World War being the most striking example, there developed great political pressure for them to do so whenever recession threatened. There were two ways for governments to finance their deficits. The hard way was to borrow money. The big drawback of borrowing was that the money had to be repaid and with interest. The easy way was to print more money. Governments generally still borrowed money, but because the loans were repaid with devalued money, the governments came out ahead.

The upshot of all this was that in the postwar period governments often had economic and political reasons to depreciate their currencies. In countries such as Germany, where the memories of the hyperinflation of the early 1920s remained sharp and painful, other influences prevailed. But in countries such as the United States, where the unemployment and despair of the great depression of the 1930s dominated economic memories, the tendency toward depreciation was strong. Price inflation, the most obvious manifestation of currency depreciation, was the frequent result.

Yet inflation in any one country has disruptive effects on the international monetary system as a whole, as international traders and investors compensate for the inflation. If the inflationary country is small, the disruption is small. But if the inflationary country is large, the disruption is large. And if the inflationary country is very large—for instance, the dominant economic power in the international system—the disruption can be so great as to wreck the system. This was what happened during the early 1970s to the Bretton Woods system.

The crisis had its roots in the 1960s when the Johnson administration attempted to pay for both the Great Society and the war in Vietnam without significantly raising taxes. The American economy was probably strong enough to fund either the domestic reforms or the war without unusual strain, but it could not handle both without generating unprecedented inflationary pressure. High government spending on medical care, urban renewal, bombers, and helicopters drove up prices as the government competed with private purchasers for goods and services. A tax increase would have bled off some of the pressure by reducing private purchasing power. But there was no considerable constituency for a tax increase (there almost never is). And so until Johnson's last year in office, when a modest surcharge corrected matters somewhat, the American government chose to borrow. Inflation, made possible by a government policy of monetary expansion, would soften the pain of repayment.

Two decades earlier America's Bretton Woods partners had had no recourse but to go along with American actions since these countries needed America's economic help and military protection; but by the early 1970s things had changed. The military threat from the Soviet Union did not occasion as much worry as before, and the Western Europeans and Japanese were far more self-reliant economically. Previously the Europeans and Japanese had needed all the American dollars they could get their hands on to purchase the American exports they required. As their economies grew stronger, however, and their own exports to the United States increased, they began earning more dollars than they knew what to do with. They started converting dollars to gold, that age-old hedge against inflation. Their demand for gold created pressure on

America's gold supply. Similar pressure had triggered the gold crisis and financial panic of 1893, which not coincidentally was the last year before 1971 that the United States had run a trade deficit.

The pressure on gold caused the Nixon administration to take drastic measures. In August 1971 Richard Nixon announced that the American Treasury would no longer fund the conversion of dollars to gold. This action knocked one prop—gold—out from under the Bretton Woods system. Heretofore, the dollar had been as good as gold; now it was only as good as the word of the American government and the strength of the American economy. Neither of these impressed America's trading partners as an adequate substitute for gold, and they grew increasingly reluctant to peg their currencies to the dollar. Nor were they impressed by the Nixon administration's imposition of a 10 percent surcharge on imports, which was designed to alleviate America's trade deficit.

The reluctance of the allies to peg their currencies to the dollar soon knocked the second prop—fixed exchange rates—out from under the Bretton Woods system. West Germany, in particular, refused to tie itself to an increasingly unreliable American dollar, and it led a revolt against fixed rates. Because the American government was no longer able to impose its will on its partners, Washington had no choice but to accept the new reality: in 1973 Washington acquiesced in an abandonment of the fixed schedule in favor of floating rates. Henceforth the dollar would be a commodity like other commodities. If people wanted dollars, the price in other currencies of dollars would rise. If people did not want dollars, the price of dollars would fall. The same applied to the other currencies: West German marks, Japanese yen, British pounds, French francs.

The collapse of the Bretton Woods system indicated how much the world economy had changed since 1945. At that time the United States had been industrially as strong as the rest of the world combined. American leaders established the rules America's trading partners played by. In the subsequent twenty-five years, the American economy grew significantly but not as fast as those of such rebounders as West Germany and Japan. By the early 1970s, the American economy had declined relatively to a position where the United States was merely the first among comparative equals. When the world abandoned the dollar standard for floating exchange rates, Americans found themselves playing by the same rules as everyone else. It did not help matters, from the American standpoint, that the other countries had been playing by these rules for years and had more practice.

The End of the Line in Vietnam

The governments of the European allies and Japan might have been more willing to follow America's lead economically had they placed more confidence in the judgment of American officials. But various American actions, particularly in Vietnam, sapped alliance confidence.

Richard Nixon entered the presidency in 1969 pledged to end the war in Vietnam. Following the Tet offensive of early 1968, Americans increasingly had demanded a change in strategy, and Nixon was prepared to give them such a change. Shortly after moving in to the White House, he announced a policy that went by the label "Vietnamization." Under this policy the United States would gradually withdraw its ground forces from Vietnam while strengthening the army of South Vietnam. Nixon recognized that Americans objected less to the war itself than to the toll the war was taking on Americans. If American soldiers no longer came home in body bags, Nixon calculated, and if American young men no longer had to fret about getting drafted, their opposition to the war would fade. Meanwhile by pumping money and military equipment into South Vietnam and by providing air support to South Vietnamese ground units, the United States would frustrate North Vietnam's efforts to conquer the South.

Nixon was shrewd enough to recognize that Vietnamization might appear to some observers as a mere fig leaf to cover an American abandonment of South Vietnam. To dispel this notion, he sought to demonstrate indisputably America's continued commitment to South Vietnam. Even as he narrowed American involvement in the fighting in South Vietnam, he widened the war geographically. He ordered American planes to bomb North Vietnamese refuges and supply routes across the border in neutral Cambodia. At first Nixon and other administration officials denied that the Cambodian bombing campaign was taking place, and the American air force was ordered to conceal evidence. But the story leaked out, undermining Nixon's already shaky reputation for integrity. To make matters worse, the bombing failed to achieve the objective of getting the North Vietnamese out of Cambodia. In 1970 Nixon felt compelled to order American ground forces into Cambodia to do the job.

The protests in the United States against the war in Vietnam had died down somewhat following Johnson's decision to seek peace, but the invasion of Cambodia provoked the largest demonstrations of the entire war. Marches took place and riots broke out all across the country. On two college campuses—Kent State University in Ohio and Jackson State in Mississippi—clashes between demonstrators and National Guard troops resulted in the deaths of a total of six young people.

The uproar in the United States indicated to Nixon that maintaining the American commitment to South Vietnam would be more difficult than he had anticipated. But Nixon was not one to back away from a challenge. In February 1971 he ordered American air support for a South Vietnamese invasion of Laos, despite expected protests. The protests materialized, though without the violence of the previous year's demonstrations. During 1971 and 1972, the president ordered the heaviest bombing raids of the war. Meanwhile, angered by the antiwar protests, officials connected to the Nixon White House started down the road of political espionage and dirty tricks against administration critics that ultimately entangled the president in the Watergate scandal and forced his resignation.

The North Vietnamese could read the signs of declining popular American support for the war effort almost as well as the Nixon administration could. Following the Tet offensive, Hanoi agreed to the commencement of peace negotiations with the United States. The talks began in Paris in May 1968 but produced little movement toward a solution. The North Vietnamese were satisfied with merely presenting the appearance of seeking peace; while events on the battlefield were moving their way, they saw no reason to give up at the bargaining table what they might soon win on the ground. They watched the Americans withdraw their troops—from 550,000 in 1969, to 400,000 in 1970, to 300,000 in 1971, to 100,000 in 1972, to a mere handful after January 1973.

Hanoi sporadically mounted large operations designed to show the South Vietnamese they would stand no chance once their American protectors had gone. In the spring of 1972, the North Vietnamese launched an "Easter offensive"—needless to say, the officially atheist but primarily Buddhist North Vietnamese did not call it that—against South Vietnam. The attack proved to be a bitter disappointment for North Vietnam. South Vietnamese ground forces assisted by American air power inflicted heavy losses on the attackers. Probably more than one hundred thousand on the communist side died in the fighting.

The failed Easter offensive strengthened the hand of those in the North Vietnamese government who argued that Hanoi ought to negotiate a settlement that would get the Americans out of Vietnam as soon as possible. Defeating Saigon and reunifying the country could be postponed until after the Americans had departed.

The Nixon administration likewise was looking for a settlement that would allow an American departure. Nixon had long believed that if Americans were still dying in Vietnam at the time of the 1972 election, he would have great difficulty getting reelected. The election was fast approaching. Nixon ordered Henry Kissinger, the administration's national security adviser and chief negotiator, to speed up the Paris talks. Several days before the election, Kissinger felt able to announce, "Peace is at hand."

In reality, it was not quite at hand, though Kissinger's prediction accomplished its short-term goal: helping Nixon win reelection, by a landslide. The South Vietnamese government, headed by Nguyen Van Thieu, did not like the terms of the deal Kissinger had struck with North Vietnamese representative Le Duc Tho. From Saigon, Thieu denounced the draft accord as a sellout of South Vietnam. Nixon and Kissinger tried to calm Thieu's fears by sending more military and economic aid, launching the so-called Christmas bombing campaign (the most intense series of air raids in the history of warfare), and pledging swift and decisive American action against North Vietnam in the event of violations of the accords.

Thieu still opposed the deal, which did not change materially by January 1973 when Kissinger and Le Duc Tho officially signed the pact. The feature most objectionable to Thieu was a provision allowing the North Vietnamese troops to remain where they were in South Vietnam, while the last American combat troops withdrew from the country. Thieu recognized, as did most

Henry Kissinger and Le Duc Tho talk in Paris. They talked long and hard before reaching the 1973 agreement that ended U.S. involvement in the Vietnam War.
National Archives: Nixon Presidential Materials

objective observers, that the Paris accords of January 1973 were chiefly a device for allowing the United States to leave South Vietnam with a modicum of grace. Few people really expected that Hanoi would give up its decades-old quest for the unification of Vietnam under communist control.

The North Vietnamese chose to abide by the terms of the Paris accords until the last American combat troops left Vietnam in March 1973. For several months thereafter, the conflict remained on hold. Time appeared to be Hanoi's agent, especially as the Watergate scandal ensnared Nixon, rendering him increasingly unable to fulfill his promise to Thieu about decisive action in the event of a resumption of fighting. In the summer of 1973, Congress barred the president from further military operations in or over Indochina. In November the legislature approved the War Powers Act, which curtailed the ability of any president to commit American armed forces to combat without explicit congressional authorization.

Nixon's paralysis, followed by his August 1974 resignation, emboldened the North Vietnamese leadership. At the end of 1974, Hanoi prepared what it trusted would be the war's final offensive and launched it early the following year. The offensive succeeded better than the North Vietnamese could have expected: the suddenness of Saigon's collapse stunned even communists, who had expected to be fighting into 1976. Wearied by years of corruption and dependence on the United States, the South Vietnamese army melted away before the North Vietnamese advance. The North Vietnamese rolled from the

central highlands toward Saigon; in late April 1975 Thieu resigned and fled
the country. The communists took the capital, which they renamed Ho Chi
Minh City, in late April, completing the reunification of Vietnam and ending
the fighting.

The fall of Saigon was accompanied by a mad scramble of Vietnamese who
had been closely connected to the Americans to get out of the city and the
country. Some succeeded at that time; tens of thousands more followed during
the next decade. A large portion of these wound up in the United States under
terms of special immigration laws recognizing the American role in creating
their plight. Their presence served as a continuing reminder of the tragic failure
of American policy in Vietnam. All told, nearly sixty thousand Americans died
in Vietnam in a vain effort to prevent Vietnamese reunification under communist control. The cost to Vietnam was far larger: as many as 2 million died
in the long struggle. Millions were rendered homeless, and cities, towns, and
villages across the length of the country were ravaged.

The Vietnam experience seared the American consciousness as nothing had
since the great depression of the 1930s. For a generation American leaders and
the American people would be exceedingly wary of military involvement in

Saigon was never as popular a destination as during the spring of 1975. These South
Vietnamese are fleeing before the advancing North Vietnamese army, hoping to find
shelter in the capital. They will be disappointed. *AP/Wide World Photos*

foreign quarrels. The Vietnam experience also caused many Americans to question the Cold War premises on which the American involvement in Vietnam had been based, and it prepared them for a new approach to superpower relations.

The Triumph of Geopolitics: Détente

If Americans found the outcome of the Vietnam War troubling, several of America's allies considered it something of a relief. It was the fighting of the war that had worried them. Not the fact that the Americans were losing: France had lost in Vietnam before the Americans; Germany and Japan had lost the Second World War. The worrisome aspect of the Vietnam War was that it betrayed a lack of American judgment. American leaders had long stressed the importance of credibility in maintaining the coherence of the American alliance system: if America's allies could not rely on the United States to meet its commitments, this reasoning went, they would begin to look elsewhere for security. There was something to this argument. Credibility certainly counted. But credibility was not everything. Judgment mattered as well, in particular the ability to judge when a cause was lost. America's European allies feared that the United States was becoming so obsessed by Vietnam that Washington would forget where the real interests of the Western alliance lay. Even if the Americans won in Vietnam, the alliance might lose if Vietnam stole resources and attention that should have been devoted to strengthening Atlantic security. The Japanese, closer to the action in Vietnam, were more tolerant of America's Southeast Asian obsession, but the Japanese similarly had to wonder whether the high cost of the war in Vietnam might turn the American public away from larger matters of Pacific defense.

Tempering allied worries, however, was the new policy of the Nixon administration toward the communist powers. For all Richard Nixon's flaws, he was the most profound thinker on geopolitics to occupy the White House in the half century after the Second World War. Henry Kissinger, an academic–turned–policy maker who cut his intellectual teeth studying the diplomacy of Metternich at the Congress of Vienna, was a suitable match for Nixon. Between them, the president and the national security adviser (later secretary of state) came to the conclusion that the bipolar premises of the postwar order no longer fit the circumstances of the world. The pledge of the Truman Doctrine—that the United States would guarantee the safety of anticommunist governments almost anywhere on earth—was now beyond America's reach. Power was diffusing rapidly: to the former colonial world, to the reviving vanquished countries of the Second World War, to allies that formerly had been almost dependents. Where America had previously secured its interests by sheer strength, now achieving such security would require cleverness.

Part of the cleverness consisted in farming out responsibilities to allies and proxies. This was the essence of Vietnamization, which placed the burden of

South Vietnamese security on the Vietnamese. America would provide the guns, but the Vietnamese would have to fill the foxholes. Nixon subsequently extended the principle behind Vietnamization, to the point that it acquired the status of a doctrine. Under the Nixon Doctrine, the United States would supply economic, military, and logistical assistance to friendly powers, but they would have to take the lead in defending themselves and their neighborhoods against communist encroachment. Besides Vietnam, the Nixon Doctrine was applied most visibly to the Persian Gulf. Washington nominated the shah of Iran to be the policeman of the gulf. The shah was allowed to purchase billions of dollars of American military equipment; thousands of American advisers trained his army and his police; hundreds of millions of American dollars helped develop his economy. In return he was expected to maintain a pro-American status quo in the region.

The Nixon Doctrine had some problems, as developments in Vietnam and later Iran showed; but Nixon and Kissinger had more tricks up their sleeves. Their most important contribution to the practice of American international relations was their willingness to admit and try to exploit the rift between the Soviet Union and China. Ever since 1947, when Truman had spoken of a global struggle between two "ways of life," American leaders had been compelled by the logic of their good-versus-evil arguments to treat Soviet communism and Chinese communism as being basically equivalent. During most of the 1950s, this identification of Beijing with Moscow had not grossly violated reality, but as the Chinese and Soviets fell out with each other, it prevented American leaders from doing what leaders of other countries in analogous circumstances had been doing for millennia: playing one rival off against the other. Had Kennedy or Johnson been able to emphasize the differences between Chinese and Soviet interests in Asia, for example, they might never have committed the United States to such an impassioned defense of South Vietnam. They could have seen that a communist Vietnam might, with Soviet help, become a thorn in Beijing's side—as in fact it did.

Geopolitically, playing the big communist powers against each other made sense, but in terms of domestic politics it was too risky for either Kennedy or Johnson to attempt. As Democrats they rightly feared the ghost of McCarthy, which surely would brand them as appeasers for anything approaching warmer relations with Red China. Conceivably, they might have succeeded in changing American policy toward China, yet they probably would have expended so much political capital in the effort that they would have bankrupted their administrations for anything else.

For this reason injecting a dose of geopolitical reality into American policy toward China was left to Richard Nixon. Like one who has had rabies before and survived—and Nixon indeed had been one of the most rabid of the anti-communists of the early postwar period—Nixon was immune to the kinds of charges that would have been politically fatal to Kennedy or Johnson. In their hearts most Americans who thought about such things understood that it did little good, twenty years after the end of the Chinese civil war, to pretend that the regime that ruled Taiwan was the true government of China. Most

Americans were prepared to accept a change of American policy on the China question. But it required a person like Nixon, whose anticommunist credentials could not be questioned, to take the fateful step.

Nixon did so in an initiative shrouded in the darkest secrecy. During a July 1971 visit by Kissinger to Pakistan, the national security adviser pleaded the sort of stomach upset that often afflicts travelers. While ostensibly recuperating in his room, Kissinger slipped aboard a Pakistan Air Lines plane and flew across the Himalayas to Beijing. There he arranged a meeting between Nixon and Mao Zedong for the purpose of seeking a normalization of relations between the two countries.

Although Nixon earlier had hinted at the prudence of an American opening to China, the announcement of the upcoming meeting stunned the world. The Soviet Union warned of "secret collusion" between the Americans and Chinese. A Kremlin spokesman declared, "This is a matter of grave consequence for the Soviet people, for world socialism, for the entire international situation, for world peace." The Japanese reeled from what they called the "Nixon shokku." Well they might have: America's rapprochement with China, of which Tokyo had received no advance warning, promised to have the most profound effects on the balance of power in Asia. The North Vietnamese were likewise worried. In 1954 the Soviets and Chinese had strong-armed Ho Chi Minh and his comrades into accepting less at the Geneva conference than they might have claimed on the basis of their battlefield victories. "We were betrayed," remembered Pham Van Dong, the chief Vietminh negotiator at Geneva. Now they feared another such power play by the big countries just as their goal of Vietnamese unification was in sight. With more hope than conviction, Hanoi declared that it was "inconceivable" that the United States and China would negotiate an end to the Vietnam War over the heads of the Vietnamese.

Nixon did not think it was inconceivable at all. In fact, a major objective of his opening to China was precisely to persuade Hanoi's communist sponsors to rein in the North Vietnamese. Nixon could hardly ask Beijing to force Hanoi simply to drop its goal of Vietnamese unification; the Chinese no less than the Americans had matters of credibility and prestige to consider. Besides, the North Vietnamese would have rejected any such demand. But Nixon *could* ask the Chinese to cut back on aid to Hanoi, perhaps as part of an overall reduction of tension in Southeast Asia. The United States was withdrawing its troops from Vietnam; China could show its good faith by some analogous action.

As things happened, Nixon's efforts with China regarding Vietnam had little observable effect. The North Vietnamese had approached too near victory for such modest pressure as Beijing brought to bear on Hanoi to turn them aside.

The other primary target of Nixon's opening to China, however, responded in a fashion more to Washington's liking. By warming to China, Nixon hoped to give the Soviet Union an incentive to warm toward the United States. The strategy worked. Lenin had once said that the road between the West and Moscow ran through Beijing; Nixon certainly found this to be true. Without his opening to China, the Soviet Union doubtless would have demonstrated considerably less interest in bettering relations with the United States. Not that a reduction in tensions between the nuclear superpowers did not make sense to the Soviets on its own terms: since the embarrassment of the Cuban missile crisis, Moscow had devoted a large portion of the Soviet Union's national resources to catching up with America in the arms race. Although the Americans retained a numerical edge in some categories of nuclear weapons, by the early 1970s the Soviets had achieved effective parity—meaning that the United States could not expect to survive a major nuclear exchange with the Soviet Union without incurring tens or hundreds of millions of deaths and comparable property damage. But the race had been costly and wearing, and the Soviet Union was ready for a rest. In addition, a relaxation would lessen the danger that someone might be tempted to use all those nuclear weapons.

Yet what put a particular edge on the Soviets' desire for détente was a fear that the Americans and the Chinese might be ganging up on them. The Kremlin had had enough worries about China and the United States when those two countries were enemies of each other; if Beijing and Washington began coordinating their actions, there was no telling the trouble they could cause. Consequently, preventing the formation of a Beijing-Washington axis became a principal objective of Soviet foreign policy. Not even an intensification of American bombing of Hanoi, or the mining of Haiphong harbor, deflected the Kremlin from this objective. Despite these provocations, Moscow refused to cancel a Soviet-American summit meeting scheduled for May 1972.

The atmosphere of the Moscow summit reflected the bland public personalities of the two summiteers, Nixon and Soviet general secretary Brezhnev; but, unusually for summits, the substance of this one mattered more than the atmospherics. Nixon and Brezhnev agreed to a set of twelve principles that should guide Soviet-American relations. Although several of the principles seemed added to round out the dozen, a few involved issues of real importance. The first called for what amounted to an ideological nonaggression pact. It said that differences in ideology and social systems should not be obstacles to the development of normal relations. The second principle came close to announcing a military nonaggression pact. It declared that the aforementioned normal relations required recognition of the security interests of the two countries, based on the principle of equality and the renunciation of the use or threat of force. The third principle extended the first and second by asserting a special responsibility on the part of the United States and the Soviet Union to avoid fanning regional conflicts into larger confrontations between the superpowers. Proxy wars, the export of revolution, and troublemaking by similar means were now out of bounds.

More specific and concrete than the declaration of principles were two arms control treaties Nixon and Brezhnev signed at the Moscow summit. The weightier of the twin Strategic Arms Limitation Talks treaties (SALT—with the label later revised to SALT I when SALT II came along) banned comprehensive antimissile defenses. Each side could build one antimissile installation near the

Leonid Brezhnev and Richard Nixon toast each other after signing the SALT I pact in Moscow in 1972. Detente made the two leaders happy, but many American conservatives thought Nixon was getting too chummy with the Soviets. *UPI/Bettman*

national capital and one near a missile field, but that was all. Because the erection of defensive systems would have spurred the deployment of additional offensive weapons to overwhelm the defenses, this antiballistic missile (ABM) treaty implicitly put a check on the arms race in offensive missiles as well. The second SALT I agreement made this check explicit, capping offensive missiles and other delivery systems, albeit at a relatively high level, for five years, pending completion of further talks.

From Moscow's side, Brezhnev's public acceptance of the American social system indicated a substantial retreat from Stalin's 1946 assertion that capitalism and communism could not coexist. To be sure, the Kremlin's ideologists still contended that communism would triumph over capitalism. But they obviously were in no hurry, and they recognized that the triumph might be a long time coming.

From Washington's perspective, an official acceptance of the legitimacy of the Soviet system signaled a similar setting aside of the premises that had undergirded American policy since the late 1940s. In the American case, it was the Truman Doctrine that had most clearly stated the conviction that the world was locked in a struggle between two mutually incompatible ways of life. The essence of détente was that the two ways of life really were *not* incompatible.

The era of détente was the most conspicuous of the geopolitical phases of the Cold War. As during earlier moments when ideology was subordinated to geopolitics, détente reflected a conviction on the part of both superpowers that the world was too dangerous to risk allowing ideological differences to get out of hand. The very survival of the two superpowers rested on their ability to coexist. The terms of the SALT I treaty represented an admission by the United States that the Soviet Union had achieved nuclear parity; whether another crisis like that surrounding the Cuban missiles in 1962 might be settled peacefully, now that the Soviets could threaten the United States as convincingly as the Americans could threaten the Soviet Union, was problematic. Neither side wished to find out.

There were other reasons for détente as well. The Soviet Union desired the opportunity to expand trade with the West, and American businesses wanted to sell more of their products to the Soviet Union. As part of détente, Washington loosened constraints on American exports to the Soviet Union. This loosening led to such transactions as the sale of American grain worth more than $1 billion to the Soviets. The Nixon administration allowed the American Export-Import Bank to extend credits to the Soviet Union for the purchase of American goods. It authorized the opening of additional American ports to Soviet ships. It pledged to seek congressional authorization of most-favored-nation status for the Soviet Union. In return Moscow agreed to pay $700 million in Lend-Lease debts from the Second World War to open Soviet ports previously off limits to American shipping, and to undertake measures designed to encourage development of Soviet markets for American products.

Détente also indicated a recognition by the United States of a trend that had been developing in Europe for several years. America's European allies had watched the expansion of Moscow's nuclear arsenal with considerable misgivings. At the time of the signing of the North Atlantic Treaty in 1949, the United States had possessed a monopoly on nuclear weapons, a monopoly that afforded the Europeans a feeling of security in the face of the conventional superiority of the Red Army. This feeling of security diminished during the 1950s, but as long as the United States remained significantly superior to the Soviet Union in nuclear weaponry, the American threat to respond to a conventional Soviet attack with nuclear arms remained credibly reassuring. The Soviets' achievement of nuclear parity during the 1960s changed the situation markedly. The Europeans could not help doubting that the American government would really court the destruction of the United States over a conflict that might otherwise be confined to Europe. Would an American president put New York and Washington on the line to save West Berlin or Paris? Europeans had to wonder. Such wondering had been behind Charles de Gaulle's insistence that France have its own nuclear deterrent; it likewise motivated de Gaulle's efforts to promote the idea of a single Europe "from the Atlantic to the Urals." To this end the French president had traveled to Moscow seeking closer ties between France and the Soviet Union, and it was with this in mind that he pulled France out of NATO.

The Germans similarly began moving toward a position more equidistant between Washington and Moscow. In September 1969 a new government assumed power in Bonn pledged to new policies. Among the foremost of the new policies of Willy Brandt's Socialists was *Ostpolitik*, a commitment to reducing tensions with the East. Until this time West Germany had resolutely refused to recognize the legitimacy of the East German government; even now it took a while for Bonn to bring itself to such an action. In 1970 Bonn signed a treaty with Moscow conceding the inviolability of the territorial status quo in central Europe. This came close to admitting the legitimacy of East Germany but did not quite. Only in 1972 did Bonn take the big step: it agreed to exchange representatives with East Germany and to base relations between West Germany and East Germany on mutual cooperation rather than hostility.

Brandt's *Ostpolitik* had multiple causes, just as détente did for both the United States and the Soviet Union. At the level of personal relations, Bonn's opening to the East was designed to facilitate the reunification of families divided by the superpower rivalry. Normalized dealings between West Germany and East Germany made it possible for people to travel back and forth across the frontier between Germany's two parts far more freely than before. At the

Thirty years earlier, when Soviet and German leaders had gotten together, a world war had shortly followed. Nothing like that seemed imminent when Soviet premier Alexei Kosygin greeted West German chancellor Willy Brandt, but Brandt's *Ostpolitik* did occasion a few flutters of concern in certain Western capitals, including Washington. *AP/Wide World Photos*

level of business and economics, West German businesses wanted to tap into the markets they saw on the other side of the Elbe: in East Germany, in Poland and the other Soviet client states, and in the Soviet Union. Brandt, a Socialist, was no tool of German capitalism, but even so he appreciated the economic and political benefits that would accrue to West Germany and to his government from expanded export opportunities. At the diplomatic and strategic level, *Ostpolitik* reflected Germany's decreasing willingness to defer to Washington's wishes. The Nixon administration did not like *Ostpolitik*, fearing that it might foreshadow German neutralism and perhaps a resurgence of German nationalism. Where earlier such American dislike might have cut short any such loosening of Atlantic alliance ties, by the early 1970s Bonn was self-confidently determined to pursue its own interests. Washington would have to do more than grumble to stop the Germans from acting as they saw fit. Yet in the meantime, the German desire for better relations with the East encouraged the Nixon administration in the direction of détente.

The European involvement in détente was additional indication of what the new arrangement between the United States and the Soviet Union was all about. Détente amounted to an admission by the superpowers that the bipolar model of international affairs, in which two superpowers dominated the landscape of world politics and guided the destinies of lesser states, was outmoded. In fact, the model had been outmoded for some time. But accepting unpleasant reality is never easy.

Some people found it particularly hard, despite détente's obvious benefits. First among the benefits was the chance it afforded the world's people to sleep a little easier at night: by all evidence détente diminished the danger of nuclear war. A second benefit accrued to a narrower group: the owners and employees of American businesses, including farms, that would gain new markets from the enhanced opportunities for trade with the Soviet Union. On the Soviet side, consumers would eat better through increased access to American farm products, and the Soviet economy as a whole would grow faster as a result of the availability of American machine tools and other industrial equipment. Leonid Brezhnev personally liked being treated as an equal by the president of the United States. In this regard the Kremlin's propaganda machine did not let it be overlooked that Nixon had come to Moscow to initiate the official phase of détente; Brezhnev had not gone to Washington.

Americans who regretted the passing of the old order missed the overwhelming power the United States had wielded during the late 1940s and 1950s; many also missed the moral and political certitude that had infused American thinking about the world. In those days communists had clearly been enemies: moral enemies of personal freedom, political enemies of democratic practices, military enemies of American security. Now Americans had to get accustomed to seeing their president take tea with Mao in Beijing and drink vodka with Brezhnev in Moscow. The 1960s had been a decade of turmoil in American domestic affairs: of race riots, antiwar protests, and the emergence of a counterculture that delighted in thumbing its nose at values most Americans cherished. Détente, with its overturning of old verities about the world beyond

American shores, extended the emotional and conceptual turmoil to global affairs.

The Arabs Strike Back: The October War of 1973

Whatever the confusion of the changes associated with détente, in some other areas of international affairs things remained much as before. In the Middle East, the Arab-Israeli dispute was as bitter as ever. During the autumn of 1973, the Arabs and Israelis went to war once again. To tell the truth, the fighting had never really stopped in the vicinity of Israel after the previous round of conflict in June 1967: the Israeli forces occupying the West Bank and the Gaza Strip continually had to deal with unrest there, and a civil war broke out in Jordan where armies of radical Palestinian guerrillas backed by Syria challenged the moderate regime of King Hussein. In the latter conflict, the royalist loyalists won, throwing the guerrillas out of Jordan and into Lebanon, to that country's sorrow. Meanwhile Egypt refused to accept the situation that had emerged out of the 1967 war. In 1969 Egyptian president Nasser denounced the 1967 cease-fire and declared what he called a "war of attrition" against Israel's presence along the Suez Canal and in the Sinai. Egyptian attacks on Israeli-held positions provoked Israel to respond with air strikes against military and civilian targets along the canal and far into the rest of Egypt.

But before much came of the renewed fighting, Nasser died. He was succeeded by Anwar el-Sadat, a co-conspirator in the 1952 revolt that had brought Nasser's group to power but lately something of an outsider. Nasser's intimates could not agree among themselves as to who should follow the great man of Arab nationalism, so they chose Sadat as an interim place filler. Sadat proved wilier than they, however, and when they tried to elbow him aside, he clapped them in jail.

Although Sadat was less the firebrand than Nasser, no Egyptian leader who aspired to stay in power long, and certainly no successor to Nasser, could forget the struggle against Israel. Three years after the 1967 war, the Israelis still occupied thousands of square miles of Egyptian territory in the Sinai. Sadat initially tried to secure the return of the Sinai by diplomatic means. He sought improved relations with Washington out of the well-founded belief that if anyone could pressure Israelis to withdraw, the Americans could. Toward the goal of improved Egyptian-American relations, and also because the Soviets made boorish guests, he evicted some fifteen thousand Soviet military advisers in July 1972.

Yet after their smashing 1967 victory, the Israelis did not feel like pulling back from the occupied territories without guarantees more ironclad than Sadat was willing to give. And with the 1972 American election campaign in full swing, Nixon did not have much desire to lean on the Israelis at the risk of upsetting pro-Israel American voters.

Sadat then decided to argue his case on the ground. During the summer of 1973, Egyptian strategists met with their counterparts from Syria, whose government wanted to regain the Golan Heights. Following an elaborate disinformation campaign that disguised war mobilization as military maneuvers, Egyptian artillery and armor attacked Israeli positions along the Suez Canal, while Syrian tanks and infantry stormed the Golan Heights.

The October War (also called the Yom Kippur War because it commenced on the Jewish holy day) caught Israelis relatively unprepared. It was obvious to them, as to much of the rest of the world, that the balance of military forces between Israel and the Arabs tilted strongly in Israel's favor. The Egyptians and Syrians surely knew that if they started a war, they would lose.

In fact, the Egyptians and Syrians *did* know this, but what the Israelis failed to appreciate was the depth of the Arab desire for revenge. The 1967 war had been an utter humiliation for the Arabs. Egypt and Syria insisted on striking a blow against Israel to reclaim their honor, even if in doing so they had little chance of recapturing their lost land.

The blow the Egyptians and Syrians struck wounded Israel badly. In the Golan Heights, Syrian armor smashed Israeli defenses; Syrian paratroops captured key Israeli positions on Mount Hermon. After twenty-four hours of fighting, the Syrians appeared poised to rush down into Israel itself. In the south, Egyptian forces leapfrogged the Suez Canal, burst through Israeli lines, and advanced into the Sinai. The fighting produced greater losses than Israel had ever suffered on the battlefield. More than one hundred Israeli planes were destroyed, along with five hundred tanks. Some five hundred Israeli soldiers were killed. These numbers were not large as battlefield statistics go, but for a small country like Israel, they hurt tremendously. After the 1967 war, an aura of invincibility had surrounded Israel's military; the beginning of the October War of 1973 pretty well dispelled the aura.

Yet despite their initial losses, the Israelis soon rebounded and counterattacked. Israeli forces split the Egyptians in the Sinai, driving to the Suez Canal and continuing twenty-five miles onto the western side. Israeli armor and infantry regained their footing on the Golan Heights and threw the Syrians back down the eastern slope of the mountains.

But Israeli supplies were running thin, and the government of Prime Minister Golda Meir called desperately to the United States for help. Fortunately for the Israelis, the fact that they had not fired the first shot this time made it easier for Washington to respond favorably than otherwise would have been the case—though it took Washington a couple of days to convince itself that the Israelis really had not fired first. The initial reports from the front were confusing, as such reports usually are, and American leaders recalled how the Israelis had lied about the beginning of the 1967 war. But as the reality of the situation grew clearer, it became evident in this instance that Israel was the aggrieved party, the victim of aggression.

Or at least such became evident to most Americans. To the Arabs and to many others who saw Egypt and Syria as simply trying to regain Egyptian and

Syrian territory seized by force in the previous war, the aggressor-aggressee question was more complicated.

The Nixon administration was willing to give the Israelis the weapons they wanted, but it preferred to keep them waiting a bit. The administration desired to avert a repetition of 1967, when the Israelis had thoroughly thrashed the Arabs and wound up occupying lots of Arab territory. Another such victory would probably ruin for a generation any chance of peace in the Middle East. Nixon hoped for something closer to an equilibrium between the two sides.

To foster a stalemate, rather than an Israeli triumph, as well as to avoid antagonizing the Arabs more than necessary, the Nixon administration doled out arms to Israel at a carefully controlled pace. At first the administration required the Israelis to pick up the weapons themselves from American military bases in Israeli planes that had had their Israeli markings painted over. As the war continued and as the Soviets began mounting a major resupply effort of their own to the Arabs (overlooking Sadat's impoliteness in sending Moscow's advisers home), the administration authorized the American air force to deliver the goods in American planes. By early in the second week of the war, the American airlift was landing one thousand tons of supplies a day in Israel. Included among the reinforcements was a new batch of American Skyhawk and Phantom fighter-bombers.

The operation succeeded too well. Confident that they would not run out of arms, the Israelis drove farther into Syria until they approached the outskirts of Damascus. In the south they threatened to encircle the Egyptian Third Army and destroy it entirely.

At this point the Nixon administration decided to press hard for a cease-fire. Secretary of State Kissinger flew to Moscow—a less dramatic trip now than in predétente days—where he and the Soviet leadership agreed on the advisability of terminating the current war before either superpower's client got humiliated.

Egypt was glad enough for a cease-fire, but Israel did not like the idea. Countries suddenly winning wars that began badly usually do not. In particular, the Israelis wanted to teach the Arabs not to pick any future fights. All the same, when Kissinger flew to Israel to impress on Golda Meir and her government the great importance Israel's chief arms supplier placed on a quick end to hostilities, and when he indicated further that the United States would wink at a little "slippage" in Israel's adherence to the deadline of a proposed cease-fire, the Israelis grudgingly obliged.

Almost immediately the cease-fire started fraying. The Israelis continued their tidying up for more than the few hours Kissinger thought he had granted them. Egyptian artillery bombarded Israeli positions. Each side blamed the other for breaking the truce first, and the war was under way once more.

Things got particularly tense when Moscow, acting on a request by Egypt's Sadat, suggested a Soviet-American peace-keeping force. Soviet leader Brezhnev said he hoped the Americans would agree to the suggestion, but if they did not, the Soviet Union would have to move alone. Brezhnev told Nixon, "I will say it straight that if you find it impossible to act with us in this matter, we should be faced with the necessity urgently to consider the question of taking appropriate steps unilaterally." To underline Soviet concern, the Kremlin ordered Soviet ships in the Mediterranean to prepare for action and placed several airborne divisions on alert.

The Nixon administration rejected the idea of Soviet troops in the Middle East. Détente or no détente, keeping the Soviets out of the region to the extent possible remained a principal goal of American policy. In the present instance, the consequences of the introduction of Soviet forces, even as peace keepers, could be imagined. If the Soviets interposed themselves between the Israelis and Egyptians, the Israelis might fire on them. If this happened, the Soviets might retaliate and perhaps escalate. The United States would be forced to decide whether to counter-intervene. If it did, it risked a major blowup with the Soviet Union. If it did not, it risked letting the Kremlin get away with intimidating its protégé Israel. In the aftermath of the American pullout from Vietnam, such intimidation could have especially harmful repercussions on American credibility worldwide.

Nixon's capacity to concentrate on the Middle East suffered at this time from concurrent impeachment hearings in the House of Representatives; the Watergate posse was closing in fast. But even so he responded vigorously. The president went Brezhnev one better in the bluff-and-bluster game: he placed American conventional and nuclear forces around the world on alert. He wrote Brezhnev saying that the United States would view unilateral Soviet action as a matter "of the gravest concern, involving incalculable consequences."

Skeptics on the subject of Nixon thought the president might be overreacting for domestic political effect. He seemed to be making the point that in a moment of world crisis, impeachment was not a good idea. Administration officials then and later vehemently denied the charge. Whatever Nixon's motivation, the highly visible combat preparations on American military bases across the globe helped persuade the Kremlin to drop whatever notions it had of landing troops in the Middle East.

At the same time, the administration warned the Israelis to quit before bigger trouble started. The Israelis resisted momentarily, hoping to place Egypt's Third Army entirely at their mercy. But when the likely consequences of a cutoff of American aid began to sink in, they agreed to stop shooting.

Getting from a cease-fire to a peace treaty was even harder than getting to a cease-fire. In the months after the fighting stopped, Kissinger shuttled back and forth between Israel and Egypt trying to disentangle the forces of the two countries along the Suez Canal and in the Sinai desert. The going went very slowly, lasting through the end of the Nixon administration and on into the Ford administration. But persistence gradually paid off. The opposing armies pulled apart, and, more important, the two sides gained confidence in each other's desire to avoid another war. During the same period, Kissinger persuaded Israel and Syria to disengage their forces in the Golan.

When Jimmy Carter entered the White House in 1977, he dedicated himself to bringing Israel and Egypt to a definitive peace settlement. Carter succeeded, due both to his dogged determination and to a confluence of factors that inclined both sides to peace. On the Israeli side, it helped matters, paradoxically perhaps, that Israel's prime minister was the conservative and suspicious Menachem Begin. Although convincing Begin to compromise was not easy, when he did finally come to terms with the Egyptians, he could be counted on to deliver the assent of the Israeli parliament, the Knesset. It was also crucial that the Sinai, the territory Egypt most wanted back, was not holy ground to anyone in Israel—in contrast to the West Bank, which many Israelis considered part of the Jewish patrimony. On the Egyptian side, President Sadat believed that the time had come to accept the reality of Israel's existence. Sadat risked a great deal in pursuing this belief, but he decided that Egypt needed to turn to other issues besides Israel. Egypt had lots of poor people and could not bear the cost of indefinite mobilization.

In September 1978 Begin and Sadat met at the American presidential retreat of Camp David, Maryland. After almost two weeks of wearing and often angry negotiations, the Israelis and the Egyptians reached an agreement. Israel would return the Sinai to Egypt, and Egypt would extend diplomatic recognition to Israel. A peace treaty would seal the agreement. To sweeten the deal, Carter promised a major program of American aid to each side.

Jimmy Carter, in shirtsleeves, did not get Egypt's Anwar Sadat (left) and Israel's Menachem Begin to relax much at Camp David, but he did get them to agree to sign a peace treaty. *Courtesy Jimmy Carter Library*

By the spring of 1979, the various parts of the peace program were in place. At the end of March, Begin and Sadat signed the peace treaty in Washington. Ratifications followed, and the promised American aid began flowing. Egypt and Israel were soon the two largest recipients of American assistance.

The Industrial World over a Barrel

While Henry Kissinger and Jimmy Carter were working to solve the political and military problems arising from the October War, the American people and many others were trying to cope with some unprecedented economic problems that emerged from that same conflict. In the second week of the October War, following the commencement of the American operation to resupply Israel with arms, the Arab members of the Organization of Petroleum Exporting Countries (OPEC) announced their intention to cut oil production 5 percent per month until the Israelis withdrew from the territories occupied in the 1967 war and until the rights of the Palestinians were restored. A few days later, when Nixon asked Congress for more than $2 billion to pay for the weapons and equipment going to Israel, the Arab OPEC members proclaimed a complete embargo of oil to the United States.

Since the late 1940s, American leaders had lain awake nights sweating over the possibility that someone might shut off the Middle Eastern oil spigot. For most of the postwar period, American concern had centered on the vulnerability of America's allies to an oil shortfall. Western Europe and Japan possessed almost no petroleum of their own (none that they could produce at reasonable cost, anyway: the British and Norwegian North Sea fields did not pay their way until after the large price rises of the post–October War period). And if the oil stopped flowing in, the economies of the allies would seize up. Under such circumstances holding the alliance together might become extremely difficult.

As for the United States itself, imported oil had amounted to a relatively small portion of the American energy picture through the mid-1950s. In 1954 imports totaled less than one-sixth of domestic production; in 1957 they came to slightly less than one-fifth, where they remained for a decade. Yet even this modest rise in imports worried American domestic producers, who lobbied for import quotas. (American companies with major production facilities overseas viewed the rise in imports, from which they profited, with comparative calm.) The domestic producers' efforts paid off: in March 1959 Eisenhower announced a schedule of quotas designed to curtail imports. The chief ostensible aim of the quotas was to enhance American security against the threat of dependence on foreign sources; but a main result was the propping up of the price of the oil the domestic producers pumped.

While the American oil economy was protected behind the walls of the quota system, world demand for petroleum grew substantially. Much of the increase in demand was the simple consequence of economic growth. As industrial production in Western Europe and Japan continued its recovery from the early postwar period, the appetites of the Europeans and Japanese for imported oil mounted. Changes in industrial and transportation technology also magnified the demand for oil. Western European countries shifted from coal-based economies to oil-based ones. In the United States, the construction of the interstate highway system facilitated the continuing shift away from railroads and toward trucks and automobiles as the chief mode of ground transport. Burgeoning fleets of airliners, especially the new jets, burned petroleum-derived fuels at unprecedented rates.

The consequence of all this was that by the early 1970s world petroleum production barely managed to stay ahead of consumption. American producers were stretched to their limit, pumping at nearly full capacity. In March 1971 the Texas Railroad Commission, the body that for decades had set production quotas for Texas oil fields and thereby indirectly set prices for American oil generally (and greatly influenced world prices), authorized production at 100 percent of capacity for the first time since the Second World War. The Nixon administration responded to the pressure on supplies by relaxing and then abolishing the import quotas. By 1973 Americans were importing 6 million barrels per day, more than one-third of their total consumption.

Western Europe and Japan were even more dependent on imported oil than the United States, and this unaccustomed Western dependence made world oil prices especially susceptible to manipulation by countries that had lots of oil to sell. Of such countries by far the most important were in the Middle East, and the most important of the Middle Eastern oil exporters was Saudi Arabia. What gave the Saudis, who controlled one-fifth of world oil exports, and to a lesser extent the other Middle Eastern producers, such leverage in the world oil market was that they could fairly easily adjust their production to suit their political or economic tastes. If they wanted to expand output, they could do so. If they chose to leave the oil in the ground, they could do that.

This flexibility in production was what had led to the birth of OPEC in the first place: producers hoped to curtail output and thereby raise prices. Yet from its founding in 1960 until the early 1970s, efforts by the cartel to increase members' income had usually got tangled up in the slack in the world oil market. If OPEC trimmed production, non-OPEC countries such as the United States could boost production, negating the upward pressure on prices. So toothless was the cartel during this early phase that the producing countries had to negotiate, more or less as equals, with the companies that purchased their oil. Dictating terms to the companies remained beyond OPEC's reach.

As the oil market stretched tight in the early 1970s, however, OPEC came into its own. Prices edged up during the first years of the decade, and when OPEC members gathered in Vienna in the autumn of 1973, they expected to push prices higher still. The fortuitous outbreak of the October War, just as the Vienna meeting commenced, intensified the upward pressure on prices even more. It also added a political dimension to the negotiations, at least for the

Arab members of OPEC, which responded to the American resupply of Israel with the progressive cutbacks in production and the anti-American embargo.

What with the tight supply situation, the shock of another Middle Eastern war (which raised insurance rates and other transportation costs and potentially threatened the oil fields with destruction), and the politically induced curtailment of output, petroleum prices went through the roof. One oil company executive, confronting the specter of a winter of short supplies, described the atmosphere that drove his firm to bid prices up: "We were not bidding just for oil. We were bidding for our life." The Arab OPEC members announced a 70 percent increase in the posted price of their oil, to a little more than five dollars per barrel. The sensitive spot market, where buyers scrambled for cargoes to fill short-term orders and top off tanks, showed still greater jumps. In November nervous buyers signed short-term contracts for oil at sixteen and seventeen dollars per barrel. One Japanese firm went as high as twenty-two dollars.

This first "oil shock" dealt the world economy a body blow. The developing countries that did not produce oil were hit the hardest. Lacking significant cash reserves, countries such as India, the Philippines, and Kenya had to choose between doing without oil or doing without other imports. They usually did without some of each, to the double detriment of current living standards and of prospects for future growth.

For the industrial countries, the oil shock produced both higher inflation and slower growth. It nailed shut the coffin lid on the Bretton Woods system, and its impact rippled down the decade. Modern economies run on energy; when the price of a principal source of energy goes up, the price of nearly everything else goes up, too. For years afterward economists debated the relative contribution of the jump in oil prices to the sharp increase in inflation in the United States and elsewhere during the latter half of the 1970s. (Government deficits and easy-money policies were also prime suspects in America.) But no one denied that the rising cost of oil contributed significantly. And when people spent more money on oil, they had less to spend on other items. (Oil prices rose much faster than wages and most other prices.) As a result, factories and businesses of all kinds laid off workers. Interest rates went up as depositors demanded an inflation hedge. High interest rates crimped credit-sensitive industries like automobiles and construction and generally discouraged investment. By the end of the decade, much of the industrial world was suffering from an unprecedented combination of inflation and economic stagnation, summarized in the newly coined term *stagflation*.

The massive transfer of wealth from the oil consumers to the oil producers provided the latter with a windfall of political power as well. The Arab oil producers, led by Saudi Arabia, found themselves courted by the industrialized countries as never before. Several oil importers—but not the United States—reconsidered their policies in the Arab-Israeli conflict and decided to distance themselves from Israel. The Saudis bankrolled such Arab causes as the Palestinian quest for a homeland, particularly as pursued by the Palestinian

Liberation Organization (PLO). Saudi support for radical Arab factions like the PLO was not entirely philanthropic: the most conservative of the Arab regimes, the Saudi ruling family paid the money partly to persuade the radicals to keep their radicalism safely away from Saudi Arabia.

The meetings of OPEC representatives became a focus of the attention of most of the world's governments. Government budgets, development plans, and fiscal initiatives hinged on the decisions of the oil cartel. How much would oil prices rise this year? Could the oil producers be persuaded to "recycle" their petrodollars: that is, purchase securities of consumer governments, provide aid to the developing nations, or buy more goods and services from the industrialized countries? To the extent the answer was yes, the world economy would be insulated from the worst damage of the oil shock. To the extent the answer was no, the industrialized nations and most others could only hold on tight and hope to ride out the quake.

The Doolittle Doctrine Discredited: Carter and Human Rights

The oil shock of 1973–1974 was part of a triple whammy for Americans. It came in close conjunction with the American defeat in Vietnam and the unraveling of the sordid story of the Watergate scandal. Americans sitting in long lines waiting to pay previously unheard of prices for gasoline had plenty of time to reflect on the sad state of both their country's foreign relations and its domestic politics. Voters' revulsion recast the composition of the American Congress in the 1974 elections, chucking out incumbents in record numbers and peopling the corridors of the Capitol with planeloads of fresh faces. The legislature determined to complete the housecleaning started by the Senate Watergate Committee, whose investigations had been instrumental in forcing Nixon's August 1974 resignation. As investigative committees delved into the secrets the American government had been keeping from the American people, they discovered piles of dirty laundry that related to American international relations, especially relations with the Soviet Union and its real and perceived agents in other countries.

Americans learned, for example, of the CIA's involvement in the overthrow of the governments of Iran in 1953 and Guatemala in 1954. They learned of the intelligence agency's efforts to assassinate foreign leaders, including Cuba's Castro and the Congo's Lumumba. They learned that the CIA had engaged in domestic intelligence gathering in direct violation of its charter. They learned that at least one president, Nixon, had used the CIA to cover up the political misdeeds of his administration.

The combined impact of these and other revelations raised new and disturbing questions about America's dealings with the world. Most Americans had long believed that their country adhered to a higher standard than other countries in conducting foreign affairs. They especially believed that American practices were more honorable and forthright than those of the communist powers they had been taught to fear and loathe. Therefore, it was with considerable anguish and dismay that many of them greeted the knowledge that American practices often had not been.

Among the documents unearthed by the congressional investigators was a report written for President Eisenhower in 1954 by General James Doolittle. Eisenhower had appointed Doolittle to review the operations of the CIA and recommend improvements. Doolittle asserted that the exigencies of international relations were such that the United States government had to set aside traditional American values. Regarding the competition between the United States and the Soviet Union, Doolittle said, "There are no rules in such a game." Americans must learn "to subvert, sabotage and destroy our enemies by more clever, more sophisticated, and more effective methods than those used against us." Twenty years later Americans discovered that their government had taken Doolittle's advice to heart. It was a discouraging discovery, and it caused many Americans to question whether America's cause in trying to contain communism had been worth the cost.

The post-Watergate revelations helped elect Jimmy Carter to the presidency in 1976. Carter reestablished a tradition in American politics that had originated with Andrew Jackson: of running successfully for president as the outsider, the man from the provinces who had not been corrupted by the ways of Washington. Carter's political approach, combined with his personal inclinations, produced an attitude toward international affairs that promised to extend and broaden détente, despite contrasting sharply with the Nixon-Kissinger school of pragmatic, sometimes cynical, realpolitik. Carter asserted that for many years American policy had been warped by an "inordinate fear" of communism. This fear had driven the United States off the high road of honor and morality and into the morass of equivocation and uncertainty. Vietnam and the sins of the CIA testified to the folly of such a course. Carter pledged to return America to the ideals of democracy, fair play, and integrity.

As a centerpiece of his campaign for a restoration of American ideals, Carter focused the attention of the United States on human rights. He refused to overlook abuses by American clients and allies of their citizens, and he created a special office in the State Department to monitor the performance of governments around the world on issues of freedom of speech, freedom to organize opposition, treatment of prisoners, and other matters Washington had usually judged to be internal matters of the countries involved. Those governments over which the United States had meaningful leverage, especially those receiving American aid, were subject to remonstrance and subsequent curtailment of aid if they failed to pass muster.

Carter's campaign for human rights did not transform the relationship between governments and people throughout the world, yet it did produce improvement in some cases. In the Philippines, American pressure was instrumental in persuading President Ferdinand Marcos to release his most prominent political prisoner, Benigno Aquino. American nudgings figured in the

South Korean government's decision to allow democratic elections. More controversially, Carter's human rights policy played a role, albeit a minor one, in the ouster of autocratic regimes in Nicaragua and Iran; the controversy turned on the question of whether the successor regimes were an improvement or a setback for American interests.

Sandino Lives! The Nicaraguan Revolution

The events in Nicaragua were a reaction to forty-five years of rule by the Somoza family. The first Somoza, the one who had been helped to power in the 1930s by the Roosevelt administration, had ruled Nicaragua until 1956, when he was assassinated by an obscure but idealistic young poet who was himself gunned down instantly by members of Somoza's National Guard. Somoza's son Luis took over as president, while Luis's younger brother, Anastasio, Jr., a graduate of the United States military academy at West Point, assumed control of the National Guard. Luis died in 1967, leaving the government to his brother.

Although Luis had at least nodded in the direction of reform, partly to tap into American Alliance for Progress aid, Anastasio wasted little effort hiding the fact that he considered Nicaragua to be his personal fiefdom. He showered favors on the National Guard, which served as his private army and was in fact always commanded by a member of the Somoza family. He filled his bank account and those of friends with money from the public coffers. Meanwhile the living standards of the Nicaraguan people slumped. By the late 1970s, half the population of the country had to survive on a per capita income of less than three hundred dollars per year.

The Somozas' excesses had triggered opposition as early as the 1950s. Some of the opposition came from within the ruling class. Pedro Joaquín Chamorro, editor of the newspaper *La Prensa* and the scion of two wealthy and well-connected families, repeatedly tried to raise a revolt against the government. (Only Chamorro's connections allowed him to live to repeat the effort after each failure.) A more radical movement took shape in the 1960s under the banner of the Sandinista Front for National Liberation, named after Augusto Sandino, the nationalist leader killed in the 1930s. The Sandinista front often went by its initials in Spanish: FSLN.

The FSLN insurgency did not really catch hold until 1972 when an earthquake leveled much of Managua and the Somozas and the National Guard raked off a large share of the international relief funds intended for those rendered homeless and destitute by the devastation. This disgraceful behavior outraged many middle-class types who despaired that anything would ever come of Nicaragua with such thoroughly conscienceless characters in charge. Many of the disaffected joined the ranks of the FSLN; many more merely sympathized with the rebels and abetted their antigovernment activities. In 1974 a spectacular mass kidnapping of dozens of prominent citizens led to a crack-down by Somoza and the National Guard. For a time the crackdown seemed to be working, but in 1978 the regime once more overstepped the limits of Nicaraguan tolerance. A government-condoned and probably government-sponsored assassination squad murdered Chamorro following a string of crit-ical revelations in *La Prensa*. In reaction the population of Managua staged a general strike. The National Guard managed to break the strike but not before alienating many more people. Several months after Chamorro's murder, FSLN commandos stormed the national palace in Managua; they captured the build-ing and seized hundreds of hostages, including members of Nicaragua's parlia-ment. After some testing of the commandos' determination, Somoza released more than fifty Sandinistas previously arrested by the National Guard and paid a large ransom in exchange for the hostages' freedom. Although the ransom helped balance the insurgents' books and the release of the prisoners raised morale, the most important effect of the raid was to demonstrate that the So-moza regime could no longer govern Nicaragua. More general strikes and ad-ditional rebel raids reemphasized the point.

Until this stage of the revolt, the United States had stuck by Somoza, albeit uneasily. The Carter administration chided the Nicaraguan government for human rights abuses, but after Somoza instituted some minor and essentially cosmetic reforms, Washington applauded his efforts as steps in the right direc-tion and eased the pressure.

To some observers American policy appeared disjointed. It was. In nearly all American presidential administrations, vigorous debates occur among groups advocating different positions on important issues. Administrations in which no such debates take place are administrations that almost surely are bound for trouble. Consensus is usually the enemy of critical, sound thinking. Too much debate, however, prolonged too long can yield policies that work against themselves. This was Carter's problem. Carter's secretary of state, Cyrus Vance, recommended policies designed to accommodate change, even revolu-tionary change, in such places as Nicaragua. Carter's national security adviser, Zbigniew Brzezinski, distrusted radical change and argued for a firmer defense of the status quo. Carter wisely encouraged the debate within his administra-tion, but he unwisely procrastinated in making decisions. In the case of Nica-ragua, he let himself be tugged back and forth between Vance and Brzezinski. One month Carter would press for reforms; the next he would back away. A principal result was that neither Somoza nor the Sandinistas knew what to expect from Washington. Another result was that the United States lost much of the influence it might have been able to exercise in mitigating the violence of the Nicaraguan revolution.

The Carter administration did try to find a middle ground between the op-posing sides. It promoted initiatives by the Organization of American States aimed at a negotiated settlement. It also tried to work with middle-class op-ponents of Somoza toward the goal of getting rid of the dictator without hand-ing Nicaragua over to the radical Sandinistas. This sort of solution was the kind American leaders have usually preferred in revolutionary situations: a compromise between a corrupt status quo and a wholesale overturning of the system. But such solutions do not always exist, and the secret to finding those that do lies in getting there early before so much blood has been spilled that the middle ground has been washed away.

By the time Carter was convinced that Somoza had to go, the middle ground was beyond salvage. The Sandinistas, with assistance from Castro's Cuba, from several noncommunist Latin American governments, and from Western European socialist parties launched their final offensive against Somoza in the spring of 1979. In June, FSLN troops entered Managua. Somoza forced them to retreat but only by bombing his own capital and thus further alienating the Nicaraguan people. The rebels proceeded to surround the city and gradually tightened the noose about Somoza. In mid-July, convinced that his career in Nicaragua was over, Somoza and his intimates flew away from Nicaragua to exile in Florida.

Although the Carter administration had failed to find a moderate solution to the problem of change in Nicaragua, the administration was determined to avoid pushing the Nicaraguan revolution any further to the left than necessary. American diplomats are often students of history, and the diplomats responsible for Carter's policy toward Nicaragua knew how Eisenhower's reactions to the Cuban revolution twenty years earlier had encouraged Castro to turn to the Soviet Union. Carter's people intended to avoid a like result in Nicaragua.

The new government of Nicaragua, controlled by the victorious Sandinistas, faced an immense task of reconstructing the country after years of civil war as well as decades of exploitation by the Somozas and their cronies. The Sandinistas showed a definite leftist tilt, with avowed Marxists holding several key positions and the government espousing a generally socialist line for the Nicaraguan economy. But the government also included representatives of business, the professions, and the Catholic church. To some degree the diversity within the government represented a sincere attempt to reach out to the various sectors of Nicaraguan society and to heal the wounds of war. To some degree it indicated a desire to put on a pluralist face for foreign donors and lenders. The United States, the Western Europeans and such agencies as the World Bank and the IMF would find it easier to underwrite Nicaragua's reconstruction if the Sandinistas made gestures in the direction of democracy.

Skeptics within the Carter administration, and among Carter's critics, doubted the bona fides of the Sandinistas. They pointed to large shipments of aid from the Soviet Union and Cuba and especially to the presence of Soviet and Cuban advisers in Nicaragua. Yet Carter held to his course. He approved plans to reschedule old loans owed by the Nicaraguan government, thereby easing repayment, and he pushed for new loans in the amount of $75 million. Carter did not know whether relations between the United States and Nicaragua would be fruitful or otherwise, but he wanted to be sure that if they were otherwise, the fault would rest with the Nicaraguans, not with Americans.

Iran and the Soldiers of the Prophet

The Nicaraguan revolution was one of two such dramatic upheavals in 1979. The other one, the one with larger consequences for international affairs, occurred halfway around the globe in Iran. During the period after the ouster of Mossadeq in 1953, the shah had consolidated his grip on Iran. American assistance of several hundred million dollars in economic and military aid had helped in the consolidation. By the late 1950s, the shah was already something of a despot. The Iranian parliament rarely challenged his authority, and his American-trained secret police efficiently silenced most dissent.

During the 1960s the shah tried to deflect what demands for change he had not silenced, by means of what he called a "white revolution," as distinguished from the "red revolution" of the communists. The shah's reforms targeted education, distribution of land, and government services, among other matters. They succeeded marginally but left unaddressed many of the basic difficulties confronting Iran's poor. At the same time, they antagonized two groups that grew increasingly influential during the next two decades. Members of the urban middle class thought the shah was reforming too timidly and too slowly. These Westernized, educated, relatively well-off people wanted more influence in the running of Iran. Islamic fundamentalists thought the shah was reforming too extensively and too swiftly. The Islamists decried the monarch's undermining of Islamic values and demanded closer adherence to the teachings of the prophet Muhammad.

The oil boom of the 1970s increased the shah's wealth and power, but it also increased the strain on Iranian society. The demands of both the middle class and the fundamentalists increased: the former for additional loosening of traditional constraints, the latter for a return to the old ways. The shah contributed to the strain by keeping the lid tight on dissent and political participation.

Throughout the various developments in Iran, America's relationship with the shah remained close. For a time during the early 1960s, the Kennedy administration encouraged the shah to loosen up a bit. The American encouragement added some impetus to the White Revolution. But Washington lost interest in Iranian reform as Vietnam consumed more of America's attention and resources. During the early 1970s, the Nixon administration chose Iran and the shah as a test case of the Nixon Doctrine. The geopoliticians in the Nixon and Ford administrations allowed the Iranian government to purchase all the American weapons it wanted, which proved to be quite a lot. And they stopped inquiring very closely about Iran's internal affairs. In return, the shah agreed to keep Iran safely in the Western camp and to help police the always volatile Persian Gulf region.

There were additional reasons, economic rather than political, for letting Iran buy so much American weaponry. These reasons applied to other potential purchasers of American weapons as well. One was that foreign weapons sales eased America's growing balance-of-payments problems. With ballooning oil prices draining dollars away from the United States, arms sales repatriated some of these dollars and lessened the trade imbalance. Selling high-ticket items like F-5 fighter planes, C-130 transports, and helicopter gunships to Iran did not close the deficit entirely, but it helped. A second objective of the arms sales was to ensure the survival of the American defense industry. In the aftermath of Vietnam, the Pentagon scaled back purchases of all manner of items, with consequent ill effects on the profit margins of major weapons contractors. Finding foreign customers such as Iran for American arms served to keep profit margins up, weapons workers employed, defense-dependent communities solvent, and—the political bottom line—legislators from defense-sensitive districts in office.

From this combination of causes, American arms flowed to Iran at a rapid rate. The shah bought more than $10 billion worth between 1971 and 1977. Recalling the atmosphere in Teheran, the chief of the American military advisory group there later declared, "It was a salesman's dream."

American solicitude encouraged the shah to think grandly of himself. In 1971 he hosted an extravagant festival celebrating twenty-five hundred years of the Persian monarchy. Estimates of the cost of the affair ran to $200 million. Some shah-watchers thought the celebration, during which Pahlavi linked himself to Cyrus the Great and other Persian demigods, pushed him off the deep end. In its wake he showed a tendency toward megalomania and a growing disconnectedness from the lives of ordinary Iranians. He tightened his security apparatus, further provoking the middle classes, even as he proceeded with the secularizing reforms that infuriated the Islamists.

It helped neither the shah nor the United States that large numbers of Americans—technicians, advisers, support staff—accompanied the American weapons and equipment delivered to Iran. By the end of 1976, nearly twenty-five thousand Americans resided in Iran. Even if they had been exemplary guests, and some were, they would have tested the patience of the millions of Iranians who knew that the shah was spending mountains of money on the Americans and their merchandise that he might have been spending on projects more essential to the well-being of the Iranian people. Earlier, in the days of British domination of Iran's affairs, Iranians had learned to distrust the West by watching British officials, soldiers, and capitalists; now their distrust focused on the Americans.

By the late 1970s, the situation in Iran was approaching a crisis. The shah's secret police corps, SAVAK, had become notorious for its common use of torture and its long reach, even to foreign countries, where SAVAK agents kept tabs on Iranian students and expatriates. Amnesty International and other human rights monitoring organizations regularly excoriated the shah's government for its abuses. The secretary general of Amnesty International declared flatly that no country in the world had a worse record on human rights than Iran.

Jimmy Carter was pulled two ways regarding Iran, as he was at the same time regarding Nicaragua. The human rights activists in his administration, and others who believed that reforms in Iran were needed to prevent revolution, advocated pressuring the shah to make changes. The United States should not throw the shah to the sharks, they said, but it should let him know plainly that continued American support depended on improvements in his performance. The hard-liners in the administration argued that the shah had been a reliable ally of the United States for twenty-five years. If he did not run Iran quite according to the preferences of the American Civil Liberties Union, his failure to do so simply showed that Iran was not Massachusetts. Especially in the Middle East, strength and stability counted for more than free elections.

Carter failed to choose between the two camps regarding Iran, as he failed regarding Nicaragua. Not that a clear choice by the American government probably would have made much difference in the way things turned out: in Iran, as in Nicaragua, events had acquired such momentum that diverting them would have been very difficult for any outside party. In any event the signals Washington sent the shah only confused the issue. In the spring of 1977, Secretary of State Vance flew to Teheran and told the monarch that the Carter administration placed great importance on human rights. The United States, Vance said, hoped and expected that America's allies would demonstrate respect for the fundamental liberties of their citizens. But when the shah essentially ignored this message, Carter refused to invoke any significant sanctions against Iran. The president allowed the shah to continue buying some of the most sophisticated weapons American manufacturers produced. Carter brought the shah to Washington for an elaborate state visit in late 1977. Several months later the president traveled to Teheran, where he gushed over the "respect, admiration and love" the Iranian people exhibited toward the shah and pronounced Iran "an island of stability in one of the most troubled regions of the world."

Within months this island of stability exploded. The few concessions the government made to popular opinion failed to satisfy the demands of ever-growing numbers of Iranians. When Islamic fundamentalists staged demonstrations in the holy city of Qom, the shah's police fired on the demonstrators. Two dozen died, and many more were wounded. The location of the shootings as well as the occupation of the casualties—Muslim theology students—aggravated the situation more than ever. Rioting against the monarchy spread across the country. Fighting rocked Tabriz during the spring of 1978, producing hundreds more martyrs to the cause. Teheran erupted in May, Meshed in July, Isfahan and Abadan in August. In September army troops fired on a large crowd gathered in Teheran's Jaleh Square. The dead and wounded totaled more than one thousand.

Still the shah held on, and Washington stuck by him. In what proved to be a gross underestimation of the strength of the opposition, American intelligence analysts predicted that the regime could contain the insurgents. There were several reasons for this intelligence failure, including three that in one form or another often characterized American perceptions of events in the Third World and to some extent elsewhere. First, American intelligence in Iran

had never been very good. American relations with Iran had not been sufficiently important to induce many American officials to devote careers to mas-
tering the Farsi language and otherwise immersing themselves in Iranian
politics and culture. Lacking their own expertise, American officials overrelied
on the shah's informants, who naturally painted a rosy picture of their boss's
prospects. As a result, American analysts looking at Iran misgauged the proportion of the unrest they could see to the proportion they could not see. They
assumed that the riots and other demonstrations indicated the alienation of a
comparatively small group of people rather than the disaffection of huge segments of the population.

Second, because American policy backed the shah, the American bureaucracy tended to filter out reports challenging the wisdom of that policy. American leaders are no more immune than anyone else to the tendency to see what
they want to see. Their subordinates encourage this tendency. The subordinates
quickly learn that although bearers of bad news do not usually get their throats
slit anymore, bearers of good news more often get promoted.

Third, while Iran was hurtling toward revolution, the Carter administration
was distracted by other developments. At the time of the Jaleh Square massacre, the president and his top Middle East advisers were holed up at Camp
David hammering out a peace accord between Israel and Egypt. With only one
president and only twenty-four hours in a day, the American government often
suffers from things falling through the cracks.

While Washington was distracted, the turmoil in Iran continued to mount.
Strikes paralyzed large sectors of the economy. Inflation and hoarding-induced
shortages pinched the middle class and ravaged the poor. Once-radical political factions came to appear moderate. The guiding spirit of the Islamic fundamentalists, Ayatollah Ruhollah Khomeini, directed his followers from exile
in France. Khomeini promised salvation to those who died struggling against
the shah, and he called on the faithful to fight harder than ever. Victory was
at hand, he said. The ayatollah insisted that the Pahlavi usurper relinquish
power at once and that secular, Westernizing Iran be remade without delay
into an Islamic theocracy. When an associate suggested that a gradual transition to Islamic rule might be better than an abrupt transformation, Khomeini
retorted that there must be no gradualism and no waiting. "We must not lose
a day, not a minute," he declared. "The people demand an immediate revolution. Now or never."

The American government still failed to perceive the significance of developments in Iran. In December 1978 Carter stated that the Iranian government
continued to enjoy America's confidence and support. The president declared,
"I fully expect the shah to maintain power in Iran and for the present problems
in Iran to be solved."

In fact, Carter may not have been quite so blind as events soon made him
appear. Even if he had strongly suspected that the shah was about to go under,
the president might well have spoken as he did. At this late date, little Washington could have done would have appeased the radicals in Iran; consequently there was not much to be gained by predicting or encouraging the

shah's demise. And on the other hand, steadfastness in defeat can be an admirable quality. America's surviving clients presumably would take courage from knowing that Washington had stood by the shah to the end. Standing by the shah would help Carter domestically as well. The drumbeat of criticism from conservatives, who from the beginning had decried his emphasis on human rights and his tolerance of radical change, was getting stronger all the time; anything that would still the drums for a while would be worth attempting.

Even with Washington's support, the shah could not get a grip on his troubles. Part of the monarch's difficulty was that he was slowly dying of cancer and knew it. Whether a healthy shah would have reacted more decisively to the challenges he faced is impossible to tell; the sick shah could not summon the energy. Another part of the shah's problem was that he did not know how far to trust his army to carry out his directives. Would the generals relay orders to fire on civilians? Would the rank and file obey such orders? In the end the shah chose not to test the army's loyalty. In December 1978 he handed power to the prime minister, Shahpour Bakhtiar, and two weeks later left the country.

The shah's departure only accelerated the pace of the revolution. Millions of people took to the streets. Many carried weapons and used them against landlords, employers, creditors, and whomever else they had it in for. Surging crowds attacked symbols of the regime and of Western influence: military and police headquarters, government offices, foreign banks and hotels, the American embassy. Islamic fundamentalists destroyed liquor stores and movie houses. Bakhtiar's government lasted only a month, swept away by the flood of emotion that accompanied the triumphal return of Khomeini to Teheran in February 1979.

Although the United States exercised almost no influence over the events of this period, the radicals in Iran found America to be a convenient scapegoat. To a degree Washington insufficiently appreciated, Khomeini and his followers actively encouraged bad feelings between Iran and the United States. When some associates voiced concern that the American-Iranian relationship was being seriously endangered, Khomeini answered, "May God cause it to be endangered. Our relations with the United States are the relations of the oppressed with the oppressor; they are the relations of the plundered with the plunderer." Khomeini went on to ask rhetorically, "What need have we of the United States?"

In fact, Khomeini did need the United States, or at least he found it handy. America became a blunt instrument for beating the moderates who hoped to halt the Iranian revolution short of the establishment of an Islamic theocracy. As in many revolutions, the radicals enjoyed the advantage of appearing more dedicated than their moderate opponents to the principles from which the revolution arose, in this case hatred for the shah and all he stood for, including close ties between Iran and the United States. Yet the moderates were not without resources. And many moderate members of the Iranian middle class desired to preserve the advantages of living in a secular society. On account of this moderate opposition, the Iranian revolution progressed more slowly than

Ayatollah Khomeini considered himself Allah's agent for redeeming Iran from the poisonous influence of the shah, America, and the godless West. Millions of Iranians agreed. *AP/Wide World Photos*

Khomeini had thought it would. To speed the pace of change, he and the other radicals sought to polarize conditions in the country.

An obvious target for the polarizers was the American embassy in Teheran. In February 1979, just two weeks after Khomeini's triumphal return from exile, an armed crowd attacked the embassy. The American ambassador, William Sullivan, recognized that a spirited defense of the embassy by the marine guards would produce large numbers of casualties and enormous quantities of bad blood. Accordingly, he surrendered the building to the attackers. They shot and killed an Iranian employee at the embassy and wounded an American marine. They also took Sullivan and some one hundred other persons hostage. On this occasion, though, the Khomeinists opposed such extreme action. The hostage takers, it turned out, were leftists who hoped to push the revolution in a Marxist direction. The Khomeinists had accepted the leftists' cooperation in throwing out the shah, but they did not want to let the leftists in on the spoils of the victory. Within hours of the embassy takeover, the Khomeinists denounced it, allowing the relative moderates who still controlled the government to negotiate with the hostage takers and free the captives.

As the revolution proceeded, however, and the leftists lost out, the Khomeinists' attitude toward hostage taking changed. Now they began to look on such dramatic action as a device to discredit the moderates who hung on to power. The Carter administration played into their hands by allowing the exiled and ailing shah to enter the United States for medical treatment. The Khomeinists derided the American statement that medical reasons accounted for the ex-monarch's visit to New York; the Americans, they said, were plotting a reversal of the revolution. As additional evidence they cited a recent meeting in Algeria between American national security adviser Brezezinski and Iran's current prime minister, Mehdi Bazargan. To protest the American moves and to further undermine the Iranian moderates, Khomeinists led huge crowds in demonstrations outside the American embassy. On November 4, 1979, hundreds of particularly committed demonstrators, some of whom evidently had planned this next step carefully, climbed the walls of the embassy compound, overwhelmed the guards, and seized more than seventy hostages.

At first the Carter administration hoped for a quick resolution of this second hostage taking, on the order of that of the previous February. But events soon blasted this hope. Khomeini applauded the action of the hostage takers, transforming them into heroes of the revolution. The ayatollah used the hostages against Bazargan: when the hostage takers, with Khomeini's blessing, ignored Bazargan's efforts to free the Americans, the hapless prime minister was forced to resign. Power passed to the hard-line Revolutionary Council. Within weeks

Pictures like this, of one of the American hostages in Teheran, convinced many voters that the United States needed a stronger leader than Jimmy Carter to deal with the crises confronting America in the 1980s. *AP/Wide World Photos*

the Khomeinists achieved their goal of reconstitutionalizing Iran as an Islamic state.

But the struggle for control of the revolution continued, and the hostages became a football between the weakening moderates and the strengthening radicals. The latter sought a continuing confrontation with America, now officially styled the "Great Satan" of the West, to prove their devotion to Iranian nationalism and the teachings of the Koran. The hostages provided the surest means of keeping the confrontation going. Several days after the takeover of the embassy, Khomeini ordered the release of the African Americans (who were supposed to be less culpable in the sins of the American imperialists) and women among the hostages, and several months later the captors let a sick hostage go. But the remaining fifty-two had too much value as guarantors of bad relations with America to be given up. They stayed in custody.

The Carter administration tried various means to get the hostages back. It halted the shipment of military spare parts to Iran. It deported Iranian students. It barred oil imports from Iran. It froze Iranian financial assets. It applied legal and diplomatic pressure through the United Nations and the International Court of Justice. It packed the shah off to Panama as soon as reasonably possible. (From there he traveled to Egypt, where he died in July 1980.) It broke diplomatic relations with Iran. It declared an economic embargo against Iran. In April 1980 Carter ordered a military rescue attempt, but the effort failed when two helicopters collided, killing eight members of the rescue team.

The Great Game Again: Afghanistan

The turmoil in Iran had a destabilizing effect on several of Iran's neighbors. Afghanistan felt the destabilization sooner and more profoundly than the others. For more than a century, Afghanistan had served as center court in the "great game" between Britain and Russia, in which the Russians tried to push south toward Persia and India, while the British tried to keep the Russians back. Neither side ever controlled Afghanistan for long, largely because the Muslim Afghans ferociously resisted dictation from outside infidels. After the Second World War, the game changed, most notably on account of the withdrawal of Britain from India and southern Asia generally. Britain's departure tempted the United States to fill in, but the temptation at this time was not exactly irresistible. Afghanistan was very far away, and Americans had more pressing matters to contend with. Besides, the Soviets were showing relatively little interest in Afghanistan. The Eisenhower administration considered sending military aid to Afghanistan, but the Pakistanis, allies Washington judged more important than the nonaligned Afghans, objected, and the administration confined itself to a modest amount of economic aid.

Eventually, however, Moscow began paying greater attention to Kabul. The Soviet Union provided economic assistance, then weapons, and though Af-

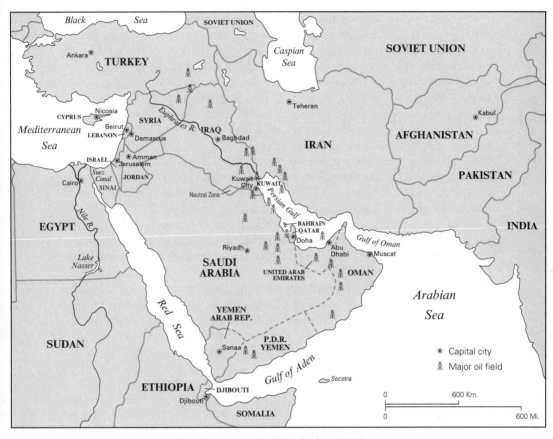

The Countries Surrounding the Persian Gulf in the late 1970s

ghanistan never abandoned its allegiance to the principle of nonalignment, by the 1970s the Soviets were on cozy terms with the government of Mohammad Daoud Khan. Unfortunately for Moscow and for Daoud, the Afghan leader had many enemies, some of whom combined to overthrow him in April 1978, massacring the entire Daoud family and the families of his chief associates to emphasize their point. All was not lost, however, from Moscow's angle, for Afghanistan's new strong men, Nur Mohammad Taraki and Hafizullah Amin, did not object to continuing Daoud's pro-Soviet policies.

But certain of those policies upset Islamic fundamentalists in Afghanistan, who were taking encouragement from the success of the Islamists across the border in Iran. Some of the Afghan fundamentalists raised the flag of revolt against the Taraki government. Amid the fighting, terrorists kidnapped and killed the American ambassador in Kabul. In September 1979, while the revolution in Iran continued to gain force, Taraki himself went down, though not at the hands of the rebels. He was done in by Amin, who preferred sole power to sharing.

The Soviets gave Amin a few months to stem the insurgency, but he did no better than Taraki. Moscow grew increasingly nervous, especially after the Iranian militants seized the American embassy and the Revolutionary Council took control of Iranian politics. The Kremlin feared that the rampaging fundamentalism sweeping Iran would spill over into Afghanistan and—much worse—into the largely Islamic provinces of Soviet Central Asia.

By the final week of December 1979, the Kremlin concluded that Amin was not up to the job of quashing the revolt. Moscow ordered a massive airlift of troops over the mountains into Afghanistan. Tanks and other ground support soon followed. Although the Soviets asserted that Amin had invited them in, he became one of the first casualties of the intervention. His replacement, Babrak Karmal, announced that Amin had not been what he claimed to be. Rather, he was an "oppressor and dictator," a "murderer," a "bloodthirsty agent of American imperialism," and a "charlatan of history"—whatever that was. The Soviet newspaper *Pravda* reported the verdict at the beginning of 1980: "Overthrown by a wave of popular indignation, the treacherous scoundrel was tried and shot."

American leaders did not shed any tears for Amin, but they worried a great deal about what the Soviet invasion of Afghanistan portended. With Iran in a weakened condition as a result of the revolution there, Moscow might be making a move toward the Persian Gulf. Détente or no détente, the West could not count on the Kremlin passing up what might be the opportunity of a lifetime to achieve the traditional Russian goal of access to the warm waters of the Indian Ocean.

Even if the Soviets did not move directly against Iran, their heavy breathing just across the border could have a disruptive effect on the Persian Gulf region, which was already in a turbulent state following the overthrow of the shah. The most convenient measure of the turbulence, the price of oil, was hitting unheard-of highs. This second oil shock started shaking the world economy during the shah's last months in Teheran when strikes by Iranian oil workers drastically cut Iran's exports; by the time the shah fled his country, the strikers had closed down the Iranian oil industry almost entirely. Since Iran had lately been the world's second largest oil exporter, the loss of Iranian oil put a severe crimp on international supplies. It also put a fright into purchasing agents, who bid oil prices sharply up: from thirteen dollars per barrel to thirty-four before relative calm returned to the markets. Although prices moderated during the first half of 1979 as the oil strikers returned to work after the shah's departure, the November seizure of the American embassy, followed by the Soviet invasion of Afghanistan in December, sent another jolt through the system. Spot-market cargoes of oil sold for as much as forty-five dollars per barrel.

* * *

The sequence of coups and revolts in Afghanistan, along with such other disruptive events of the 1970s as the collapse of the Bretton Woods system, the

October War of 1973, the oil shocks, the Sandinista revolution in Nicaragua, and the Islamic revolution in Iran demonstrated how unruly the world had grown thirty years after the Second World War. The competition between the United States and the Soviet Union, once the dominant feature of international affairs, had been relegated almost to the status of a nonstory. Other events crowded it out of the headlines.

Détente codified this downgrading of the superpower competition. The Moscow accords of 1972 and the supplementary agreements between the United States and the Soviet Union indicated a recognition by the two sides that they had problems often more pressing than each other. China was one mutual problem, though bigger for the Soviet Union than for the United States. Early in the decade, Vietnam was the principal bone in the American throat. Both the Americans and the Soviets wanted to slow the nuclear arms race, which was costing more money all the time but producing no more security.

Détente lessened tensions between the United States and the Soviet Union, yet it left nearly untouched many of the planet's most serious troubles. The Arab-Israeli conflict festered as messily as before. The oil shocks divided the world economy, not along ideological East-West lines, but according to whether countries exported or imported oil. The Nicaraguan and Iranian revolutions were homegrown affairs, with the latter being so baffling to many Westerners, and doubtless many Easterners as well, because it transcended the ordinary categories of left and right, radical and conservative. Khomeini and his followers denounced America as the Great Satan but had no more use for the official atheists of the Soviet Union.

Because the upheavals of the 1970s had little to do with relations between the superpowers, it was an open question how those upheavals would affect détente. One could argue that détente helped prevent such turbulent events as the Nicaraguan and Iranian revolutions from entangling the superpowers, as might have been the case in an earlier, more ideological phase of the Soviet-American struggle. On the other hand, judging from all the turmoil in the world, détente between the superpowers did not seem to be doing much for peace and stability generally.

Sources and Suggestions for Further Reading

The end of the Bretton Woods financial regime is analyzed in Robert Solomon, *The International Monetary System, 1945–1976* (1977); David P. Calleo, *The Imperious Economy* (1982); John S. Odell, *U.S. International Monetary Policy* (1982); and Joanne S. Gowa, *Closing the Gold Window* (1983).

On the final outcome of the Vietnam War, see the books by Karnow, Hess, Harrison, Herring, and Young cited in the previous chapter. Richard Nixon, *RN: The Memoirs of Richard Nixon* (1978); and Henry Kissinger, *White House Years* (1979), give the perspective of those two policymakers.

Nixon's and Kissinger's memoirs are a good place to start on the subject of detente, although the claims of both books have to be considerably discounted for personal axe-grinding. The most complete account of detente and what came immediately after is Raymond Garthoff, *Detente and Confrontation* (1985). William Hyland, *Rivals:*

Superpower Relations from Nixon to Reagan (1987), is also valuable, as are Richard Pipes, *U.S.-Soviet Relations in the Era of Detente* (1981); Adam Ulam, *Dangerous Relations: The Soviet Union in World Politics, 1970–1982* (1983); and Richard W. Stevenson, *The Rise and Fall of Detente* (1985). Robert D. Schulzinger, *Henry Kissinger* (1989), is objective; Walter Isaacson, *Kissinger* (1992), is more thorough. Seymour Hersh, *The Price of Power* (1983), is highly critical of Kissinger's policies and style. The biographical work that gives Nixon's diplomacy the most thorough airing (and Nixon the fairest hearing) is Stephen E. Ambrose's three-volume *Nixon* (1987–1991).

On the Middle East, William Quandt, *Decade of Decision* (1978), *Camp David* (1986), and *Peace Process* (1993) examine American policy. Kissinger's memoirs, including *Years of Upheaval* (1982), provide detail on both the October War of 1973 and the peace negotiations that followed. Frank Aker, *October 1973: The Arab-Israeli War* (1985), traces the course of the fighting. Mohamed Heikal, *The Road to Ramadan* (1975), and Anwar el-Sadat, *In Search of Identity* (1978), provide Arab (specifically Egyptian) views, while Golda Meir, *My Life* (1975), and Chaim Herzog, *The War of Atonement* (1975), give Israeli perspectives.

A prize-winning study of the transformation of the oil industry is Daniel Yergin, *The Prize* (1991). Anthony Sampson, *The Seven Sisters: The Great Oil Companies and the World They Created* (1988 ed.), is racier; while Steven A. Schneider, *The Oil Price Revolution* (1983), is duller. Dankwart A. Rustow, *Oil and Turmoil* (1982), concentrates on American dealings with OPEC and the Middle Eastern producing states.

Gaddis Smith, *Morality, Reason and Power* (1986), is an overview of Carter administration foreign policy. Jimmy Carter, *Keeping Faith* (1982); Zbigniew Brzezinski, *Power and Principle* (1983); and Cyrus Vance, *Hard Choices* (1983), are the memoirs of the three principal policymakers in the Carter administration. David S. McLellan, *Cyrus Vance* (1985), affords a more detached assessment of the secretary of state.

The Nicaraguan revolution and its effects on American policy, and the effects of American policy on the Nicaraguan revolution, are discussed in LaFeber, *Inevitable Revolutions*; Mary B. Vanderlaan, *Revolution and Foreign Policy in Nicaragua* (1986); E. Bradford Burns, *At War in Nicaragua* (1987); and Robert Pastor, *Condemned to Repetition* (1987).

On Iran and the United States, the books by Barry Rubin and James Bill cited previously are the most useful. See also Amin Saikal, *The Rise and Fall of the Shah* (1980), R. K. Ramazani, *The U.S. and Iran* (1982); Gary Sick, *All Fall Down* (1985); and Nikki R. Keddie and Eric Hooglund, eds., *The Iranian Revolution and the Islamic Republic* (1986).

A broad view of the turmoil in South Asia is Stanley Wolpert, *Roots of Confrontation in South Asia* (1982). Anthony Arnold, *Afghanistan* (1981); Rosanne Klass, ed., *Afghanistan: The Great Game Revisited* (1988); and Mark L. Urban, *War in Afghanistan* (1988), deal more particularly with that country.

Chapter 15

The Last Superpower, 1980–1990s

As matters turned out, détente did not last into the 1980s. But though both the Americans and the Soviets might have wished otherwise, the collapse of détente did not resurrect the superpower-dominated order of the earlier postwar period. Both sides were weakening: the Americans relatively, the Soviets absolutely. The Soviet weakening was the more spectacular. It produced, in stunning succession, the emergence of the first truly reformist government in Soviet history, the dissolution of Moscow's Eastern European empire, and finally, the disintegration of the Soviet Union into its constituent parts.

The weakening of the United States was quieter. America's decline relative to its allies and trading partners consisted mostly of a steady erosion of American economic vitality and self-reliance. To be sure, the collapse of the Soviet Union left the United States as the world's only full-service superpower: America's economy remained the largest in the world, and its effective military forces far overshadowed those of its closest potential rivals. But the most powerful part of America's military arsenal, its nuclear force, was almost completely unusable in any plausible situation, and the American economy sagged under the double burden of growing trade and federal deficits. The twin deficits, and what they implied about America's slipping strength compared to Western Europe and Japan, left American leaders seriously constrained in dealing with rapid changes in the international order.

Those changes were taking place faster than ever during the 1980s and early 1990s. Most of the changes were variations on old themes. Three wars roiled the Middle East, but the least dangerous was between the Arabs and Israel. The other two were among the Arabs themselves, with the last of the three directly involving the United States and additional non–Middle Eastern countries. Japan continued its remarkable economic growth, acquiring clout second only to that of the United States and sometimes not second. Several smaller Asian countries followed Japan's lead. The nations of Western Europe drew closer together; under the aegis of the European Community, they moved to create the largest single market in the world. America's power continued to grow, but the power of other countries was growing more rapidly.

Chronology

1980	Carter Doctrine; U.S. boycotts Moscow Olympics; Reagan elected; Iran-Iraq war begins; Solidarity union in Poland; civil war in El Salvador
1981	American aid to Afghan rebels; Reagan administration proposes "zero option"
1982	Israeli invasion of Lebanon; U.S. troops as peacekeepers to Lebanon
1983	Reagan announces SDI; bombing of U.S. Marine barracks in Beirut; American invasion of Grenada
1984	American troops withdrawn from Lebanon; Reagan reelected
1985	Gorbachev becomes Soviet leader; first (of several) Reagan-Gorbachev summit meetings, in Geneva
1986	Marcos driven from power in Philippines; American air raid on Libya; Iran-contra cover blown; Reagan-Gorbachev summit in Reykjavik
1987	American patrols of Persian Gulf; INF treaty signed
1988	INF treaty ratified; Bush elected
1989	Soviet pullout from Afghanistan; Tiananmen Square massacre in Beijing; unrest in Eastern Europe leads to opening of Berlin wall
1990	Elections in Nicaragua remove Sandinistas; Lithuania votes for independence from Soviet Union; Estonia and Latvia follow; Iraq invades Kuwait; Germany reunified
1991	Persian Gulf war against Iraq; Warsaw Pact disbands; Yugoslavia fractures; Soviet Union disintegrates
1992	War in Bosnia; Clinton elected on platform basically ignoring foreign affairs

Who Killed Détente?

Jimmy Carter did not have to treat the Soviet invasion of Afghanistan as a major threat to world peace. The Soviet Union's Afghan adventure, which soon bogged down into the kind of bloody morass Vietnam became for the United States, was almost certainly not part of any broad Kremlin strategy for striking south to the Persian Gulf. Instead it was probably a defensive move designed to keep militant Islamic fundamentalism at bay. Moscow's Muslim subjects were restless enough as it was; to allow a fundamentalist regime to gain control in Afghanistan, just after one had gained control in Iran, would only exacerbate the unrest.

Yet Carter *did* choose to interpret the Soviet invasion of Afghanistan as provocative. In an almost complete reversal of his earlier complaint about Americans' inordinate fear of communism, he issued the most straightforward public statement of militant opposition to the Soviet Union since Kennedy's ultimatum during the Cuban missile crisis. Calling the Soviet occupation of Afghanistan a "grave threat" to the flow of Middle Eastern oil, Carter declared, "An attempt by any outside force to gain control of the Persian Gulf region will be regarded as an assault on the vital interests of the United States of America, and such an assault will be repelled by any means necessary, including military force." To emphasize this policy, which came to be known as the Carter Doctrine, the president withdrew from Senate consideration the SALT II treaty (a follow-on to the 1972 SALT I accord), embargoed new grain shipments to the Soviet Union, suspended the sale of high-technology products to the Soviets, canceled Soviet fishing privileges in American waters, stopped a variety of cultural and academic exchange programs, and pulled the American team out of the 1980 Moscow summer Olympic Games.

Carter's strong reaction to the events in Afghanistan had more to do with the political situation in the United States than with conditions in Central Asia and the Middle East. Détente had never been popular with American conservatives, even when practiced by Republicans. They contended that détente was simply a smokescreen for continued Soviet expansionism. They pointed to Angola, where Soviet advisers and Cuban troops helped a Marxist faction take over in 1975 from departing Portuguese colonialists; to the Horn of Africa, where Soviet aid to leftist coup makers in Ethiopia and Somalia helped Moscow push the Western powers aside as the favorite foreigners; and to Nicaragua, where the pro-American Somoza had been tossed out by the radical Sandinistas. They also cited Iran, not as an example of Soviet expansionism, but as evidence of the way Carter's vacillation had doomed an American ally to defeat and fifty-two Americans to continuing captivity. In addition to the strictly political conservatives, American weapons manufacturers and their representatives tended to oppose détente as bad for business, though they usually did not say so directly. The unrelenting criticism threw Carter onto the defensive. The stagflation afflicting the American economy rendered him more defensive still.

The Soviet thrust into Afghanistan afforded the president an opportunity to answer his critics by demonstrating his capacity for forceful action and strong leadership. Carter doubtless believed what he said about the Soviet presence in Afghanistan being a grave threat to American interests; that such a statement was politically convenient made it all the easier for him to believe.

Carter's response to the Soviet invasion of Afghanistan effectively killed détente. If the killing solved some of Carter's domestic political problems, it caused a certain regret in the Kremlin. Soviet leaders understood the advantages that had accrued to their country as a result of détente. Détente had accorded the Soviet Union unprecedented prestige as the diplomatic equal of the United States; it had provided a respite from the exhausting nuclear arms race; it had helped prevent the formation of an American-Chinese alliance against the Soviet Union. Meanwhile behind the treaties and public agreements of détente, the Kremlin had reserved the right (without always saying so explicitly) to define détente as it pleased and to continue to pursue Soviet advantage in such places as Angola, the Horn of Africa, and Nicaragua. It also reserved the right to defend Soviet borders against trouble like that brewing in Afghanistan.

Moscow must have guessed that its move into Afghanistan would elicit a strong reaction from Washington. By late 1979, however, the Kremlin's America-watchers could see that détente did not have long to live. Republicans had stopped using the word "detente" in 1976, and no Republican presidential candidate for 1980 was about to go anywhere near the idea. Conservative opposition in the Senate had stalled the SALT II treaty even before Carter pulled it. Under the pressure from the right and from the crisis of confidence the continuing hostage situation in Iran was producing, Carter could hardly be expected to defend détente vigorously, if at all. Considering the circumstances, Moscow probably felt it had nothing to lose in antagonizing Washington by invading Afghanistan. Moreover, there were factions in the Soviet Union, just as in America, that had never liked détente. Just as many American conservatives held that the United States must not compromise with the evil of communism, so the hard-liners in the Soviet Union argued for continuing struggle against world capitalism. Elements of the Soviet military-industrial complex opposed détente for reasons similar to those that motivated the American defense industry and its allies.

If the Kremlin's move into Afghanistan and the Carter administration's response to that move killed détente, the election of Ronald Reagan in November 1980 buried it. Reagan's opponents often underestimated him. They spotted the shallowness of his understanding of the intricacies of international affairs and pronounced him a lightweight; they decried his skill with an anecdote and his mastery of the medium of television as Hollywood's revenge on Washington. Reagan's understanding was indeed often shallow, and his use of television and other public relations devices was certainly manipulative, but Reagan possessed a few unshakable convictions that resonated in the American public. In domestic affairs, he believed that government was too big and needed to be cut down to smaller size; in foreign affairs, he believed that communism was a powerfully malevolent force that aimed to surround and eventually strangle freedom.

Reagan attempted to frustrate the communists' designs by two methods. The first involved a large increase in American military spending. Between 1981 and 1985, the American defense budget rose by more than a third, in inflation-corrected terms. Whether the bigger budget bought Americans more defense was hard to say, but it certainly bought them more tanks, ships, and planes than ever. It also bought them the beginnings of a potentially revolutionary and definitely controversial system of outer space–based antimissile defense officially called the Strategic Defense Initiative and informally dubbed "Star Wars."

Reagan's second method was summarized by what came to be known as the Reagan Doctrine. Unlike previous presidential doctrines, Reagan's was not encapsulated in any single statement or at any single moment; instead it grew out of circumstances and ad hoc policies. The Reagan Doctrine took as its point of departure the common complaint of conservatives that the United States had allowed the Soviets to seize the initiative in the Cold War. The Soviets were constantly on the attack in Asia, Africa, and Latin America, supporting leftist guerrillas and other radicals, while the United States confined itself to defending the status quo. The Reagan Doctrine was a call for America to wrest the initiative away from the Soviet Union. Henceforth the United States would provide assistance to anticommunist guerrillas and other right-wing insurgents fighting against leftist governments. Success would mean more than merely holding the line against communist advance, which had been American policy since the days of the Truman Doctrine; success would mean rolling back the borders of the communist sphere.

Washington applied the Reagan Doctrine in several locations. In Angola, American aid assisted the antigovernment rebels of Jonas Savimbi's UNITA movement. In Afghanistan, American money and weapons helped the anti-Soviet *mujahideen* block the Kremlin's efforts to pacify the country under the rule of the Soviet Union's clients. In Cambodia, American support encouraged a coalition of anti-Vietnamese groups to resist Cambodia's forced inclusion in Hanoi's Southeast Asian sphere. In Nicaragua, American agents armed, trained, and bankrolled the anti-Sandinista *contra* rebels.

Reagan's critics lodged numerous complaints against the administration's antiradical campaign. Savimbi kept the unsavory company of the apartheid government of South Africa, and the tactics he employed in his struggle against the Angolan government were not the sort to suit the squeamish. The Afghan *mujahideen* included Islamic fundamentalists who were quite as intolerant as the most zealous followers of Iran's Khomeini. The Cambodian resistance embraced members of the Khmer Rouge, the murderous gang that under the leadership of the infamous Pol Pot had killed perhaps a third of the Cambodian people.

The most controversial aspect of the Reagan Doctrine, however, was the administration's backing for the Nicaraguan *contras*. Unlike the other three resistance movements, which had undeniable indigenous support, the contra army was largely a creation of the American CIA. American operatives trained the *contras*, American weapons armed the *contras*, and American money fed and clothed the *contras*. Even the *contras'* supporters conceded that if the United States pulled the plug, the *contra* army would probably dissolve. Moreover, the *contras* included many questionable characters who had been part of Somoza's hated National Guard; their actions during the war against the Sandinista government indicated that the ex-Somocistas had forgotten little of what had made them so hated. In the Reagan administration's support of the *contras*, Washington flouted international law, for example by mining the

Nicaraguan port of Corinto and rejecting the jurisdiction of the World Court when the Nicaraguan government complained to that tribunal. Many observers, both in America and in other countries, had difficulty accepting the Reagan administration's contention that the Sandinista government posed a serious threat to legitimate American interests in the Western Hemisphere. Many viewed the *contra* war as simply the latest manifestation of Yankee imperialism.

Whatever the weaknesses of the Reagan Doctrine, it had the signal advantage of keeping American troops mostly out of harm's way. Despite the big military buildup and despite some impassioned denunciations of the Kremlin by the president, including a widely remarked condemnation of the Soviet Union as an "evil empire," Reagan was careful to avoid direct confrontations with the Soviet Union. On two occasions during his early years in office, when the opportunity arose for a clear challenge to the Kremlin, Reagan demurred. In December 1981, following months of unrest in Poland instigated by the opposition Solidarity movement, the Polish military staged what amounted to a coup, imposed martial law, banned Solidarity, and imprisoned the opposition leaders. Although the Soviet hand was not so evident this time as it had been in Hungary in 1956 and Czechoslovakia in 1968, few Western observers doubted that the newly ruling Military Committee of National Salvation was doing Moscow's bidding, if only to forestall Moscow's doing the bidding itself. The Reagan administration responded with expressions of moral outrage, but its substantive reaction was markedly mild and was directed primarily against hapless Poland rather than against the Soviet Union. The administration's punishment of Moscow consisted chiefly of some minor economic sanctions, a refusal to renew a scientific exchange program, and a temporary denial of American landing privileges to the Soviet airline Aeroflot.

The second instance in which American outrage remained essentially rhetorical followed the shooting down of a Korean airliner by a Soviet fighter plane in Soviet airspace in August 1983. Reagan and other administration officials characterized the downing as an act of cold-blooded barbarism and murder, alleging that the Soviets had known that the straying aircraft was a civilian plane but had rocketed it anyway. Yet despite the American finger pointing and name calling, the administration confined its substantive response essentially to another suspension of Aeroflot landing privileges.

The one occasion on which the Reagan administration used direct military force in its campaign against what it deemed Soviet expansionism was an invasion of Grenada in the autumn of 1983. For two years the administration had registered concern regarding the efforts of Grenada's prime minister, Maurice Bishop, to improve relations with Cuba and the Soviet Union. When Havana and Moscow sent military aid to Grenada and assisted Bishop's government in the construction of what Washington judged a suspiciously long airport runway, one suitable for long-range military aircraft—or, as Bishop asserted, for long-range tourist airliners—Reagan complained publicly of a "Soviet-Cuban militarization of Grenada."

Washington's worries only increased when persons apparently more radical than Bishop overthrew the prime minister. Amid the uncertainty and confusion that followed the ouster, the Reagan administration discerned a threat to the safety of Americans in Grenada. Administration officials expressed particular worry about several hundred American students enrolled at a medical school in the capital, St. George's. The magnitude of the threat was debatable, but the administration was not in a mood to debate; it had no desire to risk an Iran-style hostage taking. At the same time, it had a great desire to reverse the leftward trend of events in Grenada and thereby demonstrate America's willingness to defend the Western Hemisphere against the expansion of leftist influence. Accordingly, the president ordered the invasion of Grenada.

Had the administration wanted merely to rescue the American students, the American marines might quickly have airlifted them out of the country and departed. Instead the troops stuck around to topple the Grenadian government. Doing so did not take very long since Grenada was a very small country. The Reagan administration trumpeted the action as a victory for freedom against totalitarianism. Although Washington sent some follow-up aid to help repair the damage the fighting caused, the people of the country remained about as poor as ever.

Deadly Labyrinth: Lebanon and Libya

Officials of the Reagan administration did not deny that the invasion of Grenada was supposed to send a message to the Soviets, the Cubans, and anyone else who might be watching that the United States had shaken its post-Vietnam aversion to use military force and could effectively defend American interests abroad. The message was particularly important at just this time since in certain other places American military force was proving particularly *in*effective. The Middle East afforded the most telling example of the ineffectiveness.

Although the Iranians had continued to hold the American hostages through the end of the Carter administration, they released the captives on the day of Reagan's inauguration. By this time the Khomeinists had securely fastened their hold on Iran, and the hostages no longer served much useful purpose. In certain ways they had become a distraction from the more important business of remaking Iran as an Islamic state. So the ruling powers in Teheran decided to let the Americans go.

This solved America's most pressing Middle Eastern problem, but others only grew more vexing. A war between Iran and Iraq that began in September 1980 endangered the flow of oil from the Persian Gulf to Western Europe, Japan, and the United States. Islamic fundamentalism challenged the few remaining pro-Western governments in the Middle East. A civil war in Lebanon was pulling in Lebanon's neighbors. The Lebanese war also threatened to spark another round of fighting between Arabs and Israelis, for though the

Israeli-Egyptian peace treaty of 1979 had calmed the southern front in the Arab-Israeli dispute, it had not led, as Carter and many others had hoped, to similar agreements between Israel and its other Arab neighbors. On the contrary, Egypt was treated as a pariah by other Arabs rather than as a model. Egypt could survive such treatment, being the largest and most important of the Arab countries, but the other obvious candidates for treaties with Israel— Jordan and Syria—did not enjoy such independence. Egyptian president Sadat's 1981 assassination by Muslim extremists sent an additional shudder through would-be Arab moderates. Besides, Israel was much more attached to the territory it had taken from Jordan (the West Bank) and Syria (the Golan Heights) than it had been to Egypt's Sinai.

The Lebanese civil war pushed a comprehensive peace agreement even farther into the distance. Lebanon had never really recovered from the woes that had triggered the 1958 American intervention there. The essential problem— the imbalance between the politically and economically dominant, and consequently conservative, Christian community in Lebanon and the more populous but relatively disenfranchised, and therefore more radical, Muslim community—had only gotten worse, partly on account of the Muslims' faster population increase and partly on account of the general radicalization of regional politics. The arrival of thousands of Palestinian guerrillas from Jordan after the 1970 Jordanian civil war aggravated Lebanon's troubles. The Palestine Liberation Organization used southern Lebanon as a base for operations against Israel. In addition, the PLO sided with Lebanon's radical Muslims, who took a strong anti-Israel stance, against the conservative Christians, who were more favorably disposed to their southern neighbor. In 1975 the lid blew off the situation, and Lebanon, once an oasis of cosmopolitan moderation in the Middle East, erupted into civil war. By early 1976 the government had lost control of most of the country to rival Christian and Muslim militia units.

As the opposing factions pounded away at each other, Lebanon's neighbors got worried. Syria's leaders, recalling the Ottoman days, had long considered Lebanon legitimately part of their own country, or at the minimum a country within their sphere of influence, but had nonetheless refrained from overt involvement in Lebanese affairs until the civil war began; a variety of more pressing problems relating mainly to Israel prevented Damascus from concentrating on Lebanon. But the prospective disintegration of Lebanon caused the Syrian government of Hafez al-Assad to reconsider. Nominally, Syria supported the PLO and its radical friends in Lebanon. As the leader, following the defection of Egypt, of the anti-Israel front, Syria could hardly do otherwise. But Assad did not much relish the idea of a PLO-dominated Lebanon, which might goad the Israelis into a war the Syrians did not want to fight. To prevent this happening, Assad in 1976 sent thousands of Syrian troops and hundreds of Syrian tanks into Lebanon. The Syrian forces fought on behalf of the Christians against the PLO and the Muslim militias. Yet rather than seeking a clear-cut victory for either side, the Syrians sought primarily to avert a collapse of the status quo.

Israel took more time to become directly involved in the Lebanese civil war, though Israel trigger fingers got itchy when the Syrians went in. As long as the conservative Christians had securely controlled Lebanon, Israel experienced little difficulty dealing with the Lebanese government. But after the PLO guerrillas arrived in Lebanon and serious fighting commenced in that country, the border between Israel and Lebanon heated up. The guerrillas lobbed mortar shells into northern Israel, and Israel fired back. Terrorist attacks on Israeli targets provoked Israeli forces to stage reprisals against PLO bases and associated sites—and some not so directly associated, such as the Beirut airport—in Lebanon. In most cases the Israelis hit quickly and retired back across the border. By 1982, however, the Israelis decided that their country's security required more sweeping measures. In June of that year, the Israeli army invaded Lebanon in large numbers. What the Israelis originally intended has remained a subject of considerable dispute. The official government line described "Operation Peace for Galilee" as designed to secure a PLO-free zone contiguous to Israel's northern border. But subsequent events indicated that at least some Israeli military leaders—Ariel Sharon, the defense minister, for one—had more ambitious aims, notably the annihilation of the PLO in Lebanon and the expulsion of the Syrian forces there.

The American government initially viewed developments in Lebanon with ambivalence. Some American officials interpreted the contest between Syria and Israel chiefly in terms of the reviving competition between the United States and the Soviet Union. Syria was a Soviet client, while Israel was an American client: therefore an Israeli victory over Syria would be an American victory over the Soviets. According to this reasoning, Washington ought to encourage, or at least not discourage, Israel from doing what the Israelis deemed necessary in Lebanon. Others in the American government saw the situation as more complicated. This latter group contended that a major Israeli offensive in Lebanon would irrevocably shatter what remained of the stability of that country, making peace impossible and opening the door to endless strife.

As Israeli forces drove deeper into Lebanon, everyone could see that Israel's ambitions extended beyond securing a PLO-free zone in southern Lebanon. When the Israelis reached Beirut, they undertook to crush the several thousand PLO guerrillas holed up in the mostly Muslim western portion of the Lebanese capital. Meanwhile Israel's soldiers inflicted stinging defeats on the Syrians they encountered, throwing some back into Lebanon's Bekaa Valley and trapping others in Beirut.

At this stage Reagan chose to side with those in his administration who opposed a major Israeli victory. The American president urged Menachem Begin to rein in Israel's troops and launched a diplomatic initiative to make it attractive for Begin to do so. Washington's pressure achieved its objective, but only after many more deaths in Beirut. In the deal that finally emerged, the PLO agreed to leave Lebanon for Algeria, Tunisia, and other radical parts of the Arab world, while the Israelis, following considerable last-minute pounding of PLO positions, agreed to let the guerrillas go. The United States provided a small peace-keeping force to help supervise the evacuation.

This second American intervention in Lebanon (the first since 1958) went smoothly. By mid-September more than eight thousand PLO fighters had left Beirut. Several thousand Syrian soldiers took the opportunity to go back to Syria. The American peace keepers left shortly afterward. The success of the operation and the ease with which the American troops extricated themselves allayed the fears of many in America who worried that the Reagan administration was getting the United States into something on the order of another Vietnam.

But subsequent events almost immediately rekindled those fears. During the third week of September 1982, assassins murdered the Christian president of Lebanon, Bashir Gemayel. Christian militia responded to the deed by entering two Palestinian refugee camps near Beirut and massacring some eight hundred Palestinians, including hundreds of women, children, and old people. Israeli troops occupying the area stood by and let the killing proceed.

The massacre at the Sabra and Shatila camps fulfilled the worst fears of Palestinian civilians in Lebanon who had watched with trepidation while the PLO guerrillas, their only reliable defenders, left the country; it also brought demands that American troops return to Beirut to prevent further score settling. The Reagan administration, anxious to deflect charges that it had pulled American troops out prematurely, agreed to reintroduce them.

The trouble was that this time the American marines had only a very ill-defined goal, one that possessed no obvious termination point. They would assist the Lebanese government to assert its authority over the country against the various groups currently fighting there. Just what this meant, how long it would take, and whether it was even possible, no one could say for certain.

The work went slowly but comparatively peacefully for the first few months; then things turned bad. Rebels objecting to American support for the Lebanese government began firing on American soldiers and American positions. In April 1983 a Shiite Muslim suicide bomber attacked the American embassy in Beirut, killing seventeen Americans and twenty-three other persons. Among the American dead were the CIA station chief in Beirut and the CIA's top Middle East analyst. The April attack drew the Americans more deeply into the fighting, both out of a desire for self-preservation and in hopes of quelling the rebellion. American units returned the fire of their attackers and engaged in limited efforts on behalf of the Lebanese government. The escalating American involvement only heightened rebel resentment against the American presence. In October 1983 a Shiite terrorist-martyr drove a truck filled with explosives into the American zone at the Beirut airport; when the truck exploded, it killed 241 American marines as well as 58 French soldiers.

If most Americans had perceived any significant worthy purpose in the marines' presence in Lebanon, this latest bombing might have produced a remember-Pearl-Harbor reaction. But Americans tended to find politics in Lebanon nearly incomprehensible, and few understood why American soldiers ought to get themselves killed there. After trying to put a brave face on the matter, the

Reagan administration announced in early 1984 that it was going to redeploy the American troops from Lebanon proper to American naval vessels offshore. Reagan contended that the shift did not indicate an abandonment of previous American objectives in Lebanon. "We're not bugging out," the president assured reporters. "We're just going to a little more defensible position." Whatever the explanation, most Americans were happy to see American soldiers shake the dust of Lebanon from their boots.

Pulling American troops out of Lebanon did not solve the growing problem of Middle Eastern terrorism, however. Until the early 1980s, Americans had rarely been the targets of terrorist attack. But after the American intervention in Lebanon, Americans began to be kidnapped off the streets of Beirut. In 1985 an American TWA airliner was hijacked. In 1986 an elderly American was brutally murdered and thrown overboard following the seizure of the Italian cruise ship *Achille Lauro*.

It is in the nature of terrorism that governments have difficulty responding to terrorist actions. The identity and affiliation of the terrorists are often uncertain. They are usually difficult or impossible to locate. And any reprisals against them usually entail a danger of killing or wounding uninvolved civilians. All these complications confronted the Reagan administration during the mid-1980s.

But the administration refused to be paralyzed. Unable to strike back at all the terrorists, the Reagan administration determined to go after those it *could*

Hijackers prepare to take an American plane on an unscheduled flight. *Reuters/ Bettmann Newsphotos*

reach. Among the most reachable appeared to be the Libyan government of Muammar Qaddafi. The Libyan leader had been a thorn in the American side ever since a 1969 coup that toppled the Libyan monarchy and left Qaddafi in charge. Qaddafi had thrown American military forces out of Libya and closed a conveniently located American air base in the country. He championed the causes of revolutionary movements around the world, including those dedicated to overthrowing moderate governments in Egypt, Jordan, Morocco, and Tunisia. He provided sanctuary to Palestinian terrorists of the Black September gang who killed eleven Israeli athletes at the 1972 Munich Olympic games. He was widely and plausibly suspected of complicity in a number of other terrorist attacks against Israel and countries of the West. Nor did it help his reputation in Western eyes that he established close ties to the Soviet Union.

During the last years of the Carter administration, Washington had singled Libya out for condemnation as aiding and abetting international terrorism; the Reagan administration went considerably further. The CIA under Reagan trained a group of anti-Qaddafi Libyan exiles with the evident intention of toppling Qaddafi's government or at least keeping him off balance. American ships and planes tested Libyan defenses, leading to an August 1981 skirmish in which two Libyan jets were shot down. When the Reagan administration, following the bombing of the American marine barracks at Beirut, was looking for a villain, Qaddafi fit the bill. Washington repeatedly denounced the Libyan leader for "state-sponsored terrorism" and asserted that Qaddafi's actions placed Libya beyond the pale of civilized international intercourse. After a pair of 1985 terrorist shooting sprees at the Rome and Athens airports, Reagan asserted that the American government had "irrefutable evidence" of Libya's involvement. Reagan again ordered the American Mediterranean fleet to undertake maneuvers along the Libyan coast; when Libyan shore batteries opened fire, the American task force responded by blasting Libyan radar installations and sinking or crippling several Libyan patrol boats, with dozens of casualties.

The climax of the confrontation came in April 1986. In the wake of a terrorist bombing of a nightclub in West Berlin in which two American soldiers were killed and more than two hundred other people were wounded, Reagan ordered a series of air raids against Libya. The evidence linking Qaddafi to the Berlin bombing was not exactly irrefutable, but the administration decided it was good enough to go on. American jets rocketed targets in Tripoli and Benghazi, causing considerable destruction. Whether the administration was trying specifically to hit Qaddafi remains a matter of dispute; the Reagan administration said it was not, yet American leaders certainly would not have been sorry to learn that one of the American rockets or bombs had the Libyan leader's name on it. Though they missed Qaddafi, the attacking aircraft killed dozens of Libyan civilians. Qaddafi claimed that the dead included his adopted daughter, but skeptics on Qaddafi did not rule out posthumous adoption.

The raid against Libya provoked considerable controversy, with many people in the United States and elsewhere complaining that by bombing a country with which it was not at war, the United States made itself hardly better than the terrorists it meant to combat. Most of the Arab governments, even some that privately detested Qaddafi and would have been happy to see a bomb land in his bedroom, railed publicly against the Reagan regime.

Gulf War I

The controversy would have been greater but for the fact that there was much bigger news from the Middle East: the war between Iran and Iraq. The first Gulf war began in 1980 (neutral observers often avoided the prefix "Persian" before Gulf out of deference to Iraq and the other Arabs who called the body of water in question the Arabian Gulf). Iraq's Saddam Hussein had decided to take the opportunity of Iran's revolutionary turmoil to renew the age-old struggle between Mesopotamia and Persia. The Iraqi government had initially greeted the fall of Iran's shah with satisfaction, not least because Baghdad had never thought much of the American strategy of arming the shah as an agent of the West in the gulf. But when Khomeini started preaching Islamic revolution not only for Iran but also for other Muslim countries, the secular Iraqi regime reassessed its position. And when Iran began supporting insurrectionary activities by Iraq's Kurdish and Shiite communities, culminating in assassination attempts against various Iraqi officials, Baghdad decided to teach the Iranians a lesson. Border firefights and artillery exchanges escalated until the end of September 1980, when Saddam Hussein ordered Iraqi troops across the frontier into Iran.

Americans, at that time still preoccupied by Teheran's holding of the American hostages, could not sympathize with Iran. Nor did American sympathy increase in the first two years of the war, during which Iraq generally got the better of the fighting. Washington essentially stayed out of the conflict during this period. But as the balance shifted in Iran's favor after 1982, the Reagan administration worried that Khomeini might actually have his way in toppling Saddam Hussein and the Baathists in Baghdad and replacing them with people more to his liking. The American government responded with a tilt in the direction of Iraq. Washington strengthened American representation in Baghdad and organized a blockade of weapons to Iran. Yet on the whole American participation in what was becoming an enormously bloody but indecisive stalemate remained distinctly limited. In the American view, so long as neither side seemed about to deliver a knockout blow to the other, and thereby threaten to dominate the region, there was no percentage in getting deeply involved.

The percentages changed toward the end of 1986 when Iran stepped up attacks on neutral shipping in the Persian Gulf. Iranian gunboats particularly targeted vessels calling at Kuwait, the oil-rich Arab emirate at the head of the gulf, whose government had been helping underwrite Iraq's war effort. Partly because they were so wealthy and partly because they often flaunted their wealth, the Kuwaitis counted few friends even among other Arabs. But countries that have oil do not need friends: they have customers, who tend to be more reliable. The Kuwaitis appealed for assistance to the international community, shrewdly including the Soviet Union along with the United States and other oil-consuming countries. When Moscow, glad for the chance of increased influence in the Persian Gulf, said it would oblige, the Reagan administration decided it could do no less. What the Kuwaitis had in mind was the reflagging of Kuwaiti ships under American registry and American naval protection. The Reagan administration quickly approved the reflagging plan. The Soviets by this time had already agreed to a similar scheme, but when Washington gave its assent, it pressured the Kuwaitis to back out of their arrangement with Moscow, and Kuwait partially complied. The Kuwaitis chartered a few Soviet ships for oil-carrying work rather than reflagging their own under the banner of the hammer and sickle.

The Reagan administration presented the reflagging operation as entirely in keeping with its official neutrality in the Iran-Iraq war. The Kuwaitis, after all, were neutral, even if their oil income, which was really what Teheran was trying to cut off, benefited the Arabs in Iraq and hurt the Persians of Iran. But no one watching had much difficulty determining where Washington's good wishes lay.

What little difficulty observers might have had diminished further in May 1987 when an Iraqi fighter plane patrolling the gulf fired on an American warship, the *Stark*. The attack severely damaged the *Stark* and killed thirty-seven American sailors. The Iraqis claimed mistaken identity, and the Reagan administration chose to accept the excuse, if only because no one in Washington could come up with a compelling reason why the Iraqis would hit the American ship deliberately. (Later, when Saddam Hussein remade himself into a villain, some observers would look for a deeper motive behind the *Stark* affair. They did not turn up much.)

The accident, if such it was, had two consequences. First, it convinced Iran that America remained the Great Satan, ready to side with almost anyone against the Islamic republic. Second, it warned the American Congress of the hazards of war duty in the Persian Gulf. The attack on the *Stark* came even before American warships actually commenced convoying the reflagged Kuwaiti tankers down the gulf; what those warships would encounter once they got in the thick of the tanker war was anyone's guess.

The reflagging and convoying operation turned out to be relatively uneventful. The Western Europeans led by Britain and France sent naval vessels to the gulf to help out. This expanded Iran's target list in case the Iranians decided to start shooting at ships defending the tanker traffic. It also alleviated complaints in America about American sailors defending oil destined for European cars and generating facilities. In September 1987 an American ship seized an Iranian craft caught in the act of laying mines, and a month later American forces retaliated for an Iranian missile attack on one of the reflagged tankers by destroying an Iranian communications post on an offshore oil platform;

but neither the Reagan administration nor the Iranian government particularly wanted these skirmishes to expand into a real war.

Reagan had the 1988 elections to worry about, not for himself but for the Republican party and his heir apparent, George Bush. And though Iran continued to top the American list of disliked foreign countries, almost no voters looked favorably on a war against the ayatollah and his followers.

As for the Iranians, they had a full plate dealing with Iraq. The Iranian economy was slumping drastically after seven years of fighting. Public enthusiasm for the war likewise was sagging. Starting early in 1988 and continuing through the spring, Iraq bombarded Iranian cities with missiles; these attacks did not do much for Iranian morale either. In April Iraqi troops recaptured the strategically situated Faw Peninsula, reversing one of the principal Iranian gains in the war to date.

Yet certain radical elements in Iran saw hostility against the United States as a device for maintaining enthusiasm for the war and preventing counter-revolutionary backsliding. The Iranian Revolutionary Guards stepped up minelaying activities, producing an explosion against an American destroyer. Washington ordered reprisals against a pair of Iranian oil platforms in the gulf.

The American policy of tit for tat continued into the early summer of 1988. During that time it occasioned relatively little controversy outside Iran. In July, however, a tragic accident (according to Washington) or mass murder (according to Teheran) produced a new round of questioning of American actions in the gulf. On July 3 radar operators aboard the American destroyer *Vincennes* spotted an aircraft flying out of Iran on what seemed a threatening trajectory. The American ship had just engaged Iranian gunboats, and the officers and crew were nervous. The captain ordered rockets fired and watched them destroy the plane, only to discover that it was an Iranian airliner carrying nearly three hundred passengers. All aboard died. The Iranians protested loudly, and many observers in other countries, even among those who did not like Khomeini, sympathized.

The incident would have produced greater repercussions than it did had the Iranian government not finally decided at just this time that enough was enough in the war against Iraq. On July 18, after nearly eight years of one of the most futile conflicts of the twentieth century, Iran accepted a United Nations cease-fire resolution, and the first Gulf war ended.

There was a curious sidebar to the story of American involvement in the Iran-Iraq war, one that was very embarrassing to the Reagan administration. In the autumn of 1986 a Lebanese magazine broke a story of American arms sales to Iran—sales that had taken place during the period when the United States was pressing its allies to block the sale of weapons to Teheran. The reason for this double-dealing, it turned out, was that the Reagan administration hoped to purchase the freedom of Americans who had been kidnapped in the previous few years by pro-Iranian factions in Lebanon. This made the tale doubly embarrassing since the administration had repeatedly declared in the most uncompromising terms that it would strike no deals with the kidnappers.

The arms sales originally had been proposed for other purposes. For some time American officials had pondered the possibility of improving relations with Iran. In principle the idea made sense. Whether Americans liked it or not, Iran remained the largest power in the Persian Gulf, and American interests could only suffer if Iran continued indefinitely to be estranged from the United States. In practice, though, there was serious doubt whether Iran was ready to reciprocate the American desire for improved relations and whether American efforts at improvement would not simply blow up in Washington's face. The doubters included a number of top administration officials, including Secretary of State George Shultz and Secretary of Defense Caspar Weinberger.

Nonetheless, the Reagan administration went ahead, with the staff of the National Security Council leading the way. Robert McFarlane, the national security adviser, proposed allowing the Iranian government to purchase American military equipment for use in its war against Iraq. The sales would be top secret since neither party to the arrangement wished to drop its outward attitude of opposition to the other. McFarlane won the president over to the project. Evidently, a persuasive part of McFarlane's argument was the suggestion that the arms sales might facilitate the release of some of the American hostages in Lebanon.

In August 1985 the first planeload of American arms—ninety-six antitank missiles—landed in Teheran. But no hostages were freed as a result. It was unclear whether there had been a mixup or whether the Iranians were playing the Americans for fools. Assuming the former, the administration sent another shipment, this time of more than four hundred missiles. The next day one American hostage turned up free near the American embassy in Beirut.

Although a single hostage for more than five hundred missiles might have seemed niggardly, the administration went ahead with more shipments. One reason was Reagan's sympathy for the plight of the hostages and their families and his strong desire to see the captives safe at home. Another reason had nothing to do with hostages, Iran, or even the Middle East. Certain White House officials, particularly National Security Council staffer Oliver North, had found a novel use for the profits from the arms sales to Iran. By this time American support of the *contra* rebels in Nicaragua had become highly controversial. In 1984 Congress approved an amendment (the Boland amendment) to the fiscal 1985 appropriations bill, blocking funds for the *contras'* military operations, and the president signed the bill into law. But North and his associates refused to be bound by congressional disapproval. They solicited and received donations from *contra*-friendly individuals and foreign governments. And they diverted funds from the Iranian arms sales to the *contras*.

This combination of factors kept the secret sales alive. Through the autumn of 1986, the arms continued to flow to Iran, supplemented by American satellite intelligence regarding the disposition of Iraq's military forces in the Gulf war. Three American hostages were released during this period, but several more remained in captivity.

In November 1986 the arms-for-hostages scheme came to a screeching halt when the Lebanese magazine spilled the story. Washington tried, unsuccessfully, to deny the report. The Iranian government was no less embarrassed, and those persons involved in the sales on the Iranian side had some fast explaining to do. Teheran reasserted its passion for the objectives of the Islamic revolution and denounced the American Great Satan in terms more sulfurous than ever.

The Double Deficit Crunch

Amazingly, the Iran-*contra* scandal failed to do much damage to Ronald Reagan's reputation. Most Americans apparently were willing to believe that Reagan's subordinates had planned and carried out the operation on their own, with little or no involvement on the part of the president himself. Reagan's critics coined a term for the way blame for the mistakes and follies of his administration failed to stick to him: they called him the "Teflon president."

Reagan's critics wondered hardly less at the way he evaded responsibility for what many observers judged to be the most grievous failing of the American government during the Reagan years. Running for president in 1980 as a good Republican, candidate Reagan had decried the unbalanced federal budgets of the Carter administration. Indeed, Carter's *were* unbalanced and, by historical American standards, egregiously so. But they were nothing compared to the deficits that became standard practice during Reagan's presidency.

The big federal budget deficits resulted from increased government spending without increased taxes to cover the costs. The first principle of Reaganomics—the name given to the economic policies of the Reagan administration—was that tax rates were too high and needed to be lowered. Congress can rarely resist the temptation to cut taxes when a president makes tax cuts an issue, and it did not resist now. At the same time, the administration, with similar congressional concurrence, commenced its big defense buildup. The cuts in income and corporate tax rates and the increases in defense spending were not entirely responsible for the ballooning of the federal budget deficit during the 1980s; federal spending on other programs—social security and health care, for instance—contributed considerably. But the net result was a federal budget that ran chronically and deeply in the red and a federal debt that tripled during the Reagan years.

Many economists warned that the federal deficit would have a seriously debilitating effect on the American economy. Funding the debt required dipping into savings: either the savings of the American people or the savings of foreigners. If American savings funded the debt, those savings could not be devoted to the investment necessary to make the economy grow in the future. If foreign savings funded the debt, the American economy would become at least partly dependent on the willingness of foreigners to keep buying American bonds. And in either case a big debt would tend to push up interest rates, crimping the economy across the board. It would also lessen the flexibility of the American government to deal with unexpected events and unanticipated expenses. As things turned out, the debt was funded by domestic and foreign savings alike. Both American and foreign investors valued the safety of American government bonds, which had the highest rating of any securities available.

Certain foreigners, especially Japanese and Germans, had the additional incentive of needing to find some place to put the dollars they were earning from exports to America in excess of the dollars they were spending on imports from America. During the 1980s the United States began to run consistent trade deficits for the first time during the twentieth century. American exports grew during this period but not as fast as imports from foreign countries. The largest beneficiaries of the resulting imbalance were Japan and West Germany, which consequently found themselves with more dollars than they required. The glut of dollars depressed the value of the American currency relative to other currencies (in the post-Bretton Woods regime of floating exchange values), thereby partly alleviating the problem: American exports became comparatively less expensive, while foreign imports to the United States became more expensive. This kept the trade deficit lower than it would have been otherwise, but a sizable and growing trade shortfall remained.

In the mid-1980s the United States slipped from being a net creditor of the rest of the world to being a net debtor. Not since the First World War had Americans been in the position of owing more to foreigners than foreigners owed to them. Many people found this predicament troubling. When the dollar-rich foreigners repatriated some of their dollars by purchasing American companies and American real estate, many Americans found this troubling as well. They did not like seeing the Japanese buy up such American landmarks as Rockefeller Center in New York, nor did they like the idea that decisions affecting thousands of American jobs might be made in Hamburg. Other persons contended that the nationality of capital had become irrelevant in the modern era. The new owners of the Rockefeller Center could hardly move it to Tokyo. Neither would the German directors of firms with factories in the United States be less concerned with the bottom line than the directors of American firms were. If anything, that foreign buyers were available for ailing American businesses helped preserve American jobs. Finally, those who thought the foreign debt issue was being overblown argued that the more foreigners purchased American businesses, American property, and American securities, the greater would be their stake in American prosperity; as partners in the American economy, the foreigners could only wish America well.

What almost no one questioned, however, was that the United States could not run large trade deficits forever without a decline in American living standards. For many years Americans had watched companies shift production from America to foreign countries with lower wage rates; Americans had hoped and usually expected that the jobs lost would be replaced by other and better jobs. But this confidence eroded in the face of the mounting American trade deficits, which demonstrated a decreasing capacity to compete on world markets. Only if Americans competed successfully would they be able to earn the money needed to support themselves in the style to which they had become accustomed.

New Kid on the Bloc: Gorbachev, the End of the Cold War, and the Demise of the Soviet Union

While Americans worried about their budget and trade deficits, the inhabitants of the other superpower could only wish they had such troubles. The 1980s were a sorely trying time for the Soviets. The first half of the decade was particularly hard on the country's top leadership. Three Soviet head men died within three years; there had been only four others during the entire period since the 1917 revolution. Leonid Brezhnev died in November 1982, giving way to Yuri Andropov, who died in February 1984, handing the leadership to Konstantin Chernenko, who died in March 1985, bequeathing power to Mikhail Gorbachev. There the torch passing terminated for the time being. Gorbachev was young, by Kremlin standards, and hardy, clever, and determined. Gorbachev saw what many of those around him also had seen but were afraid to admit: that the Soviet system was staggering toward its grave under the weight of a sclerotic bureaucracy and an outmoded ideology. The bureaucrats still paid lip service to the teachings of Marx and Lenin, but they did so far less out of conviction than out of an understanding that this was what legitimized their continued hold on power—and on the perquisites and privileges that power brought with it.

Gorbachev unleashed a second Russian revolution, though he intended merely to reform the Soviet system. Under the twin rubrics of *glasnost* (openness) and *perestroika* (restructuring), he challenged both the rule of the bureaucrats and the revered status of communist ideology. Critics were allowed, even encouraged, to identify deficiencies in the Soviet system. A few bold persons did so at first, often hesitantly. That they were not crushed for their temerity emboldened others. Soon Soviet publications were filled with stories of a system that served not the people in whose name it governed but those who did the governing. Soviet citizens had long since learned to be cynical, yet some of the revelations shocked even them. With each tale of corruption, public support for the system slipped further.

The point of *glasnost* was not simply to discredit corrupt bureaucrats; the point was to jolt the system sufficiently that *perestroika*'s restructuring could take place. Like a person renovating a house, Gorbachev understood that he had to do some tearing out before he could start rebuilding. Unfortunately for Gorbachev, he discovered, as many reformers had before him, that it was far easier to tear things down than to build things up. *Glasnost* continued at an accelerating pace, but *perestroika* never got far, at least not under Gorbachev.

As part of his effort to relieve the strain on the Soviet system, the Soviet general secretary adopted a favorable attitude toward arms control with the

United States. Heretofore the Soviet Union had consistently attempted to match America in nuclear strength. The Americans built the first atomic bomb; the Soviets built the second. The Americans detonated a hydrogen device in 1953; the Soviets did likewise in 1954. The Americans deployed intercontinental missiles in the late 1950s and 1960s; the Soviets followed shortly. After America introduced multiple warheads in the 1970s, the Soviet Union adopted the same technology. Now the Americans were embarked on another arms buildup, potentially including novel and exorbitantly expensive space-based weapons. Maybe the United States could afford such spending, but Gorbachev did not think the Soviet Union could. He decided to try to avert another round of the weapons race through arms control agreements.

During the early 1980s, the Reagan administration had offered a series of arms control proposals relating to intermediate-range missiles in Europe. The proposals were part of an effort to persuade the governments of the NATO allies to accept deployment in their territories of American Pershing II missiles and Tomahawk cruise missiles. Several of the allied governments were somewhat reluctant, facing considerable political pressure to reject the new missiles. An earlier clash over the so-called neutron bomb had sensitized large numbers of people, particularly in West Germany, to nuclear issues. In that case the Carter administration had initially ordered the development of a weapon that would emit huge and deadly doses of radiation but produce little blast or heat. This was supposed to make the weapon usable in defense of German cities, for example, NATO defenders could obliterate invading Soviet troops without obliterating the cities and towns they were invading. But the neutron bomb was loudly criticized as being the ultimate capitalist weapon, capable of killing people while preserving property. Despite the political uproar, the West German government gave its qualified approval to the project—only to have Carter change his mind and drop the idea.

Subsequent spats did not improve the climate in Europe for acquiescence in American initiatives. During the years of détente, Western European exporters had developed some close business connections to the Soviet Union and other countries of the Eastern bloc. They were reluctant to sever these connections when the Americans canceled détente in favor of renewed confrontation. In 1981 this reluctance produced a fierce wrangle between the Europeans and Washington over a proposed natural gas pipeline from the Soviet Union to Western Europe that would deliver gas to the West at attractive prices and diminish European dependence on Middle Eastern oil. The Reagan administration did its best to block the pipeline, arguing that the gas sales would give the Soviets excessive influence over the European governments. Washington went so far as to forbid European subsidiaries of American companies to supply critical parts for the construction of the pipeline. Several European leaders—including Margaret Thatcher of Britain and Helmut Kohl of Germany, conservatives who normally saw eye to eye with Reagan—objected vigorously to what they perceived as unwarranted interference in the affairs of their countries.

It was against this background of alliance unease that the Reagan administration sought to introduce the new Pershings and cruise missiles. The NATO council had agreed in principle in 1979 that the Europeans would accept the new missiles to offset a recent and continuing upgrading of Soviet intermediate missiles. But the agreement was conditioned on an effort by the United States to achieve an arms control pact that would remove the threat posed by the new Soviet SS-20s. In fulfillment of this condition, the Reagan administration offered what was commonly called the "zero option." According to this plan, the United States would forgo deployment of the Pershings and cruise missiles if the Soviet Union would dismantle its SS-20s.

Almost no one took the zero option at face value. The Soviets rejected it out of hand, noting that it required them to give up a weapons system that by now

During his first term, Ronald Reagan concentrated on building weapons; during his second, on scrapping them. During his first term, he disdained summit conferencing; during his second, he set a record for most meetings by an American president with his Soviet counterpart. Mikhail Gorbachev made Reagan's reversals possible. *AP/Wide World Photos*

was essentially in place in exchange for a system Americans and their allies had yet to build. Given the widespread popular opposition to the Pershings in the NATO countries, the NATO system might well never be constructed at all.

The Soviet rejection did not surprise the Reagan administration. The hard-liners who at this point controlled Reagan arms control policy were more interested in getting the new American missiles into Europe than in getting the Soviet missiles out of the Soviet Union. As Moscow pointed out, there was an imbalance in the American proposal, for whereas the Soviet missiles in question targeted only the European countries and not the United States, the American missiles were capable of hitting the Soviet Union. What Moscow saw as a drawback, the Reagan administration saw as an advantage. The zero option did, however, serve its political purpose of meeting the terms of the 1979 NATO agreement, and despite some continued misgivings in Europe, as evidenced by widespread antinuclear protests in West Germany, Britain, and elsewhere, the American missiles were duly deployed.

One result was that by the time Gorbachev achieved power in the Kremlin, the zero option had gained much appeal for Moscow. Now a zero solution would involve trading real missiles for real missiles rather than real for hypothetical. For this same reason, the proposal had lost much of the appeal it had once held for the Reagan administration. Consequently, when Gorbachev announced that the Soviet Union accepted the zero principle, the American administration began backing and filling. As part of this retreat, the Pentagon launched a flanking maneuver by proposing to eliminate *all* ballistic missiles, not just intermediate ones.

Gorbachev then raised the stakes by recommending the elimination of all nuclear *weapons,* not merely those delivered by ballistic missiles. Although this was even more utopian than the Pentagon's proposal, which no one took seriously either, it indicated Gorbachev's intention to keep up the pressure for real arms control. At a summit meeting with Reagan in Iceland in November 1986, Gorbachev urged the American president to join him in an effort to "wrench arms control out of the hands of the bureaucrats." The Americans had already rejected his plan to eliminate all nuclear weapons, but as another counteroffer he suggested substantial cuts in heavy missiles—in which the Soviet Union enjoyed a sizable advantage over the United States. In other respects as well, he tailored his proposal to suit American inclinations.

In essence Gorbachev said yes to arms control faster than the Americans could say no. Paradoxically, his very cooperativeness disposed some American officials to dig their heels in all the more. With the Kremlin in a compromising mood, they argued, the United States should see just how far the Soviet Union would go to accommodate America. But after further Soviet concessions and the departure to private life of some of the hardest of the Reagan administration's hard-liners, the American president decided to accept victory. In December 1987 at a summit meeting in Moscow, Reagan and Gorbachev put their signatures to a treaty eliminating the intermediate missiles. After Congress convened the following January, the Senate approved the INF (intermediate nuclear forces) treaty by a wide margin.

The INF treaty formed the centerpiece of a remarkable turnaround in Soviet-American relations. To some extent the resumption of détente was America's doing: after the staunchly anti-Soviet approach of his first term, Reagan softened somewhat in his second term. But to a larger degree the responsibility for the improvement in relations belonged to Gorbachev. The Soviet general secretary decided that continued confrontation with the United States was a losing game. American leaders had long assumed, and often declared openly, that the Soviet economy could not keep up with the American economy; sooner or later the Soviets would crack under the stress of the competition. When the Soviets managed to stay in the race for nearly four decades, American analysts explained Moscow's perseverance as a consequence of its ability to squeeze the Soviet people far harder than Washington could squeeze Americans. In the mid-1980s Gorbachev decided that the squeezing had to stop lest the entire Soviet system be wrung completely dry.

Cutting nuclear weapons promised only modest savings, however. Indeed, it was the inexpensiveness of nuclear weapons compared to conventional forces that had caused NATO to rely on nuclear weapons to counter the Warsaw Pact's conventional edge. If Gorbachev was to achieve big savings, he needed to look to cuts in the conventional forces of the Soviet Union. This would require scaling back Soviet commitments beyond its borders.

The first scaling back took place in Afghanistan. After almost a decade of unsuccessful Soviet effort to suppress the resistance to the pro-Moscow Kabul regime, Gorbachev chose to concede failure and give up. Prior to *glasnost* the Kremlin had been able to hide the true cost in money and lives of the Afghan intervention, but as the glare of public attention revealed the thousands of lives and millions of rubles Afghanistan had swallowed up, the war there became politically insupportable. In the early part of 1988, Gorbachev announced that Soviet troops would leave Afghanistan by the spring of 1989. He proved as good as his word, and when the snows melted in the passes of Afghanistan's mountains in 1989, the Soviets were gone. (Contrary to many expectations, Soviet protégé Najibullah held on to power in Kabul for three years, before finally being run out by the *mujahideen*, who took to squabbling among themselves.)

Liquidating the Afghanistan operation trimmed the Kremlin's costs considerably, but Afghanistan was light beer compared to the heavier brew of Eastern Europe. For forty years Moscow had underwritten the defense of East Germany, Poland, Hungary, Czechoslovakia, Romania, and Bulgaria. More precisely, Moscow had underwritten the defense of the *governments* of those countries. Everyone realized, and the Kremlin twice proved, that the Red Army troops in Eastern Europe would be used against the people of those countries if they challenged the hold of pro-Moscow regimes. Just as Gorbachev calculated that an arms race with the United States and the occupation of Afghanistan were bad investments, so he judged the continued occupation of Eastern Europe.

The first sign of a loosening of the Soviet grip was Gorbachev's encouragement of Eastern European reformers who sought to apply the concepts of *glasnost* and *perestroika* to their own countries. During the summer of 1989, Gorbachev rejected the Brezhnev Doctrine of socialist solidarity enforced by Moscow. He asserted that any interference in the internal affairs of other countries was "inadmissable." A Gorbachev spokesman summarized the Kremlin's new attitude as the "Sinatra doctrine": they do it their way.

To a certain extent Gorbachev and other reformers in the Soviet Union hoped to use the Eastern European countries as laboratories in the difficult process of refurbishing communist rule. Even the least perceptive observer could tell that change would bring pain; perhaps the East Germans, the Poles, and the others could figure out how to minimize the pain.

To a greater degree Gorbachev wanted to trim the economic and political costs associated with maintaining a large defense establishment. A big Red Army absorbed lots of money. At the same time, it helped sustain the power of some of the most adamant opponents of Soviet reform. Cutting the army down to size would also cut the right-wing generals down to size.

Not surprisingly, the generals did not like the idea, and the ruling regimes in Eastern Europe liked it even less. The East German government of Erich Honecker, for example, stoutly resisted the importation of Soviet ideas regarding reform. But without the backing of Moscow, the pressure from below for change grew too great to squelch, and the East German Communist party was forced to dump Honecker in favor of the smoother Egon Krenz. In Poland the Communist party tried to buy off the opposition Solidarity movement with elections for a minority of seats in the national parliament. The Communist party of Czechoslovakia staged a palace coup, toppling the hated old guard in favor of a new guard that no one had yet learned to hate. Nicolae Ceauşescu of Romania ordered his troops to fire on demonstrators.

Yet once Gorbachev made clear that the Eastern Europeans were truly on their own—that, as Soviet foreign minister Eduard Shevardnadze declared in October 1989, every country of the East bloc had "a right to an absolute, absolute freedom of choice"—the ruling regimes crumbled. Demonstrations demanding fundamental change erupted all along the Eastern European front. Rioters in Leipzig and East Berlin denounced the Krenz government and insisted on the right to travel to the other halves of Berlin and Germany. The government capitulated. In November 1989, in a gesture that more than any other symbolized the changes sweeping Eastern Europe, the East German government opened the gates in the Berlin Wall; subsequently it tore the wall down. In Czechoslovakia the Communist government commenced negotiations with the main opposition group, Civic Forum, an odd collection of intellectuals, students, religious dissenters, and economic reformers. The Communists agreed to let Civic Forum join the government. But before long Civic Forum had essentially taken over the government, with playwright Vaclac Havel as president and Alexander Dubček, the deposed architect of the liberalization of 1968, as leader of the legislature.

The transition in Czechoslovakia was called the "velvet revolution," after the relatively soft manner in which it occurred; by contrast, the change in Romania was brutally hard. The dictator Ceauşescu vehemently denounced

Previously, loitering atop the Berlin Wall was a capital offense, punishable by summary execution by East German border guards. But in 1989 the rules regarding the wall and much else in Germany changed. *AP/Wide World Photos*

the weak wills of the other communists in Eastern Europe and vowed to stand firm against challenges to his own rule. Ceauşescu's defiance cost him his life. After widespread fighting broke out in Romanian cities, key portions of the military defected to the opposition. Angry at the dictator and simultaneously afraid of him, some of the defectors arrested Ceauşescu and his wife and on Christmas day 1989 executed them for crimes against the Romanian people.

Both as a consequence of and as a contributor to the overthrow of communist rule in Eastern Europe, the Soviet government negotiated terms of withdrawal of Red Army troops from that region. Gorbachev might have been happy to pull all the troops home at once, except that he had no place to house them and no jobs for those he would have to muster out. The last thing he needed was a dozen armored divisions freezing in tents outside Moscow or a hundred thousand disgruntled veterans looking for work and longing for the good old days of Stalin or even Brezhnev. For their part, though the Eastern Europeans wished the Soviets would leave as soon as possible, they hesitated to press the issue. Gorbachev was the person who had put all the changes in motion, and if he needed more time, he could have it.

Moscow's relinquishment of control of Eastern Europe, coming after the INF treaty between the United States and the Soviet Union and after the various other manifestations of warmer Soviet-American relations, indicated a sea change in international affairs. In headline shorthand, the change would be called the end of the Cold War. But just as the term Cold War had been misleading from the start, to say that it had ended was hardly more enlightening. The Cold War was simply a competition between two superpowers and their respective clients and allies. It was partly ideological and partly geopolitical. It was not a war and therefore did not have a readily identifiable end, the way real wars do. When most real wars end, the two sides that have been shooting at each other stop shooting, more or less all at once. In the superpower competition between the United States and the Soviet Union, the nature of the competition changed over a long period of time. In the late 1940s the possibility of a regular war between the United States and the Soviet Union, triggered perhaps by events involving divided Germany, seemed dangerously real. Starting in the early 1950s, the developing nuclear stalemate required the superpowers to confine their belligerence to proxy fights, as in Korea and later Vietnam. During the 1960s and 1970s, the mushrooming of the nonaligned movement and the emergence of such new centers of power as OPEC rendered the superpower competition increasingly irrelevant to the lives of the mass of people on earth. By the late 1980s, both superpowers were in decline: the United States relatively so, compared to such allies as Germany and Japan; the Soviet Union absolutely so. The Soviets decided to acknowledge their decline and set about trying to reverse it. Their efforts to do so constituted what was generally called the end of the Cold War.

The end of the Cold War rendered all sorts of things suddenly possible; the most momentous, at least on first appearance, was the reunification of Germany. The German question had spawned many of the bad feelings between the United States and the Soviet Union at the end of the Second World War, and the division of Germany had provided the pattern for the division of the rest of the Continent—not to mention the division of Korea and Vietnam. Although the Atlantic allies had supported West Germany's claim to the rest of Germany, in practice they had not done anything to end the division of the country; Germany's neighbors remembered all the trouble Germany had inflicted on the Continent subsequent to the first unification in 1871, and they were in no hurry to put Germany back together again. Skeptics were sometimes heard to explain that the division of Europe between the superpowers was not about America and the Soviet Union but about Germany. The Americans kept an eye on the West Germans, while the Soviets watched over the East Germans.

On account of this history, both Washington and Moscow, and both sides' allies viewed the approach of German reunification with wary reserve. Yet the West could not easily retract its support for unification, even if for years that support had been chiefly rhetorical, given in the comfortable belief that unification was impossible. As for the Soviets, since they had recently cut East Germany adrift, they were in no position to prevent the East Germans from getting back together with the West Germans. Optimists on the subject of Germany argued that forty years of democracy in (West) Germany had cured the Germans of their authoritarian tendencies. The optimists also held that the Germans had learned an important lesson since the 1930s: that economic expansion paid much better returns in the long run than military expansion. All the same, there were plenty of people—French, Dutch, Belgians, British, Poles, Czechs, Russians, and some Americans—who could not put their worries aside.

As matters turned out, German unification was a more difficult process than most people expected. Politically, the two half countries retied the knot in October 1990 amid great fanfare and much speechmaking; but economically the rejoining required more time and an enormous investment of resources. The economy of the former East Germany was a disaster—though less of a disaster than the other Eastern European economies—and bringing it up to speed with the former West German economy meant slowing that latter economy down substantially. The fact that reunification occurred amid a slackening of world demand for German exports (and everyone else's exports, too: the early 1990s witnessed a global recession) did not help matters. But it did ease some of the foreign fears since taking care of business at home promised to keep the Germans from acting too bumptious abroad for at least a few years.

Not surprisingly, many Germans who were enthusiastic about reunification lauded Gorbachev, the man who had made it possible, as a hero; in fact, by 1990 the Soviet president was considerably more popular in Germany and many other foreign countries than he was at home. Domestically, Gorbachev found himself blasted from two sides at once. Soviet reformers castigated him for moving too slowly toward democracy and a postcommunist market economy, while the old guard denounced him for moving at all. The hard-liners in the Kremlin had been upset at the loss of the Soviet Union's Eastern European empire; they became utterly outraged when the nationalist feelings unleashed by *glasnost* and *perestroika* started to create fractures right beneath the Soviet Union's feet. The Soviet Baltic republics of Lithuania, Latvia, and Estonia showed the first separatist impulses. Those three countries had enjoyed an independent existence between the world wars and were forcibly annexed to the Soviet Union only in 1940. The Baltic peoples had never accepted their Soviet status and commonly looked on their countries as occupied territory. With Moscow letting go of the Eastern European countries, the Baltics clamored for their own independence.

Gorbachev resisted for a time, partly from his own disinclination to preside over the dissolution of the world's largest country and partly to placate the old guard. When several of the other non-Russian republics within the Soviet Union joined the Baltics in demanding independence, the old guard really took fright. In August 1991 a group of generals and reactionary civilian leaders staged a coup. They arrested Gorbachev and commenced to roll back his reforms. But the coup came unglued when Boris Yeltsin, the recently elected president of the Russian republic and a rival of Gorbachev, defied the conspirators and rallied the Russian people around him. Gorbachev was restored to office, but Yeltsin emerged from the fiasco the true winner.

During the next few months, the Soviet Union fell to pieces. The coup discredited the Soviet government, and power passed to the governments of the republics. The economic improvement that Gorbachev had held out as the goal of *perestroika* failed to materialize; indeed, living standards in the Soviet Union declined markedly. A general feeling developed that the republics could hardly do worse on their own than as part of the union. One by one the republics expanded their prerogatives at the expense of the central government. Gorbachev tried to slow the disintegration, but fewer people with each passing month listened to what he had to say. Finally in December 1991 the republics declared the Soviet Union dissolved.

Europe Uniting

The dissolution of the Soviet Union took place alongside a contrary process in Western Europe. By the standards of the other continents, Europe has long been divided into an unusually large number of separate political states. With more than two dozen major countries plus a handful of ministates, the second smallest continent has the largest number of sovereign countries outside of many-times-bigger Africa. Over the centuries, a variety of unifiers noticed that this multiplication of sovereignty was inefficient and dangerous. Julius Caesar and his successors brought most of Europe into the Roman empire; Charlemagne appropriated some of the forms of the Roman empire in building his own; Napoleon aimed to unify Europe under French rule; Hitler wanted to do so under German. Not everyone thought force would be necessary to convince the many governments of Europe to subordinate their separate interests to a larger, continental good. The English Enlightenment philosopher and economist Jeremy Bentham proposed a European parliament and a continental army. Jean-Jacques Rousseau, the French exponent of the social contract, called for a European confederation. The French utopian socialist Henri Saint-Simon supplied a charter for a United States of Europe.

But the various would-be unifiers encountered insuperable problems. The empire builders had to contend with the fact that most of the people they tried to conquer did not desire to be conquered. Their empires had to be held together by force. The successful imperialists succeeded in supplying the force for a while, but eventually they or their successors ran out of energy, and the empires fell apart. The unifiers-by-choice accomplished even less. Most of them spoke and wrote during the age of growing nationalism—whose violent excesses were what they were offering an alternative to—and few people wished to bury their national identities in an indistinct, unfamiliar, and polyglot international entity.

Yet some progress toward European unity did occur during the nineteenth century through the back door of trade. Or perhaps it was the front door. The international forces that operate between countries can be grouped into two categories: those that bring people together across frontiers and those that divide them. Broadly speaking, the bringing-together, or integrative, forces have usually been economic. Of these, international trade has been the most important. Trade creates a community of interest among those involved: because trade is voluntary, everyone involved comes out ahead. (If it is not voluntary, it is called theft. And anyone who does not come out ahead soon stops trading.) On the other hand, the most important of the divisive forces have been political in nature. Politics—particularly the nationalistic style of politics characteristic of the modern era—has been responsible for the borders between countries and for most wars.

Under the mercantilist philosophy of the eighteenth century, trade was subordinated to politics; but during the nineteenth century, the free-trading school pioneered by Adam Smith, which placed trade above politics, gained ground. The free traders' victory in Britain during the mid-nineteenth century advanced the cause of European unity by demonstrating that mercantilist protection was not a prerequisite to the prosperity of a large country. At the time, though, the demonstration did not get far beyond Britain's borders; most of the rest of Europe clung to the mercantilist model.

The hopes of European unifiers revived briefly after the First World War. The League of Nations embodied the fundamental ideals of many of the unifiers, even carrying the notion of unity beyond the continental level to the global. But the collapse of the League and the rise of the fascists knocked European unity back a generation.

The emergence of the bipolar order after 1945 had a dual effect on the concept of European unity. One part of the effect was negative: by dividing the Continent between the two superpowers, the bipolar order placed continent-wide unity beyond the pale of practical possibility. The other part was positive: the establishment of the two spheres highlighted the similarities among the nations that clustered respectively on the opposite sides of the Elbe. In the West, NATO provided a framework for joint action under American sponsorship. In the East, the Warsaw Pact functioned analogously, with the Soviet Union being first among unequals.

Even as the American nuclear umbrella sheltered the NATO allies from Soviet military power, the Western Europeans began work on a structure that eventually threatened to supplant NATO. At the time of the formulation of the Marshall Plan, American officials had strongly urged the European countries to reduce tariff barriers and other impediments to trade. The Americans wanted to get the most mileage out of their recovery dollars, and they did not want to see Europe's revival stall at the customs checkpoints at each border crossing. In addition, the opening up of Europe to cross-border trade neatly dovetailed with Washington's promotion of the free trade regime of the GATT. A number of European officials hardly needed the American prodding. Robert Schuman, the French foreign minister, in 1950 presented a plan for joint cooperative control of the French and German coal and steel industries. The Schuman plan gave rise to the European Coal and Steel Community, which included Italy, Belgium, the Netherlands, and Luxembourg in addition to France and West Germany. The basic principle behind the establishment of the

Coal and Steel Community was the elimination of tariffs and other trade restrictions in the coal and steel industries among the six members.

The six countries of "Little Europe," as they were called, found their experience in coal and steel profitable and promising enough to warrant expanding the approach to other sectors of the continental economy. In 1957 representatives of the six countries signed the Treaty of Rome, which called into existence the European Economic Community. The EEC had two purposes: to remove barriers to trade between member states and to establish common policies toward nonmember states. This would not happen all at once; such a cold turkey approach would never have passed muster with the parliaments of all six. But as the EEC members gradually lowered tariffs among themselves, they would simultaneously move toward a single tariff schedule with respect to outside countries. The two moves were closely linked: if American goods, for instance, could enter Italy more cheaply than they could enter France, and if there were no tariffs between Italy and France, then Italian importers could sell their American goods in France and undercut French merchants who imported the same goods straight from America. The rationale behind the creation of the EEC was the same as the rationale for free trade anywhere. By allowing each country to specialize in what it did best—France in making jet airplanes; Italy, clothes; and West Germany, machine tools—everyone within the community would benefit.

So successful was the concept that before long other countries were applying to join. The most important new applicant was Britain, which sought membership in the early 1960s. British membership almost certainly would have benefited both existing members and the British themselves, at least economically. But French president Charles de Gaulle blackballed the British, essentially on the political ground that Britain was too closely tied to the United States to be a good member of a European community. British membership had to await de Gaulle's departure from office; London gained admission in 1973. Ireland and Denmark joined the EEC in the same year as Britain. The community expanded again in 1981 when Greece entered. It grew still further in 1986 with the admission of Spain and Portugal.

By this time the community had acquired explicitly political functions that went beyond the original idea of an economic common market. For this reason the name European Community (shortened to EC) increasingly supplanted European Economic Community. In 1974 a European Council was established to regularize meetings among the governments of the member states. In 1979 the community took one large step further by creating a European Parliament. The largeness of the step resulted from the fact that the members of the parliament were responsible not to the governments of their countries but to the people of those countries. The step would have been yet larger had the European Parliament received significant powers. This, though, was more than most of the member governments were willing to hand over.

In 1985 the European Council adopted the Single European Act. This landmark measure, upon ratification by the twelve members, called for the creation of a fully unified European market by the end of 1992. At that point all barriers to the free flow of goods, services, capital, and individuals would vanish. There would be no tariffs or other trade restrictions. Companies and professionals licensed to do business in any country would be free to do business in every country. Investment from any country would be treated the same way as investment from any other. Workers could travel freely throughout the community looking for jobs. The fundamental objective was to create a large single market—in terms of population, the largest in the world.

Among the European Community's more enthusiastic proponents were those who hoped that economic union would lead to political union. To a certain extent a tendency in this direction was inevitable. If, as seemed likely, the community moved toward a single currency, this currency would have to be managed by a single central bank. The central bank would usurp some of the

Europe in 1993

powers that national governments had discovered they possessed at the time of the financial revolution of the eighteenth and nineteenth centuries. No longer would they be free to inflate their currencies, for example. Likewise, the logic of the single market strongly indicated a fairly uniform tax code. Otherwise people and companies would tend to seek the country with the lowest taxes. The need to move toward tax uniformity would diminish the authority of the national governments to design their tax codes as they saw fit.

Whatever the additional consequences of the creation of a single European market, which did for the most part come into existence on schedule by the end of 1992, the economic consequences promised to be dramatic. The European Community formed a huge trading area. Companies and individuals doing business there could reap maximum economies of scale. As a consequence, they were well positioned to compete vigorously throughout the rest of the world. Political power had almost always followed economic power, at least eventually, in other cases throughout history. Regardless of whether European political union would indeed follow economic unification, the European countries separately or collectively seemed nearly certain to take a greater part in world affairs than they had since before the Second World War.

Japan and the Tigers

The European Community provided one possible model for the new great power of the twenty-first century. Japan provided another. Each model, significantly, placed economic development ahead of military power. The Japanese had been doing so for more than forty years. The most obvious result, in the case of Japan, was an astonishing rate of economic growth. In 1951 Japan's per capita gross national product had been one-twelfth that of the United States. During the following decade and a half, Japan's economy grew at an average rate of approximately 10 percent per year. It continued to grow steadily, if not so spectacularly, for another ten years. By the mid-1970s Japan's per capita production was more than two-fifths that of America, despite strong growth in the United States in the meantime. Already Japan had surpassed Britain in economic power; during the next decade it outstripped Germany, France, and the Soviet Union, remaining second only to America.

The engine for Japan's astonishing economic growth was its export sector. Government policies, especially regarding taxation, and national predilections encouraged a high rate of savings. These savings were channeled by the powerful Ministry of International Trade and Industry (MITI) and other agencies into investment in state-of-the-art factories that produced goods to sell to foreign countries. Initially, Japanese firms actively sought out licensing arrangements with foreign companies, allowing Japan to produce goods invented elsewhere. This gave the Japanese a reputation as imitators rather than innovators. But it also gave them experience perfecting the techniques of production, which are often more important than the techniques of invention in winning customers for finished goods. It was soon a commonplace of world trade for Japanese manufacturers to take products invented elsewhere—color television, motorcycles, cameras, video recorders, computer memory chips—and master their manufacture, with the consequence that Japanese exports of many of these products came to dominate world markets.

The Japanese strategy of export-led economic development worked, as witnessed by the rapid growth of the Japanese economy into one of the planet's most powerful; but it also generated strains within the international economic order. During the late 1940s and early 1950s, Japan ran a large international deficit, which would have been larger but for heavy infusions of American funds, partly for aid and partly for procurement of goods and services relating to the Korean War. Between 1955 and 1965, Japan's international accounts were roughly balanced. After 1965, as Japan's exports really took off, the country ran a consistent and growing surplus. It was this surplus that played a major role in the disintegration of the Bretton Woods system and the adoption of the floating exchange rates during the early 1970s.

The oil shocks of the 1970s hit Japan harder than most other countries. Japan produced next to no oil of its own and therefore was more dependent than most other industrial countries on imported oil. This did not mean that Japan's oil bill increased more than other countries': the rise in price of OPEC oil immediately translated into comparable price rises for non-OPEC oil—making American oil producers, among others, beneficiaries of the petroleum cartel's price manipulations—so that everyone was soon paying the higher world price regardless of where the oil came from. But the price rise did underline Japan's vulnerability to disruptions of international oil markets. Japanese companies, with the encouragement of the Japanese government, determined to lessen their exposure and reduce their energy bills. The Japanese adopted energy conservation measures for themselves, and they expanded production of such items as gas-stingy automobiles. Because other countries were slower to respond, Japanese products gained a larger share of world markets. Japanese cars, to cite the most obvious example, grew increasingly popular in the United States, with Nissans, Toyotas, and Hondas driving Chevrolets, Fords, and Chryslers off the streets.

Although American automobile manufacturers did not appreciate the Japanese inroads, economic relations between the United States and Japan were not particularly problematic until the early 1980s. For years the United States had experienced a bilateral trade deficit with Japan, but this was outweighed by a larger trade surplus with the rest of the world. Only when America's overall trade balance began sticking regularly in the red did American officials and the American public pay particular attention to the large surplus of Japanese exports to the United States compared with American exports to Japan.

The Reagan administration responded in two ways. First, it moved to push the value of the yen upward relative to the dollar. High American interest rates had made the dollar more attractive to Japanese and other foreign investors than would have been the case strictly on America's trade performance. The overvalued dollar decreased American exports by making American goods relatively expensive abroad, and it increased American imports by making foreign goods relatively cheap. In the mid-1980s Washington persuaded its major trading partners to allow the dollar to fall against their currencies. In the case of Japan, the dollar dropped some 40 percent against the yen between 1985 and 1987.

The decline of the dollar against the yen afforded a modest improvement in America's trade balance vis-à-vis Japan but not enough to eliminate the deficit. Washington supplemented its exchange-rate initiative with pressure on Tokyo to allow greater access to Japanese markets. The question of access became a major bone of contention between the two countries. The Japanese government, responding to a powerful Japanese farm lobby, had long barred the import of rice, which had symbolic value even to many Japanese nonfarmers, and set quotas on beef and citrus fruits. Restrictions on other kinds of imports were less blatant but no less real. Rules on bids for public construction contracts were written to favor Japanese builders; close-knit networks among suppliers and distributors discriminated against foreign firms; bureaucratic delays hindered the licensing of foreign-owned enterprises.

Complaints against Japan—some justified, many exaggerated—came to figure centrally in American political campaigns. Legislators found Japan an easy target and Japanese trade practices an easy explanation for why workers in their districts were losing jobs. Demands for retaliation against "unfair" Japanese tactics became a regular feature in congressional hearings and debates. The Reagan administration and subsequently the Bush administration were free traders by heart, but the demands for protection against Japanese imports grew strong enough that representatives of both administrations felt obliged to threaten Japan implicitly and explicitly with higher tariffs and additional restrictions.

Japan reacted to the protectionist threats by building factories in the United States. This diminished the trade deficit, created a counterlobby of workers and suppliers in America, and offset some of the effects of the devalued dollar. In addition, Japan voluntarily curtailed auto exports to America. And it promised to promote purchases of American goods by the Japanese government and Japanese consumers.

As Americans and Japanese grappled with the changing relationship between their two countries, Japan's economic performance was imitated by several smaller Asian states. The most important of these were the so-called four tigers (sometimes dragons): Taiwan, South Korea, Hong Kong, and Singapore. During the 1980s these four experienced growth rates that paralleled those of Japan twenty years earlier. Although there seemed little likelihood that any of the four would fully reproduce Japan's success—Hong Kong and Singapore being no more than city-states and Hong Kong being scheduled to revert in 1997 from British control to that of China, itself a surprising economic up-and-comer—they demonstrated that Japan's experience was not going to be unique. In certain respects the tigers were to Japan what Japan had been to the United States. As the Japanese grew rich and showed signs of getting tired of working so hard, the hungry tigers looked likely to encroach on Japan's turf. This provided little comfort to Americans since each of the tigers enjoyed a large trade surplus with the United States. But some Americans took solace in the idea that the Japanese might now appreciate the worries Americans had been having for years.

Gulf War II

As the Red Army released its grip on Eastern Europe, as Western Europe forged a single market, and as the economies of Japan and the Asian tigers continued to grow rapidly, some sanguine types hoped that military confrontations had become a thing of the past. The new competition, they predicted, would be economic rather than military. But events soon exploded such naiveté, at least as it involved the short term. Perhaps predictably, the Middle East provided the counterexample. Not entirely predictably, it was not the Arab-Israeli conflict that flared up again but another round of intra-Arab turmoil.

For fifty years Iraq had coveted the territory and oil of Kuwait: the territory because it controlled Iraq's outlet to the Persian Gulf, the oil for the obvious reasons of wealth and power. The Iraqis complained that the British colonialists had cynically and illegitimately carved Kuwait out of Iraq on granting the latter independence in the 1930s; they asserted that Kuwait, which gained its own independence in the early 1960s, was therefore a bogus country. The Iraqi government waved aside Kuwait's counterarguments: that Baghdad had not really governed Kuwait for two hundred years and that the Kuwaiti royal family enjoyed a far better claim to rule the small country. On more than one occasion, Baghdad had pointed guns in Kuwait's direction but each time had stopped short of invasion and annexation. After fighting much-larger Iran to a draw in the Gulf war, however, Saddam Hussein was feeling self-assured, and he decided to revive his country's claims against Kuwait. In July 1990 he accused Kuwait, along with other oil producers, of conspiring to hold down oil prices, thereby depriving Iraq of revenues required to pay debts from the war with Iran. He also alleged that Kuwait was stealing oil from the Rumaila oil field, which straddled the border between Iraq and Kuwait. To lend emphasis to his complaints, Saddam sent one hundred thousand Iraqi troops to the border region.

Because Iraq had huffed and puffed against Kuwait before with no grave consequence, because bluster seemed to characterize Hussein's style on many political issues, and because most outside analysts believed that it would be a few years before the Iraqi army was up to whatever gulf-dominating schemes Hussein was hatching, a number of foreign governments did not take Baghdad's threats against Kuwait especially seriously. The American government was among these. The American ambassador to Iraq, April Glaspie, met with Hussein on July 25 for her first direct conversation with the Iraqi president since she had arrived in Baghdad two years before. Hussein ignored the late American tilt in his favor during the war with Iran and rebuked the United States for joining the ranks of Iraq's enemies: for plotting with Kuwait, he said, to keep oil prices down and Iraq impoverished. Depending on whose story was true, Glaspie either warned Hussein in no uncertain terms to keep his hands off Kuwait (her story) or indicated that Iraq's troubles with Kuwait were a matter for the Arabs to solve without America's involvement (Hussein's story).

Whatever Glaspie really told Hussein on July 25, Washington definitely did *not* adopt a highly visible stance on the Iraq-Kuwait dispute before the beginning of August. Had the American government believed that Hussein was about to order his troops into Kuwait, President Bush could have warned him that such a move would bring down on his head the wrath of the United States. But American intelligence analysts thought Hussein would settle for something less than all of Kuwait. One possibility was an agreement by Kuwait to curtail oil production and raise prices; others were a lease of the two Kuwaiti islands that blocked Iraqi access to the Persian Gulf and the transfer to Iraq of Kuwait's corner of the Rumaila oil field. Already Baghdad had consented to discuss its differences with Kuwait; the troop movements might well be just a bargaining tactic.

On August 2, however, Saddam Hussein demonstrated the wishfulness of this thinking. Probably believing that the United States would do no more than diplomatically slap his wrist, or at worst impose trade restrictions, he ordered his troops into Kuwait. The Kuwaitis were no match for Iraq's battle-hardened forces, which required less than a day to capture Kuwait City and establish control over the country. The ruler of the country, Emir Jabir Al Sabah, flew away to Saudi Arabia one step ahead of the Iraqi tanks.

Washington was surprised by the Iraqi invasion and alarmed by what it portended. The CIA warned President Bush that Hussein had his eyes on the Saudi Arabian oil fields. The agency predicted that the Saudis would not put up much more of a fight against an Iraqi invading force than the Kuwaitis had.

The Bush administration quickly decided to act. The world could live with a merged Iraq-Kuwait; such a merged entity would be an important player in the international energy market, but as long as Saudi Arabia, the largest exporter of Middle Eastern oil, remained independent, Hussein would not be able to achieve a stranglehold over supplies and prices. An Iraqi seizure of Saudi Arabia's fields, on the other hand, might turn the global oil picture upside down. Where the price of a barrel of oil, already soaring on news of the invasion of Kuwait, would stop, none could tell. In addition, an Iraqi takeover of Saudi Arabia's oil would afford Hussein enormous financial power, potentially convertible to military power. This prospect alone was enough to sober anyone.

Although the Bush administration judged it imperative to take strong measures to prevent Iraq's tanks from continuing past Kuwait into Saudi Arabia, the Saudis themselves initially appeared ambivalent about the idea. They had no desire to be Hussein's next victims, but they had some doubts regarding

America's steadfastness as a protector. They remembered how quickly the Americans had fled Lebanon after suffering a mere few hundred casualties. By nearly all predictions, a tangle with Hussein would produce a great many more than a few hundred casualties, and the last thing the Saudis wanted was to provoke Hussein by appealing to the United States for protection, only to have the Americans turn tail and abandon Saudi Arabia, leaving the country undefended. After some persuading by American officials, though, King Fahd agreed to invite American troops into Saudi Arabia.

American officials meanwhile worked on the governments of other countries to assist against Hussein. At first Washington sought the imposition of international economic sanctions against Iraq. The British needed no convincing whatsoever; indeed, British prime minister Thatcher had argued for vigorous action against Hussein from the start. The French were less demonstratively bellicose than the British, but Paris joined Washington and London in freezing Iraqi and Kuwaiti assets (the latter to prevent financial looting by the Iraqis) and in condemning Baghdad's aggression.

The key to the international united front, however, was the Soviet Union. By the summer of 1990, anyone could tell that the success of reform in the Soviet Union would require the assistance of the West, especially Western economic aid. While ties of previous diplomacy, strategy, and economics, including lucrative arms sales, linked Moscow to Baghdad, Gorbachev and Foreign Minister Shevardnadze decided that the Soviet Union needed the West at this point more than it needed Iraq. Consequently, where previous crises in the Middle East had usually found the United States and the Soviet Union on opposing sides, the 1990 crisis in the Persian Gulf arrayed them on the same side. Following the example of the Western powers, Moscow suspended deliveries of military equipment to Iraq. It voted with the rest of the United Nations Security Council to condemn the invasion of Kuwait and demand Iraq's withdrawal. It supported economic sanctions against Iraq and later approved the use of military means to enforce the United Nations sanctions.

Not having to worry about Soviet counterintervention, the Bush administration moved swiftly to place American troops on the ground in the gulf region. At first the American deployment was "wholly defensive," in the words of the president. The administration was responding to an emergency—the possibility that the Iraqi army would keep going beyond Kuwait into Saudi Arabia—and it initially acted to deal with that emergency. The president ordered the dispatch of 125,000 American troops, scores of ships, and hundreds of aircraft to Saudi Arabia and the waters nearby.

Before long, however, American officials began thinking about doing more than defending Saudi Arabia. With each week that went by, an Iraqi invasion of Saudi Arabia seemed less likely. Logic said that if Hussein had been planning such an invasion, he would have launched it before all the American forces started arriving. Yet neither did the passing weeks showed any sign of an Iraqi withdrawal from Kuwait. In fact, where Hussein had initially hinted at leaving Kuwait after installing a friendly government there, now he described Kuwait as Iraq's nineteenth province.

The United Nations sanctions were supposed to supply pressure that would compel Hussein to leave Kuwait. From the start, though, many observers questioned whether the sanctions would do the trick. During the eight-year war against Iran, Hussein had shown his ability to tighten his compatriots' belts; odds were that he would be able to tighten them again. Besides, as a self-made dictator he did not have to retain the active support of the Iraqi people; so long as the army, especially the elite Republican Guards, stayed happy, he could probably stay in power. And past experience indicated that he would not hesitate to starve the civilian population to keep the soldiers happy. Economic sanctions, even at their best, would take a long time to work.

Whether the international coalition arrayed against Iraq would hold together long enough for the sanctions to work was the big question. There were reasons for doubt. The coalition was one of the most disparate in history, including Westerners and Easterners, capitalists and communists, Christians and Muslims, Jews and Buddhists. Petroleum consumers would be tempted to cut a deal with Baghdad for cheap oil (Baghdad quickly slashed its prices); Arabs and Muslims would get fidgety in a group that included Israel (even though Israel, with strong American encouragement, kept its head low); formerly colonized countries would gravitate back toward their natural anti-Americanism (partly because the governments of coalition states were often firmer against Saddam Hussein than many people in those states, who saw Hussein as a hero challenging the hegemony of the American imperialists).

Hearing the clock ticking, the Bush administration began lobbying for stronger measures to eject Hussein from Kuwait. Bush called the Iraqi aggression an affront to a "new world order" in which small states as well as large should be free from fear of attack. The president and other American officials argued that the end of the Cold War afforded the international community a unique opportunity to establish a fresh set of guidelines regarding the conduct of nations. Unless the world joined forces to reverse the outrage committed by Saddam Hussein against Kuwait, other dictators and regional bullies would follow his obnoxious example. Additional considerations, most notably the desire to get Kuwait's oil out of Hussein's hands, added to the administration's resolve.

During the autumn of 1990, the international coalition led by the United States moved toward war against Iraq. The Bush administration increased the size of the American military force in the Persian Gulf area, working toward a total of some half million soldiers. While the military buildup was proceeding, the administration politicked at the United Nations for what amounted to an international declaration of war against Iraq. Most of the members of the Security Council had little difficulty accepting a resolution authorizing the use of force to free Kuwait since such a resolution seemed a logical extension of measures the Security Council had approved already. The Soviet government, however, had to agonize a bit before backing the resolution. The Iraqis had been Kremlin clients since the late 1950s, and treating them badly would not do much for Moscow's credibility. Nor would a defeat of Iraq by a United States–led coalition do much for the reputation of Soviet arms; because arms sales

American artillery troops take aim on an Iraqi position during the Persian Gulf War.
Reuters/Bettmann

looked like a potential moneymaker for the Kremlin, this might prove a serious problem. Finally, for Mikhail Gorbachev and the Soviet government to follow meekly behind George Bush and the United States would probably weaken Gorbachev politically against his rivals and the Soviet Union diplomatically against other countries. Eventually, however, Moscow joined the rest of the Security Council in approving a resolution insisting that Iraq clear out of Kuwait by January 15, 1991; after that date members of the United Nations could use "all means necessary" to effect Iraq's withdrawal.

Getting the American Congress to vote for war proved harder than winning the Security Council's approval. Bush's congressional critics questioned whether he was allowing the United Nations sanctions enough time to work; many hesitated to send American soldiers into battle if the economic blockade might accomplish the same end. Many wondered if Kuwait really mattered that much to the United States. But in a close decision—the margin in the Senate was only 5 votes—the legislature approved a resolution authorizing the president to use American military force to help secure the freedom of Kuwait.

The January 15, 1991, United Nations deadline passed, with Iraqi forces still in Kuwait; hours later the war began. American naval vessels fired the first shots: Tomahawk cruise missiles that skimmed the desert en route to Baghdad. Even as the Tomahawks approached their targets, American electronic-warfare aircraft blinded and overloaded Iraqi radar, allowing American and allied bombers easy access to military installations, communication centers, and assorted other targets in Iraq and Kuwait.

From the start the war was terribly lopsided. The anti-Iraq coalition quickly and completely dominated the skies above the desert and the gulf. Iraq's only important counterthrust in the first phase of the fighting was its launching of Scud ballistic missiles at Israel and Saudi Arabia. American analysts had feared that Iraq would place chemical warheads—a few real doomsayers thought perhaps even a rudimentary nuclear bomb or two—on the Scuds, which then would cause massive casualties wherever they hit. As matters turned out, the Scuds carried no chemical or nuclear warheads; the technology evidently surpassed what Baghdad commanded. But even armed with conventional explosives, the Scuds put a scare into the coalition.

The less scary of the Scuds were those that hit Saudi Arabia. The Saudis were already involved in the war against Hussein up to their necks, and unless the missiles did far more damage than seemed likely, they would not change Saudi Arabia's policy. The more worrisome were the Scuds that hit Israel. From the beginning of the crisis, Washington had feared that Hussein would try to transform the Iraq-Kuwait quarrel, a fight among Arabs, into a fight between Arabs and Israelis. To this end Hussein rhetorically championed the cause of the Palestinians—even as his ravaging of the Kuwait economy threw hundreds of thousands of Palestinians out of work—and cast his challenge to the West as a blow against the American-Zionist conspiracy. He fooled the Palestinians, or rather the leadership of the PLO, which voiced strong support for Hussein against the filthy rich Kuwaitis. But he did not fool many other people, at least not among those who ran the governments of countries with particular interest in the affairs of the Persian Gulf.

His failure to do so owed especially to Israel's forbearance in not being provoked by the Scud attacks to retaliate against Iraq. Israel's forbearance in turn owed a great deal to Washington's rapid delivery of Patriot antimissile missiles, which provided psychological insurance, if not much physical protection. How effective the Patriots were in intercepting the Scuds remained a matter of debate for years after the war. Even those Patriots that did hit Scuds allowed debris to rain down on the targeted cities. Israel's forbearance about the Scuds also reflected the billions of dollars of aid Washington had supplied the Israelis over the decades.

With Israel agreeing to hunker down, holding the rest of the coalition together proved comparatively simple. It assisted things that the war went exceedingly well from the allies' standpoint. For five weeks American and British planes flew thousands of sorties per day, aided by French, Saudi, and Kuwaiti aircraft. Together the allies succeeded in destroying nearly everything that might conceivably contribute to Iraq's ability to sustain its occupation of Kuwait. In the process they suffered exceedingly modest casualties, numbering only in the low hundreds.

After the five weeks of the air war, Bush gave the order for American ground forces to take the offensive. Troops from other coalition countries joined the Americans in a multipronged assault from Saudi Arabia across the border into

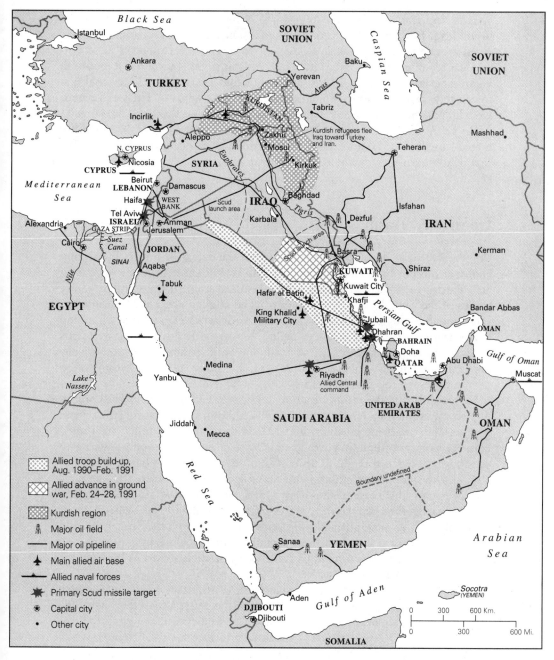

The Persian Gulf War of 1991

Kuwait and Iraq. While helicopter-borne American units landed fifty miles inside Iraq, far behind the Iraqi lines, coalition tanks and personnel carriers raced around the Iraqi defensive positions to sever retreat routes. Feared poison gas counterattacks and bitter-end resistance by Hussein's Republican Guards never materialized. With a rapidity that amazed nearly all coalition forecasters, Iraqi resistance collapsed. Tens of thousands of Hussein's troops were killed, and others surrendered in groups of several thousand at a time.

On February 27, 1991, six weeks after the war began, coalition forces liberated Kuwait City. Hours later, with coalition troops occupying a sizable portion of southern Iraq, Bush called off the attack.

Unfinished Business

Unfortunately for Bush's "new world order," the defeat of Iraq in the second Gulf war did not bring about either the fall of Saddam Hussein or the end of his capacity for mischief making. The president stopped the fighting before troops of the United Nations coalition reached Baghdad because he wanted to keep casualties down and because he and his advisers were not sure what kind of government they could install to replace Hussein. Already Iraq showed signs of disintegrating, with Kurds in the north and Shiite Arabs in the south revolting against Baghdad's rule. A seriously enfeebled Iraq would be an invitation to Iran to restart the first Gulf war.

Bush hoped that the Iraqis would oust Hussein without tearing the country to pieces, but the Iraqi leader was tenacious and infuriating. During the several months after the war, Hussein did his best to hinder efforts by the United Nations to ensure that Iraq would not develop nuclear weapons; whenever possible he acted as though his army had not been crushed in battle. The Bush administration found the situation maddening to the point where the American president took the extreme step—for American diplomatic practice—of publicly calling on the Iraqis to depose their leader. For many Americans the outcome of the war was distinctly disappointing. Kuwait was free again, and Hussein's military power had been curtailed; but with the Iraqi strong man thumbing his nose at the United Nations, peace seemed almost as far from the Middle East as ever.

Only *almost* as far: one positive side effect of the second Gulf war was to bring the Israelis and their Arab neighbors to the negotiating table. As of the middle of 1993, the negotiating table was as far as they would go, but that the Israelis and the Palestinians were talking face to face for the first time was a positive development.

The situation in the rest of the world was a similarly mixed bag. Democracy definitely appeared to be making headway against the forces that had long opposed it. In South Africa the white-controlled government was taking large steps toward abandoning the race-separating policy of apartheid and allowing blacks to participate fully in the country's politics. Toward this objective the United States had backed United Nations economic sanctions against the apartheid regime. As South Africa moved toward racial equality and democracy, Washington supported the United Nations' decision to lift the sanctions.

In Latin America the Nicaraguan Sandinistas had agreed to elections that resulted in their removal from office. The Republicans in Washington claimed victory for their policy of supporting the *contras*; critics asserted that the elections might have taken place sooner had the *contra* war not allowed the Sandinistas to plead military necessity in putting the balloting off. A long-running civil war in El Salvador ended in a tenuous cease-fire. Again the American government claimed victory for its policy, this time of supporting the (rightist) government *against* the (leftist) rebels; critics pointed to the horrendous toll of deaths in the twelve-year war and alleged that no one had won. In Chile and Peru military rulers handed power over to elected civilians, though in Peru the elected president proceeded to suspend the constitution and govern by decree.

In Panama democracy, or something approximating it, arrived with an invading force of American marines. During much of the 1980s, Panamanian dictator Manuel Noriega had cooperated with the Reagan administration's antileftist efforts in Central America; in exchange Washington supplied economic and military assistance and ignored his participation in the international drug trade. By the end of the decade, however, Noriega was getting carried away with himself, sinking deeper into corruption and treating the Panamanian people with increasing brutality. Meanwhile the blowing of the cover of the Iran-*contra* operation placed covert operations generally in a bad light and diminished Noriega's value as an agent of American policy. Additionally, the Reagan administration made a great issue of waging a "war on drugs," and as Noriega's involvement in the drug trade grew evident, he became a serious liability for the administration. When the American Justice Department, to the consternation of the State Department, which wished to handle the Noriega matter quietly, delivered two drug-trafficking indictments against Noriega in February 1988, the White House found itself under still greater pressure to ease the dictator from power.

But Noriega would not be eased, insisting on being pushed, which the Reagan administration did and the Bush administration did even more energetically. Washington levied economic sanctions against Noriega's regime and stepped up psychological pressure by increasing the size and readiness of the American garrison in the Panama Canal zone. Finally, following the killing of an American soldier in December 1989, Bush sent ten thousand American troops to seize control of the capital and capture Noriega. Capturing the general took longer than seizing the capital, but in early January 1990 Noriega surrendered and was flown to Miami, where he subsequently was tried and convicted. Panama was turned over to opposition leaders from whom Noriega had stolen national elections several months before. Although the governments of several Latin American countries decried the blatant use of American force, most found little to complain of in the end result. The Panamanians themselves seemed pleased that Noriega was gone, but many of them had qualms about the means of his departure and especially about the heavy violence that accompanied the American takeover. Whole neighborhoods were leveled, and hundreds, at least, died.

Outside the Western Hemisphere, democracy made even bigger strides. The biggest continued to take place in Eastern Europe and the former Soviet Union. By the middle of 1992, all the former satellite states and all the former Soviet republics were enjoying elected governments of their own, though some enjoyed them more than others. The overriding question in what had been the Eastern bloc was whether democracy would bring happiness. In the West people had long gotten used to democracy's deficiencies and had learned to live with them the way partners in a marriage of many years get used to the foibles of their spouses. But the Eastern Europeans and former Soviet peoples were entering the early posthoneymoon letdown. Recently infatuated, they were now starting to argue about who would take out the garbage—or, more appropriately, who would put the food on the table. Most observers believed that economic development would be crucial to planting democracy permanently where communism had been uprooted. The United States joined a consortium of industrialized nations established to provide economic aid to the new democracies. Whether the aid would meet the need and whether the formerly communist countries would live happily ever after with democracy remained for a future installment of the story to reveal.

An important exception to the democratic trend in world affairs was China. Following the 1976 death of Mao Zedong, the Chinese government gradually moved away from the communist model of economic relations. Deng Xiaoping and other reformers took a lesson from the economic progress made by Japan and the Asian tigers (of whom three—Hong Kong, Taiwan, and Singapore—derived most of their economic energy from the Chinese communities residing there) and decided that what those countries could accomplish, so could China. Deng reintroduced private property and the free market to increasingly large sectors of the Chinese economy, with the result that by the early 1990s China was showing one of the fastest rates of economic growth in the world. Yet political reforms did not keep pace with the economic liberalization. When Chinese students and other advocates of democracy staged demonstrations in Beijing's Tiananmen Square in the spring of 1989, the Chinese government sent tanks against the demonstrators. Hundreds died; thousands were wounded; large numbers of survivors were arrested. The Bush administration expressed shock at the massive use of force against peaceful protesters but, arguing that China was too important to ostracize, refused calls to break diplomatic relations or otherwise seriously punish the Chinese government.

If the Tiananmen massacre injected a disquieting note into American–East Asian relations, disquiet of another kind developed in American dealings with Japan. The demise of the Soviet Union loosened transpacific ties by shifting attention away from strategic matters, on which Americans and Japanese had long agreed, to economics, on which they often had not. A recession in the United States and a stock market crash in Japan put the peoples of both coun-

Chairman Mao meets the Goddess of Democracy in Tiananmen Square. The meeting went badly: the goddess was destroyed, hundreds of demonstrators were killed, and democracy in China was dealt a grave blow. *AP/Wide World Photos*

tries in irritable moods. American politicians and editorialists complained of Japan's unfair trade practices. American legislators, showing a protectionist streak not seen so clearly for decades, threatened to bar Japanese imports unless Japan bought more American goods. America's free traders were hard pressed to defend the gains they had made since the depression of the 1930s. For their part, the Japanese increasingly gave back as good as they were getting in the way of shouting and finger pointing. Some prominent Japanese called Americans ignorant; others said Americans were lazy. Although Japanese government officials disavowed or explained away most such comments, the remarks left a residue of bad feelings over the Pacific. Historically minded people in both countries remembered how similar bad feelings had festered during the first half of the twentieth century and feared for the first part of the twenty-first.

Americans had fewer worries regarding the possible unification of Europe. Partly this was due to a greater American cultural affinity with Europe. Partly it was due to the lack of bad memories about the countries of the European Community—Germany excepted. Partly it was due to the American trade surplus with Europe. And partly it was due to the uncertainty about what European unification would entail. Unification might be a model for a wider economic integration. Conceivably, the United States might join an expanded (and suitably renamed) European Community. On the other hand, unification might produce a Fortress Europe: a trading bloc that closed itself off to outside competition. As a hedge against this possibility, Washington negotiated to include Mexico in an existing free trade agreement between the United States and Canada.

Nothing about the future was certain, but at least one thing appeared very likely: that Americans were entering a phase of history in which their country no longer dominated world affairs the way it had in the recent past. The era just after the Second World War had been an anomaly. Other nations had been bound to recover from the war and narrow the gap with the United States. By the 1990s they clearly had. Americans who had grown up during the age of American predominance might not find their country's comparative decline easy to accept, but there was not much they could do about it.

If the recent past afforded a misleading example of where the United States fit in the international scheme, the more distant past provided a perhaps more reliable guide. For most of its history, the United States had been one power among many. It had had to accommodate its desires to the competing desires of other countries. Sometimes Americans got what they wanted; sometimes they did not. As the United States grew in size and wealth, its power grew, and Americans tended to get more of what they wanted. In the last decade of the twentieth century, the United States remained very powerful. But America's power relative to the power of other nations was less than it had recently been. Americans could expect to get less of what they wanted in relations with other countries. Even so they had a long history of dealing profitably with the world on a give-and-take basis, and there was no reason to think they could not deal with the world in such a way again.

Sources and Suggestions for Further Reading

Garthoff, *Detente and Confrontation,* traces the collapse of detente, as do the books by Stevenson, Hyland, and Ulam cited in the previous chapter. Strobe Talbott, *Deadly Gambits* (1984), examines the arms control policies of the first Reagan administration. Diana Johnstone, *The Politics of Euromissiles* (1985), looks at the INF issue. Paul Stares, *Space and National Defense* (1987), treats SDI. The rise of Gorbachev and the disintegration of the Soviet Union can be followed in such books as Barukh Hazan, *From Brezhnev to Gorbachev* (1987); Zhores A. Medvedev, *Gorbachev* (1986); Richard Sakwa, *Gorbachev and His Reforms* (1990); Stephen White, *Gorbachev in Power* (1990); Neil Felshman, *Gorbachev, Yeltsin, and the Last Days of the Soviet Empire* (1992) and David Remnick, *Lenin's Tomb* (1993).

Robert Dallek, *Ronald Reagan* (1984), provides a general interpretation of the early Reagan years. Memoirs of the Reagan administration include Reagan's own, *An American Life* (1990); Alexander Haig's *Caveat* (1984); George P. Shultz's *Turmoil and Triumph*; Caspar Weinberger's *Fighting for Peace* (1990); and Donald Regan's *For the Record* (1988), by Reagan's treasury secretary and subsequent chief of staff.

Issues in the new world economic order are dealt with by various authors. Nicholas V. Gianaris, *The European Community and the United States* (1991), covers relations between the United States and the presumptive European economic superpower. For background on Japan's economic emergence, look at Chalmers Johnson, *MITI and the*

Japanese Miracle: The Growth of Industrial Policy, 1925–1975 (1982). A more recent evaluation is Stephen D. Cohen, *Cowboys and Samurai: Why The United States is Losing the Industrial Battle and Why It Matters* (1991). See also Michael Lewis, *Pacific Rift* (1991); and Lester C. Thurow, *Head to Head: The Coming Economic Battle among Japan, Europe and America* (1992). America's trade problems are the subject of Chris C. Carvounis, *The United States Trade Deficit of the 1980s* (1987); Don Bonker, *America's Trade Crisis* (1988); and the brief Anthony M. Solomon, *The Dollar, Debt, and the Trade Deficit* (1987).

Itamar Rabinovich, *The War for Lebanon* (1984), explains the troubles in Lebanon. Zeev Schiff and Ehud Yaari, *Israel's Lebanon War* (1985), and Richard A. Gabriel, *Operation Peace for Galilee* (1984), focus on the 1982 Israeli invasion that led to American involvement. George W. Ball, *Error and Betrayal in Lebanon* (1984), critiques Reagan administration policy. Stephen Green, *Living by the Sword* (1988), examines the relationship between the United States and Israel from the late 1960s to the mid-1980s.

On the first Persian Gulf war, between Iran and Iraq, see Majid Khadduri, *The Gulf War* (1988), and John Bullock and Harvey Morris, *The Gulf War* (1989). The second Gulf war, between Iraq and the American-led coalition, is too recent to have spawned much literature that will stand the test of time, but try H. Norman Schwarzkopf, *It Doesn't Take a Hero* (1992), by the American commander; Micah L. Sifry and Christopher Cerf, eds., *The Gulf War Reader* (1991); and John Fimlott and Stephen Badsey, eds., *The Gulf War Assessed* (1992).

Index

407